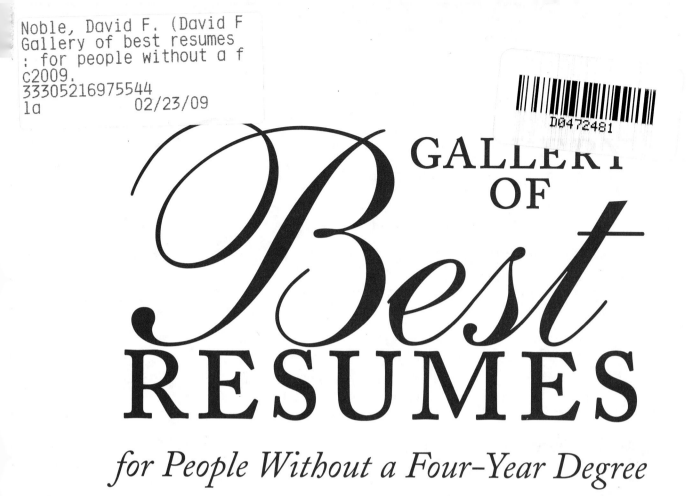

GALLERY OF *Best* RESUMES

for People Without a Four-Year Degree

FOURTH EDITION

DAVID F. NOBLE, Ph.D.

JIST Works
America's Career Publisher®

Gallery of Best Resumes for People Without a Four-Year Degree, Fourth Edition

A Special Collection of Quality Resumes by Professional Resume Writers
Originally published as *Gallery of Best Resumes for Two-Year-Degree Graduates*
© 2009 by David F. Noble

Published by JIST Works, an imprint of JIST Publishing
7321 Shadeland Station, Suite 200
Indianapolis, IN 46256-3923
Phone: 800-648-JIST   Fax: 877-454-7839   E-mail: info@jist.com

Visit our Web site at **www.jist.com** for information on JIST, free job search tips, tables of contents, sample pages, and ordering instructions for our many products.

> **Other books by David F. Noble:**
> *Gallery of Best Cover Letters*
> *Gallery of Best Resumes*

Quantity discounts are available for JIST books. Have future editions of JIST books automatically delivered to you on publication through our convenient standing order program. Please call our Sales Department at 800-648-5478 for a free catalog and more information.

Trade Product Manager: Lori Cates Hand
Proofreaders: Linda Seifert, Paula Lowell, Jeanne Clark
Interior Designer: Debbie Berman
Cover Designer: Amy Adams
Page Layout: Toi Davis
Indexer: Virginia Noble

Printed in the United States of America.

13 12 11 10 09   9 8 7 6 5 4 3 2 1

Library of Congress Cataloging-in-Publication Data
Noble, David F. (David Franklin), 1935-
    Gallery of best resumes for people without a four-year degree / by David F. Noble. -- 4th ed.
        p. cm.
    Includes bibliographical references and index.
    ISBN 978-1-59357-427-7 (alk. paper)
1. Résumés (Employment) I. Title.
    HF5383.N622 2009
    650.15'2--dc

222008051339

ISBN: 978-1-59357-427-7

In memory of my brother,
Maynard A. Noble (1929–1995),
and to Peggy, Ron, Chris, and Wendy,
who made him rich with their loving care

Acknowledgments

To all those who helped make possible this updated Gallery for people without a four-year degree, I would like to acknowledge my appreciation. I am most indebted to all the professional resume writers who sent me examples of their latest work for inclusion in this book. These writers took the time on short notice to supply a pool of examples for the 56 replacement documents selected for this book: 52 new resumes and 4 new cover letters. The purpose of these replacements is to provide documents by writers who are still members of one or more professional resume-writer organizations, who are still active as resume writers, and whom readers can contact easily for professional services. To find the writer of a particular resume or cover letter, see the List of Contributors appendix at the back of the book.

I want to express again my gratitude to Bob Grilliot, who suggested that the second edition of this book should include resumes for people without a four-year degree. I am altogether indebted to my wife, Ginny, for the many tasks she performed online, on-screen, and on hard copy for the preceding editions of this book and for the two indexes of this fourth edition.

Contents

Part 3: Best Cover Letter Tips.............379

Introduction

Like the *Gallery of Best Resumes*, the *Gallery of Best Resumes for People Without a Four-Year Degree* is a collection of quality resumes from professional resume writers, each with individual views about resumes and resume writing. Unlike many resume books whose selections look the same, this book contains resumes that look different because they are representations of *real* resumes prepared by different professionals in Australia, Canada, and especially the United States for actual job searchers. (Certain information in the resumes has been fictionalized by the writers to protect the clients' privacy.) Even when several resumes from the same writer appear in the book, most of these resumes are different because the writer has customized each resume according to the background information and career goals of the client for whom the resume was prepared.

During the past several years, the resume writing industry has matured because of the following factors:

- The increase in the number of professional organizations for resume writers.

- The ready sharing of ideas at these organizations' national conventions.

- Easy access to e-mail and the World Wide Web.

- The greater availability of higher-resolution, lower-cost printers (black-and-white and color) for personal computers.

- The increase in the number of books like this Gallery that display collections of quality resumes and cover letters by professional writers. Often these books serve as idea books that emerging writers use as they develop their own expertise.

Instead of assuming that one resume style fits all, the writers featured here believe that a client's past experiences and next job target should determine the resume's type, design, and content. The use of Best in this book's title reflects this approach to resume making. The resumes are not "best" because they are ideal types for you to copy, but because the resume writers interacted with their clients to fashion resumes that seemed best for each client's situation at the time.

This book features resumes from writers who share several important qualities: good listening skills, a sense of what details are appropriate for a particular resume, and flexibility in selecting and arranging the resume's sections. By "hearing between" a client's statements, the perceptive resume writer can detect what kind of job the client really wants. The writer then chooses the information that best represents the client for the job being sought. Finally, the writer decides on the best arrangement of the information for that job, from most important to least important. With the help of this book, you can create this kind of resume yourself.

Most of the writers of the resumes in this Gallery are members of one or more of the following organizations: Career Directors International (CDI), Career Management

Alliance™ (The Alliance), the National Résumé Writers' Association (NRWA), or the Professional Association of Résumé Writers & Career Coaches (PARW/CC). Each organization has programs for earned certifications. Writers who have CPRW certification, for Certified Professional Resume Writer, received this designation from the PARW/CC after they studied specific course materials and demonstrated proficiency in an examination. Those who have NCRW certification, for Nationally Certified Resume Writer, received this designation from the NRWA after accumulating 10 continuing education units over three years, having these units approved, and then passing two tests. Members of the Career Management Alliance work toward acquiring coveted Master Resume Writer (MRW) certification, and those who belong to Career Directors International take a series of tests to gain Certified Advanced Resume Writer (CARW) certification. For contact information for CDI, The Alliance, NRWA, and PARW/CC, see their listings at the end of the List of Contributors appendix.

Why a Gallery for People Without a Four-Year Degree?

First of all, it should be made clear that people without a four-year degree are not people without education or who go to college for a couple of years, grow tired of studying, drop out, and get a job. This stereotypical misconception is refuted by almost every resume in this Gallery. People without a four-year degree include diverse kinds of individuals:

- Those who took courses of a particular curriculum to work in a specialized field, such as paralegals

- Those who got a two-year degree as a step toward getting a bachelor's degree

- Those who are job changers—people in transition—who acquired a two-year degree and possibly additional certification(s) to move to a new field of opportunity

- Those who had to interrupt their education for various reasons

- Those who had to work for economic reasons rather than study

- Those who took different paths (military training, technical education, and so on) to their current occupation

People without a four-year degree have special resume needs. Compared to traditional four-year students, who may have more campus activities and less full-time work experience to report on a resume, people without a four-year degree may have more full-time work experience to report. This means that Skills and Achievements tend to be emphasized more than Education.

People without a four-year degree also need resumes that help them compete successfully for jobs of employers who traditionally prefer workers with four-year and higher degrees. This Gallery showcases resumes that have helped people without a four-year degree compete successfully for better jobs in today's job market.

How This Book Is Organized

Like the preceding editions, this fourth edition has three parts.

Part 1: Best Resume Tips

Part 1, "Best Resume Tips," presents resume writing tips, design and layout tips, and resume writing style tips for making resumes visually impressive. Some of these tips were suggested by resume writers who contributed resumes to *Gallery of Best Resumes* (Indianapolis: JIST Works, 1994).

Part 2: The Gallery of Professional Resumes

Part 2 is the Gallery itself. It contains 195 resumes from 84 professional resume writers throughout the United States, Australia, and Canada.

Resume writers commonly distinguish between chronological resumes and functional (or skills) resumes. A *chronological resume* is a photo—a snapshot history of what you did and when you did it. A *functional resume* is a painting—an interpretive sketch of what you can do for a future employer. A third kind of resume, known as a *combination resume,* is a mix of recalled history and self-assessment. Besides recollecting "the facts," a combination resume contains self-interpretation and therefore is more like dramatic history than news coverage. A chronological resume and a functional resume are not always that different; often, all that is needed for a functional resume to qualify as a combination resume is the inclusion of some dates, such as those for positions held. Almost all the resumes in this edition are combination resumes.

The resumes in the Gallery are presented in the following occupational categories and in a final section on electronic resumes.

Accounting/Bookkeeping
Administrative Support
Communications
Construction
Customer Service
Design
Education
Events Planning
Finance/Banking
Firefighting
Health and Safety
Healthcare
Hospitality
Human Resources
Information Systems/Information Technology
Law/Law Enforcement
Maintenance
Management
Manufacturing
Purchasing
Real Estate
Recruiting
Sales and Marketing

   Technology
   Transportation
   Electronic Resumes

Within each category, the resumes are generally arranged from the simple to the complex. Many of the resumes are one page, but a number of them are two pages. A few are more than two pages.

The Gallery offers a wide range of resumes with features you can use to create and improve your own resumes. Notice the plural. An important premise of an active job search is that you will not have just one "perfect" resume for all potential employers, but different versions of your resume for different interviews. The Gallery, therefore, is not a showroom where you say, "I'll take that one," alter it with your information, and then duplicate your version 200 times. It is a valuable resource for design ideas, expressions, and organizational patterns that can help make your own resume a "best resume" for your next interview.

Creating multiple versions of a resume may seem difficult, but it is easy to do if you have (or have access to) a personal computer and a laser printer or some other kind of printer that can produce quality output. You also need word processing, desktop publishing, or resume software. If you don't have a computer or don't know someone who does, most professional resume writers have the hardware and software, and they can make your resume look like those in the Gallery. See the List of Contributors in the appendix for the names, addresses, phone numbers, e-mail addresses, and Web sites (if any) of the professional writers whose works are featured in this book. A local fast-print shop can make your resume look good, but you will probably not get there the kind of advice and service the professional resume writer provides.

Many employers now encourage the electronic submission of resumes or cover letters because of timeliness and expediency in processing. Any of the resumes in this book can be modified for electronic transfer. If you intend to apply online for positions, be sure you follow the submission guidelines posted by the employer. If they are not clearly explained, e-mail or phone the company to inquire. You don't want to be disqualified for a job that suits you well because you did not follow the steps for successful submission. Note that most professional writers, such as those whose resumes are featured in this book, may help you develop a version of your resume for online posting. Be aware, however, that posting your resume online or in a database has some risk because of the possible exposure of confidential information to public. Therefore, be certain not to include your Social Security number and any important account numbers in your resume.

Part 3: Best Cover Letter Tips

Part 3, "Best Cover Letter Tips," discusses some myths about cover letters and offers tips for polishing cover letters. Much of the advice offered here also applies to writing resumes. Included in this part is an exhibit of 12 cover letters. Most of these letters accompanied resumes that appear in the Gallery.

The List of Contributors in the appendix is arranged alphabetically by country, state or province, and city. Although most of these resume writers work with local clients, many of them work nationally or internationally with clients by e-mail, phone, or fax.

You can use the Occupation Index to look up resumes by the current or most recent job title. This index, however, should not replace careful examination of all the resumes. Many of the resumes for some other occupation may have features that you can adapt to your own occupation. Limiting your search to the Occupation Index may cause you to miss some valuable examples. You can use the Features Index to find resumes that contain representative resume sections that may be important to you and your resume needs.

Who This Book Is For

Anyone who wants ideas for creating or improving a resume can benefit from this book. It is especially useful for active job seekers—those who understand the difference between active and passive job searching. A *passive* job seeker waits until jobs are advertised and then mails copies of the same resume, along with a standard cover letter, in response to a number of help-wanted ads. An *active* job seeker believes that a resume should be modified for a specific job target *after* he or she talks in person or by phone to a prospective interviewer *before* a job is announced. To schedule such an interview is to penetrate the "hidden job market." Active job seekers can find in the Gallery's focused resumes a wealth of strategies for targeting a resume for a particular interview. The section "How to Use the Gallery" at the beginning of Part 2 mentions how to do this. Comments at the bottom of each resume and cover letter page give you additional insights for shaping your own documents for job searching.

Besides the active job seeker, any unemployed person who wants to create a more competitive resume or update an old one should find this book helpful. It shows the kinds of resumes professional resume writers are writing, and it showcases resumes for job seekers with particular needs.

What This Book Can Do for You

Besides providing you with a treasury of quality resumes whose features you can use in your own resumes, this book can help transform your thinking about resumes. There is no one "best" way to create a resume. This book helps you learn how to develop a resume that is best for you as you try to get an interview with a particular person for a specific job.

You might have been told that resumes should be only one page long. This may be true for a high school graduate with little work experience, but this kind of advice is limiting for someone without a four-year degree but with a wealth of work experience. The examples of multiple-page resumes in the Gallery help you see how to distribute information effectively across two or more pages. If you believe that the way to update a resume is to add your latest work experiences to your last resume, this book shows you how to rearrange your resume so that you can highlight the most important information about your experience and skills.

After you have studied "Best Resume Writing Tips" in Part 1, examined the professionally written resumes in Part 2, and reviewed "Tips for Polishing Cover Letters" in Part 3, you should be able to create your own resumes and cover letters worthy of inclusion in a gallery of best resumes!

1

P·A·R·T

Best Resume Tips

Best Resume Tips at a Glance

Best Resume Writing Tips

In a passive job search, you rely on your resume to do most of the work for you. An eye-catching resume that stands out above all the others may be your best shot at getting noticed by a prospective employer. If your resume is only average and looks like most of the others in the pile, chances are you won't be noticed and called for an interview. If you want to be singled out because of your resume, it should be somewhere between spectacular and award-winning.

In an active job search, however, your resume complements your efforts at being known to a prospective employer *before* that person receives it. For this reason, you can rely less on your resume to get someone's attention. Nevertheless, your resume plays an important role in an active job search, which may include the following activities:

- Talking to relatives, friends, and other acquaintances about helping you meet people who can hire you before a job is available

- Contacting employers directly, using the yellow pages to identify types of organizations that could use a person with your skills

- Creating phone scripts to speak with the person who is most likely to hire someone with your background and skills

- Walking into a business in person to talk directly to the person who is most likely to hire someone like you

- Using a schedule to keep track of your appointments and callbacks

- Working at least 25 hours a week to search for a job

When you are this active in searching for a job, the quality of your resume confirms the quality of your efforts to get to know the person who might hire you, as well as your worth to the company whose workforce you want to join. An eye-catching resume makes it easier for you to sell yourself directly to a prospective employer. If your resume is mediocre or conspicuously flawed, it will work against you and may undo all your good efforts in searching for a job.

The following list offers ideas for making your resume visually impressive. Many of the ideas are for making your resume pleasing to the eye, but a number of the ideas are strategies to use for special cases. Other ideas are for eliminating common writing mistakes and stylistic weaknesses.

As you work on your resume, be sure to check out the writing advice in Part 3. You can apply many tips for writing cover letters to the writing of your resume, especially its text portions.

Best Resume Writing Strategies

1. **Although many resume books say you should spell out the name of the state in your address at the top of your resume, consider using the state's postal abbreviation instead.** The reason is simple: It's an address. Anyone wanting to contact you by mail will probably refer to your name and address on the resume. If they appear there as they should on an envelope, the writer or typist can simply copy the information you supply. If you spell out the name of your state in full, the writer will have to "translate" the name of the state to its postal abbreviation. Not everyone knows all the postal abbreviations, and some abbreviations are easily confused. For example, those for Alabama (AL), Alaska (AK), American Samoa (AS), Arizona (AZ), and Arkansas (AR) are easy to mix up. You can prevent confusion and delay simply by using the correct postal abbreviation.

   If you decide to use postal abbreviations in addresses, make certain that you do not add a period after the abbreviations, even before ZIP codes. Be sure to use the postal abbreviations in the addresses of references if you provide them.

   Do not, however, use the state postal abbreviation when you are indicating only the city and state (not the mailing address) of a school you attended or a business where you worked. In these cases, it makes sense to write out the name of the state in full.

2. **Adopt a sensible form for phone numbers, and then use it consistently.** Do this in your resume and in all the documents you use in your job search. Some forms of phone numbers make more sense than others. Compare the following:

123-4567	This form is best for a resume circulated locally, within a region where all the phone numbers have the same area code.
(222) 123-4567	This form is best for a resume circulated in areas with different area codes.
222-123-4567	This form suggests that the area code should be dialed in all cases. But that isn't necessary for prospective employers whose area code is 222. Avoid this form.
222/123-4567	This form is illogical and also should be avoided. The slash can mean "or" in an alternate option such as ON/OFF (ON or OFF). In a phone number, this meaning of a slash as "or" makes no sense.
1 (222) 123-4567	This form is long, and the first 1 is unnecessary. Almost everyone will know that 1 should be used before the area code to dial a long-distance number on a land line.
222.123.4567	This form, which resembles a Web address, is becoming more popular, particularly with people in computer and design fields.

   Note: For resumes directed to prospective employers *outside* the United States, be sure to include the correct international prefixes in all phone numbers so that you and your references can be reached easily by phone.

3. **If you include a Goal or an Objective statement, indicate what you hope to do for the company, rather than what the company can do for you.** See Resume 163. Resume 45 begins with a bulleted list showing what the applicant can do for the company.

4. **Near the top of the first page, consider including a focused Profile section.** If your Profile fails to grab the reader's attention, he or she might discard your resume without reading further. A Profile can be your first opportunity to sell yourself. For examples of Profiles, see Resumes 5, 44, 54, 83, 85, 113, 168, and 183. Resumes 74, 165, and 173, along with many others, include a profile without a heading for it.

5. **In the Experience section, state achievements or accomplishments, not just duties or responsibilities.** The reader often already knows the duties and responsibilities for a given position. Achievements, however, can be interesting. See, for example, Resumes 142 and 172. Resume 175 presents achievements as Benchmarks and Milestones.

6. **Consider quantifying your achievements (using dollar amounts, percentages, and so on) to make their value more visible.** See, for example, Resumes 16, 37, 38, 55, 91, 110, 152, 155, 156, 158, 161, 171, 173, and 177. Resumes 133 and 174 use charts to quantify achievements.

7. **When skills and abilities are varied, group them according to categories for easier comprehension.** See, for example, Resumes 56, 96, 106, and 181.

8. **Create a prominent Expertise section that draws together skills and abilities you have gained in previous or current work experience.** See, for example, Resumes 22, 63, 85, 89, 104, 123, and 149.

9. **Consider including a Highlights section to draw attention to special accomplishments or achievements.** See, for example, Resumes 64, 121, and 161.

10. **If you have a noticeable gap in your employment, consider omitting dates and indicating instead the number of years in each position.** See Resume 183.

11. **Summarize your qualifications and work experiences to avoid having to repeat yourself in the job descriptions.** See, for example, Resumes 2, 22, 134, 137, and 139.

12. **Instead of just listing your achievements, present them as challenges or problems solved, indicating what you did when something went wrong or needed fixing.** See, for example, Resumes 138 and 159. Resume 124 presents achievements as Results, and Resumes 45 and 135 indicate Payoffs. Resume 78 presents Outcomes.

Best Resume Design and Layout Tips

13. **Use quality paper correctly.** If you use quality watermarked paper for your resume, be sure to use the right side of the paper. To know which side is the right side, hold a blank sheet of paper up to a light source. If you can see a watermark and read it, the right side of the paper is facing you. This is the surface for typing or printing. If the watermark is unreadable or if any characters

look backward, you are looking at the "underside" of the paper—the side that should be left blank if you use only one side of the sheet.

14. **Use adequate white space.** A sheet of paper with no words on it is impossible to read. Likewise, a sheet of paper with words all over it is impossible to read. The goal is to have a comfortable mix of white space and words. If your resume has too many words and not enough white space, it looks cluttered and unfriendly. If it has too much white space and too few words, it looks skimpy and unimportant. Make certain that adequate white space exists between the main sections. For examples that display good use of white space, see Resumes 20, 30, 54, 71, 83, 85, 176, 184, 187, 194, and many others.

15. **Make the margins uniform in width and preferably no less than an inch.** Margins are part of a resume's white space. If the margins shrink below an inch, the page begins to have a "too much to read" look. An enemy of margins is the one-page rule. If you try to fit more than one page of information on a page, the first temptation is to shrink the margins to make room for the extra material. It is better to shrink the material by paring it down than to reduce the size of the left, right, top, and bottom margins. Decreasing the type's point size is another way to save the margins. Try reducing the point size of text in your resume to 10 points. Then see how your information looks with the font(s) you are using. Different fonts produce different results. In your effort to save the margins, be certain that you don't make the type too small to be readable.

16. **Be consistent in your use of line spacing.** How you handle line spacing can tell the reader how good you are at details and how consistent you are in your use of them. If, near the beginning of your resume, you insert two line spaces (two hard returns in a word processing program) between two main sections, be sure to put two line spaces between the main sections throughout your resume.

17. **Be consistent in your use of character spacing.** If you usually put two spaces after a period at the end of a sentence, make certain that you use two spaces consistently. The same is true for colons. If you put two spaces after colons, do so consistently.

    Note that an em dash—a dash the width of the letter *m*—does not require spaces before or after it. Similarly, an en dash—a dash the width of the letter *n*—should not have a space before and after it. An en dash is commonly used between a range of numbers, such as 2002–2004. If you use "to" instead of an en dash in a range of numbers, be sure to use "to" consistently in other ranges.

    No space should go between the *P* and *O* of P.O. Box. Only one space is needed between a state's postal abbreviation and the ZIP code. You should insert a space between the first and second initials of a person's name, as in I. M. Jobseeker (not I.M. Jobseeker). These conventions have become widely adopted in English and business communications. If, however, you use other conventions, be sure to be consistent. In resumes, as in grammar, consistency is more important than conformity.

18. **Make certain that characters, lines, and images contrast well with the paper.** The printed quality depends on the device used to print your resume. If you use an inkjet or laser printer, check that the characters are sharp and clean, without smudges or traces of extra toner.

19. **Use vertical alignment in tabbed or indented text.** Misalignment can ruin the appearance of a well-written resume. Try to set tabs or indents consistently throughout the text instead of having a mix of tab stops or indents in different sections.

20. **Try left- or right-aligning dates.** This technique is especially useful in chronological resumes and combination resumes. For examples of left-aligned dates, see Resumes 32 and 140. For right-aligned dates, look at Resumes 3 and 71.

21. **Use as many pages as you need to portray your qualifications adequately to a specific interviewer for a particular job.** Try to limit your resume to one page, but set the upper limit at four pages. No rule about the number of pages makes sense in all cases. The determining factors are your qualifications and experiences, the requirements of the job, and the interviewer's interests and pet peeves. If you know that an interviewer refuses to look at a resume longer than a page, that says it all: You need to deliver a one-page resume if you want to get past the first gate. For examples of two-page resumes, see Resumes 9, 75, 94, 108, 110, 156, and 189. For three-page resumes, look at Resumes 62, 66, 100, and 120.

22. **Make each page a full page.** More important than the number of pages is whether each page you have is a full page. A partial page suggests deficiency, as if the reason for it is simply that information on page 1 has spilled over onto page 2. In that situation, try to compress all your information onto the first page. If you have a resume that is almost two pages, make it two full pages.

23. **When you have letters of recommendation, use quotations from them as testimonials in your resume.** Devoting a whole column to the positive opinions of "external authorities" helps make a resume convincing as well as impressive. See, for example, Resumes 23, 47, 75, 80, 90, 94, and 167. See also Resume 79 for a single testimonial.

24. **Unless you enlist the services of a professional printer or skilled desktop publisher, resist the temptation to use full justification for text (to make each line go all the way to the right margin).** The price you pay for a straight right margin is uneven word spacing. Words may appear too close together on some lines and too spread out on others. Although the resume might look like typeset text, you lose readability. See also Tip 4 in the section "Using Good Strategies for Letters" in Part 3.

25. **If you can choose a typeface for your resume, use a serif font for greater readability.** *Serif* fonts have little lines extending from the tops, bottoms, and ends of the characters. These fonts tend to be easier to read than *sans serif* (without serif) fonts, especially in low-light conditions. Compare the following font examples:

Serif	**Sans Serif**
Century Schoolbook	Gill Sans
Courier	Futura
Times New Roman	Helvetica

Words such as *skills* and *abilities,* which have several consecutive thin letters, are more readable in a serif font than in a sans serif font.

26. **If possible, avoid using monospaced fonts, such as Courier.** A font is monospaced if each character takes up the same amount of space. For example, in a monospaced font, the letter *i* is as wide as the letter *m*. Therefore, in Courier type, iiii is as wide as mmmmm. Courier was a standard of business communications during the 1960s and 1970s because it was the font supplied with IBM Selectric typewriters. Because of its widespread use, it is now considered "common." It also takes up a lot of space, so you can't pack as much information on a page with Courier type as you can with a proportionally spaced type such as Times New Roman.

27. **Think twice before using all uppercase letters in parts of your resume.** A common misconception is that uppercase letters are easier to read than lowercase letters. Actually, the ascenders and descenders of lowercase letters make them more distinguishable from each other and therefore more recognizable than uppercase letters. For a test, look at a string of uppercase letters and throw them gradually out of focus by squinting. Uppercase letters become a blur sooner than lowercase letters do.

28. **Think twice about underlining some words in your resume.** Underlining defeats the purpose of serifs at the bottom of characters by blending with the serifs. In trying to emphasize words, you lose some visual clarity. This is especially true if you use underlining with uppercase letters in centered or side headings.

29. **Use italic carefully.** Whenever possible, use italic instead of underlining when you need to call attention to a word or phrase. You might consider using italic for duties or achievements, as in Resumes 5 and 36. Resumes 93 and 95 use italic to describe the companies where the applicant worked. Think twice about using italic often, however, because italic characters are less readable than normal characters.

30. **To make your resume stand out, consider using unconventional display type for headings.** See, for example, Resumes 49, 50, and 58.

31. **If you have access to many fonts through word processing or desktop publishing, beware of becoming "font happy" and turning your resume into a font circus.** Frequent font changes *can* distract the **reader**, AND SO CAN GAUDY DISPLAY TYPE.

32. **Be aware of the value differences of black type.** Some typefaces are light; others are dark. Notice the following lines:

    A quick brown fox jumps over the lazy dog.

    A quick brown fox jumps over the lazy dog.

    Most typefaces fall somewhere between these two. With the variables of height, width, thickness, serifs, angles, curves, spacing, ink color, ink density, and boldfacing, you can see that type offers an infinite range of values from light to dark. Try to make your resume more visually interesting by offering stronger contrasts between light and dark type. See, for example, Resumes 49, 50, 58, 73, 155, and 171.

33. **Use boldfacing to make different job experiences more evident.** See, for example, Resumes 4, 59, 71, 74, 110, and many others.

34. **If you use word processing or desktop publishing and you have a suitable printer, use special characters to enhance the look of your resume.** For example, use curly quotation marks (" ") instead of their straight, "typewriter" equivalents (" "). For a dash, use an em dash (—). Don't use two hyphens (--) or a hyphen with a space on either side (-). To separate dates, try using an en dash (a dash the width of the letter *n:* –) instead of a hyphen, as in 2001–2008.

35. **To call attention to an item in a list, use a bullet (•) or a box (❏) instead of a hyphen (-).** Browse through the Gallery and notice how bullets are used effectively as attention getters.

36. **For variety, try using bullets of a different style, such as diamond (◆) bullets, rather than the usual round or square bullets.** Examples with diamonds are Resumes 2, 39, and 182. For other kinds of bullets, see Resumes 9, 16, 20, 25, 27, 36, 45, 47, 48, 56, 58, 72, 87, 95, and 161.

37. **Make a bullet a little smaller than the lowercase letters that appear after it.** Disregard any ascenders or descenders on the letters. Compare the following bullet sizes:

    · Too small   ● Too large   • Better   • Just right

38. **When you use bullets, make certain that the bulleted items go beyond the superficial and contain information that employers really want to know.** Many short bulleted statements that say nothing special can affect the reader negatively. Brevity is not always the best strategy with bullets. For examples of substantial bulleted items, see Resumes 96 and 100.

39. **When the amount of information justifies a longer resume, repeat a particular graphic to unify the entire resume.** Resume 50, for example, displays a series of small black boxes, each containing a large letter. Resume 98 uses arrow tips repeatedly. See also Resume 146.

40. **If possible, visually coordinate the resume and its companion cover letter with the same font treatment or graphic to catch the reader's attention.** See, for example, Resumes 63, 102, and 123 and Cover Letters 2, 7, and 8, respectively.

41. **Try to make graphics match your field.** See, for example, Resumes 11, 44, 48, 72, 74, 80, 82, 84, 90, 95, 150, 180, and 185. Resume 37 includes company logos. Some of the information presented in Resume 82 is in the shape of a cake!

42. **Use a horizontal line or lines to separate your name or contact information from the rest of the resume.** If you browse through the Gallery, you can see many resumes that use horizontal lines this way. See, for example, Resumes 13, 20, 26, 75, and 182. Resume 67 contains snazzy, ornate lines in color as separators.

43. **Use horizontal lines to separate the different sections of the resume.** See, for example, Resumes 43, 61, and 67. See also Resumes 4, 8, 37, 57, 80, 114, and 162, whose lines are interrupted by the section headings.

44. **To call attention to a resume section or certain information, use horizontal lines or even a box to enclose it.** See, for example, Resumes 19, 33, 62, 65, 66, 77, 93, 99, and 148. See also Resumes 109 and 153, in which two or more sections are enclosed by horizontal lines.

45. **Use short horizontal lines to call attention to headings,** as in Resumes 64 and 106.

46. **Enclose your resume within a page border for visual interest.** See, for example, Resumes 9, 47, 52, 63, 107, 123, 157, 170, 173, and 195. Place a box around information you want to stand out, as shown in Resumes 27, 28, 107, 122, and 193.

47. **Use a vertical line or lines to spice up your resume.** See, for example, Resumes 1, 23, 44, 49, and 68. See also Resumes 44, 53, and 86, in which both vertical and horizontal lines are used.

48. **Use shaded boxes (with or without borders) to make a page visually more interesting.** See, for example, Resumes 37, 53, 94, 99, 163, 166, 167, and 169. Compare these boxes with the shadow boxes in Resumes 49, 85, and 125. Note the shaded bars used for headings in Resumes 10, 27, 131, and 154. See also the vertical black bars for headings in Resume 42, and look at the vertical black bar for displaying contact information in Resume 108.

Best Resume Writing Style Tips

49. **Avoid using the archaic word "upon" in the References section.** The common statement "References available upon request" needs to be simplified, updated, or even deleted in resume writing. The word "upon" is one of the finest words of the 13th century, but it's a stuffy word in the 21st century. Usually, "on" will do in place of "upon." Other possibilities are "References available by request" and "References available." Because most readers of resumes know that applicants can usually provide several reference letters, this statement is probably unnecessary. A reader who is seriously interested in you will ask about reference letters.

50. **Check that words or phrases in lists are parallel.** For example, notice the bulleted items in the Career Highlights section of Resume 60 and in the Highlights sections of Resume 134. All the verbs are in the past tense.

51. **Use capital letters correctly.** Resumes usually contain many of the following:

   ▨ Names of people, companies, organizations, government agencies, awards, and prizes

   ▨ Titles of job positions and publications

   ▨ References to academic fields (such as chemistry, English, and mathematics)

   ▨ Geographic regions (such as the Midwest, the East, the state of California, and Oregon State)

   Because of such words, resumes are minefields for the misuse of uppercase letters. When you don't know whether a word should have an initial capital letter, don't guess. Consult a dictionary, a handbook on style, or some other authoritative source, such as a reputable Web site. Often a reference librarian can provide the information you need. If so, you are only a phone call away from an accurate answer.

Use headline style in headings with upper- and lowercase letters. In other words, capitalize the first letter of the first word, the last word, and each main word in the heading, but not articles (*a, an,* and *the*), conjunctions (*and, but, or, nor, for, yet,* and *so*), and short prepositions (such as *at, by, in,* and *on*) within the heading. Capitalize prepositions of five or more letters.

To create a heading with small caps, first create a heading with upper- and lowercase letters. Then select the heading and assign small caps to it through the Format, Font, Small caps command. The original uppercase letters will be taller than the original lowercase letters, which will now appear as small capital letters.

52. **Check that you have used capital letters and hyphens correctly in computer terms.** If you want to show in a Computer Experience section that you have used certain hardware and software, you may give the opposite impression if you don't use uppercase letters and hyphens correctly. Note the correct use of capitals and hyphens in the following names of hardware, software, and computer companies:

AutoCAD	Microsoft Word	Photoshop
dBASE	MS-DOS	PostScript
Hewlett-Packard	NetWare	QuarkXPress
LaserJet III	PageMaker	Windows
Microsoft	PC DOS	WordPerfect

The reason that many computer product names have an internal uppercase letter is for the sake of a trademark. A word with unusual spelling or capitalization can be trademarked. When you use the correct forms of these words, you are honoring trademarks and registered trademarks and showing that you are in the know.

53. **Use all uppercase letters for most acronyms.** An *acronym* is a pronounceable word usually formed from the initial letters of the words in a compound term, or sometimes from multiple letters in those words. Note the following examples:

BASIC	Beginner's All-purpose Symbolic Instruction Code
COBOL	COmmon Business-Oriented Language
DOS	Disk Operating System
FORTRAN	FORmula TRANslator

An acronym such as *radar* (*ra*dio *d*etecting *a*nd *r*anging) has become so common that it is no longer all uppercase.

54. **Be aware of the difference between an acronym and an abbreviation.** Remember, an acronym is a combination of letters making a word that you can pronounce as a word. An abbreviation, however, may consist of uppercase letters (without periods) that you can pronounce only as letters and never as a word. Examples are CBS, NFL, YWCA, and AFL-CIO.

55. **Be sure to spell every word correctly.** A resume with just one misspelling is not impressive and may undermine all the hours you spent putting it together. Worse than that, one misspelling may be what the reader is looking for to screen you out, particularly if you are applying for a position that requires accuracy with words.

Your computer's spelling checker will catch many misspellings. It will not, however, detect when you have inadvertently used a wrong word (*to* for *too*, for example). Also be wary of letting someone else check your resume. If the other person is not a good speller, you may not get any real help. The best authority is a good dictionary.

56. **For words that have more than one correct spelling, use the preferred form.** This form is the one that appears first in a dictionary. For example, if you see the entry **trav·el·ing** *or* **trav·el·ling,** the first form (with one *l*) is the preferred spelling. If you make it a practice to use the preferred spelling, you will build consistency in your resumes and cover letters.

57. **Avoid British spellings.** These slip into American usage through books and online articles published in Great Britain. Note the following words:

British Spelling	American Spelling
acknowledgement	acknowledgment
centre	center
judgement	judgment
towards	toward

58. **Avoid hyphenating words with such prefixes as** *co-, micro-, mid-, mini-, multi-, non-, pre-, re-,* **and** *sub-.* Many people think that words with these prefixes should have a hyphen after the prefix, but most of these words should not. The following words are spelled correctly:

coauthor	midway	nonfunctional
coworker	minicomputer	prearrange
cowriter	multicultural	prequalify
microcomputer	multilevel	reenter
midpoint	nondisclosure	subdirectory

Note: If you look in the dictionary for a word with a prefix and you can't find the word, look for just the prefix. You might find a small-print listing of a number of words that begin with that prefix.

59. **Be aware that compounds (combinations of words) present special problems for hyphenation.** Writers' handbooks and books on style do not always agree on how compounds should be hyphenated. Many compounds are evolving from *open* compounds (two different words) to *hyphenated* compounds (two words joined by a hyphen) to *closed* compounds (one word). In different dictionaries, you can therefore find the words *copy editor, copy-editor,* and *copyeditor.* No wonder the issue is confusing! Most style books do agree, however, that when some compounds appear as an adjective before a noun, the compound should be hyphenated. When the same compound appears after a noun, hyphenation is unnecessary. Compare the following two sentences:

> I scheduled well-attended conferences.

> The conferences I scheduled were well attended.

For detailed information about hyphenation, see a recent edition of *The Chicago Manual of Style* (the 15th Edition is the latest). You should be able to find a copy at your local library.

60. **Hyphenate so-called *permanent* hyphenated compounds.** Usually, you can find these by looking them up in the dictionary. You can spot them easily because they have a long hyphen (–) for visibility in the dictionary. Hyphenate these words (with a standard hyphen) wherever they appear, before or after a noun. Here are some examples:

all-important	self-employed
day-to-day	step-by-step
full-blown	time-consuming

Note that *The Chicago Manual of Style,* 15th Edition, recommends that permanent hyphenated compounds should no longer be considered permanent but may be used without a hyphen (or hyphens) when they appear after a noun or are used adverbially. (See Tip 58.)

2 P·A·R·T

The Gallery
of Professional Resumes

The Gallery at a Glance

How to Use the Gallery

You can learn much from the Gallery just by browsing through it. To make the best use of this resource, however, read the following suggestions before you begin.

Look at the resumes in the category containing your field, related fields, or your target occupation. Notice what kinds of resumes other people have used to find similar jobs. Always remember, though, that your resume should not be "canned." It should not look just like someone else's resume but should reflect your own background, unique experiences, and goals.

Use the Gallery primarily as an "idea book." Even if you don't find a resume for your specific occupation or job, be sure to look at all the resumes for ideas you can borrow or adapt. You may be able to modify some of the sections or statements with information that applies to your own situation or job target.

Study the ways in which professional resume writers have formatted the applicants' names, addresses, and phone numbers. In most instances, this information appears at the top of the resume's first page. Look at typestyles, size of type, and use of boldface or italic. See whether the personal information is centered on lines, spread across a line, or located near the margin on one side of a page. Look for the use of horizontal lines to separate this information from the rest of the resume, to separate the address and phone number from the person's name, or to enclose information for greater visibility.

Look at each resume to see what section appears first after the personal information. Then compare those same sections across the Gallery. For example, look just at the resumes that have a Profile as the first section. Compare the Profiles for length, clarity, and use of words. Do the Profiles contain complete sentences or just one or more partial lines of thought? Are some Profiles better than others in your opinion? Do you see one or more Profiles that come close to matching a Profile for you? After you have compared Profiles, try writing *in your own words* a Profile for yourself.

Repeat this "horizontal comparison" for each of the sections across the Gallery. Compare all the Education sections, all the Qualifications sections, and so on. As you make these comparisons, continue to note differences in length, the kinds of words and phrases used, and the effectiveness of the content. Jot down any ideas that might be useful for your own resume.

As you compare sections across the Gallery, pay special attention to the Profile, Summary, Areas of Expertise, Career Highlights, Qualifications, or Experience sections. (Most resumes don't have all of these sections.) Notice how skills and accomplishments are worked into these sections. Skills and accomplishments are *variables* you can select to put a certain "spin" on your resume as you pitch it to a particular interviewer or job. Your observations here should be especially valuable for your own resume versions.

After you have examined the resumes "horizontally" (section by section), compare them "vertically" (design by design). To do this, you need to determine which resumes have the same sections in the same order, and then compare just those resumes. For example, look for resumes that have personal information at the top, a Profile, an Experience section, and an Education section. (Notice that the section heads may differ slightly. Instead of the word *Experience,* you might find *Work Experience, Employment,* or *Career Highlights.*) When you examine the resumes in this way, you are looking at their *structural design,* which means the order in which the various sections appear. The same order can appear in resumes of different fields or jobs, so it is important to explore the whole Gallery and not limit your investigation to resumes in your field or related fields.

Developing a sense of resume structure is extremely important because it enables you to emphasize the most important information about yourself. A resume is a little like a newspaper article—read quickly and usually discarded before the reader finishes. That is why the information in newspaper articles often dwindles in significance toward the end. For the same reason, the most important, attention-getting information about you should be at or near the top of your resume. What follows should appear in order of descending significance.

If you know that the reader will be more interested in your work experience than your education because you don't have a four-year degree, put your Experience section before your Education. If you know that the reader will be interested in your skills regardless of your education and work experience, put your Skills section at or near the beginning of your resume. In this way, you can help ensure that anyone who reads only *part* of your resume will read the "best" about you. Your hope is that this information will encourage the reader to read on to the end of the resume and, above all, take an interest in you.

Compare the resumes according to visual design features, such as the use of horizontal and vertical lines, borders, boxes, bullets, white space, graphics, and inverse type (light characters on a dark background). Use the Features Index for help here and pay attention to the comments at the bottom of each resume page. Notice which resumes have more visual impact at first glance and which ones make no initial impression. Do some of the resumes seem more inviting to read than others? Which ones are less appealing because they have too much information, or too little? Which ones seem to have the right balance of information and white space?

After comparing the visual design features, choose the design ideas that might improve your own resume. You will want to be selective here and not try to work every design possibility into your resume. As in writing, "less is more" in resume making, especially when you integrate design features with content.

Accounting

Resumes at a Glance

C. NICHOLAS DONATO, MCP, A+

8899 FORTIN ROAD
NAPLES, FLORIDA 34134

donatoc@earthlink.net

(239) 777-9999

OBJECTIVE	Position offering growth opportunity in a computer-networking environment.
SUMMARY	▶ Broad knowledge of current computer industry, including networking.
	▶ Experienced retail store manager of national footwear chain.
	▶ Highly motivated and resourceful; formal and self-taught in developing professional business acumen and technical skills.
	▶ Proven abilities in sales, merchandising, and customer service in computer industry and retail business.
EXPERIENCE	**Accounting Offices of Fritsch, Botts, Leonard, CPAs,** Naples, FL
	Accounting Clerk/Technology Specialist, 2001–present
	• Prepare worksheets, taxes, accounts payable and receivable.
	• Set up and care for computer hardware and other office equipment.
	• Install and effectively maintain general business and accounting software.
	Cordell Business Technologies, Fort Myers, FL
	Executive Teleservices Account Analyst, 2000–2001
	• Called commercial entities for copier and network integration divisions.
	• Generated leads, set appointments after discovering needs and interests.
	• Made customer calls, servicing existing accounts in database.
	• Successfully prospected for new accounts and their development.
	CompUSA, Cape Coral, FL
	Account Executive, 1998–2000
	• Sold computer merchandise from busy nationally recognized retail outlet.
	• Managed account deck of 50 private and government clients.
	• Actively participated in lucrative state and local client bidding.
	• Earned Top Seller of the Month award six times; highest commissions 1999.
	Thom Mcan Shoes, Inc., Raleigh, NC
	Manager and Assistant Manager, 1994–1998
	• Managed until corporate downsizing called for store closing.
	• Hired and trained sales staff in proper company merchandising techniques.
EDUCATION	**Southwest Florida Community College,** Fort Myers, FL
	A.S. Degree in Business Administration, Accounting, May 2000
	Accounting certificate, July 2001
	Stephens University, Raleigh, NC
	Microsoft Certified Professional, 1999
	CompTIA's A+ Certified, 1998
	Sanders-Michaelson College, Raleigh, NC
	Attended two semesters, 1992–1993

1

Edward Turilli, North Kingstown, Rhode Island

Boxes enclose the contact information, the section headings, and the body of information. Bullets point to Summary items and to duties and achievements in the Experience section.

KATRINA LARSON

7889 Forest Avenue • Huntington Beach, CA 55555 • (555) 555-5555

OBJECTIVE: Payroll Clerk

SUMMARY OF QUALIFICATIONS

- Well-organized and detail-oriented with experience in payroll, office support, data entry and billing. Computer skills include MS Word and Excel and various proprietary software programs.

- Self-motivated employee who performs diligently to accomplish business goals. Ability to learn new skills quickly and effectively.

- Adept in customer relations with the ability to handle and resolve issues. Team-oriented; thrive in fast-paced environments. Record of dependability.

EXPERIENCE

Payroll / Billing
- Maintaining up-to-date payroll data and records, including entering changes in exemptions, insurance coverage, savings deductions, job title and department transfers.
- Compiling summaries of earnings, taxes, deductions, leave, disability and nontaxable wages for report preparation.
- Calculating employee federal and state income and Social Security taxes and employer's Social Security, unemployment and workers' compensation payments.
- Researching and resolving payroll discrepancies in a timely manner.
- Maintaining accurate customer billing information and preparing invoices in an efficient, timely manner.

Reception / Customer Service
- Greeting visitors; answering busy multiline telephone systems; screening and transferring calls while handling general inquiries.
- Addressing customer concerns, researching and resolving problems to ensure service satisfaction; extensive interface with all levels of internal personnel.

Administrative Support
- Performing diverse administrative duties such as word processing correspondence, creating presentations and maintaining confidential files/records.
- Scheduling and coordinating meetings and appointments; ordering department supplies.

EMPLOYMENT HISTORY

SULLIVAN CORP., Huntington Beach, CA
Office/Billing Clerk (1996 to present)

JENSEN INC., Huntington Beach, CA
Payroll Clerk (1994 to 1996)

FINLANDIA INC., Huntington Beach, CA
Payroll Clerk (1992 to 1994)

WARNER PACKAGING, Huntington Beach, CA
Receptionist/Accounting Clerk (1989 to 1992)

EDUCATION

Fullerton Community College, Huntington Beach, CA
Accounting courses

Louise Garver, Windsor, Connecticut

Horizontal lines under the main section headings help separate the sections visually before you read any of their content. Thickening of the line under the person's name helps call attention to it.

Melissa Simon

99 Norman Road • Wellesley, MA 02481
781-555-1234 • msimon@xyz.com

Summary

Experienced and detail-oriented accounting professional, with a proven ability to perform a broad range of functions quickly and accurately in a fast-paced environment. Skilled at multitasking. Recognized for dedication, work ethic, and going the extra mile to get the job done. Excellent interpersonal skills. Expertise includes

- Accounts payable
- Bank statement reconciliations
- Expense reports
- Payroll

- Collections
- Bank deposits
- Spreadsheets
- Problem resolution

Selected Achievements

- Resolved price discrepancies and past-due balances with up to 700 vendors, including subcontractors.
- Oversaw accounts-payable functions for 10 divisions nationwide; set up and maintained new accounts for multiple divisions.
- Uncovered and reported fraudulent activities, enabling company to recover $10,000.
- Streamlined procedures to ensure timely production of all accounting reports.
- Managed twice-weekly check run of 400 checks per week and verified them manually for accuracy.

Experience

Accounts-Payable Clerk—First Data, Watertown, MA   1997–2004
Oversaw the day-to-day A/P operations for a 450-person company with 10 divisions throughout the U.S. Processed codes and supervised check runs and mailings. Input expense reports. Assisted auditors at year-end. Communicated with vendors to expedite processing of checks. Performed collection calls regarding outstanding accounts. Assisted with bank reconciliations.

Assistant to Controller—Boston Lighting Company, Brighton, MA   1991–1997
Supervised daily A/P functions for light fixture company. Detected fraudulent activities that enabled company to recover $10,000. Maintained daily cash and deposits. Performed daily audit from all payroll activity, credit cards, and accounts receivable. Issued invoices for accounts receivable. Monitored petty cash and bank deposits.

Accounting Clerk—Town of Westwood, Westwood, MA   1988–1991
Processed payments of property taxes and water/sewer bills.

Computer Skills

Deltek, Peachtree, proprietary accounting software, MS Word, MS Excel

3

Wendy Gelberg, Needham, Massachusetts

The Summary consists of a profile statement and a two-column list of areas of expertise. The Selected Achievements section contains five bulleted accomplishments—most of them quantified.

Jane Jobseeker

555 Street Address City, ST 00000	someone@resumeasap.com	Home: 000-000-0000 Cell: 555-555-5555

Targeting Positions In...

Bookkeeping / Accounts Payable / Accounts Receivable

Profile   Experienced business professional with a well-rounded skill set seeking to leverage strong background in office management, sales, customer service, and bookkeeping to obtain administrative support position. Strong computer literacy and a quick study of new technology. Proven multitasker known for attention to detail, organization, and impeccable service. Backed by solid credentials (A.S. degree in Accounting Technology).

Software Proficiency: Microsoft Office Suite, WordPerfect, Prime Time, 30% File, Wintegrate, Peachtree, HTML, and Proform Softpro.

Expertise
- Invoice Management
- Month-End Closings
- General Ledger
- Reconciliation
- Invoicing, Billing, and Collections

- Accounts Payable/Accounts Receivable
- Spreadsheets
- Expense Reports
- Financial Statements
- Payroll Processing

Experience   REAL ESTATE LEGAL FIRM—City, ST

Legal Assistant, 2007 to Present
- Prepared legal documents and collaborated with lenders, title companies, and attorneys. Assisted with real estate closings.
- Composed business letters and disbursement of funds and worked closely with clients, updating them on case status.
- Researched, reviewed, and examined legal documents involving real estate transactions and issued title policies.
- Frequently assisted office manager with payroll, accounts receivable, and general ledger responsibilities.

CONSTRUCTION COMPANY—City, ST

Office Manager, 2002 to 2007
- Oversaw company performance; directly responsible for increasing company profits by 54% in 2002, 33% in 2003, and 10% in 2004 by ensuring quality service, improved workflow, and customer satisfaction.
- Prepared company budget; verified, maintained, and reviewed payroll, accounts receivable, accounts payable, and time records.
- Supported field supervisors and managed, coached, and supervised more than 19 employees.
- Evaluated the economic trends in the area to determine the costs associated with investment, billing, and hiring.
- Managed all new and existing accounts' contract modification, mediation, and negotiation.

4

Jennifer Anthony, Woodland, Washington

This job seeker was a military spouse who moved frequently, had to take the first job she could find, and often had to settle for lower pay. She never held the actual title of accountant or book-keeper but did have an associate's degree and job experience. The writer found in every position

Jane Jobseeker

Experience Continued	MAJOR INSURANCE COMPANY—City, ST **Premium Control Administrator,** 1998 to 2002

- Processed more than $5M in annual premiums and maintained premium accounts receivable for the entire southeast region.
- Collaborated with clients and staff for all company premium correspondence.
- Prepared agency remittance reports, billing statements, and premium calculation worksheets, and generated statistical reports.
- Bookkeeping assistance; set up, maintained, and reviewed payroll, accounts receivable, benefits, and time and vacation records.
- Gained experience and trained staff in other departments such as reception, courier, data entry, typing, abstracting, scanning, and bookkeeping.
- Researched personal information; reviewed facts, data, and legal documents in preparations of title documents and policies.

Early Career History

INDUSTRIAL SERVICES RETAIL STORE—CITY, ST
Store Manager, 1996 to 1997

MAJOR RETAIL PHARMACY—CITY, ST
Data Entry / Cashier, 1995 to 1996

MAJOR RETAIL CHAIN—CITY, ST
Cashier, 1994

Education & Training

A.S. Degree, Accounting Technology—UNIVERSITY NAME, 2002
Bookkeeping and Accounting Diploma—UNIVERSITY NAME, 1998

Specialized Training:

Company Name—Certificate of Achievement, Sales Training Program, 2005
Institution Name—Certificate of Achievement, 1999
Company Name—Customer 1st Workshop (32 hours), 1999

Awards

Outstanding Leadership Award, Student Government—University Name, 2002
Leadership Award—Institution Name, 1994 and 1995

---

certain skills and responsibilities relevant to the job goal and highlighted these. To minimize dates, the writer made these less evident by placing them next to the job titles.

PENELOPE WIGGINS, EA

E-mail: pwiggins@gmail.com

Mobile: 262.334.0571

509 Ski Hill Rd #3 ◆ Grafton, WI 53024

PROFILE

➢ **Accounting and Finance Professional** with more than 25 years of experience managing a large client base and administering a successful accounting practice. Expertise includes client acquisition/retention, compilations, management services, income tax planning/preparation, and financial planning.

➢ Active licensure includes IRS Enrolled Agent; NASD Series 6, 63, 7; Wisconsin Life, Accident & Health Insurance; and Wisconsin Real Estate Broker. Extensive estate, trust, and gift taxation knowledge.

➢ Expert analysis, troubleshooting, and issue resolution skills. Technically proficient using various custom and packaged accounting systems; demonstrated ability to learn and adopt new software.

Core Competencies Include

- Monthly/Quarterly Financial Statement Preparation
- Cash Flow Analysis and Financial/Tax Planning
- A/P and A/R Reconciliations
- Individual and Corporate Federal/State Tax Returns
- Cash and Asset Reconciliation
- Property Tax/Real Property Reporting

- Sales and Use Tax Reporting
- Payroll Preparation and Reporting
- Month-End/Year-End Closing Procedures
- Workflow Planning, Process Development, and Prioritization
- Staff Training and Development

PROFESSIONAL EXPERIENCE

BLACKHAWK ENTERPRISES, INC.—Grafton, WI　　　　　　　　　　　　　　　**1982 to Present**
Accounting and tax preparation firm established in 1950.

Office Manager/Staff Accountant—1992 to Present
Hire, train, and direct a staff of 17 professionals and support personnel. Simultaneously manage a base of more than 350 small business/professional practice clients.

Key Functions and Responsibilities

- Advise on complex tax and financial planning inquiries. Review and approve more than 1,000 tax returns per season.
- Perform monthly/quarterly compilations including sales/use tax, property tax, corporate tax, and multistate returns. Reconcile accounts and prepare financial statements. Ensure compliance with GAAP and regulatory requirements.
- Develop business plans and loan package submittals, including SBA and WHEDA loans. Support business accounting processes to include various regulatory filings, implementation of software, development of procedures/controls, training of employees, and management advisory.
- Assist with business liquidations, buy-sell situations, and reorganizations. Interact with client's attorneys, bankers, investment brokers, and retirement plan administrators.

Selected Accomplishments

- Delivered bottom-line results through expert business administration skills including the implementation of successful electronic filing procedures and a paperless file management system. Local IRS E-file representative noted that the firm had the lowest rejection rate per transmission and wished to study the firm's procedures.
- Contributed to the steady growth of firm revenues—approximately 5% average annual increase in client billings—through effective business development and relationship management efforts.
- Developed a longstanding and loyal client base with approximately 75% of new business derived from satisfied client referrals.
- Gained extensive knowledge in estate, trust, and gift taxation, as well as tax-law research and compliance.

Continued

5

Michele J. Haffner, Glendale, Wisconsin

The lack of a four-year degree did not keep this individual from accumulating a wealth of experience over a 25-year career in accounting and finance. Notice how the writer displays this experience over two full pages. Right arrow-tip bullets call attention to information in the Profile, and

PENELOPE WIGGINS, EA

Resume, Page 2 of 2

E-mail: pwiggins@gmail.com

Mobile: 262.334.0571

BLACKHAWK ENTERPRISES, INC. (Continued)

Support Staff Member/Income Tax Preparer—1982 to 1992
Rotated through a series of increasingly responsible positions to achieve experience in all core functions of the firm. Functioned in a **Customer Service** capacity providing reception and clerical support; progressed into a **Marketing** role and developed/executed the firm's marketing/advertising plan. Managed **Accounts Receivable and Accounts Payable** functions to include client invoicing, budgeting, and vendor contract negotiations; simultaneously directed **Human Resources** functions to include payroll and compliance. Simultaneously performed income tax preparation duties to include, interviewing clients, gathering information, and compiling basic, individual tax returns—400 per year.

COLDWELL BANKER REALTY, INC.—Grafton, WI

1983 to Present

Full-service real estate brokerage firm.
Real Estate Broker
Function as a part-time independent contractor obtaining commercial and residential listings, as well as assisting buyers with purchases. Assist with the completion and processing of real estate contracts including the handling of earnest funds. Procure closing documents and facilitate the closing process.

LICENSURE

IRS Enrolled Agent

1986 to Present

- ◆ Completed 12-hour examination measuring knowledge of individual, partnership, corporate, estate, gift, and trust taxation.

NASD Series 6, 63, 7

Current

- ◆ Registered Representative for First Montauk Securities Corporation.
- ◆ Obtained Series 7 license in 2006.

Wisconsin Insurance Resident Intermediary for Accident & Health, Life, Property & Casualty

Current

Wisconsin Real Estate Broker, Member of the National Realtors Association

Current

Wisconsin Notary Public

Current

EDUCATION AND PROFESSIONAL DEVELOPMENT

MARQUETTE UNIVERSITY—Adult Education and Budgeting Course Work
UNIVERSITY OF WISCONSIN—Accounting 1, Accounting 2, and Managerial Accounting

Completed 60 hours per year (average) in Continuing Education

- ◆ *Tax Insight Workshop—Annual Individual Tax Seminars*
- ◆ *National Association of Tax Practitioners—Annual Tax Seminars*
- ◆ *PESI—Professional Education Seminars*
- ◆ *National Business Institute—Management Training Seminars*
- ◆ *Wisconsin Association of Accountants—Annual Tax Seminars*
- ◆ *National Association of Securities Dealers—Firm Compliance and Firm Element Educational Requirements*
- ◆ *Wisconsin Realtors Association—Continuing Education Requirements*
- ◆ *Wisconsin Insurance Association—Sponsored Continuing Education Requirements*

RECENT COMMUNITY LEADERSHIP AND VOLUNTEER SERVICE

OZAUKEE COUNTY VOLUNTEER CENTER
United Way agency linking volunteers with nonprofit organizations.
- ◆ *Board of Directors (2000 to 2006)—President and Treasurer.*
- ◆ *Compiled 15 years of Endowment Fund activity and implemented procedures for proper reporting.*
GRAFTON ADVANCEMENT ASSOCIATION
Community group sponsoring fundraising efforts to donate money for community projects/needs.
- ◆ *Board of Directors (2000 to Present)—Secretary and Treasurer.*

diamond bullets unify the two pages visually. Boldfacing directs attention to side headings, subheadings, and embedded information. Italic highlights Continuing Education on page 2.

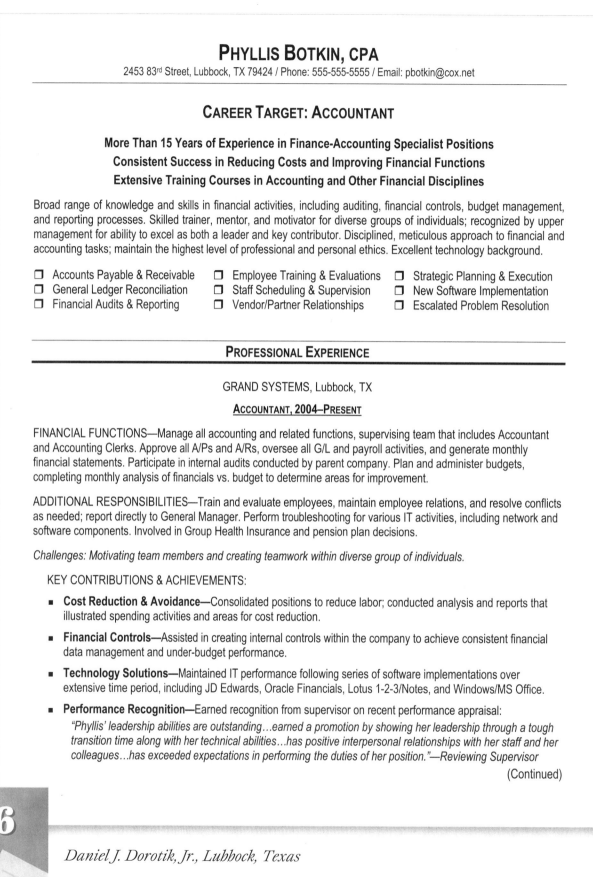

PHYLLIS BOTKIN, CPA

2453 83rd Street, Lubbock, TX 79424 / Phone: 555-555-5555 / Email: pbotkin@cox.net

CAREER TARGET: ACCOUNTANT

More Than 15 Years of Experience in Finance-Accounting Specialist Positions
Consistent Success in Reducing Costs and Improving Financial Functions
Extensive Training Courses in Accounting and Other Financial Disciplines

Broad range of knowledge and skills in financial activities, including auditing, financial controls, budget management, and reporting processes. Skilled trainer, mentor, and motivator for diverse groups of individuals; recognized by upper management for ability to excel as both a leader and key contributor. Disciplined, meticulous approach to financial and accounting tasks; maintain the highest level of professional and personal ethics. Excellent technology background.

- ❏ Accounts Payable & Receivable
- ❏ General Ledger Reconciliation
- ❏ Financial Audits & Reporting
- ❏ Employee Training & Evaluations
- ❏ Staff Scheduling & Supervision
- ❏ Vendor/Partner Relationships
- ❏ Strategic Planning & Execution
- ❏ New Software Implementation
- ❏ Escalated Problem Resolution

PROFESSIONAL EXPERIENCE

GRAND SYSTEMS, Lubbock, TX

ACCOUNTANT, 2004–PRESENT

FINANCIAL FUNCTIONS—Manage all accounting and related functions, supervising team that includes Accountant and Accounting Clerks. Approve all A/Ps and A/Rs, oversee all G/L and payroll activities, and generate monthly financial statements. Participate in internal audits conducted by parent company. Plan and administer budgets, completing monthly analysis of financials vs. budget to determine areas for improvement.

ADDITIONAL RESPONSIBILITIES—Train and evaluate employees, maintain employee relations, and resolve conflicts as needed; report directly to General Manager. Perform troubleshooting for various IT activities, including network and software components. Involved in Group Health Insurance and pension plan decisions.

Challenges: Motivating team members and creating teamwork within diverse group of individuals.

KEY CONTRIBUTIONS & ACHIEVEMENTS:

- **Cost Reduction & Avoidance**—Consolidated positions to reduce labor; conducted analysis and reports that illustrated spending activities and areas for cost reduction.

- **Financial Controls**—Assisted in creating internal controls within the company to achieve consistent financial data management and under-budget performance.

- **Technology Solutions**—Maintained IT performance following series of software implementations over extensive time period, including JD Edwards, Oracle Financials, Lotus 1-2-3/Notes, and Windows/MS Office.

- **Performance Recognition**—Earned recognition from supervisor on recent performance appraisal:
  "Phyllis' leadership abilities are outstanding…earned a promotion by showing her leadership through a tough transition time along with her technical abilities…has positive interpersonal relationships with her staff and her colleagues…has exceeded expectations in performing the duties of her position."—Reviewing Supervisor

(Continued)

6

Daniel J. Dorotik, Jr., Lubbock, Texas

A well-designed resume containing a blend of white space and much information about someone who has worked since 1985. The opening section on the first page summarizes the applicant's experience, success, training, skills, worker traits, and areas of expertise marked by square,

ASSISTANT ACCOUNTANT, 1990–2004

Promoted to assist in accounting activities and functions in joint effort with Senior Accountant. Served as key point of contact for software/hardware-related issues.

Challenges: Motivating team members and addressing problems with high turnover.

KEY CONTRIBUTIONS & ACHIEVEMENTS:

- **Process Improvement**—Transferred manual process for gathering financial data to automated database entry, allowing for the production of multiple reports to improve data analysis and decision making.

- **Technology Implementation**—Managed several technology integrations and changes throughout 14-year period, including previously mentioned Microsoft, Lotus, and JD Edwards implementations. Improved operations' capability for managing activities, resources, and information through IT contributions.

- **Additional Responsibility**—Acted as Senior Accountant during his year-long absence, meeting corporate and regulatory requirements for completing all core accounting functions on time.

- **Auditing Process**—Participated in both internal and external audits; worked effectively with outside individuals in reviewing documentation, analyzing issues, and pinpointing few-to-zero discrepancies.

- **Problem Resolution**—Maintained excellent record of identifying and resolving problems across multiple areas, including computer operations, accounts payable, accounts receivable, and financial reporting.

GENERAL OFFICE ASSISTANT, 1985–1990

Challenges: Leading turnaround for under-performing department, addressing issues with unionized personnel.

KEY CONTRIBUTIONS & ACHIEVEMENTS:

- **Process & Information Management**—Automated several accounting functions to improve accuracy, efficiency, and productivity. Created sales reports and revenue/expense analyses to support management's efforts in meeting business and operational development goals.

- **Operations Turnaround**—Created a more efficient office and decreased overtime needed for task completion. Implemented staffing decisions that eliminated problems and strengthened team performance.

- **Collections Optimization**—Worked aggressively with Collections in reducing accounts receivable.

PROFESSIONAL DEVELOPMENT

Certifications
Certified Public Accountant

Professional Training
100+ hours in Accounting, Finance, Auditing, Compliance, and Office Management disciplines

Computer Skills
Windows, MS Office, Lotus Notes & 1-2-3, JD Edwards, database programming, software installation/configuration

shadowed bullets. The corresponding spot on the second page draws attention to key contributions and achievements. Note the diverse treatment of fonts throughout the resume.

CATHERINE HARRISON

CatHarrison@email.com

5555 Swanson Avenue • Granada Hills, California 55555
(818) 555-5555 • Mobile (919) 555-0000

FULL CHARGE BOOKKEEPER

Experienced in Full Range of General Bookkeeping and Accounting Procedures
AR/AP • GL • Balance Sheet • P&L • Journal Entries • Payroll / Payroll Taxes • Reconciliations

- A hardworking professional with a strong work ethic, excellent organizational abilities and attention to detail.
- Superior record of low absenteeism and punctuality.
- Experienced in both manual and computerized systems, including conversion from manual to automated system.
- Computer skills: MS Word, Excel; Intuit Quicken, QuickBooks; Peachtree

Notary Public

PROFESSIONAL EXPERIENCE

Full Charge Bookkeeper • 1996 to Present
A. B. CHAMBERS, INC., Sherman Oaks, CA
Initially hired as receptionist for full-service insurance agency servicing broad range of commercial clients. Achieved promotions to bookkeeping positions of increasing responsibility as company grew from 6 staff members to 16.

- Perform all bookkeeping and accounting functions, including accounts receivable, accounts payable, collections, general ledger, payroll, bank reconciliations, trial balance.
- Generate financial statements and other financial reports.
- Handle licensing documentation for customer service representatives, agents and 40 nonresident insurance licenses.
- Prepare all quarterly and year-end payroll tax reports.
- Administer group health insurance and pension plan.
- Audit customer and general ledger accounts to resolve disputes and identify exceptions.
- Maintain office and computer supplies inventories; purchase as required.

EDUCATION

LOS ANGELES VALLEY COLLEGE, Van Nuys, CA; 2002
A.A. Degree; Extensive Course Work in Accounting
Graduated with Honors; Completed Studies While Working Full-Time

—*Member, National Notary Association*—

Vivian VanLier, Los Angeles, California

This candidate earned an A.A. degree concurrently with full-time employment. Her record of progressive promotions from an entry-level position is indicated in italic after her job title.

Administrative Support

Resumes at a Glance

PATRICIA THOMAS

85 Barclay Road ~ East Brunswick, New Jersey 08816
Phone: 732.678.1691

RECEPTIONIST ~ OFFICE ADMINISTRATION

Well-organized and versed in many areas of production, sales, customer service, telephone communications and overnight shipping. Computer-literate with Internet experience. Possess excellent telephone and communications skills.

• Self-disciplined	• Motivated
• Problem solver/Troubleshooter	• Telephone techniques
• Excel under pressure	• Superb memory
• Professional	• Quick learner

HIGHLIGHTS

- Detail-oriented employee with pleasant speaking voice.
- Serve as a liaison to match customers with the right staff professional.
- Perform computer data processing in Word, daily office operations and filing.

PROFESSIONAL EXPERIENCE

AMERICAN BOUQUET COMPANY, *Edison, NJ*   1987–Present
Receptionist

- Answer telephone and greet visitors.
- Schedule conference room for various meetings.
- Type letters and perform general secretarial work.
- Assist with payroll.
- Make hotel and flight reservations, finding least-expensive plans through the Internet.
- Serve as liaison between sales and manufacturing.
- Proof all product orders to ensure accuracy.

HOWARD GRAPHICS, *New Brunswick, NJ*   1977–1987
Secretarial, proofreading, receptionist, quality control

~ Excellent References Upon Request ~

8

Beverly and Mitch Baskin, Marlboro, New Jersey

A page border, three strong horizontal lines, and relatively large font sizes are the dominant visual elements. Bulleted lists throughout make the resume a quick read. Keywords are near the bottom.

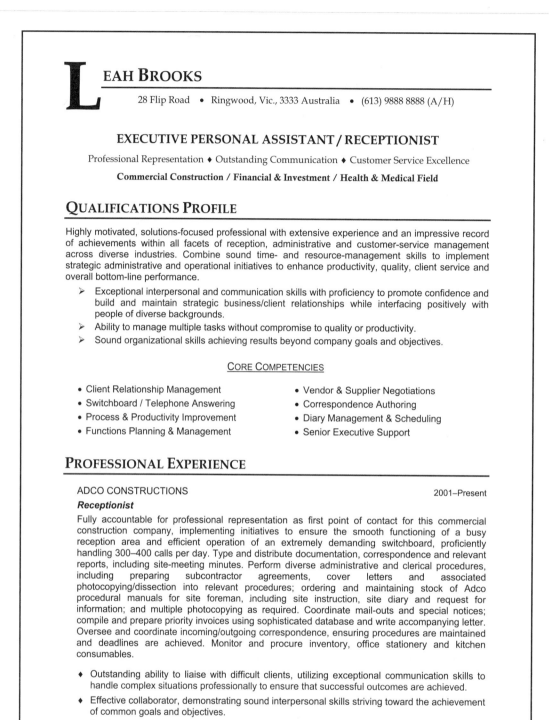

LEAH BROOKS

28 Flip Road • Ringwood, Vic., 3333 Australia • (613) 9888 8888 (A/H)

EXECUTIVE PERSONAL ASSISTANT / RECEPTIONIST

Professional Representation ♦ Outstanding Communication ♦ Customer Service Excellence

Commercial Construction / Financial & Investment / Health & Medical Field

QUALIFICATIONS PROFILE

Highly motivated, solutions-focused professional with extensive experience and an impressive record of achievements within all facets of reception, administrative and customer-service management across diverse industries. Combine sound time- and resource-management skills to implement strategic administrative and operational initiatives to enhance productivity, quality, client service and overall bottom-line performance.

- ➢ Exceptional interpersonal and communication skills with proficiency to promote confidence and build and maintain strategic business/client relationships while interfacing positively with people of diverse backgrounds.
- ➢ Ability to manage multiple tasks without compromise to quality or productivity.
- ➢ Sound organizational skills achieving results beyond company goals and objectives.

CORE COMPETENCIES

- Client Relationship Management
- Switchboard / Telephone Answering
- Process & Productivity Improvement
- Functions Planning & Management

- Vendor & Supplier Negotiations
- Correspondence Authoring
- Diary Management & Scheduling
- Senior Executive Support

PROFESSIONAL EXPERIENCE

ADCO CONSTRUCTIONS   2001–Present

Receptionist

Fully accountable for professional representation as first point of contact for this commercial construction company, implementing initiatives to ensure the smooth functioning of a busy reception area and efficient operation of an extremely demanding switchboard, proficiently handling 300–400 calls per day. Type and distribute documentation, correspondence and relevant reports, including site-meeting minutes. Perform diverse administrative and clerical procedures, including preparing subcontractor agreements, cover letters and associated photocopying/dissection into relevant procedures; ordering and maintaining stock of Adco procedural manuals for site foreman, including site instruction, site diary and request for information; and multiple photocopying as required. Coordinate mail-outs and special notices; compile and prepare priority invoices using sophisticated database and write accompanying letter. Oversee and coordinate incoming/outgoing correspondence, ensuring procedures are maintained and deadlines are achieved. Monitor and procure inventory, office stationery and kitchen consumables.

- ♦ Outstanding ability to liaise with difficult clients, utilizing exceptional communication skills to handle complex situations professionally to ensure that successful outcomes are achieved.
- ♦ Effective collaborator, demonstrating sound interpersonal skills striving toward the achievement of common goals and objectives.
- ♦ Track record in operating independently, prioritizing commitments to meet deadlines.

Continued…

Annemarie Cross, Hallum, Victoria, Australia

A drop cap in the individual's name is the first distinctive design element. Page borders and horizontal lines both in the contact information and under the section headings tie the two pages together visually. Bullets change within the Qualifications Profile but persist as diamonds

LEAH BROOKS

PERPETUAL   1995–2001

Receptionist / Telephonist

Distinguished track record within all facets of receptionist/telephonist procedures when interfacing with clients to meet/greet and respond to their needs; maintained Perpetual's overall corporate image through professionalism and outstanding customer service. Managed diaries and scheduled appointments for Financial Consultants; directed client introductions for Senior Consultants involving research and reporting of client's relevant data; and collaborated with Client Relationship Managers and Senior Financial Consultants. Supported Executive Personal Assistant with word processing, inbound/outbound mail, reconciliation of accounts, and preparation of invoices. Coordinated conference rooms and car bookings; maintained tearooms; monitored and procured supplies; and ensured reception area was well presented at all times.

- ◆ Spearheaded development and implementation of benchmarking customer liaison techniques, which secured ongoing accolades from senior executives and clients.
- ◆ Placated irate and concerned customers using diplomacy and tact, ensuring that clients' needs were addressed appropriately and professionally.
- ◆ Empowered relief staff through training, supervision and support in company procedures.
- ◆ Skillfully operated a 20-line Meridian 2000 switchboard, implementing outstanding communication skills/telephone techniques; requested to record corporate business message on answering machine and mobiles across the entire company.
- ◆ Coplanned and coordinated special corporate functions involving sourcing, qualifying and organizing caterers and facilitating the entire function to ensure successful completion.

HOSPITAL MANAGEMENT ASSOCIATION   1990–1994

Corporate / Customer Service Officer (1993–1994)

Steady promotion demonstrating expertise and professionalism through increasingly responsible positions, becoming fully accountable for the research, planning and implementation of innovative product marketing and promotional initiatives to a diverse corporate client base. Responded to technical inquiries; supported and advised companies providing Payroll Deduction Schemes to HMA clientele on a global level; provided onsite support to businesses; and assisted with general telephone inquiries.

- ◆ Enhanced corporate image of the company through continually representing HMA as a professional and committed organization, maintaining key alliances with a diverse client base of corporate customers.
- ◆ Provided strategic customer relationship management techniques to maintain client satisfaction, retention and ongoing business.

Front Desk Receptionist (1990–1993)

Maintained highest level of professionalism when greeting and assisting clients and guests; handled internal/external telephone inquiries; and coordinated internal/external deliveries. Prepared correspondence and reports using MS Word; maintained HMA's library, including distribution of daily papers, periodicals and associated literature.

EDUCATION & PROFESSIONAL DEVELOPMENT

PERPETUAL IN-HOUSE TRAINING
Professional Letter Construction / Concise Writing ◆ **First Impression**
Customer Service ◆ **Telephone Techniques** ◆ **Time Management**

Office & Secretarial Studies Certificate—BOX HILL COLLEGE OF TAFE

Word for Windows—POLLAK PARTNERS

TECHNOLOGIES

MS Word ◆ MS Excel ◆ MS Outlook

in the Professional Experience section as it extends from page 1 to page 2. The resume contains much paragraph text, but many blank lines provide white space and prevent a crowded appearance.

GRACE COLEMAN

76 COLUMBIA STREET
MOHAWK, NY 13407

gracecoleman@aol.com

H. (315) 866-2792
C. (315) 868-2272

EXPERIENCED OFFICE ADMINISTRATOR
Highly qualified, mature and dependable individual with significant experience in helping to guide daily business operations

Reliable support professional with an expert ability to multitask and a proven ability to play a key role in client services and general office operations. Consistently able to surpass production quotas through scheduling competence and a profit-driven focus. Accustomed to a fast-paced office environment that demands professionalism at every level.

Additional Highlights

- Effective in managing time, coordinating details and balancing competing demands. Proven ability to answer and screen calls, make travel arrangements, extract pertinent information and profitably schedule appointments.

- Experienced and competent in all standard office administrative functions as well as basic accounting procedures.

- Friendly and meticulous with excellent phone etiquette, a professional demeanor, a personable office presence and a demonstrated ability to convey complex/technical information in a clear and concise manner.

SPECIFIC AREAS OF EXPERIENCE

- Front Office Functions / Reception / Patient Relations
- Employee Orientation / Records Management
- Account Management / Billing / Collections
- Complex Scheduling / Travel Arrangements

- Report Compilation / Activity Analysis
- Technical Support / Marketing Activities
- Insurance Procedures / Banking Matters
- Information Gathering / Problem Resolution

EXPERIENCE

Alexandra Tamburro, DDS, *Frankfort, NY*   **1990 to Present**
(Busy dental specialty practice with six full-time employees and state-of-the-art equipment and computer systems.)

Business Assistant

Work in a team environment with direct accountability for coordinating daily business activities, maintaining a productive calendar and communicating with patients by phone and in person. Perform a broad range of administrative functions, including report compilation, collections, financial arrangements, banking, records management, travel planning and correspondence development.

Scope of responsibility also includes heavy telephone work, data entry, payment posting, file maintenance, insurance records and coordinating inbound and outbound mailings. Prepare and disseminate critical information to dentist, hygienists and other office personnel and responsibly manage confidential administrative and financial information.

- Interact extensively with patients to coordinate information and help guide them through insurance processes, serving as a direct liaison to facilitate issues and resolve problems.

- Maintain records and reports per state OSHA and other regulatory requirements.

- Ensure that the confidentiality of information / documentation is strictly maintained and regularly review patient records to ensure accuracy and appropriate billing for services.

PROFESSIONAL DEVELOPMENT

Training
Front Office & OSHA Seminars
CPR Certifications

Computer Application Skills
Microsoft Word & Excel
Industry-specific applications (Soft-Dent)

10

Kristin M. Coleman, Poughkeepsie, New York

Shading between gray lines enclosing the section headings is the distinctive design feature. The applicant lacked formal training, so the resume plays up her abilities, traits, and experience.

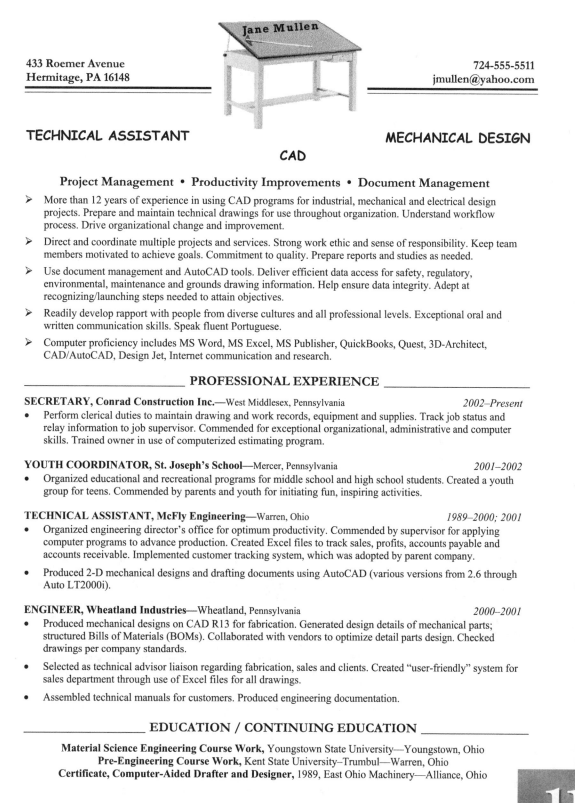

Jane Mullen

433 Roemer Avenue
Hermitage, PA 16148

724-555-5511
jmullen@yahoo.com

TECHNICAL ASSISTANT

CAD

MECHANICAL DESIGN

Project Management • Productivity Improvements • Document Management

➤ More than 12 years of experience in using CAD programs for industrial, mechanical and electrical design projects. Prepare and maintain technical drawings for use throughout organization. Understand workflow process. Drive organizational change and improvement.

➤ Direct and coordinate multiple projects and services. Strong work ethic and sense of responsibility. Keep team members motivated to achieve goals. Commitment to quality. Prepare reports and studies as needed.

➤ Use document management and AutoCAD tools. Deliver efficient data access for safety, regulatory, environmental, maintenance and grounds drawing information. Help ensure data integrity. Adept at recognizing/launching steps needed to attain objectives.

➤ Readily develop rapport with people from diverse cultures and all professional levels. Exceptional oral and written communication skills. Speak fluent Portuguese.

➤ Computer proficiency includes MS Word, MS Excel, MS Publisher, QuickBooks, Quest, 3D-Architect, CAD/AutoCAD, Design Jet, Internet communication and research.

PROFESSIONAL EXPERIENCE

SECRETARY, Conrad Construction Inc.—West Middlesex, Pennsylvania   *2002–Present*
- Perform clerical duties to maintain drawing and work records, equipment and supplies. Track job status and relay information to job supervisor. Commended for exceptional organizational, administrative and computer skills. Trained owner in use of computerized estimating program.

YOUTH COORDINATOR, St. Joseph's School—Mercer, Pennsylvania   *2001–2002*
- Organized educational and recreational programs for middle school and high school students. Created a youth group for teens. Commended by parents and youth for initiating fun, inspiring activities.

TECHNICAL ASSISTANT, McFly Engineering—Warren, Ohio   *1989–2000; 2001*
- Organized engineering director's office for optimum productivity. Commended by supervisor for applying computer programs to advance production. Created Excel files to track sales, profits, accounts payable and accounts receivable. Implemented customer tracking system, which was adopted by parent company.

- Produced 2-D mechanical designs and drafting documents using AutoCAD (various versions from 2.6 through Auto LT2000i).

ENGINEER, Wheatland Industries—Wheatland, Pennsylvania   *2000–2001*
- Produced mechanical designs on CAD R13 for fabrication. Generated design details of mechanical parts; structured Bills of Materials (BOMs). Collaborated with vendors to optimize detail parts design. Checked drawings per company standards.

- Selected as technical advisor liaison regarding fabrication, sales and clients. Created "user-friendly" system for sales department through use of Excel files for all drawings.

- Assembled technical manuals for customers. Produced engineering documentation.

EDUCATION / CONTINUING EDUCATION

Material Science Engineering Course Work, Youngstown State University—Youngstown, Ohio
Pre-Engineering Course Work, Kent State University–Trumbul—Warren, Ohio
Certificate, Computer-Aided Drafter and Designer, 1989, East Ohio Machinery—Alliance, Ohio

11

Jane Roqueplot, West Middlesex, Pennsylvania

The drafting-table graphic makes this resume unique and invites interest. Good touches are the slanted name on the drawing board, a font with drafting characters, and a good use of boldfacing.

LAURI A. MARTINGALE

000 Rising Sun Road
Salem, KY 55555

• 555-555-5555
• martingale@email.com

JOB TARGET: ADMINISTRATIVE SALES SUPPORT

Mature, proactive, results-oriented professional with extensive equine and research experience seeks position of responsibility within your dynamic organization. Possess a deep affinity for horses and **thorough knowledge of equine behavior and care,** combined with **solid business acumen** and **proficiency in customer service.** Willing to travel.

PROFILE

Equine Knowledge
- Skilled in **hands-on care, feeding, training of equine population;** owner, breeder and experienced shower with past recognition as AQHA Champion
- Experienced working **Keeneland Yearling sales** for Rolling Thunder Farm
- Knowledgeable of the **Thoroughbred industry—conformation, racing and breeding**

Research & Analysis
- Experienced **analyzing, gathering, writing, evaluating and producing reports** on varied projects
- Skilled in **synthesizing complex information** to provide concise, streamlined responses
- **Computer literate;** proficient using MS Word, MS Excel, MS PowerPoint, database and other software applications

Leadership
- Committed to **delivering personalized attention** to all customers/clients without compromising overall service and efficiency
- Able to successfully **manage multiple assignments** simultaneously

---

EMPLOYMENT SUMMARY
Highly committed, intelligent career professional with background that exemplifies a proactive customer orientation, computer proficiency and exceptional written and oral skills.

RESEARCH ANALYST PRINCIPAL   University Lab   9/2004–Present
Major Functions: Assist postdoctoral fellows and graduate students; select and maintain soybean embryos for genetic engineering while managing greenhouse and soybean tissue cultures. Organize 4-H Biotechnology camps for middle school students. Maintain inventory of stock solutions and media.

RESEARCH ASSOCIATE   Breaking Research, Inc.   5/1994–10/2003
Major Functions: Supported Field Investigator with pesticide experiments: conducted residue, efficacy, worker exposure and soil dissipation trials. Collected data, scheduled trials and ensured smooth flow of business within office environment. Served as Archivist with responsibility for indexing and filing facility data, securing the facility and ensuring quality in retrieval of archived information for audits.

EDUCATION

COURSEWORK—EQUINE MAJOR
University of Findlay—Findlay, OH

AS—INFORMATION PROCESSING / SECRETARIAL
Thomas Edison State College—Trenton, NJ

12

Tammy K. Shoup, Decatur, Indiana

The challenge was to blend the applicant's equine knowledge with her office skills. The writer used bold keywords to highlight transferable abilities. See Cover Letter 1.

Mary Labunski

306 Parker Road
Schenectady, New York 12306

Residence: (518) 353-2367
Office: (518) 458-1342, Ext. 7001
xxx@aol.com

OBJECTIVE

To obtain a challenging position as an Administrative Assistant

SUMMARY OF QUALIFICATIONS

- Ability to execute multiple tasks and projects simultaneously.
- Skilled in administrative and office procedures.
- Competent with computers and numerous software applications.
- Strong analytical and negotiating skills; ability to find cost-effective solutions.
- Excellent organization and communication skills.
- Skilled in acting as liaison between senior executives, staff/outsiders.
- Dependable, loyal, discreet, trustworthy, innovative team player who can work independently.

EXPERIENCE

TRANS WORLD ENTERTAINMENT, Schenectady, NY
With more than 1,000 stores nationwide and annual sales of more than $1 billion, Trans World Entertainment is one of the nation's largest and most successful music and movie retailers.

Administrative Assistant   1992–Present
As Administrative Assistant of MIS, report directly to Vice President/Chief Techno logy Officer, Director of Operations, and Director of Development. Perform a variety of high-priority, time-critical, confidential activities for company. Oversee department budget and vendor accounts and manage office.
Selected contributions:
- Saved $5,000 annually by selecting new phone vendor for internal phone system.
- Negotiated with phone vendors to save more than $8,000 in annual maintenance.
- Reduced long-distance phone service by $10,000 per month by selecting new carrier.
- Improve customer service for in-store and online shopping as member of E-Works Committee.
- Cut MIS spending by creating tracking report using Excel spreadsheets to track all purchases by account.
- Assisted in coordinating national meeting to introduce a Point of Sale register system to more than 800 stores.
- Participated in selection of new cabling vendor for voice and data communication upgrades.
- Participated in Y2K testing.
- Handle travel arrangements and convention planning.

Data Entry Supervisor   1987–1992
Supervised staff of 5 data entry clerks in MIS Department. Monitored accuracy and quality of all data entries. Performed data entry, typing, and filing and diverted incoming calls. Wrote and oversaw accuracy of purchase orders, new-store orders, and receiving orders. Posted catalog items in computer system.

Data Entry Clerk   1984–1987
Entered and verified data into computer system in MIS Department. Filled purchase orders, receiving orders, and catalog orders. Conducted daily billing, physical inventories, and canceled A/P checks. Handled store returns, new-release information, inventory and back-order adjustments, promo LP and cassette catalogs, gift certificates, and other miscellaneous projects.

Payroll Clerk   1982–1984
Served as Payroll Clerk in the Payroll Department, preparing weekly payroll for 150 employees. Recorded and verified hours worked by employees. Prepared quarterly, monthly, and annual taxes. Responsible for new-hire paperwork, insurance forms, and all other Payroll Department paperwork.

COMPUTER SKILLS

Thoroughly familiar with all components of Microsoft Office (Word, Excel, PowerPoint, Access), WordPerfect, and Nortel Phone System.

Highly skilled and experienced at setting up templates and organizational systems for company records and procedures.

13

John Femia, Altamont, New York

Like a resume for an experienced executive, this one-page resume contains much information through the use of a relatively small font size. Blank lines ensure adequate white space.

Norma Wood

555 Beverly Court • Alexandria, VA 22304
240-555-1297—Mobile • norma_wood@yahoo.com • 703-555-5061—Home

Professional Profile

- Office Manager and Operations Support Professional offering more than eight years of experience supporting department managers, business owners, clients, external department personnel, and laborers.
- Present history of creating order and improving customer relations by establishing office systems and procedures, implementing technology to streamline operations, and delivering timely and responsive customer service.
- Thrive in a fast-paced environment that requires organizational skills, efficiency, and ability to simultaneously manage multiple projects while ensuring consistent customer satisfaction.
- Demonstrate strong communication skills; professionally represent a company in person and on the phone. Speak fluent Spanish.
- Proficiently use computer technology, including Windows XP; Microsoft Word, Excel, PowerPoint, and Access; Adobe Photoshop; Internet marketing and research; business email correspondence.

Professional Employment

Flanagan & Rice   Reston, VA
A manufacturer and "to the trade only" wholesaler of fine custom window treatments and bed coverings.

Office Coordinator, Installation Division   2003–Present

- Provide administrative support to Installation Services Manager. Manage day-to-day office operations, oversee one office clerk, and maintain schedules for five installers.
- Coordinate projects with retailers, designers, and Richmond, VA, workroom staff. Respond to customer phone and online inquires and prepare project quotes.
- Effectively prioritize and manage as many as 40 ongoing projects throughout Maryland, Virginia, and Washington metro area.

Key Contributions

- Took leadership role in establishing office policies and procedures for emerging division; managed onsite operations for seven months prior to company hiring division manager.
- Streamlined scheduling, tracking, and reporting efficiency by collaborating with corporate IT department to develop and implement customized computer applications and tools.
- Computerized scheduling, warehouse inventory, and return-authorization tracking systems.
- Assisted division manager in creating full-color customer guide to provide new and existing clients with direction for doing business with Flanagan & Rice.
- Improved and continually maintain positive customer relations by delivering immediate followup and proactively addressing service issues to avert future problems.

Foltz Manufacturing   Rockville, MD
An industrial equipment supplier to nationwide manufacturers and small businesses.

Office Manager   2000–2003

- Coordinated daily office operations and delivered administrative support to company owner, drivers, and machinists.
- Trained and oversaw newly hired office support staff tasked with filing, data entry, and receptionist duties.

14

Norine Dagliano, Hagerstown, Maryland

To make the resume appear different, the writer used an uncommon font for the applicant's name and section headings. These are enclosed within broken horizontal lines. The applicant was a talented administrator who took on tasks beyond her basic job description. The writer highlighted

Norma Wood   240-555-1297 / norma_wood@yahoo.com   **Page 2**

Foltz Manufacturing, Office Manager (continued)
- Coordinated UPS and FedEx shipments. Input equipment specifications to company eBay account for online advertising and sales.
- Maintained company bookkeeping records, including billing customers and making bank deposits of approximately $15,000–$20,000 per day.
- Provided full lifecycle customer support, from initial inquiry to delivery, setup, and service followup.

Key Contributions
- Computerized manual bookkeeping system and recorded more than five years of accounting records on customized Excel spreadsheets.
- Tackled two-month backlog of customer records left by previous office manager and recouped thousands of dollars from unbilled accounts.

Montgomery Community   Rockville, MD
A two-year community college offering onsite and distance learning courses to traditional and nontraditional students.

Registration Office Assistant   1999–2000
- Supported registrar director and registration activities as a work-study student while maintaining full-time college attendance.
- Maintained class schedule and course specification in department database. Assisted walk-in and remote students in attaining class information and completing registration process.

Kelly Services   Alexandria, VA
Employment agency providing administrative support to corporate, federal, and municipal businesses in and around the Washington, D.C., area.

Contract Worker   1998–1999
- Completed a variety of short-term administrative assignments with numerous businesses including Department of Veterans Affairs, NIH, and Walter Reed Medical Center.
- Consistently represented Kelly Services as a professional and well-managed organization while delivering efficient data entry, filing, and customer service support.

Prior Experience: Established outstanding employment record as a waitress and bartender in the fast-paced, customer service–driven restaurant industry. Employed in various four-star and family-style restaurants in both Maryland and Virginia.

———————————————— Education ————————————————

Associate of Arts (Art History concentration), Montgomery Community College

these tasks in the Key Contributions sections. For each employer the writer supplied a descriptive statement in italic. Square bullets tie together the two pages visually.

CARA WAVERLY

58 Chelsea Way ◆ Bridgeport, CT 22222 ◆ (333) 333-3333 ◆ cara@aol.com

Executive-level administrative support professional whose accomplishments reflect excellent administrative skills and a demonstrated commitment to providing exemplary service

SUMMARY OF QUALIFICATIONS

- Capable executive assistant with extensive experience in administrative roles.
- Organized and detail-oriented with demonstrated project coordination skills. Practiced in prioritizing and managing tasks. Effective at balancing the competing demands of multiple projects.
- Excellent interpersonal skills. Able to develop easy rapport with others while building trust.
- Versatile and resourceful team player who is willing to do whatever is necessary to complete goals and meet deadlines. Polished and professional, yet warm and accommodating.
- Recognized "go-to" person for a broad range of issues and concerns.
- Committed to providing the highest levels of customer service.

PROFESSIONAL EXPERIENCE

PETPHARMA CORP., Bridgeport, Connecticut   2001 to present
Administrative Assistant

As lead administrative assistant, provide effective support to VP of Global Marketing, VP of International Operations, and three other managers. Handle administrative details such as maintaining calendars, making travel arrangements, scheduling meetings, and coordinating conferences.

Administrative Leadership

- Established strong record in developing best practices for administrative support. Proactively provide support, looking beyond immediate need to maximize effectiveness.
- Hired as first administrative assistant in newly relocated group; developed and documented group processes and procedures. Trained and mentored new administrative assistants.
- Developed administrative checklist for new hires, ensuring smooth transition for more than 20 new employees.
- Implemented filing system for all product-related literature, creating easy-to-use resource for customer inquiries. Also developed individual product binders for each sales rep.
- Effectively support group training efforts by developing manuals and presentations, and scheduling and facilitating training sessions.
- Consistently explore lower-cost options in keeping with company's "Smart Initiatives."

Project Coordination

- Successfully arranged numerous domestic and international conferences, effectively planning and coordinating events for groups of more than 100 people.
- Oversaw all administrative details to ensure flawless events. Booked all facilities, negotiating favorable pricing. Made travel arrangements and scheduled ground transportation for all attendees. Generated handouts and purchased gifts and awards. Shipped materials to site, meeting all project timetables.
- Implemented effective follow-up system to ensure all projects and tasks remain on schedule.
- Effectively supported Transition Team, collecting and collating staff résumés for timely presentation to management.

15

Carol A. Altomare, Three Bridges, New Jersey

This applicant wanted an executive-level administrative position but did not hold that title at the time even though she supported executives and was functioning as an Executive Assistant. To show that the applicant had executive-level experience, the writer organized accomplishments

PETPHARMA CORP., Westport, Connecticut   1998 to 2001

Administrative Assistant

Provided effective administrative support for Customer Development, Sales Training, and Sales Operations groups following relocation. Maintained all personnel and customer files.

- Developed guidelines and procedures for administrative assistants. Documented procedures for new hires.
- Established and managed system to track broker payments.
- Developed process for customer scorecarding, following up with clients to determine satisfaction with products, delivery times, and customer service. Developed spreadsheet to record and track response.
- Maintained divisional "dashboard"—a prominent display that tracked key performance measures and staff awards.
- Successfully planned and coordinated large-scale conferences and sales meetings.

BOYD, INC., Mullica Hill, New Jersey   1992 to 1998

Executive Secretary

Assisted president and controller in managing International Division. Prepared all correspondence and assisted in preparing all confidential salary reviews, business plans, budgets, and presentations.

- Organized office, setting up effective filing systems and archiving old files.
- Developed and implemented more efficient procedures for office operations.
- Effectively organized numerous conferences and sales meetings.
- Served as Board Member for Boyd's Federal Credit Union in addition to regular duties.

Corporate Flight Coordinator

Assisted Manager of Flight Operations and scheduled flights for corporate executives.

- As first full-time coordinator, set up effective scheduling system to accommodate increasing demand for flight services.

UNITED CHEMICALS, Clifton, New Jersey   1985 to 1992

Administrative Assistant

Assisted Region Administrative Manager, providing support in the area of marketing, administration, office services, information systems, and annual planning activities.

- Gathered background information for reports and special projects.
- Coordinated and scheduled system usage, enforcing region guidelines. Mobilized system specialists to handle problems and requests.
- Provided instruction for all software packages.

COMPUTER SKILLS

Word ◆ Excel ◆ PowerPoint ◆ Outlook ◆ Internet ◆ E-mail
DCIS (database for sales reporting)

References Available Upon Request

in the most recent job under the headings Administrative Leadership and Project Coordination. This approach pleased the applicant and proved to be a strong way to feature her relevant experience.

JUANITA SANCHEZ
jsanchez@email.com

5555 West 5th Street
Los Angeles, California 55555

Residence (323) 555-5555
Mobile (323) 555-0000

ADMINISTRATIVE/EXECUTIVE ASSISTANT
Special Expertise in Fashion Industry/Private Label

➤ Motivated self-starter who consistently goes beyond the requirements of the job to meet organizational objectives.

➤ Proven ability to multitask with attention to detail and accuracy in a fast-paced environment.

➤ Solid reputation for a strong work ethic and managing trusting relationships with public, clients and coworkers at all levels.

➤ Excellent computer skills, including Microsoft Word, Excel, PowerPoint, Access and Outlook.

—*Core Competencies*—

Multitasking • Account/Client Relations • Time & Task Management
Oral & Written Communications • Travel & Event Coordination • Problem Solving • Troubleshooting

---

PROFESSIONAL EXPERIENCE

SOUTHERN CALIFORNIA BEACHWEAR, Los Angeles, CA • 1998 to Present
Achieved fast-track promotions through positions of increasing challenge and responsibility for leading swimwear designer/manufacturer that generates $25 million in annual revenues with 300 employees.

Executive Assistant/Corporate Sales Support (2001–Present)
Pattern Maker (1999–2001); **Designer** (1998–1999)
Report concurrently to company President, Vice President/Sales Director and Vice President/Private Label Sales. Provide broad range of support, including client relations, report preparations, correspondence, overseeing shipping and inventory for private-label accounts, coordinating trade show participation and special events.

- Oversee inventories, supplies ordering and report preparation for private-label business that comprises more than 25% of annual profit.
- Manage excellent working relationships with 12 national key accounts, promoting positive company image.
- Coordinate all trade show participation, including working closely with agencies on casting calls for trade show models.
- Download routing and vendor guides for 90% of major accounts.
- *Accomplishments:*
  - Accurately tracked and ensured compliance with shipping and EDI process for major account, avoiding thousands of dollars in charge-backs.
  - Upgraded order entry processes, ensuring that appropriate inventory levels are maintained.
  - Arranged all travel and accommodations for 30+ people attending annual sales meetings in Florida.

LAGUNA LEISUREWARE, Los Angeles, CA • 1996 to 1998
Design Assistant
Provided direct assistance to swimwear designer, including developing screens, monitoring and reporting on fashion/consumer trends and interfacing with contractors and screeners.

EDUCATION

FASHION INSTITUTE, Los Angeles, CA • **AA Degree in Fashion Design,** 1996
Honors: Awarded 1st place in design category

—*Bilingual English/Spanish*—

16

Vivian VanLier, Los Angeles, California

This candidate had an A.A. degree in Fashion Design and moved from being a designer to becoming an Administrative/Executive Assistant. Her goal was to become a manager in the fashion industry.

PATRICE PACKARD

45 Chestnut Street, Cold Spring Harbor, New York 55555 • (555) 555-5555 • ppackard@mail.com

---

~ Seeking a Position in a Not-for-Profit Organization ~
Emphasis on Fundraising and Event Planning

➤ Strong skills in initiating and pulling together all aspects of projects.
➤ Meticulous with details. Capable of autonomously handling a diverse array of responsibilities.
➤ Strength in anticipating problems before they arise.
➤ Excellent computer proficiency: Windows, Word, Excel, Access, PowerPoint, Outlook, and Internet.

~NOT-FOR-PROFIT EXPERIENCE~

Executive Assistant, 2003. Alzheimer's Association, Long Island Chapter, Smithtown, NY

Assistant to the Executive Director, 2001–2003. Child Care Council, Commack, NY

Public Relations / Writing / Promotions

- Wrote press releases for television and print promotion. Designed and produced flyers for special events.
- Assisted with the preparation of grant proposals and quarterly reports delineating accomplishments relative to goals set.
- Edited/proofread materials for Web site and for voice scripts used in public service announcements.
- Initiated and composed correspondence to acknowledge donors.
- Cultivated and maintained excellent relationships with professionals from related organizations.

Correspondence / Mailings / Information Management

- Handled mass mailings for fundraising initiatives. Coordinated projects and delegated activities to volunteers and interns.
- On a monthly basis, updated a mailing list of 12,000 names. Electronically transferred information to an outside printing vendor for widespread dissemination.
- Prepared budgets and verified calculations for accuracy.
- Maintained several databases to track contact information.

Executive Administrative Support

- Supported an executive director, a managing director, board members, and other professional staff. Handled virtually every type of administrative support function.

  -Managed office supply and repair needs. Dealt with vendors and repair technicians.
  -Processed and batched credit card and check donations. Handled bank deposits.
  -Troubleshot a variety of challenging and unique office problems.

Special Events

- Assisted in the planning, promotion, and execution of numerous special events. Attended events to actively promote organizational missions.

  -Conducted community outreach to secure donations and ensure solid levels of event participation.
  -Researched, evaluated, and made recommendations regarding event activities.
  -Assessed, priced, and hired caterers in accordance with budgetary guidelines.

~EDUCATION~

Bachelor of Arts Program, Sociology. 96 credits completed. Adelphi University, Garden City, NY

Excellent References on Request

17

MJ Feld, Huntington, New York

A few years out of college without a bachelor's degree, this applicant wanted to work for a not-for-profit organization. Because she had little relevant experience, the writer played up prior activities.

KYLA WALTERS

7558 South Fremont Way • Butte, MT 55555
Home: 777.777.7777 • kyla@aol.com • Mobile: 777.777.7777

Office Management/Administrative Support

Accomplished Administrative Manager with more than 15 years of experience in instituting organizational strategies and measures for continuous improvements and efficient business operations. Self-starter who meets project deadlines and requirements while performing multiple tasks within fast-paced environments. Respond rapidly and appropriately to changing circumstances; evaluate problems, make astute decisions to effect positive change and refocus on new priorities. Thrive as team player and coordinator for special events and programs. Outstanding interpersonal communication skills; quickly establish rapport with patients, physicians and staff members. Key strengths include

- Project Control & Management
- Human Resources Functions
- Law & Regulation Compliance
- Problem Identification & Resolution
- Team Building & Leadership

- Administrative Support
- Office Management
- Scheduling & Event Coordination
- Budgeting & Financial Affairs
- Interpersonal Communications

♦♦♦

"Kyla proved to be one of the most conscientious and hard-working associates that I have worked with in many years. Her attention to detail, dedication to her job, and positive attitude helped to make her a leader and an example for her peers and a tremendous asset to our department."

— Fred Knight, Risk Operations Manager, Rhapsody, Inc.

Professional Experience

MOUNTAIN HOSPITAL, Butte, MT   2000–Present
Executive Administrative Assistant
Provide administrative support to CEO and up to 12 management team and hospital staff members. Scope of responsibility is diverse and includes patient communications, special-event coordination, operations management, executive administration, human resources and regulatory compliance.

- Designed and implemented administrative programs to reduce redundancy, streamline processes and improve daily operations.
- Led internal office training to ensure compliance with all local, state and federal regulatory agencies; extensive knowledge of HIPAA, JCAHO and HCFA laws and regulations.
- Performed and assisted with human resources functions; interviewed, recruited and conducted new general employee orientations. Built work teams that consistently exceeded goals for productivity, efficiency and quality.
- Implemented Employee Incentive Award programs designed to promote outstanding work performance, which delivered measurable improvements in employee morale and satisfaction.
- Planned and facilitated a broad range of administrative functions, including travel arrangements, calendar management, business correspondence and outlining agendas for various functions and meetings.
- Designed and instituted a new database system for marketing, enabling the department to track areas of expertise and work history of specific licensed employees. Ultimately streamlined the process of submitting documentation to become certified or provider within network.
- Trained more than 12 staff members in equipment operations and various processes; developed team members committed to optimal productivity.
- Organized all charitable functions, special events and ongoing employee activities such as Christmas parties and picnics. Managed yearly budget of $6000 and events for 240 employees and 25 physicians; consistently stayed under budget and saved $1000–$2000 annually.
- Served as backup HR Director, frequently sought out by employees to handle issues and defuse problem situations.

18

Denette Jones, Mountain View, Hawaii

This two-page resume offers much information through smaller type, wider lines from narrower left and right margins, and a variety of sections with shorter lines in the last half of the second page. The strong testimonial at the end of the opening section near the top of the

KYLA WALTERS – Page 2

Professional Experience continued…

RHAPSODY, INC., Butte, MT   1999–2000
Administrative Assistant/CRS Representative
Provided assistance to customers regarding various issues with accounts; established operational policies and procedures necessary for smooth business operations; developed recognition awards and motivational incentives for employees, which enhanced office environment.

MEDICAL SERVICES, Butte, MT   1999
Administrative Assistant
Directly reported to President and Vice President; oversaw projects and progression; prepared job costing, reports and materials; updated files; implemented new forms providing better efficiency and accuracy, clearing 2-month backlog within 3 weeks; accountable for new software installation, setup and maintenance of user profiles on NT environment; developed key database program for critical $1 million project, streamlining materials process, enhancing efficiency and ultimately saving costs.

BUTTE MEDICAL CONSULTING, Butte, MT   1995–1999
Administrative Assistant
Participated in assigning risk assessment to products inventoried, data entry, report updates and analysis, formal and informal research and manufacturer and vendor correspondence; collaborated with Project Manager during meetings to generate new ideas that would facilitate Y2K project.

BEAL TRANSPORTATION, Fontana, CA   1987–1995
OS & D Clerk/Supervisor
Developed and implemented new procedures that reduced claims by 12%; honored with award for completing Excellence Training Program within top 2%.

Education & Professional Development

A.A.S., Business Technology Administration (with honors), ITT Technical Institute, Butte, MT, 1999

Continuing in-service training courses sponsored by Mountain Hospital included

- Access Advanced Techniques
- Speak with Confidence & Clarity
- How to Discipline Employees
- Recruiting for Vacant Positions
- Workmen's Compensation Verification
- Knowledge of FLSA, FMLA & EEOC

- Management Skills for Administrative Assistants
- Coaching & Teambuilding Skills for Managers
- Basic Functions of HR
- Conducting Employee Orientations & Meetings
- JCAHO, HCFA, State & Federal Regulatory Agencies
- Computer/Business Software Applications

Technical Proficiencies

Access · Word · PowerPoint · Publisher · Excel · Windows XP · Outlook · Lotus Organizer · Transcription

Professional Associations

Member, Executive Women in Sales
Member, Business Professionals of America

Community Activities

Speaker/Volunteer, Suicide Awareness Program
Volunteer, Hope House
Volunteer, United Way

first page speaks louder than the impressive bulleted lists before it. Such a testimonial can help offset a gap in employment, questions about unrelated jobs, or doubts about a candidate's worth.

BELLA DORNO

25481 Crocker Avenue	Downey, California 90242	323 798-1418

EXECUTIVE ADMINISTRATIVE OFFICER
PERSONAL EXECUTIVE ADMINISTRATIVE ASSISTANT
Driving Organizational Change, Quality, and Continuous Improvement

Meticulous, detailed, multitasking professional with experience planning and directing executive-level administrative affairs and support to Boards of Directors and Senior Management. Combines strong planning, organizational, and communications skills with the ability to independently plan and direct high-level business affairs.

Background encompasses managing cross-functional business affairs for small and large service organizations, providing hands-on leadership, direction, and focus with positive results and outcomes. Proactive in analyzing existing operations and implementing strategies, processes, and technologies to improve organizational performance. Possess unique sense of innovation and resourcefulness with proven expertise in devising original solutions to complex problems. Effective troubleshooter whose strengths include the following:

- Administrative Policies and Procedures
- Board of Directors Meetings
- Facilities Management
- Budgeting and General Accounting
- Purchasing and Vendor Negotiations

- Regulatory Reporting and Communications
- Executive Office Management
- Confidential Correspondence and Data
- Special Project Management
- Customer Communications and Liaison Affairs

Professional and articulate; work well with all levels of management in a professional, diplomatic, and tactful manner. Delivered improvements in productivity and operating efficiency, cost reduction, and earnings. Sharp presentation, negotiation, and team-building qualifications. Outstanding interpersonal skills. Energetic and decisive business leader able to merge disparate technologies and personnel into a cohesive team-centered unit. Hardworking, dependable, trustworthy. Dedicated with a strong work ethic.

Proficient in the use of Word 2000, Excel 2000, and Access 2000. Experienced with shorthand and machine transcription.

PROFESSIONAL EXPERIENCE

EXECUTIVE ADMINISTRATIVE ASSISTANT   2001–Present
Downey Bank & Trust, Downey, CA

High-profile, executive-level administrative position supporting the Executive Vice President / Chief Lending Officer and other top management personnel throughout the organization. Scope of responsibility is diverse and includes Board affairs, customer communications, special events, regulatory reporting, and executive administration (assemble loan packages, collect reports, set appointments, keep calendar, screen calls).

- Executive liaison between Chairman, Senior Management, and employees to plan, schedule, and facilitate a broad range of corporate initiatives, company operations, and large-scale business functions. Communication is of the utmost importance in order to function independently and be self-starting in implementation.
- Built rapport with all departments and all branches. Recognized as principal Consultant.
- Handle confidential operating and financial information; maintain corporate records and minutes.
- Maintain / update files for regulatory review, oversight, and approval.

19

Myriam-Rose Kohn, Valencia, California

Two horizontal lines work together to call attention to the information between them. In this resume the two lines at the top of the first page appear together as a banner announcing the applicant's job goals and drive. The information below the banner provides a profile of the

BELLA DORNO Page 2

- Organize all bank community involvements:
  - American Cancer Society: Heart Walk, Relay for Life: selected as coteam captain, recruit people to participate, coordinate fund raising.
  - Fourth of July Parade: assist with float decoration, participate in annual parade.
  - Office holiday party: serve on the committee to organize and facilitate all activities, handle invitations.
- **Several commendations** from President and Board of Directors.

College Assistant, Communications Department 2001
Mission College, Mission, CA

Obtained significant experience in primary research; very resourceful at finding data and developing primary and secondary sources for Department Chair / Professor. Aided with brochure creation for the Communications Department. Provided general office support. Tabulated and recorded grades.

Administrator 1993–2001
Various community activities in Downey, CA

- Participated in reading programs at elementary and junior high schools.
- Acted as Recording Secretary at Franklin Roosevelt Elementary School Site Council Meetings.
- Planned and organized social events for high school sports team.
- Designed flexible administrative systems and processes for dissemination of reports to parents of confirmation students at Christ Lutheran Church. Transitioned from manual operations to complete automation.

Executive Assistant / Administrative Assistant 1990–1993
Sumitomo Bank of California, Business Development Offices, Los Angeles, CA

Executed complex administrative duties for Executive Vice President. Assisted in budget planning and monitored / analyzed monthly operating statement. Compiled reports using various research sources. Widely recognized as information source on executive policies and procedures as well as general personnel policies. Administered all personnel functions for office staff.

Executive Assistant 1979–1990
Crocker National Bank, Los Angeles, CA

Managed confidential correspondence, appointments, meetings, and schedules. Personally planned and coordinated bank and intercompany meetings. Performed executive administrative duties as outlined under current position.

EDUCATION

Currently pursuing **Associate of Arts, Business Information Management**
California State University, Los Angeles, CA

Diploma, Executive Secretarial Program
Patricia Stevens Career College and Finishing School, Milwaukee, WI

Numerous AIB Courses, Fred Pryor Seminars, and Internal Training Classes

applicant, indicates her background and strengths, and mentions some of her worker traits and job skills. Boldfacing makes conspicuous the applicant's former positions as you glance through the Professional Experience section.

Rachel Osborne

Floral Gardens, Apartment 5-C
Idaho Falls, ID 00000

000-000-0000
luckyladybug@woohoo.com

SKILLED IN
- Office Management
- Executive Assistance
- Sales and Business Support

PROFESSIONAL QUALIFICATIONS

- More than 20 years of experience as a loyal, dedicated and trusted assistant to high-level corporate executives
- Recognized by management as a perceptive and assertive problem solver who thrives in a multitasking environment and can adapt quickly to new challenges
- Extremely well organized with strong project orientation and major strength in coordinating the details of business affairs with minimal direction
- Willingness and initiative to handle the numerous clerical responsibilities that keep an office functioning smoothly
- Proficient in building solid relationships, enabling people to work together as a team
- Continually contribute new ideas to increase efficiency and add value to the organization

BUSINESS PROFICIENCIES

- Computer knowledge: Windows NT, Word, Excel, PowerPoint, Quicken, ACT customer database, Macola accounting program, PC Anywhere, Delrina Winfax and Omnipage OCR program used with HP scanner
- Keyboarding of daily correspondence, customer quotes and statistical reports
- Fast longhand note taking
- Mail routing/letter composition for routine responses
- Transcription from taped dictation
- Setup and maintenance of complex filing systems
- Safeguarding of confidential matters
- Courteous and knowledgeable telephone and interpersonal communications

ADMINISTRATIVE MANAGEMENT

- Total responsibility for office services: facility maintenance, cleaning, equipment repair, telephones and building security system
- Implementation/enforcement of policies and procedures for increased efficiency
- Purchasing/inventory control of stationery supplies, printed forms and lunchroom items
- Minor troubleshooting of various office equipment, including computers and network server
- Bookkeeping assistance: invoicing, cash receipts, expense report reconciliation and commissioned payroll
- Training of clerical assistants to assume advanced responsibilities
- Control over company credit cards, leased vehicles, telecommunications pass codes and keyholder access

PROJECT COORDINATION

- Sales staff liaison for up-to-date product information, price quotes, delivery scheduling and credit terms
- Travel and meeting arrangements, domestic and international
- Company luncheons and social events
- Office moves to larger quarters
- Comparative analysis/recommendation for new capital equipment acquisitions
- Follow through on others' assignments to ensure timely completion

(Continued)

20

Melanie Noonan, West Paterson, New Jersey

An uncluttered, hanging-indent layout provides pleasing white space and makes it easy to view this resume's chief headings and subsections. A single vertical path of square, shadowed bullets direct the reader's eyes down both pages. The first page displays the breadth of the

Rachel Osborne

Page 2

CAREER HIGHLIGHTS

U.S. PACKAGING SYSTEMS, INC., POCATELLO, ID   1992 TO PRESENT
Office Manager/Executive Assistant, *reporting directly to CEO of $10 million manufacturer of customized packaging machinery*

- ❐ Hired permanently following temporary assignment with the company, having established a positive rapport with a difficult manager in a position where prior turnover was exceptionally high.
- ❐ Took charge of all office services, previously unassigned and often neglected in the past.
- ❐ Interfaced with CFO and Controller for preparation of confidential financial reports.
- ❐ Given joint check-signing authority for up to $10,000 and was empowered to carry out corporate directives.
- ❐ Supervised a receptionist, ensuring phone coverage at all times and timely completion of clerical work.
- ❐ Organized all historical data, specifications, drawings, contracts, invoices and general correspondence related to hundreds of machine projects into orderly binders. As a result, facilitated the quotation process, provided immediate information on the progressive stages of each project and saved countless hours in responding to customer requests.
- ❐ Worked closely with consultants to implement new accounting and order entry systems, eliminating redundant steps. Trained clerical staff in the use of these systems.
- ❐ Coordinated all aspects of 2 office moves to accommodate company's growing needs, from 15 employees initially to 47 currently. Conducted both moves smoothly with no disruption to normal business routines.

BEACON POLLUTION CONTROL CORPORATION, SHELLEY, ID   1984 TO 1992
Administrative Secretary to the Senior Vice President of Finance

- ❐ In addition to normal secretarial duties, assumed responsibilities of office service manager and personnel assistant, each for a period of several months during incumbents' respective absences.
- ❐ Successfully handled a large renovation project that involved securing and working with various building tradespeople as well as arranging for movement of large machinery.
- ❐ Reorganized departmental files from a paper system to electronic access of data.
- ❐ Cross-trained clerical employees to perform accounting and human resources functions.
- ❐ Designed formats that streamlined ongoing financial reporting and contributed to more efficient monthly closings.

CONTINUING EDUCATION

Groupwise IV: *Scheduling and Project Management Program*
Computer Applications Learning Center: *Microsoft Professional Office Suite*
Dun & Bradstreet: *Effective Writing Techniques*
Fred Pryor Seminar: *Management Skills for Executive Secretaries*

applicant's experience, skills, responsibilities, and activities. The bulleted items on the second page include some of her achievements at the two companies where she has worked since 1984.

JULIE L. METZLER

1327 N. 3rd Ave. 201 ♦ Denver, CO 55555 ♦ 303.555.5555♦ Cell 303.000.0000
Metzler39@comcast.net

PROFESSIONAL QUALIFICATIONS

Highly dependable Administrative Professional with strong foundation in insurance claim adjusting. Proven ability to multitask and prioritize between day-to-day and long-term projects. Excellent ability to organize, streamline and attend to fine details. Adept at assuming new responsibilities with minimal supervision. Demonstrated skill with working efficiently under pressure and stress in a busy atmosphere. Excel at communicating effectively across a wide range of people. Possess strong work ethic.

ADMINISTRATION—Highly proficient with quickly learning and mastering different computer systems and software. Excellent ability to interact effectively with the public. Strong ability to manage complicated schedules and produce detailed reports.

CLAIM ADJUSTING—Proven track record of processing and adjusting medical claims quickly and accurately while consistently meeting and exceeding quotas. Acknowledged ability to lead teams, perform quality control, interpret plan benefits and assume difficult and/or complicated claims. Comprehensive knowledge base includes CPT, revenue, HCPC codes, Medicaid, Medicare and commercial health insurance.

COMPUTER SKILLS

Microsoft Windows, Microsoft Office, Outlook, Maccess Imaging System, Rumba, EZ-Cap, QMacs, ECura & various mainframes

ADMINISTRATIVE & INSURANCE EXPERIENCE

EASTERN HEALTH/ TEMPORARY POSITIONS   2003–2004
Claims Examiner
Performed medical claims processing. Accountable for distributing claims to appropriate adjuster and department during absence of supervisor. Compiled daily reports and performed quality control and adjustments. Searched for claim information in system. Reviewed claimant files for necessary payments and documented claims action.

➢ As temporary employee for Blue Cross Blue Shield, entrusted with training new class of temporary workers on system operations and processing. As a result of performing effective training for 20 students, attained promotion to team lead.
➢ Consistently demonstrated immediate comprehensive understanding of billing processes and procedures.
➢ Processed backlog and cleared from system during employment at Eastern Health.

INFORMATION SYSTEMS CORP, Denver, CO   1996–1997, 1999–2003
Claims Team Lead, Claims Research & Analysis, Adjustment Technician
Third party administrator of Medicaid plans and United Healthcare. Processed medical claims according to policy guidelines, including assuming responsibility for complicated or incorrectly processed claims. Delegated claims to team of 10 processors and assisted staff with problems. Created spreadsheets showing payment history and work history associated with claims. Accountable for quality control for team.

➢ Acknowledged for speed and quality during processing. Consistently attained assigned quotas, "exceeds" on evaluations and bonuses for exemplary performance.
➢ Managed Medicare processing team—consistently maintaining processing time within 10 days and preventing state-levied fines.

ATLANTIC HEALTH, Littleton, CO   1998–1999
Claims Examiner
Third party Administrator for Pacificare and HMO of Colorado. Accountable for distributing and assigning claims for processing. Downloaded electronic files from three companies. Completed claims adjustments according to contracted policies and procedures.

➢ Entrusted with additional responsibility of processing electronic claims because of high level of expertise and reliability.

21

Michele Angello, Aurora, Colorado

Each section heading is on a line completed by a partial horizontal line extending to the right margin. The all-important zone near the top of the first page is a Professional Qualifications section that indicates the applicant's skills, worker traits, administrative abilities, and claim-adjusting

JULIE L. METZLER

ADDITIONAL EXPERIENCE

AURORA POLICE DEPARTMENT, Aurora, CO   2004–PRESENT
Officer
Accountable for ensuring safety and security of facility, inmates and visitors. Responsible for running video visitation, including monitoring conversations for illegal activity. Conducted extensive computer research to develop viable visit schedules that did not allow contact between rival inmates and accounted for warrants, protection orders and visiting privileges. Oversaw and coordinated average of 24 inmates and 35 visitors simultaneously. Compiled visit reports and entered on computer for tracking.

> ➤ Noted for exceptional ability to handle argumentative clients with tact and professionalism, and provide prompt attention to problem situations. One satisfied visitor donated money to Sheriff's Foundation for these abilities and pleasant demeanor.
> ➤ Gained supervisor's commendation for assuming responsibility for and facilitating implementation of video visitation system.
> ➤ Achieved overall performance evaluation score of 49, a score 5 points above "exceeds expectations" mark. Noted for promptness, problem-solving, professionalism and good interpersonal skills.

GLENDALE POLICE DEPARTMENT, Glendale, CO   2003
Police Officer Recruit
Gained knowledge of officer safety, writing reports, defense tactics, writing reports and firearms. Recognized for excellent ability to relate to and deal with public in difficult situations.

Previous background includes experience in records and data entry for Invesco and additional experience with claims adjusting. Also completed courses in data entry and DOS.

"I am proud to recognize your duty performance... (which) has been nothing less than outstanding.... You have displayed a commitment to your duties and a level of professionalism that has become a hallmark for you. No matter what job is assigned to you, you give your best effort at all times....

The number of complaints from the public were drastically reduced while you were assigned to Visit Reservation position....

On a number of occasions you were asked to assist the Visit Supervisor in completing critical tasks. You never complained, always completing these additional tasks cheerfully and professionally....

From the feedback I have received from other staff, and members of the public, I know that you are one of our most productive and efficient officers."

—Excerpt from letter of recommendation
By Sergeant R. Davis, supervisor

Additional Excellent References Available Upon Request

expertise. Right arrow-tip bullets throughout the resume point to noteworthy accomplishments. The boxed testimonial on page 2 is a strong ending.

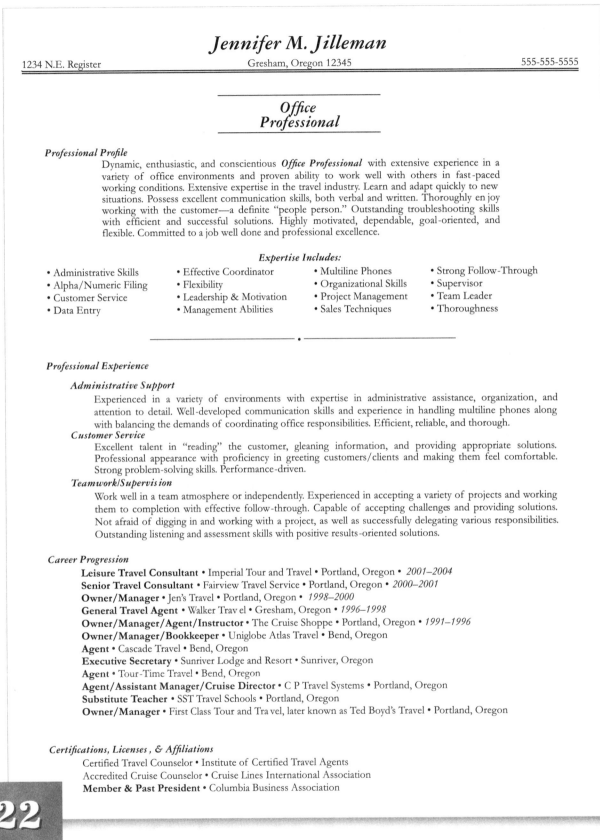

Jennifer M. Jilleman

1234 N.E. Register   Gresham, Oregon 12345   555-555-5555

Office Professional

Professional Profile

Dynamic, enthusiastic, and conscientious ***Office Professional*** with extensive experience in a variety of office environments and proven ability to work well with others in fast-paced working conditions. Extensive expertise in the travel industry. Learn and adapt quickly to new situations. Possess excellent communication skills, both verbal and written. Thoroughly enjoy working with the customer—a definite "people person." Outstanding troubleshooting skills with efficient and successful solutions. Highly motivated, dependable, goal-oriented, and flexible. Committed to a job well done and professional excellence.

Expertise Includes:

• Administrative Skills	• Effective Coordinator	• Multiline Phones	• Strong Follow-Through
• Alpha/Numeric Filing	• Flexibility	• Organizational Skills	• Supervisor
• Customer Service	• Leadership & Motivation	• Project Management	• Team Leader
• Data Entry	• Management Abilities	• Sales Techniques	• Thoroughness

Professional Experience

Administrative Support

Experienced in a variety of environments with expertise in administrative assistance, organization, and attention to detail. Well-developed communication skills and experience in handling multiline phones along with balancing the demands of coordinating office responsibilities. Efficient, reliable, and thorough.

Customer Service

Excellent talent in "reading" the customer, gleaning information, and providing appropriate solutions. Professional appearance with proficiency in greeting customers/clients and making them feel comfortable. Strong problem-solving skills. Performance-driven.

Teamwork/Supervision

Work well in a team atmosphere or independently. Experienced in accepting a variety of projects and working them to completion with effective follow-through. Capable of accepting challenges and providing solutions. Not afraid of digging in and working with a project, as well as successfully delegating various responsibilities. Outstanding listening and assessment skills with positive results-oriented solutions.

Career Progression

Leisure Travel Consultant • Imperial Tour and Travel • Portland, Oregon • *2001–2004*
Senior Travel Consultant • Fairview Travel Service • Portland, Oregon • *2000–2001*
Owner/Manager • Jen's Travel • Portland, Oregon • *1998–2000*
General Travel Agent • Walker Travel • Gresham, Oregon • *1996–1998*
Owner/Manager/Agent/Instructor • The Cruise Shoppe • Portland, Oregon • *1991–1996*
Owner/Manager/Bookkeeper • Uniglobe Atlas Travel • Bend, Oregon
Agent • Cascade Travel • Bend, Oregon
Executive Secretary • Sunriver Lodge and Resort • Sunriver, Oregon
Agent • Tour-Time Travel • Bend, Oregon
Agent/Assistant Manager/Cruise Director • C P Travel Systems • Portland, Oregon
Substitute Teacher • SST Travel Schools • Portland, Oregon
Owner/Manager • First Class Tour and Travel, later known as Ted Boyd's Travel • Portland, Oregon

Certifications, Licenses, & Affiliations

Certified Travel Counselor • Institute of Certified Travel Agents
Accredited Cruise Counselor • Cruise Lines International Association
Member & Past President • Columbia Business Association

22

Rosie Bixel, Portland, Oregon

Note how the use of italic ties together the centered and side headings and subheadings, including the individual's name in the contact information. Boldfacing makes key information stand out.

Communications

Resumes at a Glance

Rebekka Johnson

1234 Baker Road ▼ Albany, Ohio 45710 ▼ 740.698.0000 ▼ bekka0000@yahoo.com

Excerpts from Letters of Recommendation...

"...demonstrated leadership qualities and is looked up to by the other individuals in our classes...very sincere regard for relationships...will be a wonderful success at whatever career path she chooses...Rebekka is a winner!"

—Teresa South
Youth Group Leader

"...a pleasure to be around...a role model for her peers...acted responsibly, with integrity and maturity beyond her years— definitely standing out among her peers...without reservation we recommend Rebekka for any employment opportunities you may have available."

—David Kasler
Alexander Local School Board

▼ ▼ ▼

"...proven to be very dependable, responsible, and trustworthy... completed several college courses in an attempt to enter college a step ahead...her efforts are an indication of her personality because she always wants to accomplish more than what is expected...would be a great asset to any employer."

—Katie Chaney
Teacher

SUMMARY OF QUALIFICATI ONS

Outgoing and enthusiastic individual with a strong work ethic and career goals focused on the field of journalism. Highly self-motivated, as evidenced by successful college studies during high school years, including achieving Dean's List status. Innate talent for writing and experience as Senior Editor of school newspaper. Good listening skills and a sense of humor—elements of success in my chosen field!

EDUCATION

OHIO UNIVERSITY, *College of Communication,* Athens, Ohio (start Fall 2004)
Media Studies Sequence—International Communication Major

ALEXANDER HIGH SCHOOL, Albany, Ohio (May 2004)
Diploma

HOCKING COLLEGE, Nelsonville, Ohio (2003–2004)
General Studies for transfer credit while still completing high school education
- ▼ Received Dean's List Certificate of Merit for Outstanding Academic Achievement
- ▼ Phi Theta Kappa International Honor Society of the Two-Year College

OHIO UNIVERSITY, Athens, Ohio (2001–2002)
General Studies for transfer credit while still completing high school education

RELATED EXPERIENCE

Senior Editor—SPARTAN TIMES NE WSPAPER, Alexander High School, Albany, Ohio (2003–2004)
Gained valuable experience in layout and design while assisting with production of school newspaper. Assigned articles to appropriate staff members. Performed copy editing and proofreading. Coordinated sales and distribution of newspaper. Learned to work efficiently under deadline pressure.

COMMUNITY INVOLVEME NT

- ▼ Vo lunteer work with Toys for Tots, Ohio Educational Support Group, and the Athens County Sheriff's Department DARE program. Received a Certificate of Achievement for Outstanding Citizenship and Volunteer Work.
- ▼ Member of Athens Church of Christ. Active in You th Group activities and volunteer with Community Meals Program.

EXTRACURRICULAR INVOLVEMENT

- ▼ Member of Dance Team, Marching Band, Flag Corps, Spanish Club, and Cheerleading Squad at Alexander High School
- ▼ Member of NASA STARS—Co mpetitive Cheerleading Squad

23

Melissa L. Kasler, Athens, Ohio

This candidate was looking for a summer position before starting her college career in communication. The testimonials are from recommendation letters used with scholarship applications.

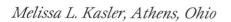

Erica C. Herman

School Address
4444 Alder Avenue
Eugene, OR 97401
(555) 444-4444
ericaherman@aol.com

Permanent Address
8888 N.W. 15th Place
Beaverton, OR 97229
(333) 555-5555

GOAL

A Public Relations Internship

RELEVANT QUALIFICATIONS

♦ Fully capable of handling assignments that require research, creativity and decision-making skills. Deadline-oriented...can produce under pressure.
♦ Exceptional language skills...good interviewer...creative writer...able to express thoughts clearly and effectively both verbally and in writing.
♦ Extensive knowledge of and experience with PageMaker, Photoshop, Microsoft Office applications and Internet communication.
♦ Achiever with an outgoing, enthusiastic personality; comfortable with individuals of all ages and professional levels.
♦ Bilingual: fluent in Spanish.
♦ Editor, high school newspaper.

EDUCATION

University of Oregon, Eugene, OR
Major: Journalism/Concentration: Public Relations
Minor: Spanish

Fall 2003–Present
Cumulative GPA: 3.5

Activities
• Chi Omega Sorority—Marketing/Public Relations Director
• Vice President, National Honor Society
• Public Relations Student Society of America
• Order of Omega

University of Georgia, Athens, GA
Major: Pre-Public Relations
Minor: Spanish

Fall 2002–Spring 2003
Dean's List honors
Cumulative GPA: 3.5

RELATED EXPERIENCE

Media Services Intern
University of Oregon Athletic Media Services, Eugene, OR

Jan. 2004–Present

Research and develop press releases covering various collegiate athletic events. Regularly update the media with information on all UO home athletic events. Write copy for team media guides; manipulate photos for media and public use. Post releases and team results on *www.goducks.com*.

Public Relations Intern
Portland Art Museum, Portland, OR

June 2003–Aug. 2003

As key media contact, coordinated media interviews for staff, curators and directors; fielded inquiries regarding current exhibitions; and assisted in coordinating and staffing special events to gain the public's interest and participation. Researched and produced press releases, public service announcements and copy for the PAM newsletter. Created exhibition press kits.

Continued....

24

Karen L. Conway, Media, Pennsylvania

The applicant hoped for an internship that would turn into a full-time position. She was successful in landing the internship for a Fortune 500 communications firm, with the promise of receiving a full-time position after she graduated. (She took a term off from school to gain this

ERICA C. HERMAN   Page 2

RELATED EXPERIENCE
Continued

<u>Oregon Public Affairs Intern</u>   Dec. 2001–Aug. 2002
XYZ Corporation, Hillsboro, OR
Participated in coordinating community and media relations events. Wrote for worldwide PA newsletter on an Internet website; monitored correspondence between the corporation and Oregon legislators. Assisted with the Strategic Investment Program.

HONORS & AWARDS

National Society of Collegiate Scholars
Ancient Order of Druids Honor Society
Outstanding Freshman in PRSSA (2001–2002)
PRSA Codispoti Technology Section Grant (2003)
Erik Elder Memorial Journalism Scholarship (2002)
Outstanding Junior: service and performance in journalism (2004)

COMMUNITY SERVICE

American Cancer Society administrative volunteer
Oregon Humane Society foster family member
Oregon Public Broadcasting telethon volunteer
Spanish tutor for mentally handicapped student
Make-A-Wish Foundation contributor

valuable experience.) Main section headings are centered with all capital letters. Underlining makes the side headings stand out. Many blank lines ensure white space. The last two sections make a strong ending.

188-17 Greenway, Salt Lake City, UT 00000
000-000-0000
jacqueline@alois.net

Jacqueline Alois

Marketing Communications ❖E-mail Template Design ❖Database Management

Profile

Sales and Marketing Support Professional with more than 14 years of experience in time-sensitive, fast-paced environments. Highly developed skills in oral and written communications, multitasking, attention to detail, and perseverance to completion. Keen insight into clients' perspectives, goals, and target audiences. Proficient with various software programs, including Word, Excel, Access, and Goldmine.

Key strengths include:

- ❖ Promotional copywriting
- ❖ Market research
- ❖ Sales lead qualification
- ❖ Proactive problem solving
- ❖ Database administration

- ❖ Internal/external customer service
- ❖ Computer and procedural training
- ❖ Project coordination
- ❖ Relationship building
- ❖ New-account development

Professional Employment History

GRAYROCK COMMUNICATIONS, INC., BEAR CREEK, UT   1999–PRESENT
Database Marketing Coordinator for trade show design firm
- ❖ Assist the President, Creative Director, and sales force of 7 in developing targeted messages to promote company's services (trade show display design and client training seminars). Contribute ideas in brainstorming sessions and translate concepts into persuasive written materials (brochures, web pages, and e-mail templates).
- ❖ Generate leads through extensive phone contact, which has facilitated the closing of numerous sales by determining clients' interests and addressing their specific needs or concerns.
- ❖ Enter and update all pertinent information for up to 500 clients and prospects on Goldmine system; create profiles and periodically send electronically distributed promotional pieces to keep company in the forefront for future business.
- ❖ Initially train new sales consultants on data mining to their best advantage as well as empower them for success in prospecting and cold calling. Organize sales assignments to avoid duplication of efforts.
- ❖ Coordinate all pre- and post-sale details with various departments.
- ❖ Demonstrated versatility and talent in several areas; was retained on staff despite 2 company downsizings.

QUIGLEY & VANCE, CARRINGTON, UT   1997–1999
Inside Sales Representative for graphic arts supply company
- ❖ Performed duties of sales liaison, assistant purchasing agent, and customer service representative.
- ❖ Streamlined department by automating the quote process and systematizing sales literature.

Education

Westview County College, Randolph, UT — A.A.S., Marketing Communications, 1997

Shelton Institute, Shelton, UT — Applied Writing and Database Administration courses, 1998

25

Melanie Noonan, West Paterson, New Jersey

Note how the fonts are enhanced. Look for boldfacing, bold italic, italic, and small caps. Note also the use of a different font (Albertus Medium) for the person's name, expertise areas, and headings.

Construction

Resumes at a Glance

Daniel L. Madigan

555 North Howard Street · Hagerstown, MD 21740 · Home: (301) 555-9413

Project Superintendent
Residential / Commercial / Government Contracts
Demolitions / Base Builds / Fit-ups

Accomplished Project Superintendent with 20+ years of experience, from initial site work through final walkthrough. Combine broad-spectrum trades knowledge with expert leadership and coordination skills to deliver on-time and under-budget projects. Recognized for exceptional professionalism and ability to interface with all types of people. Offer broad-based responsibilities in the following areas:

- subcontractor & supplier relations
- materials purchasing & management
- contract negotiations & review
- job order contracts (JOC)
- quality control & inspection

- estimating & budgeting
- scheduling & project sequencing
- reading & scaling blue prints
- MD, VA, DC codes & regulations
- OSHA, USDA & EPA regulations

solid work ethic · pride in a job well done · 10-year history of perfect attendance · excellent safety record
high commitment to quality and service

Experience

HOSE BUILDERS, Frederick, MD   2003–Present
- *Project:*   Construct $2.5M, two-story, 12,000 square-foot parts and service department for large GMC dealership.
- *Tasks:*   Oversaw 12 subcontractors and 65 personnel, while ensuring minimal disruption to daily business operations.
- *Outcome:*   Brought project from "trees to keys," 2 months and $.5M under budget.

BUTLER CONTRACTORS, INC., Rockville, MD   1999–2003
- *Project:*   Rotating demolition and reconstruction of $250K to $2.2M scientific laboratories. $10M JOC (Job Order Contract) with National Cancer Institute (Ft. Detrick, MD).
- *Tasks:*   Supervised subcontractors and crew. Oversaw plumbing, electrical, dry wall, cabinet, and equipment installations. Communicated job status to project manager and contract representatives.
- *Outcome:*   Completed 18–20 labs in conformance with researchers' specifications and government/laboratory regulations.

ROSS CONSTRUCTION COMPANY, INC., Silver Spring, MD   1997–1999
- *Project:*   Multiphase, inner-city, apartment-complex renovation project—54 building/469 units/489,000 square-foot site. Funded by Department of HUD (Housing and Urban Development) at $15M.
- *Tasks:*   Supervised two direct reports, 10 subcontractors and 60–70 workers. Demolition, roofing, masonry, and interior renovation of vacant and occupied units.
- *Outcome:*   Brought in within budget and ahead of schedule.

Education & Military Service

Graduate, Fredrick Senior High School, Frederick, MD

Three years' activity military, U.S. Army, Specialist 4, Honorable Discharge

26

Norine Dagliano, Hagerstown, Maryland

The applicant's style was direct: he had a project to do, a deadline to meet, and a budget to keep. The writer echoed this style with a direct Project-Task-Outcome format, using industry keywords.

Shawn Burleson

153 Asbury Lane   McAllen, TX 78501   915-552-1562   915-582-4635

GENERAL FOREMAN
CONSTRUCTION / PIPE FITTER

30 years of comprehensive piping experience,
primarily in chemical plants, refineries, and oil fields on both short- and long-term projects throughout the United States. Proven track record of success with an excellent reputation for
- *quality*
- *troubleshooting*
- *safety compliance*

Knowledgeable in all facets of the construction field. Effective in supervising 20- to 100-man crews.

CORE STRENGTHS

Competent, reliable, and committed professional repeatedly earning promotions throughout career history. Sound and aggressive decision maker utilizing resources and organized processes to achieve success.
- Manage safety regulations according to OSHA and EPA regulations.
- Oversee complex projects and successfully complete them on deadline while exceeding quality standards and staying within budget guidelines.

Willing to travel

Additional core competencies include:

Detail-Oriented	Multitask-Oriented	Analytical
Proficient in OSHA / EPA Regulations	Safety Compliance	Budget Management
Excellent Presentation Skills	Supervision	Quality-Focused
Excellent Communication Skills	Keen Problem-Solving Ability	Assertive Troubleshooting Ability

PROFESSIONAL EXPERIENCE

Most recent history:

General Foreman and Pipe Foreman

10 years as a general foreman in multiple locations throughout the United States.

ACHIEVEMENTS:
- Refurbished and remanufactured a disassembled plant that had been out of service for 10 years. It was eventually shipped to Trinidad.—***CORP ENGINEERING.***
- Supervision:
  - Crew of 45 fabricating and erecting piping on 3 new HRSG boilers—***TRU-COR.***
  - Pipe Support and Hanger crew—***BFM CONTRACTORS.***
  - Installation crew for steam piping in paper mill expansion—***BJ COLE CONTRACTORS.***
  - Crew of 40 fabricating and erecting piping in 865 MW power plant—***HOLCOMB INDUSTRIAL.***
  - Crew of 25 responsible for installing a cold box and associated piping—***SOL-CHEM.***
  - Crew of 34 in fabrication, erection, and weld out of all vendor-furnished piping on 5 new heaters—***J.C.C. JENKING.***
  - Crew of 85 personnel in all activities of Pipe Department—***JACKSON REINOLD.***
  - Crew of 30 in fabrication and erection of process piping, punch out, and hydro test for gas plant expansion in Amarillo, Texas—***CORP ENGINEERING.***

27

MeLisa Rogers, Shiner, Texas

This candidate had a 30-year background in the construction/pipe fitting field. Within 11 years he had worked for 16 different companies but was not a "job hopper." To avoid giving this impression, the writer presented all expertise, achievements, and core strengths that the individual could

Shawn Burleson   Page 2
Professional Experience – Continued

Pipe Fitter and Pipe Superintendent

3 years of pipe fitting background includes experience in multiple United States–based plants, primarily in power and gas settings.

ACHIEVEMENTS:
- Erected steam piping in 1100 MW generating facility—***CRAIG CONSTRUCTION.***
- Fabricated and erected small-bore piping on STG—***REON INDUSTRIAL.***
- Fabricated and erected piping in new paper machine addition—***R.P. STANLEY.***
- Fabricated piping for shutdown—***KARL-ZACHRY.***
- Pepsi plant expansion—***BILMER MECHANICAL.***
- Building of computer chip plant—***JESTER REYNOLD.***

EMPLOYMENT HISTORY

General Foreman	TRU-COR—San Antonio, Texas	Mar 2003–Jun 2003
Pipe Fitter	CRAIG CONSTRUCTION—Phoenix, Arizona	Nov 2002–Feb 2003
Pipe Foreman	BFM CONTRACTORS—Boise, Idaho	Feb 2002–Oct 2002
Pipe Fitter	REON INDUSTRIAL—Tucson, Arizona	Nov 2001–Jan 2002
Pipe Foreman	BJ COLE CONTRACTORS—Austin, Oregon	Jun 2001–Oct 2001
Pipe Fitter	R.P. STANLEY—Wharton, Texas	Sep 2000–May 2001
Pipe General Foreman	HOLCOMB INDUSTRIAL—Houston, Texas	Aug 1999–Jul 2000
Pipe Fabricator	KARL-ZACHRY—Shreveport, Louisiana	Feb 1999–Jun 1999
Pipe Fitter	BILMER MECHANICAL—Tyler, Texas	Oct 1998–Dec 1998
General Foreman	SOL-CHEM—Abilene, Texas	May 1998–Aug 1998
Pipe Fitter	JESTER REYNOLD—Wichita, Kansas	Oct 1997–Jan 1998
Pipe General Foreman	J.C.C. JENKING—Ardmore, Oklahoma	Feb 1997–Jul 1997
Pipe Superintendent	JACKSON REINOLD—Tulsa, Oklahoma	Jun 1995–Aug 1996
Foreman	CORP ENGINEERING—Amarillo, Texas	Oct 1994–Apr 1995
General Foreman / Foreman	CORP ENGINEERING—Lubbock, Texas	May 1993–Sep 1994
General Foreman	CORP ENGINEERING—Amarillo, Texas	May 1992–Jul 1993

SPECIALIZED TRAINING & CERTIFICATIONS

Interaction Management Program

Sol-Chem's STOP Program—certificate of completion

OSHA's Construction Safety Course—10 Hours—certificate of completion

Certified Pipe Fitting and Welding Teacher

bring to the table. The first page focuses on all these categories instead of referring to the numerous places where he had worked. These are mentioned all at once in the Employment History on page 2.

Dennis Rogers

12 Van Buren Drive ▪ Dix Hills, NY 55555 ▪ (555) 555-5555 ▪ dennisrogers@mail.com

BUILDING MATERIALS PROFESSIONAL

Strong Knowledge Base and Network of Contacts in the Building Materials Industry

SUMMARY OF QUALIFICATIONS

- More than 17 years of industry experience. Skilled in sales, purchasing, and operations management.
- Track record of building loyal, profitable customer relationships through excellent service delivery.
- High level of accountability, professional ethics, and dedication to profitability and organizational improvements.

SPECIFIC SKILL AREAS:

- Sales & Marketing
- Inventory Management
- New-Product Evaluation
- Strategic Business Planning

- Quality Assurance Standards
- Cost Reduction & Avoidance
- Warehouse Management
- Staff Training & Mentoring

- Problem Resolution
- Vendor Negotiations
- Delivery Coordination
- Customer Relationships

BUILDING MATERIALS EXPERTISE:

> **Gypsum, steel structural products, ceiling systems, insulation, sheet goods, plywood, lumber, roofing materials, hardware, moldings, paint, screws, and fasteners**

PROFESSIONAL EXPERIENCE

Manager	KLEET LUMBER, Syosset, NY	2000–2004
Manager	BUILDERS' SUPPLY COMPANY, Queens, NY	1992–2000
Owner	ROGERS CONSTRUCTION SUPPLY, Queens, NY	1985–1992

Maintained consistent performance and progressive growth in business development/management operations through full-career experience in wholesale/retail distribution of building materials. Diverse scope of responsibility spanned customer and vendor relationship management, sales and marketing, purchasing, shipping and receiving, warehouse and inventory coordination, and financial management functions. Kept abreast of national and global issues affecting the industry. Fostered extremely loyal customer relationships.

SELECTED SKILL AREAS AND ACCOMPLISHMENTS:

SALES & MARKETING

- Produced 75% of sales for Kleet and 90% of Builders' Supply sales as sole salesperson within each organization. Managed inside sales activities at both companies and outside sales activities, including local travel, for Kleet.
- Recaptured three large Kleet accounts by addressing prior problems in service delivery and restoring customer confidence.
- Managed complex negotiations with customers for commodity-based supplies with fluctuating price structures. Ensured profitability by buying low and selling high.
- Created marketing materials that informed customers of in-stock items. Led effort to bring in new product (lumber) for Builders' Supply that resulted in an additional, profitable revenue stream.

Continued...

28

MJ Feld, Huntington, New York

This resume has many different areas and formats. The Summary of Qualifications itself has three different areas of interest: three bulleted items, followed by Specific Skill Areas, which are followed by Building Materials Expertise items as keywords. Under Professional Experience the three

Dennis Rogers

SALES & MARKETING *(continued)*

- Explored and opened new accounts on Long Island through cold calling and lead generation strategies (Kleet).
- Overcame premium-pricing objections through the strength of customer relationships.

PURCHASING

- Worked closely with approximately 30 companies for the procurement of various building materials. Secured better pricing through negotiation of volume discounts.
- Achieved best prices for customers by keeping abreast of fluctuating markets/prices and conducting favorable negotiations with material suppliers.
- Analyzed supply versus demand and balanced existing inventory with purchasing to ensure profitability.

INVENTORY/WAREHOUSE COORDINATION

- Played key role in reorganizing warehouses at Kleet (20,000 sq. ft.) and Builders' Supply. Employed space-saving strategies at Builders' Supply warehouse to accommodate all materials and fulfill workspace needs.
- Coordinated delivery schedules, verified accuracy of orders against load, and fixed delivery problems to uphold high standards for warehouse operational performance.
- Maintained high quality standards to avoid inventory losses.
- Maximized warehouse utilization through the routine clearing of "dead" inventory, some of which I was able to sell.

MANAGEMENT

- Addressed and resolved occasional customer issues regarding damage and quality of purchased materials.
- Hired and retained skilled workforce members, conducted employee evaluations, and held team members accountable for individual performance.
- Cross-trained administrative and yard personnel to cover instances of employee absence. Improved individual capabilities of team members.
- Managed accounts-receivable and accounts-payable functions.

EDUCATION

Business Administration, 64 credits
STATE UNIVERSITY OF NEW YORK AT STONY BROOK, Stony Brook, NY

COMPUTER SKILLS

Word, Excel, Internet

Excellent References Provided on Request

positions are mentioned together to avoid repetition that would appear in detailed, separate descriptions. Presenting Selected Skill Areas and Accomplishments by categories makes them easily understood.

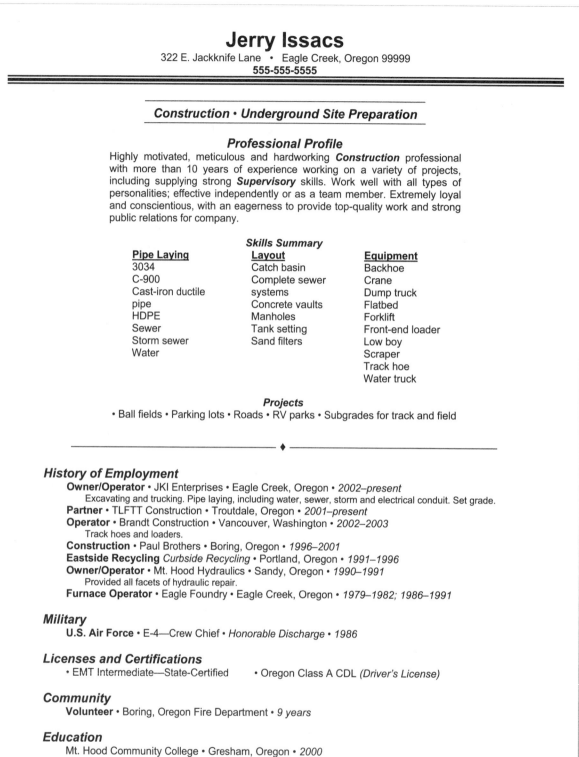

Jerry Issacs
322 E. Jackknife Lane • Eagle Creek, Oregon 99999
555-555-5555

Construction • Underground Site Preparation

Professional Profile
Highly motivated, meticulous and hardworking **Construction** professional with more than 10 years of experience working on a variety of projects, including supplying strong *Supervisory* skills. Work well with all types of personalities; effective independently or as a team member. Extremely loyal and conscientious, with an eagerness to provide top-quality work and strong public relations for company.

Skills Summary

Pipe Laying	Layout	Equipment
3034	Catch basin	Backhoe
C-900	Complete sewer	Crane
Cast-iron ductile	systems	Dump truck
pipe	Concrete vaults	Flatbed
HDPE	Manholes	Forklift
Sewer	Tank setting	Front-end loader
Storm sewer	Sand filters	Low boy
Water		Scraper
		Track hoe
		Water truck

Projects
• Ball fields • Parking lots • Roads • RV parks • Subgrades for track and field

◆

History of Employment
Owner/Operator • JKI Enterprises • Eagle Creek, Oregon • *2002–present*
  Excavating and trucking. Pipe laying, including water, sewer, storm and electrical conduit. Set grade.
Partner • TLFTT Construction • Troutdale, Oregon • *2001–present*
Operator • Brandt Construction • Vancouver, Washington • *2002–2003*
  Track hoes and loaders.
Construction • Paul Brothers • Boring, Oregon • *1996–2001*
Eastside Recycling *Curbside Recycling* • Portland, Oregon • *1991–1996*
Owner/Operator • Mt. Hood Hydraulics • Sandy, Oregon • *1990–1991*
  Provided all facets of hydraulic repair.
Furnace Operator • Eagle Foundry • Eagle Creek, Oregon • *1979–1982; 1986–1991*

Military
U.S. Air Force • E-4—Crew Chief • *Honorable Discharge* • *1986*

Licenses and Certifications
• EMT Intermediate—State-Certified   • Oregon Class A CDL *(Driver's License)*

Community
Volunteer • Boring, Oregon Fire Department • *9 years*

Education
Mt. Hood Community College • Gresham, Oregon • *2000*
Clackamas Community College • Oregon City, Oregon • *1992*

29

Rosie Bixel, Portland, Oregon

A three-column Skills Summary highlights specific skills for this Construction Professional. The History of Employment section lists all his positions together without repetitious commentary.

Customer Service

Resumes at a Glance

Samantha Rodriguez
475 Red Bridge Road
Melville, NY 11747
sam@email.com
(631) 382-2425

Customer Service Representative

Experienced in providing direct customer support by answering inbound calls and providing in-person customer service. Solid customer satisfaction and account-management skills that result in increased revenue and longstanding customer relationships.

Qualifications include the following:

- Timely assessment and understanding of customer expectations. Take a hands-on approach in clarifying customer expectations and resolve issues efficiently.
- Answer and follow up on customer inquiries, generate sales, and handle complex discrepancies related to transaction processing.
- Maintain existing client accounts and process inbound paperwork after receipt, including system update and customer notification.
- Have been described as courteous, patient, and respectful of client concerns.
- Portray a professional image and properly handle confidential information.
- Strong verbal, written, and interpersonal communication and data entry skills. Focus on detail and accuracy.
- Solid computer skills, including MS Word, Excel, Access, and Outlook.

PROFESSIONAL EXPERIENCE

CUSTOMER SERVICE REPRESENTATIVE, Advantage Banking Services, 1998–2001, Dix Hills, New York

Serviced customers, including processing and disbursing loans; opening, closing, and reconciling accounts; processing payroll deductions and direct-deposit requests; processing modifications to existing accounts; and marketing additional banking services and products to customers.

CUSTOMER SERVICE ASSOCIATE, Bank of Long Island, 1996–1998, Huntington, New York

Provided information to customers on issues such as account balances, CD rates, and loan rates. Recommended services such as stop-payment orders, check cards, and fund transfers and processed online applications. Verified deposits and answered questions regarding products and services.

SUPPORT SERVICE REPRESENTATIVE, Mortgage Homes and Loans, 1994–1996, Huntington, New York

Input member information in main system for easy, up-to-date access of data. Maintained files and documentation regarding member accounts. Carried out various clerical duties, including answering phones, distributing mail, and filing. Offered support to other members of Service Center team.

EDUCATION

Liberal Arts, Suffolk County Community College, Brentwood, New York, 1995

30

Linda Matias, Smithtown, New York

The applicant took three years off to raise her first child. The writer made three years of unemployment less evident by playing up qualifications and embedding dates in the Professional Experience section.

JULIE PETERSON

555 Park Lane, Lewiston, NY 14092   (716) 555-8837   peterj@adelphia.net

BANKING CUSTOMER SERVICE REPRESENTATIVE

Dependable, outgoing and conscientious professional seeks position as a bank teller/service representative. Experience in ensuring customer satisfaction and handling complaints and problems. Excellent organization and planning skills. Previous bank teller experience in a busy branch.

Administration	✯ Chosen to settle and restock the ATMs daily
	✯ Reorganized office filing system, updated accounts receivable and processed collections
Customer satisfaction	✯ Worked as customer service representative taking custom orders and ensuring delivery on a tight timetable
Dependable	✯ Worked overtime and unscheduled hours to make sure all holiday orders were filled in time
Managing the public, resolving unpleasant situations	✯ Ran the drive-through window as a bank teller and resolved issues
	✯ Coordinated many public fund-raisers and committees
Organization, planning & multitasking skills	✯ As President of an organization, ran a 33-board-member group with multiple projects
Computer skills	✯ Proficient in Microsoft Word and bank teller systems

PROFESSIONAL EXPERIENCE

The Village Bakeshop, Lewiston, New York, 2001–2008
<u>CUSTOMER SERVICE REPRESENTATIVE</u>
Answered phones, answered questions, resolved problems and wrote orders for custom baskets generated from this bakery's advertising and website. Developed and communicated priorities with the shipping/local delivery department and filled orders to meet customer needs. Worked overtime assisting owner with organizational challenges of running a small business.

Dentist's Office, Lowell, Massachusetts, 1985–1986
<u>RECEPTIONIST/OFFICE MANAGER</u>
Started as dental assistant, and then began completing insurance forms and directly billing insurance companies. Set up and confirmed appointments. Reorganized and improved office filing system. Dramatically improved dentist's financial situation by getting caught up on insurance payments for services already completed, as well as identifying accounts receivable and ensuring collection of balances due.

31

Gail Frank, Tampa, Florida

This candidate had been a military wife and mom for years. With her youngest child in school, she wanted to go back to work. She had been a Bank Teller long ago and wanted to be in banking again. The writer therefore highlighted experience, worker traits, and skills related to a Teller.

JULIE PETERSON

PAGE 2

Arlington Trust Bank, Lowell, Massachusetts, 1984–1985
BANK TELLER/CUSTOMER SERVICE REPRESENTATIVE

Cashed checks, managed the drive-through, created cashiers checks and money orders. Selected for additional responsibility to monitor, balance, settle and restock the ATM with supplies and cash. Verified customers' identities for transactions.

Officers' Spouses Club (OSC), Del Rio, Texas, and Grand Forks, N. Dakota, 1994–2000
PRESIDENT
1ST VICE PRESIDENT
2ND VICE PRESIDENT
CHAIRPERSON OSC WAYS AND MEANS COMMITTEE/FUNDRAISING
CHAIRPERSON OSC PROGRAMS

The Officers' Spouses Club is a nonprofit charitable/social organization composed of U.S. Air Force officer spouses. Elected President due to leadership skills, strong work ethic, ability to listen and enjoying the challenge of making more money for charitable projects.

As President, led OSC to largest amount of charitable funds collected in 3 years. Presented charitable funds to Girl and Boy Scouts troops, Red Cross, public schools and individual scholarships. Fund-raisers included a live auction, an art auction, booths at air shows, craft shows that necessitated coordination of vendors from the entire state and a murder mystery play.

Set agenda and ran monthly 33-person board meeting, ran social dinner/meetings and wrote monthly newsletter for the 200 members. Conducted biannual budget meeting to establish budget. Maintained and evaluated budget throughout year. Learned accounting/checking system and tax code requirements. Attended base hospital quarterly health care meetings and communicated changes in programs and services to OSC members.

86 Flying Training Squadron Spouses Organization, Del Rio, Texas, 1998–1999
DIRECTOR/COORDINATOR
Planned and coordinated monthly meetings to assist spouses with information and support.

PTA Grand Forks Elementary School, Del Rio, Texas, 1994–1998
SECRETARY AND FIRST GRADE VOLUNTEER

Compiled and published monthly meeting notes and assisted with fund-raisers. Volunteered in first grade classroom twice a week. Entrusted with reading groups of 4–5 children.

EDUCATION

Degree, Lowell High School, Lowell, Massachusetts, 1984. Awarded scholarship as a senior.

Bold sans serif type on both pages suggests confidence and reliability. Five-pointed stars as bullets are a different touch on page 1. Under Professional Experience, paragraphs indicate responsibilities and achievements.

BENJAMIN THOMAS MUELLER

177 Squantum Avenue
Midtown, Rhode Island 02888
(401) 000-9999

SUMMARY

➢ Highly qualified professional with extensive experience in customer service, sales, and management.
➢ Consistently maintain a high degree of effectiveness in balancing daily responsibilities with concurrent participation on special committees.
➢ High-energy, client-focused, and goal-oriented manager and team player.
➢ Proven capable and reliable in handling multiple tasks while maintaining an orderly efficiency of operations.

EXPERIENCE

1997–present   **Edgewood Sensors, Inc.,** Pawtucket, RI
Customer Service Supervisor

- Discuss, advise, and assist in selection and sale of appropriate products to satisfy customer requirements, providing formal quotes, tracking orders, and solving problems.
- Address and resolve customer issues, expedite orders, and increase business.
- Upgrade and streamline online data system, providing training in manufacturing systems, sales, and incentive programs.
- Coordinate and administer major account activities, resulting in 60% net growth and customer satisfaction.

1994–1997   **AT&T Communications,** Providence, RI
Customer Service Representative

- Responded to 70 customer calls per day, managing resolution of billing inquiries to full customer satisfaction.
- Calmed and counseled irate and difficult customers, clarifying their needs and recommending appropriate actions, thus enhancing customer loyalty, company reputation, and overall increase in annual sales.
- Contributed generously to team's success in meeting aggressive sales objectives.

1989–1994   **Victor Auto Group,** Midtown, RI
1991–1994   *General Sales Manager*

- Managed operation of auto dealership with $7M gross sales, including staffing, sales, service, and general office.
- Increased unit sales volumes by 120% and gross sales averages by 22% through rebuilding of sales staff and improved marketing procedures.
- Automated finance and insurance function utilizing PC system and TRW reporting, resulting in increased efficiency, information capture, and sales closures.
- Standardized advertising strategy and format, thus improving customer recognition and increasing sales per advertising dollar.

32

Edward Turilli, North Kingstown, Rhode Island

Although prospective employers like to read about an applicant's most recent experience first, you can view an individual's career development by starting at the end of the resume and reading to the beginning. Here you can trace the person's growth after he got out of the Air Force:

BENJAMIN THOMAS MUELLER

1989–1991   *Sales Manager and F&I Manager*

- Directed auto sales and finance and insurance departments for busy dealership.
- Established profitable finance and insurance department, representing 30% of gross sales profits.
- Implemented tracking system to provide a central standardized profile of customers and customer traffic, resulting in better utilization of sales strategies and increased sales.

1988–1989   **Rally's Auto Sales,** Dartmouth, MA
              Finance and Insurance Manager

- Negotiated financing between customers and lending institutions, leading to acceptable terms during a soft sales market.
- Coordinated auto delivery operations, including all necessary paperwork.

1986–1988   **Oldsmobile, Cadillac, GMC Auto Sales,** Midtown, RI, and Fall River, MA
              Sales

- Sold autos and trucks to individual and commercial customers, averaging 15 sales per month, or $225,000 in monthly gross sales.
- Coordinated dealer swaps and special orders for auto and truck sales, ensuring accurate, efficient sales and deliveries.

1984–1986   **The Foxboro Company,** Foxboro, MA
              Several positions held over four-year employment:

- Manager of Operations Support Services, Supervisor of Software Support Services, Associate Programmer, Software Technical Writer, and Lead Software Technician.
- Supervised and managed staffs up to 20 employees.

EDUCATION / TRAINING

- Took several courses in Business Management and Computer Science at Montana State University and Northwestern University.
- Throughout career completed numerous management programs and courses, particularly in computer technical operations, programming, and software.

MILITARY

United States Air Force, 1980–1984 (Honorably Discharged)

- Rank of Computer Specialist, First Class

– Excellent references and letters of recommendation furnished upon request –

from a Support Services Manager, to a Car Salesperson, to a Finance Manager, to a Sales Manager, and so on, until he became a Customer Service Supervisor at his present company. The Summary now makes sense.

CYD MARSTEN

15722 Arkansas Street
Newhall, California 91321

Residence: 661 253-1908
Cellular: 661 807-1171

CUSTOMER SERVICE / COLLECTIONS

Customer Service

Results-oriented, enthusiastic, creative, client-services professional with extensive experience in client relations **across broad industries** (medical, mortgage, insurance). Excellent problem-solving skills with a strong orientation in customer service/satisfaction. Able to work under pressure in fast-paced, time-sensitive environments. Demonstrated ability in assessing problem areas and offering recommendations resulting in increases in productivity and profitability. Background encompasses **strong leadership** as well as the ability to establish and build positive, solid relationships with clients and all levels of management. Outstanding listening and interpersonal skills. Energetic, with proven stamina. Computer literate.

Collections

- Expertise in reenergizing stagnant customer accounts.
- Superb negotiation skills with the ability to interact with clients, establish equitable payment policies, and resolve billing errors to maintain positive relations.
- Professional and articulate; ability to deal with clients at all levels.
- Conscientious application of policies, procedures, and systems.
- Quick and effective problem solver while dealing with new concepts, systems, and procedures.
- Knowledge of how to deal with difficult people.

SYNOPSIS OF ACHIEVEMENTS

- ◆ Captured **$160,000 within one week** by reinstating three loans.
- ◆ Collected **$112,000 within a one-month period,** the highest amount ever collected by anyone during entire history of Collection Bureau of Modesto.
- ◆ Developed program facilitating processing of **medical claims,** which was implemented company-wide. Still in use today.
- ◆ Reorganized high-delinquency, mortgage-accounts unit to lower delinquency ratios to acceptable standards.
- ◆ Reactivated key accounts using persuasion/mediation skills.
- ◆ **People's Choice Award,** Security Pacific Home Loans

HIGHLIGHTS OF RELATED WORK EXPERIENCE

COLLECTIONS COUNSELOR ● Security Pacific Home Loans—Riverside, CA
Communicate regularly and effectively with mortgagees who are delinquent on their mortgage loans. Complete documentation of collection efforts including communications, reason for default, payment plans, updated telephone numbers, and mailing addresses. Explored alternatives to foreclosures, which led to reinstatement of 25 loans in September and 10 in October. Types of loans were various conventional loans and B&C paper loans. **90% performing commitment** for September 2003.

CUSTOMER SERVICE / COLLECTIONS ● Archibald Enterprises—Santa Paula, CA
Consistently exceed collection quotas (currently **ranked No. 1** by collecting more than 50%) through diplomatic and sensitive interaction with debtors. Resolve clients' advertising difficulties. Handle all correspondence pertaining to customer service.

33

Myriam-Rose Kohn, Valencia, California

Two horizontal lines enclose the Customer Service/Collections heading, making it seen first. The two topics are then treated in turn as subheadings to describe the applicant's experience, skills, worker traits, and expertise. These assertions are reinforced by the Synopsis of Achievements.

CYD MARSTEN

COLLECTOR / SUPERVISOR • Collection Bureau of Modesto—San Jose, CA
Resolved most billing problems on behalf of policyholders while maintaining an ongoing professional relationship with most insurance companies. **Ranked No. 1** collector. Created programs that streamlined productivity and increased efficiency.

CLAIMS SUPERVISOR • Allstate Insurance—River Falls, CA
Proactive planning led to notable increase in morale in all departments and in reestablishing clients' trust and loyalty.

LOAN SERVICE / COLLECTION OFFICER • Great Western Savings—Northridge, CA
Diplomacy and assertiveness allowed for adherence to payment schedules and resolution of tax problems. Dealt with insurance queries, lawsuits, and culture/communication barriers. Handled FHA, VA, and conventional types of loans.

NON-RELATED EXPERIENCE

OWNER • L.A. Rottweilers—Modesto, CA
Bred, raised, showed, and sold Rottweilers trained as Pet Therapy Dogs to bring sunshine to patients in Children's Hospital and elderly homes.
Handled all daily administrative affairs, including A/P, A/R, general ledger, and running credit checks.

WORK HISTORY

Collections Counselor	Security Pacific Home Loans	Riverside, CA	2009
Customer Service/Collections	Archibald Enterprises	Santa Paula, CA	2001–2009
Administrative Assistant	Personnel Plus	Santa Clarita, CA	2000–2001
Server/Trainer	Mimi's Café, Birks	Modesto, CA	1995–2000
Business Owner	L.A. Rottweilers	Modesto, CA	1992–1995
Collector/Supervisor	Collection Bureau of Modesto	Modesto, CA	1989–1992
Claims Supervisor	Allstate Insurance	River Falls, CA	1987–1989
Loan Service/Collection Officer	Great Western Savings	Northridge, CA	1985–1986

CONTINUAL TRAINING
B&C 101 New Hire Training Course
B&C 102 New Hire Training Course
B&C 102 On The Job Training Course
Seminar in Customer Service

Boldfacing calls attention to significant points on both pages. The Work History on page 2 keeps the writer from having to mention similar duties at similar positions.

SHARON C. WEIGERT

5005 Burnet Creek, Twin River Valley, NJ 05500
(555) 505-5500 ▪ scweigert055@live.net

Clinical Office Manager / Senior Administrative Support

Versatile Administrative Support Specialist with Project Management (PM) training and proven skills in:

✓ **Office Administration**—Executive administrative operations, sales support operations, special projects, regulatory compliance, corporate meetings, and travel arrangements. Top-notch multitasking skills.

✓ **Customer Service and Call Center Management**—Research and analysis, inbound service operations, database management (DBM), process improvement, after-call work, fulfillment, product and launch support, and management reporting in multichannel, customer-focused environments.

✓ **Project Management**—End-to-end planning for initiatives, resource management, coordination of internal and external resources, communications with cross-functional teams and stakeholders, and problem solving.

✓ **Communications**—Effective verbal skills with strategic partners, internal and external customers, and senior management. Experienced interfacing with key clinical sales account representatives and vendors.

✓ **Training**—Software training and materials for medical office staff end users and central billing office call center on billing systems, database management, and online applications.

CLINICAL & PHARMACEUTICAL EXPERIENCE

VALLEY HEIGHTS MEDICAL CENTER, Twin River Valley, NJ   2007–Present
Premier New Jersey health organization providing comprehensive medical, diagnostic, surgical, behavioral health, rehabilitative and preventive health services for inpatients and outpatients.

Office Manager—Burnt Creek Family Healthcare Center

▪ **Office Administration:** Directed smooth-running operations for Burnt Creek Family Health Center office with 35 physicians and 15 physician assistants. Supervised and trained 10 full-time and part-time clerical staff.

▪ **Regulatory Compliance:** Ensured cost-effective operations, meeting patient and residency-training-program needs. Monitored and conducted activities directed by State of New Jersey licensing boards and provided direction for meeting state regulations and JCAHO standards.

DIAGNOSTICS GLOBAL CORPORATION, Edison Central, NJ   1992–1997
Senior Customer Service Group Leader—promoted from Customer Service Rep
Led 20-member customer service unit responsible for order fulfillment and billing. Trained, supervised, and scheduled customer service staff, including new hire orientation. Served as liaison with senior management.

▪ **Call Center Administration:** Directed high-volume, 800-line inbound service operations (order processing) from regional sales reps, hospitals, purchasing agents, and physicians.
  - Consistently resolved account escalations and achieved 98% rating for customer satisfaction.
  - Gained in-depth knowledge of pharmaceutical products, pricing, order fulfillment, claims, and credits.

▪ **Sales Support:** Served as first point-of-contact with Regional Account Managers in East Coast territory. Answered product-related inquiries, researched customer issues, and resolved order discrepancies. Initiated product-update meetings via conference calls for enhanced account relationship management.

▪ **DBM and Reporting:** Ensured accurate database management for current, divested, discontinued, and future pipeline products. Generated statistical reports on daily call volumes and breakdowns for management.

GREEN HILLS BIOMEDICAL LABORATORIES, Green Hills, NJ   1990–1992
Administrative Support to VP of Laboratories

▪ **Executive Support:** Served as key point-of-contact (POC) for 50-member Sales Force team. Coordinated in-house and off-site meetings, business calendars, and executive travel for Vice President of Laboratories.

▪ **Project Management:** Entrusted with rush assignments, as well as multiple-project management oversight. Maintained high levels of confidentiality while conducting sensitive records management and processing.

34

Susan Guarneri, Three Lakes, Wisconsin

The first section near the top of the first page is, in effect, a summary of skills indicated by embedded bold headings in five different short paragraphs. The next two major headings cover the applicant's experience (Clinical & Pharmaceutical and Telecommunications). An interest in all three

SHARON C. WEIGERT

Page 2

(555) 505-5500 ▪ scweigert055@live.net

TELECOMMUNICATIONS EXPERIENCE

APEX TRAINING TECHNOLOGIES, Peterwell, NJ   2006–2007

World's largest provider of telecommunications training services with 165 operation-support systems.

Solution Software Deployment Specialist

- **Project Management:** Led successful project management of billing and customer-care software deployment services, meeting project milestones and deadlines. Delivered software training on-site to client end users and local staff to ensure accurate order entry and billing and carrier-to-carrier message exchanges.

- **Customer Service:** Decided on new processes to improve end-user experience in automated customer-care and billing environment; 2 were adopted company-wide. Selected by VP of Training to serve on 4 cross-functional process teams to align performance improvements with client needs and business strategies.

US WIRELESS, Carrolltown, NJ   2002–2005

Leading provider of digital wireless communications in the United States with 6.3 million subscribers.

Manager, Customer Service Call Center

- **Call-Center Operations:** Promoted from Customer Service Coordinator to manage call-center operations for launch of Customer Service Call Center located in Pennsylvania. Trained and supervised team of 10 new hires in call-center operations, as well as Trouble Ticket Manager software.

- **End-User Training:** Designed and developed training materials and delivered on-site training programs for end users, field support, and managers in Trouble Ticket Manager software at multiple locations. Served on executive management team charged with improving the GUI interface entry screen for new trouble tickets.

- **Technical Documentation & Reporting:** Oversaw and monitored 7-member team in daily data collection and documentation for call-center operations. Generated activity reports and performed data analysis to determine root cause of service failures.

- **Customer Needs Analysis:** Developed interdepartmental customer-needs assessment and analysis reports for Corporate Relations and Engineering, which were rolled out enterprise-wide within 6 months.

TELECOMM GLOBAL, East Warwickshire, NJ   1997–2002
Repair Bureau Specialist—Corporate Network Operations Control Center

- **Customer Service Honors:** Promoted from Customer Care Analyst in less than 8 months. Won Customer Service Honor Award (1998) for maintaining high service levels of 100 inbound calls daily for 4 weeks.

- **Process Improvement:** Served as first point-of-contact for 800-line call center, supporting 8 domestic regional markets. Improved call-center operations and decreased call-volume escalations 40% by designing and developing one-call resolution training package for Customer Care Analysts.

- **Project Management:** Earned Award of Excellence, Outstanding Customer Service Performance for Olympic Summer Games trials by directing successful project management and implementation of 300 wireless phones for Olympic Committee members within 24 hours of initial request.

EDUCATION, TRAINING, & COMPUTER SKILLS

Medical Coding Certificate—Twin River Valley Community College, Twin River Valley, NJ—2007
Project Management Professional (PMP) Training—Project Management Institute (PMI)—2006
Personal Computers Applications Certificate—Computer Technology Institute, Edison Central, NJ

Computer Proficiency—Well versed in Medical Management, Windows, MS Office, Word, Excel, PowerPoint, Access, MS Project, MS Outlook, MS Publisher, Visual Basic, Visio, SQL Server Database, UNIX, Linux

major sections is to point out her management experience and abilities. Information about her Education, Training & Computer Skills comes last at the bottom of page 2.

JENNIFER MOORE

17422 Green Forest Drive ❖ Houston, TX 77068
(555) 555-5555 ❖ j_moore4123@aol.com

CUSTOMER SERVICE & RELATIONSHIPS SPECIALIST

Excellent Communication Skills / Bilingual in Spanish & English

Customer-driven, creative Customer Service professional offering extensive experience and consistent track record of creating strategies for new market penetration, customer base expansion, and revenue gains. Skilled in developing and executing special events and promotions that earn rave reviews and produce results. Effective communicator and presenter; maintain uncompromising focus on assessing and fulfilling customer needs. Recipient of awards for on-the-job performance.

Knowledge & Skill Areas:

- Event Planning/Coordination
- Customer Needs Assessment
- Competitor Research/Analysis
- Customer Satisfaction/Retention
- Strategic Market Planning
- Customer Communications
- Relationship Building
- New Program Development
- Workflow Prioritization
- Sales/Revenue Growth
- Problem Resolution
- Inventory Management

PROFESSIONAL EXPERIENCE

CITY OF HOUSTON, Houston, TX   1996–Present
Customer Service Representative, Houston Power & Light (1999–Present)

Promoted to drive business development objectives for HP&L in highly competitive environment, with Xcel Energy as primary competitor. In charge of planning, developing, and implementing marketing game plan to build and retain customer base, including in-person customer visits and attendance at luncheons, banquets, trade shows, business expos, and other special events. Provide comparisons between HP&L and other utility companies to highlight company's advantages and gain new business. **Selected Accomplishments:**

- *Revenue Growth*—Played key role in building business growth within heavily competitive market, securing **9,067** new meters since 1999 that represents **$7.4 million** in additional annual revenues. Contributed to one of HP&L's most productive years in 1998–1999, with **227,376** new customers, and market share representing **46%** of customers in Houston.

- *Customer Satisfaction*—Maintained high levels of customer satisfaction over 4-year period, primarily through visiting average of **67** customers per week to address and resolve problems.

- *Partner Liaison*—Serve as Organizational Representative for apartment communities and management companies regarding vacant apartments, billing, and complaints.

- *Customer Retention*—Retained **28** multi-housing communities and several commercial business customers, preventing departure to competitor.

- *Community Involvement*—Represented HP&L at major charity events, including Walk for Life, MS, and March of Dimes, to enhance company's image within community and assist those in need.

Benefits Specialist (1997–1999)

Held multiple HR responsibilities regarding benefits program for 1,850 full-time employees, including scheduling exit interviews, assisting employees/retirees/dependents with inquiries and complaints, creating notifications regarding benefit changes, and supporting Payroll department with annual budget and payroll data-entry activities, completing ad-hoc duties on request from Payroll/Benefits Coordinator. Prepared and organized all full-time employee files. **Selected Accomplishments:**

- *Event Coordination*—Planned and coordinated organization's 1st Annual Benefits Fair. Arranged logistics, selected vendors, solicited donations, and promoted event extensively to city employees; attracted **5,000+** attendees for highly praised fair that became permanent event.   *(Continued)*

35

Daniel J. Dorotik, Jr., Lubbock, Texas

A pair of parallel lines defines the all-important zone that will be read near the top of the first page. The purpose of this area is to capture the reader's attention and create interest in reading further. Casting the Knowledge & Skill Areas list as three columns of bulleted phrases makes it

JENNIFER MOORE   2

Professional Experience, Continued

- *Community Involvement*—Served as assistant to Campaign Chairperson for United Way Campaign in 1998. Prepared financial statement, pledge cards, awards certificates, and promotional materials. Contributed to reaching **91.6%** of goal for total of **$122,500** in employee contributions.

- *Management/Team Support*—Created effective reports for Payroll/Benefits Coordinator, Managing Director, and Benefits Committee using PowerPoint, Excel, Access, Word, and Lotus.

Recruitment/Administrative Assistant (1996–1997)

Assisted in various aspects of recruitment, including preparing recruiting packets, maintaining internal Job Board, writing and updating job descriptions, screening applicants, and processing hiring paperwork. For large recruiting positions, highlighted minimum qualifications and special requests from supervisor, providing recruiter with only qualified applicants to save time. **Selected Accomplishments:**

- *Advertisement Placement*—Worked closely with **Houston Chronicle, Dallas Morning-News,** and other publications to ensure proper placement of advertisements for various positions, including clerical, police, fire, library, and IT.

- *Productivity Improvement*—Created Advertising Log to provide valuable reference for methods of advertising; assisted Senior Clerks in mail-merge activities to expedite word processing tasks.

HOUSTON APARTMENT ASSOCIATION, Houston, TX   1991–1996
Administrative Assistant to the Executive Officer

Worked closely with EO in various administrative and information-management functions, including researching data for annual budget, preparing expense statements, answering phones, proofing organizational manuals/documents, maintaining files, and processing invoices. Key aspect of position involved arranging materials and promotions for special events. **Selected Accomplishments:**

- *Event Coordination*—Contributed to successful execution of events that included **Annual Golf Tournament, Installation & Awards Banquet, Annual Trade Show,** and **Members-Only Luncheons.** Prepared bulk mailers, promoted event in monthly publication, organized skits for luncheons, and managed reservation list, billing, registration, and financial statement.

- *Productivity & Efficiency*—Converted A/R from manual entry to QuickBooks/Peachtree Accounting; maintained accurate membership rosters and provided updates to Texas Apartment Association and National Apartment Association.

*Held position as Assistant Property Manager for the Utica Plaza Apartments from 1987 to 1991. Played key role in increasing occupancy from **60%** to **95%** and maintaining delinquency at less than 1% rough widespread upgrades and improved tenant relationships by creating open, friendly atmosphere.*

PROFESSIONAL DEVELOPMENT

Certifications & Designations:
Certified Apartment Manager (CAM)
Notary Public, 2nd Renewal—Expiration Date: 02/10

Awards & Recognitions:
- "Five Years of Dedicated Service," Houston Apartment Association
- "Job Well Done," City of Houston Benefits Department Award

easy for the reader to spot particular areas of interest quickly. An added value of this format is that different phrases can be substituted easily to tailor the resume to a different job target.

Debra Lockstedt

| 752 Lakewood Drive | Lubbock, Texas 79411-5838 | (806) 897-5583 |

CUSTOMER SERVICE MANAGEMENT PROFESSIONAL
with 16 years of multifaceted experience offers effective and decisive leadership in a fast-paced, results-oriented environment with an emphasis on client development and customer satisfaction.
Background includes 11 years of staff supervision and 17 years in technology.

Career Highlight
"Supervisor of the Quarter –Fourth Quarter 2008"
Presented by the Vice President of Operations of Titan Communications, Inc., in recognition of the attainment of the highest achievement of outstanding quality in customer service among a corporate supervisor team of 60 personnel.

PROFESSIONAL ACHIEVEMENTS

➢ *Achieved an A+ rating* on the research, creation and delivery of a PowerPoint presentation titled "T.E.A.M.—Together Everyone Achieves More." This presentation was graded by an audience of site management personnel and peers as part of a communication module in our operation's supervisor development training series.

➢ *Recognized as a leader in quality* by maintaining the highest team quality average of 96% for both quality and retail operations teams. These teams consist of approximately 15–18 agents each.

➢ *Managed a client dial-up project for 45 days,* resulting in client satisfaction. Implemented the following strategies: daily statistical analyses of call volume; tracked number of calls per variety of card; produced analytical reports of calls and consumer data.

➢ *Exceeded client customer service goals* through troubleshooting customer service quality issues during 6–7 client calibration conference calls per week. Quality enhancement plans are implemented as a result of these calls, and the success of these changes is measured through the daily monitoring and scoring of agent customer service skills and is reported to the client.

PROFESSIONAL TRAINING

Supervisory Skills and Certifications
- Time Management
- Sexual Harassment Recognition and Prevention
- Fundamental Skills of Managing / Communicating
- Performance Counseling I & II
- People-Trak Human Resource Information Management Systems

Technical Skills

Hardware	**Software**
PCs (IBM, Dell, Compaq)	UNIX
Liebert Datawave Battery Backup	HBO Clinical
Laser, line, dot-matrix, and barcode printers	Keane Financial
DG Hardware – MV10, 000 and MV20, 000	HBO STAR Navigator (GUI)
Clarion/Avion 8500	Rhino X Medical Communication
Interfaces	Watch Child
Modems	Physician Access
Networks (basic)	Versys
	HBO Laboratory

36

MeLisa Rogers, Shiner, Texas

The applicant had a diverse background in computer technology and customer-service management. She wanted to become an Office Manager. The writer presented all professional achievements on the first page before indicating in the Professional Experience section where the

Debra Lockstedt   page 2

PROFESSIONAL EXPERIENCE

TITAN COMMUNICATIONS, INC.
Supervisor (Customer Care and Retail Teams)   *June 2000–Present*
- Coach and develop agents through agent evaluations, reviews, and attendance records
- Process and manage payroll hours and QRP (quality reward program) monthly incentives
- Implement new products as they are introduced into the call center
- Create a productive working environment for agents through positive communication and leadership

HIGHLAND MEDICAL CENTER
Information Services Operations Supervisor   *February 1999–June 2000*
- Supervised the operations staff and assigned work duties
- Scheduled, trained, and monitored software calls/resolutions of employees
- Maintained all computer systems, backups, and networks
- Managed upgrades to computer systems
- Created Ad-Hoc reports as required (Keane Cyberquery, UNIX, SQL, and basic Crystal Reports); set up Interface Management systems—created menus and forms and wrote procedure manuals
- Worked closely with LAN/WAN administrator, PC technicians and internal departments; managed communication with outside vendors

Acting Information Services Operations Supervisor   *August 1998–February 1999*
- Upgraded computer system
- Managed inventory of all equipment, computer system backups, and report maintenance and delivery; monitored help desk, troubleshooting all computer problems
- Supervised operations Staff: assigned work duties and scheduled and trained employees
- Created Ad-Hoc reports as needed

PC Technician   *April 1998–August 1998*
- Installed and configured PCs and performed troubleshooting on PC-related problems
- Loaded software and managed delivery and setup of PCs to medical personnel
- Managed inventory of equipment and tested/ordered supplies from vendors

Computer Operator   *April 1987–April 1998*
- Provided maintenance of the HBO Clinical and Keane Financial systems which involved system backups; table maintenance; report creation, generation, and distribution; optical disk backups; data entry; creation of Ad-Hoc reports
- Processed payroll and managed employee security schedules and training
- Managed the troubleshooting of hardware/software and assisted with upgrades, system decision making, and help desk support

EDUCATION and PROFESSIONAL CERTIFICATIONS

Lakeridge High School—Graduate, Lubbock, Texas
Lubbock Christian University—One Semester September 1998
Highland Medical Center—Courses and certifications: Local-Area Network, SynOptics Communication Termserver, Ethernet connectivity DG UNIX Basic, Medical Communications software Keane Cyberquery Reporting, SQL, Crystal Reports (basic), GUI Interface Management, and Forms and Menus

person worked before. Career highlights near the top of the first page focus on her management ability in her current position as a supervisor. Technical skills are listed at the bottom of page 1.

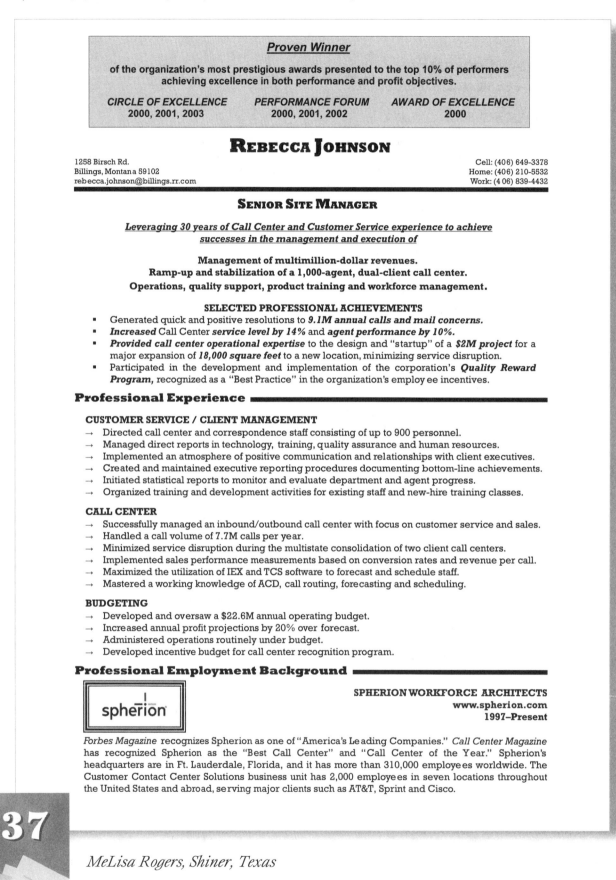

> **_Proven Winner_**
>
> of the organization's most prestigious awards presented to the top 10% of performers achieving excellence in both performance and profit objectives.
>
> | CIRCLE OF EXCELLENCE | PERFORMANCE FORUM | AWARD OF EXCELLENCE |
> |:---:|:---:|:---:|
> | 2000, 2001, 2003 | 2000, 2001, 2002 | 2000 |

REBECCA JOHNSON

1258 Birsch Rd.
Billings, Montana 59102
rebecca.johnson@billings.rr.com

Cell: (406) 649-3378
Home: (406) 210-5532
Work: (406) 839-4432

SENIOR SITE MANAGER

Leveraging 30 years of Call Center and Customer Service experience to achieve successes in the management and execution of

Management of multimillion-dollar revenues.
Ramp-up and stabilization of a 1,000-agent, dual-client call center.
Operations, quality support, product training and workforce management.

SELECTED PROFESSIONAL ACHIEVEMENTS

- Generated quick and positive resolutions to *9.1M annual calls and mail concerns.*
- *Increased* Call Center *service level by 14%* and *agent performance by 10%.*
- *Provided call center operational expertise* to the design and "startup" of a *$2M project* for a major expansion of *18,000 square feet* to a new location, minimizing service disruption.
- Participated in the development and implementation of the corporation's **Quality Reward Program,** recognized as a "Best Practice" in the organization's employee incentives.

Professional Experience

CUSTOMER SERVICE / CLIENT MANAGEMENT

- → Directed call center and correspondence staff consisting of up to 900 personnel.
- → Managed direct reports in technology, training, quality assurance and human resources.
- → Implemented an atmosphere of positive communication and relationships with client executives.
- → Created and maintained executive reporting procedures documenting bottom-line achievements.
- → Initiated statistical reports to monitor and evaluate department and agent progress.
- → Organized training and development activities for existing staff and new-hire training classes.

CALL CENTER

- → Successfully managed an inbound/outbound call center with focus on customer service and sales.
- → Handled a call volume of 7.7M calls per year.
- → Minimized service disruption during the multistate consolidation of two client call centers.
- → Implemented sales performance measurements based on conversion rates and revenue per call.
- → Maximized the utilization of IEX and TCS software to forecast and schedule staff.
- → Mastered a working knowledge of ACD, call routing, forecasting and scheduling.

BUDGETING

- → Developed and oversaw a $22.6M annual operating budget.
- → Increased annual profit projections by 20% over forecast.
- → Administered operations routinely under budget.
- → Developed incentive budget for call center recognition program.

Professional Employment Background

spherion

SPHERION WORKFORCE ARCHITECTS
www.spherion.com
1997–Present

Forbes Magazine recognizes Spherion as one of "America's Leading Companies." *Call Center Magazine* has recognized Spherion as the "Best Call Center" and "Call Center of the Year." Spherion's headquarters are in Ft. Lauderdale, Florida, and it has more than 310,000 employees worldwide. The Customer Contact Center Solutions business unit has 2,000 employees in seven locations throughout the United States and abroad, serving major clients such as AT&T, Sprint and Cisco.

37

MeLisa Rogers, Shiner, Texas

This individual had an extensive 30-year background, which had to be communicated as precisely as possible in a two-page resume. She had been laid off and therefore needed to be positioned as competitively as possible in the call center industry. Because the applicant had won multiple

REBECCA JOHNSON
– Page Two –

Senior Site Manager, Customer Contact Center—Great Falls/Helena/Billings, Montana **2000–Present**
- Increased client satisfaction scores by 22% in less than one year.
- Center was recognized by organization for top quality agents in consecutive periods.
- Maintained the highest percentage of staff promoted within the organization.
- Used several temporary agencies to meet fluctuating business demands.
- Controlled all sensitive correspondence for the business referred to Better Business Bureau, Attorney General, media or private law firms.
- Created ongoing programs to recognize achievements and participation for employees.
- Organized celebration festivities for the prestigious "Call Center of the Year Award."

Manager, Services Integrity—Fairbanks, Alaska **1999–2000**
- Identified, communicated, and implemented "best practices" in Spherion call centers.
- Assisted with start-up operations, acquiring operations transition knowledge and experience.

Manager, Consumer Relations—Fairbanks, Alaska **1997–1998**
- Responsible for all consumer relations processing for Spherion products.

BERTELSMANN MUSIC GROUP
www.bmg.com
Fairbanks, Alaska 1981–1997

BMG's company headquarters are located in New York, New York. Primary areas of business include record labels, music publishing and music distribution. BMG has offices worldwide with a total of 4,500 employees and annual revenues of $2.7 billion.

Manager, Doubleday Member Services **1994–1997**
- Coached analysts utilizing proprietary software package, M/Text, for written communications.
- Co-chaired and implemented company-wide incentive program.
- Managed six direct reports, two support staff and 150+ employees.

Manager, Customer Support Services **1981–1994**
- Oversaw the auditing process of customer transactions for scanned, data entry and CSR input.
- Managed customer correspondence generated from the site for CSR and communication inserts.
- Executed 100% of all sensitive correspondence, such as escalated concerns, BBB, Attorney General, law office and special enforcement agencies.
- Coordinated all insertion and manual club mailings.
- Supervised two correspondence analysts, eight supervisors and three support staff with 200+ employees.

RCA RECORD CLUB (*Name changed to Bertelsmann*)—Fairbanks, Alaska **1976–1981**

Supervisor, Music Service

- Processed enrollment applications for mail order music.
- Verified post office information and edited documents to set up accounts in the database.
- Mailed out and processed return correspondence from members.
- Conducted two-week new-hire training classes four times a year to meet the direct marketing spring, summer, fall and winter enrollment campaigns.
- Supervised call center activities and processed online transactions relating to customer accounts.

Education

Business and General Studies
Fairbanks Community College—Fairbanks, Alaska

Committees and Memberships
Board of Directors, Boys and Girls Club—Billings, Montana
Board Member of Montana Workforce Innovative Networking—Great Falls, Montana
Board Member of Montana Workforce Commission—Helena, Montana
International Association of Reservation Executives

awards, the writer headed up the resume with "Proven Winner" to generate interest and to intrigue the reader. The first time the applicant used this new resume, she got called for an interview.

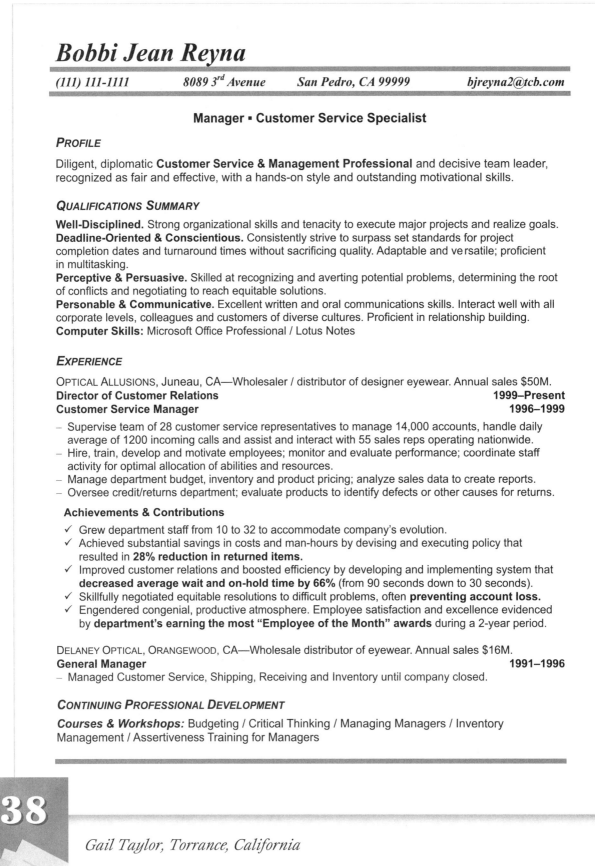

Bobbi Jean Reyna

| (111) 111-1111 | 8089 3rd Avenue | San Pedro, CA 99999 | bjreyna2@tcb.com |

Manager ▪ Customer Service Specialist

PROFILE

Diligent, diplomatic **Customer Service & Management Professional** and decisive team leader, recognized as fair and effective, with a hands-on style and outstanding motivational skills.

QUALIFICATIONS SUMMARY

Well-Disciplined. Strong organizational skills and tenacity to execute major projects and realize goals.
Deadline-Oriented & Conscientious. Consistently strive to surpass set standards for project completion dates and turnaround times without sacrificing quality. Adaptable and versatile; proficient in multitasking.
Perceptive & Persuasive. Skilled at recognizing and averting potential problems, determining the root of conflicts and negotiating to reach equitable solutions.
Personable & Communicative. Excellent written and oral communications skills. Interact well with all corporate levels, colleagues and customers of diverse cultures. Proficient in relationship building.
Computer Skills: Microsoft Office Professional / Lotus Notes

EXPERIENCE

OPTICAL ALLUSIONS, Juneau, CA—Wholesaler / distributor of designer eyewear. Annual sales $50M.

Director of Customer Relations	**1999–Present**
Customer Service Manager	**1996–1999**

- Supervise team of 28 customer service representatives to manage 14,000 accounts, handle daily average of 1200 incoming calls and assist and interact with 55 sales reps operating nationwide.
- Hire, train, develop and motivate employees; monitor and evaluate performance; coordinate staff activity for optimal allocation of abilities and resources.
- Manage department budget, inventory and product pricing; analyze sales data to create reports.
- Oversee credit/returns department; evaluate products to identify defects or other causes for returns.

Achievements & Contributions

✓ Grew department staff from 10 to 32 to accommodate company's evolution.
✓ Achieved substantial savings in costs and man-hours by devising and executing policy that resulted in **28% reduction in returned items.**
✓ Improved customer relations and boosted efficiency by developing and implementing system that **decreased average wait and on-hold time by 66%** (from 90 seconds down to 30 seconds).
✓ Skillfully negotiated equitable resolutions to difficult problems, often **preventing account loss.**
✓ Engendered congenial, productive atmosphere. Employee satisfaction and excellence evidenced by **department's earning the most "Employee of the Month" awards** during a 2-year period.

DELANEY OPTICAL, ORANGEWOOD, CA—Wholesale distributor of eyewear. Annual sales $16M.

General Manager	**1991–1996**

- Managed Customer Service, Shipping, Receiving and Inventory until company closed.

CONTINUING PROFESSIONAL DEVELOPMENT

Courses & Workshops: Budgeting / Critical Thinking / Managing Managers / Inventory Management / Assertiveness Training for Managers

38

Gail Taylor, Torrance, California

The writer needed to highlight the applicant's best skills. The Continuing Professional Development section shows the candidate's enthusiasm for learning and her attempts to increase her value as a worker.

Design

Resumes at a Glance

jason blue

433 darby drive, huntington, new york 11743 ◆ bluemagic@mail.net ◆ 555.555.5555

award-winning graphic designer

top-notch creative skills … project management & production … graphics business management

full advertising campaigns ◆ corporate identity/communication packages
business-to-business & business-to-consumer project design and management

brochures ◆ logos ◆ sales kits ◆ newsletters ◆ direct mail ◆ posters ◆ press kits ◆ sell sheets ◆ signage

professional experience

graphic designer, The Design Team, Northport, NY (2001–Present)

◆ Assess clients' needs and develop successful designs for promotional, marketing, and collateral materials across a wide variety of industries. Utilize an intuitive knack for appreciating clients' business goals as well as distinguishing clients' campaign from the competitive field.
◆ Establish rapport with clients, communicating vision of project with ease and passion. Through confident interpersonal interactions, secure sales and ensure clients' ultimate satisfaction with finished product.
◆ Meet client deadlines through judicious project management, orchestrating and coordinating milestones against timetables.
◆ Ensure profitability and competitiveness on projects through astute pricing of jobs.
◆ Evaluate and choose vendors for select outsourcing and materials purchasing. Credited with negotiating favorable prices, saving clients thousands of dollars.
◆ Brought in on several client projects requiring expert-level guidance. Provided consultation on conceptual and technical approaches, which ultimately allowed the client's in-house design staff to proceed with minimal supervision.

senior designer/art director, The Regional Letter, Melville, NY (1985–2001)

◆ Hired and supervised designers, interns, photographers, and freelance illustrators for Newsday's promotion & marketing department.
◆ Developed content-driven marketing programs that generated millions in new revenue for Newsday. Successes of these programs were noticed and subsequently rolled out as a model for all Tribune Media companies.
◆ Oversaw production scheduling and traffic management, ensuring that the tight weekly deadlines of the newspaper business were always met.
◆ Managed the department's budget for projects (allocation between departments, printing, studio rentals, and outside vendors).
◆ Designed special-events sections for the paper's city editions. Directed photo shoots and created illustrations to complement written material.
◆ Implemented new software/hardware and brought in products that enhanced the efficiency of the creative team. Trained staff on new technologies.

awards

Numerous Best of Long Island (BOLI) Ad Club Awards ◆ Art Directors' Club of New York Award ◆ Society of Illustrators Award ◆ NMA/Editor & Publisher Award ◆ 57th AGC Graphic Arts Award ◆ General Excellence Award, Newspaper Association of America

software proficiencies

Quark — Illustrator 10 — Photoshop — Acrobat — Flatbed scanning technology
Word for PCs and Macs

39

M J Feld, Huntington, New York

The original version of this resume lacked visual appeal. The writer replaced many initial caps with lowercase letters, and the resume became a hit—one of the nicest formats seen.

Thomas Black

5560 Sunny Point Lane ◆ Fayetteville, AR 72567
Thomas_Black@yahoo.com
679.467.9485

Graphic Arts... Audio/Visual & Multimedia Production...Merchandising

Twelve years of creative experience applied within various work environments. Objective as a graphic designer is to provide creative visual and audio media support to successfully communicate and enhance the overall message to target audiences. Unique value to the organization stems from a willingness to continually learn and master new skills coupled with a commitment to achieving excellent project results through dedicated commitment and consistent effort.

Skills Summary

- ◆ Logo Design, Multimedia Presentations, Custom Illustrations, Website Design, Flyers, Posters, Promotional Materials, CD/DVD Design, Merchandise Displays, Trade-Show Booths, Stage Sets.
- ◆ Digital Photo Retouching, Color Correction, and Special Effects Using Adobe Photoshop.
- ◆ Website Design and Graphics Including Animated Gifs and Rollovers Using Flash and Dreamweaver.

Computer Skills (Windows and Macintosh OS)

Microsoft Office (Word, Excel, Outlook, PowerPoint) ◆ Macintosh iWork (Pages, Keynote, Numbers, Mail)
Windows Movie Maker ◆ iMovie ◆ Preview ◆ Adobe Acrobat ◆ Adobe Photoshop CS ◆ Adobe (Macromedia) Flash
Adobe (Macromedia) Dreamweaver ◆ HTML Kit ◆ Magix Music Studio ◆ Garage Band (Mac) ◆ Pro Tools (Digidesign)
Quick Time Pro ◆ Media Shout (Presentation Software) ◆ Easy Worship (Presentation Software)

Experience/Work History

Worship Music & Visual Arts Leader | *Calvary Crossing Church* | *Fayetteville, AR* | *Jan 06 to May 09*
Coordinated worship teams (musicians, A/V, ministers, servers) and led worship services. Designed and created weekly worship materials and multimedia presentations. Created themed graphics and advertising/marketing collateral. Developed videos. Designed and constructed stage sets. Arranged musical scores for worship teams. Demonstrated strategic vision, leadership skill, and teamwork while collaborating with volunteers and paid staff.

Christian Musician | *Various Groups* | *Nashville, TN* | *Nov 97 to Dec 05*
Managed merchandise sales while traveling. Arranged performance events with public relations representatives. Created marketing collateral and trade show displays. Collaborated with design professionals and managed outside vendors for CD/DVD production, apparel, and website construction. Functioned successfully as a freelance road manager, sound manager, and recording engineer. Functioned as a freelance merchandise manager for 19 Christian artists.

Carpenter | *Best Construction* | *Nashville, TN* | *Feb 02 to Feb 04*
Performed rough and finish carpentry for a residential construction firm with a three- to five-person team specializing in new homes and remodeling projects. Accurately interpreted blueprints/architectural drawings.

Special Education Paraprofessional | *Nashville Special School District* | *Nashville, TN* | *Aug 99 to Feb 02*
Assisted 12 to 15 students (grades K-6) with basic and fine motor skills, reading, language arts, and mathematics within the special education and regular classrooms. Organized daily art and music activities. Directed the classroom in absence of teacher. Designed and constructed bulletin boards within the classroom and throughout the school.

Landscaper | *LawnPro* | *Springfield, MO* | *Apr 98 to Aug 99*
Interpreted architectural drawings, identified/gathered planting materials from nursery, delivered equipment/plants to work sites, prepared sites for planting, installed sprinkler systems, and installed planting materials adhering to quality standards.

Youth Minister | *Northbrook Church* | *Springfield, MO* | *May 97 to Aug 99*
Coordinated, prepared, and led youth retreats, lock-ins, church camp, weekly Bible classes/devotionals, individual counseling sessions, and other church activities.

Education

Music Education | *Libscomb University* | *Nashville, TN* | *Aug 96 to May 97*

Professional and Personal References Furnished on Request

40

Michele J. Haffner, Glendale Wisconsin

The writer wove this applicant's varied background of jobs into a search for a position in visual arts and media. Blue and brown colors in the original resume met with much success.

Dee Provard

555 West Cedar
Apt. 2034
Roanoke, VA 24018

555.000.3627
dee.provard@hotmail.com

Personable, artistic, highly
organized, motivated to succeed

High potential for success in
customer relations, product
promotion, business support

Skill sets include

MS Word and Excel
Customer Service
Filing & Keyboarding
Project Management
Team Supervision
Inventory Management
Trade Show Participation
Mixing Paints/Stains
Oil/Acrylic Painting
Faux Finishes
Statuary & Fountain Designs

Education

Midlothian High School
Midlothian, VA

Employment Background

Artist Assistant/Business Manager

Jason Eckner, Roanoke, VA   2006–Present

- Organize and manage business operations for this independent artist of abstract paintings, murals, and faux finishes.
- Handle customer relations, materials ordering, filing, preparing bills of sales, and prospecting new business through cold calls and personal visits.
  - ✓ Increased market exposure and contributed to more than $25,000 in sales by booking, organizing, and staging show at a local coffee shop.
  - ✓ Lend artistic talents and knowledge of various media in helping to create stencils, murals, plasterwork, and marbleizing of faux finishes.

Painter/Shipping & Receiving Manager

Jeter Manufacturing, Richmond, VA   2003–2006

- Oversaw shipping and receiving activities, including supervising eight employees, for this $3.4M manufacturer and distributor of decorative fountains and statuary.
- Secured employment as a painter; promoted to manager within first year of hire. Ensured smooth operation throughout 25,000-square-foot warehouse.
- Loaded and unloaded 52-foot delivery trucks; received and stocked raw materials while ensuring proper storage of materials with low shelf life.
- Interfaced with mold-making and casting departments to verify receipt of products and performed quality control inspections of incoming products.
  - ✓ Learned to operate pallet jack and forklift through videotape self-study.
  - ✓ Created inventory management system to organize and manually track incoming and outgoing shipments against product orders.
  - ✓ Worked extra hours to assist office manager with completing sales orders, making phone calls, typing, and filing.
  - ✓ Showed creativity and initiative in developing sketches for new product design; created one fountain design selected for wholesale distribution.
  - ✓ Visited commercial customer sites to match paint colors to existing structures and custom-mixed colors following formulas provided by stain manufacturers.
  - ✓ Assisted with setting up and creating attractive displays at trade shows.
  - ✓ Personally painted all fountains and statuary featured in product catalog; proofread and performed color and quality checks of catalog.

Snavely's Garden Center, Richmond, VA   2002–2003
Customer Service Representative/ Stock Yard Attendant

- Operated forklift and pallet jack to unload monthly shipments of international pottery; displayed products throughout retailer's large outdoor stockyard.
  - ✓ Touched-up paint on products with minor imperfections and damages.
  - ✓ Assisted customers in choosing right products for their design scheme; handled cash transactions; loaded purchased products in customers' vehicles.

41

Norine Dagliano, Hagerstown, Maryland

This resume's creative design was for an artistic applicant who wanted a job that would use her creative design talents. She now works part-time in a framing shop and runs a TV news camera.

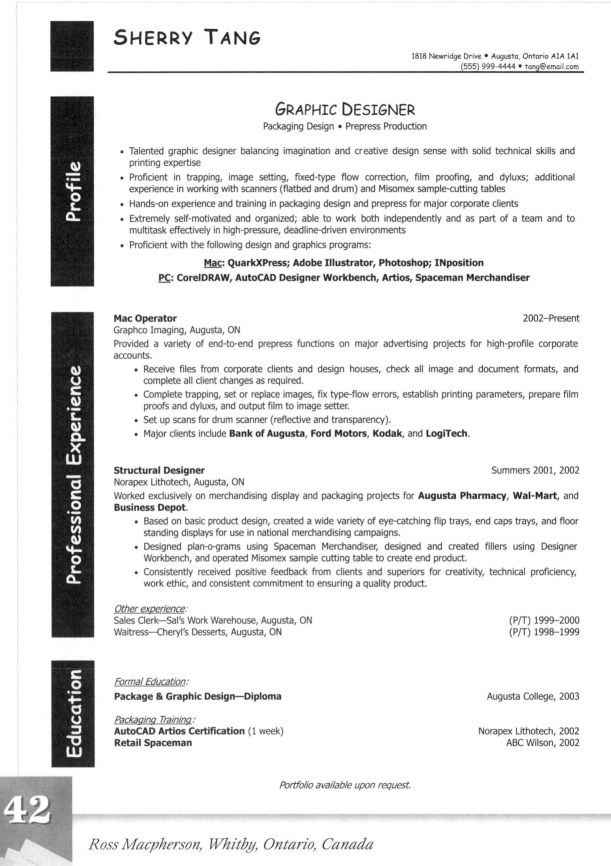

SHERRY TANG

1818 Newridge Drive • Augusta, Ontario A1A 1A1
(555) 999-4444 • tang@email.com

Profile

GRAPHIC DESIGNER
Packaging Design • Prepress Production

- Talented graphic designer balancing imagination and creative design sense with solid technical skills and printing expertise
- Proficient in trapping, image setting, fixed-type flow correction, film proofing, and dyluxs; additional experience in working with scanners (flatbed and drum) and Misomex sample-cutting tables
- Hands-on experience and training in packaging design and prepress for major corporate clients
- Extremely self-motivated and organized; able to work both independently and as part of a team and to multitask effectively in high-pressure, deadline-driven environments
- Proficient with the following design and graphics programs:

Mac: QuarkXPress; Adobe Illustrator, Photoshop; INposition

PC: CorelDRAW, AutoCAD Designer Workbench, Artios, Spaceman Merchandiser

Professional Experience

Mac Operator   2002–Present
Graphco Imaging, Augusta, ON
Provided a variety of end-to-end prepress functions on major advertising projects for high-profile corporate accounts.
- Receive files from corporate clients and design houses, check all image and document formats, and complete all client changes as required.
- Complete trapping, set or replace images, fix type-flow errors, establish printing parameters, prepare film proofs and dyluxs, and output film to image setter.
- Set up scans for drum scanner (reflective and transparency).
- Major clients include **Bank of Augusta**, **Ford Motors**, **Kodak**, and **LogiTech**.

Structural Designer   Summers 2001, 2002
Norapex Lithotech, Augusta, ON
Worked exclusively on merchandising display and packaging projects for **Augusta Pharmacy**, **Wal-Mart**, and **Business Depot**.
- Based on basic product design, created a wide variety of eye-catching flip trays, end caps trays, and floor standing displays for use in national merchandising campaigns.
- Designed plan-o-grams using Spaceman Merchandiser, designed and created fillers using Designer Workbench, and operated Misomex sample cutting table to create end product.
- Consistently received positive feedback from clients and superiors for creativity, technical proficiency, work ethic, and consistent commitment to ensuring a quality product.

Other experience:
Sales Clerk—Sal's Work Warehouse, Augusta, ON   (P/T) 1999–2000
Waitress—Cheryl's Desserts, Augusta, ON   (P/T) 1998–1999

Education

Formal Education:
Package & Graphic Design—Diploma   Augusta College, 2003

Packaging Training:
AutoCAD Artios Certification (1 week)   Norapex Lithotech, 2002
Retail Spaceman   ABC Wilson, 2002

Portfolio available upon request.

42

Ross Macpherson, Whitby, Ontario, Canada

Adding a little flair for a Graphic Designer with little experience, this resume shows creativity, illustrates her technical skills, and highlights some big-name client projects she has worked on.

CAROLINE KOZYNSKI

11-17 LINCOLN AVENUE, MILWAUKEE, WISCONSIN 53203

414-555-5555 / ckdesigner@email.com

PROFILE

Award-winning **Kitchen and Bath Designer,** offering solid, well-rounded experience to sell and manage clients' projects from concept to final details, positively influencing company performance, profitability, and operations. Areas of expertise include:

- Creative interior design
- Sales agreement negotiations/closings
- Space planning with precise measurements

- Architectural and construction knowledge
- Computer and hand drafting
- Budget development and monitoring

QUALIFICATIONS

- Totally committed to exceptional service and quality work for both new home construction and remodeling projects.
- Thoroughly handle the entire process of sales, design, construction, and follow-through of projects.
- Collaborate effectively with individuals at all levels, including coordination with trade professionals.
- Enjoy extensive one-on-one contact with clients throughout all project stages, proactively resolving issues to ensure timely completion and client satisfaction.
- Possess exceptional listening skills to assess customers' real needs and translate their vision into the completion of projects.
- Suggest design alternatives to maximize clients' functionality and aesthetic requirements while respecting their budgetary limitations.
- Acknowledged as a highly organized, articulate professional who maintains excellent relationships with clients, staff, and senior management.
- Stay current with the latest kitchen and bath design trends through industry publications and showroom visits.
- Proficient in AutoCAD R-12, 20/20 Graphic Design, National Estimator 2001, and MS Word programs.

PROFESSIONAL EXPERIENCE

Home Expo
Designer, Kitchens and Baths

Milwaukee, WI
2005–Present

- Met one-on-one with customers and provided them with creative ideas for remodeling their kitchens and baths, using 20/20 Graphic Design package effectively to showcase design ideas to potential customers.
- Developed strong organizational and administrative skills in order to properly service the large number of information requests and projects per day.
- Instrumental in the creation of the location's first-ever in-store appointment chart and Design Center class, allowing customers greater personal time with design professionals that resulted in higher closing ratios and improved overall satisfaction.
- Received Shining Star Award conferred by Kraft Maid Cabinet Company and Home Expo Gold Sales Achievement in 2007.

Pavlik Associates, Residential Architects
Draftsperson/AutoCAD Operator

Racine, WI
2002–2005

- Transferred freehand architectural drawings into AutoCAD for final presentation.
- Gained design experience, made on-site inspections, gathered information, and ultimately had full autonomy over design and layout of areas within projects.

EDUCATION & TRAINING

Associate's degree in Computer-Aided Interior Design—Milwaukee Community College   2002
Kitchen and Bath Design courses through NKBA   2006–Present

Portfolio of designs available on request

43

Melanie Noonan, West Paterson, New Jersey

This applicant gained recognition with her kitchen designs and wanted a new job to continue her education. Keywords in the Profile correspond to qualifications called for in advertised jobs.

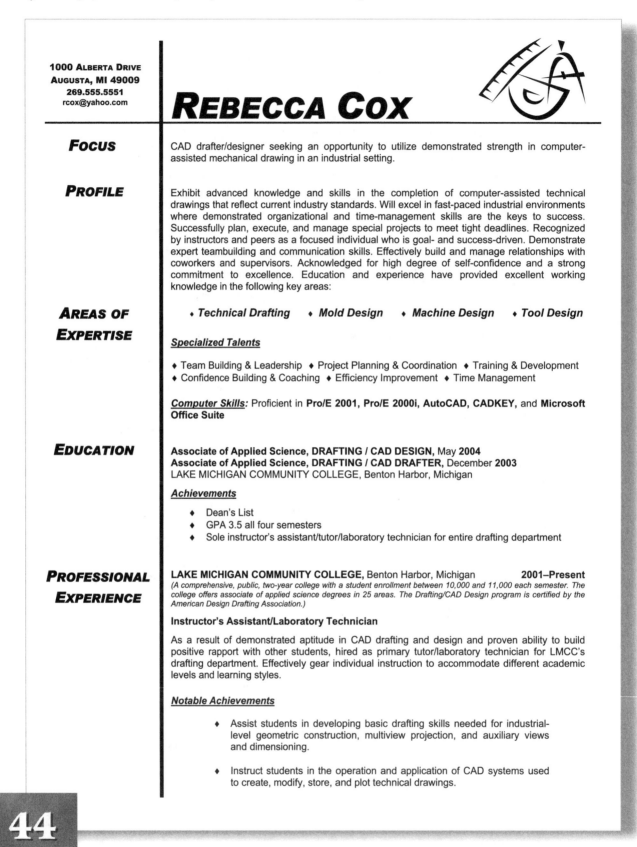

1000 ALBERTA DRIVE
AUGUSTA, MI 49009
269.555.5551
rcox@yahoo.com

REBECCA COX

FOCUS

CAD drafter/designer seeking an opportunity to utilize demonstrated strength in computer-assisted mechanical drawing in an industrial setting.

PROFILE

Exhibit advanced knowledge and skills in the completion of computer-assisted technical drawings that reflect current industry standards. Will excel in fast-paced industrial environments where demonstrated organizational and time-management skills are the keys to success. Successfully plan, execute, and manage special projects to meet tight deadlines. Recognized by instructors and peers as a focused individual who is goal- and success-driven. Demonstrate expert teambuilding and communication skills. Effectively build and manage relationships with coworkers and supervisors. Acknowledged for high degree of self-confidence and a strong commitment to excellence. Education and experience have provided excellent working knowledge in the following key areas:

AREAS OF EXPERTISE

♦ *Technical Drafting*   ♦ *Mold Design*   ♦ *Machine Design*   ♦ *Tool Design*

Specialized Talents

♦ Team Building & Leadership ♦ Project Planning & Coordination ♦ Training & Development
♦ Confidence Building & Coaching ♦ Efficiency Improvement ♦ Time Management

Computer Skills: Proficient in **Pro/E 2001, Pro/E 2000i, AutoCAD, CADKEY,** and **Microsoft Office Suite**

EDUCATION

Associate of Applied Science, DRAFTING / CAD DESIGN, May **2004**
Associate of Applied Science, DRAFTING / CAD DRAFTER, December **2003**
LAKE MICHIGAN COMMUNITY COLLEGE, Benton Harbor, Michigan

Achievements

♦ Dean's List
♦ GPA 3.5 all four semesters
♦ Sole instructor's assistant/tutor/laboratory technician for entire drafting department

PROFESSIONAL EXPERIENCE

LAKE MICHIGAN COMMUNITY COLLEGE, Benton Harbor, Michigan   **2001–Present**
(A comprehensive, public, two-year college with a student enrollment between 10,000 and 11,000 each semester. The college offers associate of applied science degrees in 25 areas. The Drafting/CAD Design program is certified by the American Design Drafting Association.)

Instructor's Assistant/Laboratory Technician

As a result of demonstrated aptitude in CAD drafting and design and proven ability to build positive rapport with other students, hired as primary tutor/laboratory technician for LMCC's drafting department. Effectively gear individual instruction to accommodate different academic levels and learning styles.

Notable Achievements

♦ Assist students in developing basic drafting skills needed for industrial-level geometric construction, multiview projection, and auxiliary views and dimensioning.

♦ Instruct students in the operation and application of CAD systems used to create, modify, store, and plot technical drawings.

44

Richard T. Porter, Portage, Michigan

This applicant was a student graduating with an Associate of Applied Science degree in CAD Drafting and Design. As a top-flight student who was recognized for her skills, she was hired by the drafting department of the community college to tutor other CAD students—the only

REBECCA COX   **PAGE 2**

PROFESSIONAL
EXPERIENCE
(CONTINUED)

PRINTING PLUS PRINTING COMPANY, Augusta, Michigan   **1998–2000**
(Midsized commercial printing company specializing in layouts, typesetting, high-resolution scanning, and single- and multiple-color offset printing.)

Assistant Manager

Responsible for helping manage the day-to-day business activities of the print shop. Scheduled projects and used printing software to design brochures, business cards, letterhead, newsletters, and other business-related projects. Effectively worked with customers to fulfill orders. Used creative and critical-thinking skills to approach and resolve problems.

Notable Achievements

    ◆ Constantly monitored quality control/customer satisfaction issues, seeking new ways to improve customer service.

    ◆ Effectively assumed responsibilities as office manager, meeting with customers, selling products and services, and performing day-to-day general office management duties, including bookkeeping and ordering supplies.

COMMUNITY
OUTREACH

Secretary, Judson Middle School PTA, 2003–Present

Volunteer, Kalamazoo County United Way, 2000–Present

Volunteer tutor, English as a Second Language, Community Outreach Center, 2001–2004

Nursery school teacher for family church, 1999–Present

Assistant coach for AYSO girls soccer association, 1999–2000

Assistant Cub Scout den leader, 2001–Present

— *Outstanding References and CAD Drafting Samples Available on Request* —

◆ ◆ ◆

student in the department considered for this position. Although she does not have field experience in her search for an industrial position, her teaching experience attests to her aptitude and abilities.

Howard J. Charles

4412 Millhaven Road, Conner City, Alabama 35000
☎ 256.555.5555 📠 hjchjc@lakeone.net

WHAT I CAN OFFER **YOUR ORGANIZATION** AS YOUR NEWEST **FACILITIES MANAGER**

❑ Capable leader with a proven track record of **maximizing ROI** and ROE (return on energy) by matching your facilities to employees' and customers' needs

❑ Skilled facilities professional who helps people tie their personal success to your **corporate growth**

❑ Thoughtful workplace planner who can turn your vision into **rising productivity** and profits

❑ Effective communicator whose written and spoken words get **results**

RECENT WORK HISTORY WITH EXAMPLES OF PROBLEMS SOLVED

❑ Draftsman *promoted over four competitors, some with six years more experience, to be* **Manager of Design and Drafting** (CAD Department Supervisor), Conner Corporation, Conner City, Alabama   86–Present

Conner is an international manufacturer of sportswear and textiles.

Sought out by senior management to get a stalled office space reorganization plan moving again. Folded in the views of 10 department managers. Then wrote and briefed every detail. *Payoffs:* Work done **five months early** and **50 percent below budget.**

Found a better way to install a critical material-handling system. My ideas were approved by the manufacturer and our leadership team. The vendor's plan: $75K in materials and lots of labor. *Payoffs:* My modular approach **saved $45K** in material and **cut labor** needs in half. My system is now our corporate standard—and the worldwide vendor's as well.

Tapped by CFO and COO to play a key role in designing and building three new plants in Mexico—without ever leaving my office and with no ability to speak Spanish. Worked everything from bidding to construction. *Payoffs:* Dropped design time **from two months to two weeks.** Not a single change order. Our work was the **most cost-effective ever.**

Helped keep us competitive when transition to new technology nearly crippled our ability to reply to RFPs. Wrote new foolproof procedures that let unskilled temps do the work accurately. Transformed skeptics into strong supporters. *Payoffs:* Converted more than 1,100 drawings a month. **Vendors wanted $300K;** I did it for only **$20K.**

CONFIDENTIAL   *More indicators of performance your organization can use …*

45

Don Orlando, Montgomery, Alabama

This individual was being downsized in two ways: his field of drafting was being displaced, and his company was letting him go. He learned through career coaching that Facilities Manager would be an ideal position for him. The writer focused on the benefits the applicant could offer

Howard J. Charles	**Facilities Manager**	256.555.5555

Chosen by our CEO over four more-senior people to help a community college produce a drafting curriculum from scratch. Wrote the lesson plans and exams and then taught the classes. ***Payoffs:*** Everything was **ready in six weeks.** Eighty percent of students passed this challenging course.

EDUCATION

❑ Associate of Applied Technology, Patterson State Technical College, Montgomery, Alabama · 86

Paid my own way to earn this degree by working full time and carrying a full academic load at night.

❑ Course work in Industrial Design, Auburn University, Auburn, Alabama · 82–83

❑ Course work, Chattachoogee Valley Community College, Phenix City, Alabama · 80–81

❑ Course work in Building Science, Auburn University, Auburn, Alabama · 78–79

COMPUTER SKILLS

❑ Expert in AutoCAD, Photoshop, Word, Excel, Windows XP, Internet search protocols

❑ Proficient in PowerPoint; Adobe Acrobat; MS Project; Windows 3*x*, 9*x*, 2000, XP, NT; UNIX

❑ Working knowledge of Means Data Estimating Software, Adobe Illustrator, Access, **Aperture CAFM software**

PROFESSIONAL AFFILIATIONS

❑ Member and former Secretary (92–94), Alabama Design & Drafting Association · 86–Present

❑ Member, National Association of Photoshop Users · 98–Present

❑ Chairman, Committee for the Drafting and Design Technology Department, Trenholm State Technical College, Montgomery, Alabama · 00–03

an employer, because competing applicants might focus instead on narrow task-based experience alone. For the benefits, look for "Payoffs" and boldfacing in the resume in connection with each problem solved.

25 Deerfield Court
Burlington, VT 05401
(802) 555-0000

slopedog@mindspring.com

Glen Weston

career goal   To contribute innovative ideas and graphic design skills to a marketing organization with particular focus to outdoor sports enthusiasts.

personal and professional qualifications

- Versatility to participate in all creative stages—conceptualization through production of advertising design. Expertise encompasses:
  – on-site photography as well as work from camera-ready art
  – graphic illustration in pencil, pen and ink, or watercolor
  – image scanning and computer manipulation in a combination of programs
  – four-color processing
  – typeface selection to convey client's message with style
- Well-read in design industry publications such as *HOW* magazine, *I.D.,* and *Art Forum,* especially attentive to aesthetics and ad layouts.
- Precise with details while conscious of project tracking and deadlines.
- Avid interest in seasonal sports that include skiing, snowboarding, surfing, rock climbing, and mountain biking.
- Relate easily to young adults in pursuit of outdoor activities; know what they look for when purchasing equipment and accessories.

education   Associate of Science in Graphic Design   August 2008
The Art Institute of Pittsburgh Online Division

mac computer skills

Illustrator	Photoshop	Freehand MX
Painter X	QuarkXPress	MS Word

related experience

Freelance graphic design and photography	ADVERTISING COMPS	Burton Snowboards *Mocha Java* magazine
Freelance graphic design and illustration	RETAIL LAYOUT/ CATALOG DESIGN	Slalom Ski Shops Sports Authority Empire Stores
	LOGO DESIGN	AllStar Tech Solutions

other experience

SALES ASSOCIATE at Slalom Ski Shop, Burlington, VT   2003–Present

- Advised customers on selections best suited to their needs
- Met with sales representatives and evaluated new equipment for store inventory
- Attended promotional demos, which afforded opportunities for photography

46

Melanie Noonan, West Paterson, New Jersey

The applicant had little work experience but did have artistic ability that he wanted to combine with outdoor sports. The graphic helped him to stand out from more advanced candidates.

Education

Resumes at a Glance

Heather Hammond

52 Lancaster Avenue
Newbold, AR 00000
(000) 000-0000
heatherhammond@email.com

QUALIFICATIONS

*More than 7 years of experience working in private preschool settings
with exposure to all childhood development stages*

Early Childhood Education Certificate, 1997
Willis County College

Certified in CPR and First Aid

TESTIMONIALS

"Heather has a natural talent for building immediate rapport with children. Her patience, confidence, and commitment make her a valuable member of our day care staff."
—Liz Kaufman, Director

"It is such a pleasure to work with Heather. She always stays calm, even in stressful moments with the children."
—Maryann Bradley, Teacher's Aide

"Kelsey loves you, and we can certainly tell she means the world to you. What we didn't realize was that you would bring out the musician in her."
—Linda and Greg Mills

"The following two words are simple but truly express our feelings for the fine job you did in helping Justin enjoy his first experience with academics. Thank you!!!"
—Sean and Deanna McFarland

"We came to you last year with our precious rosebud and have watched her bloom. We alerted you of her thorns, but you overcame most of them with your tender pruning and weeding."
—Annette and Frank DeMartino

"Thank you so much for all of your love and nurturing. Jolie loves coming to school every day, and I know you play the greatest role in her happiness."
—Janet Tremain

"Because of your gentle, kind and patient love for Rico, he has become more interested in learning. Thank you for keeping cool in the face of such great challenges."
—Consuelo and Pedro Cortez

"Thank you so very much for looking after our precious angel Adrianna. As a working mother, words can never express how thankful I am for your patience and guidance."
—Karen Fortner

"We, the parents of Kirit, wish to thank you from the bottom of our hearts for nurturing our child and expanding his horizons, opening his mind and heart in a caring and affectionate way."
—Pradeep and Naila Ashrani

PROFESSIONAL EXPERIENCE

SESAME STREET CHILDREN'S ACADEMY
Newbold, AR   1997–2004

Preschool Teacher
Promoted from Teacher's Aide after 1 year

✴ Taught 3 classes of 12 children each, ages 3–4, and supervised 2 teacher's aides.

✴ Used a variety of hands-on activities to instill an early love of learning in culturally diverse children.

✴ Created a safe, relaxed environment, which allowed the development of social and physical skills as well as creativity.

✴ Encouraged reading and writing through innovative alphabet games. By end of each school year, all children were able to print their names and orally spell them.

✴ Helped to build self-esteem by designating helpers and pairing shy children with assertive ones in play activities such as "Caterpillars and Butterflies."

✴ Contributed to a friendly, family-type work environment, sharing ideas with other teachers.

HOUSEHOLD OF MITCH AND DELIA BASCOMB
Newbold, AR   1994–1997

Nanny

✴ Assisted with educational and after-school activities for 3 children.

✴ Recommended by Mr. Bascomb for employment at Sesame Street Children's Academy.

47

Melanie Noonan, West Paterson, New Jersey

This resume shows the value of testimonials. If you read just the Professional Experience column, you read typical information. If you then read the Testimonials, you're ready to hire the person.

JAY B. GABRIEL

5451 SR 338   740.247.0000 (H)
RACINE, OHIO 45771   740.248.0000 (W)

 ## OBJECTIVE

Alexander Varsity Boys Basketball Coach
Talented basketball coach offering a lifetime of involvement in and broad knowledge of the game of basketball

 ## SUMMARY OF QUALIFICATIONS

- Alexander graduate and district resident with 17 years of successful coaching experience ranging from Biddy League through junior varsity level at Alexander
- Demonstrated talent for motivating players and building cohesive teams focused on a common goal
- Excellent communication skills—proven ability to work effectively with all parties, including players, parents, community, and administration
- Effective fundraising skills—organize various fundraisers, including recruiting numerous volunteers; oversee all expenditures
- 22 years of experience as a basketball referee

COACHING HISTORY AND ACCOMPLISHMENTS

- Achieved first-ever undefeated season in the history of Alexander Basketball
- 12 years of coaching experience with a combined 135–80 record
  - 3 years of coaching at the junior varsity level—undefeated season
  - 3 years of coaching at the freshman level—won 2 freshman tournaments
  - 6 years of coaching at the 8th grade level—won the 8th grade tournament

 ## COACHING PHILOSOPHY

Coaching philosophy is based on fundamentals. Promote fast-paced, exciting game of getting the ball up and down the court quickly with a mixture of offensive and defensive strategies. Firm believer in teaching fundamentals while motivating players to perform at peak levels. Continuously promote sportsmanship and mutual respect in all aspects of program.

48

Melissa L. Kasler, Athens, Ohio

Because the resume was more of a formality, the writer decided to have some fun with the design. Using basketballs as the focus, the writer integrated the graphics with the layout.

Events Planning

Resumes at a Glance

Benjamin Hall

86 Sunny Knoll Drive ✦ Poughkeepsie, NY 12601 ✦ 845.454.9900

Experienced Event Planner & Promotions Specialist

Energetic and progressive-minded individual with financial aptitude and a special strength in cause-related marketing. Consistently successful in generating philanthropic support through superior communication skills, excellent writing abilities and a service-oriented philosophy. Vast experience in planning, marketing and executing local and national events involving VIP relations, high-profile galas and corporate functions.

Summary of Qualifications

✦ Able to perform in highly visible roles, capitalize on opportunities and deliver strong results
✦ Skilled at concepting events, enhancing promotional efforts and designing ad and collateral materials
✦ Consistently successful in blending creative and administrative abilities to deliver seamless events
✦ Function well in a multidimensional role and can perform under a great deal of pressure
✦ Proven ability to assemble cohesive staffs and build consensus among groups with conflicting interests

Selected Highlights

▸ Recruited by the Beautiful Foundation with the challenge to strengthen its annual event and advance its overall philanthropic efforts. Initiated a shift in the Foundation's focus that tripled corporate sponsorships, doubled event revenues and secured celebrity involvement for its annual gala.

▸ Provided strategic direction, administrative guidance and financial oversight for Clairol's "Color Can Make a Difference." Coordinated a national media tour as well as several cause-related fundraising and marketing campaigns. Increased campaign participation while simultaneously reducing the budget by 10%.

▸ Coproduced Beautiful's annual gala fundraiser, which generated $80,000. Successfully raised $375,000 for "Color Can Make a Difference" and obtained $100,000 in corporate donations.

▸ Directed media relations and helped complete fundraising events for the Hudson Valley Film Festival. Executed a large media campaign, enlisted celebrity cochairs and coordinated a fundraising gala ($67,000).

▸ Established b•cause, a professional beauty industry foundation that supports specific causes including Count-Me-In (online lender dedicated to helping women-owned businesses) and Locks of Love (organization that provides wigs and hairpieces to children with long-term illnesses).

Employment History

b•cause Foundation, *Poughkeepsie, NY*	National Program Coordinator	**2000 to Present**
Les Cheveaux Group, *White Plains, NY*	Salon Manager	**2001 to 2002**
Beautiful Foundation, *New York, NY*	Director of Special Events	**1999 to 2000**
Peter Coppola, *New York, NY*	Front Desk Manager	**1998 to 2001**
Hudson Valley Film Festival	Director of Media Relations	**1996 to 1997**
Clairol Professional, *New York, NY*	National Program Director	**1992 to 1995**
Heidi's Salons, Inc., *New York, NY*	Assistant Manager / Salon Promotions	**1990 to 1992**

Professional Development

Member of the Association of Fundraising Professionals   NYS Licensed Hairdresser & Cosmetologist

---

Special Skills

Promotions

Press Releases
Media Relations

Event Planning

Fund Development
Media Participation
Industry Partnerships
Event Coordination

Financials

Operational Budgets
Activity Analysis
Expense Forecasting

Public Relations

Celebrity Support
Corporate Sponsors

Management

Staff Development
Employee Supervision
Scheduling/Training

Honors

Award of Distinction
Corporate Leadership
Honored by WEPR
Social Responsibility
Beauty Industry Hero
American Salon
Magazine, 2001

49

Kristin M. Coleman, Poughkeepsie, New York

This two-column resume has a shadowed page border and a vertical line separating the columns. The vertical positioning of the text lines in the left column matches that in the right column.

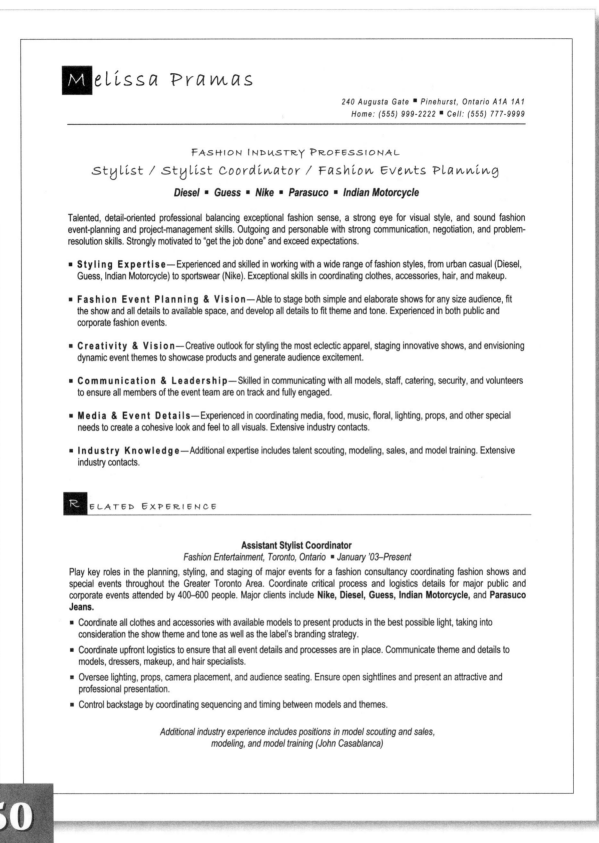

Melissa Pramas

240 Augusta Gate ▪ Pinehurst, Ontario A1A 1A1
Home: (555) 999-2222 ▪ Cell: (555) 777-9999

FASHION INDUSTRY PROFESSIONAL
Stylist / Stylist Coordinator / Fashion Events Planning

Diesel ▪ Guess ▪ Nike ▪ Parasuco ▪ Indian Motorcycle

Talented, detail-oriented professional balancing exceptional fashion sense, a strong eye for visual style, and sound fashion event-planning and project-management skills. Outgoing and personable with strong communication, negotiation, and problem-resolution skills. Strongly motivated to "get the job done" and exceed expectations.

▪ **Styling Expertise**—Experienced and skilled in working with a wide range of fashion styles, from urban casual (Diesel, Guess, Indian Motorcycle) to sportswear (Nike). Exceptional skills in coordinating clothes, accessories, hair, and makeup.

▪ **Fashion Event Planning & Vision**—Able to stage both simple and elaborate shows for any size audience, fit the show and all details to available space, and develop all details to fit theme and tone. Experienced in both public and corporate fashion events.

▪ **Creativity & Vision**—Creative outlook for styling the most eclectic apparel, staging innovative shows, and envisioning dynamic event themes to showcase products and generate audience excitement.

▪ **Communication & Leadership**—Skilled in communicating with all models, staff, catering, security, and volunteers to ensure all members of the event team are on track and fully engaged.

▪ **Media & Event Details**—Experienced in coordinating media, food, music, floral, lighting, props, and other special needs to create a cohesive look and feel to all visuals. Extensive industry contacts.

▪ **Industry Knowledge**—Additional expertise includes talent scouting, modeling, sales, and model training. Extensive industry contacts.

RELATED EXPERIENCE

Assistant Stylist Coordinator
Fashion Entertainment, Toronto, Ontario ▪ January '03–Present

Play key roles in the planning, styling, and staging of major events for a fashion consultancy coordinating fashion shows and special events throughout the Greater Toronto Area. Coordinate critical process and logistics details for major public and corporate events attended by 400–600 people. Major clients include **Nike, Diesel, Guess, Indian Motorcycle,** and **Parasuco Jeans.**

▪ Coordinate all clothes and accessories with available models to present products in the best possible light, taking into consideration the show theme and tone as well as the label's branding strategy.

▪ Coordinate upfront logistics to ensure that all event details and processes are in place. Communicate theme and details to models, dressers, makeup, and hair specialists.

▪ Oversee lighting, props, camera placement, and audience seating. Ensure open sightlines and present an attractive and professional presentation.

▪ Control backstage by coordinating sequencing and timing between models and themes.

*Additional industry experience includes positions in model scouting and sales,
modeling, and model training (John Casablanca)*

50

Ross Macpherson, Whitby, Ontario, Canada

This applicant wanted to transition to the fashion industry. The writer wanted the resume to have some creative design elements to complement the transition. Note the two Experience sections: Related Experience, which contains information of importance to the target industry, and

CORPORATE EXPERIENCE

Major Accounts Service Representative
telNET, Toronto, Ontario ▪ December '99–December '02

Personally selected by VP Sales and Marketing to provide elite-level account service for major corporate clients and Fortune 500 companies. Responsible for managing 12 major corporate accounts, resolving all client issues, ensuring account retention, and upselling on new service offerings. Client accounts include **Xerox, Coca-Cola, Dynamex, Loomis, Netricom, University of Toronto,** and **Durham Regional Police.**

Commercial Senior Accounts Representative
telNET, Toronto, Ontario ▪ July '97–December '99

Provided single point of contact in the resolution of billing, credit, and collection issues for a client portfolio of up to 3000 accounts (dealer, consumer, and commercial). Worked effectively with coordinating areas, including Client Care, Dealer Care, Credit, and Activation, to resolve common issues.

Process Coordinator
telNET, Toronto, Ontario ▪ March '96–June '97

Finalized financial month-end for 6 branches. Supervised client care representatives to ensure proper procedures and processes were followed, reconciled accounts to keep accurate financial records, and liaised with team leaders to ensure consistently high quality of client care.

COMPUTER SKILLS

- Proficient in all MS Office applications, including **Word, Excel, Outlook,** and **Explorer.** Particularly strong in developing and presenting **PowerPoint** presentations.
- Additional experience using Corel WordPerfect, AccPac, and specialty applications including Boss 1-2, BSCS, Clarity, AFP Viewer, DSS, and BOA.

EDUCATION

Broadcasting—Radio & Television, *Pinehurst College*   1992
Business Management, *Pinehurst University*   Ongoing

REFERENCES

Outstanding professional and personal references can be provided upon request.

Corporate Experience, which tells of the applicant's responsibilities and achievements as an Accounts Representative. White space makes the resume easy to comprehend at a glance.

Addie Brown

555 Person Court, Island Top, SC 55555
Home: 000.000.0000 Cell: 000.000.0000
addbro@comcast.net

KEY QUALIFICATIONS

Hardworking Event Planning Associate with solid educational foundation in hospitality management and hands-on experience in guest/customer service. Reliable and strong team member, coupled with proven ability to work independently. Motivated, energetic employee capable of handling heavy workload. Interacts well with a wide range of people/staff in order to expedite tasks; including communicating effectively with high-end clientele. Demonstrated ability to work under pressure and stress in busy atmosphere. Dedicated to completing assigned projects on time and on budget through careful attention to detail and follow-through. Recognized expertise in:

Organization   Client/Guest Service   Multitasking   Time Management

EDUCATION

Associate's Degree, Applied Science/Hospitality Management

Core Community College, Island Top, SC, May 2009
<u>Coursework:</u> Event Planning I & II, Banquet Operations, Menu Planning, Vendor Sourcing

PROFESSIONAL EXPERIENCE

Sea Side Hotel, Hilton Head, SC   5/09–10/09
Front Desk Clerk & Guest Relations
Entrusted with guest service experience for hotel with 100 suites. Accountable for checking guests in and out. Performed daily sales and completed correct billing using checks, cash and credit cards. Arranged for services with other hotel departments in order to ensure optimal guest experience.
- ❖ Successfully performed as sole staff person on-site during late shift, effectively managing operations and guest services.
- ❖ Displayed strong ability to problem-solve and correct inaccurate reservations while accommodating guests needs, resulting in high guest satisfaction.
- ❖ Gained excellent feedback from supervisor, including ability to relate effectively to guests and provide attentiveness to their needs and concerns.

Campbell Family, Hornets, SC   Summers 07, 08, 09
Nanny
Responsible for welfare and well-being of five children aged 4 to 14. Oversaw and adhered to complicated schedule of activities and ensured on-time arrivals. Prepared nutritionally balanced foods. Supervised activities and obtained well-rounded sources of entertainment.
- ❖ Noted for ability to responsibly care for children, gaining the trust and respect of employers.
- ❖ Demonstrated proficiency with time management, as shown by successfully performing two jobs simultaneously.

51

Michele Angello, Aurora, Colorado

This applicant was a new graduate with an associate's degree in event planning but no direct experience. The writer emphasized first transferable skills as qualifications and then education.

Finance/Banking

Resumes at a Glance

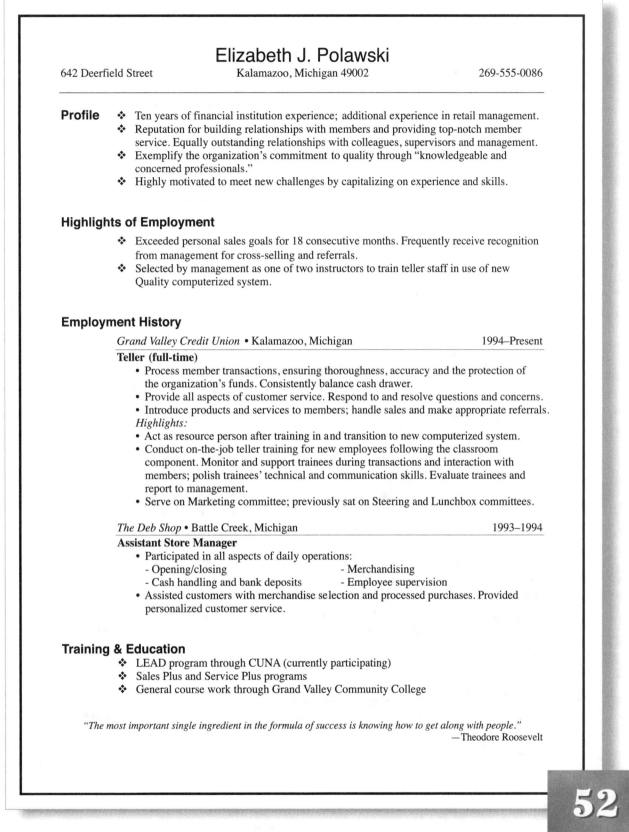

Elizabeth J. Polawski

642 Deerfield Street   Kalamazoo, Michigan 49002   269-555-0086

Profile
- ❖ Ten years of financial institution experience; additional experience in retail management.
- ❖ Reputation for building relationships with members and providing top-notch member service. Equally outstanding relationships with colleagues, supervisors and management.
- ❖ Exemplify the organization's commitment to quality through "knowledgeable and concerned professionals."
- ❖ Highly motivated to meet new challenges by capitalizing on experience and skills.

Highlights of Employment
- ❖ Exceeded personal sales goals for 18 consecutive months. Frequently receive recognition from management for cross-selling and referrals.
- ❖ Selected by management as one of two instructors to train teller staff in use of new Quality computerized system.

Employment History

Grand Valley Credit Union • Kalamazoo, Michigan   1994–Present
Teller (full-time)
- Process member transactions, ensuring thoroughness, accuracy and the protection of the organization's funds. Consistently balance cash drawer.
- Provide all aspects of customer service. Respond to and resolve questions and concerns.
- Introduce products and services to members; handle sales and make appropriate referrals.
Highlights:
- Act as resource person after training in and transition to new computerized system.
- Conduct on-the-job teller training for new employees following the classroom component. Monitor and support trainees during transactions and interaction with members; polish trainees' technical and communication skills. Evaluate trainees and report to management.
- Serve on Marketing committee; previously sat on Steering and Lunchbox committees.

The Deb Shop • Battle Creek, Michigan   1993–1994
Assistant Store Manager
- Participated in all aspects of daily operations:
  - Opening/closing   - Merchandising
  - Cash handling and bank deposits   - Employee supervision
- Assisted customers with merchandise selection and processed purchases. Provided personalized customer service.

Training & Education
- ❖ LEAD program through CUNA (currently participating)
- ❖ Sales Plus and Service Plus programs
- ❖ General course work through Grand Valley Community College

"The most important single ingredient in the formula of success is knowing how to get along with people."
—Theodore Roosevelt

52

Janet L. Beckstrom, Flint, Michigan

This candidate loved her job as a Credit Union Teller and wanted to position herself for promotion within the company. Acronyms are not defined because they are known within the industry.

Jane Jones

5555 Street Address
City, ST 00000
Home: 555.555.5555
Cell: 000.000.0000
info@resumeasap.com

Career Goal: Bank Teller

Seeking to use seven years of experience in administrative support to achieve a career shift as a bank teller.

- Knowledge of principles and processes for providing customer and personal service, including customer needs assessment, meeting quality standards, and evaluation of customer satisfaction.
- Results-driven; known for strong work ethic and the ability to work unshaken under pressure.
- Strong attention to detail and thoroughness in completing work tasks.
- Skilled at building relationships with customers from all walks of life.

KEY SKILLS

- Customer Service
- Cash Handling
- Complaint Resolution
- Phone / Front Desk Reception

- Organization and Follow-through
- Creative Problem Solving
- Switchboard / Multiline Phones
- Appointments / Scheduling

EXPERIENCE

CAR DEALERSHIP—City, ST—10/07 to Present
Accounts Payable / Cashier

- Properly code and record expenses to the correct accounts.
- Receive payments by cash, check, credit cards, or automatic debits.
- Enter all invoices into the computer for processing in a timely manner.
- Resolve purchase order, contract, invoice, or payment discrepancies.
- Perform vendor reconciliation and produce checks monthly.

AUTOMOTIVE BODYSHOP—City, ST—8/02 to 10/07
Accounts Payable Clerk

- Verified accounts by reconciling monthly statements.
- Reviewed invoices and purchase orders for errors.
- Matched, batched, and coded invoices within company standards.

CAR DEALERSHIP—City, ST—4/01 to 7/02
Head Cashier

- Assisted customers and provided information on procedures and policies.
- Wrote work schedules, maintained records, and scheduled appointments.
- Maintained accurate cash drawer and receipts.

53

Jennifer Anthony, Woodland, Washington

This applicant did not have much work experience, so the writer created this layout to narrow the area for the work history. A print shop made the shading in the left column a royal blue.

Raynell Gardner

125 N.E. Woods Street • Boring, Oregon 88888

000-000-0000 *cell*   *home* **999-999-9999**

Commercial Loan Officer

Professional Profile

Top-producing, results-oriented **banking professional** with more than 20 years of experience in the banking industry. Strengths include business development, loan analysis, problem solving and top-quality customer service. Experienced in **Commercial Loans,** with a thorough understanding of the real estate business, construction loans, and business and consumer lending. Have expertise in procuring clients, analyzing needs, cross-selling, and a strong track record of "going the extra mile" to ensure client satisfaction and bank profitability. Possess outstanding communication skills. Personable, self-motivated, analytical, committed, an effective listener, and committed to a job well done.

Outstanding Achievements and Accomplishments

- Started with $0 and built portfolio to $3.5 million in loans—*largest portfolio of the Business Banking Officers.*
- Assisted in opening three branch offices.
- Top producer in referring to bank's strategic partners.
- Ranked in top three nationally in production—*2008.*

- Achieved above 130% of goal—*2004; 2005.*
- Retained 95% of book of business clients—*2006.*
- Received Chairman's Award for Outstanding Service.
- Top producer in Oregon—*1998; 2005.*

Career Progression

Umpqua Bank • Sandy, Oregon
Business Development Officer • *2002–present*

Centennial Bank • *purchased by Umpqua Bank,* Portland, Oregon
Business Banking Officer • *1998–2002*

Keybank • Portland Metropolitan area • Portland, Oregon
Small-Business Relationship Manager • *1992–1998*
Credit Analyst • *1989–1992*
Commercial Loan Assistant • *1983–1989*
Operations Assistant • *1981–1983*

Affiliations

Member • Soroptomist International • Sandy, Oregon
Chapter Secretary • LeTip International • Sandy, Oregon
Member of Mentor Committee • Gresham Area Chamber of Commerce • Sandy, Oregon

Certifications

Certified • Lending and Small Business
Licensed • Credit Life and Disability Insurance

Education

Small-Business Classes for certifications • Numerous training programs • Portland, Oregon
Accounting • Northwest College of Business • Portland, Oregon • *1972*

54

Rosie Bixel, Portland, Oregon

Two challenges were the age of this applicant and her being overqualified. The writer decided to play up the person's achievements. These appear within horizontal lines below the Profile.

Pamela Hernandez

7676 Royal Drive
Gainesville, GA 20144

Home Phone: (603) 744-6315
Cell Phone: (603) 318-6492
kygirls@aol.com

PROFILE

Loan Officer with more than 11 years of real estate and auto industry experience within increasingly responsible positions. Expertise in revenue generating, sales, employee training, recruiting, customer service, and relationship and team building. Recognized as top producer for consistently maintaining high monthly sales volumes and maximizing profits. Able to design and implement highly efficient business processes and programs and motivate teams of professionals toward achieving company goals. Results-oriented with keen eye for detail and perfect customer satisfaction ratings. Strong organizational skills with ability to manage multiple tasks and priorities simultaneously.

PROFESSIONAL BACKGROUND

First Horizon Home Loans, Centreville, VA   2001–Present
Loan Officer for home mortgage lending company with $450 million in annual sales.
- **Generate average sales volume of $1.5 million in loans per month.**
- Coordinate all details and phases of clients' loan process from application to closing.
- Maximize clients' credit rating by working with 3 credit bureaus.
- Boost sales by working with Real Estate Agents in selling property listings.
- Train Real Estate Agents on mortgage products and services.
- Seek ways to successfully move up homebuyers by exploring all financial options.
- Designed training course for new agents—specifically, Keller Williams Realty.
- Instituted highly successful mortgage application process.

Koons of Manassas, Manassas, VA   1999–2001
Finance Director for auto dealer with 3,000 new and used car sales per year.
- Oversaw average of 300 auto loans per month with 17 different lenders, including First Virginia Bank, GMAC, and First Union.
- **Doubled average profit per each car sold within 90 days after being hired.**
- Achieved most profitable GM dealer finance department on East Coast.
- Reduced sales costs by collaborating with accountants.
- Managed more than $4 million of contract dues per month.
- Supervised 4–6 Settlement Agents on a daily basis; hired, trained, and motivated agents on auto lending and selling finance products to customers.
- Assisted Sales Managers in selling cars and trained Car Salesmen.
- Planned and presented training programs and manuals for Auto Sales Staff and Settlement Agents and Sales Managers.

Continued...

55

John Femia, Altamont, New York

Read this resume from the end to the beginning, and you will recognize immediately the truth of the statement in the Profile that this candidate has had a career of increasingly responsible positions. In the Professional Background section, boldfacing calls attention to a notable

Pamela Hernandez   Résumé / Page 2

Tyson's Ford, Tysons Corner, VA   1997–1999
Settlement Agent for auto dealer with 2,500 car sales per year.
- Ranked as top producer in sale of auto loans during entire time with dealer.
- **Handled nearly 50% of dealership's auto loans per year; processed and sold auto financing to 100 customers per month.**
- Controlled all finance deals and placed loans with lenders.
- Cut outstanding debts by working closely with accountants.
- Increased profits by finding best rates with various banks and leasing companies.
- Registered cars and processed titles with DMV and helped Sales Managers with sales.
- Liaised with Ford Motor Credit in developing a sales training process.
- Established more efficient sales process for customers by improving relationships with Managers.

Landmark Honda, Alexandria, VA   1993–1997
Settlement Agent for auto dealer with 3,000 car sales per year.
- **Top producer for American Honda for 2 consecutive years, receiving Top Gun Award 1995 and 1996 for highest profitability per car financed.**
- Sold greatest number of finance contracts for American Honda Finance throughout country in 1994 and 1995.

EDUCATION & TRAINING

NVAR, Fairfax, VA   2001
Certificate in Real Estate Sales

First Horizon University, Dallas, TX   2001
Certificate in Call Sales Reluctances

First Horizon University, Dallas, TX   2001
Certificate in Mortgage Lending, *Top Honors*

GM Training Center, Scottsdale, AZ   2000
Certificate in Maximizing Profit, *Best Auto Presentation Award*

Geneva, Arlington, VA   1999
Certificate in Showtime Sales and Lending

Honda Training Center, Arlington Heights, IL   1996
Certificate in Professional Selling

PROFESSIONAL AFFILIATIONS

Social Committee Chairperson, Keller Williams Realty

LANGUAGES

Working knowledge of Spanish

KEYWORDS: New Home Sales, Sales Representative, Sales Manager, Mortgage Loan Officer, Senior Loan Officer, Business Manager, Financial Analyst

achievement in each position held. Bold italic makes it easy to spot the positions held. Keywords at the end of the resume make it scannable for storing in a resume database for online searches.

Noreen Filbert

555 Drakewood Avenue	**Brandon, Florida 33702**	**(813) 555-7901**	**nfilbert@yahoo.com**

More than 10 years of experience in banking and finance. Dependable and conscientious professional who is attentive to detail and produces quality work. Ambitious team player who enjoyed increasing responsibility levels during NationsBank/Huntington Bank career.

Attending college at night to get a B.A. degree with specialization in Management and Quality tracks. Previous entrepreneurial experience as 6-year owner and business manager of small business. Ready and eager to assume management training duties in Finance Department.

Skills and Accomplishments

Analytical and Detail-Oriented	☑ Conducted analytical procedures on financial data, spread financial data and tax returns, and calculated financial ratios to determine compliance.
	☑ Researched media sources such as *Wall Street Journal* to gather external data on large corporate borrowers.
Cash Management	☑ Provided service and help for 50 Cash Management Program accounts pertaining to setup, wire transfers, and disbursement of funds to accounts.
Customer Service	☑ Resolved 10–15 customer problems per day due to changing corporate customer requirements and product limitations.
Trustworthy	☑ Created new position as Credit Associate to provide continuity and attention to detail in monitoring loans of less than $500,000.
Credit Policies	☑ Prepared Credit Review Committee meeting minutes and compiled essential reports for senior management.
Reports	☑ Significantly refined, improved, and regimented reports used by loan officers and senior management to determine when borrowers were out of compliance.
Accounting	☑ Completed Accounting I and Principles of Banking through American Institute of Banking (AIB).
	☑ Mastered Financial Accounting for Managers, Management Accounting and Control (Cost Accounting), Financial Management, and Investments during B.A. program.
New Accounts	☑ Wrote procedures, communicated, and corresponded with new statewide accounts to set up customized account profiles and requirements.
Budget & Financial Statements	☑ Grew small business to profitable status and managed operations as Business Manager. Developed annual budget, administered payroll, administered banking, coordinated mailing, did purchasing, and developed advertising and public relations strategies.
Management	☑ Hired, trained, and managed 4 employees in addition to teaching 20 one-hour classes per week.
	☑ Managed all aspects of annual and quarterly art shows: secured facility, sold advertising, contracted with artists, and created program.

56

Gail Frank, Tampa, Florida

This candidate worked her way up through banking with only an A.A. degree. She was told that to get into management training, she needed a B.A. degree. She is in the process of getting it; however, her job was eliminated. Wanting to get into a management training program

Noreen Filbert Page 2

Presentations	☑ Earned designation as Competent Toastmaster (CTM) after creating and delivering a number of successful oral presentations.
Office Management	☑ Coordinated physical move of entire banking department with minimal downtime: directed movers and utilities, developed floor plan and requirements, and notified employees about plans and progress.
Decision Making	☑ Thoroughly interpreted and made recommendations regarding financial position of borrowers.
Total Quality Management (TQM)	☑ Completed TQM training, including Foundations of TQM, Quality Implementation, Operations Management and Quality Enhancement, and Advanced Quality Management.
Leadership	☑ Voted "Educational Vice President" of Barnett Toastmasters due to strong organizational skills and trustworthiness.
Problem Solving	☑ Created system for loan officers to monitor financial loan covenants through design and implementation of standard compliance reports.
Computer Literate	☑ Competent in Microsoft Word and Excel 97, Lotus 1–2–3, Ami Pro, WinFast, WordPerfect. Familiar with Paradox and Word Pro.

Performance Review Excerpts

Noreen meets deadlines
Noreen is very meticulous
Noreen makes sound decisions
Noreen maintains excellent documentation
Noreen has easily met the targets set for her
Noreen's reports are readable and to the point
Noreen has been proactive in obtaining what is needed
Noreen is quickly able to serve as a resource to credit analysts
Noreen has very high standards regarding the accuracy of her work
Noreen does a good job of recognizing unclear requirements and obtaining clarification
Noreen demonstrated increased confidence in completing assignments that were not always "routine"

Professional Experience

HUNTINGTON BANK (formerly NationsBank)	**TAMPA, FLORIDA**	**1984–2003**
Credit Reporting Analyst, Credit Policy Administration		2002–2003
Credit Associate, Commercial Credit Department		1996–2002
Account Coordinator, Corporate Cash Management		1989–1996
Administrative Assistant to Senior Vice President and Branch Manager		1984–1989
MAJESTIC ART GALLERY	**BRANDON, FLORIDA**	**1980–1986**
Founder, Co-owner, and Business Manager		

Education

UNIVERSITY OF SOUTH FLORIDA	**TAMPA, FLORIDA**	**A.A.**
CONNECTICUT COLLEGE	**NEW LONDON, CONNECTICUT**	**2 YEARS**
SPRINGFIELD HIGH SCHOOL	**SPRINGFIELD, DELAWARE**	**HIGH SCHOOL**

immediately while working toward her B.A., she hoped that this resume would help her in her search. The writer showcased the person's experience and current B.A. work, plus excerpts from outstanding reviews.

Christian Sadler

1234 Any Drive ◆ Indian Trail, NC 28079 ◆ (704) 555–1212

Current Objective

Position in **Inside Sales** capitalizing on successful retail and financial product sales while leading to promotional opportunities.

Qualifications

- More than 5 years of successful banking and finance-related experience.
- Proficient in all areas related to customer service.
- Solid work ethic; proven ability to meet deadlines.
- Proven ability to manage staff and achieve positive results.

Home Management

Relocation
- Launched interstate relocation of entire family, coordinating moving services, trucks and packing schedules.

Budget and Purchasing
- Managed family finances, including budgeting, medical, dental, insurance packages, expenses and taxes.

Conflict Resolution
- Arbitrated personal and related business issues. Effective interpersonal skills.

Additional Professional Experience

Personal Banker (1997–1998)   My Bank   Orlando, FL
Customer Service Supervisor (1995–1997)

- Regularly managed 8 customer service employees in absence of immediate supervisor.
- Provided customer service in opening of new accounts as well as normal banking transactions.
- Lead teller responsible for preparing daily bank deposit and branch account summary.
- Posted daily rejects from the ACH credit/debit report.
- Experienced in providing the following services: checking, savings, money market and share loan accounts, CDs, IRAs, consumer loans, home equity loan closings and home equity lines of credit.

Retail Sales Associate (1994–1995)   Army and Air Force Exchange Services   Europe Operations

- Advised customers with product selections, processed customer sales and prepared nightly deposit slips.
- Proven ability to work accurately with large amounts of cash.

Bank Operations Processor (1992–1994)   Lender Bank Connecticut   Hartford, CT

- Researched, prepared and distributed requests for copies of documents for legal cases.
- Extracted and processed data from company's mainframe system for research purposes.
- Experienced in preparation of remittance and adjustment documents.

57

Nathan J. Adams, Indian Trail, North Carolina

This individual was a stay-at-home mom who needed to return to the workforce. The writer pulled out her home-management experience to show that she had developed skills while not being formally employed. Horizontal lines enclose the contact information. Partial lines

Christian Sadler
Page Two

Awards and Recognition

My Bank (1997–1998)

- Recipient of numerous cash awards for outstanding customer sales.

Valley High School (1988)

- Graduated with honors and received the Binkel Business College Award.
- Maintained the highest average in Business Administration.

Community Involvement

- Participant in the Juvenile Diabetes Foundation Walk (1995–1997)

Professional Development

1997
- Supervisory and Leadership Training
- Client Services and Sales Seminar
- Individual Retirement Accounts Training

Technical Ability

Fax ◆ Multiline Phone ◆ Data Processing ◆ Data Key Operations ◆ Microsoft Windows

Education

New Valley Vocational Technical Institute, Fairfield, CA
Studied Accounting and Marketing (1988)

---

extend from the end of each section heading to the right margin and so make more evident the overall design. Diamond bullets in almost all the sections tie together the resume's parts visually.

Sam T. Chapman

PO Box 1462, Winchester, VA 22602
540.555.0111 ♦ stc@hotmail.com

Business Management & Sales Professional
Client Relationship Specialist

❧ overview

Conceptual thinker with ability to define an overall vision and develop appropriate strategies and tactics to obtain end results.

Resourceful, decisive and persistent. Aggressive in financial dealings. Extremely self-confident; focused under pressure.

Dedicated to providing high-quality performance for a high-quality product, service or company.

❧ strengths

Background encompasses leasing and finance second-generation entrepreneurship; Marine Corps service and training; sales and leadership. Common thread of key skills:

- negotiation & problem solving
- verbal & written presentation
- organization
- autonomy
- adaptability
- financial & business acumen
- computer literacy

> Motivator
> > People Reader
> > > Risk Taker

❧ self-educated

"Anything worth knowing can not be taught in the classroom."

Oscar Wilde

❧ Skillfully employing the fine art of client-vendor relationships, which are firmly grounded in the principles of respect, open communication and trust.

Creator of customer loyalty. Executor of increased profits.

❧ professional experience

The Chapman & Rich Lending Company, Gaithersburg, MD
1998–present

- Vice President and Managing Partner of a financial lending firm, delivering customized financing solutions for individual and corporate clients, both domestic and international.
- Created an unconventional network of private lenders and business professionals to better service clients and ensure consistent referrals, transactions and closings.
- Manage financial transactions ranging from $10K to $5M; assess client needs, secure requested funds and negotiate/monitor payment terms.

ABC Financial Group, Baltimore, MD
1994–1998

- Consumer Finance Analysis and Lease Administration Manager for a financial firm negotiating automobile lease programs for credit-challenged individuals.
- Recruited by the Regional Business Development Manager to manage day-to-day operations, including staff management and training, marketing, customer service, portfolio and asset management and tactical business planning.
- Interfaced with the company comptroller, banks and credit lending institutions to ensure sufficient cash flow to support $1.5M in monthly operating costs.
- Collaborated with the company attorney in representing ABC Financial in legal proceedings.
- Made final determination on qualifying up to 300 applications per month, from a monthly applicant pool of 1500 to 2000 consumers.
- Managed a $20K monthly advertising budget; collaborated with radio and TV advertising personnel to design and execute an effective marketing campaign.
- Created and managed pay-plans and monthly bonuses for 10 independent brokers and 10 company sales personnel.
- Conceived and implemented a client monitoring system, which strengthened client relationships by proactively engaging them in self-monitoring of their lease status.

58

Norine Dagliano, Hagerstown, Maryland

This unique individual insisted on a unique design for his resume. The writer wanted the resume to be a window on the applicant's personality. Note the Education ("self-educated") section.

Thomas M. Worthington

123 Prince Road • Marlboro, NJ 07746 • 732.964.7790 (H) • tmw6762@aol.com

FINANCIAL SPECIALIST

Investments ~ Portfolio Management

Results-driven and well-organized *Investment Specialist* with extensive experience in stocks, bonds, securities, and other investment instruments. **Possess a talent for understanding market trends and emerging markets. A self-motivated professional with a proven record of financial success. Achieved significant positions through hard work, honesty, and a commitment to the workplace. Member of New York Stock Exchange.**

Excellent leadership, team-building, communication, and problem-solving skills. Provide superior customer service by cultivating strong relationships with clients.

Competencies

- Investment Management
- Portfolio Management
- Economic Forecasting
- Troubleshooting

- Financial Planning
- Financial Services
- Customer Relations and Retention
- Packaged Investment Products

Professional Experience

New York Stock Specialists, *New York, NY*   **(1986–2004)**
Managing Director—Specialist NYSE (2001–2004)
- Appointed as Managing Director when Morris Hart & Schultz merged with Merrill Lynch, forming the third-largest specialist firm on the New York Stock Exchange.
- Made fair and orderly markets in several securities at one time.
- Represented the firm in meetings with major clients, utilizing interpersonal communication skills, extensive business networking, and persuasive salesmanship.

Morris Hart & Schultz, *New York, NY*
Partner—Specialist NYSE (1995–2001)
- Promoted to Partner when Morris merged with Hart & Schultz.
- Earned increasing responsibilities as a partner maintaining close relationships with CEOs and CFOs of Fortune 500 firms such as Southern Company, Ingersoll-Rand, Navistar (International Harvester), and Puritan Funds.
- Trained and developed numerous employees to maximize their productivity in the services that they provide to traders.

Morris Partners, *New York, NY*
Associate—Specialist NYSE (1994–1995)
- Promoted to Associate when BET merged with Morris; received steady advancement, demonstrating achievement of company goals and a strong professional work ethic.
- Executed trade orders for clients specializing in 8 to 10 firms simultaneously.
- Assigned to desks with largest currency volume and consistently received the top bonus for performance. Knowledgeable regarding pricing and quick mathematical computations to trade a variety of equities earning the most profits for clients and the company.
- Developed excellent research skills and an intuitive sense regarding equities and the market. Identified and advised brokers of current trends reflecting buy and sell orders.

BET Partners, *New York, NY*
Trading Assistant NYSE (1986–1994)
- Promoted to First Assistant, having increased responsibilities, including the position of "Fireman," assisting traders when things got particularly hectic by providing a calm, detail-oriented manner to put out the fires.
- Recorded transactions, verified orders, and verified sales commissions.
- Researched questionable trades, analyzed trade data, and recorded all stock splits.

AL Colman, *New York, NY*   **(1985–1986)**
Trading Assistant NYSE
- Assisted the specialist, performing multiple tasks.
- Performed record keeping of trades and commissions.

United States Marine Corps   **(1981–1984)**

59

Beverly and Mitch Baskin, Marlboro, New Jersey

Follow the bold, and you will gain a quick overview of this well-designed resume with a page border and useful lines to separate the main sections. Note also the use of bold italic and regular italic.

MARGARET VENETTA
1500 South 22nd Place • Phoenix, AZ 85044
(480) 855-3710 • mvenetta@cox.net

PROFESSIONAL QUALIFICATIONS

- Proven history of achievements in **Loan Processing / Funding** for consumer and commercial credit organizations.
- Areas of expertise: **auto financing, mortgage loans, account management, market penetration, customer service, relationship development and office administration.**
- Ability to sort through broad range of financial options to find products best suited to customer=s needs.
- Organized, focused problem-solver who remains calm during stressful situations.
- Professional manner and appearance; able to easily build rapport with customers, peers and management.
- Computer skills: MS Windows, Word, Excel; Internet and intranet.

State of Arizona Insurance Sales License

CAREER HIGHLIGHTS

Office Management
- ◆ Performed all administrative functions, including A/P, A/R and bank deposits; organized bookkeeping records for accountant; purchased supplies and equipment; developed and implemented procedures. (Stanford)
- ◆ Conceived and installed showroom displays; interacted with walk-in customers. (Stanford)

Finance / Loan Administration
- ◆ Arranged consumer financing and performed credit analyses; administered and documented loans and leases; processed loans for 50–60 new and used cars per month. (Maxwell)
- ◆ Interfaced with loan officers of major banks and credit unions. (Maxwell)
- ◆ Completed commercial credit transactions and funded commercial loans against discounted notes. (Carnegie)
- ◆ Processed paperwork for home loans and interfaced with mortgage bankers. (A-Z Mortgage)
- ◆ Managed buy rates and reserves; promoted add-ons to generate maximum profit per transaction. (Maxwell)
- ◆ Tracked penetration into high-profit areas, reserves and total transactions on monthly basis, generating reports for corporate management. (Maxwell)

Sales / Customer Service
- ◆ Consistently achieved personal index of 97–98% for customer satisfaction. (Maxwell)
- ◆ Achieved Department CSI of 80%+ (1998, 1999), compared to company overall national average of 70–75%.
- ◆ Balanced profitability for company with customer needs, creating win-win situations and satisfied customers.
- ◆ Developed and implemented customer contact plans that significantly impacted sales. (Safety Plus)
- ◆ Assisted sales consultants in preparing individual marketing plans. (Maxwell)
- ◆ Used proven sales strategies to establish relationships with key accounts to expand territory. (Safety Plus)
- ◆ Interacted with vendors and sales representatives to promote sales. (Safety Plus)
- ◆ Built territory from 0 to 20 accounts in Nevada within one year, opening territory to allow addition of full-time sales representative for state. (Safety Plus)

PROFESSIONAL EXPERIENCE

Finance Director / Financial Consultant, MAXWELL CORPORATION, Tempe, AZ	1995 to Present
Office Manager / Sales Representative, SAFETY PLUS, Phoenix, AZ	1990 to 1995
Administrative Assistant—Funding Department, A-Z MORTGAGE, San Diego, CA	1986 to 1987
Office Manager, STANFORD & SONS, San Diego, CA	1980 to 1986

Prior to 1980:
Loan Administrator, CARNEGIE FINANCIAL CORPORATION, St. Paul, MN	7 years

---

EDUCATION / PROFESSIONAL DEVELOPMENT

- **University of Minnesota,** Minneapolis, Minnesota—Undergraduate studies
- **Training Courses**—Consultative Sales & Financial Consultative Sales Process
- **Anthony Robbins**—10-Hour Seminar

60

Wanda McLaughlin, Chandler, Arizona

This person had worked in jobs relating to mortgage and auto loans. She wanted to move into a banking or administrative position. The writer emphasized various skills for a flexible job search.

Firefighting

Resumes at a Glance

PHILLIP KNIGHT
71 Crater Avenue · Springfield, Oregon 99999 · (555) 555–5555

DIVISION CHIEF — SPECIAL OPERATIONS

Proactive leader and manager of personnel and programs, offering more than 14 years of experience as a firefighter. Extensive experience as a motivator and coordinator; able to focus the efforts of diverse groups to a common goal. Committed to providing innovative protection programs that reflect the values, diversity, aspirations, and priorities of the community they serve. Effective combination of interpersonal, analytical, and organizational qualifications with strengths in

› Coordination with Existing Organizations	› Administration & Reporting
› Public Speaking & Community Outreach	› Federal & State Regulatory Compliance
› Team Building, Training, & Management	› Strategic Planning & Critical Thinking
› Program Development & Direction	› Design of Policy & Procedures

PROFESSIONAL EXPERIENCE

SPRINGFIELD CITY FIRE DEPARTMENT; Springfield, OR   **1989–Present**
Captain — Operations Division
Currently supervise Engine 1B, Dive 1B, and coordinate shift manning as Captain of Operations. Scope of responsibility is broad and includes supervision, direction of fireground activities, tactical operation of emergency scenes, safety of firefighters, and the protection of life and property. Additionally responsible for ensuring continued compliance with all OSHA, NIOSH, and NFPA standards and regulations. Promoted on several occasions due to knowledge, skills, and high level of integrity and dedication.

- Developed extensive knowledge of all emergency response program plans, including Dive Rescue, Technical Rescue, Hazardous Materials, Airport Rescue Firefighting, and Special Events.
- Instrumental team member developing policies and procedures, including safety and minimum standards for Dive Rescue Company.
- Managed extensive firefighter training program for Recruit Academy and assisted in development of Firefighter II program currently being utilized, resulting in improved standards and operations.
- Proven ability to develop and maintain productive relationships and partnerships with a wide variety of organizations, officials, and individuals, including businesses and local citizens.
- Cooperatively worked with local government agencies such as EPA, DEQ, Springfield City Public Works, Springfield Parks and Recreation, and Springfield Police Department.
- Conducted public education classes on fire prevention, water rescue, CPR, and first aid training through gained knowledge of instructional methodologies.

PROFESSIONAL DEVELOPMENT & SPECIALTY TRAINING

Fire Officer I
Red Cross Lifeguard Instructor
American Heart Association BLS Instructor Trainer
Instructor Trainer National Fire Academy Leadership Series

Dive Rescue	**Technical Rescue**	**Hazardous Materials**	**Airport Rescue**
· Public-Safety Diver	· Rope Rescue Technician	· Awareness Level	· Operations Level
· Swift-Water Rescue	· Confined-Space Rescue	· Operations Level	
· Ice Diving	· Trench Rescue	· Technician Level	
· Ice Rescue		· Incident Command System	
· Current Diving			
· Deep Diving			

61

Denette Jones, Mountain View, Hawaii

The opening section is a profile, a summary of qualifications, and areas of strengths without being titled as such. The bottom section lists areas of training grouped by rescue categories and materials.

JOHN J. JONES

555 Ridge Court • East Demarest, Illinois 00000 • (555) 555-5555 • jjones@aol.com

Combine a diverse background in fire ground operations, fire prevention, public education, organizational leadership, training & development with a commitment to achieve governmental agencies' short- & long-term goals & objectives

Management Capabilities

Team Leadership—Demonstrate qualities that positively motivate business owners, students and employees and foster a spirit of cooperation in team environments. Willingly mentor coworkers, citizens, government officials and others in achieving goals and objectives.

Public Education—Instruct students of all ages on fire prevention and safety practices and procedures including first aid, swimming, disaster planning, fire safety, fire-fighting, vehicle extrication, hazardous materials operations, fire inspections and preplanning.

Program Development—Develop fire prevention and safety programs for municipalities and their employees from idea stage, through design and implementation. Successful in reducing employee claims and insurance costs.

Administration—Plan, organize, coordinate and control departmental services and programs. Manage the budget. Interface with all levels of management, insurance carriers, government agencies and officials. Accomplish major tasks within established time deadlines.

Procurement—Budget, order, inspect, test and repair safety and hazardous materials supplies and equipment.

Interpersonal Strengths

Decisiveness—Observe and analyze situations quickly and initiate prompt, effective action. Act calmly and decisively during emergencies and in stressful situations.

Problem Resolution—Identify problems and opportunities for process improvement; arbitrate conflicts fairly and develop workable solutions; maintain confidentiality in performance of job duties. Use available resources to meet deadlines.

Articulate Communication—Express complex data clearly and concisely, both orally and in writing, to ensure understanding. Record information completely and accurately. Interview witnesses and testify in court.

Meticulous Organization—Possess excellent planning skills, pay strict attention to details, follow assignments through to successful completion, and organize and prepare detailed reports.

Self-motivation—Work well independently and effectively within confines of standard operating procedures. Eagerly learn and actively seek self-improvement.

Professional Image—Communicate and interact positively with elected and appointed officials, community leaders, business owners, fellow employees, and citizens. Demonstrate a solid work ethic and willingly accept challenges and added responsibility. Maintain a high standard of ethics, conduct and honesty. Flexible and adaptable.

Computer Savvy—Skilled operating computer software, including MS Office, NFIRS, and Fire House.

SUMMARY OF EXPERIENCE

MANAGEMENT

Acting Fire Officer—Managed day-to-day operations of a suppression & EMS crew responding to emergency calls. Participated in developing and implementing Fire Prevention and Safety goals and objectives, work plans, priorities, and policies and procedures. Assisted with fire investigations.
- ➢ Implemented a departmental Hazardous Materials Team.
- ➢ Developed and conducted a Household Hazardous Waste Collection Site.

62

Rosemary Fish Justen, Schaumburg, Illinois

The applicant wanted to call attention to his management and interpersonal strengths to find a higher position in firefighting or fire inspection. Three pages are not only appropriate but also

John J. Jones _____ Page Two

Safety Coordination—Developed, implemented and managed safety programs to ensure compliance with OSHA and IDOL standards. Established excellent rapport with village employees, the insurance carrier and village administration. Immediately troubleshot and resolved departmental problems and deficiencies.

➢ Taught safety awareness courses to employees that resulted in fewer accidents and a 14% reduction in claims.
➢ Recognized by village officials for superior performance in managing safety programs.
➢ Prepared and maintained the annual safety budget.

Facility Management—Managed all aspects of recreational facility. Hired, supervised and trained staff. Maintained and serviced equipment. Developed and enforced safety policies and procedures. Troubleshot and resolved problems and deficiencies.

FIRE DEPARTMENT ACCOUNTABILITY

Fire Inspector—Conduct inspection, re-inspection and pre-fire planning of commercial, industrial, institutional, residential and public buildings to ensure compliance with applicable building, property maintenance, health, fire and life safety codes, including NFPA 101 Life Safety Code and International Fire Code. Inspect and witness testing for proper installation and operation of fire protection systems including sprinklers, fire alarms and kitchen hoods. Perform periodic and follow-up inspections of new and existing buildings, structures and installations for compliance with fire clearance, fire protection systems and fire alarm standards.

➢ Participate in fire investigations and Juvenile Firesetters Intervention interviews. Conduct and assist with fire cause determinations.
➢ Simplify complex fire and safety problems and generate timely and effective solutions.

Code Enforcement/Plan Review—Assist Bureau Manager in researching and reviewing regulations, codes, and standards for designing village ordinances. Interpret and enforce code standards and pursue legal remedy for noncompliance (pre-citation notices, citations, legal complaints, court testimony). Review plans to ensure fire and life safety requirements comply with applicable fire protection and building code standards. Audit plans, specifications and calculations on building, fire protection equipment and systems and hazardous-equipment installations.

Training—Conduct training with shift personnel on basic fire-prevention skills, fire system operations and building preplans. Deliver public education demonstrations and presentations to community and school groups.

➢ Adjunct Faculty, Illinois Fire Inspectors Association, teaching NFPA Fire Inspector I classes.

Administrative—Maintain fire prevention bureau records and reports. Prepare inspection reports, logs and inspection activities, and file information for future reference and/or follow-up.

➢ Develop new programs and reports from idea stage through design and implementation to improve accuracy, productivity and timeliness of information dissemination.

Firefighting—Perform fire suppression/fire prevention duties; assess and treat acutely ill and injured citizens; perform rescue procedures, operate emergency fire apparatus and emergency medical equipment; assist in prevention programs; regularly participate in Fire/EMS training exercises; maintain station and equipment; and perform related duties as assigned.

➢ Department Diver and M.A.B.A.S. Team member.

Dispatch—Received, assessed, prioritized and classified calls for service on a variety of emergency and nonemergency situations. Dispatched emergency units. Simultaneously managed telephone and radio traffic while inputting and extracting data from computer systems. Prepared clear and concise records and reports with comprehensive documentation.

necessary for the amount of important information presented here. The idea that a resume should be no longer that one or two pages makes no sense when there is an important story to tell to seize a significant opportunity. Boxes enclosing contact information and the major, centered headings help to tie together the

<u>John J. Jones</u>   Page Three

WORK HISTORY

Fire Inspector	Village of Sweetflower, IL	03/02 to Present
Firefighter	Village of West Demarest, IL	10/97 to Present
Fire Inspector/Safety Coordinator	Village of Lakewater, IL	07/97 to 02/02
Safety Coordinator/Acting Fire Officer	Village of Lincoln, IL	09/94 to 07/97
Fire Officer	Yorktown Fire Department, IL	10/90 to 05/95
Facility Manager	Trails Assoc. Pool, Rosedale, IL	05/89 to 09/94
Firefighter/911 Dispatcher	Woods Fire Department, IL	04/80 to 08/96

AWARDS AND HONORS

1986	American Red Cross Community Health Education Safety Service Award
1997	Village of Lincoln Achievement Award
2001	Nominee for the Village of Lakewater Government Employee of the Year Award
2003 & 2004	Edgewater Community College, William College Academic Honors List

MEMBERSHIPS

Illinois Fire Inspectors Association	Since 1992
Northern Illinois Fire Inspectors Association (Executive Board Member, 2000–2003)	Since 1997
Pyrotechnical Guild International	Since 2003
International Code Council	Since 2004

EDUCATION

Edgewater Community College, Edgewater, IL	A.A.S. in Fire Science and Safety
William College, Prince, IL	Certificate in Building Codes and Enforcement

Office of the State Fire Marshal Certifications include

Firefighter I, II & III	Fire Certified Fire Apparatus Engineer
Fire Officer I, Provisional Fire Officer II	Fire Service Vehicle and Machinery Operations
Certified Fire Investigator	Fire Prevention Inspector II & Plan Examiner I
Fire Prevention Officer I	Juvenile Firesetters Intervention Specialist
Fire Instructor I & II	Hazardous Materials First Responder
Hazardous Materials Awareness	Hazardous Materials Incident Command
Fire Service Vehicle Operator	Hazardous Materials Technician A
Rescue Spec-Confined Space/Trench Rescue	Licensed Emergency Medical Technician B

National Fire Protection Association & International Code Council

Certified Fire Inspector I, II	Certified Plans Examiner I

REFERENCES

References, both professional and personal, are available upon request.

three pages visually. Judicious use of boldface, italic, and bullets helps to avoid monotony across the pages. The third page exhibits considerable white space at a time when the reader may be becoming overloaded with information.

Health and Safety

Resumes at a Glance

William S. Beyer

78 Holcomb Drive • Franklin Park, NJ 08823 • 732-378-1972 • wsbeyer7@aol.com

DISTRIBUTION / WAREHOUSING SPECIALIST

Top-performing and motivated manufacturing professional with 12 years' experience in distribution, warehousing, line production, supervision, team building, and equipment operation.

Successful track record of ensuring that the plant was in compliance with all local, state, and federal safety regulations. Self-disciplined administrator with the ability to troubleshoot and resolve problems in a timely manner. As **Safety Leader,** managed all monthly safety meetings and safety training programs for the 125 workers at the plant.

Experienced in supervising, mentoring, and training staff. Address process improvement issues to find better methods to get the job done with fewer injuries. Computer-proficient in Microsoft Word, email, and use of the Internet.

Areas of Expertise:

- OSHA Compliance
- Warehouse Operations
- Shipping/Receiving
- Good Manufacturing Practices (GMP)

- Real Time Control Inventory System (RTCIS)
- Ergonomics/Safety
- Problem Identification/Troubleshooting
- Licensed Fork Lift Driver

Professional Experience

Procter & Gamble—Warren, New Jersey (1991 to 2003)
Safety & Ergonomics Leader (1996 to 2003)
Fork Lift Technician/Materials Handler (1991 to 1996)

- Loyal, dedicated, efficient employee. Accepted an early retirement package from Procter & Gamble after a 12-year career.
- Knowledge of RTCIS inventory control system.
- Performed physical inventories using bar code scanners.
- Extensive knowledge of the processes and equipment in the food, beverage, bottling, and packaging industry. Calculated, weighed, and verified exact amount of ingredients per batch.
- Served as a forklift technician and driver on a computerized forklift.
- Thorough knowledge of procedures and techniques used for shipping and receiving and materials handling.
- Some of the many safety programs managed were
  ♦ Job Safety Analysis (JSA)
  ♦ Job Task Analysis (JTA)
  ♦ Safety Inspections
  ♦ Personal Protective Equipment (PPE)
  ♦ Material Safety Data Sheets (MSDS)
  ♦ Lock Out Tag Out (LOTO)
  ♦ Ladders and Safety Climbing Devices
- Considered reliable and honest, with excellent follow-through. Ability to work alone and to build excellent rapport with employees, vendors, and customers.

Education

Orange High School, Orange, NJ
Bloomfield College, Bloomfield, NJ

Military

United States Army, Specialist 4th Class—Honorable Discharge, Vietnam Service Award

63

Beverly and Mitch Baskin, Marlboro, New Jersey

Boldfacing establishes down the page a path for seeing, in turn, key information and the main headings. A switch to a serif font in the final section adds a formal note. See Cover Letter 2.

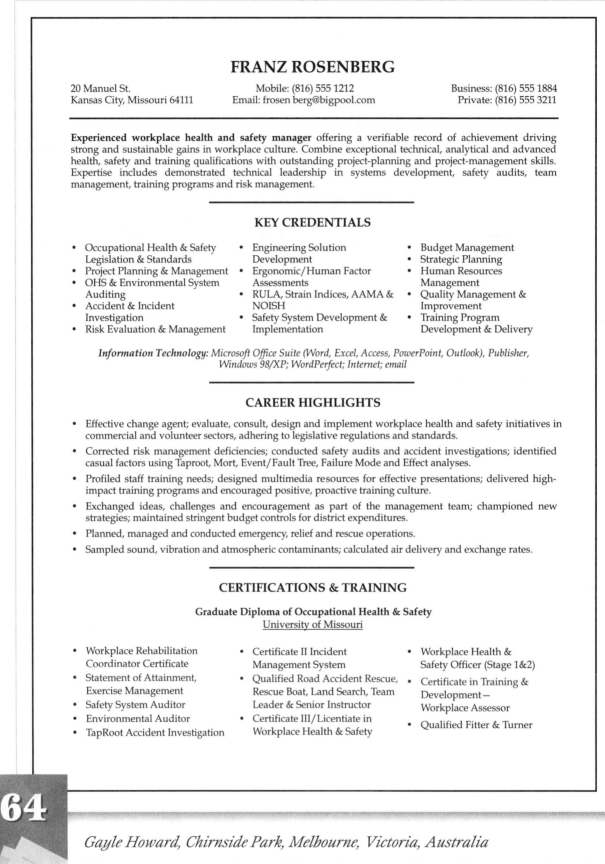

FRANZ ROSENBERG

| 20 Manuel St.
Kansas City, Missouri 64111 | Mobile: (816) 555 1212
Email: frosen berg@bigpool.com | Business: (816) 555 1884
Private: (816) 555 3211 |

Experienced workplace health and safety manager offering a verifiable record of achievement driving strong and sustainable gains in workplace culture. Combine exceptional technical, analytical and advanced health, safety and training qualifications with outstanding project-planning and project-management skills. Expertise includes demonstrated technical leadership in systems development, safety audits, team management, training programs and risk management.

KEY CREDENTIALS

- Occupational Health & Safety Legislation & Standards
- Project Planning & Management
- OHS & Environmental System Auditing
- Accident & Incident Investigation
- Risk Evaluation & Management

- Engineering Solution Development
- Ergonomic/Human Factor Assessments
- RULA, Strain Indices, AAMA & NOISH
- Safety System Development & Implementation

- Budget Management
- Strategic Planning
- Human Resources Management
- Quality Management & Improvement
- Training Program Development & Delivery

Information Technology: Microsoft Office Suite (Word, Excel, Access, PowerPoint, Outlook), Publisher, Windows 98/XP; WordPerfect; Internet; email

CAREER HIGHLIGHTS

- Effective change agent; evaluate, consult, design and implement workplace health and safety initiatives in commercial and volunteer sectors, adhering to legislative regulations and standards.
- Corrected risk management deficiencies; conducted safety audits and accident investigations; identified casual factors using Taproot, Mort, Event/Fault Tree, Failure Mode and Effect analyses.
- Profiled staff training needs; designed multimedia resources for effective presentations; delivered high-impact training programs and encouraged positive, proactive training culture.
- Exchanged ideas, challenges and encouragement as part of the management team; championed new strategies; maintained stringent budget controls for district expenditures.
- Planned, managed and conducted emergency, relief and rescue operations.
- Sampled sound, vibration and atmospheric contaminants; calculated air delivery and exchange rates.

CERTIFICATIONS & TRAINING

Graduate Diploma of Occupational Health & Safety
<u>University of Missouri</u>

- Workplace Rehabilitation Coordinator Certificate
- Statement of Attainment, Exercise Management
- Safety System Auditor
- Environmental Auditor
- TapRoot Accident Investigation

- Certificate II Incident Management System
- Qualified Road Accident Rescue, Rescue Boat, Land Search, Team Leader & Senior Instructor
- Certificate III/Licentiate in Workplace Health & Safety

- Workplace Health & Safety Officer (Stage 1&2)
- Certificate in Training & Development—Workplace Assessor
- Qualified Fitter & Turner

64

Gayle Howard, Chirnside Park, Melbourne, Victoria, Australia

This two-page resume contains much information because of a small font size, long lines of text, and compact three-column lists. Horizontal lines and centered headings make it easy to see at a

---

CAREER EXPERIENCE

CONSOLIDATED MINING   1/2001–Present

Health & Safety / Training Manager

Brief: To establish a portable and adaptable safety management system applicable to multiple projects.

Reviewed and improved safety management mechanisms, enforced compliance with contemporary legislative practices and spearheaded across-the-board organizational training systems. Presided over adherence to workplace health and safety training and revamped complete rehabilitation program design and delivery.

Core accountabilities include safety management, advice and legislative compliance; accident investigation and reporting; policy/procedure and management systems development/review; risk assessment; safety and compliance auditing; rehabilitation planning and management; strategic planning; training design, delivery and evaluation; training/safety record maintenance and analysis; external training/safety service procurement and human resources management.

Highlights:

- Reduced *"Lost Time Injury Frequency Rate"* from 45 to 0; reduced *"Disabling Severity Rate"* by 34.5% employing behavior modification principles at both manager and employee levels.

- Pioneered organizational shift to a "no blame" culture; reengineered accident investigation policy, spearheading an organization-wide investigation system (Tap Root).

- Introduced a more streamlined, user-friendly training and safety record system adopted throughout the organization that met stringent internal/external auditing requirements.

- Optimized early hazard identification and corrective action status tracking by developing a contemporary risk management system.

DEPARTMENT OF CRISIS SERVICES, Counter Disaster & Rescue Service   3/1998–1/2001

District Operations & Training Officer / Acting District Manager

GABSTONE BREWERIES   12/1997–3/1998

Service Department Supervisor

SELECTED PROJECTS & RESULTS

- Investigated ergonomic hazards and metabolic rate expenditure during night shift supermarket environment; considered extreme temperatures and workers' primary occupations.

- Examined potential effects of Sodium Azide from deployed vehicle restraining systems on panel beaters and tow truck drivers and potential hazards of inadequately storing faulty devices.

- Conducted extensive risk assessment report for cabinet manufacturing workshop, leading to company embracing comprehensive safety policy, including staff training, job descriptions, machine guarding and exhaust ventilation installations.

- Assessed operational competencies of small construction company from site preparation to handover. Company adopted and implemented all recommendations, including site-specific work plans, strict enforcement of safety on building sites and weekly inspections by external consultant.

- Investigated staff complaints of headache and nausea within an administrative building. Conducted detailed ventilation survey, concluding that contaminated air was returned to air-conditioning unit for recycling.

Franz Rosenberg   Page 2   Confidential

glance the sections of the resume and thereby its overall design. Careful use of white space between sections prevents this resume from appearing crowded. Note where italic is used effectively.

Joe Mitchum

555 Rose Drive
Delray Beach, Florida 33483

Fax (561) 555-8566 (561) 555-5095 JMSafety@comcast.net

More than 10 years of experience in the Safety/OSHA field as a manager and problem solver. Previous military career created special experience in management and training with additional accomplishments in OSHA, safety, risk management and logistics. Experienced fixed-wing/helicopter pilot.

Dependable and hardworking professional who solves tough problems and is attentive to detail. Multifaceted manager who analyzes needs, creates structure, develops systems, implements training and unifies staff. Strong mechanical ability.

Selected Management Accomplishments

OSHA
- Developed first-ever OSHA program in 3 different locations/companies and drastically improved safety compliance each time. Reduced hazards in areas of electrical, storage, fire detection, lighting, hazardous and flammable materials, medical equipment, first aid and airplane safety.
- Created first-ever safety inspection checklist for supervisors, resulting in ongoing detection of issues. Facility then established periodic inspections for prompt problem resolution.

Safety Manual Creation
- Selected to be on Safety Committee for independent aviation company that initially served the Rockefeller family and Chase Manhattan Bank. Created, researched and wrote 30-page safety supplement and inspection checklist for General Operating Manual.

Safety Program Development
- Developed system for 400–500-person organization to track injuries on the ground and begin measuring output and impact of injuries. After measuring, implemented safety program and drastically decreased auto, recreational and on-the-job injuries.

Management
- Appointed Airfield Manager in addition to Safety Director due to organizational and leadership abilities. Developed schedules for shift personnel and tower operations, maintained fuel and material inventories and assisted visiting air crews with accommodations.
- Managed workforces ranging from 30 to 350 people in variety of positions requiring training, standard setting and monitoring versus objectives.

Risk Analysis
- Initiated first risk analysis of the workplace, prioritized deficiencies for correction and instituted ongoing evaluation of deficiencies.

Logistics
- Organized and developed logistics for mock aviation accidents and mock invasions: contacted military police, fire departments and area hospitals; prepared reports; and secured airspace from the FAA. Coordinated all aspects of Present Reagan's base visit with Secret Service and Military Police to ensure smooth and safe exhibition.
- Selected as Air Mission Commander for nuclear warhead movement throughout Germany, Italy, Greece and Turkey. Also appointed member of Nuclear Inspection Team.

Instructional Design
- Developed objectives, program content and lesson plans for more than 25 different training courses.

Trainer
- Master Trainer for air safety. Tested instructor pilots on their ability to teach. Instructed them in methods and knowledge.
- Provided instruction on OSHA safety requirements to 20 participants.
- Created Training Board to track all required training courses and completion of courses. Developed and maintained weekly training schedule.

65

Gail Frank, Tampa, Florida

This candidate was an ex-military pilot and a private pilot who was laid off from his job of piloting small planes. He tinkered around with several different jobs and tried to find a new piloting job, but he was considered too old. He was trying to use safety/OSHA experience to land a job in

J. MITCHUM PAGE 2

Creativity	• Conceived and implemented innovative closed-circuit television system throughout company. Improved reach and accessibility of required training courses.
Mediation	• Started and currently run company representing homeowners in insurance arbitration. Inspect properties, create written report, present facts and evidence to arbitrator and insurance company, negotiate terms and approve settlement for client. 98% success in obtaining money for clients.
Quick Learner	• Completed intensive ground school training to become certified to fly Boeing 737 aircraft. Passed comprehensive 5-hour oral test, simulator checkride and flight test by FAA examiner.
Mechanical Ability	• Designed and remodeled bathrooms for area builder and construction company. Performed plumbing, electrical, carpentry and tile work in homes valued from $250K to $3M.
Bookkeeping	• Selected as political campaign Treasurer. Provide accounting to City Clerk for contributions and expenditures for City Council candidate. Approve all campaign checks and monies.
	• Perform all bookkeeping, billing and tax filing for Johansen-Hale Associates, a consumer research company.
PR and Marketing	• Developed, wrote and produced training video that received attention from top officials.
	• Secured extensive press coverage in radio and television for the high-priority Project Partnership in Europe. Arranged filming and briefings for press.
Inventory Management	• Tracked and maintained appropriate inventories for $10M worth of aviation parts and equipment.

PROFESSIONAL AND EDUCATIONAL BACKGROUND

ALTERNATIVE DISPUTE RESOLUTION	Delray Beach, Florida	1998–Present
Owner of business that assists in arbitration, insurance appraisal and family mediation		
CITY COUNCIL CAMPAIGN	Delray Beach, Florida	1998–Present
Treasurer for Candidate		
TROPIC ISLE CIVIC ASSOCIATION	Delray Beach, Florida	1995–Present
Vice President, Board Member		
PRIVATE CONTRACTOR	Delray Beach, Florida	1997–1998
Designer for area builder and remodeler		
CARNIVAL AIRLINES	Dania, Florida	1995–1996
Student/Pilot		
WAYFARER KETCH, INC.	White Plains, New York	1988–1994
Corporate Pilot/Safety Manager		
UNITED STATES ARMY		
Airfield Safety Manager/Airfield Operations Manager/Pilot—Fort Campbell, Kentucky		
Safety Manager/Airport Manager/Pilot—Germany and Italy		
Pilot—second tour/Infantry—first tour/Maintenance Supervisor—Vietnam		
Parts Supply Manager—Fort Riley, Kansas		
Drill Sergeant Instructor—Fort Jackson, South Carolina		

SPECIAL TRAINING AND EDUCATION

Aviation Officer Safety Course
OSHA Safety Course
Warrant Officer Senior and Advanced Course
Method of Instruction and Instructor Pilot Course
Saint Martins College—2 Years Liberal Arts

that field. Side headings in the Selected Management Accomplishments section make the long list of bulleted items easier to understand. Without those headings the long list would be overwhelming.

JACK S. JORDAN

555 Bass Lane • Littleton, CO 80000 • Home: (303) 555.5555 • Cell: (303) 000.0000
jacksjo@aol.com

INSTRUCTOR & FIRST RESPONDER

Emergency Medical Treatment, Weapons of Mass Destruction Response, Diving Instructor

SUMMARY OF QUALIFICATIONS

Diverse expertise in Emergency/Incident Response, Business Management and Hyperbaric Therapy. Comprehensive knowledge base includes Weapons of Mass Destruction response, detection and protection; emergency response and treatment; hazardous materials transportation and handling; antiterrorism and incident preparedness. Extensive training and experience with SCUBA safety, emergency medical response and diving injuries. Proven career record of responding to and managing emergency situations, including quickly and effectively directing team efforts. Highly motivated self-starter. Demonstrated ability to develop and implement emergency protocols. Exceptional skill as instructor and public speaker.

EMERGENCY/INCIDENT RESPONSE EXPERIENCE

INSTRUCTION & AFFILIATIONS

STATE OF COLORADO, DENVER, CO   2005–PRESENT
SAFETY DIVISION
National Incident Management System (NIMS) Instructor
COLORADO REGIONAL INSTITUTE
Safety Instructor
  ◆ Delivered Weapons of Mass Destruction (WMD) Instruction.

CENTER FOR DOMESTIC PREPAREDNESS, CLOVIS, NM   2005–PRESENT
WMD General Instructor

UNITED STATES DEPT. OF HOMELAND SECURITY   2001–PRESENT
NATIONAL DISASTER SYSTEM (NDS)
DISASTER ASSISTANCE TEAM (DAT)
Logistics Professional
NATIONAL RESPONSE TEAM (NRT)
PPE Instructor, Logistics Professional, WMD First Responder
  ◆ Directed in-house maintenance of all Personal Protective Equipment (PPE). Oversaw motor pool.
  ◆ Recognized as Volunteer of the Year, 2002.
  ◆ Served on NMRT as only airborne team in the nation for WMD DHS/FEMA.

INTERNATIONAL AIRLINE TRANSPORTATION ASSOCIATION (IATA)   2002–PRESENT
Hazardous Materials Air Transportation Officer, on call

NATIONAL CENTER FOR BIOMEDICAL TRAINING
ACADEMY OF COUNTER TERRORIST EDUCATION
Law Enforcement Response to Weapons of Mass Destruction, Certified Field Instructor

EDUCATION & PROFESSIONAL DEVELOPMENT

U.S. Dept. of Homeland Security, Domestic Preparedness Equipment Technical Assistance Program,
WMD Detection Technologies, 2005
WMD Mass Casualty Personnel Decontamination, 2005

Montana Tech, Energetic Materials Research & Testing Center
Incident Response to Terrorist Bombings Technical Operations Course, 2005
  ◆ Certified as Instructor for Incident Response to Terrorist Bombings Awareness Level Program.
  ◆ Certified as Instructor for Incident Response & Prevention of Suicide Bombings.

66

Michele Angello, Aurora, Colorado

Documentation for this resume was in a folder an inch thick. The writer's challenge was to select from this material the information that would best market the applicant effectively. His objective was to become an instructor and a responder in emergency medical treatment and in response

JACK S. JORDAN

EMERGENCY/INCIDENT RESPONSE EXPERIENCE

> **EDUCATION & PROFESSIONAL DEVELOPMENT** (continued)

U.S. Dept. of Homeland Security, Office for Domestic Preparedness
WMD Law Enforcement Protective Measures, 2005
WMD Law Enforcement Protective Measures Train-the-Trainer course, 2005
WMD Technical Emergency Response, 2005
WMD General Instructor, 2005
WMD Radiological/Nuclear course for Hazardous Materials Technicians, 2005
WMD Live Agent-Cobra, 2004
WMD Incident Command, 2004
WMD Hands-on-Training, 2004
WMD Incident Complexities, Emergency Medical Services, 2004
WMD Responder Operations Radiological/Nuclear, 2004
WMD Hazmat Technician, 2005
WMD Radiological Nuclear Awareness Train-the-Trainer course, 2004

TUV: National Emergency Response & Rescue Training Center
Public Works: Preparing & Responding to WMD Terrorism Incidents, 2004
Public Works WMD Basic Concepts, 2004
EMS Operations and Planning WMD, 2004
WMD/Terrorism Incident Operations Course for Emergency Responders, 2004
Senior Officials Workshop for WMD/Terrorism Incident Preparedness, 2004
Enhanced Incident Management Unified Command, 2004

Jossey Air Force Base
Hazmat Technical Specialist certification, #FEMA-005, 2004

Emergency Institute
Department of Homeland Security IS 700, National Incident Management System, 2004

New Mexico Office of Emergency Management
Mass Fatalities, 2004

Department of Homeland Security, Federal Law Enforcement Training Center
Land Transportation Antiterrorism, 2003

Montana Training Institute
Hazardous Material Awareness Training, 1984

Littleton Fire Department
L.P. Gas Fire Training, 1983

American Hospital Systems, Institute of Emergency Medical Training
Emergency Medical Technician, 1977

ENTREPRENEURIAL EXPERIENCE

A STEP ABOVE SHADE & DRAPERY, FORT COLLINS, CO   1983–PRESENT
Owner & Manager
Directed operations of successful drapery business. Supervised six employees. Accountable for ordering and procurement. Oversaw marketing campaigns and conducted sales with internal clients.
- ◆ Attained numerous awards from manufacturer for attaining excellent dealer sales. Awards included cruise and all-expense-paid vacation to New York.
- ◆ Propelled continual improvements to sales methods, resulting in successful endurance of small business.

to weapons of mass destruction. Each horizontal line is the clue to understanding the sections of the resume. It has four major parts: Summary of Qualifications, Emergency/Incident Response Experience, Entrepreneurial Experience, and SCUBA & Hyperbaric Experience. Centered subheadings in boxes make it easy to spot the

JACK S. JORDAN

SCUBA & HYPERBARIC EXPERIENCE

WORK EXPERIENCE & SHORT-TERM CONTRACTS

COLORADO DIVING EXPERIENCE, BLUE LAKE, CO — 1977–1985
Instructor, Dive Medic, Dive Control Specialist, Retail Sales
Supervised and trained new instructors. Performed commercial dive work.
- Developed State of Colorado diving injury protocols.

IVY LEAGUE MEDICAL CENTER, PHILADELPHIA, PA — 1981–1984
Associate Regional Coordinator, Diving Alert Network
Instructed courses on treating diving injuries.

UNIVERSITY OF CALIFORNIA, SAN DIEGO, CA — 1981–1984
Hyperbaric Therapy Team
Performed hyperbaric treatments using multiplace systems. Treated patients for decompression sickness, arterial gas embolism, radiational necrosis and osteomyelitis. Completed periodic, month-long contracts to operate hyperbaric chamber and treat divers for injuries.

UNDERWATER CONCRETE AUTHORITY, ALBUQUERQUE, NM — 1978–1980
Dive Medical Technician, Surface Coordinator, Commercial Diver
Developed system to coordinate organization's dive plans with Hospital Flight for Life program. Provided training to medical staff. Performed commercial dives for Colorado Diving Experience.
- Noted for taking initiative to obtain additional training in field of dive medicine and for implementing new safety precautions for ice diving and diving protocols.

INSTRUCTION & CERTIFICATIONS

PROFESSIONAL ASSOCIATION OF DIVER MEDICS
Diver Medical Technician, 1983

NATIONAL ASSOCIATION OF DIVING INSTRUCTORS (NADI)
Open Water SCUBA Instructor, 1982

SCUBA INTERNATIONAL (SI)
Advanced Open Water Instructor Certification, 1982
Dive Control Specialist Instructor Certification, 1982
Dive Rescue Specialist I & II, 1981

SPEAKING ENGAGEMENTS & PUBLICATIONS

PACIFIC MEDICAL CENTER, AIR LIFE FLIGHT TEAM, HONOLULU, HI
Presentation —Diving Accident Management & multiplace vs. mono-place hyperbaric treatment, 1984

MARGOLIS HEALTHCARE SYSTEMS, COLORADO SPRINGS, CO
"Through their unique efforts and those of Jack Jordan, another problem of providing responsible health care to Colorado citizens was overcome."   —Quotation in Flight Log publication, 1984

PROFESSIONAL UNDERWATER INSTRUCTORS (PUI), SACRAMENTO, CA
Honorary Speaker, 1982

UNDERSEA HEALTH ASSOCIATION, ROCKY MOUNTAIN REGION
Secretary Treasurer, 1982

COLORADO DIVISION OF WILDLIFE, DENVER, CO
Presentation—Emergency Management, 1980

subsections of the first and third parts. Boldfacing helps you to see at a glance the considerable amount of information in each subsection.

Healthcare

Resumes at a Glance

ANNE BARGER

Reliable, Service-oriented, Intuitive, Compassionate Negotiator

16721 Twp. Hwy. #22
Carey, OH 43316
Phone: 419-396-7135

Seeking position in Medical Office as…
* Medical Billing and Coding Specialist *

Immediate Value Offered

Professional integrity, a detail-oriented focus, and solid understanding of the medical billing and insurance industry are the hallmarks of a Specialist who can streamline processes in dynamic medical office environments. **Solution-driven with refined negotiation skills** and a proficiency to facilitate change through **comprehensive problem solving.** Certified EMT / CPR / First Aid.

Transferable skills include the following:

⇒ Research, develop, and manage insurance claim forms (HCFA, 1500s, EDI, ICD-9, CPT and HIPAA) to ensure proper posting, collection, and privacy amidst ever-changing governmental and managed-care regulations. **Well organized and versed in medical terminology.**

⇒ **Relationship management** to effectively interface with physicians, patients, coworkers, insurance reps, governmental agencies, and other healthcare professionals to obtain and transmit information and diagnoses.

⇒ **Team motivation and commitment.** Skilled in supporting staff and employees through effective communication within office environments. **Set high standards for self and others** to produce accurate, compliant documentation and to provide excellent customer service.

Education & Medical Certifications

Millstream Career & Technology, Findlay, OH
Medical Office Program—Billing and Coding
*376-hour medical coding and billing program providing the skills to succeed in the
Health Information Technology industry*

Certified Billing & Coding Specialist (CBCS), February 2009
Certified Medical Administrative Assistant (CMAA), February 2009
Administered by National Healthcareer Association

Excelsior College, Albany, NY
Associate in Registered Nursing
Anticipated Graduation: June 2009

Terra State College, Fremont, OH
Associate in Law Enforcement—GPA 3.2
Ohio Peace Officer's Training Certification
Ohio State Patrol Academy, Columbus, OH

Internship & Work Chronology

Blanchard Valley Women's Center, **Billing & Coding Intern,** Findlay, OH	*96 hours*—2009
Barger Apiaries, **Marketing / Bookkeeping,** Carey, OH	1999–Present
Toledo Hospital Dialysis Unit, **Nursing Internship,** Toledo, OH	*Full-time 4-month internship*–2005
Hamilton County Community Action Agency, **Executive Secretary,** Hamilton, OH	1997–1999
Grandview Hospital, Dayton, OH	
Respiratory Technician / Cardio-Pulmonary Department	1994–1997
City of Fostoria, Police Officer, Fostoria, OH	1978–1994

"Anne is conscientious, a hard worker, and knows her stuff—professionally for both nursing and medical billing and coding. She would be an asset for any medical office."

—Linda Stricker, RN, BSN, Nursing Instructor, Terra State College

67

Sharon Pierce-Williams, Findlay, Ohio

Three ornate horizontal bars in varied colors and corresponding headings in a matching color indicate at a glance the main sections. An instructor's boxed testimonial is a strong ending.

Jacob L. Hilliard

555 Edgecove Way
Henderson, NV 89015
jacob.hill@aol.com

Primary Phone: (702) 555-5438
Alternate Phone: (702) 555-2922

Vocational Training and Credentials

Nevada State Board of Nursing
License # LPN 55555

◆

Virginia Department of Health
and Mental Hygiene
License # LP 00055

◆

LPN Certificate
St. Phillips College
San Antonio, TX

◆

CPR and First Aid Certified

◆

First Responder Certified

◆

Additional training
AIDS, nutritional care, epilepsy,
and suicide prevention

Skill Sets

Military Intensive Care

Acute/Chronic Mental Illness

Vehicle Accident Triage

Patient Assessments

Alzheimer's, Huntington's and
Multiple Sclerosis Care

Choking Emergencies

Drug & Alcohol Treatment

Medication Maintenance

IV Blood Draws

Injections

Profile

- Trusted and competent health care professional with more than 18 years of nursing experience in a variety of facilities, including an adult detention center, military hospital, nursing home, and state-run mental hospital.
- Demonstrate impeccable attention to detail in maintaining uniform, equipment, and patient records.
- Illustrate clear and concise written communication skills in completing incident reports, memos, and log entries—on time and error free.
- Earned respect of internal and outside agency staff for professional knowledge, competence on the job, calm demeanor, and positive attitude.

Recent Professional Experience

County Sheriff's Department, Leesburg, VA   1990–2009
Security Division & Community Service Division
Transportation Officer (1999–2009)

- Transported inmates from county detention center to and from court and community appointments. Supervised and transported groups of up to 14 adult offenders performing court-assigned community-service activities.
- Assessed arrested detainees' medical conditions and advised arresting officers of suitability for transport to jail or to hospital for treatment.
- Responded to roadside medical emergencies by stabilizing accident victims, controlling bleeding, and administering basic first aid and CPR prior to arrival of emergency medical team.

County Adult Detention Center
Correctional Nurse/Officer (1990–1999)

- Performed on-site medical care and treatment—in eight-bed medical ward and on the floor—as key member of medical team supporting up to 500 inmates.
- Responded to onsite medical emergencies, performed triage, stabilized trauma patients, set broken bones, treated dog bites and stab wounds, administered injections and medications, performed blood draws on IV drug users.
- Supervised and maintained safety and security of assigned inmates. Escorted inmates throughout facility and to and from community appointments.

Prior Nursing Experience

- *Charge Nurse/LPN,* **Longwood Nursing Home,** Reston, VA
- *LPN,* **United States Army Reserve, 117th Combat Support Hospital,** San Antonio, TX
- *LPN,* **Walter Reed Army Medical Center,** Washington, D.C.
- *LPN,* **Virginia State Hospital,** Ashburn, VA

68

Norine Dagliano, Hagerstown, Maryland

The applicant had been a nurse in a detention center and also a security transporter. He wanted to be either a nurse or a security driver. This resume is written for his search for a nursing position.

Ellen Evans

203 Marler Boulevard • San Diego, CA 92100 • 555.555.5555 • ellenevans@aol.com

Medical Laboratory Management

Certified Medical Laboratory professional with achievements in team leadership, policy development and management in a major medical center environment. Solid background in staffing, training, developing and supervising emergency and lab personnel. Budget planning and administrative expertise includes successes in cost reductions while maintaining highest quality standards.

Career Milestones

- **Selected to establish, staff and manage medical lab operations at an overseas clinic. Developed policies/procedures and led operations to attain licensure and certification in only 14 months.**
- **Chosen to lead the startup of medical laboratory functions at naval hospitals in 2 states, coordinated staffing and procurement of state-of-the-art equipment.**
- **Achieved and maintained 100% safety record in laboratory operations through effective staff training, team building and supervision in all clinical areas.**
- **Initiated the first blood DNA collection program for Naval Academy and Department of the Navy to be launched organization-wide. Credited by senior management for "phenomenal planning, meticulous attention to detail and flawless program execution."**
- **Annually awarded and achieved 5 promotions for superior performance record and initiative in the development of staff educational and other programs.**

Experience & Accomplishments

UNITED STATES NAVY
Assistant Medical Laboratory Supervisor, Naval Hospital, San Diego (1999 to present)
Medical Laboratory Technician, Clinic & Naval Hospital, New Mexico (1993 to 1999)

Lab Operations & Management

- Supervise medical laboratory operations and staff of 24 technicians in performing more than 2,000 procedures weekly, utilizing state-of-the-art equipment.
- Plan and administer $150,000 annual budget for laboratory operations, successfully reducing costs and maintaining budget well under 20% through training and accountability.
- Involved in administrative functions, including medical billing, patient medical records, purchasing, and inventory/stock control.
- Coordinate and prepare all documentation required by JCAHO and OSHA regulatory agencies.
- Develop, implement and monitor adherence to laboratory department policies and procedures.
- Ensure stringent compliance to standards on quality control, infection control, safety, and disposal of hazardous materials.

Staff Training, Development & Supervision

- Supervise and develop teams of up to 45 personnel, motivating and evaluating performance to maximize efficiency and productivity.
- Train staff on laboratory equipment procedures and protocols to improve productivity while maximizing safety.
- Develop and conduct training programs for new recruits on infectious diseases and preventive medicine.
- Implement training curriculum for health science students on nursing, laboratory policies, procedures and operations.

Education / Certifications

AS, Laboratory Science, 1993   Morris Community College, San Diego, CA

Certifications: Laboratory Technician, Emergency Medical Technician, Phlebotomy, CPR/First Aid

69

Louise Garver, Windsor, Connecticut

Horizontal lines below side headings make clear the overall design. The first section serves as a profile, and Career Milestones are important achievements. More are in the Experience section.

MADISON GIBSON

555 West 120th Avenue, #000, Denver, CO 55555
Cellular (555) 555-5555, Home (555) 555-5555, lester@aol.com

Job Target Long-term association with a radiology facility that will benefit from academic preparation, radiology experience and a driving work ethic.

Skills

> Highly skilled in many modalities of radiology, including digital and regular fluoro, portables, c-arms, diagnostic, surgical, trauma, tomography and PACS. Eager to receive training on any additional modalities.
> Comprehensive knowledge of daylight and darkroom film processing.
> Capable in hospital environment, currently having completed 2,048 hours of clinical experience.
> Effectively manage multiple complex tasks simultaneously. Highly analytical, organized and detail-oriented.
> Consistently go the extra mile to ensure patient care and comfort.

Education

Associate, Radiography   August 2003
DPS Medical Institute, Denver, Colorado. GPA: 4.0.
Representative course work: Pathology, Radiography, Medical Ethics, Positioning, Physics, Anatomy, Patient Care and Medical Terminology. Hold CPR card.

Professional Experience

Radiography Technician Assistant   January 2003 to Present
Centura Health One, Aurora, CO—Accountable for taking radiographs, including operating portables, patient care, patient protection and positioning, operating x-ray machines and processing films in the darkroom. Conduct filing, answer phones, and schedule patients promptly. Commended by ER and clinical doctors, who went out of their way to call supervisor with appreciation for initiative and skill.

Radiography Technician Assistant   December 2001 to January 2003
Columbia Hospital, Thornton, CO—Performed all duties of radiology technician. Was hired before graduation based on superior performance in clinical work.

Item Processing Operator Level III   June 1999 to December 2001
Wells Fargo Bank, Denver, Colorado—Balanced customer transactions and large items, applied debits and credits accurately, audited transactions for customer and bank employee errors and met Federal Reserve deadlines. Consistently given raises, promotions and excellent reviews.

Bank Teller   September 1998 to June 1999
Wells Fargo Bank, Boulder, Colorado—Demonstrated efficiency, accuracy and speed when processing customer transactions. Assisted customers with inquiries about problems and banking products. Displayed ability to recognize forgery, counterfeit currency and kiting operations and observe security protocols. Recognized for speed, accuracy and dependability with promotions and raises.

Accomplishments

Received letter of recommendation from Dr. Anthony Stephen: "... skilled technologist... responsible, dedicated worker... great deal of energy... pleasant personality... utmost compassion for patients"

Worked 25 to 30 hours a week at bank, 32 hours per week on clinical requirement and 24 hours per week at Columbia Hospital while attending classes for Radiography degree and maintaining 4.0 GPA.

70

Michele Angello, Aurora, Colorado

This resume emphasizes academic preparation, clinical hours completed, and an impressive work ethic to make up for a lack of paid work experience. Testimonials are from a recommendation letter.

Lily A. Lucas

111 2nd Street
Racine, Wisconsin 00000
(333) 444-4444

PROFILE

- More than 5 years of experience in **social service** and **health care** positions requiring the ability to work with patients and customers of all ages and backgrounds.
- Reputation as a patient and sympathetic individual with a strong ability to troubleshoot emergency situations.
- Knowledge of computer software, including MS Word, WordPerfect and company database software.
- Proven telephone skills. Experience using multiline telephone.

EXPERIENCE

Childcare of Wisconsin   Milwaukee, Wisconsin
Child Care Provider   2006–2009
- Worked for residential program for teen mothers and their children.
- Monitored activities of mothers and children and recorded on daily charts.
- Advised mothers on parenting skills. Participated in planning for goals and career development.
- Provided court and field supervision.
- Oversaw clients in their daily living activities and housekeeping tasks.
- Administered medications and carried out medical treatments as instructed.

Kenosha Family Care   Kenosha, Wisconsin
Home Health Care Aide   2004–2006
- Assigned to clients who were elderly, disabled, or infirm.
- Visited clients in their homes and assisted them as needed with shopping, housecleaning, and child care.
- Administered medications as instructed. Assisted clients with bathing and feeding as necessary.
- Acted as liaison with nurses, doctors and other medical staff assigned to patient.

Dil Computer Corporation   Milwaukee, Wisconsin
Production Clerk   1994–2004
- Updated and maintained production schedules on computer.
- Performed intermediate full systems backup for three computers and peripherals.
- Responsible for timely and accurate printing of documentation for United States military personnel.
- Coordinated activities with other offices.

TRAINING

College of Kane County   Milwaukee, Wisconsin
Completed college course work in customer service, basic computers and MS Word

71

Eva Locke, Waukegan, Illinois

The applicant was concerned about having held jobs in many different fields. The writer noticed that previous positions had the common quality of serving others. The resume highlights this theme.

ANTHONY DUBOIS
162 OXFORD AVENUE, RENO, NV 89501

775.555.9479 ADFIT@YAHOO.COM

Fitness Specialist

**A hands-on professional / goal-oriented strategist
whose confidence, perseverance and vision promote success**

GOAL: An opportunity to serve as a **Youth / Athletic Director**
employing my abilities to improve and motivate the physical fitness / rehabilitation of individuals

GENERAL QUALIFICATIONS

Recognize client's needs and set goals
Utilize initiative, achievement and independent judgment
Demonstrate record of high performance standards
Detailed attention to schedules, deadlines, budgets and quality results
Track record of creativity and innovation

PROFESSIONAL FITNESS EXPERTISE

20 years of progressive experience and responsibility with documented success in the areas of health / fitness

❖ Successfully develop, initiate and coordinate individual and group exercise programs
❖ Demonstrate correct and safe use of exercise equipment and routines
❖ Observe participants during exercise sessions for signs of physical stress; adjust pace
❖ Conduct group and independent aerobic, strength and flexibility sessions
❖ Supervise other instructors

MAJOR PROJECT: "TONY'S KIDS"

Developed franchised program implemented nationally in public / private schools

❖ Innovative fitness education program for improving overall health of at-risk children
❖ Encourage positive lifestyle choices to offset school violence and nutrition problems
❖ Detailed curriculum designed for infusion into school districts nationwide
❖ Utilize behavior style profiling and customized physical fitness equipment for children

SPECIALIZED TRAINING

Certifications: Strength & Conditioning / CPR / Athletic Trainer / American Red Cross
A.C.S.M. Exercise Specialist / Respiratory Technician

EXPERIENCE

DuBois & Associates, LLC	*Owner / Personal Trainer*	Barstow, NV
Reno Health & Rehabilitation	*Co-owner / Personal Trainer*	Reno, NV
Tower Fitness Industries	*Fitness Consultant / Wellness Center Program Director*	Las Vegas, NV
Reno Medical Center	*Respiratory Therapy Technician* (American Red Cross Certified)	Reno, NV

BODYBUILDING / WEIGHTLIFTING CHAMPIONSHIPS

1999	Western Power Lifting	*2nd Place*	1997	Beast of the Southeast Dead Lift	*2nd Place*
1998	Northeastern Power Lifting	*2nd Place*	1996	Nevada Strongest Man (lightweight)	*2nd Place*
1998	State Bodybuilding	*5th Place*	1995	Mid-Pacific Strongman (middleweight)	*1st Place*
1997	State Bodybuilding	*2nd Place*	1991	Northeastern Texas Bodybuilding	*3rd Place*

GYM DESIGN / LAYOUT · EQUIPPED / SET UP GYMS

GYM DESIGN / LAYOUT	EQUIPPED / SET UP GYMS
Kansas City Royals	Washington Redskins
St. Joseph's Hospital	Ford Motor Company
J.T.O. Corporation	Phoenix Cardinals
McDonald Rehabilitation	Greenville Wellness Center
World Gyms	University of Missouri
Gold's Gyms	Texas State University
Federal Correctional Institute	Police and Fire Departments

72

Jane Roqueplot, West Middlesex, Pennsylvania

This resume uses blue ink for the contact information, the word Goal, and the section headings in small caps. The appearance is classy.

Darlene K. Jepson

1923 Church Road   Columbus, Michigan 48063   313-555-3098

Profile
- ❖ Physical Therapist Assistant **with more than 500 hours of clinical experience in sports medicine, outpatient, inpatient, and acute-care settings.**
- ❖ Recognized by supervising physical therapist as working and communicating effectively with other health care professionals, staff, and especially patients and their families.
- ❖ Proven ability to work with minimal supervision.
- ❖ Volunteered with the Michigan Special Olympic Games; provided one-on-one support and assistance to physically challenged children.

Education

Oakland Community College • Rochester, Michigan

Associate in Applied Science—Physical Therapist Assistant   May 2004

Clinical Skills

Treatment Modalities & Related Responsibilities

- • Ultrasound
- • Electric stimulation
- • Cervical and lumbar traction
- • Hot and cold packs
- • Fluidotherapy

- • Manual techniques including
  - - Range of motion
  - - Stretching
  - - Soft tissue
- • Patient transfers
- • Patient charting

Patients & Diagnoses

- • Traumatic brain injuries
- • Cerebral vascular accidents
- • Spinal cord injuries
- • Gunshot and other wounds

- • Total knee and hip replacements
- • Amputees
- • Burns
- • ICU

Clinical Experience

- ❖ *Acute Care:* University of Michigan Medical Center—Ann Arbor, Michigan (240 hours)
- ❖ *Outpatient Rehabilitation/Sports Medicine:* Healthwise Rehabilitation Services—Ypsilanti, Michigan (240 hours)
- ❖ *Inpatient Rehabilitation:* Harper Hospital—Detroit, Michigan (80 hours)

Professional Affiliations

- ❖ Oakland Community College Physical Therapist Assistant Club—President
- ❖ American Physical Therapy Association—Member

Employment

Lord & Taylor • Troy, Michigan   1997–Present

Estee Lauder Consultant / Cosmetics Stock Handler / Shoe Department Clerk
- • Earned Employee of the Month designation (2001)
- • Named Most Valuable Team Player (2000)

*Additional experience as **Nanny** (seasonal 1994–2000)*

– References available on request –

73

Janet L. Beckstrom, Flint, Michigan

This individual had just completed her two-year program and had minimal experience (just clinicals through the college). The writer emphasized the person's skills and types of patients served.

CATHY PIPER CFC, PTS

46 Augusta Heights
Pinehurst, Ontario
A1A 1A1
(555) 444-7777

CERTIFIED FITNESS & WELLNESS PROFESSIONAL

Expert in sports, fitness, health, and wellness training and education

ENERGETIC, DRIVEN, AND PASSIONATE FITNESS PROFESSIONAL dedicated to promoting the benefits of health and wellness. Advanced communication and interpersonal skills, with a well-developed ability to motivate others to set and achieve realistic fitness and health goals. **Certified Personal Trainer and Fitness Consultant** experienced in working with athletes, teams, and individuals at all levels. **Women's "A" Ranked Squash Player.** Combine fitness expertise with a strong corporate background demonstrating outstanding customer service, leadership, and organizational skills.

RELATED EXPERIENCE & QUALIFICATIONS

WALKING WOMEN / THE ACTION FACTORY, Augusta, Ontario
Co-Owner / Co-Founder (P/T) April 2001–Present

> Conceived and developed entire walking program, marketing plan, and promotional materials for start-up health and fitness company.
> Lead instructor and consultant responsible for acquiring client health history, assessing fitness levels and goals, and leading biweekly walks.

THE FITNESS FACILITY, Augusta, Ontario
Owner / Trainer & Fitness Consultant (P/T) 2000–Present

> Founded and successfully operate a sole proprietorship offering specialized sports training programs for individuals, athletes, and teams.
> Personally consult with athletes to determine specific fitness levels and goals, and create customized programs designed to motivate clients to achieve success.

PINEHURST WOMEN'S FITNESS, Pinehurst, Ontario
Personal Trainer / Fitness Consultant (P/T) 1999–2000

> Offered customized fitness testing and consulting for local women's fitness centre with more than 700 members.
> Tested individual clients to ascertain fitness level, assembled a realistic plan based on individual needs and goals, and conducted orientation on all gym equipment.

PROFESSIONAL TRAINING

Certified Fitness Consultant (CFC)—OASES	2000
Personal Trainer Specialist (PTS)—Can Fit Pro	1999
CPR, Heart & Stroke Foundation of Ontario	Current

74

Ross Macpherson, Whitby, Ontario, Canada

The applicant wanted to make a full-time transition to her passion for fitness and health. The writer placed all relevant information up front and created two experience sections: Related Experience & Qualifications and Professional/Corporate Experience. The graphic captures

CATHY PIPER   (555) 444-7777   Page 2

PROFESSIONAL TRAINING, *continued*

Courses and seminars include

➤ Personal Training Psychology	➤ Personal Training Program Design
➤ Heart Rate Training	➤ Manual Resistance Training
➤ Core Training on the Ball	➤ Healthy Eating on the Run
➤ Total Towel Training	➤ Training for Prime Time
➤ Motivating the Inactive Market	➤ Make It FITT for Kids
➤ Body Walk	➤ Fat Loss

ATHLETIC ACHIEVEMENTS

Championship Squash:

➤ Canadian National Championships Masters—4th (2003)
➤ Bronze Medalist—World Masters Games (2000)
➤ Ontario Masters Squash Champion (1999)
➤ Ontario Women's "A" ranked

PROFESSIONAL / CORPORATE EXPERIENCE

DUPUY CANADA, Augusta, Ontario
Senior Customer Service Representative   1988–Present
Promoted to manage and service critical "performance coating" accounts with large automotive manufacturers and automotive suppliers throughout North America.

➤ Ensure that all customer orders are completed on time and to exacting specifications. Requires advanced customer service and organization skills and ability to accurately reconcile production schedules with forecasted customer requirements.

➤ Assemble and lead cross-functional teams from product support, technical, product scheduling, manufacturing, and planning to effectively manage multimillion-dollar accounts, meet tight deadlines, and solve customer problems.

➤ Consistently recognized and commended by clients and superiors for outstanding customer service, leadership, and organizational skills.

➤ Nominated for and awarded a variety of Employee Recognition Awards.

Previously promoted through a variety of increasingly responsible customer service and purchasing positions:

Customer Service Representative—Polyethylene Pipe Division, Pinehurst, Quebec
Purchasing Representative—Energy & Materials Division, Pleasantville, Quebec
Purchasing Control Clerk—Accounting and Finance Division, Pinehurst, Quebec
Control Clerk—Real Estate & General Services Division, Pinehurst, Quebec

---

attention instantly. Boldfacing pulls the reader's eyes to key information, including the various positions held, training certifications, and side headings that introduce additional education and athletic achievements.

SALLY K. JONES

1234 Oak Road
Portland, OR 55555
(000) 000-0000 Residence
sallyjones@yahoo.com

Medical Office Specialist

Professional Summary

Enthusiastic, dependable Medical Office Specialist with 6 years of experience in medical settings. Received superior ratings by employer for attendance, dependability, and availability to assist as needed. Recognized as an excellent communicator. Winner of customer service award. Demonstrated skill in training clients and patients. Fast learner. Computer literate.

Endorsements

"Demonstrates skill in fee-for-service collections with patients, which in part led to ending fiscal year 'in the black'..." Former Supervisor, Providence Hospital

"Outstanding customer service on phones." Former Supervisor, Binyon Optical

"We wish we had more employees that we could write a review like this for." Former Supervisor, Victorinox

Professional Experience

PROVIDENCE HOSPITAL, Portland, OR   2002–2004
Office Specialist

Managed office duties for contact lens clinic within one of Portland's largest employers, a 300-bed hospital with 8,500 employees. Answered phones, took messages, and scheduled appointments. Handled front desk reception and patient check-in. Trained patients in contact lens insertion / removal. Ordered and received contact lenses and solutions.

- Acknowledged by management for assistance in eliminating $100K deficit by requiring patients to pay before receiving products.
- Won Providence Award for patience in training customers in contact lens insertion / removal.

BINYON OPTICAL, Tigard, OR   1999–2002
Optometric Technician / Assistant Manager

Reported to optometric physician for single office within firm with nine locations and approximately 80 employees. Greeted and checked in patients, answered phones, scheduled appointments. Administered patient pretests, including autorefraction, noncontact tonometry, automatic neutralization of eyeglasses, Humphrey visual fields testing, and fundus photography. Taught patients how to insert / remove and care for their contact lenses.

- Promoted to assistant manager after only two years as optometric technician.
- Embraced additional duties, including ordering supplies, resolving patient customer service issues, and managing store operations.

75

Jennifer Rydell, Portland, Oregon

The challenge for this resume was to minimize multiple jobs and virtually no education after high school. The writer eliminated unnecessary jobs, using years only (instead of months and years), and left out the education section altogether, focusing on the applicant's wonderful performance

SALLY K. JONES

Professional Experience, Continued

PALM HARBOR HOMES, Portland, OR   1998
Receptionist

Reported directly to owner of respected family-owned operation, the largest manufactured-home dealership in the Portland / Vancouver metro area. Greeted customers and answered phones. Took messages and directed them to appropriate individual. Photocopied and faxed documents. Assisted customers in filling out required forms. Answered customer questions.

- Acknowledged by supervisor as "delightful" to work with.

VICTORINOX / PORTLAND, Portland, OR   1995–1997
Stockroom Clerk / Quality Control

Hired to clerk stockroom for the original manufacturer of Swiss Army Knives, a company with 350 employees. Coordinated shipping and receiving. Weighed and prepared parts for shipment. Loaded and unloaded trucks. Provided production support. Issued supplies in lockdown environment. Inspected parts to blueprint specifications. Used calipers, micrometers, Rockwell hardness tester, and optical comparator.

- Handpicked to serve on communication and product development committees.
- Made several suggestions regarding existing drug testing policies that were implemented company-wide.
- Acknowledged by human resources manager for having "best communication skills in the company."
- Took on extra duties as quality control technician, helping to establish quality control department.
- Trained temporary staff to assist in implementing new quality control measures.

ANIMAL MEDICAL CLINIC, Portland, OR   1995
Veterinary Assistant / Technician

Assisted veterinarian in small-animal practice. Restrained animals during physical examinations. Prepared pets for surgery. Monitored and cared for hospitalized animals, administering medications and changing fluids. Sterilized instruments with autoclave. Prepared surgery packets. Greeted customers and answered phones. Checked pets in and out of office.

- Learned and excelled at job duties in a matter of weeks.

Computer Skills

MS Windows, MS Word, Novell GroupWise, SMS Health, Internet, and email

■ ■ ■

reviews, customer service award, and current computer skills. Testimonials under Endorsements build confidence and interest in the applicant and more than offset the absence of an education section.

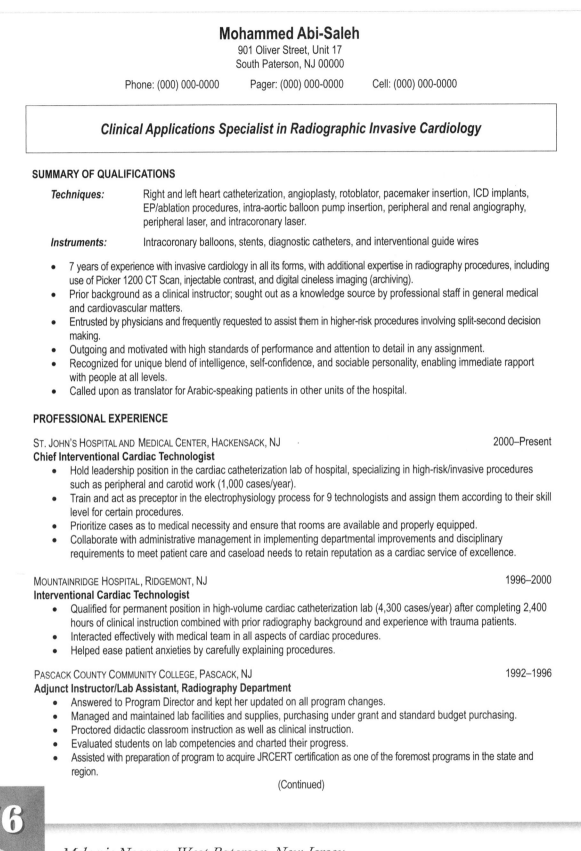

Mohammed Abi-Saleh

901 Oliver Street, Unit 17
South Paterson, NJ 00000

Phone: (000) 000-0000   Pager: (000) 000-0000   Cell: (000) 000-0000

Clinical Applications Specialist in Radiographic Invasive Cardiology

SUMMARY OF QUALIFICATIONS

Techniques: Right and left heart catheterization, angioplasty, rotoblator, pacemaker insertion, ICD implants, EP/ablation procedures, intra-aortic balloon pump insertion, peripheral and renal angiography, peripheral laser, and intracoronary laser.

Instruments: Intracoronary balloons, stents, diagnostic catheters, and interventional guide wires

- 7 years of experience with invasive cardiology in all its forms, with additional expertise in radiography procedures, including use of Picker 1200 CT Scan, injectable contrast, and digital cineless imaging (archiving).
- Prior background as a clinical instructor; sought out as a knowledge source by professional staff in general medical and cardiovascular matters.
- Entrusted by physicians and frequently requested to assist them in higher-risk procedures involving split-second decision making.
- Outgoing and motivated with high standards of performance and attention to detail in any assignment.
- Recognized for unique blend of intelligence, self-confidence, and sociable personality, enabling immediate rapport with people at all levels.
- Called upon as translator for Arabic-speaking patients in other units of the hospital.

PROFESSIONAL EXPERIENCE

ST. JOHN'S HOSPITAL AND MEDICAL CENTER, HACKENSACK, NJ   2000–Present
Chief Interventional Cardiac Technologist
- Hold leadership position in the cardiac catheterization lab of hospital, specializing in high-risk/invasive procedures such as peripheral and carotid work (1,000 cases/year).
- Train and act as preceptor in the electrophysiology process for 9 technologists and assign them according to their skill level for certain procedures.
- Prioritize cases as to medical necessity and ensure that rooms are available and properly equipped.
- Collaborate with administrative management in implementing departmental improvements and disciplinary requirements to meet patient care and caseload needs to retain reputation as a cardiac service of excellence.

MOUNTAINRIDGE HOSPITAL, RIDGEMONT, NJ   1996–2000
Interventional Cardiac Technologist
- Qualified for permanent position in high-volume cardiac catheterization lab (4,300 cases/year) after completing 2,400 hours of clinical instruction combined with prior radiography background and experience with trauma patients.
- Interacted effectively with medical team in all aspects of cardiac procedures.
- Helped ease patient anxieties by carefully explaining procedures.

PASCACK COUNTY COMMUNITY COLLEGE, PASCACK, NJ   1992–1996
Adjunct Instructor/Lab Assistant, Radiography Department
- Answered to Program Director and kept her updated on all program changes.
- Managed and maintained lab facilities and supplies, purchasing under grant and standard budget purchasing.
- Proctored didactic classroom instruction as well as clinical instruction.
- Evaluated students on lab competencies and charted their progress.
- Assisted with preparation of program to acquire JRCERT certification as one of the foremost programs in the state and region.

(Continued)

76

Melanie Noonan, West Paterson, New Jersey

This easy-to-read resume uses font enhancements to lead the reader through the resume. Boldfacing makes the person's name stand out in the contact information and highlights the section headings and the positions held. Bold italic calls attention to the position and field

Mohammed Abi-Saleh
Page 2

St. John's Hospital and Medical Center, Hackensack, NJ   1984–1991
CAT Scan Technologist
- Performed all diagnostic CAT scan procedures, including invasive procedures (needle biopsy, aspirations, and tumor localizations).
- Disclosed potential problem areas to physicians.

Assistant Chief Technologist
- Worked closely with and assisted the chief technologist and held full responsibility for the Radiological Department in the chief's absence, which included supervising up to 24 full- and part-time personnel on 2 shifts.
- Oversaw patient care, ensured appropriate procedures, and served as troubleshooter in resolving any problem areas.
- Assisted with time analysis, upgrading of equipment, and scheduling of staff.
- Managed the darkroom (film processing and development) and ensured proper inventory levels of supplies. Negotiated with vendors to obtain best price and value-added features.

Senior Radiographer
- Answered to the chief technologist and assumed some staff and departmental duties during the chief's absence.
- Trained new staff in existing and new procedures.
- Worked effectively in a high-pressure, demanding environment, consistently earning excellent performance reviews.

EDUCATION/CERTIFICATION

Pascack County Community College, Pascack, NJ
- Associate of Applied Science in Radiography, 1984
- Registered Radiographer/Board Certified AART
- Basic Life Support (BLS) Certification

CONTINUING EDUCATION

- Use of GPI Inhibitors in Acute Coronary Syndrome
    St. John's Hospital and Medical Center, January 2002

- Cardiac Catheterization 2000: Diagnostic and Interventional Symposium for Cardiac Catheterization Laboratory Professionals
    HMP Communications, LLC, September 2001

- Siemens Coroskop Plus Clinical Applications
    Siemens Medical Systems, Inc., July 2000

- Intraoperative X-Ray Imaging
    OEC Medical Systems, Inc., February 2000

- Siemens ACOM Net PC Clinical Applications
    Siemens Medical Systems, Inc., July 1999

- Listening: Interpersonal Effectiveness
- Building Healthy Relationships
    Mountainridge Hospital, July 1998

- A Live Symposium of Complex Coronary Cases Focusing on Rotational Atherectomy
    The Mount Moriah Hospital School of Medicine, June 1998

- Multi-Link—Inservice, Mountainridge Hospital
    Guidant Corporation, October 1997

information in the box and to the subheadings under Summary of Qualifications. The workplace names and locations appear in small caps. Bullets throughout direct attention to the beginning of each new information item.

Mary Jane Martha Barclay
135 Killdeer Road, Apt. 721, Ewing, NJ 08628
(609) 771-7665 Residence Phone / Fax ▪ mjmbarclay@yahoo.com

Medical Billing / Medical Records Technician

Dedicated, experienced professional with recent training in medical billing, medical terminology, and ICD-9-CM coding. Strong organizational, communications, and project management skills. Calm demeanor under stress; cooperative team leader. Proven multitasking / operations support skills. Adept in

☑ Client Relationship Management	☑ Medical Records Terminology	☑ Budget Controls
☑ Customer Needs Management	☑ Administrative Support	☑ Project Coordination

---

KEY SUPPORTING SKILLS

- **Administration:** Diverse administrative expertise includes directing nationwide CHART (California Hospital Association Review Team) Program for American Hospital Association, managing seven-county sales territory in south central California, and maintaining large, upscale apartment complexes.

- **Time Management:** Demonstrate top-notch organizational skills, with ability to prioritize and multi-task. Developed records management systems to expedite back-office operations for sales generation, residential and retail property management, and meeting and event planning.

- **Communications:** Employ proactive problem-solving communications skills to generate "win-win" scenarios. Effectively communicated special situations and potential problem areas to management.

- **Personal Strengths:** Conscientious in following through on commitments and deadlines. Mature, discreet team player with experience interfacing with high-level executives and corporate clients.

EDUCATION
Medical Records Technician Program, The College of New Jersey, Ewing, NJ—2006
Courses: Medical Terminology, Advanced Medical Terminology, Medical Billing, ICD-9-CM Coding
Associate of Arts Degree, San Diego Community College, San Diego, CA

PROFESSIONAL EXPERIENCE

Estate and Health Care Management, Princeton, NJ   2004–2009
- ✓ **Administrative Management.** Acted as prime interface with 60 physicians, nurses, hospice, attorneys, CPA, stockbroker and insurance companies for elderly parents with progressive, debilitating illnesses. Managed health care appointments and treatment, and daily living arrangements on-site.

- ✓ **Records Management.** Submitted insurance claims and tracked insurance reimbursements. Oversaw distribution of $1 million estate. Arranged sale of house and distribution of all household goods.

Manufacturer's Representative   2001–2004
Pacific Printing, San Diego, CA, and Elegant Communications, Inc., San Francisco, CA
Independent contractor representing fine gift, paper/stationery, and greeting-card lines for two businesses.

- ✓ **Account Management.** Grew accounts by 45% (from 175 to 250) and increased sales by 20% in seven-county south central California territory. Generated 25 new key accounts (such as Yellowstone Park gift shops) through thorough market research, competitive market analysis and persuasive prospect interaction. Provided personalized customer service that generated 100% customer retention.

- ✓ **Customer Relationship Management.** Developed strong client-communications networks, building relationships with 250 buyers for retail stores, museums, hospital gift shops and nurseries. Educated buyers in 60 lines of merchandise, updating them on retail trends and demographics-driven marketing.

Susan Guarneri, Three Lakes, Wisconsin

For two and a half years, the applicant took care of her ill parents until they passed away. She completed certification in medical records billing and wanted to become a technician in that field. The writer provided a summary upfront, emphasizing the applicant's recent training as well as her

Mary Jane Martha Barclay

(609) 771-7665 Residence Phone / Fax ▪ mjmbarclay@yahoo.com   Page 2

PROFESSIONAL EXPERIENCE (continued)

Residential Property Management   1999–2001
Excelsior Properties, San Raphael, CA (2000–2001), and Seaside Views, San Diego, CA (1999–2000)

✓ **Administrative Management.** Managed two upscale apartment communities (up to 516 units), with monthly rent collections of $432,000. Supervised on-site leasing, as well as 18 maintenance and grounds staff. Closely controlled $2,500 per month expense budget, monitoring five vendor services. Oversaw renovation of 35 apartment units, coordinating workflow and scheduling of carpet, flooring, paint, and fixture vendors with tenants.

✓ **Customer Service.** Maintained 92% residency rate and achieved 98% on-time rent collection by developing proactive tenant-relationships programs. Initiated educational newsletter for tenants, as well as open-door policy for tenant complaints. Credited with stabilizing the tenant community through lawful evictions of known drug dealers.

Retail Property Management   1994–1999
Townsend Group Companies, San Diego and San Francisco, CA

✓ **Administrative Management.** Initiated and developed specialty leasing programs for three major developers (12 regional shopping centers) in high-profile metropolitan areas. Maintained high occupancy rates (95%) by actively recruiting retailers for year-round common area, as well as developing long-term, favorable leases for in-line sales operations.

✓ **Program Management.** Conceptualized and supervised design projects for kiosks and store décor, as well as for marketing communications (brochures, print advertising and directories). Developed and met program budgets, generating in excess of $500,000 for each shopping center annually.

Meeting and Event Management   1993–1994
California Hospital Association, San Diego, CA

✓ **Program Management.** Served as Director of CHART (California Hospital Association Review Team) Program. Traveled statewide conducting peer review meetings for 8 to 10 state hospitals. Wrote reports based on participant feedback and critical observations and analysis of policies and procedures. Recommended policy and methodology changes, 90% of which were implemented by the Boards of the state hospitals.

✓ **Customer Service.** Facilitated in-house discussions on-site of hospital personnel and management at all levels to increase quality assurance, strengthen employee relations, improve customer service and streamline processes and procedures. Initiated and encouraged constructive dialogs among groups that had a history of communication breakdowns.

COMPUTER SKILLS

☑ Training in Medical Billing software, Medical Records databases, and ICD-9-CM coding.
☑ Experienced in composing and editing letters, memos, marketing communications and reports.
☑ Use Windows XP, MS Office 2003—Word, Excel, PowerPoint, Access, Internet Explorer, e-mail.

---

transferable skills. After a section on Key Supporting Skills, the writer supplied sections on Education and Professional Experience, stressing management and client skills in each position.

Lanina Crowne, RN, CLNC
legal nurse consultant

1111 New London Road
Montgomery, Alabama 36100
bnw002@soma.net ✆ 334.555.5555

WHAT I CAN OFFER DEWEY, CHEATAM & HOWE

Gathering "bulletproof" support to assess the quality of medically based cases

Building and maintaining a "stable" of expert witnesses

Anticipating adversaries' theories

Controlling costs and limiting liability

Conducting fully documented discovery based on court-tested standards of nursing care

Serving as an expert witness in nursing care

EXAMPLES OF PERFORMANCE

Stepped in quickly to **correct a potentially actionable situation** involving a critically ill patient. With the family present, calmly corrected the situation and then fully documented every action. *Outcomes:* House counsel said he could have used my report without change because it was so complete and accurate.

Corrected a liability that had been present for years. Redesigned how we documented suicide precautions for patients. *Outcomes:* Situation resolved in just two weeks. My new system also saved $5K in labor costs annually.

Got control of expensive instruments with a **low-cost solution** that required no additional staff training. *Outcomes:* Treatments more efficient. Chronic misplacing of instruments stopped and never returned.

Redesigned the security measures we relied on to track movements of psychiatric patients. *Outcomes:* **Reduced** our **liability** and **increased** the **safety** of our staff and patients in a hurry.

RECENT WORK HISTORY

Office Nurse, Arista Psychiatric Services, Montgomery, Alabama Jan 03–Present
APS is a statewide corporation offering services through four providers.

Staff Nurse *with additional duties as* **Relief Charge Nurse,** Central Medical Center South, Montgomery, Alabama Oct 00–Jan 03
Served as direct supervisor of three registered nurses, a licensed practical nurse, and up to four mental health technicians.

Staff Nurse, Central Medical Center East, Montgomery, Alabama Nov 98–Nov 00
Handled pre-admitting for surgical patients in wards with censuses of about 30.

Nurse, Top Shelf Home Health, Montgomery, Alabama Aug 98–Jan 99
Provided at-home care for patients ranging from infant to adult with diabetic and wound care. Instructed patients and care providers in safe and accepted basic healthcare procedures.

More indicators Dewey, Cheatam & Howe can use…

78

Don Orlando, Montgomery, Alabama

A common weakness of a resume Goal statement is that it expresses the hope that the company will do something for the applicant (such as "I'm looking for a place where I may improve my skills"). The first section of this resume clearly indicates how the candidate can benefit the

| Lanina Crowne | **Legal Nurse Consultant** | 334.555.5555 |

Charge Nurse *promoted to* **Charge Nurse Supervisor,** Manor Nursing Home, Montgomery, Alabama   Aug 96–Aug 98
Supervised two licensed practical nurses and seven nursing assistants to care for 90 elderly patients.

Staff Nurse, Quality Care, Montgomery, Alabama   Feb 90–May 96

Dental Health Technician and **Hygienist,** Dracon Air Force Base, Louisiana   Oct 83–Sep 89
Supported eight dentists in a comprehensive practice that cared for thousands of patients annually.

RELEVANT PROFESSIONAL DEVELOPMENT

A.S., Nursing, Central State University, Montgomery, Alabama   93
Awarded Registered Nurse. Paid my own way to earn this degree while working seven days a week. Commuted 1,000 miles a week. One of 10, from a class of about 200, to be inducted into a national academic and service honorary society.

Certificate of Nursing, Norton College, Montgomery, Alabama   77
Awarded LPN.

"Crisis Prevention Intervention for Psychiatric Patients," Horizon Corporation, one day   02

PROFESSIONAL CERTIFICATIONS

Certified Legal Nurse Consultant   02
Certification awarded by the Medical Legal Consulting Institute, Inc.

Registered Nurse   Expires 04
Registered to practice in the state of Alabama.

PROFESSIONAL AFFILIATIONS

Member, National Alliance of Certified Legal Nurse Consultants   Since Oct 02

COMPUTER SKILLS

Expert in medical support software; working knowledge of WordPerfect, Quicken, and Internet search protocols

LANGUAGE SKILLS

Working knowledge of spoken Spanish and Italian.

prospective company. The Examples of Performance section presents significant achievements and their outcomes, which suggest additional benefits for a company. Study the italic comments as informative explanations.

JENNIFER U. SMITH

9631 Dallas Avenue, Houston, TX 77068
Home: (555) 555-5555 / Cell: (555) 555-5555 / jusmith234@aol.com

CAREER TARGET: NURSING

Earned Degree in Nursing; Current Experience as Patient Care Associate

Met All Core Goals and Objectives in Providing Superb Patient Care, Demonstrating Proficiency in Procedures, and Exhibiting a Positive Attitude

Dedicated, resourceful health care professional with success in providing basic and more advanced patient treatment. Developed and expanded knowledge of principles, methods, and procedures of medical care. Work effectively with physicians, nurses, and other professionals within health care environments. Knowledge and skill areas include:

*JCAHO & Quality Assurance Standards • Team Member Support • Medical Equipment Use & Maintenance
Patient Assessment & Evaluation • Patient Tracking & Charting • University Health System Standards
Emergency Service Processes • Professional Nursing Standards • Patient Confidentiality Measures*

Education & Credentials

Associate of Applied Science Degree in Nursing
Houston Community College, Houston, TX, 2008

Associate of Arts Degree
North Harris Community College, Houston, TX, 2004

Professional Experience

ST. JOSEPH HOSPITAL, Houston, TX, 2008–Present
Patient Care Associate

Provide patient care on individual and teamwork basis, ensuring highest level of care and comfort for patients from broad range of backgrounds. Assist patients with meals, personal hygiene, and range of motion exercises. Perform procedures as directed by the registered nurse.

Change surgical wound dressings, provide care for patients with nasogastric tubes, conduct in-and-out urinary catheterizations, and supply oxygen as ordered by nasal cannula, face mask, or tracheotomy. Perform NT suctioning, routine care for tracheotomies and colostomies, enemas and douches, post-mortem care, and specimen collections. Verify vital signs and conduct accu-checks.

KEY CONTRIBUTIONS & ACHIEVEMENTS:

- **Recognized by supervisors for meeting and exceeding goals in patient care and satisfaction.** Demonstrated high level of competency and skill in performing assigned patient-care responsibilities in line with organizational mission.

- **Adapted various patient assessment, treatment, and care methods** to accommodate unique physical, psychosocial, emotional, and other developmental needs of each patient.

- **Maintained excellent relationships with patients, family members, and colleagues.** Influence positive reactions and behaviors through encouraging patients to work proactively toward improving health.

- **Contributed to the achievement of high-quality scores in the hospital** through strict adherence to proper organizational procedures, patient protocol, and health care practices.

79

Daniel J. Dorotik, Jr., Lubbock, Texas

The new associate's degree was important to this applicant, so the Education & Credentials section was put just after the opening profile with bulleted areas of expertise.

215 Lincolnshire Lane
Findlay, OH 45840
419.420.1258
sspieker@msn.com

Seeking position as ...
✴ REGISTERED NURSE ✴

PROFILE

A **dedicated, compassionate** individual with the ability to maintain personal high-level-of-care standards by taking whatever steps necessary to ensure patient safety, comfort, and medical care. Recognized by supervisors and instructors for **team orientation, critical-thinking skills,** and a desire for continuous learning. **Problem-solving skills** gleaned by identifying solutions to challenging problems that arise when providing individualized care to those in need. Additional core competencies include

Charting by Exception—Meditech Software	Patient Relationship Management
Concise Written & Verbal Communications	Resourcefulness / Flexibility
Organizational / Time Management Skills	Accurate Report Documentation
Pharmacologic Knowledge	Patient Assessment / Analytical Judgment

EDUCATION

OWENS COMMUNITY COLLEGE, Findlay, OH
Associate in Applied Science Degree, May 2003
Major: Nursing Technology   GPA: 3.3

CLINICAL ROTATIONS

3/03–5/03	**OB,** Blanchard Valley Health Association, Findlay, OH
2/03–3/03	**Pediatrics,** Wood County Hospital, Bowling Green, OH
2/03–4/03	**Med/Surg and Peds**—Precepting
	Blanchard Valley Health Association, Findlay, OH
1/03–2/03	**Geriatric,** Winebrenner, Findlay, OH
11/02–12/02	**Psychosocial Dysfunction**—Inpatient Psychiatric Stress Unit
	Fulton County Hospital, Wauseon, OH
8/02–10/02	**Med/Surg, Oncology, PCU, ER, ICU**—Adult Health II
	Blanchard Valley Health Association, Findlay, OH
1/02–5/02	**Med/Surg, ER, OR**—Adult Health I
	Blanchard Valley Health Association, Findlay, OH
8/01–12/01	**Med/Surg and Bilio Floor**
	Wood County Hospital, Bowling Green, OH

> "As a clinical instructor for Susan in the acute medical–surgical setting, as well as long-term care of the elderly patient, I have found Susan to be very knowledgeable of disease process, medications, and treatments. She is well-prepared and organized and continues to build her confidence and experience with various nursing skills as well as nursing judgment."
> Erin Iglehart, RN, BSN
> Owens Community College
> Clinical Instructor

Responsibilities during the above rotations included

- Working cooperatively with patients, families, and other members of the healthcare team to provide individualized care.

- Providing a full range of patient care in the medical/oncology unit—monitoring vital signs and labs; working with ports, IV piggybacks, push meds, and heplocking; bathing; kinetic dosing; communicating patient status to nursing team; and delivering end-of-life care with empathy and compassion.

- Prioritizing patient care to deal with concerns and complex medical issues while making well-thought-out decisions and utilizing consultants and reference tools appropriately.

- Facilitating patient well-being by systematically assessing short- and long-term goals and by educating patients and their families about medical conditions and nursing procedures.

WORK EXPERIENCE

THE PHARM PHARMACY, **Pharmacy Technician**	2000–PRESENT
SKIP TATE APPLIANCE, **Secretary/Bookkeeper**	1999
SEARS & ROEBUCK, **Sales Associate**	1998–2001
OLD MILL DAIRY, **Cashier/Server**	1997–1998

Consistently worked part-time jobs to pay for college expenses.

80

Sharon Pierce-Williams, Findlay, Ohio

The applicant had only part-time jobs and clinical rotations. The writer included the testimonial and supplied much information. An HR director judged this "the best resume...in quite some while."

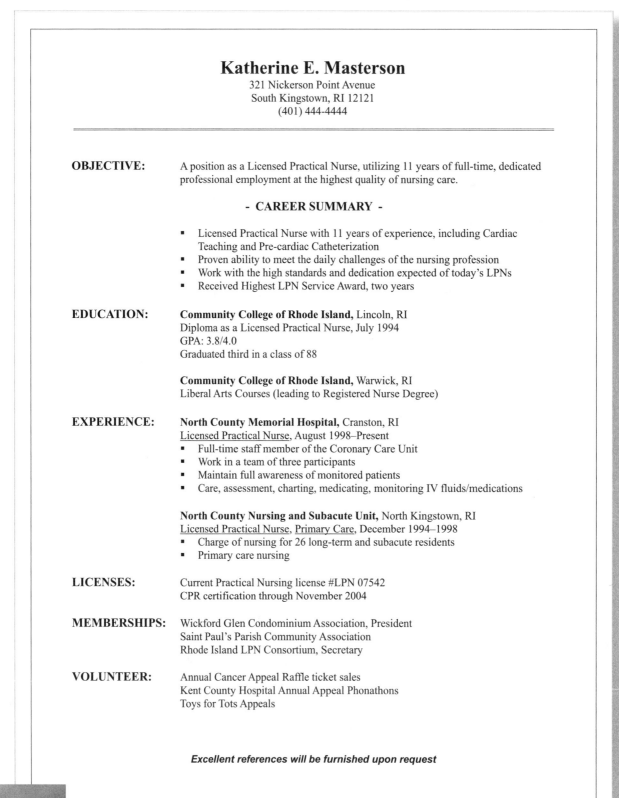

Katherine E. Masterson

321 Nickerson Point Avenue
South Kingstown, RI 12121
(401) 444-4444

OBJECTIVE: A position as a Licensed Practical Nurse, utilizing 11 years of full-time, dedicated professional employment at the highest quality of nursing care.

- CAREER SUMMARY -

- Licensed Practical Nurse with 11 years of experience, including Cardiac Teaching and Pre-cardiac Catheterization
- Proven ability to meet the daily challenges of the nursing profession
- Work with the high standards and dedication expected of today's LPNs
- Received Highest LPN Service Award, two years

EDUCATION: **Community College of Rhode Island,** Lincoln, RI
Diploma as a Licensed Practical Nurse, July 1994
GPA: 3.8/4.0
Graduated third in a class of 88

Community College of Rhode Island, Warwick, RI
Liberal Arts Courses (leading to Registered Nurse Degree)

EXPERIENCE: **North County Memorial Hospital,** Cranston, RI
Licensed Practical Nurse, August 1998–Present
- Full-time staff member of the Coronary Care Unit
- Work in a team of three participants
- Maintain full awareness of monitored patients
- Care, assessment, charting, medicating, monitoring IV fluids/medications

North County Nursing and Subacute Unit, North Kingstown, RI
Licensed Practical Nurse, Primary Care, December 1994–1998
- Charge of nursing for 26 long-term and subacute residents
- Primary care nursing

LICENSES: Current Practical Nursing license #LPN 07542
CPR certification through November 2004

MEMBERSHIPS: Wickford Glen Condominium Association, President
Saint Paul's Parish Community Association
Rhode Island LPN Consortium, Secretary

VOLUNTEER: Annual Cancer Appeal Raffle ticket sales
Kent County Hospital Annual Appeal Phonathons
Toys for Tots Appeals

Excellent references will be furnished upon request

81

Edward Turilli, North Kingstown, Rhode Island

A thin page border and a two-line horizontal line under the contact information are the two chief design elements. The centered Career Summary heading breaks up for variety the list of headings.

Hospitality

Resumes at a Glance

TAMMY PARSONS
1422 HARTFORD ROAD • FOWLER, OHIO 44418 • (330) 555-0000

~ ~

CAKE DECORATOR

~ ~ Creative ~ ~

~ ~ Eye for detail ~ ~

~ ~ Flexible to changing priorities ~ ~

~ ~ Excellent organizational skills ~ ~

~ ~ Noteworthy interpersonal skills ~ ~

~ ~ Establish and maintain well-organized work area ~ ~

~ ~ Comply with all food safety and sanitation standards ~ ~

~ ~ Maintain high-quality standards and product integrity ~ ~

~ ~ Exceptional reading, writing and communication skills ~ ~

~ ~ Use production list to meet product needs throughout the day ~ ~

~ ~ Effectively merchandise all cake items according to plan-o-gram ~ ~

~ ~ Versatile, enthusiastic, hardworking individual; driven to meet or exceed expectations ~ ~

~ ~ Assist customers with bakery products or purchases using suggestive selling techniques ~ ~

~ ~ Work well as a team member with people of all professional levels and of various cultures ~ ~

~ ~ Computer systems knowledge includes Art Deco, Kopy Kake, Telxon, ACR and Label Machine ~ ~

~ ~ ~ ~ ~ ~ ~ ~ ~ **PROFESSIONAL EMPLOYMENT** ~ ~ ~ ~ ~ ~ ~ ~ ~ ~

Shop-a-Lot, Hermitage, Pennsylvania
CAKE DECORATOR, 2002–Present

Receive special orders from customers for cakes, pies, tortes, and cookies. Decorate cakes and pastries; duplicate customer-supplied drawings freehand or with Kopy Kake.

Prepare a wide variety and assortment of fresh and appealing cake items. Assist bakery manager when ordering ingredients and decorator supplies. Rotate product to ensure optimum freshness.

Introduced use of airbrush to cake business. Incorporated use of popular character images and recommended placing picture cakes in showcase. Saw immediate increase in cake business.

Farrell Bakery, Farrell, Pennsylvania
CAKE DECORATOR, 1996–1997

Produced quality, appealing cakes to customer orders with consistent, on-time delivery.

Tastee Bakery, Hermitage, Pennsylvania
CAKE DECORATOR, 1989–1995

Constructed beautiful cakes for special orders. Skilled in creating royal icing flowers. Reputation spread by word / taste of mouth, resulting in significant increase in volume of orders.

~ ~ ~ ~ ~ ~ ~ ~ ~ ~ **EDUCATION / TRAINING** ~ ~ ~ ~ ~ ~ ~ ~ ~ ~ ~

Certificate, 1986, Advanced Cake Decorating, Trumbull County Joint Vocational School, Warren, Ohio
Graduate, 1984, Badger High School, Kinsman, Ohio

82

Jane Roqueplot, West Middlesex, Pennsylvania

This creative resume is for a creative applicant, and its design illustrates the applicant's occupation. Center justification and controlled line width create the cake's layers.

Valerie W. Butler

333 S.E. Riveredge Drive • Vancouver, Washington 33333

222-222-2222 *cell*   *home* 555-555-5555

Server

Professional Profile

Energetic and highly motivated **Food Server** with extensive experience in the food service industry. Expertise lies in working with the fine-dining restaurant, providing top-quality service, and maintaining a professional demeanor. Solid knowledge of the restaurant business, with strengths in excellent customer service and food and wine recommendations.

Get along well with management, coworkers, and customers. Well-developed communication skills. Known as a caring and intuitive "people person," with an upbeat and positive attitude. Highly flexible, honest, and punctual, with the ability to stay calm and focused in stressful situations. Committed to a job well done and a long-term career.

Outstanding Achievements & Recommendations

• Served notable VIP clientele, including clients associated with Murdock Charitable Trust.
• History of repeat and new customers requesting my service as their waitress.
• Known for creating an atmosphere of enjoyment and pleasure for the customer.

*"...Valerie was warm, friendly, kind, and very efficient.
We didn't feel rushed. She handled our requests, and
we appreciated her genuine 'May I please you' attitude...."*

Related Work History

Waitress • Banquets • Heathman Lodge • Vancouver, Washington • *2002–present*
Northwest seasonal cuisine.

Banquets • Dolce Skamania Lodge • Stevenson, Washington • *2001–2002*
Casual fine-dining restaurant.

Waitress • Hidden House • Vancouver, Washington • *1993–2001*
Exclusive fine-dining restaurant.

Waitress • Multnomah Falls Lodge Restaurant • Corbett, Oregon • *1992–1993*
Historic Columbia Gorge Falls restaurant serving authentic Northwestern cuisine.

Waitress • The Ahwahnee at Yosemite National Park • California • *1 year*
World-renowned, award-winning fine-dining restaurant—sister lodge to Timberline Lodge.

83

Rosie Bixel, Portland, Oregon

The applicant wanted to work for an upscale, fine-dining restaurant. The writer included a customer recommendation as a testimonial. Horizontal lines enclose each of the section headings.

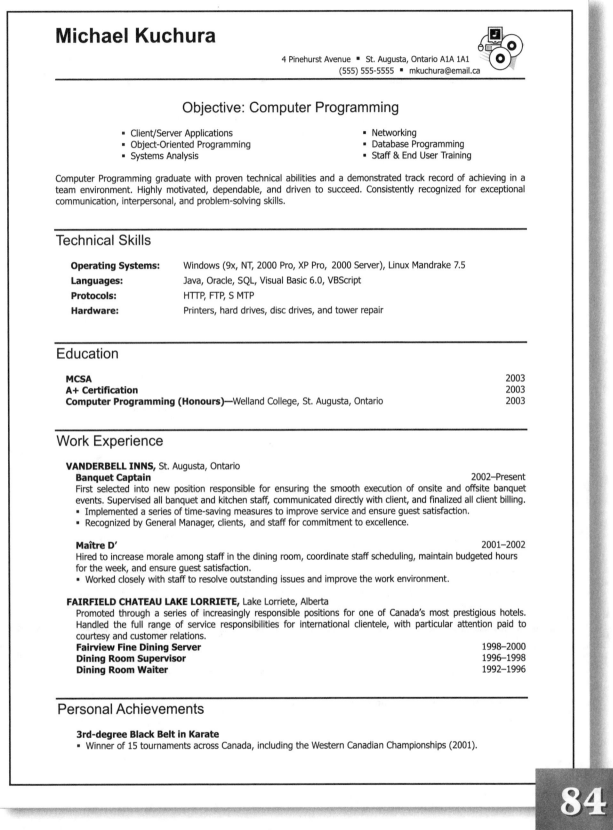

Michael Kuchura

4 Pinehurst Avenue ▪ St. Augusta, Ontario A1A 1A1
(555) 555-5555 ▪ mkuchura@email.ca

Objective: Computer Programming

- Client/Server Applications
- Object-Oriented Programming
- Systems Analysis
- Networking
- Database Programming
- Staff & End User Training

Computer Programming graduate with proven technical abilities and a demonstrated track record of achieving in a team environment. Highly motivated, dependable, and driven to succeed. Consistently recognized for exceptional communication, interpersonal, and problem-solving skills.

Technical Skills

Operating Systems:	Windows (9x, NT, 2000 Pro, XP Pro, 2000 Server), Linux Mandrake 7.5
Languages:	Java, Oracle, SQL, Visual Basic 6.0, VBScript
Protocols:	HTTP, FTP, S MTP
Hardware:	Printers, hard drives, disc drives, and tower repair

Education

MCSA	2003
A+ Certification	2003
Computer Programming (Honours)—Welland College, St. Augusta, Ontario	2003

Work Experience

VANDERBELL INNS, St. Augusta, Ontario
Banquet Captain   2002–Present
First selected into new position responsible for ensuring the smooth execution of onsite and offsite banquet events. Supervised all banquet and kitchen staff, communicated directly with client, and finalized all client billing.
- Implemented a series of time-saving measures to improve service and ensure guest satisfaction.
- Recognized by General Manager, clients, and staff for commitment to excellence.

Maître D'   2001–2002
Hired to increase morale among staff in the dining room, coordinate staff scheduling, maintain budgeted hours for the week, and ensure guest satisfaction.
- Worked closely with staff to resolve outstanding issues and improve the work environment.

FAIRFIELD CHATEAU LAKE LORRIETE, Lake Lorriete, Alberta
Promoted through a series of increasingly responsible positions for one of Canada's most prestigious hotels. Handled the full range of service responsibilities for international clientele, with particular attention paid to courtesy and customer relations.
Fairview Fine Dining Server	1998–2000
Dining Room Supervisor	1996–1998
Dining Room Waiter	1992–1996

Personal Achievements

3rd-degree Black Belt in Karate
- Winner of 15 tournaments across Canada, including the Western Canadian Championships (2001).

84

Ross Macpherson, Whitby, Ontario, Canada

This applicant had solid hospitality experience but wanted to transition to IT. The writer used a graphic, a Technical Skills section, and relevant education to show his technology skills.

Rachel Marie Lindahl

227 N.E. 99th Street • Vancouver, WA 77777

555-555-5555 *cell*   home **555-555-5555**

Restaurant Management

Professional Profile

Driven, results-oriented, and energetic *professional* with 14 years of experience in *Restaurant Management,* offering an exceptional teamwork spirit and a positive attitude.

Experienced in managing within budget guidelines, maintaining an effective flow of inventory, and developing a strong team attitude among employees. Proven skills in setting and achieving goals, supplying above-average training skills, and adding to the bottom-dollar profit margin by improving service, reducing waste, and increasing efficiency.

Work well with all types of personalities; able to perform hiring and termination duties effectively and professionally. Conscientious, customer-service-oriented, and highly focused, with strong follow-through skills and effective time-management abilities. Loyal, possess strong common sense with a keen sense of humor, and committed to a job well done.

Expertise Includes

• Bookkeeping/Deposits	• HIV Awareness Training	• Quality Assurance
• Cash Handling	• Inventory Management	• Schedule Management
• Customer Service	• Operating within Budget	• Staff Training
• Event Planning	• POS Knowledge	• Supervisor
• Excellent Facilities Presentation	• Public Relations	• Team Player

History of Employment

Assistant Manager • Shari's Restaurant • Vancouver, Washington • *2001–current*

Chef / Manager • Van Mall Retirement • Vancouver, Washington • *1996–2001*
    250 residents—supplied full meal services.

Kitchen / Assistant Manager • Carrows Restaurant • Vancouver, Washington • *1989–1995*

85

Rosie Bixel, Portland, Oregon

The elaborate box around each main section heading is distinctive. The darker sides of the box create the illusion of a shadow. Without a box the Expertise Includes heading seems part of the Professional Profile.

LYNDA ROSEN

67533 NW Elm Street
Seattle, WA 88888
(555) 666-9999
2343856@lpst.com

QUALIFICATIONS

- Extensive experience in all aspects of restaurant operations, including supervising, food and dessert preparation, catering, inventory management, supplier relations, and service excellence.

- Skilled in training, motivating, and developing new staff members.

- A talent for identifying and developing new and creative business opportunities.

- Continually seeks ways to share knowledge and vitality.

- Thrives in a team-oriented environment that honors creativity and experience.

- Passionate about creating innovative food and dining experiences.

- Developed a comfortable management style based on integrity, excellence, and trust.

EDUCATION

WYOMING STATE UNIVERSITY
Undergraduate course work in business, art, and drama

EXPERIENCE

SEAFOOD GRILL & WINE BAR, Seattle, WA   **2000–present**
Front-of-the-House Supervisor for 125-seat seafood restaurant.
Promoted rapidly from initial position of **Server** *to* **Daytime Maître d'** *to* **Floor Supervisor** *and on to current position.*

- Manage, supervise, and set up floor.
- Ensure restaurant's high standards are being met.
- Provide training, labor management, and maintenance scheduling.
- Assist in budgeting and cost controls.

LA PRIMA TRATTORIA, Seattle, WA   **1998–2000**
Server and Pastry Chef for 75-seat Italian restaurant.

- Created and prepared in-house desserts, sauces, cookies, and special-order desserts.
- Trained new waitstaff, tracked dessert inventory, and gained experience on point-of-sale computer system.

HANES BAKERY, Renton, WA   **1997–1998**
Pastry Chef and Server for Cannon Beach bakery.

- Supervised sandwich counter and served when appropriate.
- Developed pastries, desserts, and special-order desserts.
- Improved staff scheduling and overall organization to maximize peak traffic flow.
- Introduced new lunch menu items to retain bakery vitality.
- Researched and developed wedding cake division that significantly increased overall revenue. Created marketing pieces, including product descriptions and price lists.

CAFÉ DE LA MER, Renton, WA   **1982–1997**
Assistant Manager and Co-Chef for 36-seat fine-dining restaurant (serving Northwest cuisine and wines) that became known as one of the most highly rated and exclusive restaurants on the West Coast.

- Provided business experience to new owners.
- Supervised and trained wait team and prep staff.
- Helped develop menus, prepare food, and create desserts.
- Introduced new signature items such as bouillabaisse, cassoulet, and scallop serviche.
- Planned and tracked inventory; ordered all food and wine.
- Prepared payroll and managed accounting.
- Managed restaurant in absence of the owners.

86

Rosie Bixel, Portland, Oregon

The writer wanted this resume to be creative for the creative Chef/Baker/Manager applicant. One vertical line crossing one horizontal line produced unequal quadrants suitable for the sections.

WILLIAM KENT

5555 North Orange Avenue • Los Angeles, CA 55555
(310) 555-5555 • wmkent@email.com

FOOD SERVICE MANAGEMENT—15 YEARS OF EXPERIENCE

RELATED SKILLS

- Multisite Operations Management
- Customer Service
- Menu Formulation
- Food & Labor Cost Control

- Purchasing & Inventory Management
- Warehouse Supervision
- Sanitation Control
- Facilities Management & Maintenance

QUALIFICATIONS

✓ Industry-wide reputation for superior leadership and team-building skills. Gain loyalty through ability to instill confidence and encourage growth in coworkers. Skilled in hiring, training and motivating team members.

✓ Track record of exceptional productivity and expense reduction. Effectively manage costs, consistently operating within or below budget.

✓ Work well independently and as a part of a team. Interface well with public and all levels of corporate and store management.

✓ Thorough in solving problems and taking preventative actions.

✓ Consistent award winner, including *Most Improved Sales, Most Improved Operating Profit, #1 in Sales Increases, #1 in Operating Profit Improvement.*

PROFESSIONAL EXPERIENCE

GOLD STAR RESTAURANT OPERATIONS   1992 to Present
Restaurant Operations District Manager (2000–Present)
Restaurant Manager, San Fernando Valley (1998–2000)
Previous Positions: Lead Cook, Assistant Restaurant Manager (1992–1997)
Achieved fast-track promotions through a series of increasingly responsible positions. Advanced based on consistent revenue production, earnings and customer satisfaction ratings.

- Coordinate corporate food service activities, policies and procedures for up to 40 diverse units encompassing cafeterias, grills, deli counters, fast food and snack bars. Territory extends throughout Los Angeles, Orange, Ventura and San Luis Obispo counties.
- Direct management team with up to 140 employees. Screen management applicants; hire, train, supervise, motivate and conduct performance evaluations.
- Consistently achieve revenues within top 5% company-wide with annual sales of $4 million.
- Secure vendors; negotiate contracts per corporate buying specifications and standards.
- Develop and implement creative promotional programs that have contributed to district-wide success.

JENNY'S RESTAURANT, Laguna Hills, CA   1990 to 1992
Lead Cook/Cook Trainer

EDUCATION

UNITED STATES NAVY
Mess Management, Class "A"
Honorable Discharge 1989

Vivian VanLier, Los Angeles, California

The Qualifications section highlights this candidate's strong record of food management skills and notable accomplishments. The list of Gold Star Restaurant positions shows his record of promotions.

CARMELLA MONTEZ

20 Annabelle Court • Marathon Shores, FL 33050
Cell: 305.555.1128 • Home: 305.555.1129
CarmellaMontez@gmail.com

Career Focus	**HOSPITALITY • TOURISM • EVENT PLANNING**
Competencies	Self-motivated communicator with experience dealing with diverse populations/cultures through background in the public marketplace, international travel, and team competition
Studies in	Hospitality Financial Management • Strategic Management • Finance • Competitive Analysis • Management and Marketing • Marketing Statistics • Consumer Research

EDUCATION & CERTIFICATION

UNIVERSITY OF FLORIDA; Gainesville, FL
Bachelor of Science in Hotel, Restaurant, Tourism Management • 2009 *(expected)*
   Minor in **Business Administration**

   Projects: 1) Financial Analysis of Landmark Corporation—researched and charted stock prices, observed major financial ratios and calculated financial standing of the company within the industry and also the industry position. 2) Landmark Resorts International—analyzed future trends and growth strategies and created a SWOT analysis.

ACADÉMIE INTERNATIONALE DE MANAGEMENT–AIM; Paris, France • 2007–2008

Certifications

   ServSafe—Science of food safety and best practices used in the industry; critical food safety practices and their operation

   TIPS® Alcohol Awareness—Program establishes acceptable standards of practice for serving alcoholic beverages and provides intervention strategies for handling difficult situations

EXPERIENCE & INTERNSHIPS

SIMION AXIS; Miami, FL—**Premium Seating Intern** • Summer 2008
Assisted Premium Seating Manager and Premium Seating Director with daily activities and communication; liaison with Premium Seat Holders. Worked with the ticket office to organize tickets for events.
   ▸ Created PowerPoint presentations for club and suite holder's evaluations and club and suite holder's evaluations from the Brad Paisley Concert.
   ▸ Worked on implementing new seating brackets for Club Seat Holders.

FLORIDA CLASSICS; Gainesville, FL—**Recruiting Host/Assistant to the Director** • 2006–07
Recruited high school and junior college players; assisted in the recruitment of Florida Classics.

FRENCH/AMERICAN CHAMBER OF COMMERCE; Paris, France—**Office Clerk** • Summer 2007
Played a support role in the organization of The French/American Chamber of Commerce in Bastille Day Celebrations in Paris.

CELLULAR COMMUNICATIONS; Gainesville, FL—**Sales Associate** • 2005–2006
Responsible for customer relations activities for retailer of cellular phones. Managed customer service issues, handled merchandising and marketing concerns for store. Trained and advised new employees.
   ▸ Increased sales of prepaid cellular phones; improved sales of postpaid cellular phones.

COMMUNITY SERVICE

Member of • Chi Alpha Omega • Series IV • American Cancer Society, Relay for Life • Clean up Florida • Meals on Wheels • University Charity Golf Tournament • UFGA

88

Lorie Lebert, Brighton, Michigan

The applicant was studying for a bachelor's degree but had no background in hospitality. The writer focused on international experience, communication abilities, and diverse work experience.

TODD RANDOLF

MANAGER
ENTREPRENEUR / MARKETER
INNOVATIVE PRODUCT DEVELOPMENT

BUSINESS EXPERTISE

- Problem Identification/Analysis
- Logistical Planning
- Product Specification
- Operations/Administration

- Process Optimization
- Troubleshooting/Problem Resolution
- Manufacturing Strategies/Techniques
- Patent Application Process

MARKETING EXPERTISE

- Lead Generation
- Account Development
- Customer Care

- Marketing Campaigns
- Publicity and Public Relations
- Sales Strategies/Incentives

PROFESSIONAL HISTORY

CANYON RESTAURANT, MORRISON, CO   **1987–PRESENT**

Todd has been the manager of Canyon since 1995 following a series of promotions in a career spanning 17 years. As manager, Todd manages the daily operations and monitors quality control and time management. He is responsible for guest relations, scheduling, staff management and development, point-of-sale administration, inventory control, and bookkeeping. Most notably, Todd has contributed in the following ways:

Employee Motivation and Retention: Closely managing a staff of up to 65 employees at peak times. Effectively motivating the staff through incentive programs and promoting a strong family atmosphere to achieve established sales objectives through performance improvement and increased customer satisfaction levels. Canyon enjoys a long-standing, loyal staff—many employees have been there for 17 years.

Tip/Gratuity Administration: Designed an innovative tip-tracking system to comply with IRS regulations. Employees receive their tips in their regular biweekly paychecks.

Reservation Matching: Implemented a successful reservation-matching system that eliminates overbooking, minimizes table wait times, and maximizes seating at Canyon.

FOUNDER AND PRESIDENT, FORMATIVE TECHNOLOGIES, MORRISON, CO   **1998–PRESENT**

Formative Technologies specializes in custom fabricated accessories for point-of-sale systems in the hospitality, grocery, and retail industries. The flagship product is a point-of-sale printer protective cover (patent pending) used to prevent damage caused by airborne particles, grease, spills, and foreign objects.

Faced with the ongoing problem of spills disabling the printers at Canyon Restaurant, Todd unsuccessfully searched for an off-the-shelf product to protect the printer. Further investigation revealed the problem was widespread in the hospitality industry, and a protective cover could serve the grocery market as well.

Todd enlisted the help of a product designer, and together they designed and specified a protective cover. After careful consideration, a manufacturer and thermal forming manufacturing process were selected. Production began. Word of the product spread, and orders for the protective cover were booked prior to launch.

A successful marketing campaign using advertising, trade press articles, and word of mouth won key accounts such as IBM, Micros, King Soopers, and P.F. Chang's. The printer cover has been so successful that the line will be extended to include other custom accessories for point-of-sale equipment and systems.

TGR TECHNOLOGIES INC., LITTLETON, CO   **1999–PRESENT**

TGR Technologies designs and fabricates self-contained housing units for ATMs. Todd is a hands-on technician, building and installing the housing units.

EDUCATION AND CERTIFICATIONS

Business Program, Arapahoe Community College, Englewood, CO
Computer Science and Business Programs, Red Rocks Community College, Lakewood, CO
CPR Certification
Dealing with Difficult Customers Certificate

1234 W. Cheyenne Drive • Morrison, CO 55555
555.555.1111 • truser@aol1.com

89

Roberta F. Gamza, Louisville, Colorado

This candidate—also an entrepreneur—was looking for a position with a start-up manufacturer or another entrepreneur. The writer used a narrative format to attract the right type of employer.

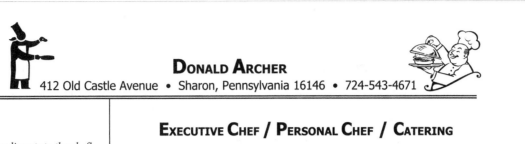

DONALD ARCHER
412 Old Castle Avenue • Sharon, Pennsylvania 16146 • 724-543-4671

"Compliments to the chef!
This is the best prime rib
I've ever eaten." — Ralph B
Monte Cello's, Sharon, PA

"Superb steak . . . cooked
to perfection . . . excellent
seasonings. My thanks to
the chef."   — Actress
Debbie Reynolds
Radisson Hotel, Sharon, PA

Knowledgeable in:
➢ Food Preparation
➢ Menu Creation
➢ Inventory
➢ Ordering Supplies and
   Food
➢ Event Planning
➢ Serving 1–2,500
➢ Nutrition
➢ Sanitation
➢ Security
➢ Policies & Procedures
➢ Personnel Management
➢ Staff Training
➢ Record Keeping
➢ Preparation of Reports

EDUCATION

Culinary Arts
International Culinary
Academy—Pittsburgh,
Pennsylvania

Winner Institute of Arts &
Sciences—Transfer,
Pennsylvania

Food Competitions and
Food Shows

Liberal Arts
Criminal Justice/
Pre-Law Course Work
Kent State University—
Champion, Ohio

EXECUTIVE CHEF / PERSONAL CHEF / CATERING

- Select menu items with an eye toward quality, variety, availability of seasonal foods, popularity of past dishes and likely number of customers. Collaborate with owner(s) to plan menus to attract specific clientele.

- Estimate food consumption. Select and appropriately price menu items to cost-effectively use food and other supplies.

- Oversee food preparation and cooking, examining quality and portion sizes to ensure dishes are prepared and garnished correctly and in a timely manner.

- Proficient knowledge of computer programs, especially to create menus; analyze recipes to determine food, labor and overhead costs; and calculate prices for various dishes.

- Hardworking, self-motivated individual with proven record of responsibility. Equally effective working independently as well as in a team effort. Work well with a wide range of people at all levels; comfortable leading, collaborating or training.

- Able to view situations/issues in a positive way and propose solutions to streamline operations. Organized and detail-oriented. Identify and resolve challenges using available resources.

- Effective communicator. Monitor actions of employees to ensure health and safety standards are maintained. Represent an organization in a professional manner and appearance.

- Receptive to relocation.

EXPERIENCE

EXECUTIVE CHEF, Monte Cello's—*Sharon, Pennsylvania*
SOUS CHEF, Mr. D's Food Fair—*Brookfield, Ohio*
KITCHEN MANAGER, Sidetrack Inn—*Warren, Ohio*
STORE MANAGER, Pit Stop Pizza—*Cortland, Ohio*
GRILL AND SAUTÉ CHEF, Radisson Hotel—*Sharon, Pennsylvania*
PREP CHEF, Avalon Inn—*Howland, Ohio*
ASSISTANT MANAGER, Moovies, Inc.—*Cortland, Ohio*
PERSONAL SECURITY TECHNICIAN, Independent Contractor—
various locations

MILITARY

Military Police, 1984–1987, Honorable Discharge
United States Marine Corp.

90

Jane Roqueplot, West Middlesex, Pennsylvania

As a printout from a color printer, this resume is two-color. The contact information, section headings, and round bullets are dark blue. The arrow-tip bullets are white over blue.

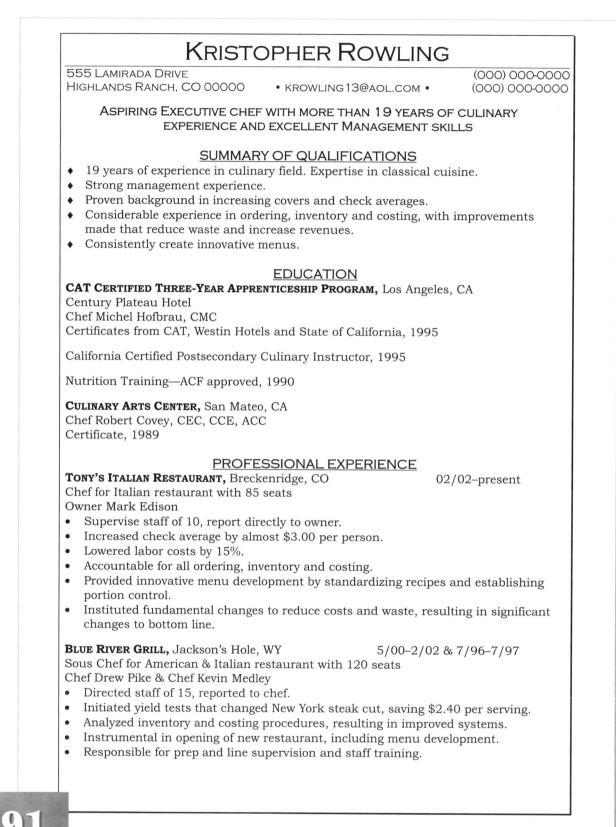

KRISTOPHER ROWLING

555 LAMIRADA DRIVE   (000) 000-0000
HIGHLANDS RANCH, CO 00000   • KROWLING13@AOL.COM •   (000) 000-0000

ASPIRING EXECUTIVE CHEF WITH MORE THAN 19 YEARS OF CULINARY EXPERIENCE AND EXCELLENT MANAGEMENT SKILLS

SUMMARY OF QUALIFICATIONS

- 19 years of experience in culinary field. Expertise in classical cuisine.
- Strong management experience.
- Proven background in increasing covers and check averages.
- Considerable experience in ordering, inventory and costing, with improvements made that reduce waste and increase revenues.
- Consistently create innovative menus.

EDUCATION

CAT CERTIFIED THREE-YEAR APPRENTICESHIP PROGRAM, Los Angeles, CA
Century Plateau Hotel
Chef Michel Hofbrau, CMC
Certificates from CAT, Westin Hotels and State of California, 1995

California Certified Postsecondary Culinary Instructor, 1995

Nutrition Training—ACF approved, 1990

CULINARY ARTS CENTER, San Mateo, CA
Chef Robert Covey, CEC, CCE, ACC
Certificate, 1989

PROFESSIONAL EXPERIENCE

TONY'S ITALIAN RESTAURANT, Breckenridge, CO   02/02–present
Chef for Italian restaurant with 85 seats
Owner Mark Edison

- Supervise staff of 10, report directly to owner.
- Increased check average by almost $3.00 per person.
- Lowered labor costs by 15%.
- Accountable for all ordering, inventory and costing.
- Provided innovative menu development by standardizing recipes and establishing portion control.
- Instituted fundamental changes to reduce costs and waste, resulting in significant changes to bottom line.

BLUE RIVER GRILL, Jackson's Hole, WY   5/00–2/02 & 7/96–7/97
Sous Chef for American & Italian restaurant with 120 seats
Chef Drew Pike & Chef Kevin Medley

- Directed staff of 15, reported to chef.
- Initiated yield tests that changed New York steak cut, saving $2.40 per serving.
- Analyzed inventory and costing procedures, resulting in improved systems.
- Instrumental in opening of new restaurant, including menu development.
- Responsible for prep and line supervision and staff training.

91

Michele Angello, Aurora, Colorado

Education and the names of "chefs studied under" are important in the field of hospitality, even when a candidate like this one has had extensive experience as an Executive Chef. The writer therefore placed Education after the Summary of Qualifications and before Professional

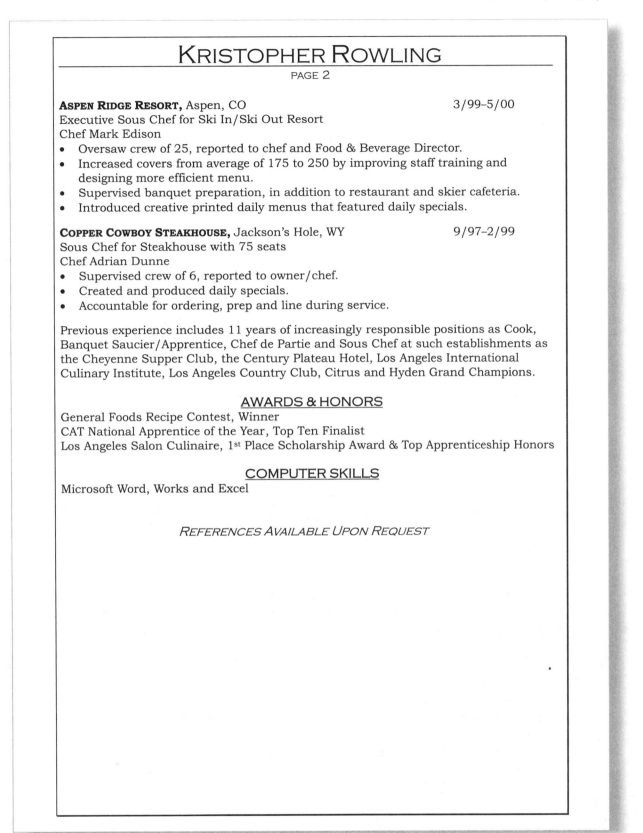

KRISTOPHER ROWLING
PAGE 2

ASPEN RIDGE RESORT, Aspen, CO   3/99–5/00
Executive Sous Chef for Ski In/Ski Out Resort
Chef Mark Edison
- Oversaw crew of 25, reported to chef and Food & Beverage Director.
- Increased covers from average of 175 to 250 by improving staff training and designing more efficient menu.
- Supervised banquet preparation, in addition to restaurant and skier cafeteria.
- Introduced creative printed daily menus that featured daily specials.

COPPER COWBOY STEAKHOUSE, Jackson's Hole, WY   9/97–2/99
Sous Chef for Steakhouse with 75 seats
Chef Adrian Dunne
- Supervised crew of 6, reported to owner/chef.
- Created and produced daily specials.
- Accountable for ordering, prep and line during service.

Previous experience includes 11 years of increasingly responsible positions as Cook, Banquet Saucier/Apprentice, Chef de Partie and Sous Chef at such establishments as the Cheyenne Supper Club, the Century Plateau Hotel, Los Angeles International Culinary Institute, Los Angeles Country Club, Citrus and Hyden Grand Champions.

AWARDS & HONORS
General Foods Recipe Contest, Winner
CAT National Apprentice of the Year, Top Ten Finalist
Los Angeles Salon Culinaire, 1st Place Scholarship Award & Top Apprenticeship Honors

COMPUTER SKILLS
Microsoft Word, Works and Excel

REFERENCES AVAILABLE UPON REQUEST

Experience. Boldfacing makes it easy to spot the certifications and the restaurants served. Bullets in the Experience section point to responsibilities and achievements.

MAURICE K. DONOFRIO

66 ADAMS STREET, BROOKVILLE, NY 55555 ● 555-555-5555 ● CHEFMAURICE@MAIL.COM

EXECUTIVE CHEF
FOOD SERVICE OPERATIONS MANAGEMENT

Accomplished and extensive culinary and management career of twenty years. Directed high-volume restaurant and catering operations. Strong leadership and management qualifications combined with interpersonal and team-building skills. Significant contributor to cost reductions and profit growth through productivity, operational efficiencies, and quality improvements.

Expertise includes:

- Food & Beverage Cost Controls
- Procurement & Vendor Relations
- Inventory Management
- Efficiency Improvements
- Quality Assurance & Control

- Kitchen Staffing & Training
- Special-Events Management
- Renovations & Capital Projects
- County Health Code Compliance
- Nutritional, Dietary, Ethnic & Organic Cooking

PROFESSIONAL EXPERIENCE

EXECUTIVE CHEF   2000–Present
Carrie's, Woodbury, NY

Oversee all food operations of a 100-seat restaurant, on- and off-premises catering service, gourmet deli, and bakery.

- Plan menus and create innovative food selections. Oversee all details to ensure quality.
- Reduced food expenses 25–30% through effective price negotiations with vendors and improved inventory management and control. Consolidated procurement activities and reduced vendor accounts from 12 to 5. Secured more favorable delivery schedules and enhanced quality of provisions.
- Hire, train, schedule, and supervise a kitchen staff of 20. Provide dotted-line supervision to a waitstaff of 45.
- Optimize work flow by regularly evaluating individual and team productivity and modifying staff responsibilities as needed.
- Conduct performance evaluations, motivate staff, and provide opportunities for advancement.
- Increase staff retention by encouraging camaraderie and fostering a pleasant work environment.
- Assisted with a kitchen renovation and upgrade. Evaluated alternative plans and selected appliances and major kitchen items.
- Set standards for food and kitchen operations. Passed all county health code inspections.

EXECUTIVE CHEF   1990–2000
The Watermill, Nesconset, NY

Directed on- and off-premises catering events for this top Long Island catering establishment serving groups of up to 600.

- Planned and designed menus for breakfasts, brunches, luncheons, and dinners.
- Cut food costs approximately 25%.
- Enhanced food preparation efficiency by providing comprehensive staff training.

Continued…

92

M J Feld, Huntington, New York

The challenge was to tell about each past job without being repetitive. Using a functional format (merely listing the workplaces in one part of the resume and summarizing elsewhere the candidate's common activities) was unsatisfactory because it was important to indicate

MAURICE K. DONOFRIO

Page Two

EXECUTIVE CHEF, **The Watermill,** *Continued*

- Handled and coordinated procurement activities, cooking, and assembly of catered orders.
- Instituted food protection/sanitation program for all cooking and food preparation activities.
- Participated in philanthropic functions for Save Our Strength and other local charities.
- Assisted with a $300,000 construction project providing input for kitchen layout and equipment.
- Supervised 7–15 direct reports.

PRIOR CULINARY EXPERIENCE

SOUS CHEF   1987–1989
Muttontown Country Club, Muttontown, NY

Handled menu planning, cooking, station work, and ice carvings for this full-service golf and country club with several food service facilities on its grounds. Ran main kitchen in chef's absence.

EVENING A LA CARTE CHEF   1986–1987
Weisbord Inn, Southampton, NY

Created innovative nightly specials and directed menu planning and food preparation for this German restaurant. Cooked up to 300 meals nightly.

SOUS CHEF   1984–1986
The Bay Club, Huntington, NY

Gained extensive experience under the tutelage of a fine European-trained chef. Supervised a kitchen staff of 8–10.

EDUCATION / AWARDS

ASSOCIATE OF ARTS, CULINARY ARTS
Le Cordon Bleu Program Diploma
Atlantic Culinary Academy, Dover, NH

PROFESSIONAL AFFILIATIONS

American Culinary Federation (ACF)
International Chef Association Federation (ICAF)

ADDITIONAL

Several first and second place awards for cooking

pertinent information about each establishment (the number of seats, type of food served, and so on). The writer made certain that the information about each workplace was different—precisely to avoid repetition.

JOSEPH BUCHEL, CCM

10400 N. Port Reserve Rd.
Mequon, WI 53092

buchelj@gmail.com

Day: (262) 241-0500
Eve: (262) 243-4534

EXECUTIVE PROFILE

Hospitality Industry Professional with more than 20 years of experience and a demonstrated track record of top- and bottom-line performance improvements.

Strategic and Tactical Business Planner—Background in the conception, planning, and implementation of cost-efficient, high-quality food/beverage programs. Ability to capitalize on market trends and deliver results through membership improvements, special events, promotions, and merchandising. Experience turning around losses through process improvements and cost containment without jeopardizing service or product quality.

General Manager and Team Builder—Hands-on manager committed to coaching/guiding staff in obtaining objectives and delivering the highest quality/service. Extensive experience in staff recruitment/hiring, talent development, and the creation of effective training programs. Broad-based experience managing major facility and grounds renovation projects.

Core Competencies Include

- Profit and Loss Management
- Cost Controls: Labor, Food, and Portions
- Menu Planning and Pricing
- Vendor Sourcing and Purchasing
- Commodities Timing and Purchasing

- Staff Training and Leadership
- Meetings and Special Events Planning
- Advertising, Media, and Promotional Communications
- Guest Relations and Satisfaction

PROFESSIONAL EXPERIENCE

WISCONSIN COUNTRY CLUB—Mequon, WI

2003 to Present

General Manager

Recruited to direct a peak-season staff of 140 with seven department heads for a 420-member private club, considered to be a premiere club in Wisconsin. Position reported to a seven-person board of directors.

- Manage a food and beverage budget of $1.2 million; significantly reduced food and beverage losses ($233,500) without jeopardizing service or quality.

- Facilitated the completion of a $7.5 million club renovation and directed the reopening after a five-month closure.

- Former supervisor wrote, *Joseph successfully reopened the club and quickly established himself as an in-charge manager. He worked on many fronts to restore the confidence of the members...he improved food quality and service levels...he reduced labor and food costs...he increased the banquet business significantly and has done so with quality...he has brought in outside entertainment and new events that have proven [to be] financially successful...and continued to make improvements in operations.*

GRAND RAPIDS COUNTRY CLUB—Grand Rapids, MI

2001 to 2003

General Manager/Chief Operating Officer

Directed a peak-season staff of 50 with five department heads for a 300-member privately owned club. Managed a $1.4 million operating budget. Established quality and service standards.

- Completely revamped service and food quality. Initiated public relations efforts and hosted a highly successful black-tie event showcasing club improvements. Results included a 65 percent membership increase.

- Opened food and beverage operations to the public, improved top-line revenue, and received positive press from *Grand Rapids Magazine* as "the best kept secret in town."

- Improved pro shop sales with new clothing items and a greater selection of golfing equipment.

Continued

93

Michele J. Haffner, Glendale, Wisconsin

This applicant was applying for high-profile positions in the West. He had no four-year degree, so the writer emphasized the individual's extensive experience and certification. PGA tour experience was important to his search, which is why the resume goes far back with his work history. Strong

BELMONT COUNTRY CLUB—Belmont, MI   1990 to 2001

General Manager/COO

Directed a peak-season staff of 150 with six department heads for a 450-member private club. Clubhouse contained three dining rooms, a lounge, and banquet facilities seating 300. Golf building included a kitchen, mixed grill, and pro shop. Assumed full profit-and-loss accountability for a $3.5 million operating budget with $1.2 million in food and beverage sales. Worked closely with board of directors to set quality/service standards, formulate directives, and enact club policies.

- Established guidelines for capital appropriations. Oversaw a two-year, $3.5 million club renovation and brought project in under budget. Oversaw a $450,000 project to reshape golf course sand bunkers.

- Revamped all menus and improved food and beverage service. Hired the McMahon Group to survey membership satisfaction in service, food quality, and menu variety. Achieved an 84 percent overall satisfaction index, seven points higher than the average of 110 other clubs surveyed during the period.

- Achieved a stellar reputation community-wide for delivering exceptional dining, private receptions, and catered parties.

FRANKLIN COUNTRY CLUB—Franklin, WI   1989 to 1990

General Manager

A 418-member private club. Managed a $1.2 million food and beverage budget. Coordinated the club's hosting of the Greater Milwaukee Open golf tournament (PGA tour) broadcast on network television.

BLUE VALLEY COUNTRY CLUB—Blue Valley, MN   1986 to 1989

General Manager

A 650-member private club. Managed a $3.9 million operating budget with $1.6 million in food and beverage. Hosted the USGA 40th Junior Girls Championship. Facilitated the completion of a $500,000 renovation project.

BADGER COUNTRY CLUB—Madison, WI   1976 to 1986

Manager

A 600-member private club. Managed a $900,000 food and beverage budget. In 1984 *Madison Magazine* readers voted it "the best country club in Madison."

EDUCATION AND PROFESSIONAL DEVELOPMENT

Certified Club Manager (CCM) Designation through the Club Managers Association of America   Current
- Examination covered food/beverage, cost controls, hotel law, and finance/accounting principles.
- Completed recertification every two years since 1984 through the Club Managers Institute.

American Hotelier Restaurant Management Certificate Program—Lausanne Hotel School—Switzerland   1981

PROFESSIONAL AFFILIATIONS

Club Managers Association of America   Current
- Served three years as president of the Wisconsin Chapter and served on seven national committees.
- Inducted into the CMAA Honor Society in 2001.
- Published several articles in *Club Management Magazine.*

features on page 1 are the Executive Profile, bulleted Core Competencies, and the testimonial in italic. Equally strong are the quantified achievements in the Experience section.

Jean Paul Rosseau, Chef

53 Goodfood Street
Seattle, WA 98122
206-888-1234 Cell
ccuisine1@yahoo.com

★ Qualifications ★

20+ years of experience in country clubs, bistros, resorts and hotels, and high-volume fine dining. Full P&L for $8M budget. Proven trainer and leader. Record of creating profits for new/stagnant ventures.

Versatile and resourceful Chef, creating exciting, cost-effective menus, including Caribbean, Italian, Northwest, Spanish, Classic French and Fusion bistro fare.

★ Reviews ★

Murphy's
"Murphy's: great food at a great price" —Rave review, *The Weekly*, 2003

★ - ★ - ★ - ★ - ★

La Place
"Far from concept dining, La Place is ideal for any neighborhood. It serves espresso and morning pastries (not to mention satisfying pear tarts for dessert).... There is a French spin on eggs for brunch, quiche and a well-respected bouillabaisse for dinner—all without pretense or stuffiness. I hope more restauranteurs follow suit." —The Weekly, 2001

★ - ★ - ★ - ★ - ★

The Mariner Restaurant
"Chef Jean Paul Rosseau has been around Boca Raton for years.... Rosseau's flare for turning ordinary dishes into tasty meals is unchanged.... Rosseau specializes in Conch-based entrees and Caribbean crab cakes."

—The *Boca Raton Citizen*, May 21, 2000

★ - ★ - ★ - ★ - ★

Objective: Head Chef for a high-volume corporate kitchen

Experience

HEAD CHEF ▪ Murphy's, Seattle, WA Opened December 2002–Present
Hired for ability to control food costs and construct a well-priced Northwest cuisine dinner menu for this neighborhood restaurant and nightclub. Rehired entire crew. Created first profitable month for restaurant 04/03.

HEAD CHEF ▪ Tapatia ▪ La Place, Seattle, WA   07/01–12/02
Spanish Tapa Neighborhood Café ▪ French Bistro
Rated "Top 10 Restaurant" —Seattle Dining Guide

Retained to develop tapa-based menu for Tapatia. Breakup between owners caused birth of La Place. Set up kitchen, hired a 4-person team, developed menu and handled all buying and planning, growing business from 80 to 120 entrees nightly in first six months. Trained Sous Chef from ground floor.

- Transitioned Spanish restaurant to a French bistro, receiving rave reviews.
- Delivered classic French dishes for a reasonable price (average entrée: $16).
- Grew loyal clientele on strength of "special sheet" offering upscale entrées at well-valued prices ($19–$25).
- Features included venison chops, steaks with Roquefort, halibut cheeks and rack of lamb. Served breakfast, lunch, brunch and dinner.

HEAD CHEF ▪ L'Opera Cafe, Seattle, WA   06/00–07/01
High-Volume French Bistro
Selected "100 Favorite Restaurants" —The Weekly, *2001*

Developed a well-trained kitchen staff that could surmount any theater rush. Served 100 covers in an hour, providing high-quality, fast-serve, full-course dinners to patrons of the neighboring Seattle Opera House prior to show time. Managed 2 salad chefs, a grill and a fryer chef. Handled all sauté and expediting tasks. Tapped by owner to create Spanish menu for new Tapatia venture.

- Reduced food costs from 30% to 25%.
- Adjusted scheduling, cutting staffing costs by 30%.
- Solved prior walkout problem 100%, serving all theatergoers promptly.
- Cut food and labor costs by 10% and increased sales by 20%. Went from 80 people nightly to 120 people nightly.

EXECUTIVE SOUS CHEF ▪ The Marina Resort ▪ Mariner Restaurant ▪ Hyatt Resorts ▪ Hyatt Casa Marina & Resort, Boca Raton, FL 09/99–06/00
Brunch Chef 09/99–12/99

Promoted to P.M. Chef in 3 months, overseeing a $.5M banquet kitchen, a full-service fine-dining restaurant and room service for a 150-room hotel. Completed formal hotel management training course. Handled full P&L for an $8M budget, hiring and supervision of a 15-person staff, menu planning, presentation and food quality assurance, purchasing and inventory and kitchen efficiency. Recreated historic 1950 upscale beach restaurant in location where four restaurants had previously failed. Established a solid local reputation in a tourist town as a quality place to eat. Did more with less, upgrading formula menu

94

Alice Hanson, Seattle, Washington

A unique design, together with different levels of shading, sets this resume apart. Other original design elements are the staggered horizontal lines and the use of rows of five-pointed stars as dividers. The use of stars picks up on the five-star *Mobil Travel Guide* rating on page 2. Important

EXPERIENCE (continued)

EXECUTIVE SOUS CHEF ▪ **The Marina Resort** ▪ **Mariner Restaurant** ▪ **Hyatt Resorts** ▪ **Hyatt Casa Marina & Resort** (continued)

to include fresh items, polenta, tuna and a 16 oz. steak for an average $16.95 entrée price. Grew local reputation for outstanding specials: Featured steak au poivre, rack of lamb and higher-end specials to attract a better clientele.

- Consistently delivered "four-star" presentations at a "two-star" restaurant.
- Received champagne toast by GM for achieving first $1M month and first profitable year for restaurant in ten years.
- Increased revenues per hotel guest: Average guest started "eating in" at the hotel restaurants at least three times a week.
- Decreased food costs 10% while increasing quality.
- Grew thriving banquet business based on local reputation.

CHEF / OWNER ▪ **Café Cuba Viva,** Boca Raton, FL   05/96–09/99
Ten-percent owner of a Caribbean café that introduced conch dishes to Boca Raton. Ran kitchen, including hiring, food costing, inventory and all aspects of kitchen efficiency. Served 200 diners, realizing $4,000–$5,000 nightly.

Mid-priced menu featured sautéed conch with fresh pineapple and ginger, conch piccata, steak-fried Martinique, calypso suite chicken, grilled pork tenderloin with cimicurri sauce, Barbados-style fried fish and a full range of appetizers. Bar featured authentic Cuban mojitos/Caribbean cocktails.

- Retained food and labor costs between 25–28% of overall revenues.
- Opened restaurant from ground floor, breaking even in a year.
- Promoted restaurant on local cable channel, quickly building clientele.

CHEF ▪ **Café Soleil,** Boca Raton, FL   10/93–05/96
Working chef handling all menu planning, personnel scheduling, food ordering and inventory. Introduced gallettes, creating $6,500 daily revenue and 350-order business with lines outside from 7 a.m.–3p.m. daily.

- Profitably introduced dinner menu to a "breakfast-lunch" tourist café.

CHEF ROUNDSMAN ▪ **La Belle Chateau,** Boca Raton, FL 09/92–09/93
★★★★★ Mobil Travel Guide. *Repeatedly listed as "Top Ten Restaurant."*
Pastry Chef 09/92–10/92

Classic French and Italian 150-seat fine-dining restaurant in a 1920 mansion, featuring a Grand Menu with 2 fixed seatings at 6 and 9:30 p.m.

- Formally trained to expedite a 10-person line. Maintained quality, handled large volumes yet always presented consistent quality.

NIGHT SOUS CHEF ▪ **Café Fleur,** Boca Raton, Florida 07/89–07/90
Nationally famous French restaurant

- Worked for chef trained by Paul Bocuse.
- Offered full chef position.

BANQUET CHEF ▪ **Alder Heights Golf Club,** Sarasota, Florida
Banquet Chef—Beach Grill ▪ High-end poolside banquets and events.

★ Reviews ★

Café Cuba Viva
"Rosseau fuses Indian, French and Spanish flavors to create an exciting café….Café Cuba features a nice mix of flavors and textures, perfectly fresh and attractively presented at a fair price. The appetizer list is simply delightful…." —Boca Raton News, 1997

★ - ★ - ★ - ★ - ★

La Belle Chateau
"The food is a throwback to the time when elegance was synonymous with French…. The kitchen emphasizes presentation….I came to La Belle Chateau fearful of pretentiousness….I leave having savored well-prepared foods with roots in the past. It is a pleasant relaxed event that comes at a high—but not unconscionable—price."

—Food review, *Florida Sentinel,* 1993

★ - ★ - ★ - ★ - ★

Education
Culinary Arts Degree
(French College 3 years)
Vannes, France

Apprenticeship: Le
Meaban, Baden, France

Engagements in France
Charcuterie (Lyon)
First Cook, Garde Mgr.

Venezia Restaurant
Versaille, France
Chef de Partie Saucier

The Red Door Restaurant
Vannes, Brittany
First Cook, Saucier,
Garde Manager

---

to this resume is the use of italic. Note where it appears: in the contact information, in ratings comments in the Experience section, and in the review excerpts in the right columns of both pages.

PAUL M. BEATTY

23 Gates Road
Quincy, MA 55555
(555) 555-5555

CHEF/PRODUCTION MANAGER

Highly qualified and creative chef with more than 15 years of professional experience in managing, organizing, and executing the full spectrum of intensive catering in elite private boarding schools, college environments, and prestigious corporations. A successful and dedicated professional whose top concern is quality and client service while respecting budget mandates. Associate Degree in Culinary Arts.

- ▶ Managed catering teams in high-volume, fast-paced, multiunit facilities.
- ▶ Developed and executed record-breaking fund-raising and special-event dinners.
- ▶ Hired, trained, and supervised back-house operations and total food service staff.
- ▶ Traveled extensively to solve problems and troubleshoot in various locations.

PROFESSIONAL EXPERIENCE

NOVEAU INTERNATIONAL
An international food service management and public restaurant company with 600 institutional accounts generating revenues of $750 million.

Chef/Production Manager, Nichols Brown School, Nichols, MA	1999–2004
Regional Executive Chef, Plymouth Academy, Plymouth, MA	1996–1999
Regional Executive Chef, Massachusetts State College, Boston, MA	1992–1996

Chef/Production Management
- Oversaw an annual food budget of $800,000 with complete responsibility for all aspects of menu planning, preparation, presentation, special events, inventory, and purchasing.
- Managed all back-house operations and the coordination of buffet and banquet setups, maximizing kitchen productivity and staff performance while ensuring quality control and minimizing waste.
- Created and developed exciting new menus for special events, such as President's luncheons and banquets, Trustees' dinners, Chamber of Commerce breakfasts, and Alumni weekends.
- Increased client sales by marketing and promoting new accounts and making presentations of new, creative setup styles and menus to prospective clients.
- Supervised and implemented fund-raising events, organizing and coordinating multiple banquets and menus simultaneously, always meeting time requirements.

Personnel Management
- Managed food service production staff of 25 cooks and crew serving meals to 1200+ people daily.
- Trained and supervised new and existing culturally diverse staff to meet and exceed company standards of performance while conforming to strict procedures of safety, sanitation, and storage.
- Solved problems by troubleshooting existing accounts, traveling to facilities at various locations to assist in management and production.
- Initiated and promoted relationship building with all departments, collaborating and advising them in planning special events and menus.

95

Carol Nason, Groton, Massachusetts

The writer wanted to give this Chef/Production Manager "an aura of creativity," so she used at the top a food graphic that would appeal to vision and taste. Horizontal lines enclose the section

SANTORINI FOOD SERVICE CORPORATION
A national food service management and public restaurant company generating revenues of $300M.

Chef, Prudential Travelers Insurance Company, Boston, MA   1990–1992
Chef/Supervisor, Rhodes Investment International, Boston, MA   1985–1990

- Supervised and implemented the setup and operation of cafeteria food line, serving more than 2,000 employees extensive luncheon menus within a two-hour time span.
- Scheduled, coordinated, and monitored staff assignments for back-house and dining room.
- Catered and organized special-event banquets and luncheons for executive staff and guests.
- Launched and developed a new menu for "Health Thyself" program, an awareness program for healthy eating that was highly praised and very successful.

EDUCATION

Associate Degree in Culinary Arts
Culinary Institute of New York, Lake Park, New York
Graduated 1985

PROFESSIONAL TRAINING

Cambridge Culinary Institute, Cambridge, MA
Food Show and Competition Buffet Presentations
Restaurant Desserts

National Hotel & Motel Association
Human Relations and Supervisory Development

National Institute for Food Service Administration
Applied Food Service Sanitation

headings and thus make them more noticeable. After an opening profile, triangular bullets point to key activities. In the Professional Experience section, bold italic statements describe each company, and bullets point to a mix of responsibilities and achievements. Training appears at the end.

Jay T. Mooney

520 Locust St., Apt. 2B, Columbus, OH 43215
Phone: (513) 294-2813 | jmooney@jitaweb.com

Restaurant & Retail Manager of a Multimillion-Dollar Operation
Personnel Management and Training / Multi-Shift / Facility Operations
History of Cutting Food Expenses, Labor Costs, and Shrinkage

Hospitality manager with an extensive background working within the food industry, including a retail operation. Track record of increased company revenues and customer satisfaction levels matched by a decrease in monthly overhead, food expenses, and labor costs. Handle all business logistics, from comparing daily revenues to sales quotas and workforce scheduling to securing customer satisfaction.

EDUCATION

A.A.S., Hotel and Restaurant Management, 1982
State University of New York (SUNY), Plattsburgh, NY

Certificate, Safety Practices for General Industry, 1993
OSHA Training Institute, New York Education Center

KEY ABILITIES

Personnel—Scheduling · Staffing · Work Flow Optimization · Employee Training & Supervision · Labor Relations · Turnover Reductions · Employee Evaluations

Operations—Restaurant Design & Layout · Floor Plan Optimization · Stock Levels · Vendor Relations · On-site Training · Waste Reduction

Financial—Goal Setting · Profit & Loss Statements · Weekly & Monthly Forecasting · Budgeting · Cash Management · Cost Avoidance · Operating Expenses · Payroll Analysis

Business Development—Staff Levels · Customer Satisfaction · Start-up / Grand Opening · Market Share Expansion · Safety Management

PROFESSIONAL EXPERIENCE

SENIOR ASSOCIATE MANAGER, 1998–2003
Rosewood Restaurant, Toledo and Columbus, OH
Oversaw a start-up location from the preliminary details to include staffing and scheduling for this restaurant and retail operation. Hired, trained, and scheduled up to 350 employees consisting of shift supervisors and support personnel (cleaning crew and stock personnel) manning $350,000 in yearly inventory. Tracked and compared all financial numbers, from retail to food sales. Concentrated employee training on providing 100% customer care to ensure a solid return client base. Checked/ordered stock and monitored levels closely to curtail employee theft and shrinkage issues.

- Promoted to senior status and transferred to the Columbus store for the grand opening and to manage the operation; opened one of the most successful operations in company's history with $323,000 in sales the first week, serving 28,000 people

- Assisted with new store location, from initial setup and budgeting to store stock levels, staffing requirements, and grand-opening event

- Selected to revisit and cut costs at the Toledo location; reduced food cost from 39.2% to 26.7% by implementing proper food preparation procedures and adequate food proportions while lowering labor cost by 5.8% and increasing staff levels by 48% after utilizing employment retention practices

- Trained employees on all aspects of the facilities operations: OSHA rules and regulations, Dept. of Health guidelines, HAACP, guest services, suggestive selling, safety and sanitation procedures, serve safe, workplace issues, and workman's compensation

96

Teena L. Rose, Springfield, Ohio

A thin horizontal line under each main section heading helps make apparent the resume's overall design. Boldfacing directs attention to the target occupation, the section headings, the degree and certification, the skill areas under Key Abilities, and the positions held. The key abilities are

Mooney, Jay T.

- Mentored other facility managers and supervisors on dealing with day-to-day concerns that plagued them and hindered revenues

- Added 6% to overall revenues by cutting labor, supplies, and food; reducing shrinkage; and conducting seminars that taught house staff about up-selling to guests, the benefit of knowing the products, and being conscious of politeness and common courtesies

- Worked with third-party contractors, including the negotiation of details surrounding contracts for landscaping, fresh produce, linen, equipment, and cleaning supplies

- Assisted with the creation and implementation of a "Best Practices" program that trained staff members on providing above-average guest services that also increased productivity; resulted in a sales record of $2,900 in sales per hour

- Reduced customer complaints by 68% at the Toledo store

- Utilized area media forums for grand openings and participated in a breakfast kick-off with community members and the mayor

CHEF, 1998
Juneau Cruise Ships, Juneau, AK
Six-month assignment aboard *Adventure Alaska* as a chef to prepare gourmet meals for 7- to 10-day cruises leaving the coast of Alaska. Addressed and attended to all aspects of kitchen management, from shopping list and meal preparation to staffing and management relations to ensure guests received high-end treatment. Prepared meals from scratch using top-quality and the freshest ingredients that "wowed" passengers.

- Promoted to chef (from assistant chef) within 2 weeks of joining the ship

DIRECTOR, FOOD AND BEVERAGE, 1991–1998
East Coast Parks and Resorts, Columbia, SC
Secured a number of promotions, from bar and pizza manager to a food and beverage management position and finally to a director position. Managed and supervised 80–190 employees at a food and beverage facility with up to $500,000 in monthly sales.

- Authored the Loss Control Program that focused on, informed, and trained on-site personnel in key OSHA safety standards

SOFTWARE

MS Word, MS Publisher, MS Excel, Lotus Notes, WordPerfect, SYSFLEX, Micros, Labor Pro, GS Order

presented as scannable keywords. In the Professional Experience section, both the paragraphs and the bulleted items under each workplace contain achievements as well as responsibilities.

Richard Johnson

2222 Indiana Avenue
Ocean Shores, WA 98343

(360) 888-1234
rjohnson3241@aol.com

GENERAL MANAGER
Hospitality – Class 3 Casinos – AAA Hotels – Fine Dining – New Venture Start-ups

Senior Hospitality Manager with more than 10 years of broad-based leadership history in gaming, luxury hotel management and fine-dining operations. *Strengths:* Finding efficiencies, motivating teams and creating on-time results.

Fast-track promotion record through all aspects of leading and operating large service-oriented businesses. Hands-on management style. Multitask easily. Strong supervisory, analytical, computer, and process-improvement skills.

Highly effective leader, guiding all business cycles: start-up, turnaround and stabilization. Proven ability to streamline systems, drive revenues, shrink staff turnover, build customer loyalty and restore profit centers. Expertise includes:

- **Design & Construction**
- **Policies, Staffing & Performance**
- **Food & Beverage**
- **Start-ups & Turnarounds**
- **Facilities & Security**
- **Regulatory Compliance**
- **IT & Communications Systems**
- **Marketing & Community Relations**
- **Vendor Management / Full P&L**

Professional Experience

HIGHLAND CASINO, Ocean Shores, WA   2000–present
Director, Support Services

Retained as part of a 5-person board and fast-track senior start-up team to plan, budget, design, license, contract, and open a $10 million class 3 casino in less than eight months.

Report to Chairman of the Board. Oversee all non-revenue functions (Housekeeping, Engineering, IT, Security, and Human Resources) for the largest casino in the state, operating 300 slot machines, 6 gaming tables, a full restaurant, a lounge with tabletop games and a bar with live entertainment 3 times a week.

Facilities, Security, IT & Construction Management: Selected vendors and negotiated contracts. Originated and monitored project budgets. Acted as sole point of contact for more than 50 vendors and contractors during construction phase, ensuring quality construction, promised price, and timely delivery of all construction services, communication systems (IT, security, telephones and cameras), hard lines, furniture and fixtures. Arranged construction and configuration for a 5,000-stall parking lot.

Regulatory Compliance: Quickly learned requirements posed by 3 casino regulators: National Indian Gaming Association (NIGA), Washington State Gambling Commission, and the Quilcene Tribe. Responded to 3 sets of requirements, writing policy and procedures manuals for each regulatory body. Addressed requests for further information, made revisions and successfully processed all licensing requirements in a tight 6-month period.

Staffing, Leadership & Human Resources: Manage 3 supervisors and 2 managers, overseeing a 46-person staff. Monitored the hiring for all personnel, pre-employment testing and establishment of all human resources procedures and policies. Trained all staff members in accordance with Casino Procedures Manual and Washington State Gambling Commission rules. Maintain positive relationships with the community and local law enforcement bodies.

- Handled buildout and securing of entitlements for $10 million casino, opening on time and under budget.

- Authored Standard Operating Procedures manual for casino, complying with 3 regulatory bodies.

- Commended by state as being the only casino in recent history to achieve regulatory review, compliance and licensing as scheduled and budgeted. Performed role as part of a tightly-knit 5-person management team.

97

Alice Hanson, Seattle, Washington

The contact information is presented in a balanced format, and the profile includes bold and bulleted areas of expertise. Boldfacing makes it easy to spot the positions held at the two workplaces.

Professional Employment (continued)

EXECUTIVE SUITES HOTEL, Seattle, WA 1992–2000

Privately held, AAA-rated, 3-star, 400-suite luxury hotel encompassing award-winning restaurant, high-energy nightclub, full-service banquet and catering facilities and 130 employees.

Assistant General Manager / Acting General Manager, 2000

Oversaw daily operations, including F&B Director and all internal financial reporting for the most profitable of 30 hotels held by Janus Capital Group in a 10-state region. Reported directly to the GM / Area Manager. Assumed decision-making and planning for facility, averaging 1 week out of every month, in GM's absence.

Accountable for revenues of $4 million, supervising performance of 10 department managers of the hotel's 12 departments, including Engineering, Housekeeping, Accounting, Front Office, Food and Beverage and Human Resources. Led by example. Built strong teams through improved recruiting and training. Complied with all local and federal laws. Managed security contracts and personnel.

Monitored and reviewed all department budget forecasts; P&L statements; STAR, promotions, marketing and sales projections; staffing plans; vendor contracts; and purchase log, inventory and expense reports. Identified and facilitated cost-saving measures with managers. Formulated short- and long-range marketing and budget plans for capital expenditures, construction / renovations and regular operations.

- Increased overall net revenues 6%, repeating 5-year record as top-producing hotel.
- Selected by Chief Operating Officer to serve on the elite Janus Capital Group Standing Committee, creating operations and food and beverage "best practice" policies for all 30 hotels.
- Reduced employee turnover 66%.
- Standardized and computerized purchase order tracking system, creating centralized managerial approval of all costs, accounting efficiencies and adherence to projected budgets.
- Incurred the fewest repair and maintenance costs company-wide.

Assistant General Manager / Food and Beverage Director, 1996–1999

Managed Food and Beverage Division, a vital profit center, producing 12% of the hotel's overall net revenues. Oversaw food service quality and profitability for 7 departments: kitchen, restaurant, lounge, banquet, comp breakfast, comp bar and suite service.

Oversaw quality and service of products within F&B outlets. Developed, marketed, rewrote and produced 8 weekly menus for restaurant, lounge and banquet service. Offered complimentary full cooked-to-order breakfast, Northwest casual fine dining, lunch and dinners in busy state-of-the-art kitchen facility.

Managed food, beverage and room items related to banquet service with banquet room that seated 350 diners, 500 theater-style, and provided 10,000 square feet of meeting space.

- Monitored food costs, producing lowest food cost budget in the company.
- Realized company's second-highest net beverage income figures for three years running.
- Increased sales 34% by upgrading menu. Won Executive Suites cuisine award for customer satisfaction.
- Contributed 60% of division's revenues by revitalizing banquet business.

Other Executive Suites positions: **Front Office Manager,** 1996; **Restaurant, Lounge and Banquet Manager,** 1993–1995; **Executive Chef,** 1993, and **Sous Chef,** 1992.

CERTIFICATIONS

Washington State Health Card Trainer   CPR Trained, July 2000   Sersafe Certified Trainer #000000000
Class 12, Class 13 Liquor Awareness Certification   Washington State Gambling Commission

EDUCATION AND TRAINING

Seattle Central Community College, Seattle, WA. Food Production Management Certificate and Hospitality Production Certificate. Programs accredited by American Culinary Federation. GPA 3.5

Activities at the casino are grouped according to underlined categories. Bulleted items throughout the Professional Experience section point to achievements, many of them quantified. The resume ends with sections on Certifications and Education and Training.

SAMUEL PECKHAM, CHME, CSP

60 Augusta Drive
Pinehurst, Ontario A1A 1A1

555.222.7777
speckham@email.com

SENIOR SALES & MARKETING EXECUTIVE
SPECIALIST IN DRIVING HOTEL & HOSPITALITY PROFITABILITY

Business Development / Strategic Planning / Key Account Sales & Management
New-Market Development / Marketing Campaigns & Initiatives / Business Planning & Forecasting

---

Dynamic sales and marketing career driving consistent revenue gains in the hotel and hospitality industry throughout Canadian and U.S. markets. Comprehensive understanding of hotel operations, sales, and profitability. Achieved strong revenue, market, and profit growth through expertise in business development, executive-level sales, and creative marketing initiatives. Extensive expertise supported by professional certification in the following:

➢ National & Executive Sales Management	➢ Hospitality Marketing
➢ Hotel Management	➢ Travel & Tourism
➢ Food & Beverage Controls	➢ Dining Room & Catering Management

★ CERTIFIED HOSPITALITY MARKETING EXECUTIVE (CHME) ★
★ CERTIFIED SALES PROFESSIONAL (CSP) ★

PROFESSIONAL EXPERIENCE

CENTENNIAL FALLS RESORT HOTEL, Niagara Falls, Ontario
(Exclusive 260-room "boutique-style" hotel and Centennial's flagship hotel in Niagara)

DIRECTOR OF SALES   May 2002–Present
Directed the strategic repositioning of the hotel following a $17 million renovation. Hired to optimize operations and rebuild the strategy to ignite growth across Domestic, Corporate, and International sales.
> ➢ Profiled the entire Sales Division to identify key areas for improvement and refocus areas of strength. Introduced dedicated Corporate and Domestic Sales Managers and augmented training division-wide.
> ➢ Developed a comprehensive AAA/CAA Travel Trade database and quickly launched a new promotion to more than 500 AAA/CAA offices across Canada and the Northeastern U.S.
> ➢ Redesigned all critical Corporate marketing tools and collateral materials and introduced simplified sales forms and operational contracts to focus more directly on F&B revenue protection and product upselling.
> ➢ Introduced a successful Preferred Rate Program with the Pinehurst Professional Sales Association (PPSA).

SELECT HOTELS INTERNATIONAL, Pleasantville, Maryland (Head Office)
(Largest international franchise hotel organization with over 5,000 locations and sales in excess of U.S. $1 billion)

NATIONAL SALES DIRECTOR—WORLDWIDE SALES   1999–2002
Selected to develop key association and consortia accounts throughout Canada and the Midwest/Western U.S. (American Express, Rosenbluth, World Travel, and Carlson Wagonlit). Scope of responsibility included all Canadian and U.S. regional sales and marketing initiatives, strategic sales and market planning, and the coordination of a team of Field Service Directors across North America.
> ➢ Exceeded annual revenue projection by $1 million within first 6 months.
> ➢ Primary accountability for $60 million CAA/AAA account, the largest single revenue-producing leisure account in the company.
> ➢ Developed highly successful joint marketing initiative between AAA Nebraska, AAA Colorado, and Alberta Motor Association (AMA) that increased gross room nights by 81%, increased gross revenue by 77%, and secured largest market share (14.83%) of any hotel company with AMA.
> ➢ AAA/AMA joint marketing initiative nominated for 3 distinguished MARQ Awards. AAA Nebraska initiative recently awarded top prize in competitive SYC&S category.
> ➢ Created CAA/AMA promotion that increased revenue from a 9.83% decline to a positive growth of 21.5%.
> ➢ Introduced two successful national marketing events designed to recognize high-performing CAA partners.
> ➢ Developed and produced all collateral marketing and training materials for Choice Hotels Canada.

98

Ross Macpherson, Whitby, Ontario, Canada

The writer aggressively highlighted keywords, professional certification, and expertise up front to help this Executive position himself as an expert in his field. The resume has features found in many executive resumes: relatively small print, giving the appearance of reduced leading

SELECT HOTELS CANADA, Augusta, Ontario (Head Office)
(Largest hotel franchise organization in Canada, operating 250 locations nationally under 8 leading brands.)

NATIONAL SALES MANAGER—TRAVEL INDUSTRY & CORPORATE   1997–1999

Hired to spearhead introduction and development of new corporate and consortia account portfolio, while revitalizing growth of leisure accounts nationally. Coordinated all strategic sales and marketing initiatives, market analysis, incentive management, budget planning, and management of largest-volume corporate account portfolio.

➤ Developed sales and marketing initiatives, promotions, and market education that assisted the licensee in increasing Revpar and developing yield management techniques.
➤ Personally secured 30 key corporate accounts from ground zero within 2 years.
➤ Grew major Quixstar/Amway corporate account by 2000% within 1 year.
➤ Generated exponential growth and dramatically improved product awareness within leisure market through aggressive sales and marketing strategies.

REGENCY VACATIONS, Augusta, Ontario
(Boutique travel business servicing high-end personal and corporate clients throughout Greater Niagara.)

PRINCIPAL / SALES & MARKETING DIRECTOR   1991–1997

Successfully built business from start-up into solid revenue generator with 2 years. Developed strategic direction, built infrastructure, and initiated all marketing, image development, sales, and public relations directives.

➤ Identified and capitalized on market trends through highly successful direct mail, presentations, and local promotional campaigns.
➤ Dramatically increased revenues by successfully targeting and penetrating lucrative corporate market.
➤ Grew sales from $0 to $1.5 million in less than 18 months and quickly established position as industry leader throughout Niagara.

ADDITIONAL EXPERIENCE

HOUSEWARE FINANCIAL CORP., Augusta, Ontario—**FINANCIAL ACCOUNT EXECUTIVE**   1996–1997
➤ Awarded "Top Sales" Ontario wide and ranked 3rd across Canada.
AUGUSTA COLLEGE, Augusta, Ontario—**AIRLINE TRAINING INSTRUCTOR**   1988–1995
WORLDWAYS LTD., Pinehurst, Ontario—**IN-FLIGHT SERVICE MANAGER**   1985–1991

INDUSTRY CERTIFICATION & EDUCATION

Certified Hospitality Marketing Executive (CHME) —Hospitality Sales & Marketing Association   2003
Executive Program in Sales Management—Sabbath School of Business, Yorktown University   2001
Skills for Sales Success—Pinehurst Professional Sales Association   2001
Certified Sales Professional (CSP)—Pinehurst Professional Sales Association   1999
National Professional Sales Manager Certification—Ontario Tourism Education Inc. (OTEI)   1998
Travel & Tourism—Augusta Business School   1983
Hotel Management: Food & Beverage Controls / Dining Room & Catering Management—Augusta College   1982

INDUSTRY AFFILIATIONS

Hospitality Sales & Marketing Association International (HSMAI)   2003
Canadian Hotel Marketing & Sales Executives (CHMSE)—Ontario Chapter   1998–Present
Pinehurst Professional Sales Association (PPSA)   1998–Present
Ontario Tourism Education Corp. (OTEC)—Hospitality Sales Manager Industry Evaluator   1998–Present

(less space between lines); wide lines of text; a variety of font enhancements (boldfacing, bold italic, regular italic, all caps, and small caps); horizontal lines that define main sections; and bullets pointing to many achievements.

JAMES JOBSEEKER

000 Street Address
City, ST 55555

555-555-5555
info@resumeasap.com

GENERAL MANAGER—HOSPITALITY INDUSTRY

Offering Extensive Hotel and Restaurant Operations Experience

Accomplished manager offering 25+ years of hands-on experience in every facet of the hospitality industry. Solid understanding of business management; able to meet the needs of a fast-paced, high-turnover industry. Strong ability to assess operational needs and establish strategies that increase productivity, enhance customer satisfaction, and improve cost-effectiveness.

Respected leader known for improving quality and consistency by utilizing well-honed and proven team building and motivation skills. Excellent communicator who draws on finely tuned interpersonal skills to influence critical business decisions.

Computer proficient and familiar with several POS systems including Squirrel, PosiTouch, Micros, and NEC.

KEY SKILLS

- Operations Management
- Budget Control
- Cost Reduction Strategies
- Regulatory Compliance
- Facilities Management

- Policy Implementation
- Training and Development
- Workplace Safety
- Scheduling and Payroll
- Accounting / Bookkeeping

- Vendor Relations
- Ordering and Inventory
- Contract Negotiations
- Customer Service
- Conflict Resolution

PROFESSIONAL EXPERIENCE

UPSCALE RESTAURANT—City, ST
180-Seat Restaurant
Owner/Manager, 2003 to Present

- Launched new restaurant developing and implementing marketing and PR strategies to increase awareness and bring in business.
- Interviewed, hired, and trained all staff members; currently supervising 35 employees.
- Developed menu based on guest preferences and seasonal considerations.
- Sourced vendors and negotiated inventory costs.
- Standardized portions and implemented labor cost controls.
- Created, developed, and implemented all formal operational systems and procedures.
- Known for the highest quality food and best service within a 60-mile radius.

99

Jennifer Anthony, Woodland, Washington

The applicant was selling his restaurant to move out of state with his spouse, who had taken a new position. He wanted a resume for his own job search. He had too much information for one page but not enough for two full pages. The writer stretched the resume by using a slightly

JAMES JOBSEEKER

PROFESSIONAL EXPERIENCE CONTINUED...

PROPERTY NAME—City, ST
50-Room Resort Hotel, 190-Seat Restaurant, 150-Seat Lounge, and 80-Seat Bar.
Owner/Manager, 1993 to 2001

- Purchased restaurant with suffering revenues and increased income by 300% within the first two years by doing a complete remodeling project, negotiating prices with new vendors, and placing tighter controls on food and labor spending.

- Increased menu items to offer more variety, up from 42 to 80 items. Added "honored" menu.

- Collaborated with the city and the state to develop a strategy for redevelopment and restoration of the entire property (property is on the National Register of Historic Places).

EARLY CAREER HISTORY

MAJOR HOTEL CHAIN—City, ST
Experience includes opening a new property, major renovations, managing very large meeting facilities, financial analysis, budgeting, marketing, and sales.

Director of Food and Beverage, 1987 to 1992
500 Rooms, 3 Restaurants, 2 Bars, Banquet to 1500

Assistant Director of Food and Beverage, 1985 to 1987
250 Rooms, 2 Restaurants, 1 Bar, Banquet to 600

Banquet Manager, 1985 to 1987

Banquet Server/Shift Supervisor, 1982 to 1985

ADDITIONAL INFORMATION

- Founding Member <City> Tourism Bureau
- Rotary Club Member
- Board Member, <City> Area Chamber of Commerce
- Nominated on AOL's "City's Best" list 2006 and 2007.

larger font, adding lines to section headings, and creating more white space through wider top and bottom margins and wider space between lines and paragraphs and before section headings.

Michael J. Fisher, C.M.C.

56 Madison Avenue
Summit, New Jersey 07901
908-277-8796

Profile

Experienced Food Services Professional. Developed extensive management skills. Capable of speed and organization in a highly productive setting. Work cooperatively with a wide range of personalities. Successful executive chef and hotel/restaurant manager. Responsible for all aspects of culinary management catering to a discerning clientele. Ability to handle a multitude of details at once and meet deadlines under pressure.

Strengths and Abilities

- Profit and Loss
- Staffing and Supervision
- Forecasting
- Hotel/Restaurant Administration
- Training and Development
- Accounting and Controlling Functions

Experience

Hague Nieuw-York, New York, NY   1999–Present
Corporate Executive Chef/Promoted to General Manager

- Hague is a Dutch-style eatery that specializes in casual dining. The restaurant is part of Avanti Brands, owner of several well-known restaurant chains and the three top restaurants in London. Avanti Brands is partnered with Hague, PLC. Hired as corporate executive chef for North America. Developed key control systems and thorough inventory-control procedures.

- Responsible for the start-up of a 225-seat restaurant. Purchase all food and supplies. Manage a staff of 50 front-of-the-house, back-of-the-house, and marketing employees. Designed the facility and the kitchen, and coordinated all aspects of new construction with six professional trades during remodeling. Oversaw renovation of the entire property.

- Involved in yearly profit and loss and all financial reporting to Hague PLC, U.K., and Avanti Brands, Inc., USA. Accountable to the CEOs for accounting forecasting, projections, and cash flow. Develop all menus. Maintain a 27% cost of goods for beverages, wine and liquor, and food. The restaurant produces $4 million in yearly sales.

- Responsible for sales and marketing projections to attract target populations. Network with professional event planners to arrange major special-events functions. Involved in New York openings and premiers. Participate in large fashion shows for major designers and publishers. Oversee preparation of food for New York City food festivals.

- Travel internationally to the other locations to evaluate properties' performance. Worked in London and Dublin to facilitate a turnaround in failing restaurants. Studied Belgian cuisine in Brussels, Bruges, and Antwerp.

100

Beverly and Mitch Baskin, Marlboro, New Jersey

This resume is for an Executive Chef/General Manager. In the earlier part of his career, he was an Executive Chef, but in 1986 he assumed the dual roles of Executive Chef and Vice President of Operations. In 1990 his work shifted into management as Director of Operations of an upscale

Michael J. Fisher, C.M.C.   Page 2

Achievements

- Established direct purchase from farm to restaurant from Maine and Nova Scotia.
- Presented First Friday Dinner at James Beard House.
- Worked with advertising people to market in-house beer seminars.
- Appeared on national syndicated television with Martha Stewart on NBC.
- Scheduled to appear on NBC's *Today* show to promote the restaurant and present a cooking demonstration.
- Made appearances on radio.
- Revised U.K. version of *Hague Cook Book* to include Signature Dishes Nieuw-York.
- Hague was reviewed in the *New York Times*.

Times Square Restaurant, Hoboken, NJ   1995–1999

Town Square Katering, Dover, NJ   1990–1999

Director of Operations

- Managed an upscale catering business and operated all phases of an American Cuisine theme restaurant. Obtained bookings for parties ranging from 10 to 4,000 people.

- Purchased all food and restaurant supplies. Responsible for marketing, purchasing, and directing 75+ kitchen staff, service staff, and maintenance employees.

- Combined Katering Operation still known as Town Square Katering with Times Square Restaurant (80 seats). Designed kitchen and restaurant layouts. Directed all kitchen, service, sales, and management.

- Taught Cooking School—Basic & Advanced & Pastry Courses M-W-F (weekly).

Pine Ridge Golf Course and Restaurant   1986–1989

Vice President of Operations
Executive Chef—American and International Cuisine

- Oversaw in excess of 10 department heads for both corporations. Responsible for profit and loss, including all accounting and controlling functions. Monitored capital expenditures of $350,000 with a gross of $4.5 million.

- Directed 152 employees and all administrative functions, including forecasting, budgeting, marketing, advertising, entertainment, and promotions.

- Directed a 1,000-seat banquet facility and a 165-seat a la carte restaurant. Responsible for operations of an 850-member golf club. Maintained excellent interpersonal relationships with members.

- Monitored standards of performance for all key control systems. Involved in developing a standard operations manual and employee manual.

catering business. His dual roles of Executive Chef and General Manager emerged again in 1999, and both were aspects of his career to the present. To gain a sense of his career path, you should read the resume from the end to the beginning. The Profile and Strengths and Abilities sections play up the person's management

Michael J. Fisher, C.M.C.   Page 3

Ordini's, Wellington, New Zealand   Prior to 1986
Executive Chef (Five-Star Rating) New Classical Cuisine
- Elevated the level of cuisine and service with a clientele including the Prime Minister, heads of state, and visiting dignitaries. Restaurant was booked 4 months in advance with a 50-seat cover.

Sheraton Corporation, *Executive Pastry Chef,* Kaanapali, Maui, Poipu Beach Kauai, Hawaii
Lahaina Yacht Club, *Executive Chef,* Lahaina, Maui, Hawaii
Summit Hotel, *Executive Chef,* Summit, New Jersey

Education

A.O.S. Culinary Institute of America, Hyde Park, NY

Awards

New Zealand Master Chef Certification
Certified Executive Chef
President, Les Amis d' Escoffier Society of New York, Inc.
Member, Société Culinaire Philanthropique De New York, Inc.

1988 NJRA Award-Winning Menus
    First Place   Best Banquet Menu
    Second Place Best a la Carte Menu

expertise. White space between the main sections and also between the bulleted items in the Experience section makes the layout pleasing. See Cover Letter 6.

Human Resources

Resumes at a Glance

WAYNE AYE

Location: Primarily the East Coast and CN
Address available upon request.

Phone: (703) 264-1171
Email: WayneAye@hotmail.com

CAREER PROFILE

METAPHYSICAL MEDIA / COMMUNICATIONS & PRODUCTION

Objective: To bring knowledge, creativity, and communication to the field of media and metaphysical science.

Well-versed consultant and speaker with 20 years of experience in media production and personal development. Strong track record and wins in every job held. Creative resource with diverse experiences. Motivated by variety and challenge. Outstanding communicator and collaborator.

➢ Extensive documentation and presentations to corporate, university, human potential, and Native American audiences.

➢ Knowledge areas in motivation, realization of human potential, the human side of productivity, and consciousness in creating.

➢ Direct experience in television and radio. Able to shape, manage, and deliver coordinated programming and motivate people to action. Strong desire to make a difference.

Strong interest in documentaries and media productions on human potential, the mind/psyche, Native American myths and practices, shamanism, motivation, energy, and the metaphysical.

TOP SKILLS

➢ Presentations & Programming
➢ Satisfying Diverse Audiences
➢ Program Development & Marketing
➢ Media Production & Oversight

➢ Communication & Motivation
➢ Creativity & Collaboration
➢ Research & Documentation
➢ Motivational Training & Coaching

CAREER HIGHLIGHTS

Experienced with all forms of media—from books to film production, as follows:

TV & RADIO MEDIA

➢ **Regular radio guest** on CFRB (Canada) and other radio stations on the East Coast. Discussed taking responsibility for shaping our own lives—and owning our own dissatisfactions, so that we can take action.

➢ **Featured guest** with a top morning-radio host in Canada. Interviewed about the sweat lodge and past-life regression, and the benefits of both.

➢ **Featured TV guest** on "The Prosperity Show" and other TV shows for a decade, on personal development, life leadership, and human potential.

➢ Currently volunteering to help start up a radio station, to strengthen production experience.

PRODUCTION & MARKETING

➢ **Coproduced a series** of 7 meditations on stillness and relaxation.
   ★ **Wrote the script** and created the meditations.
   ★ **Designed and created the artwork,** labels, and inserts for the packaging—and planned and executed the marketing. Drew on my experience in sales and commercial photography.
   ★ **Did 4 annual book signings** and presentations at the Lily Dale center in NY.
   ★ **Collaborated with the studio technician** to record and coproduce the CD series, marketed as "Visualization for Growth." Sold 10K copies in North America.

➢ **Executed a three-tiered marketing plan of** web-based marketing, catalog distribution (through an agent), and big-name bookstores, and alternative centers. Also did signings and presentations at Unicorn Books, The White Light, The Omega Centre, and Lily Dale Books.

➢ **Marketed series** to Native Americans to teach about their own tradition of sweats for healing the past. Adopted for use by The Institute for Native Advancement.

101

Helen Oliff, Reston, Virginia

This former chemistry student looked away from chemical engineering recruitment and toward the development of human potential. After 20 years of self-employment, experience as a TV and radio guest and producer, and early experience as a Career Placement Specialist and Recruiter, the

WAYNE AYE

Résumé—Page Two

RECENT WORK HISTORY	WAYNE AYE PRODUCTIONS (WAP)—East Coast and CN **Motivational Speaker & Publisher,** 1985 to Present Launched and managed a practice focused on human potential and motivation. Performed all product development, marketing, and service for this business. ➤ Spoke to more than 500 audiences in 20 years—with 25 to 700 participants. Emphasized the effect of personal responsibility on career and life motivation and satisfaction. ➤ Presented on relaxation and empowerment at trade shows—in between working the WAP booth. ➤ Helped open and widen the business mind-set toward relaxation and meditation in the workplace. ➤ Published periodic newsletters for nearly 10,000 subscribers.
DIVERSITY OF EXPERIENCE & INTERESTS	*Developed multiple pockets of specialized metaphysical knowledge—in topics of current interest—by facilitating or actively participating in all the following:* ➤ Motivation and personal development ➤ Meditation and relaxation techniques—and their benefits ➤ Sweat lodges and talking circles—and their benefits ➤ Healing the past and creating the future ➤ The effects of the mind on reality and realization of potential ➤ Energy and personal energy utilization
EARLY EXPERIENCE	AGRICHEM STAFFING—East Coast and Canada **Career Placement Specialist & Recruiter** Recruited and placed sales, marketing, and scientific executives in top-100 agricultural and environmental companies. ➤ Placed more than 300 executives in 15 years—by matching "people with people." ➤ Worked primarily with the environmental-protection, industrial-chemical, and wastewater-treatment sectors—growth markets in Canada. ➤ Interviewed, hired, and fired employees on-site, locally and across the U.S., for clients. ➤ Transitioned disengaged employees into outplacement and assisted them personally. ➤ Collaborated with senior managers at Hoechst, Alchem (now Nalco), Betz, Monsanto, and other agricultural or environmental leaders. ➤ Developed career paths for agricultural and environmental candidates and aligned them with selected companies. INDUSTRIAL CHEMICALS—PA **Sales Representative** Managed sales territories for industrial and commercial chemicals and specially formulated products. ➤ Managed relationships with management and buyers of chemical products. ➤ Coordinated extensive sales trips and actively participated and presented at trade shows.
Training & Education	Professional training in presentations, sales, motivation, writing, productivity, and leadership. Specialized training in radio production, as a volunteer with CFRB in Canada. Early studies in chemistry at Pennsylvania State University (60 hours completed).

Contact Data—E-mail: WayneAye@hotmail.com | Phone: (703) 264-1171

applicant and the writer forged this resume, targeting media and production related to human potential, Native American healing traditions, and so on. The resume attests to his diversity.

SHEILA PARKER, SPHR

16222 Settlers Way • Sugar Land, TX 77479
(555) 555-5555 • sparker210@yahoo.com

HUMAN RESOURCES MANAGEMENT

—More Than 13 Years of Management Experience, Including 10+ in Human Resources—
—Completed "Conducting an Effective Internal Investigation" Seminar in 1998 & 1999—
—Strong Knowledge of EEO, Affirmative Action, ADA, OSHA, and Other Employment Laws—

Consistent track record of maintaining extremely thorough documentation to protect organizations against legal action and audit findings. Well-versed in HR generalist and organizational development functions. Interact effectively with staff members from diverse backgrounds and at various career levels, from senior management to administrative/technical team members. Additional knowledge and skill areas include

- Procedures & Policies Design/Integration
- Benefits & Compensation Implementation
- Regulatory Compliance Files & Records
- Human Resources Information Systems
- Employee Relations & Team Building

- Information Gathering & Report Writing
- Performance Evaluation & Management
- Internal & External Investigative Functions
- Federal, State & Local Employment Laws
- Statistical Collection, Analysis & Reporting

PROFESSIONAL EXPERIENCE

FALSTAFF, INC.—Houston, TX

Director of Human Resources (1999–2009)

Oversaw all HR functions for staff of 155. Negotiated and administered health, dental, life, disability, liability, and occupational injury insurances, implemented employee recognition and benefits programs (including 401(k) and ESOP), and developed policies/procedures for all departments and functions. Ensured compliance with federal and state laws, including FLSA, OSHA, EEOC, Affirmative Action, COBRA, FLMA, ADA, HIPAA, FTA, and DOT regulations. Conducted research for HR matters, including employee requests for additional information.

- **Internal Investigations**—Conducted multiple investigations throughout 5-year period, ranging from minor to escalated issues. Maintained perfect record in addressing/resolving concerns, with zero lawsuits.

- **External Audits**—Led department to achieve exemplary results on annual Texas audits (5 total), with zero findings and commendations for up-to-date record-keeping.

- **Staff Relationships**—Earned respect and trust from diverse workforce (including managers, administrative staff, drivers, and automotive technicians) through fair, yet firm, management.

XYZ COMMUNICATIONS—Boulder, CO

Project Coordinator (1998–1999)

In charge of creating database programs for technical team based on client specifications, serving as liaison between customers, sales, and technical staff to meet requirements. Configured systems, coordinated telecommunications, provided customer support, and conducted end-user training. Gained technical proficiency and knowledge of Norstar, Mitel, Nitsuko, Active Voice, and Tie products.

- **Employee & Customer Relations**—Held extensive Q&A sessions with executives and team members to determine actual vs. perceived needs, resulting in increased efficiency for telecom segment of business and improved management-employee relations.

Continued

102

Daniel J. Dorotik, Jr., Lubbock, Texas

This job searcher's career record, evident in reading the Professional Experience section from the end to the beginning, displays continual growth in knowledge and responsibilities, plus a minimum of complaints—a condition significant to an HR manager. The all-important opening

MARRIOTT—Denver, CO

Human Resources Manager (1994–1998)

Recruited to instill stability within HR function. Administered benefits, worker compensation, liability, and unemployment programs. Recruited, hired, and conducted orientation/training for all positions. Interpreted HR policies/procedures and trained management for compliance. Collected information and prepared thorough reports (e.g., EEO 1) to prevent cost- and time-consuming government audits.

- **Dispute Resolution**—Handled 2 EEO claims filed at beginning of tenure, securing dismissal for both through comprehensive research and discovery activities. Subsequently maintained record of zero employee complaints and no escalated grievances throughout remainder of tenure.

- **Team Building**—Coordinated employee relations activities and incentive/recognition programs to develop team unity and camaraderie, foster confidence in team members, and increase productivity.

- **Staff Development**—Delivered training for broad range of topics and issues, including sexual harassment, discrimination, workplace safety, OSHA requirements, and customer service, with wholly positive results.

OFFICE OF THE ATTORNEY GENERAL, STATE OF TEXAS—Austin, TX

Program Coordinator, Victim Rights & Witness Assistance (1991–1994)

Promoted from volunteer position to direct all aspects of department's volunteer program, including recruiting, hiring, training, supervision, evaluation, and retention. Established program policies and procedures, evaluated program performance, assisted in grant writing initiatives, and created reports on program statistics.

- **Policy Development**—Created methods for implementation of laws that ensured proper service for thousands of crime victims, including quick communications and easily understandable descriptions of their rights.

- **Program Retention**—Faced with potential loss of program, gathered/reported statistics, cowrote grant requests, and represented program effectively to responsible parties, sustaining program as a result.

PROFESSIONAL DEVELOPMENT

Human Resources Management Certification Program
TEXAS A&M UNIVERSITY, 2001

Additional Professional Training
Conducting an Effective Internal Investigation, McKinsey, 1998 & 1999
Human Resources Southwest Conference, 2000 & 2001
Multiple Continuing Education Courses, 1991–Present

Affiliations & Community Activities
- Society of Human Resources Management (SHRM): National and Houston Chapter, 1999–Present; Houston Chapter, Board Diversity Chair 2007 & 2008
- Goodwill Industries, Job Creations Program, Employer Advisory Committee, 2005–2008
- Leadership Houston: Class 2003; Steering Committee 2004 & 2005
- United Way, Program Review & Funding Allocation, 2004–2008
- Meals on Wheels Volunteer, 2000–2002

section serves as a profile and a summary of skills. Adequate white space and consistent use of boldface make headings, side headings, and subheadings easily visible.

Information Systems/Information Technology

Resumes at a Glance

JIM JOBSEEKER

555 Street Address
E-mail: info@resumeasap.com

Home: 555-555-5555
Cell: 000-000-0000

Uniquely qualified for positions as...

IT CONSULTANT ■ NETWORK ADMINISTRATOR

Hands-on experience and solid foundation in network administration and workstation setup/troubleshooting. Experience establishing security protocols for employees and expertise in hardware/software issues, analysis, installation, maintenance, and support. Able to resolve quickly and accurately various functionality issues. Adept in technology skills with the ability to quickly learn, master, and apply new technical concepts. Articulate communicator, adept in conveying complex issues to nontechnical groups. Excel in project management and problem-solving roles.

TECHNICAL KNOWLEDGE AND EXPERTISE

OS/Environments: Windows 95/98/2000/XP; 2000 and 2003 Server; NetWare 6.5; Linux

Software: ACT; Bloomberg; Thompson One; ILX; Reuters Plus; Triton; Microsoft Office; VMware Workstation/Server; Backup Exec; pcAnywhere; VNC

Hardware: PCs; servers; motherboards; hard drives; tape library backup solutions; SCSI drives; memory; peripherals; expansion cards; PDA devices (Palm, Treo, Blackberry)

Networking: TCP/IP, IPX/SPX, VPN, DHCP, DNS, FTP, HTML, POP, SMTP

PROFESSIONAL EXPERIENCE

COMPANY NAME—City, ST—4/2005 to Present
IT Consultant / Project Management Assistant
o   Partner with clients to overcome their business challenges through the application of technology, determining their needs, defining the scope of the project, and recommending practical solutions.
o   Design, test, install, and monitor new systems or applications for clients.
o   Training other IT consultants on ACT! (specifically the networking aspects of the application).

COMPANY NAME—City, ST—5/2003 to 6/2004
Network Administrator
o   Created IT department; upgraded network to handle more clients and wrote computer usage policies on security and maintenance.
o   Provided end-user support for applications such as MS Office, Day-Timer, ACT, and QuickBooks.
o   Prepared remote connections using VPN and performed regular backups of file server and databases.

COMPANY NAME—City, ST—5/2002 to 5/2003
PC Tech / Network Administrator
o   Managed special project involving digitizing 1,200 folders for archiving.
o   Established security protocols to be followed by all employees, maintained peer-to-peer network, and conducted weekly backups.

EDUCATION AND TRAINING

Microsoft
C E R T I F I E D
Professional

VOCATIONAL SCHOOL—City, ST—5/2002
Major: MCSE, A+

VOCATIONAL SCHOOL—City, ST—12/1999
Certificate: Computer Programming

103

Jennifer Anthony, Woodland, Washington

This resume is the writer's remake of an older resume that had been updated many times. It contained much work experience that was irrelevant. New technical knowledge is put first.

Shultz Griggs
Computer Professional

1234 Valentine Street
Towers, WA 71234
Mobile Phone: (777) 777-7000
Fax: (777) 777-7001
email: Schultzie@email.com

Established reputation for expertise within the computer industry—more than 25 years of experience.
Personable, conscientious, resourceful.
Strong aptitude for learning.
Willing to relocate.

EXPERTISE

- Set up, configure, enhance, upgrade, and support computers, computer systems, and peripherals—including server clusters and networks.

- Develop custom software for clients; resolve software compatibility issues.

- Develop programs that interface with computer-controlled test equipment.

- EXPERT in use, installation, configuration, troubleshooting, and problem-solving of the following:

Software

Operating systems: Windows NT 4.0, Windows XP, Windows 2000 Pro, Windows 95/98, and Windows 3.1; exposure to UNIX (various) and Linux

Protocols: TCP/IP, NetBIOS, and NetBEUI

Applications: MS Word 2002, MS Excel 2002, MS Access, MS Outlook, Photoshop, Macromedia Dreamweaver, MS FrontPage, Adobe PageMaker, MS Visual C++ 6.0, MS Visual Basic 6.0, MS J++, and Borland JBuilder

Languages: C++, C, BASIC, HTML, Java, JavaScript, XML, and Assembly Language

Hardware

Desktop computers and small to midsize servers

HP servers, workstations, and RAID products; Adaptec SCSI and Fiber Channel Controllers; 3COM hubs, switches, and network cards; and SMC hubs and network cards

IDE, SCSI, and Fiber Channel hard disk drives and tape backup products from various manufacturers. Exposure to SAN and NAS storage devices.

EXPERIENCE

Computer Professional, Computer Service, Towers, WA   1991–present

Evaluated, tested, and recommended networking, storage, and server hardware to clients; provided problem resolution for MIS departments. Developed testing methods to ensure reliability and compatibility; performed testing of computer, storage, and networking products. Configured new computer, network, and storage hardware for clients. Installed and configured operating systems and drivers for workstations and servers. Configured server clusters, network software, RAID arrays, and other storage options. Aided clients with operating system and application upgrade rollouts. Undertook small to medium-size customer software development projects.

- *Major clients included* Texaco, Alcoa Aluminum, County Community College, City of Towers, and State University.

Lead Programmer, Rioters Insurance Group, Wooden, WA   1982–1991

Managed the development, installation, and support of software applications used by banks and automobile dealers. Provided technical support by phone for software. Installed and configured networking hardware and software on site. Resolved software problems on site.

- *Exemplary accomplishments:* Developed applications in C and BASIC to perform loan calculations and to print forms and contracts; developed algorithms to calculate various types of loans; developed basic email system for loan approval.

CERTIFICATIONS / EDUCATION

CompTIA A+ in progress; Network+ in progress; Microsoft MCSE in progress

State University, B.S. Program, Major in Technology and Mathematics
Community College, A.S. Program, Electronics and Technology

104

Janice Shepherd, Bellingham, Washington

Instead of a horizontal line above each section heading to divide the resume into three sections, the two horizontal lines have the effect of enclosing the Expertise section and calling attention to it.

JOHN WILLIAMS

382 White Elm Road • Unionville, NJ 07083
(222) 222-2222 • jwilliams@aol.com

Hands-on network engineer with strengths in diagnostic troubleshooting and customer satisfaction

SUMMARY OF QUALIFICATIONS

- More than 11 years in technical-support positions, including nearly one year as a network engineer.
- Skilled in configuring, networking, and troubleshooting computer systems in Windows NT & Novell environments.
- Outstanding diagnostic skills. Systematic and methodical in solving problems.
- Very strong work ethic with demonstrated commitment to providing outstanding customer service.
- Easy-going and accommodating personality. Known for going the extra mile to get the job done.

TECHNICAL SKILLS

Operating Systems: DOS, Windows NT 4.0, Windows XP
Software: Microsoft Office XP, NetWare, ProjectWise, Honeywell, proprietary refinery applications
Networking Protocols: TCP/IP, NetBEUI
Certifications: Microsoft Certified Professional

EXPERIENCE

<u>United Oil</u>, Port Murray, New Jersey   2002 to present
Contract IT Support Specialist
Provide on-site hardware and software support for 130 users throughout refinery. As part of two-person support team, build and network computer systems, install and configure software, and troubleshoot and repair all computer problems.

- Established reputation for prompt and effective response to service requests from customers, guaranteeing continued operation of workstations, servers, and refinery computer systems. Systematically troubleshoot problems to ensure quick and accurate resolution, collecting high customer satisfaction ratings.
- Effectively resolved problem with software used to allow remote downloads to networked computers, conducting research to identify possible causes and then pinpointing and addressing the source problem.
- Developed strong rapport with users, earning recognition as the "go-to" support person among users.
- Created Access database application to track inventory of computers and peripherals, monitor purchases and costs, and optimize allocation of computer resources.
- Effectively used ghost software to create and update machine images, improving speed and accuracy of custom computer configurations.

<u>ACS</u>, South Hills, New Jersey   1999 to 2002
Repair Technician
Provided on-site and in-house technical support for this distributor of automated warehouse equipment. Installed and repaired computer-based warehouse equipment and power supplies, effectively diagnosing problems.

- Worked closely with customer to determine and review scope and cost of repair projects.
- Consistently completed projects in accordance with established deadlines and customer expectations.

<u>PT Technologies</u>, South Hills, New Jersey   1997 to 1998
Repair Technician
Assembled, tested, and repaired telephone and peripheral equipment for this leading telecommunications firm.

- Worked with technicians and engineers to resolve complex technical problems. Trained new technicians.

<u>General Nissan</u>, Freeport, New York   1991 to 1996
Service Representative
Provided technical and customer support functions for this automobile dealership.

- Serving as liaison, interacted with customers to assess needs and recommend appropriate services.

EDUCATION & TRAINING

<u>Computer Institute</u>, Newark, New Jersey
Network Engineering Diploma, October 2000
- ✓ As part of team, networked classroom computers and effectively diagnosed problems introduced by instructor.
- ✓ Configured client workstations, servers, and peripherals.
- ✓ Gained hands-on experience in LAN/WAN configurations, hubs, routers, and networking protocols.

<u>Technical Institute</u>, Woodridge, New Jersey
Digital Electronic Technician Certificate

105

Carol A. Altomare, Three Bridges, New Jersey

This one-page resume offers much information through small type (10-point Perpetua) and narrower top and bottom margins. Note the use of bold, bold italic, italic, small caps, and underlining.

BRADLEY CUMMINGS
90 Parkway Road
Croton, NY 55555
555.555.9866
irwcu45@compuserv.com

Profile

Computer Operations Professional

- Skilled technical professional with 6 years of computer operations experience in mainframe systems, as well as leading and training staff.
- Desktop support includes installation and troubleshooting of PC hardware, operating systems and software applications.
- Recognized by management for dedication, strong service orientation and consistent record of quality performance.

Technical Skills

Hardware/operating systems: IBM 3083 and ES/9000; IBM 3880 disk drives; IBM 3203 printers; IBM-PC compatibles; Windows 97, 2000 and XP

Software: MVS, JES2, IDMS, CICS, PANVALET, TSO, DOS, MS Office (Word, Excel, PowerPoint and Access)

Programming languages: JCL, COBOL

Experience

HARTWELL INDUSTRIES, Croton, NY   1990 to present
Computer Operator (1998 to present)

Promoted to computer operator in Information Systems with oversight of 3 other operators on IBM ES/9000 mainframe system, using MVS, JES2, IDMS, CICS, PANVALET and TSO. Generate timely reports to all departments; perform daily and weekly system backups.

- Provide first-level technical support to internal users and monitor hardware to ensure effective operations.
- Selected to lead a continuous improvement team to enhance computer operations efficiency.
- Train and develop new operators in system procedures and processes.
- Support users on PC hardware, operating systems (Windows XP) and software (MS Office products) installation and troubleshooting.

Tape Librarian (1990 to 1998)

Performed all tape library functions to support daily computer operations in a timely manner.

- Monitored and filed tape media for midrange operations; scanned tapes for vaulting.
- Assisted with disaster recovery and media handling for backup/recovery operations.
- Maintained up-to-date documentation of tape and library operations.
- Supported customer requests for off-site storage or other needs.

Education

Certificate in Computer Technology/Programming, 1995
Dutchess Community College, Croton, NY

106

Louise Garver, Windsor, Connecticut

This person had only a certificate but wanted to apply for an internal position that would be a promotion. To offset his lack of education, the writer showcased his experience and technical skills.

TERRENCE C. JONES

99 Madison Street • North Andover, MA • 55555
Office: 555-555-5555
Email: Jones@massmainframesoftware.com

IT CONSULTING & STRATEGY: MAINFRAME COMMERCIAL SOFTWARE
CONSULTING • SUPPORT • APPLICATION DEVELOPMENT • TRAINING

Mainframe Technology Consultant with 20+ years of success in project management and mainframe systems programming and applications development

High-level strategic vision, strong business perspective, and deep detail-level technology expertise

VALUE OFFERED

Rapid-access, quick-response technology solutions to save downtime & cut costs

• • •

Comprehensive enterprise solutions in mainframe environments

• • •

Mainframe systems software design, development, & fixes

• • •

Software solutions for enterprise output management systems

• • •

JES2 / JES3 interfaces

• • •

Assembly language programming

• • •

z/OS systems software

CAPABILITIES STATEMENT

One-stop provider offering full design and development services for mainframe software solutions from innovative application concept development and programming, through project management, to long-term support.

Provide a comprehensive, 360-degree viewpoint for IT strategy within the mainframe environment. Combine bottom-line business perspective with superior technical competencies. Strong specialized expertise in the enterprise output management market. Build long-term relationships with clients, including Fortune 100 companies.

REPRESENTATIVE CONSULTING PROJECTS

• Developed FSS and SAPI Toolkits to translate JES spool files. These interfaces are **foundational intellectual property used in commercial software throughout the corporate world—Mainframe Software Services, Inc.**

• Designed/Developed/Implemented software to maximize timely, secure data throughput. **Eliminated need for mainframe staff and created new revenue stream—Boston Software Associates.**

• Streamlined mainframe operation, **drastically increasing output** while insourcing a variety of functions and netting substantial cost savings—**Wilson Software Systems / Chicago Software.**

• **Salvaged multimillion-dollar technology development at the 11th hour:** Developed FSS interface, enabling mainframe-to-print server communication when print facility was moved to remote location **with zero-downtime.** Enhancements also vastly increased user-friendliness—**Charles Investments.**

PROFESSIONAL HISTORY

As Managing Partner of Mainframe Software Services, Inc. (N. Andover, MA) since 1997, hold full P&L responsibility for this niche IT consultancy. Direct and train flexible team of up to 20 technicians, providing clients with strategic technical solutions and rapid response at 1st, 2nd, and 3rd levels of support.

Representative list of clients: [High name recognition software companies.]

Previous employment:

Solid Resources (1988–1997): Systems Programmer / Consultant
Cabot Jewelry, Inc. (1985–1988): ALC Programmer / Systems Programmer
IIT Inc. (1984–1985): COBOL Programmer / Systems Programmer
FoodKing (1981–1984): Computer Operator / Junior Programmer
Mass. Commerce Bank (1980–1981): Computer Operator

107

Jean Cummings, Concord, Massachusetts

This applicant received a bachelor's degree not long before this resume was created, so virtually all of the information pertains to his career before he received the degree. Borders around the box and columns on the first page, and around the page itself on the second page, tie the two

TERRENCE C. JONES

REPRESENTATIVE CONSULTING PROJECTS

Challenge #1—**Cabot Jewelry, Inc.:** Previously, the company had outsourced credit-information verification required for each sale. Customers tired of the long wait for credit approval opted to make purchases elsewhere.

Actions: Negotiated buy-in from management to purchase hardware and move this function in-house. Wrote applications to configure verification process, developing both front-end and back-end configurations. Delivered system in time for Christmas sales season.

Results: **Saved corporation millions of dollars in service bureau usage costs and lost customer sales in first holiday season alone.**

Challenge #2—**Softsolve, independent software vendor:** To develop multitasking capability on a CICS platform on which users had to shut down operations each time they needed to add FCT entries.

Action: Designed, developed, and implemented an innovative Dynamic FCT support.

Results: **Beat IBM by five years** in enabling users to add entries seamlessly while operations remained active. Increased system availability and reduced operational errors.

Challenge #3—**Andover Resources:** To rescue IBM mainframe prior to its planned obsolescence in order to reduce operational costs.

Action: Brought in to implement one final upgrade after mainframe experts had abandoned a key upgrade effort. Led team of programmers in the seemingly undoable upgrade of OS/390, ADABAS, DB2, and all OEM software.

Results: **Achieved full, named "impossible" upgrade in allotted 4 months.** Enabled client to correct multiple operational issues before migration, allowing streamlined support for new system and saving labor costs.

Challenge #4—**TierOne, leading identity management software provider:** To rescue client from major hardware failure that disabled OS.

Actions: Moved quickly to restore mainframe OS; reconfigured software.

Results: **Minimized productivity losses due to mainframe downtime.** Served as a 24/7 resource for both systems programming and software development for a fraction of the costs of employing an employee.

CONSULTING SERVICES OFFERED

Project Management ▪Systems Programming ▪Applications Development ▪Professional Services / Presales Support ▪CICS / Transaction Server Installation, Configuration, Diagnosis, Repair, and Support ▪Networking Support ▪Database Support ▪USS / Websphere / JAVA Configuration and Development

TECHNOLOGY SUMMARY

Hardware: 370 Series, 30XX Series, 43XX Series, 308X Series, 309X Series, ES/9000, 390 Series, 9672, P/390, R/390, Integrated Server, MP3000, Z900 Series, Sysplex, AMDAHL 58XX, IBM 37XX, AMDAHL 47XX communications, various protocol converters, and personal computers.

Operating Systems: OS/VS2, MVS/SP, MVS/XA, MVS/ESA, OS/390, Z/OS, VM, VM/SP, DOS/VSE, VSE/ESA, SSX

Software Products: POWER, JES2, JES3, ACF/VTAM, ACF/NCP, TCP/IP, CICS, CICS/VS, CICS/MVS, CICS/ESA, TRANSACTION SERVER, IMS/DB, IMS/DC, PANVALET, LIBRARIAN, OMEGAMON, ROSCOE, SAS, VSAM, SYNCSORT, DFSORT, TSO, ISPE, PDF, SDSF, ENDEVOR, UCC1, UCC7, ISAM, BDAM, BTAM, IMS/DB, CA-INTERTEST, EXPEDITER, CA-VERIFY, CA-DADS, CAFC, FILE-AID, ABEND-AID, SUPER/SESSION, TPX, CA-ACF2, RACF, CA-TOP-SECRET, DB2, ADABAS, NATURAL, NETPASS, ODE, PLATINUM UTILITIES, DATA INTERCHANGE, SMARTBATCH, BATCHPIPES

Languages: ALC, COBOL, REXX, CLIST, C/C++, Java

---

pages together visually. Shading in the box and at the top of the first column on the first page gives the resume added appeal. The Technology Summary on page 2 is an impressive end.

WEB DESIGNER • WEBMASTER

i n t e r n e t   &   i n t r a n e t   s o l u t i o n s   •   c r e a t i v e   •   b u s i n e s s - f o c u s e d

Vibrant web design professional driving design innovations, implementations, and long-term strategies and projects for maximum business exposure. Distinctively creative—engaging a rich mix of conventional and contemporary ideas that seamlessly integrate with business image, market trends, demographics, and current business climates. Gregarious, expressive, and diligent; expert in inspiring others to build on ideas, refine concepts, and connect in a spirit of consensus and imagination. Acknowledged "firefighter"—able to steer projects through the inevitable minefields of issues, changing priorities, and disparate viewpoints for on-time and on-budget project completion. Reputed for visually appealing design, smart content, crisp layouts and navigation, and delivering improved efficacy, quality, and functionality.

professional strengths

- Client Relationship Management
- Stakeholder Management
- Graphic Design & Programming
- Research and Evaluation
- Cross-Browser Functionality Solutions
- Multimedia Web Interactivity
- Productivity Enhancements

- Project Coordination
- Issues Management/Strategic Planning
- Concept Development/Modeling
- Resource Allocations & Budgeting
- Client Briefs
- Supplier Negotiations
- Change Management

---

technology snapshot

HTML • JavaScript • DHTML • ASP • PHP • MySQL • Perl • VBA • Visual Basic • Delphi • Dreamweaver • Lotus Domino • Flash • Adobe Photoshop • PaintShop Pro • Adobe Premiere • Windows NT/XP/9x • Linux • Microsoft Office Pro • MS Project • MS Publisher • Lotus Notes • IE/Netscape • Streaming media • Xara & Asymetrix products • WISE • Install Shield • FrontPage • MS Visio • Linkbot Professional • Maximine • PC Anywhere

---

project showcase

Track record of accomplishment consulting for prominent companies, including UPS, Coles Myer Group, City of Rocklin, Collins Street Company, Direct View Consulting, Department of State Development, and more.

GLOBAL ONLINE TRADING & GLOBAL MARGIN LENDING
"MY WEALTH"
Website Assistant Manager

Projects: Multiple website projects ranging from $1K–$3.6M, including Global Online Trading, Global Margin Lending, My Wealth, and intranet.
Report to: Website Manager; Direct Reports: 2 (Content Administrator and Data Business Analyst)
Technologies: Lotus Domino, ASP

Leveraged the talents of the web design team to assess multifaceted user and system needs and institute strategic short- and long-term plans for developing an end solution. Expandable website environments were critical in meeting the organization's growing needs.

Produced the creative design and content for three websites. Documented site hierarchy, server structure, third-party relationships/processes, and work request procedures. Produced comprehensive briefings on recommended navigation flows and style guides for web content. Created all graphic optimization work and page mock-ups to reinforce the vision. Controlled all brainstorming sessions, tackled potential issues, and compiled solution reports for internal business analysts that provided a snapshot of project progress.

Special Contributions

- Transformed manual work request system plagued with inadequate instruction areas, slow processing, erroneous or missing data, and sign-off inadequacies into an automated electronic system based on Lotus Notes that cut instances of complaints by 96% and reduced personal clarification visits to the requester by 80%.

- Elevated the usability and quality of websites, and arrested growing incidents of complaints regarding out-of-date content and errors, by developing a maintenance model that cemented biannual schedule dates exclusively for total website page reviews.

- Acknowledged "guru" appointed to investigate and resolve Internet-related software issues— from routine URL errors through complex browser configuration and plug-in anomalies.

- Selected to preside over proposed $3.6M website rebranding to mirror the Global image and transition to a new website platform. Collaborated with consultants on hardware/software needs and devised strategy for website redesign.

Page 1

108

119 Gowan Drive, Rocklin, CA 91677 • Mobile: (916) 632 4545 • Website: http://anita.rosario.name • Email: anita@rosario.name

Anita Rosario

Gayle Howard, Chirnside Park, Melbourne, Victoria, Australia

This applicant was an Administrator by day but wanted a job as a full-time Web Designer. She had formed her own freelance company for night and holiday work. The challenge was to play down her day work and showcase the minimal amount of design work she had performed for

Anita Rosario

119 Gowan Drive, Rocklin, CA 91677 • Mobile: (916) 632 4545 • Website: http://anita.rosario.name • Email: anita@rosario.name

---

project showcase
continued

PARKINSON'S SOCIETY
Webmaster

Project Scope: *Live national convention broadcast across the Internet*
Reported to: *Multimedia and Information Services Manager*
Technologies: *Windows Media*

With an "impossible deadline" of just 2 months from concept to delivery, presided over solution development and implementation for broadcasting the society's national convention across the Internet to a global audience.

Researched available technologies, interviewed and appointed specialist consultants, documented requirements, and collaborated on developing preseminar web pages for testing webcast signals and advertising prior to "go-live" date.

The project, delivered exactly to plan, was broadcast to a worldwide audience.

Special Contributions

- Seamlessly and successfully recorded and produced the seminar for live webcast.
- Devised multimedia PowerPoint slideshow that complemented the convention's theme. The seminar, live satellite connection, and slideshow seamlessly integrated to provide a premiere Internet broadcast.
- Offered real-time support for isolated users struggling to access the broadcast. Quickly identified individual browser plug-ins as the primary issue, providing instructions for download and installation.
- Seamlessly resolved one-time slideshow glitch by establishing alternative views on screen while re-establishing the lost connection.
- Collaborated with external companies to establish sponsorship technologies. Researched, pursued key decision-makers, presented case, and created/presented documents.
- Spearheaded e-commerce solution for donations, raffles, and merchandise. Recommended system that offered expandability, noninvasive implementation, and cost-effective pricing.
- Engaged children with the "Read-a-thon" website, designed to maximize children's enjoyment through interactivity, bright colors, and simple navigation.

---

career snapshot

THE WEB GURUS **Contractor/Consultant**	1999–Present
CITY OF ROCKLIN, Rocklin CA **Contract Administrator / Technical Administrator Coordinator**	1996–1998
MODEL SYSTEMS, Rocklin, CA **Computer Consultant**	1995–1996

---

education

Bachelor of Business (Accounting)
2 years successfully completed
Recipient, Faculty of Business Award (Computing)
Averaged Distinctions & High Distinctions in Computing & Accounting
<u>University of California</u>

Hundreds of hours devoted to ongoing professional development via formal short courses, workshops, information sessions, and meetings. Includes Dreamweaver MX, Photoshop, XML, Project Management, Time Management, Conflict Resolution, Introduction to Windows NT, Outlook and Office 97, Negotiation Skills, Software Testing, Workplace Communications, Designing User Documentation, Advanced Visual Basic, and more.

Page 2

---

her clients. The "technology snapshot" is a novel way to display her software expertise. Achievements are labeled "Special Contributions." The white-on-black contact information makes the resume stand out.

JEANNIE DANIELS

1639 Canyon Avenue • San Jose, CA 77777 • (555) 555-5555 • jdaniels@aol.com

A highly motivated, results-focused **Program Manager** with more than 8 years of information technology experience in the semiconductor industry. Encompasses strong leadership and successful team-building capabilities combined with excellent technical, communication, presentation, and customer-service skills. Resourceful problem solver with proven ability to bring quick resolution to challenging situations as well as building lasting relationships with vendors and customers.

Manufacturing Operations ◆ **Continuous Process Improvement** ◆ **Global Partnerships**
Strategic Planning ◆ **Business Development** ◆ **Customer Relationship Management**
Financial Analysis ◆ **Team Building** ◆ **Product Development**

ACHIEVEMENTS

◆ **Instrumental in becoming top service provider for Novellus Systems, Inc. in Asia (China, Taiwan, and Singapore).** Developed a service program in an effort to become the exclusive service provider for Novellus around the world. Hired resources, trained personnel, and implemented and managed program, ensuring customer and OEM satisfaction. Tracked equipment utilization and resource performance and established customer relationships.

◆ **Recognized as service provider with customer needs in mind.** Implemented new pricing structure based on client feedback from numerous meetings addressing past concerns about support and pricing. Established close customer relationships that increased revenues 90% and first-year revenues by more than $600,000.

◆ **Significantly improved practices and procedures throughout manufacturing area, increasing revenues from less than $100 million to more than $700 million annually.** Implemented ISO 9000, improving repair times and training processes, which reduced manufacturing cycle times and discrepancies while increasing mean time between failures, system availability, and on-time shipments.

PROFESSIONAL EXPERIENCE

AXIOM MECHANICAL, San Jose, CA
$35 million semiconductor services group with 480 employees throughout the United States, Asia, and Europe

NOVELLUS PROGRAM MANAGER 2000–Present

Manage operational and manufacturing personnel, continuous process and product improvement, and customer service program, creating overall operations efficiency. Play a key role in hiring, training, and scheduling, as well as implementing and supporting service plan.

- Negotiated use of Novellus training facility and equipment at no cost to company, resulting in comprehensive training and savings of $2,500 per student.
- Established database that allowed needed documentation to be retrieved for support field service efforts and training classes 24/7. Collaborated within organization to develop procedures that could be expanded on after contract agreement with Novellus.
- Increased service calls by 150% by developing strong customer relationships.
- Established accounts with key suppliers in U.S., Taiwan, and Singapore to provide nonproprietary parts, resulting in additional sales with 37% profit margin for material sold.
- Implemented new response time policy from 4- to 2-hour maximum, creating additional daily service and reduced average response time from 4 an hour to less than 1 an hour.

109

Denette Jones, Mountain View, Hawaii

The resume gets off to a strong start with a profile and center-justified areas of expertise in bold-face and separated by diamond bullets. Big numbers justify a separate Achievements section. Each entry in the Professional Experience section has a company description in italic, a paragraph

JEANNIE DANIELS

page two

JABIL, San Jose, CA
Fortune 500 company providing equipment leasing and financing services to venture capital-backed companies

TECHNICAL SERVICE MANAGER 1993–2000

Full authority over the remanufacturing, testing, and shipment of front-end fabrication equipment, including AMAT, Lam, and Novellus capital equipment. Ensured that refurbished equipment met OEM and customer specifications while targeting efforts toward quality equipment, reduced costs, on-time shipments, and improved manufacturing cycle times.

- Reduced manufacturing cycle times by 30%. Recruited technical writer to create procedures during manufacturing process, enabling staff to cross-train effectively and allowing trainees to work without constant supervision.

- Established material supply chain, improving employee morale and reducing manufacturing costs by more than 40%.

- Utilized original OEM to rebuild specific components to ensure quality and reduce costs over purchasing new, resulting in a warranty same as new and a 4-week lead time for rebuilds.

- Reduced crating times by 2 days, improving efficiency and on-time shipments. Coordinated partnership with shipping and crating vendor with prefabbed crates available for all company equipment.

NOVA CORPORATION, San Jose, CA
$1.3 billion supplier of sophisticated manufacturing systems employing more than 2,500 people in 26 locations worldwide

MANUFACTURING MANAGER 1987–1993

Responsible for all manufacturing activities and up to 104 personnel, ensuring quality and on-time delivery for more than 150 systems per quarter. Created operational budgets that consistently met or exceeded scheduled goals.

- Developed programs and employee incentives to promote quality, resulting in assembly discrepancies being reduced from 9 per module to less than 1, and final test discrepancies being reduced from 14 per system to less than 2 in 2 years.

- Achieved 100% on-time delivery 3 years in a row by reworking assembly procedures and training for better efficiency.

- Provided in-depth classroom training on ISO practices as well as Novellus workmanship standards that met production and shipment goals without increased discrepancies, which reduced cycle times by 40%.

- Reduced employee turnover rate to less than 5% a year. Encouraged employees to cross-train, increasing job challenge and employee morale.

EDUCATION / TRAINING

Completed numerous **professional training courses,** including Conflict Management, Managing to Stay Legal, Time Management, Problem Solving/Decision Making, Strategic Management, Project Management, ISO9001 Element Training, Concept I Operation and Maintenance, Capital Expenditure Linkage and Evaluation, Resource Management and Financial Performance, and Clean Room Training.

Proficient in several computer applications—Microsoft Word, Excel, Visio, Project, PowerPoint.

indicating key responsibilities, and bulleted items containing achievements. Each achievement is quantified in some way (with a dollar amount, a percentage, or some other figure). White space is used throughout.

BRUCE KATOSHI

2222 Pinehurst Crescent
Augusta, Ontario A1A 1A1

Phone: (555) 333-7777
Email: brucekat@email.com

PROFESSIONAL PROFILE

★ *Recipient of the highest corporate distinction for commitment to excellence* ★

Award-winning professional combining top-quality strategic, operational, and management expertise. Distinguished 24-year career providing high-level information security solutions designed to safeguard technology investments, services, facilities, and databases. Dynamic and results-oriented leader with outstanding communication, consulting, and team-building skills. Recipient of distinguished Wall of Winners Award for excellence.

Information Security & Disaster Recovery

- Expert in Information Security, Disaster Recovery, and Business Continuity
- 24 years of expertise planning and implementing enterprise-class security and recovery solutions to ensure integrity and protection of all critical corporate data and technology services
- Expert in mainframe and enterprise LAN/WAN technologies (Alpha, VAX, HP, Novell, and Unix)

Vendor Management & Contract Negotiations

- Outstanding contract procurement and negotiation skills—proven ability to secure comprehensive, top-quality, cost-effective vendor agreements
- Particularly skilled in managing long-term vendor relationships in a consistent and professional manner

Team Leadership & People Management

- Reputation for building and leading strong, high-performance teams
- Ability to create high team morale and to motivate teams to consistently meet and exceed corporate and departmental objectives
- Recognized for ability to create a positive and productive environment that effectively reduces staff turnover

PROFESSIONAL EXPERIENCE

TIRECO CORPORATION, Augusta, Ontario
Rapid advancement through senior technology and information security positions on the strength of advanced strategic planning, team leadership, process improvement, cost control, and vendor negotiation and relationship management capabilities.

CHIEF INFORMATION SECURITY OFFICER
1999–2004

Senior technology position charged with the strategic planning, maintenance, implementation, administration, and interpretation of all Information Security policies, standards, guidelines, and procedures across the organization to safeguard the corporation's vital technology services, facilities, and databases. Concurrently tasked with managing key technology projects and vendor negotiations.

- Revitalized the integrity of all security privileges and established comprehensive security and disaster recovery protocols that exceeded all audit security recommendations.
- Mandated disaster recovery procedures and offsite storage solutions for midrange and distributed systems (Alpha, VAX, HP, Novell, and Unix).
- Successfully renegotiated major outsource printing contract with Xerox Canada, securing more than $725,000 in savings for Canadian Tire over the term of the agreement, and further identifying a $100,000 cost avoidance opportunity for Xerox.
- Renegotiated critical Comdisco disaster-recovery contracts, resulting in cost savings of more than $700,000, improved client coverage, and the additional elimination of all 6% annual contract increases.
- Successfully managed implementation of a new fibre ring designed to reroute voice and data traffic in event of failure to the primary fibre option.

110

This resume focuses on three areas that the candidate wanted to highlight and puts them up front in the Professional Profile, enclosed in horizontal lines. Even though he received his awards earlier in his career, they also are highlighted at the top of page 1 for greater impact. In the

MANAGER—
Disaster Recovery, Data Centre Security, Facilities Management, and Health & Safety 1997–1999
Challenged with safeguarding all enterprise technology services, security, and data in the event of a physical disaster. Included comprehensive planning and coordination of all network and mainframe recovery testing, physical security of computing facilities, environmental controls, and executive transportation to recovery site.

- Established infrastructure and procedures to ensure network connectivity to all business clients within 48 hours of disaster and relocation of corporate executive to recovery site in Andover, NJ, within 3 hours.
- Spearheaded implementation of SAE, effectively reducing erase time by 66% and resolving outstanding audit security issues.
- Successfully audited five corporate computing facilities to ensure integrity of environmental and employee safety controls, including fire alarm systems, air conditioning, environmental alerts, and use of UPS/diesel generators.
- Reduced mainframe and network recovery times by 25% and card authorization (Stratus) recovery by 50%.
- Re-evaluated and/or eliminated card access to secured areas and initiated weekly and monthly audits, reporting, and procedures to ensure security issues.

MANAGER—Program Delivery 1995–1997
Selected to build and manage key Project Management Team and coordinate multiple ongoing enterprise initiatives on time and within budget. Direct management of five Project Managers and resource pool of 40 technical specialists.

- Built and maintained an efficient and highly regarded professional unit through solid team leadership, process improvement, and priority management skills.
- Effectively controlled staffing costs through judicious training and redeployment within the resource pool.

MANAGER—Network Planning and Support Data & Voice 1993–1995
Coordinated all planning, support, and applicable outsourcing for enterprise telecommunications, voice (BPX), and WAN services across the corporation.

- Recommended technology improvements and outsourcing opportunities that allowed for significant cost savings while improving level of service.
- Effectively managed seamless crossover to outsourced voice services.
- Managed ongoing support of newly implemented Spacepac satellite communications system throughout all Associate stores and Express Auto Parts facilities.

MANAGER—Spacepac Satellite Information Systems 1992–1993
Concurrently seconded by Senior Technology Team to lead strategic planning and implementation of Spacepac satellite system across 400+ Associate Dealer network. Challenged to establish entire infrastructure and manage cycle through preinstallation, installation, training, and ongoing support.

- Doubled senior management mandate by signing all 400+ Corporate Associate Dealers in first year (met expectation of 200 signed orders within 6 months).
- Successfully managed all hardware and software installations without disruption to day-to-day operations.
- Established key service level agreements with corporate sponsors and associated vendors.

MANAGER—Computer Operations / Disaster Recovery 1990–1992
Coordinated all online computer services, computer planning, disaster recovery, and system development throughout the organization. Additionally accountable for all negotiation and relationship management with third-party vendors and technology partners. Managed 42-person team with 7 direct reports.

- Successfully instituted a number of industry and corporation firsts, including the first online automated cartridge system in Canada, the largest Amdahl single image processor in Ontario, and a new Data Centre Help Desk.
- Replaced and renegotiated more than 50% of current vendor relationships unable to meet business needs, resulting in significant cost savings and service improvements.
- Renegotiated all Micrographics contracts to reduce annual costs and turn around first profit of $500,000 for Operations department.

EDUCATION

Business Administration—Marketing, Augusta College, Augusta, Ontario

Professional Experience section, each entry exhibits the popular pattern of a paragraph with responsibilities that is followed by a list of bulleted achievements. The short Education section appears at the end.

John H. Damon

SENIOR-LEVEL SALES EXECUTIVE
FOR TELECOM / CABLE / BROADBAND SALES
KNOWN AS INDUSTRY PIONEER / SALES STRATEGIST
SPECIALIZE IN STARTUP & TURNAROUND SALES OPERATIONS
EXPERTISE IN NEW PRODUCT / SERVICE / CHANNEL LAUNCH

124 Commonwealth Ave.
Raleigh, NC 27606
H: (555) 555-5555
C: (555) 500-5000
E: damon55@hotmail.com

SALES LEADER—transforming sales organizations into lean, powerful, differentiated engines for driving revenue, market share, and profitability growth. 15 years with telecom giants. Built motivated teams (100+ staff). Managed multimillion-dollar budgets, P&L, and all channels. **Consistently exceeded sales goals. Achieved double-digit percentage point increases in channel revenue. Made industry history with groundbreaking initiatives.**

Professional Highlights

Century Telecom, Houston, TX   **2003–Present**

REGIONAL SALES DIRECTOR

Manage multiple regional sales channels for the fifth-largest broadband subscription service provider nationwide. Hold full P&L accountability for residential and commercial direct sales. Develop and manage $8.3 million annual budget. Direct a regional sales manager and 135 dotted-line sales team members. Provide strategic guidance for product launches, sales contracting, and affinity programs.

- Turned around under-performing residential direct sales channel, achieving **55% increase in year-over-year sales ($2.8 million in new revenue)** while simultaneously decreasing cost per sale by 20%.

- Designed a competitive sales program that increased customer win-backs from the competition in residential direct sales channel by 75%, increasing contribution **from 4% to 7% of the total direct sales.**

- Developed a performance management report used by top management to target the most cost-effective channels: switched resources from inbound to outbound telemarketing, **saving $1 million.**

Integrated Systems, Inc., Raleigh, NC   **2001–2003**

SENIOR SALES AND ACCOUNT MANAGER

Developed relationships with service providers and retail partners to expand market share for an innovative media distribution software platform for the networked home. Directed first proof-of-concept field trials with major corporations (AT&T Broadband, Sears, etc.) leading to deployment of 150+ home server platforms.

Universal Broadband (acquired MediaControl)   **1999–2000**

NATIONAL SALES MANAGER—Etail & OEM Channels

Key member of the corporate sales team and active contributor to strategic planning efforts. Directed implementation of sales programs with online retailers and OEMs. Propelled cost-effective sales of broadband services to achieve market share and revenue goals. Project-managed product launches.

- Built relationships with online retailers and OEM partners (Gateway, HP, Coolsavings.com, etc.).

- Achieved **$73,000 in new monthly sales.**

MediaControl, Durham, NC   **1996–1999**

NATIONAL RETAIL SALES MANAGER—Broadband Internet Services (1998–1999)

Played pivotal role in strategy planning as first National Retail Sales Manager. Directed implementation of retail sales and marketing program in an industry-leading initiative to sell broadband services across multiple national markets. Negotiated / managed relationships with retail partners (i.e., Circuit City, Radio Shack). Administered $5 million channel budget. Fulfilled year-end customer-count goals. Managed brand change.

- Generated 8% of all sales in the region within 3 months of launching retail channel; **grew contribution to 12% of all sales a year later,** for a total of $46,600 in new monthly revenue.

- Catalyst for multiple enterprise-wide, value-added sales and merchandising programs.

111

Jean Cummings, Concord, Massachusetts

This IT professional was also an independent consultant. An unusual feature of this resume is profile information at the top of the page and opposite the contact information. This format hits the reader right away with sure-to-be-seen information just under the applicant's name. To get an

John H. Damon

REGIONAL SALES MANAGER (1996–1998)

Directed conversion project to connect customers' homes to newly upgraded cable plant. Managed outbound contact process to sell customers advanced analog products and services. Oversaw branding and customer communications. Monitored customer service and ensured quality control. Controlled contract costs and administered $8 million annual operating budget. Liaised with key stakeholders.

- Opened 4 sales offices across the region. **Delivered $16 million in new annual revenue.**

- Led a sales force of 80+ and a cable construction crew of 12+ that completed 294,000 in-home presentations and 109,000 set-top box installations in more than 130 different communities.

- **Doubled sales closure rates in one year to 21% rate** by improving product training, performance standards, and staff reviews.

- Orchestrated brand transition from CableNation to MediaControl.

CableNation Durham, NC   **1988–1995**

AREA TELEMARKETING MANAGER (1994–1995)

Rebuilt and directed regional outbound telemarketing department. Strategist for long-range growth plans. Created innovative sales strategies. Participated in budget administration. Hired, motivated, and evaluated all telemarketing personnel. Managed performance goals to meet cost-per-unit budgets.

- **Captured 18% annual sales increase** by maximizing efficiency and productivity of sales staff.

- Designed training programs, performance standards, and feedback mechanisms for continuous improvement that led to **sales representative retention rate of 93%.**

CUSTOMER SERVICE SUPERVISOR (1993–1994)

Directed evening and weekend inbound call center group in handling customer inquiries about services and technical issues. Managed staffing and scheduling. Tracked and sustained productivity levels.

- Surpassed customer expectations and FCC standards by maintaining a focus on excellence.

- Spearheaded a sales program designed to make transactional sales part of every customer call.

- Peer-selected winner of the **Team of the Year Award for 2 consecutive years.**

Education, Training, & Affiliations

Business Management Coursework: University of Houston, Houston, TX (2000)

Additional Training: LAN/WAN Networking Courses—University of Houston, Houston, TX

Professional Affiliations: Cable & Telecommunications Association for Marketing (CTAM)

idea of the progression of the applicant's career, start with the last position indicated at the bottom of page 2 and read upward to the current position near the top of page 1.

JAMES L. TIERNEY

1450 Greenwood Drive • Chelmsford, MA 01824
Home: (222) 222-2222 • Mobile: (333) 333-3333 • E-Mail: jltiern3@attbi.com

SENIOR LAN ADMINISTRATOR / SYSTEMS ENGINEER

- **Certified Novell Engineer** with more than 15 years of experience in installing, upgrading, troubleshooting, configuring, and supporting network operating systems, hardware, software, servers, desktops, and a wide variety of computer peripherals.
- Highly proficient at establishing user accounts, implementing network security protocols, installing and supporting backup strategies, and planning/executing disaster recovery solutions.
- Excellent troubleshooting skills; tenaciously committed to the thorough resolution of technical issues.
- Exceptional ability to grasp and master new technologies quickly and easily.
- Strong communicator; able to interact effectively and positively with individuals of all technical abilities.

TECHNICAL SKILLS AND QUALIFICATIONS

- Novell NetWare 3.1x, 4.1x, 5.x
- TCP/IP, IP X
- IBM OS/2 2.x and 3.0
- BackupExec/Arcserve Administrator
- Lotus Notes

- Microsoft Windows NT 4.0, 2000, XP
- Microsoft Windows 95, 98, Me, XP
- Microsoft Office 4, XP
- Microsoft Exchange/Outlook/Express
- Microsoft Visio

PROFESSIONAL EXPERIENCE

Signet, Inc., Westford, MA   2000–2004
Start-up IT consulting firm offering high-end technology solutions to Fortune 1000 clients.
Systems Engineer/Technical Consultant

Provide NetWare operating systems support, file server installation, troubleshooting, and technical consultation to client companies with complex networking environments. Consult with clients to determine the optimal application of technology solutions to meet their current and future IT needs.
- Participated in the application of security policy standards to NetWare and NT servers at a leading New England financial institution to ensure their compliance for an upcoming FDIC audit.
- Planned, coordinated and implemented the relocation of 20 NT and NetWare servers to a new location over two weekends for a major New England Medical facility with zero loss in user productivity.
- Led the effort to upgrade 20 laptops from Compaq to Dell at a local New England medical center. Migrated user-specific data, mail, and software applications to the new laptops. Instructed users on VPN login, network access, and e-mail retrieval procedures.

Bryant Technologies, Concord, MA   1996–2000
National Professional Services firm providing Help Desk Support and Field Service Engineering to Fortune 1000 client companies.
Systems Engineer

Provided on-site technical support and network administration for clients, including installations, maintenance, upgrades, troubleshooting, and support for servers, fiber optics, printers, software applications, and workstations.
- Managed the upgrade of a NetWare 3.12 server to 4.11 for a global securities and lending firm. Administered and stabilized all other servers and developed and implemented a data backup solution.
- Installed 18 new servers and migrated all user-specific data to increase a client's network user storage space from 10 MB to 200 MB per user. Replaced 11 aging NetWare 4.11 servers, increasing total storage to 3.6 TB.
- Instrumental in the remediation of 12,000 desktops to ensure Y2K compliance for a New England financial institution. Provided technical support for hardware, DOS, Windows 3x and 95, and Y2K software.

112

Jeanne Knight, Westford, Massachusetts

The strong opening profile, Technical Skills and Qualifications section, and Professional Experience section display this applicant's outstanding capabilities, offsetting his not having a four-year degree. In the Professional Experience section, each italic company description is useful to any

PROFESSIONAL EXPERIENCE (continued)

Larkus Corporation, Tyngsboro, MA   1992–1996
Consulting firm specializing in Novell Networks and computer support for small businesses.
Network Engineer (1993–1996)
Lead Technician (1992–1993)

Provided network systems administration for client Novell networks, including installations, troubleshooting, configuration, upgrades, support, and maintenance. Administered disaster recovery plans.

- Installed and configured NetWare 3.12 server supporting 40 users for a client divesting from its corporate headquarters. Migrated user and corporate data, created login scripts, and maintained desktops.
- Provided technical support and on-site preventive maintenance of computer hardware and peripherals for client companies.

Grenoble Information Services, Needham, MA   1992
National service provider of on-site computer repair service for PCs and peripherals supporting medium to large companies.

Field Engineer

Performed service calls and maintained spare-parts inventory for client companies. Performed lead engineering duties for two automotive manufacturer contracts supporting desktops and peripherals.

Centel Information Systems, Inc., Waltham, MA   1987–1992
National service provider of on-site computer repair service for PCs and peripherals supporting medium to large companies.

Branch Manager (1991–1992)
Lead Technician (1987–1991)

Performed service calls and diagnosed, troubleshot, and repaired computers and peripherals. Maintained spare-parts inventory. Dispatched technicians to service calls and tracked the status of those calls.

TECHNICAL CERTIFICATIONS

Certified Novell Engineer, CNE5
Certified Novell Engineer, IntranetWare
Certified Novell Administrator, CNA5
Certified Novell Administrator, IntranetWare

Microsoft Certified System Engineer, MCSE 2000
Microsoft Certified Professional, MCP (in progress)

EDUCATION

Associated Technical Institute, Woburn, MA—Certificate in Electronics and Computer Technology

reader who may not be familiar with the company. Boldfacing makes the positions held stand out. Bullets point to significant responsibilities and notable achievements. The Education section appears last.

BRUCE T. THOMAS

98 Ben Franklin Drive • Austin, TX 78734
Home: (555) 222–2222 • ThomasB@aol.com • Work: (555) 333–3333

QUALIFICATIONS PROFILE

Proactive, high-energy individual with more than 25 years of experience in law enforcement principles and practices, as well as state and federal laws relating to correctional and law enforcement agencies. Adept at building trust and developing effective relationships with county agencies and officials. Excellent organizational, time-management, and leadership skills, coupled with the ability to build and manage creative teams. Ability to think clearly and objectively, rapidly assessing the problem at hand while remaining calm in difficult situations.

☑ Penal Code

☑ Emergency Operations

☑ Community Awareness

☑ Educating & Mentoring

☑ Multi-Agency Coordination

☑ IJS & RDMT

☑ Public Speaking

☑ Technical Projects

☑ Hostage Negotiations

☑ Local Government Rules & Procedures

KEY ACHIEVEMENTS

- Pioneered the successful implementation of the RDMT project, an $11 million regional radio system and communications center involving 4 separate government entities. Liaised with Sheriff's office staff and county budget personnel for approval; developed specifications for vendors, and collaborated with attorneys over a 3-month period to write contract.
- Championed project management of IJS (Integrated Justice System) computer system, a $20 million project bringing together the Sheriff's office, Adult Probation, Constables, District Attorneys, County Attorneys, County and District courts, and elected County and District Clerks offices.
- Spearheaded writing of the Standard Operating Procedures (SOPs) for the SWAT unit, ensuring awareness by all parties (SWAT and uniformed patrol) of procedures for SWAT callout, arrival, deployment at scene, use of tactically trained medics, and handling of all victims and witnesses.
- Instrumental in leading more than 50 successful SWAT missions, ensuring the safety of all hostages, civilians, and team members.
- Played a pivotal role in Austin County agency's receiving parity pay with other local law enforcement agencies and retaining experienced staff; researched and created a detailed report to government officials, demonstrating that staff were relocating to other agencies due to pay issues.
- Wrote and submitted a successful grant request for the creation of a Warrant Research unit; unit still exists today.

PROFESSIONAL EXPERIENCE

AUSTIN COUNTY SHERIFF — Austin, TX   1987–Present
Director of Information Systems *(1999–Present)*
Report directly to Major of Austin County Sheriff's office overseeing all technical projects. Act as single point of contact for more than 20 government agencies, handling all data exchange and technology requests from staff. Execute all decisions on vendors used; develop specifications for vendors and recommendations for purchases; authority to handle all disciplinary matters up to, but not including, termination.

- Selected to research, develop, and write a successful budget request for a $5 million Training Facility; gathered outside support from numerous elected officials.
- Determined fiscal requirements and prepared budgetary recommendations for replacement PCs, staff promotions, and recruitment of new staff members.

113

Jennifer Rushton, Sydney, New South Wales, Australia

Printed on a color printer, this resume displays color (light blue) in the e-mail address in the contact information and light gray in the horizontal lines. A strong Qualifications Profile contains checked-box bullets next to areas of expertise. A Key Achievements section is put before a

Professional Experience Continued

- Independently coordinated complex "gap analysis" of the IJS, measuring differences between versions 6 and 7; saved thousands of dollars in maintenance fees and standardized growth ability with software. Collaborated with staff members in presenting results to Austin County agencies, resulting in successful conversion to version 7.
- Successfully rallied community support for the building of a radio antenna in the Austin School District; antenna is 1 of 17 towers in the new RDMT radio system, enabling full county coverage for all public safety agencies—Police, Sheriff, EMS, and Fire Department.

Lieutenant of Tactical Operations *(1994–1998)*

- Successfully led SWAT team to third place in SWAT Police Olympics; SWAT team achieved and maintained the highest level of physical fitness in the agency for 3 consecutive years.
- Planned and executed specialized training with other agencies for SWAT team; involved specialized training from the military in dignitary protection, hostage negotiations, drug lab raids, the use of helicopters in SWAT missions, raid planning, and bomb recognition.
- Independently gained authorization from Fiscal and Command staff to purchase the first "threat level 3 vests" and other costly essential equipment for the SWAT team.
- Collaborated with Sheriff's office and officials in opening a third "courthouse" in the Marks building due to growth; ensured Courthouse security and the safety of all court participants by determining security needs and establishing procedures, becoming the benchmark for Austin Courthouse security.

Lieutenant of Personnel & Training *(1990–1994)*

- Instrumental in managing grant providing Basic Peace Officer Training to students from a 10-county region, with 17 groups successfully graduating. Austin County held the State grant for Basic Peace Officer training and held the state record for 3 years, with a 100% pass rate.
- Played a key role in writing and implementing four annual promotion examinations for Corrections Sergeant, Corrections Lieutenant, Patrol Sergeant, and Patrol Lieutenant.

Sergeant of Special Operations *(1990)*

Sergeant of Patrol *(1987–1989)*

EDUCATION

University of Texas—Austin, TX
Criminal Justice (1994)

CERTIFICATIONS

Graduate of FBI National Academy, 2001
Professional License: Master Peace & Instructor License—TCLEOSE

PROFESSIONAL AFFILIATIONS

Member, Austin County Sheriff's Officers Association
Member, CLEAT

COMMUNITY ACTIVITIES

Original Founder/President—Employee's Association for the Sheriff's Office
Cadet Training Coach—University of Texas

REFERENCES AVAILABLE UPON REQUEST

Professional Experience section to ensure that these achievements will be seen. If you read the resume from the end to the beginning, you will better understand the applicant's growth in his career.

Carrie Anne Montgomery

1711 Lincoln Street, Princeton, NJ 08540

(609) 973-1331 Home ▪ (510) 259-7599 Mobile ▪ camont987@patmedia.com

---

Application Support Administrator / Technical Support Specialist / Desktop Support

Technologically sophisticated and bilingual (Spanish/English) IT Support/Training Specialist with hands-on experience in project life-cycle management for technical and intranet applications, website development, workgroup support, and desktop and network troubleshooting. Certificate in Computer Programming. Skilled in

☑ Help Desk & Hardware Support	☑ First-Level PC Support	☑ Project Management
☑ System Upgrades / Conversions	☑ LAN / WAN Architecture	☑ Escalation Resolution
☑ Peer-to-Peer User Groups	☑ Web Content Upgrades	☑ Customer Service

---

TECHNOLOGY SUMMARY

Networking—LAN / WAN, Windows 2000 / NT 4.0 Server, Windows 95 Server, TCP/IP, SQL Server

Operating Systems—Windows 95 / 98 / 2000 / XP, Windows 2000 / NT 4.0 Server, DOS 6.0

Applications—MS Office Suite 97/2000/2002 (Word, Access, Excel, PowerPoint), MS FrontPage 2000, Macromedia Dream Weaver 3.0, Adobe Acrobat 5 and PDF, Flash 4.0, Novell GroupWise 5.5, Adobe Pagemill 3, Lotus Suite 96, Corel Suite 96, Corel 9, Adobe Photoshop, Kodak digital software, Symantec pcAnywhere 32, Internet Explorer, Netscape Communicator, and WinZip

Programming—HTML code, CGI, Java, JavaScript, C Programming, RPG 400, SQL, Visual Basic 5.0, Visual InterDev 6.0, AS/400, ASP code

---

PROFESSIONAL EXPERIENCE

STATE OF PENNSYLVANIA, TREASURY DEPT., DIV. OF TAXATION, Philadelphia, PA   1995–present
Senior Technician, MIS—Technical Support Activity (2001–present)
Promoted to provide help desk support for 2,000+ end-users (including remote users) in 9 locations throughout Pennsylvania, as well as project management team leadership for special technical assignments. First-point-of-contact (Tier 1 Help Desk Technician) for support incidents, as well as end-user training.

- **Help Desk.** Ensure effective 24-hour "one-stop" technical support for mainframe, WAN, LAN, and remote system. Install and update software. Set up, configure, and troubleshoot Technology Center equipment. Track and de-escalate technology and workflow problems, collaborating with 10 cross-functional IT groups.

- **Website Development.** Project-managed Division of Taxation's website redesign to text-only version, enabling fast and easy access for all users, including vision impaired. Supervised staff of 8.

- **Intranet Development.** Key player in creation, launch, and maintenance of Division of Taxation intranet site, providing management with easily retrievable, up-to-date information for operations decisions. Initiated, created, and maintain Access users group intranet to facilitate information sharing and learning.

- **Project Management.** Led PAX CD-ROM project for 2 years, delivering interactive CD-ROMs with 1,000+ tax-law-verified documents for simplified tax preparation (tax years 2001 & 2002) on schedule.

- **ASP Development.** Played pivotal role in beta-test programming and development of causal sales application (upgraded Alpha 4 database into back end of Access 2000 and SQL Server, front end into Internet Explorer via ASP programming).

- **End-User Training.** Expanded Technology Center offerings by designing, developing, and delivering advanced programs and manuals for MS Office, GroupWise, Novell Network, and Internet, increasing usability. Currently manage 12 Access courses, training and supervising 5 adjunct team instructors.

114

Susan Guarneri, Three Lakes, Wisconsin

The applicant had a long work history going back to 1983. She worked for the state government for 12 years, and the draft of her resume had a lot of abbreviations and acronyms that only other state employees would understand. The writer eliminated or "translated" most of these terms

Carrie Anne Montgomery
(609) 973-1331 Home ▪ (510) 259-7599 Mobile ▪ camont987@patmedia.com   Page 2

STATE OF PENNSYLVANIA—continued

Technical Assistant, MIS—Technical Support Activity (1999–2001)
First-level technical support for software installation, as well as setup and configuration of new equipment used in Division of Taxation (PCs, laptops, printers, scanners, projectors, digital, & video).

- **IT Software Training.** Designed curriculum and materials, and delivered technical training, for introductory programs in Microsoft Office Suite (Word, Excel, Access), as well as Windows 95, keeping staff motivated and focused while improving job satisfaction and productivity. Personally trained more than 800 end-users.

- **Website Support.** Functioned as Web Editor for Division of Taxation's Internet/Intranet website, proofing and updating website information daily (fastest turnaround of any PA State department).

- **Database Maintenance.** Upgraded and maintained link-shared employee Access database with Chief of Staff's office, ensuring data integrity for training. Created database reports for management evaluation.

- **Technical Development Project.** Pioneered development and implementation of storage, archive, and retrieval system for 500+ electronic presentations used throughout Division of Taxation.

Principal Clerk—Technical Education (1997–1999)
Promoted to provide installation, configuration, and troubleshooting support for new equipment and software in Technology Center, as well as evaluation and modification of skills assessment.

- **Training Center Database.** Initiated and implemented Access-based data gathering system to compile, store, and retrieve statistics on computer training classes. Researched and wrote monthly reports used to evaluate training trends and staff training needs.

- **NJ Saver Rebate Program.** Key team player in initial, large-scale data compilation for PA Saver Rebate Program, including retrieval, distribution, quality control, and storage of tens of thousands of data files.

Senior Clerk Typist, Clerk Typist—Corporation Business Tax (1995–1997)
Assisted 8 auditors by researching taxpayer information on mainframe, ordered work files for Supervising Auditor using HLLAPI information system, and prepared report statistics using Excel spreadsheets.

STATE OF PENNSYLVANIA, DEPT. OF BANKING, Philadelphia, PA (temp contract)   1994–1995
Data Entry Specialist / Legal Secretary
Front office support for 5 attorneys and 3 accountants: records management, legal document preparation, purchasing, and equipment maintenance. Used IS software for research and to process taxpayer complaints.

AMERICAN COMMERCIAL BANK, Edison, NJ   1990–1993
Customer Service Representative / Supervisor Teller
Instructed 35 employees in use of computerized banking systems and procedures. Verified and audited financial reports and balance sheets. Cash management responsibility exceeded $100,000.

EDUCATION

Instructor Certification, HRDI, Philadelphia, PA—2000
Courses: Curriculum Design, Performance Consulting, Training Presentations, Design Surveys and Questions, Determining Training Needs, and Active Techniques for Teaching.

Certificate in Computer Programming, DeVry Institute, New Brunswick, NJ—1999
Courses: HTML, CGI, Java Programming, JavaScript Programming, RPG 400, C Programming, SQL, Visual Basic 5.0, AS/400 Subfiles & Common Language Queries, MS Office, Windows NT 4.0

Ongoing Professional and Technical Development in-house and at vendor locations (1995–present)

and created instead a Technology Summary to give credibility to her goal of becoming a technical support administrator or specialist. The opening section indicates her bilingual abilities.

R. K. Ashburn

156 Whittle Circle
Ashburn, GA 31714

rkashburn@AshburnIT.com

Home: (229) 555–2222
Work: (229) 555–3333

| TECH PROFILE | **IT WEB CONTRACTOR / JAVA PROGRAMMER** |

IT WEB CONTRACTOR / JAVA PROGRAMMER
Web-focused Application Developer & Database Specialist

- **Strong technical lead and Web consultant** with nearly 10 years of experience in Java, Perl, JavaScript, Java Servlets, HTML, XML, C++, and Visual Basic programming.
- **Accomplished developer of Web-based systems** for e-commerce, monitoring and notification, problem tracking (PTS), multitiered architectures, distributed databases, business automation, and other client/server applications.
- **Versatile team leader and project manager** capable of managing the full application development life cycle for both corporate and government projects.
- **Knowledgeable database manager** skilled in MySQL, Microsoft SQL Server, and Paradox, as well as Windows Advanced Server/Active Directory/NT/CE/2000 and Linux Slackware/RedHat environments.
- **Reputation for self-taught, production-level skills** in more than 75 languages, protocols, application development packages, databases, APIs, IDEs, and operating systems.

AREAS OF EXPERTISE

- Web-based Multitiered Systems
- Java, C++, Perl, and Visual Basic
- Application Development Life Cycle
- Monitoring & Notification Systems
- E-Commerce Capability

- Active Directory Management
- XML / XSLT Programming
- Problem Tracking Systems / Help Desks
- Software Development Bids
- Team & Project Leadership

EXPERIENCE

ASHBURN IT CONSULTING (ASHBURN IT)—Ashburn, GA
Independent provider of Web, database, and related applications for regional businesses, large to small.
IT Consultant/Senior Software Engineer, 2001 to Present
Design, develop, test, and implement database, connectivity, and Web-based strategies.

WEB CONTRIBUTIONS

- **Delivered the full development life cycle of a Web-based multitiered PTS** (problem tracking system), including enhancements and streamlined base code. Used Java and MySQL on a Linux platform. (Georgia Postal)
- **Was tech lead for development of a multitiered XML-based Web site.** Used a MySQL database that was written using Java servlets. (Ashburn IT)
- **Bid/designed/tested/implemented a MANS alert system for the MIRS platform.** Sends alerts via e-mail, paging, and remote pop-up boxes for hardware carousel. Uses Visual Basic, XML, and MySQL. Developed for Northrop Grumman. (Georgia Postal)
- **Led redesign/implementation of the entire backend and database for a Web site** for accountants. Used a Perl backend and Microsoft SQL Server database. Currently maintain the production system to serve 100 affiliates with 1,000 end-user customers. (Ashburn IT)
  o **Added e-commerce capability to the Web site.**
  o **Automated the Web site's system administration and Active Directory tasks.** Integrated Microsoft Terminal Services and Active Directory components into the Web site using WSH, Visual C++, and Perl. Also automated the Active Directory tasks by creating WSH scripts in VBScript and Visual Basic.
  o **Created a Windows-based client/server application and installation script** to transfer files via batch and process remote updates.
  o **Currently developing a next-generation eXML-based Web site with a distributed multitiered architecture.** Involves components in Java, Perl, and C++.

115

Helen Oliff, Reston, Virginia

E-mail and Web addresses appear in light blue in this resume. A small font (11-point Garamond) allows quite a bit of information on each page. Not shown is a third page—a Technical Addendum—that indicates in detail the more than 75 Web languages and protocols,

R. K. Ashburn
Résumé — Page Two

EXPERIENCE

DATABASE & CONNECTIVITY CONTRIBUTIONS

- **Enforced uniform logging by the distributed components of an online system.** Created a centralized logging system, and integrated SOAP (simple object access protocol) into the applications written in Perl, Visual Basic, and Visual C++. Also created interface to display and filter logging data. (Ashburn IT)
- **Developed the systems and software to support creation, ingestion, and publication of survey metadata** for the Census Bureau. (AIS)
  - o   In Java, created a rules-based system to ingest MIF files into a MySQL database.
  - o   Developed a stand-alone Visual Basic interface to create MIF files.
  - o   In Visual Basic, created a setup program to install the MIF ingestion application.
  - o   Designed/implemented a spreadsheet to help create MIF files that used VBA.
  - o   Created a Java wrapper to replicate MySQL data to different databases/providers/sites.
- **Helped bid a $900,000 contract to develop an MCD device for a vending machine** to enable credit card transaction processing and connectivity for remote maintenance. (GPS)
- **Helped design/develop a machine conversion device (MCD),** including ANSI C and microprocessor development, on a PBSM-624 vending machine. Designed/implemented the SSE messaging capability. Also ensured network connectivity and enhanced MCD functionality—as a key developer. Used Windows CE and eMbedded Visual C++. (GPS)

GEORGIA POSTAL SOLUTIONS, INC. (GPS)—Atlanta, GA (www.gapostal.com)
Global contractor of IT hardware, software, support, and training to postal services and corporations.
Software Engineer, 1998 to 2001
Provided technical development of mainly postal applications for contract clients.

- **Co-led the upgrade of a legacy IRT system from DOS to Windows** for the U.S. Postal Service. Developed Visual C++ device drivers and a Visual Basic GUI.
- **Customized Visual Basic applications for integration into a Remedy PTS,** including DLLs with the Remedy API in C++.
- **Created a change-of-address system for a self-service kiosk for the PMC/NT.**

ATLANTA INTEGRATION SYSTEMS (AIS)—Atlanta, GA (www.ais.net)
Regional contractor of IT, engineering, and logistics services for government and private industry.
Computer Programmer, 1995 to 1997
Participated in development teams/projects for major problem-tracking and database systems.

- **Helped the development team design a computer-based solution for a manual PTS** with 250 end-users. Used Remedy Help Desk.
- **Supported the development/maintenance of a Visual Basic app for economic data** from the Census Bureau. Included creating a WYSIWYG reporting interface from scratch.
- **Developed Java applets** and created/converted Visual Basic graphics into Java applets.

GEORGIA TECHNICAL COLLEGE (GTC)—Atlanta, GA (www.gatc.edu)
Educator of 15,000 students annually in architecture, engineering, science, technology, and liberal arts.
Computer Programmer, 1993 to 1994
Provided programming, GUI, and tech support services for the College's dining hall service.

- **Developed RMIS maintenance system from scratch for a dining service operation.** Replaced the existing system. Tracked equipment repair status using Paradox and Delphi.
- **Helped support a campus-wide information system for credit card processing** and tracking using Pascal and C.

application/development packages, programming interfaces, databases, and operating systems the person knows through self-teaching. He is working on becoming a Sun Certified Programmer (Java 2 platform).

Mike Galvez

ORACLE | CERTIFIED PROFESSIONAL

5346 78th Street • Atlanta, GA 50495
Cell Phone: (555) 555-5555
mgalvez3458@yahoo.com

CERTIFIED SENIOR ORACLE DATABASE ADMINISTRATOR

Profile

Detail-focused database administrator with strong knowledge base in database design, development, administration, migration, and support. Oracle Certified Professional in 9i and 8i DBA and Oracle Internet Application Developer certifications. Excellent communication and support skills; able to explain complex database management processes in easy-to-understand terms. Adept at leading teams in various database management and administration projects.

Core Skills/Areas of Knowledge

- Database Administration
- Database Maintenance
- Systems Implementation
- Systems Analysis/Design

- Data & Systems Integrity
- Testing & Troubleshooting
- Disaster Recovery Planning
- Customer Communications

- Object-Oriented Modeling
- Logical/Physical DB Modeling
- User Training & Support
- Database Configuration

Technical Summary

**Oracle10g OCP DBA (in progress) ◆ Oracle8 OCP DBA ◆ Oracle8i OCP DBA ◆ Oracle9i OCP DBA
Oracle OCP Internet Application Developer ◆ Sun Certified Solaris8 System Administrator
Microsoft Certified Professional ◆ Microsoft Certified SQL Server 2000 DBA**

Technical Skills

RBDMS:	Oracle7.3/8/8i/9i/10g; MSSQL7.0, MSSQL2000, PL/SQL, T-SQL, Data Mart, Data Mining, SQL*Loader, SQL*PLUS, Oracle iDS 6i—Forms, Reports, Designer, Oracle Financial
Tools:	VERITAS Volume & Cluster Manager, Erwin, TOAD, XML Spy, Access, Java2, JDeveloper, SAS, Visual C++, ColdFusion, ASP, Perl5, UltraEditor, Tomcat, Rapid SQL, Crystal Reports, JacORB
Languages:	Java, XML, PL/SQL, PRO*C, T-SQL, HTML, C++, PERL, Shell Script, VB, C#
Platforms:	Windows 2000, Windows NT, Solaris2.6, Solaris7, Solaris8, Red Hat Linux

Professional Experience

XYZ COMPUTER CORPORATION, Duluth, GA   2001–Present
Database Administrator

Provided database solutions for client companies to meet broad range of objectives, including DB performance optimization, data maintenance, backup planning, split-second problem resolution, and increased accessibility to key data from both traditional and online channels. Coordinated and led broad range of projects and initiatives that included:

- **High Availability Solutions**—Provided "No Data Loss Standby Database System" and "VERITAS HA System" to meet major cable company's goal of 100% uptime for video-on-demand system. Established generic HA solution for all clients using Sun Raid Manager and Dell PowerEdge Cluster.

- **Disaster Recovery/Backup**—Implemented Oracle backup/recovery mechanism through hot-cold backup and export, used SQL Server DB Maintenance Plan Wizard for backups, and participated in on-call rotational DB support during off hours.

- **Database & Data Mart Design**—Designed and modified DB logical structure using Oracle Designer and Erwin, convincing clients of optimal framework for database. Built Data Mart for reporting purposes, using Data Mining to model data and provide clients with means for revenue/profit gains.

116

Daniel J. Dorotik, Jr., Lubbock, Texas

The Profile section contains Core Skills and Areas of Knowledge listed as bulleted items in three columns. This kind of layout is useful for substituting other skills and knowledge areas for other job targets. Technical information is important to an IT professional, so a Technical Summary is

Mike Galvez   **Page 2**

Professional Experience

XYZ COMPUTER CORPORATION, continued

- **Database Installation**—Supplied response files for installing Oracle DB in silent mode that allowed for installation on multiple machines without attendance.

- **Web Database Reporting**—Used JSP, Tomcat, and Servlet to build online Database Report that expedited data management through web access.

DB SOLUTIONS, Newark, NJ   2000–2001
Oracle Consultant

Consulted with client companies to provide expertise and support for various Oracle-based initiatives, with emphasis on improving productivity, costs, and data management through DB system solutions. Completed key system development and implementation projects that included:

- *Data Warehousing System*—Designed data warehouse and created Solaris-based Oracle8i DB. Used SQL*Loader, Crystal Reports, and Erwin; wrote PL/SQL stored procedures to extract, transform and load data to DW tables. **Result: Client was able to retain critical historical data and generate key reports.**

- *Financial Management System*—Developed system in Oracle 8.1.6 Enterprise Edition. Migrated data from Access DB using Oracle Migration Assistant. Built various applications and GUI using Visual Basic. **Result: Client reported improved capacity and performance from new system.**

- *Timesheet & Billing System*—Involved in full-lifecycle system development for insurance company; tools included JSP and Java Servlets, Apache web server, Tomcat servers, XML, JDBC, Oracle8i, and FrontPage2000. **Result: Client was able to reduce costs through system use.**

AI COMPUTER SYSTEM, Nanjing, China   1997–1999
Software Engineer

Key Project: Ticket Reservation System

- **Scope**—Railway client company needed Ticket Reservation system to manage tickets. Designed and developed DB aspect of system on UNIX-based Oracle7 DB to manage daily reservations.

- **Result**—Created "Ticket Reservation System"; implemented Data Modeling, created PL/SQL stored procedures and functions, and wrote detailed report, improving ticket management as a result.

Professional Development

Professional Development Courses
Web Component Development with Servlet and JSP Technologies
Administering a Microsoft SQL Server 2000 Database
Implementing Microsoft Windows 2000 Clustering
Oracle9i: Data Warehouse Administration

Affiliations
Member of IOUG (International Oracle Users Group)
Member of SSWUG (SQL Server Worldwide Users Group)

put next. Technical skills can look bewildering when they are listed in a paragraph, so they are placed instead in a Technical Skills table with side headings to group skills by criteria.

JOHN STRONG

555 South Lynn Road
Pasadena, California 55555

(626) 555-5555
jstrong@email.com

APPLICATIONS PROGRAMMER—VISUAL BASIC

❏ Technical training plus more than 2 years of experience in program design, development, documentation, implementation and debugging.

❏ Able to understand and interpret needs of end user to design quality software. Consistent attention to detail with an ability to analyze and interpret the implications of decisions to minimize bugs and create user-friendly programs. Skilled in troubleshooting and problem solving.

❏ Quick learner who enjoys challenges and possesses a high level of energy and motivation. Dedicated to seeing projects through to completion.

❏ Experienced collaborating with clients and team members. Ability to convey technical information at all levels.

Computer Applications: Visual Basic... ADO... SQL... Crystal Reports... Windows... Word... Excel... Access... Outlook... FoxPro... Citrix... PC Anywhere... HTML (basic knowledge)... Internet

PROFESSIONAL EXPERIENCE

Application Programmer • 2006 to Present
APPLICATION LEADERS, INC., Pasadena, CA
Write programs in Visual Basic for company providing software solutions to manufacturing industry.
Representative Projects:
- Created, debugged and perfected entry screens for new release of company's main product.
- Produced reports providing critical information on gross profit, inventory transactions/projections, sales forecasts and purchase requirements.
- Wrote program to read EDI documents and generate sales-related reports.
- Collaborated on development of program that enables manufacturer to directly transfer orders to banks for approval using FTP.
- Developed customized programs to meet customer needs.

EDUCATION

PASADENA CITY COLLEGE, Pasadena, CA
Associate of Arts, Social Science May 2008
Honors: Deans List, Honors for Superior Achievement in Economics Award

COMPUTER LEARNING CENTER, Los Angeles, CA
Certificate in Client/Server Programming 2006
Relevant Course Work: Visual Basic, Integrating a Visual Basic Front-End with a SQL Server Back-End, Access, C, C++, Oracle, Client/Server Architecture
Honors: Awarded National Vocational Technical Honors Society Membership

UCLA EXTENSION, Los Angeles, CA, 2007
ActiveX Component Development with Visual Basic 6

117

Vivian VanLier, Los Angeles, California

This applicant completed a certification in client/server programming and wanted to become a Visual Basic Applications Programmer. Lines enclosing Computer Applications promote their readability.

Law/Law Enforcement

Resumes at a Glance

Tracy Holland

8956 59th Street ▪ Stafford, TX 77079
Home: (555) 555-5555 ▪ tholland@cox.net

LAW ENFORCEMENT OFFICIAL

Dedicated law enforcement officer with extensive experience in planning and managing investigations, security, public service, and police force activities. Strong qualifications in program development, personnel affairs, training, resource management, public safety, and emergency response. Confident public speaker, with experience in delivering presentations to small and large groups in formal/informal settings. Reputation for strong work ethic and uncompromising devotion to service. Uphold highest professional ethics.

"As a result of her proactive professionalism, I have assigned her as Acting Chief of Police…I know I can trust her judgment because her knowledge, skills, and ability are exceptionally strong…She has been an asset to this department." — Charles Johnson, Chief of Police, Stafford Independent School District

- Public Safety Programs
- Emergency Response
- Internal Investigations
- Crisis Communications
- Team Building & Leadership

- Community Event Coordination
- Policy & Procedure Development
- Budget Planning & Management
- Staffing, Training, & Retention
- Time & Resource Allocation

- Formal Presentations
- Community Outreach
- Police Report Writing
- Regulatory Compliance
- Hostage Negotiations

PROFESSIONAL EXPERIENCE

STAFFORD INDEPENDENT SCHOOL DISTRICT — Stafford, Texas   1986–Present
Peace Officer

Manage broad range of law enforcement and public service responsibilities within large school district with 49 campuses and 29,000 students. Conduct investigations; detain suspects; write reports; develop programs; and communicate with parents, students, and administrators regarding minor and serious infractions. Maintain strong focus on student safety and preventive programs, including peer intervention and vocational training.

SELECTED CONTRIBUTIONS & ACCOMPLISHMENTS:

- Hand-selected to serve as **Acting Chief of Police** during absence of existing Chief of Police, holding full decision-making authority for entire law enforcement functions.

- Planned, developed, and implemented **Law Enforcement Magnet Program** in 1994 (still in existence today) that provides students with career training and field work in criminal justice fields and disciplines.

- Created and introduced highly successful **Secretarial Investigator I Program** that provided instruction for administrative assistants and school administrators in proper reporting of criminal activities.

- Earned **Top Award for Special Olympics** for 4 consecutive years based on fund-raising efforts, including finish as 4th top-performing fund-raiser in entire state of Texas.

- Delivered well-received presentations to **Texas Educators Support Staff Association** on variety of public safety and criminal justice topics.

EDUCATION & TRAINING

Professional Development Coursework
Completed more than 4,000 hours of training coursework throughout career. Former FBI certification.

Certifications & Recognitions
Master Peace Officer, 2000 / Advanced Peace Officer, 1992 / Basic Peace Officer, 1981
Academic Recognition Award, 2000 / Crime Prevention Officer, 1986 / Instructor Certificate, 1994

118

Daniel J. Dorotik, Jr., Lubbock, Texas

A testimonial, such as the one embedded in the opening section, is one of the best ways to off-set a disadvantage a candidate may have, such as not having a four-year degree preferred for the job.

William T. Henry

16394 Clark Road   Charles City, IA 50616   henry@internet.com
                                                                              641-555-8721

Qualifications Summary

❑ Veteran law enforcement officer/Iowa Highway Patrol lieutenant.
❑ Strong tactical background with expertise in narcotics and critical-incident response.
❑ One who leads by example and works to build a consensus among independent interests.
❑ Additional specific experience includes

- Program implementation and administration   - Grant writing
- Building collaborative relationships with local,   - Officer training
  state and federal agencies   - Arms and ammunition

Selected Accomplishments

❑ Prepared and coordinated grant submissions generating $495,000 for narcotics investigations in Floyd and Butler counties.
❑ Earned designation as Expert Witness in Floyd and Johnson counties regarding clandestine methamphetamine labs.
❑ Sat on Office of Drug Control Policy (ODCP) committee charged with strategizing and developing policy on legal handling of methamphetamine labs in the state of Iowa.
❑ Received citations for Bravery and Professional Excellence.

Career History

<u>IOWA HIGHWAY PATROL (IHP)</u> • Statewide   1978–Present
Section Commander—Butler Area Narcotics Group & Rural Narcotics Unit (2003–Present)

- Manage two multijurisdictional drug enforcement teams (representing 14 agencies) in Floyd and Butler counties. Act as liaison with local agencies and ISP.
- Manage administrative functions, including employee supervision, fiscal management, vehicle fleet and facility maintenance.
- Develop and monitor $2.4 million budget with reporting responsibilities to local, state and federal officials.
- Coordinate and control forfeited property and funds totaling $196,000 per year. Ensure distribution to appropriate agencies.
- Monitor and participate in large-scale, multiple-agency narcotics investigations.
- Prepare grant submissions and oversee expenditures of funded grants.

Team Commander—Methamphetamine Investigation Team (2000–2003)

- Established, coordinated and supervised the state's first methamphetamine investigation team. Led team to become fully functioning within 6 months of appointment.
- Collaborated with local, state and federal law enforcement officials from multiple agencies to assist with policy development and provide training for clandestine lab response and investigation across the state. Also assisted with implementing area task forces.
- Acted as officer in charge on more than 140 investigations and subsequent raids of clandestine labs across the state. Collected evidence, dismantled equipment and coordinated clean-up activities in collaboration with the federal Drug Enforcement Agency and in adherence with OSHA requirements.

119

Janet L. Beckstrom, Flint, Michigan

The applicant had a career in the State Police/Highway Patrol. He was considering retirement to pursue a position with a little less stress, such as Police Chief of a small community. Read this person's Career History from the end of the resume to the first page to get a sense of his

William T. Henry   641-555-8721

Career History

IOWA HIGHWAY PATROL (IHP) • Statewide

Team Commander—Methamphetamine Investigation Team   *(continued)*

- Introduced equipment pool concept to methamphetamine investigation team to minimize need to purchase expensive OSHA-required equipment, thereby saving significant funds.
- Selected to make presentation to judges, law enforcement representatives and community leaders at Methamphetamine Strategy Summit hosted by the Iowa Department of Community Health Office of Drug Control Policy.
- Cowrote grant that received $50,000 to fund federal High-Intensity Drug Trafficking Area program.
- Coordinated the training of 100 local, county and state clandestine lab responders.

Assistant Team Commander—IHP Emergency Support Team (1997–2000)

- Helped supervise and develop team.
- Provided response planning and supervision at critical incidents across the state, including high-profile civil-disturbance events.
- Personally responded to several hundred critical incidents such as barricaded gunmen and hostage situations.
- Coordinated the team's training and equipment needs. Planned, coordinated and purchased equipment for a six-week (240-hour) basic training school.
- Implemented *less lethal use of force* training with the goal of reducing fatal-force incidents.

Shift Supervisor—Mason City IHP Post (1994–1997)

- Supervised post operations and 10 MSP troopers during shift.
- Served as Firearms Instructor. Researched and implemented "simmunitions" firearms training for post personnel.
- Conducted performance appraisals.
- Supervised property/evidence room.

Commanding Officer—Ordnance & Marksmanship Training Unit, IHP Training Academy (1993–1994)

- Oversaw firearms training for in-services and recruits.
- Implemented state-of-the-art decision shooting training and equipment.
- Researched and implemented ammunition changes for departmental rifle; participated in handgun selection.

Trooper—IHP Flint Post (1978–1993)

- Assigned to Floyd County to provide traffic enforcement and criminal investigation.

Training & Education

- ❏ Iowa Highway Patrol Training Academy (including credits from University of Northern Iowa)
- ❏ Iowa State University
- ❏ Selected training on relevant topics (comprehensive list available on request):
  - Leadership Development
  - Supervisor Development
  - Terrorism Responder
  - Hazardous-Materials Site Safety Officer
  - Technician-Level Hazardous-Materials Responder
  - Firearms Instructor
  - Less-Lethal Instructor
  - Chemical Munitions Instructor
  - Weapons Armorer (SigSauer, Remington, and H&K)

career path. Two levels of bullets are used in the Qualifications Summary. The Selected Accomplishments section put early helps ensure that special accomplishments will be seen and read.

John L. Sullivan

674 Loganberry Lane • Freehold, New Jersey 07728
732-467-1512 (Home) • 732-782-4576 (Cell) • 732-782-4579 (Fax) • JLSul@aol.com (Email)

Objective

I wish to utilize my leadership, management, and organizational experience to continue my career in the areas of <u>Operations</u>, <u>Inventory Management</u>, <u>Logistics</u>, and <u>Loss Prevention</u>.

Summary of Qualifications

Broad-based career with experience in the following:

- Supervisory/Management
- Surveillance
- Security and Safety
- Training and Development

- Inventory Control
- Interviewing/Interrogations
- Project Management
- Loss Prevention

Profile

A highly professional individual with diverse experience in law enforcement.....known as a results-oriented professional.....supervised major investigations leading to final solutions including apprehension or restitution.

Obtained state-of-the-art education in criminal justice techniques and technology.....developed excellent communications and data-collection abilities to assist in investigations.

Excellent interpersonal skills utilized to disseminate information to individuals at all levels.

Professional Experience

Bergen County Sheriff's Office, Jersey City, NJ   **1970–Present**

Lieutenant of Detectives   **1991–Present**
Sergeant   **1985–1991**
Officer   **1970–1985**

- Supervise a staff of 25 police officers, including patrolmen, detectives and plainclothes officers. Prepare work schedules, assign duties, and develop and revise departmental procedures.

- Train new personnel, setting goals and objectives and evaluating performance; administer budgets; handle employee relations, labor relations and grievances; write policies and procedures; conduct in-house investigations/oversee disciplinary actions and coordinate public/community relations activities.

- Assist with and monitor arrests; review major reports and collaborate with officers regarding investigative procedures.

- Utilize aggressive investigative work for successful apprehension of suspects; confirm that proper legal procedures are followed for possible judicial presentations.

- Obtain suspect information, apply for search warrants or subpoenas and, when necessary, travel nationwide to apprehend fugitives.

- While on loan to the Prosecutor's Office, performed homicide investigations. Surveillance and investigative process included identifying and locating suspects and proper handling of evidence.

- Knowledge of laws, legal codes, court procedures, precedents, government regulations, executive orders, agency rules and the democratic political process.

120

Beverly and Mitch Baskin, Marlboro, New Jersey

This resume begins with an Objective statement, a resume opener that was common a decade ago but is seen less in contemporary resumes. One reason for the Objective statement's decline in popularity is that, in the hands of an amateur, a poorly worded or too narrowly focused

John L. Sullivan

Page 2

Pennsylvania Railroad, Newark, NJ   **1960–1970**

Electrician

- Served a 4-year apprenticeship from entry level to completion as a first-class electrician.

- Maintained and repaired or replaced wiring, equipment and fixtures at Pennsylvania Station in Newark.

- Inspected systems and electrical parts to detect hazards, defects and need for adjustments or repair. Maintenance was approximately 80% of the job.

- Installed electrical wiring, equipment, apparatus and fixtures using hand tools and power tools. Performed new installations approximately 20% of the time.

Awards

Executive Member of New Jersey Police Honor Legion

Member of New York City Police Honor Legion

Twelve commendations for exceptional performance, bravery and superior investigative work

Affiliations

Past President, Policeman's Benevolent Association Local 109

Trustee, Fraternal Order of Police Lodge 127

Military

United States Air Force
Master Sergeant

Active Duty	1956–1960
Reserves	1954–1956, 1960–1965

Education

Jersey City Junior College, Jersey City, NJ—attended for criminal justice courses

New York University, New York, NY—attended for criminal justice courses

Objective statement can lead to an early screening out of the applicant. The Objective in this resume exhibits breadth in declared areas of interest. Another notable feature in this resume is the third page, which lists continuing professional seminars in ascending chronological order from 1970 to 1988. The applicant participated

Continuing Professional Seminars

FBI Combat Firearms	1970
Jersey City Police Dept. Combat Shotgun	1971
Jujitsu for Police	1971
Hudson County Prosecutor's Office—Firearms	1972
45 Thompson SMG	1972
9 MM Uzi	1972
M1 Carbine	1972
Electronic Surveillance—Wiretap	1973
Jersey City Police Academy	1973
Photo Surveillance School	1974
Jersey City Police Department Narcotics	1974
Homicide Investigation	1975
Hostage Confrontation Seminar	1976
Criminal Investigation New Jersey State Police	1976
Defensive Driving	1977
Introduction to 2C	1978
Investigation Refresher Jersey City Police Dept.	1982
New Jersey State Police Breathalyzer School	1984
Emergency Medical Technician	1984
Civil Liability	1986
Methods of Instruction	1986
Breathalyzer Refresher	1986
Managing a Detective Unit	1988

in these continuing-education events while he was first an Officer and then a Sergeant with the Bergen County Sheriff's Office in Jersey City, New Jersey.

Maintenance

Resumes at a Glance

KATHRYN TAMBURRO

76 Columbia Street
Frankfort, NY 00000

(555) 555-5555
kart@aol.com

EXPERIENCED HOUSEKEEPING PROFESSIONAL
Offering an excellent customer service philosophy, a professional attitude and proven skills in project coordination

PROFILE

Hardworking and self-directed individual with vast experience in providing comprehensive housekeeping services for a multibuilding apartment complex. Qualifications include strong organization skills, a good eye for detail and a bottom-line focus. Effective time manager with great people skills and a reputation for high-service standards. Able to function in a multidimensional role and can perform under pressure.

HOUSEKEEPING SKILLS & EXPERIENCE	AREAS OF SUPERVISORY EXPERIENCE
■ Identifying Deficiencies / Damage Assessment	■ Work Order Management & Scheduling
■ Investment Protection / Quality Control	■ Inspection Procedure Improvement
■ Carpet & Surface Care Techniques & Systems	■ Owner Relations / Personnel Training
■ Move-Ins / Move-Outs & Inspection Reports	■ Contractor Selection & Scheduling

HIGHLIGHTS

➔ Highly skilled at organizing time, resources and workload to maximize daily productivity

➔ Able to meet client expectations and overall objectives despite sudden setbacks and changing priorities

➔ Experienced in responding to demanding situations and tactfully resolving difficult issues

➔ Maintain a high degree of awareness of property owner/tenant sensitivities

➔ Skilled at communicating with work crews and able to facilitate cooperation among all groups

EMPLOYMENT EXPERIENCE

1990 to Present <u>Housekeeping Department</u>   *Guy Prindle Apartments—Frankfort, NY*

Provide housekeeping services for this 835-unit garden-style apartment complex. Accountable for maintaining all common areas, 31 in-house laundry rooms, main office and the gym. Inspect vacant units to assess overall condition and identify any deficiencies. Prepare inspection reports, formulate damage estimates and schedule work. Coordinate contractor crews (paint, maintenance, carpet) and direct daily efforts to maintain cost and schedule guidelines necessary for apartment turnovers.

Accepted increased responsibilities (3/03) to include some supervisory functions. Oversee work order management and contractor coordination, which includes distributing maintenance calls among seven Maintenance Techs and two Porters. Coordinate maintenance requests and daily tasks to comply with owner's expectations. Credited with resolving a three-month work order backlog despite a staff shortage.

1998 to Present <u>Owner</u>   *Kat's Cleaning Service—Frankfort, NY*

Built business from start-up to a consistent client base acquired through referrals only. Provide weekly and biweekly cleaning services for single-family homes, apartments and townhomes. Achieved high levels of customer satisfaction based on honesty, reliability and thorough work.

ADDITIONAL INFORMATION

QUALITIES   Detail-oriented / Persistent / Patient / Good Judgement / High Energy / Friendly Personality

OTHER   Cleaning Product Knowledge / Appliance Life Expectancy / Carpet Wear Issues / Quality Factors

CIVIL SERVICE   Completed the General Custodian Civil Service Test (5/02)

121

Kristin M. Coleman, Poughkeepsie, New York

A pair of horizontal lines acts as a banner that attests to the person's excellence and professionalism. Small type (10-point Times New Roman) makes it possible to fit much information on one page.

Jared Davis

320 Fayette Road   Beaumont, Texas 77683   H: (409) 227-3854   C: (409) 929-4512

PROFESSIONAL PROFILE

Multifaceted construction, operations and customer service background includes experience in supervision, plant equipment operations, construction, safety, maintenance, project management, customer service and product sales.

Summary of Skills

Supervision	Organization	Inventory Control
Equipment Maintenance	Scheduling	Problem Solving
Chemical Treatment	Customer Relationships	Sales / Customer Service
Mechanical Troubleshooting	Bid Estimates	Residential Trades

PROFESSIONAL EXPERIENCE

POOL MAINTENANCE TECHNICIAN / CHEMICAL ANALYST   April 2001 to Present
BEAUMONT POOL SERVICES—Beaumont, Texas—Beaumont Pool Services specializes in the construction / installation, maintenance, structural / equipment repair and product sales of residential and commercial pools and spas.
- Manage 24 residential accounts on a biweekly basis.
- Provide customer service and sales for pool / spa chemicals and supplies.
- Coordinate and follow up on equipment repair.
- Retain customer accounts by providing excellent customer service.
- Recognized in a letter of commendation from a "difficult" customer, resulting in "saving" the account.

SALES ASSOCIATE   **August 1997 to April 2001**
LACK'S—Beaumont, Texas—Lack's is Texas' largest supplier of quality home furnishings, bedding, electronics and appliances, with more than 60 years of dependable family-owned service from 39 home furnishing centers.
- Recognized in the following achievements:
  o *TOP 10% SALES CLUB,* Sealy Posturepedic Mattress, national level
  o Number one sales team, corporate level
  o Highest number of sales generated in a specific period, local level
- Accomplished a 50% ratio of repeat and referred customer database.
- Achieved high closing ratio by gauging customer response and adjusting presentations to resolve customer concerns. Proven success in overcoming resistance to close sales.
- Established a successful sales record in a strictly commission-based environment.
- Enhanced customer satisfaction through continuous implementation of communication and problem-solving techniques.
- Generated $380,000 worth of merchandise sales in the first 12 months.
- Initiated customer financing and maintained database for follow-up.

SALES REPRESENTATIVE   May 1996 to August 1997
COLOR TILE, INC.– Beaumont, Texas—Color Tile was founded in 1953 and is the most recognized name today in the flooring industry with stores nationwide. Color Tile partnered with CarpetsPlus in 2002 to create a national chain of premier floor covering design centers. Color Tile closed the Beaumont store in August 1997.
- Achieved **PRESIDENT'S CLUB** status within 2 months of employment.
- Enhanced production in the areas of negotiating sales, closing sales and customer satisfaction.

122

MeLisa Rogers, Shiner, Texas

The applicant had a multifaceted background in construction, inside retail sales, and part-time domestic work, and he wanted to present it all together in an attractive package. The writer summarized all the applicant's skills early in the resume and then—in the Professional Experience

Jared Davis

Résumé page two

OWNER / MANAGER / SUPERVISOR   May 1994 to December 1996

FRONTIER CONSTRUCTION—Jackson, Mississippi—Frontier Construction consisted of a four–man framing crew specializing in residential home construction in the Northern Mississippi area.

- **Project Management:** Managed up to four concurrent new-construction projects ranging in value from $50,000 to $250,000. Increased business by 20% through positive client relationships and a positive reputation. Secured bid estimates, purchased supplies, hired and trained personnel.
- **Bid Management:** Reviewed and selected bids and proposals, with a proven history of bringing projects in on time and at budget. Developed construction schedules for all phases of work and delegated duties to site lead personnel. Secured various trade crews for 75% of the projects.
- **Safety Management:** Achieved a zero accident rate for crew as a result of follow-through and the implementation of all safety regulations at every project site in a variety of environmental conditions.

CREW SUPERVISOR   October 1990 to May 1994

KRUEGER FRAMING—Jackson, Mississippi—Krueger Framing consisted of two four–man framing crews specializing in residential home construction in the Northern Mississippi area.

- Supervised a four-man crew in residential framing jobs.
- Processed contract bid and negotiation under direction of owner.
- Fielded customer complaints and renovations.
- Assisted in project management of a new venture awarded in a commercial assignment.

OPERATOR / LEAD MAN   February 1988 to October 1990

JENSON FOODS—Biloxi, Mississippi—Jenson Foods was the third-largest poultry operation in the U.S. with corporate offices in Birmingham, Alabama. The Biloxi facility processed approximately 173,000 birds in two production shifts. Tyson Foods acquired Jenson Foods in 1997.

- **Whole-bird Line Lead Man:** Operated bagging /stapling equipment, rerouted non-A-grade birds to packing lines, stacked and moved product to 28-degree room and managed rework process. Assisted supervisor in setting up department for the shift, assigning/motivating department personnel, training new employees and communicating with USDA Grader.
- **Weldatron:** Stacked multiple product lines, managed rework process, moved product to 28-degree room, and trained new employees.

ADDITIONAL TRAINING AND EXPERIENCE

- Currently facilitate employment workshops for a vendor trainer for the State of Texas for the Orange County Development Board. These workshops consist of job search techniques, interviewing skills, career assessments and positive work habits training.
- Achieved Bronze and Silver Award for Sealy Bedding training.
- Completed multiple courses in product knowledge for appliances, technology, fabric types, furniture lines/styles, bedding and floor coverings.
- Completed multiple courses in sales and customer service training.
- Proficient in data entry software programs.
- Knowledge of food processing equipment operations and maintenance.

section—detailed each business, listing under each any corresponding achievements. Notice the use of horizontal lines, the box, and underlining in this resume. Notice, too, the second level of bullets.

Robert Render

147 Englishtown Road ~ Old Bridge Township, NJ 08857
(732) 555-5555 (H) ~ E-mail: render538@aol.com

MAINTENANCE SPECIALIST

Top-performing and motivated maintenance professional with 20 years of experience in manufacturing, distribution, warehousing, line production, maintenance, and equipment operation. Strengths include excellent communication with all levels of personnel. Known as a results-oriented professional with attention to detail.

Self-disciplined leader with the ability to troubleshoot and resolve problems in a timely manner. Enjoy performing multiple tasks/projects while keeping an eye on bottom-line profits for the company.

Experienced in supervising, mentoring, and training staff. Address process improvement issues and find better methods to complete the job with fewer injuries.

Areas of Expertise:

- Project Management
- Equipment Maintenance
- Budget Management
- Preventive Maintenance
- Hydraulic Maintenance

- Low-Pressure Boiler License
- Electrical Maintenance
- Troubleshooting
- Maintenance Supervision
- Licensed Forklift Driver

Experience

PROCTER & GAMBLE, Dayton, NJ   1996–2004

Maintenance Leader

- Perform preventive maintenance and repair of equipment and facility grounds for this food and beverage manufacturing operation with seven manufacturing lines.
- Responsible for machine ownership during product changes, including maintenance and process adjustments.
- Recommend process machinery improvement projects.
- Familiar with conveyors, bottle cleaners, labelers, packers, palletizers, and filling machines.
- Perform work as an electrician, millwright, plumber, and forklift mechanic.
- Thorough knowledge of mechanical, electrical, hydraulic, and plumbing systems for process equipment, as well as for building and grounds.

PHILIPS WAREHOUSE, Bridgewater, NJ   1991–1995

Facility Maintenance Supervisor

- Managed five people at this public warehouse, which stored everything from hazardous chemicals to pencils.
- Responsible for eight different facilities, ordering supplies and scheduling manpower and boiler operations.
- Saved the company $5,000 by upgrading the electrical panels using in-house labor.
- Thorough knowledge of procedures and techniques used for shipping, receiving, and materials handling.

Continued

123

Beverly and Mitch Baskin, Marlboro, New Jersey

A two-line page border ties together visually the two pages of this resume. One thick line appears below the contact information, and two thinner lines enclose the Areas of Expertise. The result is that these areas are easily spotted on the first page. In the Experience section,

Robert Render

Page 2

LARRY'S ELECTRICAL SERVICE, Helmetta, NJ 1987–1991

Electrical Technician

- Installed electrical wiring, equipment, apparatus, and fixtures for both residential and commercial customers.
- Inspected systems and electrical parts to detect hazards, defects, and need for adjustments or repair.
- Tested electrical systems and continuity of circuits in electrical wiring, equipment, and fixtures using testing devices such as ohmmeters and voltmeters.
- Diagnosed malfunctioning systems, apparatus, and components using test equipment.

LOUIS FAMILY FOODS, Lansdale, MD 1986–1987

Facility Maintenance

- Responsible for daily maintenance of the facility and grounds, as well as the process equipment for the manufacture of food.
- Skills necessary to perform the job were the functions of a welder, pipe fitter, rigger, and millwright.

AMERICAN STRUCTURAL STEEL, Manville, NJ 1984–1986

Welder / Blueprint Coordinator

- Daily duties included layout of parts, interpreting locations from the blueprints; welding; and fabrication of steel structures.

Special Training/Licenses

EAST BRUNSWICK VOCATIONAL TECHNICAL SCHOOL, East Brunswick, NJ
Electrical Career Path

Black Seal Low-Pressure Boiler License, State of New Jersey

Forklift License

CPR and First Aid Training, Procter & Gamble, Dayton, NJ

bullets point to a mix of responsibilities and achievements. Boldfacing helps the reader spot key information, such as headings, company names, job positions, and dates. See Cover Letter 8.

C O N F I D E N T I A L   *Ready to relocate to the Clovis area*

Charles Henry Kraft

2102 Sledgeway Street   ✆ 907.555.5555 (Cell)
Anchorage, Alaska 99517   apmaster@whiz.att.net

WHAT I CAN OFFER TOPLINE AIRLINES AS YOUR NEWEST AIRCRAFT MAINTENANCE SUPERVISOR

❑ Credibility at every level, from management to line mechanic ❑ Skill to find, interpret, and act on trends to build productivity and limit liability ❑ Focus that removes every distraction from the workplace ❑ Skill to find, reward, and retain the best in aircraft maintainers ❑ Knowledge to separate symptoms from problems

LICENSURE AND CERTIFICATIONS

❑ Airframe & Powerplant License Number 44409976

RECENT WORK HISTORY WITH EXAMPLES OF PROBLEMS SOLVED

❑ **A & P Mechanic** *promoted from 10 eligibles (all with years more experience) to* **Alternate Lead Mechanic.** *Promoted from 3 eligibles in just 90 days to* **Lead Mechanic** *and* **RII Inspector,** Alaska Wings, Anchorage, Alaska   Dec 90–Present
Alaska Wings operates nine all-cargo aircraft, primarily in state. Annual sales approach $45M.

Supervise six A & P professionals.

Serve as the **only maintenance decision maker** on my shift. Regularly guide pilots in assessing write-ups that occur hundreds of miles from our home base. *Results:* Consistently **strike the right balance** between **maximizing time in the air** and operating in **complete safety.**

Made myself the key person in bringing on a new model aircraft critical to a major expansion. Oversaw the cargo conversion. Plowed through half a room full of boxes of records to **ensure compliance** and convert MX records to our standard. *Results:* **Easily trained our people on a type they had never seen before.**

Zeroed in on a **tiny indicator of a potentially large problem:** a newly painted-over screw. Quickly realized my finding pointed to a missed critical inspection of flight control surfaces. Got the right checks done fast. *Results:* We placed our **new airplane online with complete confidence.**

Removed a major frustration for our mechanics: reference materials that were too far from our work area. Created a mobile library. *Results:* **Saved nearly $4K** in lost labor hours alone. New arrangement made it easier for me to **help new people** find just the references they needed.

C O N F I D E N T I A L   *More indicators of performance TopLine Airlines can use…*

124

Don Orlando, Montgomery, Alabama

This individual wanted to leave Alaska for the warmer climates of the lower 48. The writer wanted to set the applicant apart by showing "the unusually harsh conditions under which he succeeded." A company wants to know what a prospective employee can offer the

CONFIDENTIAL

| Charles Henry Kraft | **Aircraft Maintenance Supervisor** | 907.555.5555 |

Used my "systems view" to fix a critical write-up that had not only stumped our maintainers, but also threatened a late departure. *Results:* Not only fixed the problem in 30 minutes, but **made certain everybody in the shop could do the same thing.**

Make training a part of everyday operations. My regular follow-ups help us **find and reward the best.** *Results:* **Directors** of Maintenance and Quality Control **accept my recommendations** for task assignments without change.

❏ **A & P Mechanic** *with later additional duties as* **RII Inspector.** Northern Lights Air, Kenai, Alaska   Dec 87–Dec 90
Northern Lights Air operated eight aircraft to carry passengers and mail as a commuter service.

Supervised three A & P mechanics.

PROFESSIONAL DEVELOPMENT

❏ "Line Maintenance for the PW100 Series Engine," SECA, one week, 03
My employer chose me as one of 6 (from a group of 18) to attend this training funded by my company.

❏ "Updating Hot Section Inspection of the Pratt & Whitney PT6 Engine," Pratt & Whitney, one day, 02.

❏ "Maintaining the EMB 120 Aircraft Propeller," Hamilton-Sunstrand, two days, 02.
One of 5 selected from a group of 18 eligibles.

❏ "EMB 120 Aircraft Line Maintenance," Skywest, one week, 99. *Paid for by my employer.*

❏ "Hot Section Inspection of the Pratt & Whitney PT6 Engine," Dallas Aeromotive, one day, 99.

❏ "Maintenance Procedures for the Beechcraft 1900 Airliner Series," Flight Safety International, two weeks, 87. *I paid for this program myself.*

COMPUTER SKILLS

❏ Proficieint in **proprietary aircraft maintenance software suite**

❏ Working knowledge of Word and Outlook

PROFESSIONAL AFFILIATIONS

❏ Member, Professional Aviation Maintenance Association, since 99

company. The resume begins with this issue and meets it head on. A company also wants results, not a lot of talk. The Recent Work History section presents, one after another, results of problems solved. See Cover Letter 9.

ALAN JOHNSON

60-90 James Avenue • East Islip, NY 11730
(H) 631-000-0000 • (C) 631-555-5555

COMMERCIAL BUILDING MAINTENANCE

Hardworking, mechanically inclined commercial building maintenance professional with 10+ years of experience providing building maintenance services for high-rise apartment buildings and major commercial building in the Metro New York area. Select areas of qualifications include

- Building Maintenance and Repairs
- Janitorial Services
- Office Relocations
- Supplies Inventory Tracking
- Work Space Improvements
- Employee / Visitor (Tenant) Relations

- External Maintenance / Groundskeeping
- Light Electrical and Plumbing Work
- Incident Reporting / Recordkeeping
- Painting (Offices, Corridors and Unit Areas)
- Carpentry Work
- Renovations / Remodeling

PROFESSIONAL EXPERIENCE

HAMPTON HOUSE, Patchogue, NY
Senior Maintenance Associate, 2004–Present

Reporting directly to Facilities Coordinator, manage the maintenance operations of a modern independent living facility with 120 apartment units with the assistance of three porters.

- Prepared building for grand opening to present it in fully operating and pristine condition.
- Conduct building inspection tours and weekly fire and alarm systems testing to ensure the safety of residents and compliance with building codes.
- Work with punch lists and blueprints to ensure the thorough and on-time completion of cleaning, painting, repairs, snow removal and minor electrical and plumbing work.
- Perform HVAC work on 300 P-TAC units in areas of preventative maintenance and repair.
- Remain on call 24/7 as point person for management, inspectors and Fire Marshall to coordinate emergency response procedures.
- Foster relationships with seniors and families by responding to a broad range of requests.
- Stand in for kitchen and dining room personnel; assist with food prep and cooking chores.

THE SILVERMAN BUILDING, New York, NY
Assistant Engineer, 2000–2004

Working under a licensed engineer, carried out electrical, plumbing and HVAC work on package units throughout 49 floors across a one-million-square-foot commercial building space.

- Conducted daily building tours to check the temperature and pressure of cooling towers.
- Responded to emergencies and routine house calls for hundreds of corporate tenants that partially included *Rock and Roll* magazine, Greeting Cards and American Credit Card.
- Performed general and preventative maintenance in areas of cleaning, painting and repairs for tenants and 70 mechanical rooms, including Switch Gear, House Pump and Fuel Tank rooms.

Continued

125

Ann Baehr, East Islip, New York

The applicant had extensive building maintenance experience in both senior residences and large commercial buildings. To showcase how well rounded the applicant was, the writer created a comprehensive list of keywords (see the shaded box of bulleted items) that would qualify him

ALAN JOHNSON

Resume, Page Two
(H) 631-000-0000 • (C) 631-555-5555

TECHNOLOGY LEADERS, Bay Shore, NY
Building Maintenance Mechanic, 1996–2000

Performed maintenance services for the Company's corporate headquarters with six floors accommodating more than 2,000 employees, including a childcare center and employee cafeteria.

- Handled service calls and projects ranging from broken keys to large-scale interoffice relocations of office furniture, file cabinets, computer equipment and floor plants.

- Maintained the condition of office spaces and leased apartments allocated for business clients and out-of-town/international employees during corporate meetings and special events.

- Worked with, and often supervised, a team of six maintenance crew members.

- Used schematics to determine furniture placement to picture-hanging alignment.

- Ensured compliance with building codes and both OSHA and Fire Department regulations.

SUPPLIES WAREHOUSE, East Islip, NY
Receiving Clerk, Evening Shift, 1994–1996

- Unloaded lumber, plumbing supplies, sheetrock and related home improvement products from trucks and transport to respective departments for restocking before store opening.

- Assisted all department personnel and early-morning customers with requests about plumbing, building supplies, lighting fixtures and millwork.

EDUCATION

MECHANICS HIGH SCHOOL, Flushing, NY
Diploma in Mechanical Applications

OSHA Safety Compliance Training

Local 23 Training Center
Fundamental for Applied Electricity for Building Equipment
Introduction to Valves, Pumps and Heating Equipment
Introduction to Commercial Office Buildings

TECHNICAL SKILLS

Operate power tools, table saw/vise,
forklifts and key machines; interpret floor plans

Professional References and Letters of Recommendation Presented at Time of Meeting

quickly to a hiring manager. For each workplace, a summary statement in italic indicates briefly the scope of the applicant's activities. Education and further training appear on page 2.

Lewis Smith

4702 NW 1659 SE, Seattle, WA 99999
Home: (555) 555–5555 ◆ Mobile: (777) 777–7777

Experienced Ground Support Equipment Technician with more than 20 years of experience in the airline ground maintenance industry. Extensive hands-on expertise in performing and supervising minor and major maintenance for airline ground equipment. Key strengths include:

▪ Maintenance Operations	▪ Project Management	▪ Staff Training & Leadership
▪ Vendor Relationship Management	▪ Program Coordination	▪ Inventory Control
▪ Hazardous Materials Awareness	▪ Fabrication	▪ Team Building

Outstanding troubleshooting ability and a proven track record of high levels of quality assurance, cost savings, productivity, and overall equipment readiness. A skilled training instructor with expertise in parts management and interpretation of system schematics. Committed to quality workmanship and ethical conduct.

Professional Experience

ALASKA AIRLINES, Seattle, WA   **1987–Present**
Progressed to Senior-level Technician in Seattle. Rated #2 GSE shop in the Northwest for Alaska Air Group in 2002 and 2003.

Lead Ground Maintenance Technician
- Oversee and coordinate service operations for more than 300 pieces of ground equipment for up to 20 city stations throughout Washington, Idaho, California, and Canada.
- Substantial mechanical and electrical systems training and experience aid in immediate repair of breakdowns, avoiding air flight delays.
- Trained more than 25 agents on correct operation of ground equipment, resulting in proper safety and injury-prevention practices.
- Awarded the Top Performer bonus for first-class commitment and service in 2001 and 2002.
- Instrumental in development of ongoing out-station repair and maintenance program.
- Provide courtesy technical support to other airlines, establishing solid relationships with station managers and agents.
- Recognized mechanical resource person. Interpret nontechnical descriptions, aiding in troubleshooting and correcting problems over the phone to outstations.
- Compose maintenance flow sheets and parts ordering sheets; maintain detailed documentation records on all equipment and parts.
- Fabricate various ground equipment, including bag carts, tow bars, LAV carts, deicers, truck flat beds, and bulk tanks with heat systems.
- Basic hands-on computer knowledge, including Windows and the Internet.
- Rapid advancement through series of progressively responsible positions in recognition of leadership capabilities, performance, and technical expertise. Other positions included On-Call Ground Maintenance (1994–1996), Ground Service Agent (1988–1994), Aircraft Groomer (1987–1988).

Continuing Education

Lektro Maintenance and Troubleshooting—model AP8850SDA-AL-100
Aero Specialties—Hobart models 600 & Jet-Ex4D
Maintenance and Troubleshooting—Hobart models GPU-600, Jet-Ex4D, & 90CU24P5
Charging Systems & Starting Circuits
Automotive Painting
Delta Weld 451-641
GPU Training, Welding, & Basic Hydraulics

126

Denette Jones, Mountain View, Hawaii

The horizontal lines enclose and thereby call attention to the applicant's key strengths that are relevant to aircraft maintenance. Under Professional Experience, bulleted items include achievements.

Management

Resumes at a Glance

DONOVAN A. THOMAS
555 Water Tower Street ● Boise, ID 00000 ● 555-555-5555 ● thomas.donovan@email.com

OPERATIONS MANAGEMENT PROFESSIONAL
"Enhance revenues and profitability via the identification & resolution of diverse operational challenges"

OBJECTIVE

Seasoned management professional with extensive leadership skills and experience over a broad range of operations and management functions seeks career opportunity within your dynamic organization. Offering solid understanding and execution of administrative, human resources, budgeting and resource management initiatives combined with track record of consistent contributions to increase quality, cost effectiveness and profitability.

Areas of Expertise

- Operations Management
- Leadership & Team Building
- Budget Planning & Review
- Regulatory Oversight (OSHA, EPA, CDL, CFR, DNR)

- Project Planning & Execution
- Business Relationship Management
- Resource Management
- Collective Bargaining
- Inventory Control

ACCOMPLISHMENTS

- Independently investigated, planned and **wrote project proposals with values up to $250K**
- **Experienced in advanced technologies;** direct operation and maintenance of all electronic equipment, transmission lines, antenna / emergency power systems and fleet equipment
- **Valued advisor and requested consultant** to the Director of Technical Services during collective bargaining sessions
- Over career, has supervised as many as 30 employees **fostering team-based environments, which promote high morale**

PROFESSIONAL EXPERIENCE

SITE MANAGER /   **Technology Avenue, Inc &**   **1999–Present**
FACILITY SECURITY OFFICER   **Security Engineering, Inc.**
Deliver consistent bottom-line results while directing operation and maintenance programs that ensure optimal performance and compliance of all technical initiatives. Handle all administrative and managerial tasks for smooth flow of daily business and review planning and budget expenditures, authorize CLIN expenditures and administer collective bargaining agreements and associated benefits. Consistently ensure adherence to OSHA, WI OSHA, EPA, CDL, CFR and DNR regulations and serve as corporate representative on behalf of site employees.

TECHNICIAN II (ELF)   **Naval Systems & Satellites**   **1993–1999**
Accountable for the operation, maintenance and repair of extremely low frequency (ELF) high-power transmitters and all associated equipment; served as watch supervisor.

FIELD ENGINEER   **Sky High Aerospace, Inc.**   **1991–1993**
Key member of the engineering team involved with repairing and manufacturing circuit boards and canvas harnesses for the U.S. Army's MILES Program. Maintained strict quality control of goods; investigated, ordered and maintained spare parts inventory and set up warehousing operation for support of the F-15 / 16 training devices and the MILES supply depot.

Prior to 1991, promoted through a series of increasingly responsible positions with the U.S. Navy including
Leading Chief Petty Officer, Department Head, Leading Petty Officer, Chief-in-Charge and Technician

PROFESSIONAL TRAINING
Extensive coursework and training in

- Automated Test Equipment
- Miniature Repair 2
- KWR-37 / KG-14 "C"
- AN/WSC-3 "C"

- COSAL Maintenance
- Microwave / Terminal "C"
- ET "A"
- NATO BID-610 Cryptographic

127

Tammy K. Shoup, Decatur, Indiana

The header states clearly the applicant's career focus and gives an idea of what he offers. The Areas of Expertise and Accomplishments capture attention and offset his lack of relevant education.

ELAINE MIRAMONT
78 Norwalk Street
New York, NY 00000
(555) 555-5555

QUALIFICATIONS SUMMARY

Offering 19 years of **MEDICAL OFFICE** experience. Excellent planning, organizational and administrative skills combine with strong performance in staffing, productivity improvement and patient service/satisfaction. Demonstrate high level of professionalism and compassion with patients. Equally comfortable with front or back office. Qualifications include the following:

- Medical Assistant Skills
- Patient Appointments / Surgical Scheduling
- Medical Office Terminology & Transcription
- Purchasing & Inventory Management
- ICD-9 Codes
- Physician & Provider Relations
- Staff Training & Development
- Files & Records Management

PROFESSIONAL EXPERIENCE

Executrix, Edward Jones Trust, Dublin, CA (2001 to present)

Wilson Group, New York, NY (1988 to 2001)
Office Manager

Managed administrative activities at a surgical practice with 6 surgeons and several support personnel. Maintained well-organized, efficient office operations. Oversaw human resources, office systems, purchasing, finance/accounting, patient relations, record keeping and regulatory affairs. Clinical functions encompassed assisting physicians with minor surgical procedures, patient exams, disposal of hazardous materials, patient flow and preparation of tissue samples and cultures.

Contributions

- Conducted phone triage, booked surgeries and surgical assistants, obtained pre-authorization from insurance companies and scheduled patient pre-op appointments.
- Directed human resources functions of interviewing, hiring and training in office procedures and sterile techniques.
- Managed physicians' monthly production reports that involved tracking number of referrals, referrals source, and accounts receivable.
- Spearheaded new office opening, including layout of business area, reception room, 3 exam rooms, 2 physicians' offices, lab and kitchen and installation of phone service; established office procedures.
- Enrolled physicians with 15 insurance companies.

Richard Murray, M.D., New York, NY (1980 to 1986)
Office Assistant & Receptionist

Assigned to 3 dentists in a practice with 5 dentists, 2 hygienists, 2 insurance secretaries and 5 dental assistants. Fielded a high volume of telephone calls in a fast-paced, demanding environment.

Contributions

- Spearheaded the initial computerization to fully automate record keeping, appointments, insurance, billing and patient database functions; assisted in entering patient data for more than 2000 patients.
- Managed Capitation Program that encompassed managing appointments and enrollment verification of patients serviced with accounts receivable.
- Recommended and implemented new filing system that increased efficiency and accessibility.

EDUCATION

A.S., Medical Assisting, Valmore Community College, New York, NY

128

Louise Garver, Windsor, Connecticut

This person had to take a leave from her career to serve as a Trust Administrator in another state. She was now ready to resume her career. The resume focuses on her strengths and accomplishments.

Pamela Heshe ◆ Katherine Heshe

1234 SE 23rd Avenue   Rhododendron, Oregon 55555   555-555-5555

Apartment Managers

Professional Profile

✓ Highly motivated, dynamic and energetic, with more than 30 combined years of experience successfully working with diverse personalities.

✓ Experienced management and maintenance of various houses and plexes.

✓ Possess strong organizational skills and effective paper-processing techniques.

✓ Expert bookkeeping abilities.

✓ Skills include minor repairs, simple plumbing, light electrical, painting, pool maintenance, landscaping, strong maintenance and clean-up experience.

✓ Effective in prequalifying new lease applicants and collecting rents in a timely fashion.

✓ Personable, loyal, honest, committed and creative. Able to maintain property impeccably and get along well with tenants and management.

✓ Able to be bonded if necessary.

✓ Computer-literate.

Pamela Heshe

Employment History

Medical Assistant • Portland, Oregon • *1990–2004*

• OHSU Sellwood/Moreland Clinic • *1999–2004*

• Medical Temporary • *1990, 1991, 1995, 1997, 1999*

• Mount Tabor Medical Group • *1996–1997*

• Dr. Samuel Miller • *1991–1995*

Education

Medical Emphasis • *1988*
• Clackamas Community College • Oregon City, Oregon

Graduate
• Portland Community College • Portland, Oregon

Graduate
• Oregon X-Ray Institute • Portland, Oregon

Katherine Heshe

Employment History

Accounting Manager/Administrative Assistant
• National Metal Distributors, Inc. • *2000–2001* Vancouver, Washington

Bookkeeper • *1998–2000*
• Aerospace & Corrosion International Vancouver, Washington

Letter Carrier • *1976–1997*
• United States Postal Service Portland, Oregon

Military

United States Air Force • *1971–1975*
• Disbursement Accountant

Education

Elliott Bookkeeping School • *1998*

Portland Community College
Accounting • *1976*

129

Rosie Bixel, Portland, Oregon

This is a rare resume because it is for two people: members of an apartment management team. The writer combined their skills in one Profile but presented their individual backgrounds separately.

Roger Grant

2345 N.E. 302nd Lane • Portland, Oregon 33333

555-555-5555 *cell*   rg32812@easystreet.org   *home* 555-555-5555

Project Manager

Professional Profile

Hardworking, disciplined, and energetic ***Project Manager*** with extensive experience in all aspects of the electrical industry. Proven strengths in effective Project Management with a history of finishing projects ahead of schedule and under budget while increasing company profits. Possess great "people" skills and a well-developed sense of humor. Strong business networking skills with a commitment to professionalism and a job well done while thoroughly enjoying a challenge.

Outstanding Accomplishments

- Advanced from Purchasing Agent to Management in four years, increasing sales from $8 thousand to $4 million per year.
- Tripled business in two years while managing Dynaelectric Service Department.
- Produced largest profits in twenty years while at Siriani.

Selected Projects

Lloyd Center Mall—Security camera installation
Most sophisticated system on the West Coast—Finished **ahead of schedule** and **under budget**
City of Portland—Portland Building electrical retrofit
Class A high-rises and various other projects for City of Portland and Multnomah County
Port of Portland—Portland International Airport
Duty-free Stores • Hudson News • Satellite Installations • Tenant Installs
Tyco—various projects—Honored as outstanding Project Manager
Oregon Health Sciences University—Primate facility
Nike—various projects

Related Employment History

Manager • Service Department • Dynaelectric, *a division of Emcor* • Portland, Oregon • *1998–present*
Emcor is the largest specialty contractor in the world.

Start-up Assistant • Team Electric • Portland, Oregon • *1998*
Assisted in development of service division. Extensive estimating and project management.

Service Manager • Siriani Electric • Portland, Oregon • *1994–1998*
Developed service department to $500,000–$700,000 with an approximate gross profit of 35%.
Dispatched, scheduled, estimated and billed using "Estimation" and "Contest" computer programs.

Purchasing Agent • Grasle Electric • Portland, Oregon • *1989–1994*
Functioned as Interim Service Manager and purchased all items as necessary for service department.

Deliveries / Customer Service • Pepco Electric • Portland, Oregon • *1983–1989*
Drove route truck, pulled orders and supplied customer service.

Training

Graduate • NECA *(National Electrical Contractors Association)*
Project Management *and* **Estimating Classes** • NECA

130

Rosie Bixel, Portland, Oregon

The writer sought to display this Electrician's major projects and outstanding accomplishments with well-known corporations. The Professional Profile makes clear his status as a Project Manager.

M.A. VANDERWIEL

64 Oswego Avenue
Saratoga, NY 12866

(845) 555-1212
maryv@optonline.net

LOGISTICS / WAREHOUSE OPERATIONS MANAGEMENT
Accomplished at utilizing strong operational, logistical and inventory knowledge to improve efficiencies and increase productivity

---

Experienced manager with a strong sense of company loyalty and a record of success for building cohesive teams and reducing costs. Offering proven sales skills, an approachable leadership style and expert analysis abilities. Consistently able to enhance operations through a substantial knowledge of warehouse practices and a clear understanding of the functioning of carriers.

- Highly ethical manager who is able to balance a dual role as a member of management and employee advocate
- Proven ability to establish mutual respect with staff and develop incentives that build cooperation and morale
- Can be counted on to work side-by-side with staff, serving as a positive influence and leading by example

SPECIFIC AREAS OF STRENGTH & EXPERIENCE

- Current Warehouse Standards & Practices / Computerized Systems
- Detailed Logs / Database Management / Activity Analysis
- Staff Motivation / Cross-Training / Teambuilding / Hiring
- Materials Movement / Quality Assurance / Order Fulfillment
- Sales / Trade Shows / Customer Service
- Scheduling, Routing & Workload Delegation
- Safety Training / Accident Prevention
- Vendor & Carrier Relations / Negotiating Tariffs

EMPLOYMENT EXPERIENCE

SARATOGA COUNTRY FURNITURE, *Saratoga, NY*   **1996 to Present**
(Privately owned furniture company with four retail showrooms and a factory that includes a residential division and a commercial sales division that serves the restaurant and hospitality industry nationwide.)

Shipping Department Manager *(1/00 to Present)*   **Assistant Foreman** *(2/99 to 9/99)*
Assistant Shipping Department Manager *(9/99 to 1/00)*   **CDL Driver / Dispatcher** *(9/96 to 2/99)*

Oversee all shipping and receiving including prioritizing shipments, determining route assignments, managing a 45,000 sq. ft. warehouse and supervising up to 15 employees. Accountable for scheduling freight carriers, commercial orders and residential deliveries while simultaneously managing inventory, expediting orders, processing paperwork and handling customer service. Plan daily workload based on available labor, adjusting priorities according to staff ability levels. Monitor safety status and constantly inspect facility and equipment to identify operational inefficiencies or safety hazards. Manage the flow of information among various departments to ensure that orders are properly scheduled, packed, tracked and shipped.

Work closely with customers to establish service quality expectations and standards. Also travel nationwide to help coordinate sales and visit client locations to handle repairs. Plan routes and schedules to maintain critical delivery timetables and manage the fleet maintenance and operational records. Analyze performance reports to identify areas in need of improvement, manage labor budgets and maintain detailed activity records. Also, serve as a sales representative and product expert when needed.

- Recognized by management and staff as a skilled problem solver who is able to quickly resolve situations before they escalate.
- Constantly make recommendations to increase productivity, reduce costs and improve efficiencies.
- Created several process improvements that improved product quality, customer service and staff capabilities.
- Initiated, developed and implemented the centralization of the delivery process, which represents 30% in annual savings.
- Consistently achieve all production goals *while* maintaining the high standard of quality required.

SPECIALIZED TRAINING

Herkimer Community College, *Herkimer, NY*
Major: Computer Information Systems

Herkimer Training (Furniture Repair / Damage Assessment Specialist)
Lockout—Tagout Certified / Forklift Certified / CDL License

131

Kristin M. Coleman, Poughkeepsie, New York

This applicant was relocating and wanted to pursue similar opportunities in warehouse management/logistics. He had no formal business training but did have successful experience.

JEFF GOLDMAN

Performance-driven executive with a wealth of operations and management experience whose accomplishments reflect outstanding leadership skills and a long-term focus on maximizing efficiency and productivity

SUMMARY OF QUALIFICATIONS

Goal-oriented executive with extensive experience in retail operations and administrative management. Demonstrated expertise in orchestrating performance turnarounds. Long-standing track record of success in identifying and exploiting key improvement opportunities to drive sales and increase profits. Open, honest, and respected manager who leads by example and is effective at motivating team to achieve outstanding results. Demonstrated commitment to efficiency and productivity that carries through entire organization. Driven leader with passion for excellence.

PROFESSIONAL EXPERIENCE

GREAT AMERICA SUPERMARKETS, Mountainview, Pennsylvania   1985 to present
President, Southern Region (6/02 to present)
Currently oversee network of stores in southern region, directing 4500 staff members through team of direct reports. Worked way up through organization, holding a series of management positions of increasing responsibility.

Performance Excellence

- Recognized for ability to effect change and improve profitability. Brought in to turn around performance of troubled Southern Region.
- Led New England team that earned ranking as top-performing group in the company.
- Effectively orchestrated new-store openings in Pennsylvania. Oversaw opening of seven stores in seven months, each of which exceeded all performance goals.
- Established long-standing record of productivity excellence, leading teams ranked best nationwide. Consistently maintain shrink at levels that are among the lowest in the industry.
- Implemented seasonal programs throughout 900 stores, achieving 25% growth in two years.

Operations Improvement

- Analyze and organize all areas of operations, instituting plans, policies, and controls to support business goals.
- Developed planning technology and operating guidelines for unit, district, divisional, and chain-wide operations that took into account the unique challenges and requirements of individual locations.
- Coordinated with merchandising management to implement strategies to exploit unique local opportunities.
- Integrated technology and education to dramatically elevate productivity, cultivating an environment for the successful implementation of new processes and procedures that substantially improved operations.
- Instituted shrinkage control measures that consistently reduced losses through the establishment and communication of team goals, enhanced staff training, and improved monitoring.
- Introduced proactive customer service culture, elevating service levels, enhancing company profile, and contributing to profit growth and competitive advantage.

Administrative Management

- Prepared and administered annual operating and expense budgets of up to $3 billion, applying skill in financial forecasting and analysis.
- Observed and evaluated consumer and market data to discover emerging trends, determine competitive position within the industry, and identify future opportunities.
- Developed and implemented performance management initiatives that used incentive programs to communicate performance expectations and motivate staff to attain them.
- Planned, organized, and directed comprehensive staff and management training programs. Successfully trained 65 new corporate managers and 12 new store managers within twelve-month period.
- Organized and administered employee recruitment and retention programs, including efforts successful in consistently reducing turnover.

8 WILSON AVENUE ▪ MIDDLEBORO, PA 22222 ▪ (333) 333-3333

132

Carol A. Altomare, Three Bridges, New Jersey

This Supermarket Executive had no degree but had worked his way up through the organization. He wanted to keep things simple and direct. He liked grouping his accomplishments under headings.

Jason J. Gill

9803 Clinton Avenue • Houston, TX 77068 • name@yahoo.com
home: 000-000-0000 • mobile: 000-000-0000

Career Target: Retail Management

Results-driven, customer-centered manager with 3 years of experience in store-management positions. Verifiable talent for maintaining profitable retail operations, with success in capitalizing on growth opportunities, implementing promotional/marketing strategies, and upholding fiscal efficiency. Articulate communicator and effective trainer skilled in achieving employee buy-in on organizational goals. Respected, trusted manager who upholds the highest ethical and professional standards. Core skill areas include

- Customer Management
- Inventory Control/Shrinkage
- Customer Service/Loyalty
- Staff Training & Mentoring
- Financial Management
- Loss Prevention/Security
- In-Store Promotions
- Performance Management
- Buyer Behavior/Awareness
- Visual Merchandise Displays
- Specialty Retail Operations
- Profit-and-Loss Management

Relevant Experience

Retail Outlet—Houston, TX

GENERAL MANAGER, 2002–2004 / **ASSISTANT MANAGER,** 2000–2002 / **ASSOCIATE,** 1999–2000

Earned promotion to GM position based on performance in Assistant Manager role, directing sales and customer service activities for team of 15 employees in fast-paced mall location. Scope of management accountability included financial management, staff training and evaluation, inventory management and loss prevention, marketing and promotions, and general management functions. *Selected Accomplishments:*

- **Performance Improvement**—Demonstrated ability to produce results and drive year-to-year increases in core revenue and profit categories, illustrated by the following:

	Inventory Shrinkage	Store Revenues[*]	Pre-Order Sales
2001 Totals	2.1%	$667,000	30
2002 Totals	0.4%	$691,000	310
Increase	1.7%	10.3%	1033%

  [*]*Generated sales increase despite downturn market and against totals of –21.3% company-wide average, –26.5% in region, and –28.35% in district.*

- **Business Development**—Led store to earn distinction as only mall store ranked in top 50 for 2 months. Store achieved exemplary company rankings following my promotion, including #1 overall in district, #1 in Texas (3 months), #1 in region (2 months), and #21 in company for 10/02 among 410 stores.

- **Profit Enhancement**—Maintained profitability by reducing operating costs 39%, performing inventory procedures that earned location excellent audit ratings, and identifying employee theft incidents.

- **Marketing & Promotions**—Secured approval from Marketing Manager for in-store promotions and sponsorships for local musical groups. Managed successful "appreciation day" programs.

- **Performance Recognition**—Groomed assistant manager to take over general manager position; requested promotion to District Manager position prior to company's Chapter 11 filing.

- **Customer & Employee Relations**—Built and sustained excellent relationships with customers, leading to frequent repeat business. Demonstrated fair, respectful treatment of team members.

PRIOR EMPLOYMENT:
LABORER—Enterprises, Santa Fe, NM (1998–1999)
FILE CLERK—Collections, Santa Fe, NM (1997–1998)
DELIVERY DRIVER—Office Equipment, Santa Fe, NM (1996–1997)

Education & Technical Skills

UNIVERSITY OF HOUSTON, Houston, TX / 106 Hours, Emphasis in Business Management & Graphic Design

Technical Summary: Microsoft Word, Excel, Access, FrontPage; Adobe Illustrator, Photoshop, Streamline, Acrobat; CorelDRAW, QuarkXPress; proprietary applications used in retail environments

133

Daniel J. Dorotik, Jr., Lubbock, Texas

Accomplishments don't need to be a list of bulleted items. The writer of this resume liked the use of a table and an italic note to illustrate revenue and profit increases. Gray shading simulates color.

TOMI SPRINGFIELD

1000 Page Blvd., Springfield, MA 01151 ▪ Tspringfield@aol.com ▪ Home: 413-788-2008

OFFICE MANAGER ▪ LOGISTICS ▪ SALES SUPPORT
*Objective: To provide office or project management, logistics, and/or sales support
for a high-tech, security, or financial services firm.*

CAREER PROFILE & SKILLS

Versatile people person and problem solver with 20 years of experience in field support, office management, logistics, and project management. Organized facilitator with excellent follow-through. Analytical self-starter able to think on her feet.

▪ Office Management	▪ Customer Service	▪ Special Events
▪ Logistics & Coordination	▪ Credit Management	▪ Meeting Planning
▪ Operational Support	▪ Proposals & Job Costing	▪ Marketing Support
▪ Project Tracking/Reporting	▪ Purchasing & Procedures	▪ Field Sales Support
▪ Training & Supervision	▪ Budget Management	▪ Account Management

Cited for *"diligence, competence, a positive attitude, and being a team player on a consistent basis"* by MA-Logistics President while providing logistics for a Homeland Security contract.

Cited as a *"competent and recognized contributor in a stressful environment with minimal supervision"* by Broadband Cable's President while supporting SASR—the federalization of high-risk airports.

OFFICE & PROJECT MANAGEMENT HIGHLIGHTS

- **Comanaged a team of 25 account clerks in a commercial credit/loan environment** as Credit Manager for Cambridge Credit Corporation. Included team scheduling, performance reviews, and credit training. Also reviewed, analyzed, and investigated credit applications and contracts.

- **Managed a 5-person customer service department that handled 1500 transactions per week** for Cambridge Credit Corp. Included hiring, training, and evaluating employee performance; managing budgets, payroll, and scheduling; and developing customer service manuals and procedures.

- **Tracked/reported the status of multimillion-dollar fiber optic network construction** for Broadband Cable Corporation. Used MS Project 2000.

- **Developed tracking/reporting procedures for hundreds of millions of dollars of equipment purchases** for Broadband Cable fiber optics business.

- **Managed entire office for an exhibits design and fabrication firm** in the President's absence. Included accounts payables/receivables, collections, proposals and job costing, invoicing, travel, and meeting plans for NE Trade Show Products. Helped administer two other companies in shared office space.

LOGISTICS & SALES SUPPORT HIGHLIGHTS

- **Helped manage logistics to federalize 429 airports in 180 days** for SASR (the Strategic Airport Security Rollout). Provided customer service and operational support for 1700 mobile/permanent airport screeners. Used AIM Help Desk Software to analyze, track, and report problems for MA-Logistics.

- **Provided customer service, inventory management, and high-volume sales to 200 retail accounts** quarterly for Kraft Foods. Assisted special promotions, set up new stores, and sold marketing programs.

- **Won two All Star Awards for 1st Place in regional sales/support** from Kraft Foods.

- **Provided field support for merchandising, marketing, sales, and service** for Helene Curtis.

- **Planned and managed special events and Board of Directors meetings** for Broadband Cable Corporation. Backed up the senior administrator who supported the Vice President of Sales.

134

Helen Oliff, Reston, Virginia

The writer demonstrated this candidate's "strength through versatility" and diminished her job hopping by using the variety and short length of multiple jobs to show progressive skills and responsibilities. Look for the comment in italic after each position indicated in the Chronological

TOMI SPRINGFIELD
Page Two

CHRONOLOGICAL EMPLOYMENT HISTORY

Junior Logistician, Task Force Homeland Security, 2002 to Present
MA-LOGISTICS, INC.—Springfield, MA
Provides solutions for supply-chain logistics challenges and project management to public/private businesses.

Project Administrator, Network Planning, 2000 to 2002
Office Manager, Network Services, 2000 to 2002
BROADBAND CABLE CORPORATION—Medford, MA
A start-up that provides bundled cable, Internet, and telephone services for broadband customer networks.

Office Manager, President's Office, 1999 to 2000
NEW ENGLAND TRADE SHOW PRODUCTS—Portland, MA
Provides millwork, casework, graphics, and fabrication for exhibit/museum displays and trade show marketing.

Office Support Specialist, 1995 to 1998
MASSACHUSETTS DESIGN ASSOCIATES—Portland, MA
Provides architectural design for both commercial and residential structures and spaces.

Sales Representative/Sales Support
SHISEIDO COSMETICS AMERICA, LTD.—Cambridge, MA Office, 1993 to 1995 (job share)
SMOKELESS TOBACCO COMPANY—Cambridge, MA, 1993 to 1995 (job share)
Major distributors of retail and consumer products and services distributed worldwide.

Sales Representative/Sales Support
KRAFT FOODS, CONFECTIONERS DIVISION—Dorchester, MA, 1990 to 1993
Major distributor of retail and food products and services to consumers worldwide.

Customer Service & Credit Manager, 1986 to 1989
Marketing & Collections Representative, 1984 to 1986
CAMBRIDGE CREDIT CORPORATION—Cambridge, MA
Provides credit services and credit management to hardware and other retail stores.

PROFESSIONAL TRAINING

Marketing & Sales Training—Kraft Foods
Customer Services & Selling Symposium—Cambridge Credit Corp.
Motivation & Productivity—Cambridge Credit Corp.

Computer Skills: MS Office 2000/97 (Word, Excel, and PowerPoint), MS Project 2000, PageMaker, AIM help desk software, e-mail, Web browsers, and Windows 2000/98

E-mail: Tspringfield@aol.com ▪ Home: 413-788-2008

Employment History. The three expertise areas of office management, logistics, and sales support, indicated at the top of page 1, are illustrated by highlights in two sections at the bottom of the page.

CONFIDENTIAL

Carol Trona

400 Conch Drive, Pacifica, California 94044
ctrona1111@aol.com 650.555.5555 (Home) — 650.555.6666 (Cell)

What I can offer TopLine as your newest Business Manager

❑ Bringing in projects on time and on budget ❑ Knowing the difference between symptoms and problems ❑ Maximizing profits by getting the right resources to the people at the right time ❑ Serving customers so well they become our unpaid "sales force" ❑ Limiting liability ❑ Controlling costs ❑ Building and maintaining excellent, motivated teams ❑ Freeing senior management for things only they can do

Recent work history with examples of problems solved

❑ *Hired away to become* **Office Manager,** *and then given additional responsibilities as* **Project Coordinator,** *and later promoted with additional responsibilities to* **Project Manager,** Carter Winslow, General Contractor, Punta Gordita, California

Sep 99–Present

This custom builder of high-end homes in the Bay Area has annual sales of more than $1.5M.

As **Office Manager,** have **near-total P&L responsibility** for this small office. As **Project Coordinator** and **Project Manager,** control all the resources—people, time, equipment, money, cooperation, and facilities—for every major project we have.

Turned around an operation that ran on handshakes—and increasing lawsuits—for six years. Built a complete system for documenting business from scratch. *Payoffs:* **Costly disputes replaced by amicable relationships** with customers and vendors. Owner freed for things only he could do.

Put management in complete control of critical resources. Helped employees draw the straight line from their responsibilities to our corporate success. *Payoffs:* Disputes over scarce resources disappeared. More than **doubled the number of projects** we worked on simultaneously. **Sales rose more than 100 percent.**

❑ *Hired away to be* **Office Manager** *with later additional responsibilities as* **Event Planner** and Event Planning **Sales Professional,** Crux & Associates, Pinetop City, California

Sep 97–Aug 99

Crux & Associates is a complete event-planning solutions provider serving major corporate clients in the Bay Area. Annual sales topped $2M.

Won over what later became a major account. Got them to buy into the "perfect" vision of the product we could provide—then realize we were best suited to deliver the goods. *Payoffs:* Customer so pleased that **we became their "sole service provider."**

CONFIDENTIAL   *More indicators of performance TopLine can use ...*

135

Don Orlando, Montgomery, Alabama

This applicant had been taken for granted too long by her current company. Her job search was an opportunity for her to "spread her wings" and proceed to the next level. The "What I can offer…" section summarizes the individual's most significant abilities, which are documented in

Carol Trona   **Business Manager**   650.555.5555 (Home) — 650.555.6666 (Cell)

Stepped in smoothly to work with demanding musicians as we planned a major event 2,500 miles away. By listening carefully, found just what the y wanted. *Payoffs:* **Used differential costing** to meet their needs yet **get their services at considerable savings.**

Pulled together — **single-handedly** — every detail of what would normally be a week-long project for four people. Did it all over a three-day weekend. Tracked down suppliers even though their businesses were closed. Convinced vendors I could provide promotional value in exchange for **moderate pricing.** *Payoffs:* **Customer was thrilled** with the event we planned for 500 people at such short notice.

❏ **Office Manager,** Triangle Company, Inc., S an Francisco, California

Nov 92–Sep 97

This public financial advisory firm helped customers across the state prepare to float school bond issues. Sales: $5M.

Transformed a challenge into new revenue. Persuaded owner to create a subsidiary to handle the mountain of publications we produced each quarter. *Payoffs:* **Netted $100K** in new revenue in the first year alone — **from an investment of $20K.**

Volunteered to rescue a "small" account ot hers said couldn't be serviced when workload threatened to overcome our staff. Made the time to master our customers' needs. *Payoffs:* Of five major efforts running at the same time, mine was **the only successful venture** — even though I had no experience in this field.

Language skills

❏ Read, write, and think in fluent German

Computer skills

❏ Expert in Word

❏ Proficient in Excel, QuickBooks, FileMaker Pro (database software)

❏ Working knowledge of Outlook and Internet search protocols

the "Recent work history…" section. In that section, look for shadowed square bullets as pointers to companies where the candidate distinguished herself by performing tasks beyond expectation.

FRANK JOHNSON

15711 Autumnbrook Drive • Houston, TX 77068
Home: (555) 555-5555
Cell: (555) 555-5555
fjohnson243@yahoo.com

CAREER TARGET: EQUIPMENT/OPERATIONS MANAGEMENT

More Than 15 Years of Management Experience, Including Current/Recent Positions as Program Manager with the NDT Corporation and Operations Manager with Fremont Corporation

Consistent Track Record of Success in Achieving Business, Operational, and Bottom-Line Objectives Within Start-up and Established Environments

Management professional with progressively responsible supervisory experience. Proven leadership credentials and significant success in building and maintaining loyal customer / vendor relationships. Deep understanding of critical business drivers; skilled in resolving problem areas, motivating diverse groups of employees, and delivering on customer commitments.

**Equipment Leasing Contract Management / New Program Implementation / Budget Planning & Administration
Vendor Negotiations & Relationship Building / Client-Account Management / Merger & Acquisition Integration
Staff Training & Mentoring / Financial Forecasting & Modeling / Policy & Procedure Implementation**

PROFESSIONAL EXPERIENCE

NDT CORPORATION (2002–Present)
Program Manager

Transitioned following acquisition of Fremont to hold full P&L responsibility for all aspects of Vendor Leasing program, including customer / client relations, credit analysis and approval, documentation, and funding activities. Completed Accounts Receivable and Accounts Payable functions.

KEY CONTRIBUTIONS & ACCOMPLISHMENTS

- **Built successful vendor program for XNY Tires Supply and generated repeat/referral business through** exemplary service to customers. Leveraged multiple capabilities and skills areas to bring additional value to the position, bringing in key clients that included primary account.

- **Protected against unnecessary risk by auditing customer portfolio and analyzing credit reports/statements.** Gained credibility with clients through forthright, respectful approach to yes/no credit decisions, particularly denials.

FREMONT CORPORATION (1998–2001)
Operations Manager

Oversaw all functions within startup operations, emphasizing relationships with funding sources, vendors, and lessees.

KEY CONTRIBUTIONS & ACCOMPLISHMENTS

- **Built value-driven company that gained interest from competitor Bow Corporation, leading to eventual** acquisition/merger.

- **Implemented and maintained procedures and processes, including vendor and customer relationships, to** facilitate successful startup organization. *(Continued)*

136

Daniel J. Dorotik, Jr., Lubbock, Texas

The resume begins with two unlabeled sections: first a summary of experience in boldface and then a profile with areas of expertise in boldface and separated by slashes. All of this important information is placed in the sure-to-be-seen zone just under the contact information at the top.

FRANK JOHNSON—PAGE 2
Home: (555) 555-5555
Cell: (555) 555-5555
fjohnson243@yahoo.com

SYSTEMS FINANCIAL (1991–1998)
Credit Analyst

Performed credit analyses and approved lease transactions, coordinated documentation and funding, and maintained sustainable relationships with vendors throughout processes.

KEY CONTRIBUTIONS & ACCOMPLISHMENTS

- **Developed and maintained vendor/customer relationships while effectively managing heavy workload.** Formed Fremont with CFO of SF following acquisition by Texas-based firm.

PROGRAM RESOURCES (1980–1990)
Manager, Investor Services / Manager, Joint Interest Auditing

As Investor Services Manager, led all corporate investor relations and financial management activities as part of master limited partnership obligations. Prepared annual/quarterly and management reports, as well as news releases and responses to investor inquiries. As Joint Interest Auditing Manager, conducted financial and operational audits for oil and gas joint venture firms. Reviewed and evaluated documentation on revenues and expenditures, directed auditing processes, and supported legal counsel during protracted litigation proceedings.

KEY CONTRIBUTIONS & ACCOMPLISHMENTS

- **Played key role in conversion of 25 limited partnerships into $36 million Master Limited Partnership traded on** AMEX, overseeing distribution of ballots, prospecti, and informational documents.

- **Maintained and developed partner and financial community relationships, communicating with partners to** address and resolve issues. Gained trust and solicited cooperation from multiple parties to meet objectives.

- **Implemented company's 1st joint interest oil-gas accounting function, leading to higher degree of accuracy** and expedited accounting processes, as well as underlying cost reduction/avoidance.

- **Developed windfall profit tax reporting system that affected 5,000+ limited partners, deploying system in all** 35 partner companies to meet regulatory requirements. Established reporting and software to produce statements.

- **Led audit that uncovered significant discrepancies within financial records, leading to recovery of $2 million.** Worked jointly with legal counsel on various tasks within the proceedings.

PROFESSIONAL DEVELOPMENT

Associate of Arts in Finance
SOUTH PLAINS COLLEGE—Levelland, TX

Computer Skills Summary
Microsoft Excel; LeasePlus; WiredCapital

Each workplace in the Professional Experience section contains a paragraph about duties and then a bulleted list of key contributions and accomplishments. These are essential in a resume.

James Howard

7777 Tracer Downs ♦ Perry, GA 00000 ♦ (H) 000-000-0000 ♦ (C) 000-000-0000

Operations Management ♦ Personnel Management ♦ Materials Management
Inventory & Logistics ♦ Purchasing & Procurement

Goal-oriented management professional with more than 20 years of progressive and stable experience in executive-level management positions. Offer background and qualifications in personnel and human resources administration, facilities management, operations administration, budgeting, materials, team leadership, security management, problem resolution, professional development, training and education analysis, public and motivational speaking, customer relations, research and investigation, international travel, and report and forecast development. Understand intricacies of regulations governing personnel issues. Ensure that subordinates remain in continual compliance with all health, safety, and security directives and specifications, including those of OSHA and the EEOC.

CAREER ACCOMPLISHMENTS

☑ Managed facilities maintenance team responsible for the upkeep of 490,000 square feet of commercial building space.
☑ Managed all aspects of logistics, transportation, and delivery support functions for assigned U.S. Marine Corps units.
☑ Spearheaded and implemented cost control measure resulting in $40,000 in annual savings for assigned unit.
☑ Chosen from 2,000 qualified candidates to serve as liaison aboard the USS Tripoli in support of logistics operations between Marine Corps and Navy personnel.

PROFESSIONAL EXPERIENCE
OPERATIONS MANAGEMENT

- Planned, directed, and coordinated human resources management activities, maximizing the strategic use of human resources and maintaining facilities maintenance department.
- Provided supervision for the equipment and supply manager, the maintenance supply manager, and all personnel responsible for the performance and management of equipment maintenance.
- Analyzed maintenance management and personnel functional areas, proficiently utilizing equipment and materiel.
- Assigned to the completed functions required by the maintenance information systems coordination office to ensure the proper functioning of the field maintenance subsystem of the Marine Corps Integrated Maintenance Management System.
- Interacted with management to formulate and implement administrative, operations, and customer relations policies.
- Analyzed expenditures and other financial reports to develop plans, policies, and budgets for increasing profits.

PERSONNEL MANAGEMENT

- Supervised and monitored the work activities of subordinates and staff.
- Developed employment policies, processes, and practices, and recommended changes to executive management personnel.
- Met with team leaders and supervisors to resolve grievances.
- Conducted new-employee orientation to foster positive attitude toward company objectives.
- Wrote directives advising department managers of organizational policy in personnel matters.
- Maintained records and compiled statistical data to identify and determine causes of personnel problems.
- Analyzed statistical data and reports to identify and determine causes of personnel problems and develop recommendations for improvement of organizational personnel policies and practices.
- Planned, directed, and coordinated the training activities of all personnel under personal authority.
- Analyzed training needs to develop new programs or to modify and improve existing programs.

TRANSPORTATION & LOGISTICS

- Reviewed transportation schedules, personnel assignments, and routes to ensure compliance with standards for personnel elections, safety, and contract terms.
- Orchestrated activities relating to dispatching, routing, and tracking of transportation vehicles, aircraft, and railroad cars.
- Monitored the process of investigation and response to complaints relating to operations department.
- Directed team responsible for tariff classifications, billing preparation, mode of transportation, and destination of shipment.
- Inspected and supervised the maintenance of equipment, vehicles, and facilities and enforced all applicable regulations.

MATERIALS MANAGEMENT, PURCHASING, & PROCUREMENT

- Oversaw procurement process, including research and testing of equipment and vendor contacts and approval of requisitions.
- Negotiated and authorized contracts with equipment and materials suppliers.
- Formulated, implemented, and interpreted policies and procedures.
- Developed plans to meet expanded needs, such as increasing capacity of facilities or modifying equipment.

137

Lea J. "Laila" Clark-Salaam, Atlanta, Georgia

The first page of this resume has design elements found in many executive resumes: narrow margins, wide lines, and small type (here, 10-point Times New Roman). Areas of expertise (in boldface and separated by diamond bullets), a profile, and Career Accomplishments

James Howard

Page Two

MATERIALS MANAGEMENT, PURCHASING, & PROCUREMENT (Continued)

- Authorized repair, movement, installation, and construction of equipment, supplies, and facilities.
- Analyzed data, trends, reports, consumption, and test results to determine adequacy of facilities and system performance.
- Investigated and evaluated new developments in materials, tools, and equipment.
- Forecast consumption of utilities to meet demand or to determine construction, equipment, or maintenance requirements.
- Developed, prepared, and distributed reports, directives, records, work orders, specifications for work methods, and other documents.

EMPLOYMENT HISTORY

Hazardous-Waste Manager, Environmental Outsourcing	**2003–present**
Inventory Support Supervisor, U.S. Air Force Logistics Center	**2001–2003**
Operations and Project Management, Facilities Management Corp.	**1999–2001**

MILITARY SERVICE

Transportation/Facilities/Communications/Operations Management, U.S. Marine Corps	**1978–1999**

EDUCATION
Graduate, Austin High School, Chicago, IL

TRAINING
Chapman College, Twentynine Palms, CA
Public Speaking, Communications, English, Math

U.S. Marine Corps, Various Locations
Advanced Staff NCO Administrative Academy, Personnel Administration, Marine Corps Leadership, Advanced Staff NCO
Non-Resident Program, Ground Safety Managers Training, Logistics and Embarkation Specialist Course,
Substance Abuse Information Program, Maintenance Management Course

Additional Employment-Related Course Work
Total Quality Management, Equal Opportunity Representative, Public Speaking,
Written Correspondence, Assertiveness Training, Safety, First Aid

COMMUNITY SERVICE AND AFFILIATIONS
Local Coordinator, Habitat for Humanity, Cobb County, GA
Volunteer Driver, Meals on Wheels, Marietta, GA
Volunteer Team Member, Boy and Girl Scouts of America, various international locations
Little League Basketball Coach, Gwinnett County

HONORS & AWARDS
United States Armed Forces
Meritorious Service Medal ◆ *Navy Achievement Medal* ◆ *National Defense Service Medal*
Armed Forces Expeditionary Medal ◆ *3 Letters of Commendation* ◆ *8 Letters of Appreciation*

Cobb County Division of Habitat for Humanity—Letter of Appreciation

are all placed just below the contact information to be the first information seen. The Professional Experience section lists items by categories rather than by workplaces. See Cover Letter 10.

Charles Gladstone

555 Franklin Drive
Ramsey, NJ 55555

(555) 555-5555 (Cell)
(555) 555-5555 (Home)
myname@mysite.net

OPERATIONS MANAGEMENT

PROFILE: Multifaceted, proactive operations manager with more than 10 years of experience in managing all aspects of warehousing and inventory control. Skilled at designing and implementing new systems and procedures to increase efficiency and decrease costs. Combine outstanding management skills with strong qualifications in distribution, budgeting, and human resources. Excellent computer skills.

- Inventory Processes & Controls
- Quality Control
- Expense Control
- Purchasing
- Contract Negotiations
- Traffic Control
- Production/Assembly Planning
- Compensation Incentives
- Testing & Sampling

PROFESSIONAL EXPERIENCE

<u>DICKINSON, INC.</u>

Warehouse Manager

Paterson, NJ
7/02–4/09

International distributor of hand-tooled instruments. Reported to Operations Manager. Promoted to this position because of knowledge of warehouse operations. Managed staff of three, including Shipping Manager, Receiving Manager, and Production Assembly Manager, and workforce of 22. Managed all facets of warehouse operations. Responsible for maintaining inventory and reducing costs. Scheduled deliveries of inbound receipts to all 3 departments. Planned daily workloads for each department. Developed and scheduled weekly production/assembly plan. Produced weekly stockout report covering more than 2,500 items.

- Improved inventory accuracy from 92% to 99.5% on $2 million inventory.
- Reduced operating expenses by $100,000 annually by reducing staff 30% and combining positions.
- Improved space utilization by introducing blanket order/release system for corrugated purchases that resulted in lower on-hand inventory, less wasted space, and improved tracking of expenses.
- Received overall rating of "Outstanding" on last 2 performance reviews.

Challenge: Ensure that all sales orders received by 2:30 p.m. were picked, packed, and shipped the same day. Initially, 50% of orders (on volume of 300 orders per day) were not being shipped the same day.
Action: Revised inventory locations, designed more efficient pick/pack flow, implemented incentive program, increased training, and designed and installed powered conveyor system.
<u>Results</u>: All sales orders received by 2:30 p.m. are now shipped the same day.

Challenge: Reduce shipping costs by 25%.
Action: Identified and introduced new equipment (strapping machine) and identified and implemented better void fill system (sealed plastic bag filled with air).
<u>Results</u>: Reduced labor and material costs by $34,000 annually (30% less than prior year).

Challenge: Develop better reports regarding daily business workloads for top management.
Action: Designed (with MIS) and implemented information tracking system that kept track of current workload on daily/hourly basis.
<u>Results</u>: Provided in-depth reports that allowed management to respond to changing patterns quickly. Also provided means for evaluating pick/pack personnel.

Assistant Operations Manager/Special Projects Coordinator

7/00–7/02

Reported to Operations Manager. Oversaw activities of 25. Responsible for monitoring and maintaining company-wide inventory levels. Monitored backorder levels. Negotiated rates and contracts with small package and common carrier freight companies. Formulated plans for reducing costs and increasing efficiencies.

138

Igor Shpudejko, Mahwah, New Jersey

This individual did not go to college but has done very well for himself with an A.A.S. degree in Electronics. Because the applicant is a "doer," the writer wanted to focus on his many accomplishments and to use the CAR (challenge, action, results) format to present achievements. This

Charles Gladstone

Page 2

- Saved more than $10,000 in annual costs by replacing old shipping manifest system with new system provided free of charge by United Parcel Service.

Challenge: Identify causes of $700,000 in backorders and reduce them.
Action: Discovered flaw in releasing backorder documents to warehouse. Designed backorder report (with MIS) that reported backorders by sales territory and released product as needed.
Results: Reduced backorders to $250,000 in 2 months.

Challenge: Conduct study to determine whether California public warehouse was cost-effective.
Action: Studied cost per item for storage and handling and shipping. Analyzed work flow in Paterson warehouse to determine possibility of absorbing extra volume.
Results: Shut down facility after it was determined that $25,000 could be saved annually without sacrificing customer satisfaction. Extra freight charges to customers were reduced.

Challenge: Obtain compensation from vendors for defective returns.
Action: Designed report (with MIS) that identified and tracked vendor defective returns over 18-month reporting period. Data showed items returned because of manufacturing defects. Presented data to vendors for defective return compensation. Initiated monthly defective return report.
Results: Recovered more than $56,000 in initial discovery and more than $40,000 on annual basis.

ONSITE GRAPHICS, INC.   Fairlawn, NJ
Plant Manager   8/97–7/00
A wholly owned subsidiary of Nu-Kote International, a leading remanufacturer and supplier of premium-quality laser printer cartridges. Directed all aspects of the East Coast pick/pack distribution and recovery center through staff of 15. Managed 15,000-square-foot facility and 2,000 SKUs. Shipped $1.5 million of merchandise monthly. Ensured that 97% of orders shipped same day. Maintained entire computer system.
- Increased distribution from 20% of total company distribution to 50% without increase in staff.
- Saved more than $50,000 annually by negotiating better international and domestic freight rates.
- Developed workable inventory and raw materials min/max levels, which decreased warehousing freight costs by 20%.
- Designed and implemented new pick/pack operation using conveyor and pallet rack systems that reduced picking time.
- Cross-trained all personnel on one other position, which improved productivity and staff morale.
- Improved operational efficiency by moving invoicing into shipping department and all receiving department data entry into receiving department.

PC SYSTEMS   Norwich, CT
Field Service Manager   8/94–8/97
Regional company specializing in service and maintenance of PC-based computer systems. Directed staff of 6 field technicians responsible for troubleshooting and resolving routine and complex service calls. Handled large volume of inbound technical questions. Maintained extensive parts inventory.

Field Technician   8/92–8/94
Responsible for handling both on- and off-site repairs of computers and peripherals.
- First technical person hired in this branch. Played key role in launching business.

COMPUTER SKILLS
- **Software:** MS/PC DOS, WordPerfect, Lotus 1-2-3, Symphony, Q&A, ProComm, Carbon Copy, Sidekick, and Smartcomm
- **Hardware:** IBM PCs and clones, HP, Epson, Okidata, and Citoh printers

EDUCATION
- **AAS in Electronics,** DeVry Technical Institute, Woodbridge, NJ, 1992

format appears in the Professional Experience section at the end of the information about the first two jobs mentioned. An italic explanation of each workplace is helpful information.

DARLENE DAVIS

123 Main Street ▪ Philadelphia, PA 19000
215-555-5555

ADMINISTRATIVE / BUSINESS MANAGER

Start-Up, Turnaround, and High-Growth Organizations

PROFILE

MANAGEMENT PROFESSIONAL with more than 10 years of experience in increasingly accountable positions requiring a high level of business operations knowledge. Recognized for consistent success in developing systems, processes, and methodologies to reorganize/revitalize purchasing operations, increase revenues, and enhance profit performance.

Demonstrated accomplishments with strategic planning, organizational development, key account management, and general management expertise. Cross-functional background in corporate communications, vendor negotiations, resource allocation, and project management. Proficient with MS Office 2000 (including advanced training in Word and Excel), Solomon System, Fourth Shift ERP/MRP, and Crystal Reports.

CORE COMPETENCIES

PURCHASING MANAGEMENT & BUSINESS ADMINISTRATION

Key player in the launching of a fast-paced, worldwide, interactive television Internet company from start-up to a public company by successfully managing major production purchases and building purchasing/materials department.

- Reduced freight costs by 15% by renegotiating rates with carriers, taking advantage of free shipping, marking up/invoicing all freight for customer shipments, and reducing volume of overnight shipments. Significantly decreased costs on mature products by sourcing alternate vendors, renegotiating existing prices, and obtaining preferred payment terms with key vendors.

- Successful in liquidating inventory as cash problems developed and sales dropped. Negotiated the return of $270,000 in excess inventory to vendors, sold specific items to cable industry vendors, and sold nonindustry items generating $800,000 in cash.

PROJECT PLANNING & MANAGEMENT

Skilled at leading cross-functional teams in the planning and execution of special projects. Able to critically evaluate project requirements and coordinate delivery of appropriate resources to meet operating demands.

- Instrumental in administering procedures and processes to streamline flow between sales, material planning, manufacturing, and materials from start to finish (inventory to time of shipment). Execution of new processes resulted in inventory accuracy moving to less than 1% (from 9% variance).

- Researched ERP/MRP software packages ranging from $300,000 to $1 million and justified product selection and cost savings to executive team. Oversaw project implementation teams, ensuring sales, IT, engineering, materials, finance, and manufacturing departments met project objectives and deadlines.

139

Darlene Dassy, Sinking Spring, Pennsylvania

This individual was laid off because of a company bankruptcy. She had extensive corporate experience but was afraid that her lack of a four-year degree would prevent her from getting a challenging job. The writer emphasized the applicant's most important qualifications on the

CORE COMPETENCIES (continued)

PERSONNEL MANAGEMENT & LEADERSHIP
Excellent qualifications in providing flexible leadership in a fast-paced work environment. Demonstrated proactive leadership practices and directed staff to be reactive when projects were altered to meet corporate deadlines.

- Consistently met and exceeded department objectives. Oversaw administrative efforts to bring various products into organization with unrealistic deadlines, which resulted in the deployment of product into field, allowing it to "go public" before originally scheduled timeframe.

- Built work teams that continually exceeded goals for productivity. Instrumental as a team leader who promoted employee ideas/input and implemented newly suggested procedures to help department run more smoothly and effectively.

CUSTOMER SERVICE & CLIENT RELATIONS
Served as the direct liaison to maintain cooperative relationships and resolve operating problems for sales administration and order fulfillment departments.

- Effectively handled customer reconciliations, ultimately restoring tenuous customer relations on many critical overseas shipments.

- Troubleshot various issues within the organization and was considered the "go-to person" among staff for solving problems within different areas of the company.

EDUCATION AND CERTIFICATIONS

Pursuing <u>Bachelor of Business Administration</u> at **Anytown College USA**

Attended **The American Institute of Paralegal Studies** for Paralegal Program

Continuing Professional Education & Seminars sponsored by the Management Development Institute of the MidAtlantic Employers' Association (1999–2000):

- Supervisory Skills Certificate
- Coaching and Team Building
- Human Resources Overview
- Basics of Supervision
- Leadership Skills for Today's Workplace
- Time Management Systems
- Successful Communication
- Managing People

CAREER EXPERIENCE

<u>Manager—Purchasing and Materials</u>	**WorldWide Communications**	1997–2004
<u>Purchasing & Inventory Control Manager</u>	**Corporate Data, Inc.**	1995–1997
<u>National Account Contract Specialist</u>	**Corporate Data, Inc.**	1991–1995

first page and placed her education and career experience at the end. The writer also beefed up the Education section with certifications and management seminars.

MARIA D. SCHERING

832 Sandy Lane   Corpus Christi, Texas 78132   361-275-4739

National Workforce Manager—Call Center Industry
offers eight years of global experience in workforce planning and management

Technology Background
TCS versions 4.0, 5.0, and 6.0; IEX; Lucent (CMS) ACD Administration; CentreVu Supervisor; Administration for Expert Agent System (EAS); WinQSB; Crystal Reports

Value-Added Competencies
Generate $50K in additional annual revenue as an external workforce management consultant to Fortune 100 and 500 companies. Own a reputation as a polished, organized, enthusiastic professional with excellent communication skills and a high level of expertise in the workforce management arena.

Professional Achievements

- ***Increased efficiency in and span of control*** over eight remote call center operations as a result of establishing an effective Global Support Center for the Workforce Management sector located in Phoenix, AZ. Functioned in the capacity of project manager from ground zero implementation of this operation.
- ***Empowered 1200 agents*** in personal performance management through the implementation of the Performix Reporting Integration System. Served in capacity of project manager and corporate liaison for multiple site implementations.
- ***Generated an additional $50K in revenue for 2002*** in role of external consultant to Dell Home Sales, La Quinta Reservations, and Humana Service Centers. This assignment required a dynamic relationship with the client. ***Solutions were created in software implementation, best practices in workforce management, forecasting, staffing, and process reengineering.***

Professional Profile

CORESTAFF
February 2003 to present
Corporate office, Boise, Idaho

Director of Resource Planning Group—On Site—Corpus Christi, Texas. Manage a staff of 30 support personnel: Staffing and Scheduling, Traffic Desk Coordinators, Telecommunications, Reporting, and Time and Attendance.
- Lead Resource Team in planning, recommending, implementing, and tracking of hiring plans and productivity for 1,000 agents networked in a "virtual" call center consisting of three multisites.
- Provide analysis and consultative support to cross-functional partners and other lines of business.
- Implemented an escalation procedure within call center for recovery and escalation notification.

CRICHTON TECHNOLOGIES—GLOBAL NETWORK SOLUTIONS
1994–February 2003
Corporate office, Cincinnati, Ohio

National Workforce Manager—Remote Office—Corpus Christi, Texas   **2000 to February 2003**
- Managed a staff of 11 workforce support personnel in both domestic and international customer service centers.
- Created and generated forecasting models for existing and newly acquired operations.
- Identified and implemented programs to improve service, performance, and productivity.

140

MeLisa Rogers, Shiner, Texas

The candidate had a strong background in workforce management with promotions, but her resume did not display the level of management she had attained and her knowledge of technology. The writer remedied this situation by making certain that this new resume

2

Site Resource Manager—Call Center, GNS—Corpus Christi, Texas　　　　**1994 to 2000**
- Administered TCS and workforce management for a multiskilled, 24/7, 250-seat center.
- Incorporated Real Time Adherence, Vacation Planner, and Meeting Planner modules.
- Presided over the hiring strategies, which supported the client volume forecast on a daily and annual basis.
- Managed and trained a team of administrators designated to manage call center operations and a real-time traffic center.
- Established procedures to deliver budget-conscious solutions while meeting the forecast expectations of the client and senior management.

DAMSON GENERAL FOODS
1992 to 1994

Corpus Christi, Texas

Territory Sales Manager—Successfully expanded the Corpus Christi market for this purveyor to hotels, restaurants, hospitals, and institutions.
- Through aggressive sales and marketing, doubled monthly revenues, expanded customer base, increased market penetration, and established a track record of strong customer service.
- Selected as the Gross Profit Leader for the Texas Region.

Prior Professional Experience

Restaurant Manager	RED LOBSTER—Houston, Texas	4/91 to 11/91
Catering Manager	BARNACLE CATERING, INC.—Houston, Texas	9/89 to 11/90
Kitchen Manager	SPAGHETTI WAREHOUSE—Houston, Texas	8/86 to 11/88
Assistant Manager	HOLIDAY INN—Beaumont, Texas	9/84 to 7/86

Professional Training and Certifications

Crystal Reports—40 hours of classroom training—2002
Benchmark Portal—Certified Specialist 2002
Lucent Custom Reports—2000
IEX Database, Process, Real-Time Adherence, and Skill Training—Certified
TCS versions 4.0 and 5.0—Certified
TCS and IEX Users Forum—1999, 2000, 2001
ICCM Forecast and Scheduling Seminar—1999
Microsoft Office Suite—Excel, Word, Outlook, PowerPoint, Access, Project
Visio

Education

Texas A&M University, College Station, Texas—Finance—1982 to 1986

Military Experience

Active-Duty USAF—Honorable Discharge—1976 to 1980—Medical Administration
Assignments:
　　Inactive Reserves—Lackland AFB—1980 to 1984
　　Clerk Office of Professional Education
　　Highest rank attained: Sergeant—Active Duty
　　Staff Sergeant—Inactive Reserves
　　Lackland AFB—1978 to 1980
　　Inspector General Specialist, Medical IG Office
　　Elmendorf AFB—1976 to 1978
　　CHAMPUS Clerk, Budget Office AAC (Alaskan Air Command)

M A R I A   D .   S C H E R I N G

8 3 2   S A N D Y   L A N E   C O R P U S   C H R I S T I ,   T E X A S   7 8 1 3 2   3 6 1 - 2 7 5 - 4 7 3 9

communicated early the applicant's position, her level of technology, and her global experience. With this resume she got the new position she was seeking, and her salary increased by approximately $30,000!

MARY ANNE SMITH

7777 West Main Street, Anytown, ST 55555
masmith@aol.com • (555) 555-5555

PROFESSIONAL PROFILE

Visual Merchandising Manager with a broad base of retail experience, including strategic concept planning for national corporations, fiscal responsibility for multimillion-dollar budgets, product development and importation and major account development to drive sales and profits. Innovative visionary with fresh ideas, a keen sense of style and fashion, trend intuition and creative design techniques. Motivational presenter and articulate public speaker who trains store management and educates corporate executives to deliver consistency of merchandising concepts throughout large retail networks. Self-sufficient and resourceful problem solver with meticulous organizational, planning, problem identification and decision-making skills.

AREAS OF EXPERTISE

National Retail Corporations	Marketing Communications	Project Management
Brand Strategy/Imaging	Executive Presentations	Training Programs
Retail Merchandising	Channel Management	Vendor Negotiations
Visual Presentation Standards	Strategic Partnerships	Team Building

SAMPLE OF CAREER ACHIEVEMENTS

➢ Directed a major collateral rollout for a nationally known merchandise brand that far surpassed corporate expectation and created consumer-recognized brand identity throughout the United States.
➢ Developed merchandising standards to maintain visual consistency throughout large retail network that optimized fashion apparel assortments, maximized sales revenue, promoted product/category awareness and improved in-store traffic patterns.
➢ Devised guidelines for implementing visual merchandise concepts, including training videos and written marketing communications.
➢ Prepared and delivered compelling, persuasive presentations to win senior executive approval of and support for new concepts, corporate direction and program rollouts.
➢ Primary visionary for new and innovative visual merchandising concepts for specialty departments of two Fortune 500 retailers throughout the United States.
➢ Redesigned and implemented a new specialty department for a major retailer at an upscale mall in San Juan, Puerto Rico, that targeted the Hispanic consumer and featured a tropical theme.
➢ Managed multimillion-dollar budgets and directed field visual merchandising teams in the development of presentation concepts and installation of 500 specialty departments in new and remodeled stores.
➢ Initiated and designed the *Innovative Concept I* and *Innovative Concept II* merchandising concepts.
➢ Created original branding concepts for private-label merchandise product lines.

PROFESSIONAL EXPERIENCE

ABC COMPANY, Anytown, ST   1998–present
Senior Account Manager
Develop new business and deliver exemplary service to existing accounts to increase market penetration, annual revenue and profit margins.

• Develop respected customer relationships through comprehensive industry knowledge, keen understanding of visual merchandising, superior customer service and meticulous attention to detail.
• Grew account base by 54% through targeted research, trade show participation, persistent prospecting and highly successful sales techniques.
• Formulate cohesive, sales-driven marketing plans and presentations based on client profiles and a thorough understanding of customer needs and what motivates consumer purchases.
• Manage the entire sales process from prototype design to in-store installation using exceptional communication and project management skills to deliver best results on time and within budget.

XYZ COMPANY, Anytown, ST   1997–1998
Manager, Merchandise Presentation—Corporate
Directed the development of visual presentation strategies for all apparel divisions nationwide. Managed a multimillion-dollar budget and coached a team of 12 direct reports. Reported directly to the Division Vice President.

• Developed merchandising standards to maintain visual consistency throughout 236 stores by defining space, adjacency, zone and fixture orientation to optimize fashion assortments, maximize sales, promote product/category awareness and improve traffic patterns.
• Corroborated with senior management, division merchandise managers, buyers and trend office personnel to create new merchandise assortments to quickly respond to changing trends and consumer buying preferences.
• Initiated and implemented product placement and visual presentation plans for all categories of merchandise to promote special sales and highlight targeted merchandise.
• Mentored creative merchandising team in designing and installing visual components, including in-store signage, trend graphics, POS collateral and POP fixture concepts.
• Provided visual merchandising direction and training for all 138 remodeled stores nationwide.

141

Rosemary Fish Justen, Schaumburg, Illinois

This applicant had a long career in retail with increasing levels of responsibility; however, without a four-year degree, she worried about progressing further in the industry. After an extensive interview and fact-gathering session, the writer presented the applicant's qualifications in a

MARY ANNE SMITH_____

LMN AND COMPANY, Anytown, ST   1994–1997
Category Creative Manager—Corporate   (1996–1997)
Responsible for strategic development of visual merchandising initiatives for entire specialty category in 573 full-line stores with $695 million annual revenue throughout the United States.
- Primary visionary for creating new and innovative visual merchandising concepts.
- Corroborated with Senior Vice Presidents to develop a visual support plan for respective businesses consistent with sales and profit objectives, marketing goals and customer perception.
- Designed fixtures, collateral elements and graphic programs. Delivered persuasive presentations of conceptual prototypes to win approval and support of the President and Senior Executives.
- As point of contact for architectural firm of record, engaged design firms, production vendors, outside consultants and contractors to meet clearly stated build-out objectives on time and within budget.
- Drove transition of projects to successful completion through articulate written and verbal communication, anticipation of obstacles and timely resolution of problems.

National Visual Presentation Manager—Corporate   (1994–1996)
Developed and directed visual presentation and merchandising concepts for specialty departments nationwide. Fiscally responsible for multimillion-dollar operating budgets, maintaining bottom-line control without sacrificing high quality of visual presentation programs and materials. Coached a team of three direct reports. Dotted-line management and training responsibility for a field implementation team who installed more than 500 specialty departments in new and remodeled stores.
- Directed all design, development and implementation of fixture programs, POP marketing materials, signage and visual collateral to create a compelling environment for the customer.
- Coordinated all elements of project initiatives with planning, fixture purchasing, construction, marketing and outside sources to maintain phasing schedules and control project expenditures.
- Initiated all merchandising standards and traveled nationally to educate region and district management to ensure consistency and seamless execution.

ANY COMPANY, INC., Anytown, ST   1990–1994
Vice President
Directed sales, product development and marketing functions for import of private-label packaging and gift items with annual sales of $162 million. Developed key packaging items for major accounts and national retail clients.
- Managed overseas sourcing and the design of decorative containers and gift items for promotional marketing programs, traveling to Hong Kong, China and the Philippines.
- Designed and delivered persuasive sales presentations to major gift accounts and specialty markets.
- Created original branding concepts for private-label merchandise product lines.

BEST CORPORATION, Anytown, ST   1984–1990
Specialty Visual Manager—Corporate   (1987–1990)
Responsible for creative design, strategic planning, vendor relations and visual program implementation to contribute to the profitability of all specialty promotions for major merchandise brands.
- Initiated gift-with-purchase and purchase-with-purchase merchandise promotion, developed visual and merchandising concepts, directed in-store implementation and monitored financial results.
- Coordinated all aspects of celebrity appearances and special events in store's most heavily promoted department. Personally presented category seminars to audiences of up to 400 key managers.

Assistant Director—Visual Presentations/Merchandising / Assistant Fashion Director / Staff Visual Positions—
Flagship Store—Best Corporation, Anytown, ST   (1984–1987)

EDUCATION AND AFFILIATIONS _____

Industry Standard **Magazine** • *Editorial Board*   **2000–2002**
Recognized School of Art, Anytown, ST • Associate in Arts Degree   **1987**

Computer Skills: ACT • Goldmine • MS Office Suite • Adobe Photoshop, PageMaker and Illustrator

Professional Profile that emphasizes her innate abilities. The writer also included industry keywords in the Areas of Expertise section and highlighted her industry successes in the Sample of Career Achievements section.

TREVOR HUTCH

555 5th Street NE, Byron, Minnesota 55555
(555) 555-5555 ▫ Email: thutch@network.net

Management ▫ Customer Service ▫ Operations

High-energy, goal- and results-oriented manager with fifteen years of experience in a customer service environment and a track record of performance and sales turnarounds. Leadership style includes team motivational techniques, training and staff development, mentoring and coaching, and individual accountability. High school Spanish courses and direct experience interacting with Hispanic, Asian, Somali, Arabic and other cultures and customs.

AREAS OF EXPERIENCE

- Execution of corporate directives … Policy planning and implementation … Retail operations
- Budget management and implementation … Finances
- Loss prevention … Inventory management … Shipping and receiving
- Customer service and community relations
- Sales, marketing, merchandising and promotions
- Employee retention … Salary determination … EEO adherence … Recruitment, interviewing and hiring of management personnel … Scheduling and work flow … Staff motivation

MANAGEMENT EXPERIENCE

♦ **LEIFSON STORES, Minnesota, 1998 to 2009**

STORE MANAGER, 2003 to 2009, Ralston, Minnesota: Provided oversight of store, pharmacy and optical center with sales volume of $23 million, 150 regular staff, 12 hourly supervisors and management team of 10.

STORE MANAGER, 2001 to 2003, Bresden, Minnesota: Led store, pharmacy and optical center consisting of 85 employees, 7 managers and 6 hourly supervisors.

ASSISTANT STORE MANAGER, 1998 to 2001, Ralston, Minnesota: Accountable for success of apparel, front end, hard lines and backroom operations.

Results and Achievements

TURNAROUNDS: Proven track record of turning around poorly performing stores in profits and execution of customer service, resulting in promotion from small- to large-volume store. Sent to store failing to meet profits and sales goals (Bresden), achieving 5% sales and 15% profit increases (exceeding goals) and transforming store from 138th in customer service corporate-wide to 8th in 1 year (earning large bonus).

HEAVY COMPETITION: Achieved success during highly competitive and rapidly expanding community retail growth involving new superstores, department stores and home-improvement megastores. Exceeded corporate goal of 15% annual sales decrease, losing only 5% of previous sales during the first year of store-to-store competition. Kept employee retention at 100% in both markets, receiving 2006 corporate award and garnering status of #1 in region and #10 nationwide. Recognized as #8 in "average store sale" company-wide.

OPERATIONS and PROGRAMS: Assisted in developing updated in-store marketing program involving merchandising presentations, displays and logistics that was adapted for use by other company stores. Decreased inventory loss last 3 years through loss prevention program that was acknowledged corporate-wide for shrink reduction.

EXECUTIVE DEVELOPMENT: Mentored numerous employees to management-level promotions and was assigned to train managers in other stores.

142

Beverley Drake, Hot Springs Village, Arkansas

The individual wanted to get away from retail management and move to some other type of management. Three areas of expertise appear in a heading above the profile. The Areas of Experience section elaborates on the person's abilities. In the Management Experience

TREVOR HUTCH, Page 2

MANAGEMENT EXPERIENCE, continued

◆ **DIVERSE PRODUCTS, Dixon, Minnesota, 1994 to 1998**

MANAGER: Oversaw 54-employee, 6-manager team and coordinated $4.5 million sales base. Trained new managers.

Results and Achievements

TURNAROUNDS: Transitioned previously unprofitable store from losing money to break-even stage within 2 years of being hired—turning a profit by the 3rd year.

OPERATIONS and TRAINING: Assigned to assist store managers in other locations to get back on track and improve operations.

◆ **SUPERIOR LTD., Minnesota, 1991 to 1994**

MANAGER, 1993 to 1994, Rochester, Minnesota
MANAGER, 1992 to 1993, Rochester, Minnesota
ASSISTANT MANAGER, 1991 to 1992, Faribault, Minnesota

ONGOING EDUCATION and PROFESSIONAL DEVELOPMENT

GRADUATE of Corporate Leadership Program, with courses covering Diversity, Leadership, Motivation, Problem Solving and Troubleshooting, Employee Disciplinary Action, Interviewing, Hiring and Peer Leadership

OTHER TRAINING: Change Management … Team Motivation and Planning … Positive Thinking … Using Employee Strengths … OSHA Communication and Compliance … MSDS Sheets … Hazardous Materials … Bloodborne Pathogens … Workplace Safety

TECHNOLOGY

PC in Windows XP environment … MS Word, Excel and Outlook … Norton AntiVirus … Email … Internet and intranet … Customized Merchandising Control and Inventory Programs … Computer Programming

COMMUNITY INTERACTON

Guest Speaker, Ralston Community and Technical College—Retail Management Program

Coach, Ralston Youth Soccer Association

Classroom Volunteer, Chimron Elementary School

Member, Neighborhood Watch Program

Member, Chimron Sportsmen's Club

Member, Church Council

section, Results and Achievements are grouped according to the categories at the beginning of the paragraphs. A diamond bullet directs your attention to each new workplace.

Tony L. Carr

P.O. Box 555
Denver, CO 80555

Cell 000.000.0000
carr00@aol.com

Summary of Qualifications

Forward-thinking, dynamic manager with more than 15 years of successful experience in the automotive industry. Proven ability to establish, build and direct a successful dealership. Documented track record of accepting challenges and producing stellar results despite minimal prior experience. Possess solid background in all aspects of dealership operations, including management of Sales, Service and Parts Departments. Strong skill with leadership, including mobilizing sales and maintaining high employee performance and morale. Skilled at dealing effectively with public and providing excellent customer service. Strengths include:

Management

Demonstrated ability to oversee all aspects of day-to-day retail sales operations, including P&L, purchasing and inventory controls of vehicles, parts and accessories; cash and credit management; personnel training and supervision; customer financing; facilities management and continuous quality improvement. Strong ability to assess, control and ensure financial success of operations.

Sales, Marketing & Merchandising

Proven expertise in serving a leadership role in creating and implementing a wide range of promotional strategies to advance sales, including direct mail, promotional events and special sales. Excellent sales skills including negotiation, follow-up and closing. Highly effective in creating vehicle displays.

Brand Expertise

Possess extensive knowledge base of autos and luxury vehicles, including BMW cars and motorcycles, Land Rover SUVs & Porsche, Audi, Volvo and Mercedes Benz cars.

Management Experience

Washington BMW
General Manager

Bellevue, WA
12/99–4/05

Entrusted with full profit and loss accountability for successful launch and management of BMW motorcycle dealership with minimal prior similar experience. Administered six employees, including hiring, training and performance evaluation. Established and managed Parts Department inventory and Service Department equipment and tools. Oversaw warranty claims process. Performed and supervised sales and marketing for new/used cars and motorcycles. Ordered and managed new-vehicle inventory. Appraised, wholesaled and managed used vehicles. Managed finance process. Coordinated advertising for sales and special promotions.

- Propelled all start-up tasks for new dealership, from construction to grand opening.
- Oversaw consistent yearly increase in sales of 30% over each previous year and held highest unit sales for new vehicles outside of area of responsibility (AOR).
- Attained recognition as top-ten BMW dealership in America by BMW Riders Association International in recognition of outstanding service and sales.
- During national sales competition, significantly exceeded sales goal by 200%, resulting in being awarded first-class air travel and accommodations to international BMW dealer conference in Cape Town, South Africa.
- Consistently achieved 95%–100% warranty index.
- Successfully bid and gained New Mexico State Police Motorcycle contract.

"Tony has a very good management style...he motivates his employees, is supportive of company objectives and brings his own management ideas to create new business.... I highly recommend Tony Carr as a valuable asset" —Shane Kuhn, General Sales Manager / BMW of Pocatello, former supervisor

143

Michele Angello, Aurora, Colorado

The applicant was feeling stuck in positions that seemed beneath his abilities and past accomplishments. The writer emphasized his past dealership-management accomplishments and reorganized his experience so that these would be seen first. He accomplished much in his career even

Tony L. Carr Page 2

─────── Management Experience (continued) ───────

Kenn Auto Corp.   Santa Fe, NM
Service Manager   9/94–12/99

Directed operations of service department for New Mexico's largest Land Rover dealership. Oversaw performance of eight employees, including hiring, training, performance evaluation, motivation and coaching. Coordinated marketing campaigns. Completed purchasing in order to ensure correct balance and availability of tools, equipment and parts. Developed training program for service employees.

- ❑ Attained promotion from BMW/Land Rover Service Advisor to Service Manager within 14 months of hire because of excellent performance.
- ❑ Achieved designation to Service Manager's Guild for top 10% performance.
- ❑ Maintained consistently high customer satisfaction index (CSI), surpassing competing dealerships.

─────── Additional Automotive Experience ───────

Hamm Motors, Inc.   Broomfield, CO
Service Advisor   05–present

Provided excellent customer service. Reviewed, analyzed and processed repair orders.

Guy Imports, Inc.   Littleton, CO
Sales Consultant   05

Performed sales of Porsche and Jaguar cars. Conducted prospecting and follow-up. Interacted with customers extensively in order to close sales.

Previous background includes additional Service Advisor experience with Mercedes Benz North America in Hollywood, CA. Established and managed new Parts Department for new Porsche/Audi dealership. Ordered initial Porsche inventory. Inherited significantly obsolete Audi parts inventory and subsequently put into balance. Additionally performed as Registered Investment Executive Paine Webber/New York Stock Exchange.

─────── Education & Professional Development ───────

College of Santa Fe   Albuquerque, NM
Bachelor of Science Degree Program, Business Management

Dale Carnegie Sales Management
Karass Seminars: Effective Negotiating
Joe Verde Sales Training
Porsche Sportdriving School, Leipzig, Germany
Mike Nichols Institute: Parts Management Seminar
UCLA: Total Quality Management

> "Tony turned a brand new, inexperienced dealership into the motorcycle dealership of choice for all existing and new BMW riders in New Mexico. Dealing with Tony you always know that you will be treated fairly...he deeply appreciates the importance of repeat business and exceeding the expectations of customers."   —Roger Feidler, Santa Fe, NM, former customer

though he did not complete his bachelor's degree when his career was taking off. The boxed testimonials help to offset the lack of the bachelor's degree.

GARY KILBURN

1743 Dickinson Place
Amarillo, Texas 79109

806-555-9211
gkilburn@aol.com

MANAGER/CONSULTANT/TRAINER
**Customer Service • Human Resources • Financial Management • Operations • Sales
Merchandising • Inventory Management • Payroll • Purchasing • Loss Prevention**

➤ Solid P&L management, training, strategic planning, budgeting, financial reporting, and leadership qualifications. Lead companies to substantial revenue gains by establishing sales goals, initiating cost containment processes, providing hands-on training, and motivating personnel. Well-informed in current best practices.

➤ Self-motivated, results-driven manager; understand overall industry position and appropriate competitive strategies in market development. Readily visualize target and identify steps required to attain goal. Creative and effective at capturing cost reductions through performance training, employee retention, and strict inventory controls.

➤ Skilled in staff training, development, and performance management to meet/exceed operational and financial goals through performance/quality improvements and adherence to established procedures. Team player; establish standards for self and others, embrace visions, and see the "big picture."

➤ Computer-literate; proficiency includes MS Excel, MS Word, PeopleSoft, LRT scanner, and Internet research and communication.

RETAIL STORE MANAGER

Howe's Home Improvement Warehouse   *1996–2004*
Profitably managed 114,000–118,000 sq. ft. home improvement stores with 150–220 employees and annual sales volume of $25 million–$45 million with a product inventory of $6 million (45,000 SKUs). Oversaw $600K weekly inventory purchasing to procure merchandise mix specific to location's demographic needs. Tracked inventory and implemented systems to reduce inventory shrink.

    STORE MANAGER, #372, Houston, Texas *(2001–2004)*
    STORE MANAGER, #80, San Antonio, Texas *(1999–2001)*
    CO-MANAGER, #372, Houston, Texas *(1998–1999)*
    OPERATIONS MANAGER, #173, Austin, Texas *(1996–1998)*

- Achieved $45 million in annual sales and $6.7 million in net-before-taxes. Managed operating budget up to $7 million at approximately 15.5% to sales. Consistently improved sales performance and produced bottom-line profits in each facility by ensuring superior customer service, efficient staff scheduling, and appropriate product merchandising while maintaining facility's appearance.

- Spearheaded numerous cost-saving initiatives:
  ➤ Employee Turnover/Retention—Achieved best rate out of 60 stores in region.
  ➤ Inventory Shrink—Reduced inventory shrink from $500K at 2% to sales to $220K at .97% to sales by introducing new programs and executing existing procedures. Maintained this standard in all facilities.
  ➤ Labor Scheduling—Implemented effective automated labor scheduling, reducing man-hours while improving productivity. Introduced night stocking of merchandise, decreasing labor to process freight by 25%.
  ➤ Supply Management Program—Resulted in 35% savings in supply expense.
  ➤ Delivery Income/Expense—Turned around significant loss in delivery to break-even status by accurately calculating load, time, and distance.
  ➤ Bad Checks/Cash Over-Short—Introduced in-store campaign with expectations and rewards, reducing losses by as much as $10K annually.

144

Jane Roqueplot, West Middlesex, Pennsylvania

A color printer prints this resume in black and brick red. The brick red is evident in all the contact information, the information between the top two horizontal lines, the arrow-tip and round bullets, and the section headings. For each corporation, work positions are clustered to avoid

Howe's Home Improvement Warehouse, continued

- Implemented operational and management changes to dramatically boost profits in every facility under my management. For example, in store #372, increased profits 48% ($2 million). Oversaw several expansion projects as well as numerous major remerchandising efforts in excess of $500K each.

- Hired best possible staff; facilitated appropriate training and emphasized customer service. Drove customer service standard in each store.

- Boosted customer satisfaction through numerous initiatives:
  ➢ Through proper scheduling, eliminated major front-end operations problem (long lines at cash registers) as well as sales floor department coverage issues.
  ➢ Created program to verify customer received product in undamaged condition.
  ➢ Improved communication and accountability by adding missing element to corporate Manager On Duty Program, providing direct access to manager.

Century Supermarkets   *1987–1996*
Managed 12,000–62,000 sq. ft. grocery stores with 25–300 employees and annual sales volume of $6 million–$35 million with a product inventory of 60,000 SKUs.

STORE MANAGER, #904, Wichita Falls, Texas *(1995–1996)*
STORE MANAGER, #897, Vernon, Texas *(1990–1995)*
STORE MANAGER, #901, Wichita Falls, Texas *(1987–1990)*

- Achieved highest volume of $35 million in sales and $2 million in profits out of 50 stores in chain.

- Succeeded in challenge to keep store productive while overseeing 12-month, $7 million construction project adjacent to facility being replaced. New facility recorded profit in first financial reporting period—a first in company history.

- Spearheaded use of computerized staffing program, which optimized efficient use of employee time during peak and off-peak store hours.

SEMINARS/TRAINING/WORKSHOPS

Recent training topics:
- Conflict Management Training
- Harassment Training
- Diversity Training
- Essentials of Communicating with Diplomacy and Professionalism

- Excelling as a Manager or Supervisor
- Substance Abuse in the Workplace
- Dale Carnegie, Effective Public Speaking

PERSONAL HIGHLIGHTS

Descriptive terms of personal strengths in the workplace based on professional Personality Profiling

Objective ~ Realistic ~ Looks for Logical Solutions ~ Competitive ~ Excellent Troubleshooter
Goal-oriented ~ Ambitious ~ Innovative ~ Responsible ~ Accurate

EDUCATION

Business Management, Texas Tech University, Lubbock, Texas

repetition in describing common duties. Attention is directed instead to achievements, cost-saving initiatives, and other initiatives for each cluster.

Tom S. Richards   1297 Silver Creek Road, Fort Worth, Texas 78413
(H) 817-897-1153 (W) 817-828-2236 (C) 682-442-6258 e-mail: tsr5125@yahoo.com

---

RETAIL STORE OPERATIONS DIRECTOR
Regional Director of Diversity

*Proven career history as a **market-driven store director** with an outstanding background in **managing multimillion-dollar retail operations**. Recognized for **increasing sales volumes, consistently beating expense goals** and successfully leading the region's 5,000 partners in corporate diversity initiatives.*

CORE STRENGTHS

Visionary Leadership / Innovation Management	Strategic-Alliance / Partner Development
Production and Efficiency Optimization	Regional Initiatives / Location Management
Customer Service and Retention Management	Human Resources Management
Organization / Team Leadership	Financial Forecasting
Sales & Shrink-Inventory Control	Staff Supervision & Management
Profit & Loss Management	Stringent Cost Control Measures
Strategic Planning	Safety / Sanitation / Premises Liability
Facility Maintenance	Training & Development

SELECTED PROFESSIONAL ACHIEVEMENTS

- Significantly increased community volunteerism and partnerships resulting in increased sales volume.
- Increased sales per man-hour 13% with no impact to service levels.
- Slashed store losses 50% by implementing systems and controls in premises liability.
- Reduced employee turnover 50% by transitioning to a fair and equitable management style, penetrating the store's leadership team from the top down.

PROFESSIONAL EXPERIENCE

H·E·B   **STORE DIRECTOR**   **May 2001–Present**

H.E. BUTT GROCERY COMPANY, Fort Worth, Texas
H.E.B. is a $10 billion company with 300 stores operating throughout Texas, Mexico and Louisiana with corporate offices in San Antonio, Texas.

Manage retail operations, inventory control, premises liability, safety/sanitation, overall facility maintenance, human resources, and revenue / cost control with full P & L responsibility in a 24/7 operation consisting of 10 departments and 250+ partners. Support and implement regional objectives, including the execution of targeted advertising efforts.

- Yield a net profit of 7–9% of total sales while managing an annual sales volume of $3–6 million per year with a bottom-line profit of $300,000 to $400,000 per quarter.
- Achieved a first-time-ever expense record of 17.99%, and consistently maintain an average of 18.33%, comparable to a corporate goal of 18.50% and store history of 19.20%. This was accomplished through an effort to refocus attention on expenses and educate store partners in the identification of opportunities to reduce waste such as electricity.
- Reduced inventory from 22 to 16 days as a result of incorporating tighter management practices combined with the successful implementation of SRS—Store Replenishment System.
- Increased achievement of strategic operating goals though the implementation of a partner-centered leadership philosophy.
- Quadrupled participation in community volunteerism activities such as Junior Achievement as a result of assembling diversity programs and building community relationships.

145

MeLisa Rogers, Shiner, Texas

This candidate did not have a college degree but did have director-level responsibility in his current position. He wanted to relocate to a major metropolitan area in another part of the country but had only an outdated, amateurish resume. The writer constructed from scratch this

Tom S. Richards   page 2

Regional Director of Diversity   **January 2002–Present**
In conjunction with Store Director responsibilities
- Spearheaded the corporate diversity program on the regional level for 29 stores and 5000 partners. Led the region's management team in "getting excited" about diversity. Installed a 12-member council and 29 diversity champions (one representative per each location) to promote diversity throughout the region. As a result, HEB has gained a reputation as an active volunteer leader in each of its respective communities in the South Texas Region.

 STORE DIRECTOR   **1999–2001**

<u>ALBERTSON'S INCORPORATED</u>, Seattle, Washington
Albertson's is an NYSE $38 billion retail grocery company consisting of 2,300 stores operating in 31 states with the corporate office located in Boise, Idaho. Albertson's merged with Lucky Stores, a division of American Stores, Inc., in 1999.

Store located in heart of Seattle with 80–100 partners.
- Saved $920,000 in annual premises liability expense—$20,000 to $250,000 per quarter—through the execution of community-based initiatives that led to increased community support and operational awareness.
- Founder of Diversity Group Leadership Committee, which assisted the regional marketing team in implementing diversified community advertising campaigns that were previously nonexistent.
- Transitioned a store with a history of incurring losses of up to $300,000 per quarter to profitability within one year of promotion to store director.

ASSISTANT STORE DIRECTOR   **1995–1999**
AMERICAN STORES, INC. (LUCKY STORES DIVISION), Portland, Oregon
- Promoted every six months within four years to Assistant Store Director.
- Created and spearheaded a marketing initiative to enhance the store's snack program, "Snacks Across Your Tracks." This resulted in .4–.6 base points in profitability and margins.

ENTRY-LEVEL MANAGER / CASHIER / COURTESY CLERK   1988–1995

AWARDS AND RECOGNITIONS

2002 – Leadership for Diversity – HEB
2002 – Retail Grocery Industry – Diversity Edge – TAMU Sorority – Fort Worth – Plaque

EDUCATION AND PROFESSIONAL TRAINING

UNIVERSITY OF TEXAS "ON-LINE"—Course of Study: Business Administration, 1996–1998
WASHINGTON STATE UNIVERSITY, Seattle, Washington—Liberal Arts, 1987–1989

Diversity   Career Advancement Program
Behavior-Based Feedback   Store Management Training
Store Operating Statement Analysis

CERTIFICATIONS

Forklift Operation   Food Preparation and Safety State Certification
Anti-Money Laundering   AST—Alcohol Sellers Training

resume, which describes the candidate's extensive background, so that he could be competitive in achieving a position he was seeking in a preferred demographic area. The logos are in bright colors.

ROBERT SEATON

One Rogers Court
Barrie, Ontario • LOG 1A1
705-555-1819 • Messages: 905-555-5693
Email Robert-Seaton@my-email.com

RETAIL MANAGER

Profile

"Customer-first" professional with nearly 10 years of increasingly responsible experience selling an assortment of products to individuals from all demographic and economic backgrounds. **Can be entrusted by senior management to take on—and complete— extra duties, all the while striving to exceed customer and Company expectations.** An effective communicator, able to foster and maintain positive ties with clients, staff, and management from all walks of life. WHMIS certified. Computer knowledge includes in-house programs, Word, and Windows XP. **Strive to apply unique blend of flexibility, high energy, and maturity in order to inspire employees to achieve bottom-line success.** Willing to relocate.

Areas of Strength

Customer Relationship-Building, Loyalty, & Retention • Buyer Awareness
Diplomatic Compliant Resolution • Closing Techniques • Employee Scheduling
Goal-Setting & Incentive Planning • Inventory Control • Loss Prevention
Mass-Merchandising Techniques • Opening & Closing Procedures • Warehousing Operations
Problem Resolution & Critical Decision Making • Senior Staff & Vendor Relations
Staff Training & Team Building • Till Setup & Reconciliation • Competitive Analysis

Professional Experience

Tires R Us, Port Elgin   2009
Assistant Store Manager
Recruited to collaborate with store manager in running entire operations—consisting of 3 departments—spanning 9,800 sq. ft. Specific accountabilities included store opening and closing, managing shipping / receiving / warehouse departments, and addressing a myriad of customer concerns.
Achievements
- Tapped to reorganize all aspects of store—including stockroom, sales floor, exterior grounds, and shop—that had not received proper attention since store opening in year 2000. Completed this ambitious project in only 3 months
- Eliminated all metal throwaways by contacting a local recycler who could haul away such material; also recouped an extra $500 that the recycler was happy to pay
- Took the initiative to instruct staff on proper up-selling techniques; as a result, consistently exceeded revenues based on preceding year's performance
- Successfully identified, organized, and sold "discontinued" merchandise valued at $20,000—a first at this location
- Instituted a ruling whereby staff would electronically log off at the end of their shift, thereby easing the end-of-day closing process

146

Marian Bernard, Aurora, Ontario, Canada

The applicant reported that he received remarkable responses to this resume. The multiple-arrow graphic (in alternating yellow and vivid red in the original) captured everyone's attention. Powerful keywords appear in the first third of the resume, and the applicant's achievements motivated

R O B E R T   S E A T O N

705-555-1819 • Messages: 905-555-5693
Email Robert-Seaton@my-email.com

Page Two

P r o f e s s i o n a l   E x p e r i e n c e *(continued)*

Pasco Furniture, Newmarket   2002–2009
  2003–2004: Senior Sales Consultant / Acting Manager
Promoted—based on history of "repeatedly going the extra mile"—to assume broader level of responsibilities such as staff training, solving an array of problems as they arise, and selling product from entire floor consisting of audio/video, furniture, and appliances departments.
  Achievements:
- Credited with generating highest revenue levels for 3 consecutive months in audio / visual and appliance departments
- Repeatedly persuade vendors to prioritize repairs for customers based on top-notch commitment to customer satisfaction
- Handpicked by Store Manager to serve on the storewide Health & Safety Committee consisting of managers and non-managers
- Tapped both by Store Manager and District Manager to travel to Quebec for 2 weeks and open 2 new stores; specific accountabilities included staff support, management, sales, warehouse operations, and customer service
- Awarded an incentive (out of 45 employees) for exceptional Electronic Product Knowledge
  2002–2003: Sales Consultant—Audio/Video and Appliances

Tires R Us, Aurora   2001
  Installer
Performed minor repairs and basic service (e.g., oil changes and tire rotations), picked up and delivered customers to specific areas, maintained neatness and orderliness in work area, and oriented new hires.
  Achievement
- Captured extra revenues 85% of the time by seizing the opportunity to "sell up" related products and services

Hydrogas, Newmarket   2000
  Equipment Maintenance Representative (contract basis)
Assembled, cleaned, tested, and maintained equipment to ensure top performance; assisted in customer setups and deliveries, and ensured cleanliness of warehouse.

Precision Detailing, Aurora   1997–1999
  Automotive Detailer
  Achievement
- Chosen by President—because of ability to meet time-critical deadlines—to work on dealership cars; specific tasks included shampooing and polishing. Repeatedly commended by owner of local dealership for commitment to top quality; "Seaton" cars were always sold within 7 days

Office Supply Store—Carrville Mall, Richmond Hill   1995–1997
  Sales Associate

---

prospective employers to invite this individual to an interview. Note the effective use of spaced characters in boldface and the separate Achievement section for most positions held.

STEPHANIE LEIGH BIXBY

555 Farmington Lane ◆ Anytown, ST 00000
555-555-5555 ◆ mysearch@mynet.com

ACTION-ORIENTED MANAGEMENT PROFESSIONAL OFFERING EXPERIENCE IN RETAIL OPERATIONS, MERCHANDISING, CUSTOMER SERVICE AND HUMAN RESOURCES

PROFILE

*Team Builder with proven record of motivating staff to achieve peak performance. Able to develop credibility and confidence with the public. Solid organizational and multitasking skills. Troubleshooter with demonstrated ability to identify problems and implement solutions. Excellent interpersonal and communication skills. Bilingual–English and Spanish. Computer literacy includes **Word, Excel, PowerPoint** and **Internet applications.***

EMPLOYMENT HISTORY

ALMOST FAMOUS   Watertown, CT   11/95 to Present
Store Manager

Orchestrate all facets of daily operations for upscale retail apparel and accessories store with annual sales of $3 million.

- Oversee activities and efforts of 23 full-time sales associates. Train staff in providing superior customer service.
- Coordinate work and vacation schedules. Arrange coverage for absences.
- Manage recruiting efforts, including screening resumes, interviewing and hiring personnel. Refer for termination. Conduct exit interviews.
- Evaluate staff and deliver constructive performance appraisals. Compensate employees based on corporate guidelines and policies.
- Maintain, monitor and troubleshoot computer sales and inventory programs. E-mail weekly reports to District Manager.
- Coordinate creative merchandising efforts by adapting corporate-provided materials to customer demographics.
- Address and resolve problems with vendors and suppliers.
- *Spearheaded efforts to resolve and correct overstock problems, resulting in $2,000 monthly additional sales along with improving efficiency.*
- *Reduced employee theft 100% by developing and instituting team sign-out policy. Received $500 bonus and commendation from company President. Policy now implemented in all stores nationwide.*

BOX OFFICE VIDEO   West Hartford, CT   7/90 to 11/95
Customer Service Manager

Oversaw operations for independently owned video rental store with average weekly revenues of $15,000.

- Supervised 12 Service Representatives in establishing memberships, processing rentals, arranging merchandise and dealing with customer service issues.
- Handled recruiting functions, including reviewing applications, conducting on-site interviews, hiring and performance reviews. Counseled, disciplined and terminated staff in appropriate instances.
- Maintained, monitored and updated sales and inventory records on customized software program.
- *Reduced employee turnover and enhanced morale by instituting store-sponsored health insurance plan along with monthly bonus program.*
- *Increased sales by more than 45% by instituting Favorite Customer Reward Plan.*

EDUCATION

NAUGATUCK VALLEY COMMUNITY COLLEGE, Waterbury, CT
Associate's Degree in **Management**

147

Ross Primack, Wethersfield, Connecticut

This person had been in retail operations/management, but she wanted to keep her options open. The writer indicated her other areas of experience so that she could pursue other opportunities.

Manufacturing

Resumes at a Glance

JOE JOBSEEKER

555 Street Address
City, ST 55555

E-mail: info@resumeasap.com
Bilingual Spanish/English

Home: 555-555-5555
Cell: 000-000-0000

Targeting Positions as...

LOGISTICS / WAREHOUSE/MANUFACTURING / OPERATIONS MANAGEMENT

Accomplished manager with a diverse and flexible skill set applicable to multiple industries. Specialty expertise in imports/exports between the U.S. and Mexico combined with broad knowledge of business management, logistics, and sales. Highly respected team leader and facilitator with excellent communication, organizational, and problem-solving skills. Able to identify redundancies and general inefficiencies to maximize resources and streamline operations. Computer proficient in Windows, including MS Word and MS Excel.

Key Skills

- Operations Management
- Strategic Planning
- Budgeting / Cost Control
- Leadership & Supervision

- Materials Management
- Inventory Control
- Customs / Tariff Regulations
- Warehouse / Distribution

- Safety (OSHA, DOT, etc.)
- Regulatory Compliance
- Transportation Coordination
- Computer Literate

Related Experience

COMPANY NAME—City, ST

Manager / Owner, 1996 to 2006

Provided third-party logistics for companies such as General Motors, Ford, Delphi, GE, Dal-tile, Great Lakes Chemicals, Detroit Diesel, Goodyear, Caterpillar, and Mack. Directed all operations, sales, inventory and equipment control, transportation, traffic, administrative details, daily operating procedures, and safety training.

- Increased gross monthly sales from $285,000 to $944,000 during tenure.
- Managed 10–15 employees, including warehouse associates, truck drivers, office assistants, and contract personnel.

REGIONAL RETAIL WAREHOUSE—City, ST

Operations Manager, 1992 to 1996

Set up the <City> location. Coordinated all transportation, managed inventory, supervised dispatching, and oversaw daily operations.

Additional Career History

REAL ESTATE CHAIN—City, ST

Realtor, 2006 to 2009

Year-over-year sales performance improvements in spite of weak economy with 2008 sales of $2.8M and 2009 sales of $1.9M.

Certifications & Affiliations

- Certified forklift operator and certified HAZMAT handler.
- Member <City Name> Transportation Association.

148

Jennifer Anthony, Woodland, Washington

This applicant wanted to transition out of the declining real estate industry and return to warehouse management. The focus is on his skills, moving his real estate experience to the end.

Jennifer D. Perrozi

116 Simpson Road • Jamesburg, NJ 08831 • 732.521.3929 (H) • 609.510.4823 (C)

MANUFACTURING ~ PRODUCTION ~ MANAGEMENT ~ CUSTOMER SERVICE
Supervisor/Team Coordinator/Trainer

Top-performing and motivated manufacturing professional with 28 years of experience in line production, supervision, team building, and machine and equipment operation.

Successful track record of maximizing resources to increase production capacity with the ability to troubleshoot and resolve problems in a timely manner. Computer-proficient. Assigned numerous projects with oversight of staff training, mentoring, diversity training, and production improvement. Aided in the design of new processes for production; excellent mediator.

Modeled customer service attitude and strong ethics within the work environment. As **team leader,** developed daily production schedule and served as a liaison between plant employees and management.

Experienced in supervising and training staff, addressing process-improvement issues, **production scheduling,** and adherence to quality standards. Mastered and implemented Good Manufacturing Practices (GMP).

Areas of Expertise:

- Manufacturing Operations
- Management & Supervision
- Production Scheduling
- Process Improvements
- Statistical Analysis
- Training/Mentoring/Team Building
- Communications/Presentations

- Good Manufacturing Practices (GMP)
- Quality Assurance/Inspection
- Problem Identification/Troubleshooting
- Customer Relationship Management
- Calibration & Instrumentation
- Lean Manufacturing
- Business & Strategic Planning

Professional Experience

General Foods—*Dayton, New Jersey (1976 to Present)*
Team Coordinator & Leader/Production & Line Technician

Challenged to supervise and coordinate 15 staff members working in manufacturing line production. Cross-trained and assisted in all business aspects by writing production schedules, attending production strategy meetings, and calculating production statistics. Functioned as Line Technician, Equipment Operator, and Quality Inspector. Known for excellent communication skills. Ability to resolve conflicts and motivate staff.

- Recognized by management for excellent product knowledge, supervisory skills, and plant machinery and equipment operation.
- Liaison between technicians and executive staff.
- Promoted to Team Coordinator for exemplary work and appointed as Diversity Trainer.
- Chosen to conduct training and development operations for various plants as Site Coordinator. Training workshops include diversity, process management, production, quality control, and project management training programs.
- Completed and facilitated Zenger-Miller training and team building operations with company departments.

Education and Training

Zenger-Miller, High Performance Workshop (HPO), and Team Development Workshop

---

149

Beverly and Mitch Baskin, Marlboro, New Jersey

This applicant had worked at the same company since 1976. Four areas of activity are indicated at the top of the resume. In the profile a paragraph is devoted to each of these areas in some way.

LEONARD COLLETTA

926 Augusta Blvd.
Pinehurst, Ontario A1A 1A1
Phone: (555) 888-3333

Assembly / Factory Production / Light Industrial
Quality Control / Team Supervisor

- Extremely **hardworking** and **dedicated,** with the ability to work in **physically demanding and high-pressure environments**
- Ability to **read blueprints** and complete **precision work** to exacting technical specifications
- Excellent **problem-solving skills**—able to quickly determine and repair source of problem
- **Highly reliable, self-motivated,** and **focused** on achieving tasks to highest standards
- Demonstrated ability to **meet and exceed production** quotas while maintaining standards for **accuracy and safety**
- Comfortable and proficient working in a **team** or **team-leader** capacity
- Solid **communication and interpersonal skills** interacting with coworkers and suppliers, with additional experience in customer service and sales

Experience

Quality Inspector / Supervisor
AVENUE METALS, Augusta, Ontario   1999–Present
- Supervise staff and monitor quality in the production of precision sheet metal components for the electronics industry.
- Produce and insert hardware components based on blueprints and specific technical requirements. Includes setup and use of punch press, kick press, and pemserter machines.

Installer
DESIGN WAVE, Pinehurst, Ontario   1998–1999
- Working from floor plans, installed entire offices for government departments around the GTA. Included all cubicle assembly and furniture installation.

Sales / Service Advisor
COLLETTA CORVETTE, Augusta, Ontario   1991–1998
- Sold new and used Corvettes to walk-in clients. Managed the store during night shifts.
- Served as Service Advisor and assisted in car detailing as needed.
- Appraised and bought used cars, handled customer service, and supervised service staff.

Education

Precision Sheet Metal Fabrication
AUGUSTA COLLEGE SKILLS TRAINING CENTRE, Augusta, Ontario   1998–2000

O.S.S.G.D.
MAJOR OAKS SECONDARY SCHOOL, Augusta, Ontario   1992

References available upon request

150

Ross Macpherson, Whitby, Ontario, Canada

A bold one-page presentation and graphic turn an otherwise blue-collar resume into an eye-catcher that had the applicant's phone ringing off the hook. Note the use of boldfacing.

ANDREW G. LANE

0505 OLD MISSION DRIVE • KALAMAZOO, MICHIGAN 49505 • HOME: 505.555.0050 CELL: 505.005.5505

WELDING SUPERVISOR / MANAGER
Specialty: Manufacturing in an Automotive-Related Industry

Well-qualified, proficient welding technician with demonstrated success managing quality, productivity improvement, and product development. Experience and practical knowledge of MIG welding in a high-volume automotive manufacturing operation. Complete understanding of various pieces of welding equipment, their performance, and operation. More than 12 years of experience ensuring that company welders perform their duties in strict compliance with company, state, and federal regulations. Self-motivated, but also able to function effectively in a team setting. Recognized among peers and management as the "in-house expert" Provides strict attention to detail. ISO-9001 and QS-9000 savvy. Proven solid organization and problem-solving skills. Successfully interacts with diverse individuals and groups. **Areas of expertise include the following:**

- **Quality Assurance / Quality Control**
- **Quality & Performance Improvement**
- **Special Welding Processes / Techniques**
- **Plasma Cutting**
- **Just in Time**
- **Robotics**
- **Team Building**

- **Internal Quality Audits**
- **Manual Writing / Documentation**
- **Welder's Qualifications**
- **Blueprint Reading**
- **Lean Manufacturing**
- **Computer Programs**
- **Team Training / Leadership**

- **ISO-9001 / QS-9000**
- **Regulations & Codes**
- **Inspection Codes**
- **TS 16949**
- **TPS**
- **Supervision**
- **Equipment Maintenance**

PRODUCTION EXPERIENCE

LEXINGTON AUTOMOTIVE, Three Rivers, Michigan   **1994–Present**
(The U.S. automotive parts manufacturing outpost of BMW's Lexington Group of manufacturers, which are responsible for manufacturing chassis, vehicle safety components, and exhaust systems. The Lexington Group's automotive operations include more than 60 locations in 20 countries.)

QUALITY TECHNICIAN / WELDER

TECHNICAL SKILLS

▸ Complete knowledge of welding symbols, blueprints, MIG welding processes, metallurgy, and welding methods used to minimize structural fatigue failure.

▸ Over the years has developed superior operator techniques to produce uniform welds of high quality.

▸ Determines the proper welding process to be used and the equipment best suited for the specific jobs.

▸ Plans layout, assembly, and welding of automotive structures; applies knowledge of geometry, physical properties of metal machining, and weld shrinkage to ensure solid, safe structures.

QUALITY CONTROL

▸ Currently the Zone Leader assisting the Line Coordinator/Supervisor for the company's BMW line.

▸ Works closely with company welders to ensure that their welds meet quality standards and adhere to regulations and codes.

▸ Supervises technicians to ensure that the company's ABB robotic system is making quality welds.

▸ Developed, implemented, and monitored ISO-9001 and QS-9000 standards for the Quality Department.

▸ Worked closely with quality engineers in the development of the PPAP and QS-9000 guidelines for certification of the Luxor 2000 control line arm.

▸ When assigned to the Luxor crossover line, responsible for packing and inspecting parts for structural defects.

▸ While assigned to the company's Quality Laboratory, developed a plan to unify all departments' cut-up areas.

▸ Developed a comprehensive system for all shifts to follow to test weld quality.

▸ Heavily involved with the company's computer program "Turnkey" that scopes and records data for weld analysis.

151

Richard T. Porter, Portage, Michigan

The applicant wanted to be a welding supervisor for a group of welders in a large automotive-parts manufacturing operation but didn't have any direct, large-group supervisory experience. The writer accentuated the individual's management skills and included a detailed section on major

PRODUCTION EXPERIENCE (CONT.)

TRAINING & DEVELOPMENT

▸ Encourages open communications to ensure effective interchange of information between workers and support resources within the company.

▸ Monitors workforce performance and implements corrective action to maintain consistent standards of quality.

Project Highlights, Achievements & Performance Improvements

Spearheaded Initiatives to Expand Quality Commitment Throughout Three Rivers' Entire Manufacturing Operation

▸ Determined a way to reduce overhead through employment reduction. On the Luxor crossover line, suggested to management that two people could work more effectively and efficiently than three in packing and inspecting parts. In the company's Quality Laboratory, saw redundancy in personnel and responsibilities. In both cases, management accepted the recommendations. Staff in the Quality Laboratory was reduced from 15 to five.

▸ In response to a rash of substandard welds noted during training sessions, developed a team to prepare and implement an associate training manual to train associate welders on the basics of weld operation before they were assigned to the shop floor. In addition, developed and implemented a weld inspection manual to train associates how to identify inferior welds.

▸ While assigned to the Quality Laboratory, researched and developed a plan to unify all the department's cut-up areas. This plan currently saves the company more than $150,000 per year in wages.

▸ Suggested that welders during their downtime rework parts that would have been scrap parts, resulting in a significant reduction in scrap.

▸ Selected to lead a team of associates charged with developing a pre-orientation training manual. This was the first time an hourly employee was asked to lead a team.

▸ Received continuous improvement nominations for quality improvement ideas for five consecutive years.

▸ As major contributor toward continuous improvement activities performed while on BMW's Luxor crossover line, the company was awarded BMW's Blue Star Award for zero PPMs for six consecutive years.

EDUCATION/PROFESSIONAL DEVELOPMENT

SAGINAW COMMUNITY COLLEGE
Saginaw, Michigan
Coursework toward Associate Degree Technical Trades

Specialized Coursework in the Following

Sheet Metal Fabrication	Structural Steel Metal Fabrication	Structural Steel GMAW
FCAW Welding	TIG Welding	GMAW MIG Welding
Pipe Welding Fundamentals	Advanced Arc Welding	Advanced GTAW (TIG) Welding
Advanced Pipe Welding	Advanced GMAW (MIG) Welding	Special Topics in Welding Technology

CERTIFICATIONS

AWS/ANSID 8.8-97
Welding Light Trucks and Cars, 1994–2005
Weld Inspection, 2004
Forklift Operation, 1994

accomplishments to back up his qualifications. The opening section serves as a profile and an areas of expertise section combined into one section. See Cover Letter 3.

ROBERT W. PETERS

1078 Monet Lane
Edisto Bay, Nova Scotia 99999
Home: (777) 555-6767
Cell: (904) 555-7272

- Operations Turnaround
- Product Line Transitioning
- EDI Stock Replenishment
- KANBAN & CFM
- Capital Improvements
- JIT & Cell Manufacturing
- TQM & MRP

Results-driven **Manufacturing Operations Executive** with 14 years of management experience. Strong general-management skills in strategic business and market planning, quality and performance improvement, customer-relationship management, contract negotiations, capital improvements/renovations, cost reduction and revenue gains and multisite manufacturing operations.

Delivered strong revenue and profit gains at an international facility
while reversing a $9.4 million loss in 8 months.

CUSTOMER-FOCUSED ▪ COST-CONSCIOUS ▪ SOLUTION-ORIENTED

PROFESSIONAL EXPERIENCE

ABBA MANUFACTURING CORPORATION (ABBA)—Sydney, Australia   1990–Present
Formerly Piccadilly Design Co., the company was acquired in 1997 by ABBA, a $500 million, global, NYSE-traded (ABBA) manufacturer of printed circuit boards.
Vice President and General Manager—Caribou, Nova Scotia/Chinchilla, Mexico (2000–Present)
Senior operating executive with full P&L responsibility for a 120,000 sq. ft., 600-employee manufacturing facility with revenues of $120 million annually. Plant operates within a high- and medium-volume, complex, box-built, system-integrated production environment. Promoted to Vice President, August 2000.

Hold full accountability for all strategic and business planning, production control and master scheduling, manufacturing engineering, materials management, purchasing, inventory control, QA/QC, finance, marketing and human resources. Lead a 7-person management staff.

- Challenged in January 2002 by corporate COO and President to plan and direct the turnaround and return to profitability of a manufacturing center in Chinchilla, Mexico, while simultaneously managing the Caribou facility. Achieved all turnaround objectives, returning the Chinchilla operation to profitability within 8 months. Contributed strong and sustainable operating gains:
  - Reduced labor costs by 15% at this then-1,200-employee facility.
  - Improved product quality by 61%.
  - Increased on-time customer delivery from 65% to 85% in 90 days.
  - Reversed $9.4 million revenue loss, generating $4.1 million in operating revenues.

- Oversaw transition of $120 million contract from Caribou to full-scale production in Mexico. Transferred 2 major accounts from Caribou over 15 months. In Mexico, transitioned several new accounts from 3 sites and new assemblies from 4 long-term customers.

- Spearheaded introduction of a series of continuous flow manufacturing (CFM) initiatives for the Caribou facility that strengthened productivity, product quality and customer satisfaction. Reduced work-in-process (WIP) from 10 days to 5 days.

- Delivered significant improvements in quality, production time and cycle time for a major customer through implementation of KANBAN scheduling. Restored credibility and resolved long-standing quality and delivery issues. Achieved and sustained 100% on-time delivery for this high-volume line.

- Pioneered introduction of process changes, such as microBGA, cell manufacturing and EDI.

152

Doug Morrison, Charlotte, North Carolina

With an A.A.S. degree in Electronic Engineering from a community college, this individual had risen through the ranks the old-fashioned way—sweat equity. He started as a Test Engineering Technician at one company, became a Manufacturing Manager at another

Robert W. Peters, page 2

- Implemented time analysis studies and SMED procedures that reduced production setup time by 83%.

- Directed $750,000, 20,000 sq. ft. renovation, including multiple conference, training and break rooms. Monitored costs for leasehold improvements.

- Negotiated contracts and letters of understanding (LOUs) with major computer and server vendors, covering materials, pricing, payment terms and related liability, warranty and disclaimer issues.

- Delivered operating cost reductions totaling $480,000 over 9 months to accelerate profit gains. Led team toward brainstorming creative solutions.

- Created and managed a focus team for scrap-reduction program. Reduced scrap from 1% to .3%.

- Played key role in winning 3 major contracts in 2½ years. Worked closely with sales, production and customer in consummating agreement. Built sales from $6 million to $22 million for one account.

Operations Manager—Caribou, Nova Scotia (1990–2000)

Managed production controls, including materials allocation, scheduling, shop floor tracking and inventory control. Supervised 3-person production planning team.

- Reduced production cycle time from 10 days to 6 days.

- Decreased indirect costs by 30%.

- Established process controls that improved and maintained test yields above 97.2% in-circuit and 98.5% functional.

GREEN BAY ELECTRONICS—Green Bay, Wisconsin   1989–1990
Manager of Manufacturing and Testing

Led 18-person team (6 supervisors, 12 technicians) for this electronics facility with 130 production employees responsible for auto-insertion, SMT, wave-soldering, burn-in and testing operations.

RONSICO, INC.—Hoboken, New Jersey   1980–1989
Quality Assurance Engineer (1987–1989)

Identified and resolved negative trends in production.

- Reduced quality defects within electromechanical assembly from 1.2 per unit to .23 per unit.
- Implemented wave-soldering techniques that improved soldering and decreased solder defects.

Manufacturing Supervisor (1985–1987)
Quality Control Technician (1982–1985)
Test Engineering Technician (1980–1982)

E D U C A T I O N

A.A.S., Electronic Engineering, Manhassett Technical Community College, Long Island, New York, 1980
Professional Development—(APICS Courses, 1998–1999): Basics of Supply Chain Management; Inventory Control Management; Master Scheduling

company, and then secured a position of Vice President and General Manager at a third company. The writer framed the contact information in a box at the top left and placed the keyword section to the right.

SHINGO T. KAIZEN

5555 East Town Road ▪ Pennsylvania, Indiana 00000 ▪ myemail@myaddress.com ▪ (555) 555-5555

MANAGEMENT PROFESSIONAL
Specialist in Production Efficiency / Quality Assurance / Project Management

Results-driven manufacturing professional with more than 10 years of management experience seeks career advancement within dynamic, high-growth organization that welcomes **fresh ideas, initiative, dedication, and experience** and demands excellence in consistently **meeting business objectives.** Exceptional ability to work under high pressure, offering **expertise in troubleshooting, problem solving,** and **management of multishift production operation.** Possess **outstanding interpersonal skills** complemented by **solid management acumen** and proven **ability to make sound, time-critical decisions**.

AREAS OF EXPERTISE

- Strategic Planning
- Budgeting
- Assembly
- Training & Leadership

- Production Scheduling
- Inventory/Material Control
- Performance Improvement
- Crisis Management

- Project Management
- HR Affairs
- Team Building
- Presentations

MANAGEMENT PROFICIENCY

PROVEN METHODOLOGY
- Drive business growth through aggressive initiatives that result in increased revenue growth
- Balance production initiatives with leadership via conceptual thinking and strategic planning
- Identify, establish, and manage strategic relationships to leverage significant long-term business opportunities
- Ensure customer service and satisfaction is afforded highest attention and priority
- Successfully build and maintain key corporate relationships

DEMONSTRATED RESULTS
- Skillfully **reduced labor costs** by 30%
- Participated in **work-flow redesign to increase production efficiencies** and reduce cycle time
- Successfully and dynamically consolidated valve designs to **reduce supply base** with an annual **savings of more than $1.5M**
- Implemented **one-person final assembly line,** reducing the need for three operators online and **realizing an annual savings of $1.2M**
- Participated in **transition of production facility** from Town, New York, to This Facility, Ohio, skillfully **absorbing new business without affecting customer** or current plant operations

CAREER PATH

PRODUCTION FACILITY—This Facility, Ohio   **1991–Present**
Fast-track promotion through a series of increasingly responsible manufacturing leadership positions

PRODUCTION MANAGER   **1998–Present**
Challenge: Coordinate production priorities with team leaders while ensuring cost efficiencies
Responsibility: Foster continuous improvement through Toyota Production System Methodology
Selected Accomplishments:
- Substantially increased production outputs
- Drove a series of successful productivity, quality, and operating improvement programs
- Facilitate team meetings, Quality Operation System (QOS) meetings, and problem-solving teams
- Motivate production employees to achieve team goals

153

Tammy K. Shoup, Decatur, Indiana

This applicant had a great deal of experience in manufacturing and management but never completed the business degree that many organizations require. To overcome this obstacle, the writer highlighted the applicant's methodology and then showed the results achieved.

SHINGO T. KAIZEN

CAREER PATH CONTINUED

SCHEDULER   **1996–1998**
Challenge: Prioritize production schedules based on capacity requirements planning (CRP) and communicate with Sales, Manufacturing, and suppliers
Responsibility: Meet customer demand for shorter lead times
Selected Accomplishments:
- Introduced Lean Manufacturing Principles such as one-piece flow cells, Kanban, and Heijunka Scheduling to New Haven Plant
- Reduced work-in-process by 60%

PROCESS TECHNICIAN   **1994–1996**
Challenge: Analyze work flow and develop processes to standardize work
Responsibility: Streamline processes and procedures for increased efficiencies
Selected Accomplishments:
- Assisted with development and launching of new products

TEAM LEADER   **1991–1994**
Challenge: Communicate work directives to employees and provide leadership necessary to accomplish goals
Responsibility: Ensure productivity of work cell
Selected Accomplishments:
- Ensured quality of parts built

MY BUSINESS—Anytown, Ohio   **1988–1991**
Entrepreneurial venture with full-charge responsibility for all aspects of business and growth initiatives

GENERAL MANAGER
Challenge: Build profitable business from ground up
Responsibility: All aspects of operations management
Selected Accomplishments:
- Increased customer base by 500% over 4-year period

THE QUICKSTOP SHOP—Corner Lot, Ohio   **1985–1988**
Recruited to plan and implement strategies that would increase market share

GENERAL MANAGER
Challenge: Motivate employees, maintain low turnover rate, and increase store profitability
Responsibility: All store HR functions and operations management for four locations
Selected Accomplishments:
- Improved profitability for each location

TECHNOLOGY

- MS PowerPoint
- MS Word
- MS Excel

EDUCATION & PROFESSIONAL DEVELOPMENT

Ongoing professional development through seminars and classes in

- Excellence in Manufacturing I & II
- Strategic Financial Decision Making
- Facilitation & Coaching
- Shingo Prize Cell Redesign
- Workplace Organization
- Physical Inventory Control

BS in Business Management in Progress
Business School University

The individual received an offer the first time out with this resume. Boldfacing of important information in the profile, the Demonstrated Results section, and the Career Path section help sell the candidate.

T.B. O'BRYAN

664 Herkimer Road
Dover Plains, NY 12522

(845) 555-1212
tbo55@hotmail.com

MANUFACTURING / WAREHOUSE OPERATIONS
Multidisciplined professional with exceptional customer-contact skills and strong mechanical troubleshooting abilities.
Offering an advanced understanding of manufacturing processes and an expert ability to resolve issues in the field.

Highly competent and productive individual with a proven ability to integrate into the work environment and serve as a positive influence. Leadership style emphasizes teamwork, safety and professionalism. Background includes vast experience with assembly projects (installation, testing, maintenance, repairs, upgrades, customer training). Highly skilled at communicating across project groups and leading complex installation projects. Equally skilled at interpreting blueprints and schematics.

———————— *Areas of Special Strength* ————————

- Workload Delegation / Installation Planning / Field Support
- PLC Programming / Inventory Control / Customer Training
- Custom Fabrication (wood, metal) / Welding (Arc & Mig)

- Machine Assembly, Installation, Testing & Debugging
- Facilities Maintenance / Predictive Maintenance
- Interpreting Blueprints & Schematics

EMPLOYMENT

ASSEMBLY COMPONENT SYSTEMS, *Herkimer, NY*   **1989 to PRESENT**
(Leading supplier to the automation industry, specializing in large and complex projects that address specific applications and provide project engineering and custom design solutions to clients worldwide.)

Assembly Manager / Field Support *(2006 to Present)*   **Component Repair Support** *(1990 to 2005)*
Manager—Production Floor *(2005 to 2006)*   **Precision Assembler** *(1990 to 1993)*
Field Service Technician *(1990 to 2005)*   **Machinist** *(1989 to 1990)*

Accountable for the installation, upgrade and repair of complex systems and machines. Position required production planning and weekly inspection/reconciliation of components received from corporate headquarters. Maintained direct accountability for scheduling machining and assembly assignments for staff of ten. Serve as a liaison with inside sales, project managers, spare parts sales and design departments to ensure a consistent workflow. Manage the flow of information among the departments to ensure that projects were properly scheduled, staffed and completed.

Actively involved with assessing, repairing and maintaining equipment, tools and machinery within the facility. Monitor safety status and constantly inspect facility and equipment to identify deficiencies (operational inefficiencies or safety hazards).

Collaborate with internal teams to resolve customer issues, coordinate projects and provide a seamless installation. Provide technical field support to nationwide customers. Work closely with customers to diagnose problems and resolve issues by phone and in person.

CORTLAND CONSTRUCTION, *Alfred, NY*   **1989 to PRESENT**

Handyman / Residential Construction (part-time)

Handle all types of home construction and renovation projects. Involved with all aspects of ground-to-roof building practices, including plumbing, electric and HVAC. Coordinate plans, tasks and timelines to adhere to owner's expectations and prevailing building codes.

PROFESSIONAL DEVELOPMENT

Education / Certifications
Herkimer High School, *Herkimer, NY*
Herkimer BOCES Machine Shop Program
Forklift Operation and Safety Certification
Festo Pneumatics Certificate

Additional Skills
Custom Fabrication & Welding
Preventive & Predictive Maintenance
Auto Custom Restoration & Rebuilding
Equipment Repair & Rebuild

154

Kristin M. Coleman, Poughkeepsie, New York

This person was downsized and wanted a position like his last. The writer showed the diversity of his experience, his progression with the company, and his commitment to mechanical trades.

Purchasing

Resumes at a Glance

Mary J. Sanders

111 East End Avenue • Elmhurst, New York 55555 • (555) 888-0000 • shop2drop@retailworld.net

Assistant Buyer

Skilled in areas of

- Wholesale / Retail Buying
- Product Merchandising
- Information Systems Training
- Product Distribution and Tracking
- Sales Analysis & Reporting
- Regional Marketing Campaigns
- Inventory Replenishment
- Vendor Relations
- Order Management

Computer Skills: Windows 2000; MS Word/Excel; Management Information Systems

Professional Experience

Merchandise Buying / Coordination

- Report directly to LAC's Director of Sales, providing support in areas of commodities buying and merchandising activities that reach annual sales volumes of $3 million for the division.
- Collaborate with multiple buyers to facilitate the marketing efforts of new products and the development of promotional calendars, product launches, and employee incentive programs.
- Maintain open lines of communication between manufacturers, sales teams, vendors, and warehousing personnel to expedite product orders, distribution, and problem resolutions.
- Reported directly to the Senior Buyer of Steinway Bedding in charge of day-to-day retail merchandise buying and merchandising activities impacting bedding sales across 37 Northeast locations.
- Successfully trained more than 45 Steinway employees on a complex LAN database management system.

Sales Tracking, Analysis, & Reporting

- Perform LAC's weekly sales analysis activities on regional/local transactions, achieving a recovery of $1,800,000 from 1998 to 2004 resulting from identification and resolution of accounting discrepancies.
- Develop sales books reflecting product lines, monthly promotions, discontinued items, order forms, and transparencies used by sales teams and personnel throughout 26 store locations.
- Formulate price breakdowns and track sales levels to determine product volume adjustments, replenishments, and allocations with a demonstrated proficiency in internal networking systems.
- Researched, compiled, and recorded Steinway's historical data to develop innovative sales strategies through close examination of inventory and product availability, pricing, and store promotions.

Work History

Assistant Buyer / Sales Analyst   7/97–present
LONDON-AMERICAN COMMODITIES, LTD. (LAC), Valley Stream, New York

Assistant Buyer / Merchandise Coordinator   4/93–7/97
STEINWAY BEDDING, Woodbury, New York

Education

Associate's Degree in Science, Business Management, 1993
STATE UNIVERSITY *of* NEW YORK *at* COBLESKILL

155

Ann Baehr, East Islip, New York

Because the applicant had held two positions in 15 years, the writer split the Professional Experience section into two categories for impact and clarity. Note the easy-to-read keywords at the top.

ELIZABETH GREEN

5555 Oak Tree Lane • Northridge, CA 55555
(818) 555-5555 • egreen@email.com

PURCHASING • MERCHANDISING MANAGEMENT

Results-oriented Purchasing / Merchandising Management Professional with demonstrated success in streamlining operations and reducing costs of multimillion-dollar purchasing units. Proven ability to develop long-term partnerships with key suppliers. Highly responsive to organization objectives and customer needs.

—Core Competencies—

Project Management • Systems Development & Implementation • Product Development
Team Building & Leadership • Vendor Selection & Negotiations • Purchasing of Imported Goods
International Transportation • Letters of Credit • International Wire Transfers • Foreign Trade Documentation
U.S. Customs Regulations • Customer Relations • Communications • Hiring, Training & Supervision

PROFESSIONAL EXPERIENCE

WEST COAST ENTERTAINMENT COMPANY, Burbank, California • 1990 to Present
Achieved fast-track promotions from initial hire as Purchasing Assistant through positions of increasing responsibility, challenge and complexity.

Manager, Import Purchasing (1999 to Present)
Full accountability for day-to-day operations of $200 million unit, including managing staff of six. Report to Vice President/Global Controller. Oversee broad range of functions, including production sourcing, material planning, shipping and receiving, vendor contract negotiations and purchasing of resale and promotional inventory for seven divisions.

Specific Areas of Accountability
- Oversee issuance of all import purchase orders for merchandise supplied by foreign agents and factories.
- Consult with various business units on establishing and/or maintaining successful import programs. Provide expertise on complete import process, including supplier selection, product development, quality control, export documentation requirements, payment options, international transportation and U.S. Customs and other government agency clearances.
- Communicate corporate importation guidelines and requirements to all foreign suppliers, ensuring compliance with all applicable international and U.S. laws.
- Approve all international Letters of Credit to support $160 million annual import purchasing volume. Coordinate daily activity with outside banking partners, ensuring timely transmission of critical data.
- Partner with internal sourcing, merchandise and logistics departments to leverage combined purchasing and shipment volumes, gaining significant efficiencies and cost savings.
- Review and approve all open account (non–letter of credit or wire transfer) payment transactions.

Representative Accomplishments
- Developed and executed automated download of purchase order transactions to letter of credit system, improving on-time issuance from 20% to 75% in less than two years.
- Streamlined operations by consolidating merchandise supplier base from 1200 to 850 in twelve months.
- Implemented adoption of buying agent agreement representing approximately 50% of current international vendors and manufacturers.

Continued...

156

Vivian VanLier, Los Angeles, California

This individual had strong competencies and accomplishments as a purchasing manager, including expertise in import purchasing. She also had held several positions of increasing responsibility over a ten-year period. The writer, however, described only the past two positions

ELIZABETH GREEN
PAGE TWO

WEST COAST ENTERTAINMENT, *continued…*

Assistant Manager, Import Purchasing (1994 to 1999)
Introduced new programs for internal/external clients, including product launches and special promotions. Primary interface between customer and internal operations. Provided recommendations and organized conversion to a new integrated software program for import purchase order generation.

Representative Accomplishments
- Instituted new infrastructure to support distribution to foreign drop-ship destinations required for third-party promotional needs.
- Created new client checklists with a standardized format that provided consistent flow of information throughout the import transaction, reducing time and costs associated with error resolution and rework.
- Participated in contract and settlement negotiations with European suppliers to develop, purchase and install theme park equipment in excess of $100 million.

Prior Positions at West Coast: Promoted through four positions from Purchasing Assistant to Buyer.

EDUCATION

CALIFORNIA STATE UNIVERSITY, Northridge, CA
Major: Communications

PROFESSIONAL DEVELOPMENT

Letter of Credit Rules and Regulations—Los Angeles Bank, CA (Annually 1999 to Present)
Laws of Letters of Credit Workshops— Bank of America, Los Angeles, CA (1994, 1997)
United States Customs Broker Examination Course—Foreign Trade Association, El Segundo, CA (1996)
International Trade Regulations—Women in World Trade Association, Irvine, CA (1995)

PROFESSIONAL AFFILIATIONS

Foreign Trade Association
Women in World Trade

COMPUTER SKILLS

Windows, Microsoft Office (Word, Excel, Outlook, PowerPoint)

—Available for Travel and/or Relocation—

because the earlier positions were a progression of nonmanagement responsibilities. Nevertheless, a broad range of responsibilities and representative accomplishments are indicated in the resume. See Cover Letter 11.

Nora T. Collins

56 MacArthur Road • Somerset, NJ 08873 • 732.958.4791 • noracol7@prodigy.net

SENIOR BUYER

Procurement ~ Materials Management ~ Sourcing ~ Inventory

Performance-driven, dynamic professional with demonstrated abilities in procurement, out-sourcing, and negotiating for manufacturing or wholesale distribution environments.

An independent self-starter with a solid history of utilizing out-of-the-box approaches, adapting to new business environments, and negotiating win-win agreements.

Competencies

- Purchasing/Buying
- Stock Control/Leveling
- Customer Relations
- Organizational/Project Management

- Material Distribution/Supply Chain
- Inventory Control/Management
- Resource/Materials Management
- Contract Negotiations/Vendor Relations

Professional Experience

American Bouquet Company, Inc. *(1984–Present)*
Purchasing Manager

Performed all buying functions for the New Jersey, Florida, and South America manufacturing facilities. Promoted numerous times over a 20-year career with the company.

Continually acknowledged for dramatically improving the firm's profitability with each assignment.

Handle disposition of defective merchandise and determine inventory levels in the warehouse while analyzing new order trends and then conducting precise inventories.

With a solid knowledge of hard-goods pricing, designed and created several new products and product lines that were significant revenue earners for the company.

Coordinated vendor operations with factory and shipping schedules and developed "Just in Time" procedures.

Improved quality and consistency of incoming merchandise by taking a tough stance with vendors.

Final authority for approving all vendor invoices for payment.

- Reduced a $1 million inventory by 50% with improved delivery scheduling.
- Reduced costs and price levels by selecting innovative vendors and changing the inventory system to augment production.
- Pioneered a company import program to purchase hard goods, reducing manufacturing costs substantially.

157

Beverly and Mitch Baskin, Marlboro, New Jersey

A pair of horizontal lines draws attention to the applicant's competencies. Bullets at the bottom of the page point to achievements. Extra-large type makes the applicant's name and position stand out.

Real Estate

Resumes at a Glance

DENISE WEYLAND

6666 Ralston Commons
Sunnyvale, CA 94080

dweyland2000@aol.com

408-555-0000 (home)
408-555-0001 (cell)

COMMUNITY SALES MANAGER

Versatile, goal-oriented new-home sales manager with a track record of producing successful results in challenging market conditions. Proven ability to establish rapport and trust with diverse individuals, including home buyers, lenders, construction staff and warranty staff. Strong negotiating and closing skills.

REAL ESTATE SALES EXPERIENCE

Elegance Homes   2000–Present
Community Sales Manager, Atlantia Creek,   Foster City, CA (2001–Present)

◆ Despite a difficult economy, lack of model homes and a less-than-desirable location, sold and closed 26 of 27 homes in the $600,000–$700,000 range between May 2001 and May 2002. Generated approximately $18 million in gross revenue.

◆ Interacted with both an in-house lender and outside lenders to overcome numerous obstacles and complete the closings.

◆ Joined the community as the fourth sales manager in approximately two months.

Sales Associate, Sunrise Shores,   Santa Clara, CA (2000–2001)

◆ Performed selling and closing for a top-producing Community Sales Manager during a period when the home-buying situation changed from long waiting lists to a challenging sales market.

◆ Played a key role in assisting the manager to close approximately 50 of 84 homes in the $600,000–$800,000 range.

◆ Recommended by the manager for promotion to Sales Manager at Atlantia Creek.

Home Resale Experience:

Richardson Mortgage, Palo Alto, CA   1998–2000
Sales Representative

Porter-Martinson, Woodside, CA   1997–1998
Sales Representative

Previous Experience:

Employed in the South Bay and Sacramento-area real estate industry in a non-sales capacity, including office management and agent assistance, 1985–1997.

LICENSE

California Real Estate License obtained in 1997

PROFESSIONAL AFFILIATIONS

Member: Home Builders Association of Northern California
Former member: National Association of Realtors®, California Association of Realtors
and Woodside Association of Realtors

158

Georgia Adamson, Campbell, California

This person wanted a new job in a highly competitive field—new-home sales. The writer saw that the person could produce exceptional results in a difficult business climate. This becomes the lead idea.

JOSEPH K. THORNSTEIN

400 Rindge Avenue
Worcester, MA 55555

thornstein42@earthlink.net

Office: (555) 555-5555
Mobile: (555) 555-5555

REAL ESTATE DEVELOPMENT CONSULTANT

Strong record of completing more than 35 development projects, from the development review, licensing, and permitting process through to final approvals. Recruited to manage the most high-profile, controversial, and environmentally sensitive projects.

- Exceptional ability to build agreement with town boards and community groups and to guide projects through complex regulatory and litigation processes on time and on budget.
- Broad and deep expertise in the industry. Able to quickly develop a feel for the community and assess whether a project is likely to be a "go," saving time and money and improving the company's bottom line.
- Excellent reputation within the New England real estate development industry. Extensive network of positive relationships with town officers, planning boards, and state and federal agencies.
- Politically and interpersonally savvy with expert conflict-management, communication, and presentation skills. Adept at breaking down barriers and turning opposing stakeholders into allies.

Development Projects

- Skilled Nursing & Alzheimer's Facilities
- Medical Office Buildings
- Corporate Office Centers
- Industrial Facilities

- Single-Family Homes
- Condominiums & Apartment Complexes
- Assisted Living Facilities
- Multiuse Facilities

Real Estate Development Skill Set

- Development review, permitting, & licensing
- Liaison with federal, state, & local agencies
- Negotiate option / purchase agreements
- Perform due diligence
- Develop & administer budgets

- Hire & manage development consultants
- Make presentations to town planning boards & community groups
- Conduct real-estate & construction-loan closings
- Siting & land acquisition

PROFESSIONAL EXPERIENCE

WORCESTER PROPERTIES, Worcester, MA
Real Estate Development Consultant

2001–Present

Representative Project

- **Southbridge Corporate Center,** Southbridge, MA
  A $110 million project to develop an 82-acre stone quarry into a high-end corporate office building.

  Full development review, licensing, and permitting accountability from day one to final approvals.

  Challenge: Lay the groundwork for developing a controversial project in a strongly anti-development town. Solve zoning and jurisdictional problems concerning wastewater treatment. Work against a December 2001 deadline to avoid the company's having to negotiate a costly new land option.

  Actions: Successfully drove the project through a land court, an appeals court, and the State Supreme Court. Hired corporate consultants who could communicate well with town planning boards and community groups. Represented the project at 120 public hearings and neighborhood-group meetings. Negotiated with selectmen. Built relationships with local board members. Cleared a major roadblock—resulting from a decision by a neighboring town not to accept other towns' waste—by developing a plan for a $1.2 million on-site treatment plant. Completed entire MEPA, DEP, MHD, and ACOE processes.

  Results: Won all final permits and approvals for the development of "the most-litigated land parcel in the Commonwealth of Massachusetts going back 45 years."

159

Jean Cummings, Concord, Massachusetts

The individual did not have a bachelor's degree but did have exceptional gifts that made him effective in his field. The writer sought to make clear what those special skills were and to give examples of how he achieved results in the face of community opposition and other

JOSEPH K. THORNSTEIN

BERTRAND COMPANIES, Worcester, MA 1992–2001
Second-largest nursing home developer in the U.S.
Development Officer for Massachusetts

Accountable for project development from inception to final approvals. Projects included nursing home facilities, medical office buildings, high-end single-family homes, and corporate office centers. Performed due diligence; hired and managed development team of architects, engineers, and other specialists; and made presentations.

Representative Project

- **Southbridge Nursing Home,** Southbridge, MA

  Challenge: Site is a $15 million facility in a suburban town. Overcome strong neighborhood and community opposition by developing negotiated solutions. Determine optimal use for the 40% of the existing structure not required by the architectural plans.

  Actions: Hired the development team. Researched possible sites. Met with town officials and planning boards. Established a "good neighbor" relationship by allowing $1-a-time use of the auditorium. Made a strategic decision to install a CORF (comprehensive outpatient rehabilitation facility) and medical offices in the 32,000 sq. ft. of space not required by the nursing home. Neutralized strong opposition from the planning board and neighbors by negotiating creative solutions such as lowering the height of light poles, moving the parking lot, and building buffers.

  Results: Achieved buy-in from all necessary groups and gained project approval within a tight nine-month time frame and within the development process budget.

SANDERSON ASSOCIATES, INC., Manchester, NH 1986–1992
Vice President

Charged with developing the NH and MA markets for the company's real estate acquisition / development business. Staffed a 10-person acquisition department. Managed the development review process.

- Instrumental in growing sales from $2 million to $115 million in four years.
- Established new divisions in NJ, CT, ME, FL, and DC/VA.

Representative Project

- **Residential / Multifamily Condominium Housing,** Salem, NH

  Challenge: Overcome strong community opposition to the proposed 204-unit housing development. Address concerns about the tax increases and quality-of-life impacts resulting from a large influx of new residents using the roads and requiring costly town services (schools, police, fire).

  Actions: Actively listened to citizen concerns and then performed in-depth research on actual impacts. Hired a finance specialist to determine costs and benefits. Made a convincing case in a public presentation that the project would result in a financial net gain.

  Results: Successfully achieved all approvals within nine months.

EDUCATION

MOUNT MONADNOCK COMMUNITY COLLEGE, Princeton, MA
A.A. Degree in Mathematics

roadblocks to successful development. His special skills are indicated in the extended profile. His successes in spite of opposition are shown in the Challenge…Actions…Results portions.

ANN T. SHERMAN

555 North Main Boulevard • Sweetwater, IL 00000 • (847) 397-0012 • home555@sbcglobal.net

OBJECTIVE ... REAL ESTATE BROKER / AGENT

QUALIFICATIONS

Experienced, knowledgeable, and results-generating producer with extensive experience in the real estate industry. Demonstrated proficiency in evaluating and prequalifying buyers, analyzing property values, and understanding market trends.

➢ Diplomatic and articulate communicator able to develop positive rapport and maintain allegiance within diverse customer populations.

➢ Reputation of maintaining honesty and integrity during all business transactions, adhering to all industry-specific laws, guidelines, and rules.

STRENGTHS

- Business Development
- Industry Knowledge
- Product Knowledge

- Meticulous Organization
- Relationship Building
- Follow Through

- Prospecting
- Networking
- Persistence

LANGUAGES

Fluent in English and Spanish

EDUCATION

REAL ESTATE AGENT   2005
- Academy of Real Estate
  Accredited by the Board of Realtors, Sweetwater, IL

MEET ALL REQUIREMENTS FOR ILLINOIS LOAN ORIGINATOR CERTIFICATION   2006
- Association of Mortgage Brokers, Lincoln, IL

REAL ESTATE AGENT LICENSE, State of Ohio (expired)   1996
REAL ESTATE ASSISTANT APPRAISER LICENSE, State of Ohio (expired)   1998

POLYTECHNICAL INSTITUTE, Madrid, Spain   1979–1981
- Civil Engineering Curriculum

EXPERIENCE

REAL ESTATE AGENT   2005–present
Ethical Realtors, Inc., Sweetwater, IL
- Research, inspect, and identify investment real estate properties for private investors.
- Evaluate condition and value of property; analyze profit potential vs. risk exposure.
- Execute purchase agreements, secure financing, and prepare documents.
- Negotiate contracts with subcontractors; monitor quality and timeliness of renovations.
- Monitor market conditions and list properties to capitalize on profitable market conditions.

ASSISTANT REAL ESTATE APPRAISER   1998–2000
Capital Appraiser Services Associates, Lincoln, IL
John M. Smith & Associates, Lincoln, IL
- Conducted physical inspections and evaluated value of real estate property.
- Recorded measurements, created drawings, and took photographs of properties.
- Evaluated property values of surrounding areas.
- Documented findings and analysis and prepared reports for financial institutions.

REAL ESTATE AGENT   1996–2000
Matthews Real Estate, Ltd., Cincinnati, OH
Cincinnati Real Estate, Cincinnati, OH
- Built a client base of real estate buyers and sellers through dedicated hard work, industry knowledge, and outstanding customer service delivery.
- Evaluated property values, prepared extensive paperwork, and closed transactions.
- Analyzed financial qualifications of buyers to maximize prequalifying position.
- Interacted with mortgage lenders and attorneys to ensure timely execution of paperwork and facilitate problem resolution.

160

Rosemary Fish Justen, Schaumburg, Illinois

The applicant wanted to stay in real estate but focus on investment opportunities. Emphasis is on the applicant's knowledge of the markets and expertise in evaluating property values.

Recruiting

Resumes at a Glance

Steven Brooks

1111 Lawrenceville Road ◆ Haven, CT 00000 ◆ 000–000–0000 ◆ user@adelphia.net

SUMMARY
An energetic, motivated and highly effective Recruiting Manager and Consultant with more than 20 years of experience in building teams of Sales, IT and Staffing professionals. Achieve astonishing success in developing and maintaining cohesive sales units, designed to fulfill organizational staffing needs. Employ extensive experience in areas of departmental operations, budget administration, lead generation and contract negotiation to directly affect financial growth and bottom-line profitability. Possess excellent command of written and verbal communication, as well as public speaking, sales presentation, staff development and resource allocation skills.

CAREER ACCOMPLISHMENTS
- Redesigned and transformed Sales and Recruiting processes for 3 geographic locations, resulting in up to 60% increase in full-time hires.
- Created diversified, motivated and innovative sourcing team responsible for filling 100 open positions nationwide.
- Integrated standardized applicant tracking, Internet posting procedures, timeline reporting and costing processes, increasing staff proficiency through detailed metrics.
- Directly contributed to hiring of more than 500 professionals on behalf of SAP America in 1998, positioning company to grow revenues from $1 billion to $2 billion in 1-year timeframe.
- Negotiated and closed contracts with Fortune 100 organizations, growing revenues for assigned branch by $3 million.

QUALIFICATION HIGHLIGHTS
- Multitasking professional with background in business development, recruiting management, personnel training and resource allocation.
- Interact and effectively communicate with executive and management personnel with decision-making authority to successfully generate client base and increase profit margins.
- Build and foster progressive, continuous business relationships, directly affecting overall bottom-line profitability.
- Utilize extensive, diversified lead-generation processes such as networking, cold-call prospecting and sales presentations to grow recruiting success and increase client base.
- Successfully interact with top-line professionals to negotiate and close employment contracts and establish qualified, motivated, cooperative and successful Sales, IT and Recruiting teams.
- Spearhead, create and implement departmental processes to increase efficiency and decrease expenditures.
- Plan and prepare for industry-specific job fair attendance.

PROFESSIONAL EXPERIENCE
IT Recruiters   2000–2004
Recruiting Consultant
- Successfully redesigned all Sales and Recruiting structures and processes for 3 national regions of $200 million IT consulting firm.
- Spearheaded and monitored restructuring of Internet and "brick and mortar" Recruiting Centers in Philadelphia, Chicago and Washington, DC.
- Created and conducted effective recruiting and sales presentations and designed employment packages to attract and retain top-quality professionals.
- Developed and integrated processes to streamline applicant tracking, Internet posting, timeline and metrics report generation to ensure recruiting and sales team met and exceeded personal, departmental and organizational goals.
- Implemented innovative interviewing and hiring processes to maintain compliance with new Affirmative Action Plan.
- Researched and contracted personnel development training, resulting in all recruiting staff being AIRS-certified, as well as improving interpersonal skills and increasing contract closures and continuous compliance with organizational/governmental regulations.

Continued…

161

Lea J. "Laila" Clark-Salaam, Atlanta, Georgia

This resume has a couple of design elements that avoid an impression of sameness: section headings that are bold, underlined, all caps, and without a blank line below them; and a staggered indentation pattern for three sets of bulleted statements under the section headings.

Steven Brooks   **Page Two**

Technology Resources, Inc.   1999–2000
Operations Manager
- Instrumental in the establishment and growth of IT consulting firm.
- Prospected and grew accounts, leading to strong, foundational client base.
- Developed, conducted, researched and contracted personnel development training, ensuring that all team members remained knowledgeable in cutting-edge industry advancements.

Staffing America, Inc.   1996–1999
Recruiting Consultant
- Maintained responsibility for the recruitment and staffing of all departments in division, including product development, instructional design and data center.
- Improved and integrated company-wide recruiting processes, resulting in the hiring of more than 500 professionals in 1998 alone.
- Managed and administered $2 million advertising budget in support of marketing plan designed to enable timely fulfillment of open requisitions.

US Technologies   1995–1996
Manager of Recruiting
- Spearheaded and implemented nationwide recruiting strategy for start-up IT project organization.
- Researched, evaluated and integrated online applicant tracking system.
- Recruited, interviewed and hired applicants with n-Tier, OO application infrastructure and architecture qualifications.
- Administered recruiting budget of $500,000.
- Interacted with market researchers and print media to develop and implement strategic recruiting campaigns.

ACME Limited, Inc.   1992–1995
Recruiting Manager
- Managed and monitored activities related to recruiting and staffing, as well as new account development.
- Created and integrated new and innovative recruiting processes, leading to contract acceptance with globally recognized firms.
- Identified, evaluated and negotiated contracts with professional development and training companies to increase productivity, efficiency and knowledge of administrative management and technical contract employees.
- Developed and trained recruiters at 12 nationwide geographic locations.

Tech Search, Ltd.   1982–1992
Founder/Operations Manager
- Built and grew successful organization from ground floor, negotiating and retaining accounts with high-end organizations such as Franklin Mint, Lotus Corp., and PECO Energy.

COMPUTER SKILLS
Microsoft Office

In the Professional Experience section, bold italic makes it easy to spot the various positions held for the different companies. Bullets point to a mix of duties and achievements. See Cover Letter 12.

TED CARMICHAEL

1652 Toad Hill Road ▪ Newfoundland, PA 00000

(555) 555-5555 ▪ tedcarmichael10@mydomain.com

OBJECTIVE

BANKING/FINANCE position requiring hard work, sound business ethics, professionalism and innovation.

PROFESSIONAL SKILLS/KNOWLEDGE

- Leadership
- Documentation
- Quality
- Methods and Procedures

- Project Management
- Supervisory Skills
- Interpersonal Skills
- Customer Service

TECHNICAL SKILLS

Strong working knowledge of Microsoft Word and Microsoft Excel

PROFESSIONAL EXPERIENCE

THE INVESTMENT GROUP, Stroudsburg, PA
Recruiter/Trainer, 2004–Present

Initiate recruiting efforts for new telemarketers and stockbroker trainees. Arrange training sessions for entry-level staff specific to successful telemarketing, customer service and general telephone techniques.

ILC MANAGEMENT GROUP, East Stroudsburg, PA
Account Executive, 2001–2004

Complete management, development and service of diversified, nationwide client base. Designed customized short- and long-term financial plans based on clients' objectives by customizing questions and providing appropriate programs and services designed to meet financial goals.

- Increased understanding of asset allocation, risk management and risk tolerance of the client as they apply to the client's long-term goals and needs
- Built relationships with high-net-worth individual accounts
- Developed structured prospecting techniques, including cold calling, mailings, computer tracking, follow up, rapport building, persistence and closings
- Established niche marketing techniques
- Established standards for customer service, including sales, advisement and problem resolving

WJP PART NERS, Warren, NJ
Investment Advisor, 1998–2001

Made contact with prospective customers, presenting corporate capabilities and offerings. Opened new accounts, advised clients on available financial options, educated clients on market trends and customized financial solutions designed to achieve short- and long-term

162

Patricia Duckers, Edison, New Jersey

Partial horizontal lines on each side of centered section headings are a distinctive design element in this resume. In the Professional Experience section, bold capital letters make the company names stand out. Italic for the job positions makes it easy to spot them if you look for italic only.

TED CARMICHAEL
Page 2

customer goals. Assisted with completion of complex paperwork. Trained new customer service representatives and brokers on ways to attract new customers. Expanded dealings to global market. Advised customers on buying/selling and performed detailed market analysis.

- Obtained required Series 7 and 63 licenses on first attempts
- Opened ten new accounts within two-week period
- Managed portfolios of high-net-worth individuals and corporate accounts

EZ CREDIT, Allentown, PA
Data Entry Operator, 1995–1998

Entered and modified orders for high-volume call center; resolved customer disputes and trained new employees.

- Handled more than 200 calls per shift, recognized as the highest of Quarter 1, '98
- Created online templates to expedite call resolution and increase personal productivity 50%

EDUCATION

Diploma, William Penn High School, Radnor, PA—1995

Dates are just after the job position so that you can associate the two items quickly. The paragraph below each job position indicates responsibilities, and bullets point to accomplishments. Education is last.

Sales and Marketing

Resumes at a Glance

Tammy Wilson

| P.O. Box 8215 | Richmond, Texas | H: 832-449-5182 |

OBJECTIVE

SALES SUPERVISOR
To lead, coach, and teach a team of sales associates in the winning techniques of achieving sales that result in the increased commission and revenue for the associate, corporation, and client.

SUMMARY OF MARKETING SKILLS

Sales	Customer Service	Product Promotions
Personnel Training	Vendor Contract	Inventory Control
Cash Accountability	Displays	Order Processing
Computer Processing	Data Entry	Problem Solving

SALES and CUSTOMER SERVICE EXPERIENCE

Long Distance Service
- Achieve 85% of sales goals on a regular basis.
- Demonstrate winning sales techniques to client's corporate personnel.
- Negotiate and close sales for long distance services and miscellaneous packages for a leading telecommunications firm.
- Proven success in overcoming resistance to achieve sales.

Cellular Sales
- Generated sales of $.5 million annually in communication products and services.
- Managed an in-house inventory of a minimum of $75,000.
- Utilized manufacturer's literature in sales presentations.
- Trained sales staff on current and changing technology.
- Dealt with vendors while selecting products.
- Achieved high closing ratio by gauging customer response and adjusting presentations to resolve customer concerns.
- Initiated customer financing and maintained database for follow-up.
- Managed customer satisfaction by addressing customer complaints and solving problems.

Furniture Sales
- Generated annual sales of $216,000.
- Monitored sales in market trends of interior design to maximize sales and customer satisfaction.
- Achieved a 50% ratio of repeat and referred customer database.

Customer Service
- Maintained customer satisfaction and sales in a fast-paced, multitasked environment.
- Achieved daily sales of $2,000.

EMPLOYMENT HISTORY

Sales Associate, Precision Telecom, October 2001–present
Sales Representative, Fort Bend Communications, June 1999–December 2000
Sales Consultant, Zarowsky Furniture, January 1998–June 1999
Customer Service Representative, various organizations, May 1994–January 1998

EDUCATION and TRAINING

General Office Operations: fax, ten-key calculator, copy machines, Microsoft Office suite
Houston Baptist University, Houston, Texas, 1998–2001

163

MeLisa Rogers, Shiner, Texas

This person did not have supervisory experience in sales but wanted to be promoted to a supervisory position to double her salary. The writer focused on achievements. The person got the promotion.

Gloria James
5555 Princeton Lane
Hometown, IL 00000
555-555-5555 home
555-222-2222 cellular
gj5555@aol.com

Summary of Accomplishments

Consistent top sales producer for new-home developments in the Chicago area.
Responsible for more than $150 million in closings since 1993.

Professional Experience

Jansen Homes, Hometown, IL
1999 to Present
On-Site Sales Manager. Recruited by the founder of Jansen Homes to manage the sales of various home-development projects, with price points ranging from moderate to upscale. Prepare marketing plans, set up model homes, hire staff and manage sales results.

- Played a key role in the company's growth from 80 to 400 average closings per year.
- Earned "Diamond" or "Gold" level sales awards each year.

Supreme Homes, Westerville, IL
1993 to 1999
On-Site Sales Manager. Originally hired as a Model Homes Hostess. Promoted to Sales Associate and then Sales Manager within the first two years with the organization. Prepared marketing plans, set up model homes, hired staff and managed sales results.

- Earned "Manager of the Month" designation nine times in five years.
- Earned "National Salesperson of the Year" award from the National Association of Home Builders, 1997.
- Earned "Diamond" level sales award for 1998; "Gold" for 1997, 1996 and 1995; and "President" for 1994 and 1993.

Gained early career experience as a Retail Staff Assistant for Global Oil, helping to manage company-owned stations, and as an Associate for Mega Real Estate Relocation Corporation.

Education

Continuing education through industry conferences and seminars.
Real Estate License, Illinois, 1994

State College, Stateville, IL
Completed two years of general and business courses.

164

Christine L. Dennison, Lincolnshire, Illinois

This applicant kept current with her knowledge of the industry by attending seminars and conferences. The writer emphasized the applicant's energy, initiative, and sales accomplishments.

AMBER PATRICK

amberpatrick@email.com

5555 Central Avenue, #1
North Hollywood, California 55555

Residence (818) 555-5555
Mobile (818) 555-5554

SALES PROFESSIONAL

Expertise in Client Development / Sales Management / Sales Training

- Motivated sales professional with seven years of experience; includes three years of outside sales as well as experience in sales management and training. Experienced in working with organizations of all sizes, including national and high-revenue accounts.

- Natural communicator and team leader with strong motivational and interpersonal relations skills. Easily establish and maintain strong working relationships with clients and coworkers at all levels. Outstanding networking abilities.

—Strengths—

Account Development & Retention • Client Relations • Sales Training • Coaching
Time & Task Management • Negotiations • Strategic Alliances & Business Partnerships
Cold Calling, Prospecting & Closing • Event Planning & Coordination

PROFESSIONAL EXPERIENCE

SOCAL CREDIT ASSOCIATION, Burbank, CA • 2000 to Present
Senior Sales Representative
Cold call, prospect and forge relationships with business owners to generate new clients for leading credit card processing company. Conduct presentations, analyze profitability of credit card volume and respond to questions. Actively network at chambers of commerce and community organizations to increase company visibility and develop new business.

- Generated highest revenues in state, first quarter 2003.
- Achieved #1 in district production two consecutive years: 2000, 2001.
- Named "rookie of the year," 2000.
- Selected to represent company at job fairs to recruit new hires.

GOLDEN STATE DEPARTMENT STORE, Glendale, CA • 1997 to 2000
Department Manager, Junior Sportswear
Advanced from Sales Associate within six months to manage apparel department catering to trend-oriented, high-end clientele. Trained new hires, scheduled and supervised staff of six, oversaw merchandising and displays, assisted customers with selections and processed purchases.

- Surpassed 1999 sales targets by 12%—the highest in region.
- Recommended merchandising enhancements that maximized product visibility.
- Monitored client preferences and communicated with buyers.

EDUCATION

CENTRAL HIGH SCHOOL, Burbank, CA
Graduated in 1997

PROFESSIONAL AFFILIATIONS / COMMUNITY ACTIVITIES

Burbank Chamber of Commerce, Member—Ambassador Committee, Education Committee
Red Cross Blood Bank, Volunteer

165

Vivian VanLier, Los Angeles, California

This individual did not have a college degree and hadn't completed college-level course work, but she proved herself in the workforce. The writer built on the person's track record of accomplishments.

BETSY LEADERQUEST

IN-STORE SUPPORT LEAD

555 Pebble Ave., South Creek, Texas 55555
(555) 555-5555 ✷ **bquest5550@aol.com**

Industry Knowledge

Customer Satisfaction

Team Development

Associate Coaching

Customer Retention

Strategic Planning

Merchandising

Prioritization

Attentive Listening

Deadline Consciousness

Troubleshooting

Decisiveness

Innovative Ideas

Diplomacy

Flexibility

Exemplary Work Ethic

Transactional Efficiency

Point-of-Sale Discipline

Policy and Procedure

Adherence to Standards

QUALIFICATIONS

Visionary leader with six years of progressive experience in retail sales ✷ Creative supervisor with marketing, planning, implementation, troubleshooting, and follow-up skills needed to ensure a smooth-running operation ✷ Outstanding RELATER with attentive listening skills ✷ Focus on quality and accuracy ✷ Accommodating achiever eager to assume increased responsibility ✷ Energetic, optimistic spirit ✷ Strong orientation toward empowering others to achieve at higher levels ✷ Life-learner who enjoys growth opportunities

ACHIEVEMENTS

- **Action Team Leader, 2005–2006**
- **Certified Manager On Duty, 2004–2006**
- **Falcon Team Leader, 2005 Holidays**
- **Above and Beyond Award, 2005**
- **Top ten in region on gift box sales, 2005**
- **Top credit performer as seasonal, part-time, and full-time employee**

PROFESSIONAL EXPERIENCE

SEARS, South Creek, Texas   *2000–Present*

Lead, Center Aisle Cash / Wrap, 2003–Present

Oversee the day-to-day center aisle cash / wrap activities, directing 20 associates, managing efficient work / customer flow, and providing premium customer service. Hire, train, coach, and schedule associate team, ensuring transactional efficiency and point-of-sale discipline. Provide professional development and performance management. Successfully increase bottom lines of credit protection and account care programs, ensuring departmental performance standards are met or exceeded. Resolve customer-related issues when associate needs assistance. Lead meetings and implement Q12 surveys.

- Created multiple time-saving forms to increase reporting efficiency
- Promote interaction with licensed in-house businesses
- Created candy incentive for credit sales that spread store wide
- Plan quarterly meeting events and coordinate logistics and activities

Part-Time Cashier, 2001–2003
Seasonal Cashier, 2000 & 2001

Owner/Operator, RBD Quality Health Care, Cedar Place, Texas   *1992–1999*

Purchased existing agency with 40 employees. Increased locations to seven across Texas, employing LVNs, RNs, Aides, Office Personnel, Director of Nurses, and CFO. Traveled among locations. Added services as company grew.

- Built organization into large, reputable agency generating $5M–$6M annually
- Empowered others to greater heights with encouragement and support

EDUCATION

- *Coursework in Business,* Superior Learning University, Riverbed, Texas

166

Edith Rische, Lubbock, Texas

The distinctive feature of this resume is the shaded left column that displays the individual's industry knowledge. Qualifications and Achievements fill the important zone near the top.

Marty Clayton

Sales Director
Fractional Aircraft Sales

"I have been amazed at, surprised by, and appreciative of the number of hours you work and your accessibility....We reviewed many options for partial jet ownership, but you helped us decide that Flying Options was the absolute right choice." Tom M., Senior V.P., Morgan Stanley, Retired	"Marty has been a joy to work with at the company and has done a great job in terms of accommodating my needs with the utmost professionalism and integrity.... I look forward to working with him again." Jerry P., Capital Management, Founder

Strengths

- Leading and building high-performance teams, driving market share and revenue growth.
- Applying innovative marketing strategies to increase client acquisition, retention, and penetration.
- Building a solid client pipeline through referrals and focused efforts to create awareness and preference.
- Identifying customer issues to achieve customer satisfaction levels that enable further sales.
- Ability to adapt to changing business requirements, market conditions, and emerging technologies.

Expertise

- Strategic Planning - Needs Assessment - High-Impact Presentations - Persuasive Communications - Closing Skills	- Strategic Alliances - Customer Acquisition/Retention - Marketing Strategies - Building Relationships - Strategic Planning/Implementation	- Leadership - Business Development - Budget Management - Time Management - Territory Management

Professional Experience

Flying Options, Denver, CO   **August 1999–Present**

Sales Director, Rocky Mountain Sales Territory   April 2000–Present

Navigator (Sales Lead Coordinator and Inside Sales Rep)   August 1999–April 2000

- ✓ Managed the toughest U.S. territory (Rocky Mountain) and achieved the second-highest closing rate (61% compared to company average of 23%) of 11 sales directors.
- ✓ Achieved the highest demo-to-sales conversion rate (64% compared to average of 37%) in the company.
- ✓ Turned the Rocky Mountain Territory (RMT) into a significant contributor to the bottom line.
  RMT received only 2.6% of the qualified leads and contributed
    - 4.5% of the Total Earned Revenue
    - 6.5% of the Total Hours Sold
- ✓ Doubled the Rocky Mountain region's sales revenue within 12 months of taking over the territory.
- ✓ Promoted to Sales Director within 6 months of joining the company as Navigator and Inside Sales Rep.
- ✓ Assistant to Vice President of Sales and Marketing while working at corporate headquarters.

Marty Clayton Excavating, Inc., Tampa, FL   **1984–1999**

Founder and Chief Operating Officer

Owned and operated business for 15 years. Built business from the ground up. Recruited, managed, and developed staff. Managed the daily operations, planned and implemented marketing and sales activities, and supervised all accounting tasks and tax filings. Sold business in 1999.

- ✓ Achieved profit within 12 months. Doubled annual gross revenue in both the first and second years.

Education

Attended University of Miami, Miami, FL 1980–1983

123 Ristal Place • Castle Rock, CO 00000 • 555.555.5555 • marclay@hotmail.net

167

Roberta F. Gamza, Louisville, Colorado

This person had the company's worst sales territory. Instead of comparing him with peers, the writer compared his closing and conversion ratios, which show him maximizing his territory results.

Jamie Anderson, Jr.

1672 North Riding Drive • Spring Oak, AL 99999
(555) 555–5555 • janderson@att.net

Profile

Management professional with 14 years of experience in the Class-8 Vehicle Parts industry, including general management, human resources, and general sales. Background includes the establishment of programs to increase sales, improve productivity, reduce costs, and enhance customer relations. Decisive and direct, yet flexible in responding to the constantly changing demands of staff members, customers, and operations throughout the company. Key strengths include the following:

- Customer-Driven Management
- Marketing & Sales
- Leadership & Team Building
- Human Resources
- Recruitment & Training

- Efficiency Improvement
- Strategic Planning
- Organizational Development
- Policies & Procedures
- Labor Relations

Use excellent communication skills to maintain positive relations with customers; provide outstanding customer service and follow-through. Bring dedication and commitment to the highest level of service within the industry.

"Jamie looks for economical alternatives when purchasing for stock…he does a good job looking out for improving our branch. He has proven he can be trusted and charged with important duties and responds positively to working with other managers and employees. He is a good addition to management."

—Ken Brooks, Baker Transport Equipment

Professional Experience

GREENWOOD SALES & SERVICE, Spring Oak, AL   1999–Present
Parts Counter Sales

- Instrumental in establishing solid customer base, including dealer-level customers, for new company through expansive network of contacts. Set up more than 150 new customers, building customer base to more than 300 within region.

- Consistently surpass set sales goals by servicing up to 50 customers daily through e-mail, telephone, and outside parts sales communications.

- Handle stock, customer special orders, and repair shop orders with 500 various vendors nationwide, providing technical information regarding equipment, order parts, returns, and special orders.

- Design monthly sales flyers, brochures, and line cards featuring all heavy equipment products sold.

- Established shipping and receiving procedures, which streamlined operations and increased efficiency.

Continued…

168

Denette Jones, Mountain View, Hawaii

Horizontal lines enclose the Profile, which ensures that it will be seen. The Profile not only contains a quick sketch of the applicant but also includes a two-column list of bulleted key strengths.

Jamie Anderson, Jr. Page 2

Professional Experience Continued

BAKER TRANSPORT EQUIPMENT, Spring Oak, AL   1989–1999
Outside Parts Sales *(1998–1999)*
Office Manager *(1996–1998)*
Assistant Parts Manager / Purchasing Agent *(1989–1996)*

- Defined and streamlined human resources systems; coordinated all HR functions, including recruiting, employee evaluation, and yearly sexual harassment awareness courses.

- Instrumental in branch gross sales increasing from $2.5 million to $4.8 million annually.

- Supervised and trained office personnel; total branch accountability during Branch Manager's absence.

- Integrated branch planning in compliance with corporate mission statement; assisted in defining branch mission and vision.

- Served as secretary for company. Directly involved during collective bargaining contract negotiations and employee contractual agreements.

- Negotiated with vendors to arrange optimal pricing and service for all departments.

- Researched and determined best shipping methods to distribute parts to customers and vendors, utilizing UPS, USPS, Federal Express, Air Freight, and Common Carrier.

Professional Development

Participated in several courses and workshops to ensure skills were up-to-date and professional education was ongoing. Courses included

- The Art of Hiring Smart
- Sales Territory Management
- Refining Interview Techniques
- Understanding Unemployment
- Basic Air Brake Systems
- Notary Public Training

- Taking Physical Inventories & Cycle Counts
- ADP Payroll Systems
- Employment Law Update
- Forklift Training & Safety
- Confined-Space Safety
- Basic First Aid & CPR

Technical Skills

Microsoft Office · Word · Excel · Publisher · PowerPoint · Photoshop · MS–DOS

The testimonial below the Profile helps dispel any reservations a reader may have about the applicant's worth. In the Professional Experience section, bullets point to accomplishments for each employer. Grouping positions under the second employer prevents unnecessary repetition.

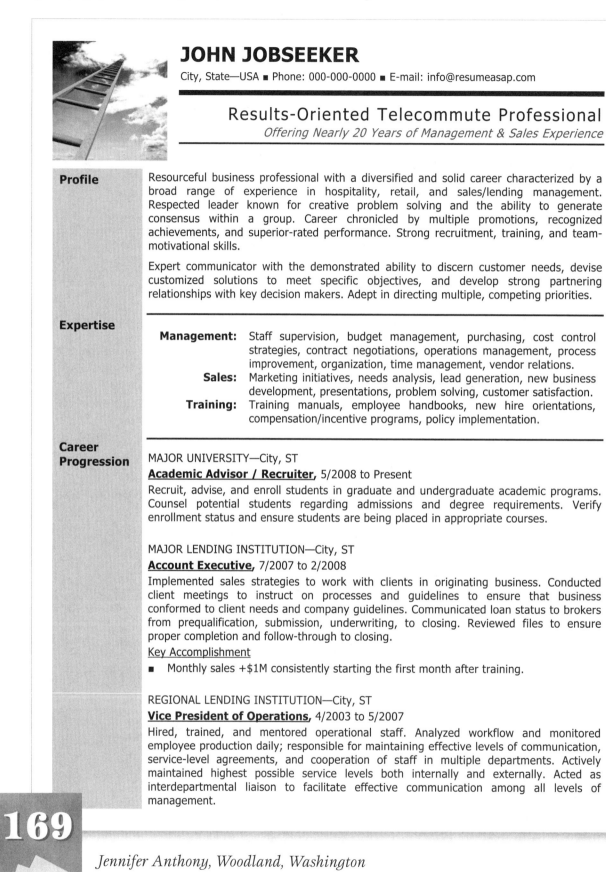

JOHN JOBSEEKER

City, State—USA ▪ Phone: 000-000-0000 ▪ E-mail: info@resumeasap.com

Results-Oriented Telecommute Professional

Offering Nearly 20 Years of Management & Sales Experience

Profile

Resourceful business professional with a diversified and solid career characterized by a broad range of experience in hospitality, retail, and sales/lending management. Respected leader known for creative problem solving and the ability to generate consensus within a group. Career chronicled by multiple promotions, recognized achievements, and superior-rated performance. Strong recruitment, training, and team-motivational skills.

Expert communicator with the demonstrated ability to discern customer needs, devise customized solutions to meet specific objectives, and develop strong partnering relationships with key decision makers. Adept in directing multiple, competing priorities.

Expertise

Management:	Staff supervision, budget management, purchasing, cost control strategies, contract negotiations, operations management, process improvement, organization, time management, vendor relations.
Sales:	Marketing initiatives, needs analysis, lead generation, new business development, presentations, problem solving, customer satisfaction.
Training:	Training manuals, employee handbooks, new hire orientations, compensation/incentive programs, policy implementation.

Career Progression

MAJOR UNIVERSITY—City, ST
Academic Advisor / Recruiter, 5/2008 to Present
Recruit, advise, and enroll students in graduate and undergraduate academic programs. Counsel potential students regarding admissions and degree requirements. Verify enrollment status and ensure students are being placed in appropriate courses.

MAJOR LENDING INSTITUTION—City, ST
Account Executive, 7/2007 to 2/2008
Implemented sales strategies to work with clients in originating business. Conducted client meetings to instruct on processes and guidelines to ensure that business conformed to client needs and company guidelines. Communicated loan status to brokers from prequalification, submission, underwriting, to closing. Reviewed files to ensure proper completion and follow-through to closing.
Key Accomplishment
▪ Monthly sales +$1M consistently starting the first month after training.

REGIONAL LENDING INSTITUTION—City, ST
Vice President of Operations, 4/2003 to 5/2007
Hired, trained, and mentored operational staff. Analyzed workflow and monitored employee production daily; responsible for maintaining effective levels of communication, service-level agreements, and cooperation of staff in multiple departments. Actively maintained highest possible service levels both internally and externally. Acted as interdepartmental liaison to facilitate effective communication among all levels of management.

169

Jennifer Anthony, Woodland, Washington

The individual wanted to transition to working as a recruiter at home. He was starting to work on his bachelor's degree because the lack of it was holding him back. The writer made this resume stand out by giving it a face-lift with a contemporary design to demand attention. The graphic

REGIONAL LENDING INSTITUTION Continued...

<u>Key Accomplishments</u>

- Developed a process to ensure compliance standards were met according to company, state, and federal guidelines.
- Considered an integral part of the development team for PMC Lending; worked as a loan officer and underwriter before being promoted to Vice President of Operations.
- Implemented training programs and job descriptions for each position.

REGIONAL SALON—City, ST

President / Owner, 10/2001 to 10/2003

Directed daily operations of a full-service salon.

<u>Key Accomplishments</u>

- Purchased the salon immediately following September 11, 2001, when business was declining. Rapidly increased sales 65% by setting performance levels to achieve sales volume and profit objectives.
- Recruited and hired a talented staff of hair designers and increased the clientele by 40% in one year.
- With an innovative approach to increasing operating efficiency, was able to sell the business, making those two years very profitable.

REGIONAL STAFFING AGENCY—City, ST

Assistant Branch Manager, 3/1999 to 10/2001

Coordinated staffing office, which offered placement for local companies and national firms such as Walt Disney World, SeaWorld, Universal Studios, and other hospitality venues. Supervised payroll, hiring, and training for employees. Managed sales team and oversaw human resources duties. Maintained high levels of communication between corporate office and local branch.

<u>Key Accomplishment</u>

- Suggested an automatic dialer system to be implemented companywide to save time and allow more productivity on other tasks.

MAJOR HOTEL CHAIN—City, ST

Food and Beverage Manager, 12/1989 to 7/1999

Managed several departments including room service, lobby, bar, restaurants, and banquets. Hired, trained, evaluated, and terminated employees. Maintained a high level of communication between departments and managers.

<u>Key Accomplishments</u>

- Organized and managed the best citywide brunch for three years in a row.
- Promoted several contests with the staff to encourage sales and repeat business.

Education

University Name—City, ST

Bachelor's degree—Business Management, expected completion: 2010

University Name—City, ST

Associate degree—Business Management, 1999

("The sky's the limit") is eye-catching and upbeat. The original document had two different shades of blue and a contrasting thin orange line. The resume drew compliments every time it was sent.

KAREN COPELAND

12 Augusta Street
Pinehurst, Ontario A1A 1A1
(555) 555-5555

RETAIL MANAGEMENT
SPECIALIZING IN FOOD SERVICES & CONSUMER GOODS

☑ Strategic Planning   ☑ Merchandising & Promotions
☑ Staff Leadership & Development   ☑ Inventory Management
☑ Customer Service   ☑ Budgeting & Cost Control

Retail Sales Manager with more than 12 years of experience in all phases of retail operations. Consistently successful in achieving P&L, sales, productivity, budget, inventory, and shrinkage goals. Skilled in marketing, merchandising, management, accounting, budgeting, staffing, and overall profitability. Motivating and results-oriented leader who balances commitment to revenue growth with outstanding interpersonal and people-management skills. Persuasive sales and customer-service skills.

KEY STRENGTHS

➤ **Staff Management**
- Extensive people management and human resources experience with full-time, part-time, and seasonal staff. Includes hiring/firing, training, performance management, policy enforcement, and salary/promotion decisions.
- Known for approachable management style and ability to motivate employees to meet performance goals.

➤ **Merchandising & Business Growth**
- Extremely creative approach to promotional events and customer incentives that attract new business, build visibility, encourage repeat business, and increase sales.
- Skilled in creating eye-catching merchandising solutions to boost sales and increase impulse purchasing.

➤ **Finances & Cost Control**
- Strong financial planning, budgeting, and profit-and-loss management skills.
- Able to maintain and optimize profitability through effective scheduling, inventory maintenance, and shrinkage control.

WORK EXPERIENCE

ST. AUGUSTINE SPRING WATER TO WINE, Pinehurst, Ontario

GENERAL MANAGER   1998–Present
Hired and quickly promoted to manage all day-to-day operations for local distributor of high-quality springwater and U-Brew wines. Selected to manage new retail facility on the strength of retail expertise and track record of increasing sales revenues.
- Opened and currently manage all day-to-day operations for U-Brew retail franchise in Oshawa. Developed marketing plan, implemented processes and procedures, handled all administration and staffing, and grew loyal customer base to more than 1500.
- Selected to coordinate transition from St. Augustine's water distribution business to retail franchise operations following purchase by Crystal Springs in 1999. Responsible for all staff release, rehiring, and administration associated with the dissolution of the company.
- Assumed full responsibility for all marketing, sales, distribution, and business development for new biodegradable soap product line in 1995. Quickly expanded territory stretching from Pickering to Cobourg.

Achievements...

170

Ross Macpherson, Whitby, Ontario, Canada

This applicant had made a career change into retail management just a few years ago. The writer wanted to focus heavily on retail management as the target on page 1. He provided a strong profile, featuring the applicant as a Retail Sales Manager, and he made Key Strengths

ST. AUGUSTINE'S SPRING WATER TO WINE, *continued*

Key Achievements:

➢ Successfully increased annual revenues for U-Brew wine franchise by 8–10% annually.

➢ Conceived successful Fall & Winter wine campaigns that consistently increase sales by 300–400%.

➢ Enhanced company image through effective customer and employee relations.

➢ Spearheaded successes in annual trade shows, including Canada Blooms and The Cottage Show. Coordinated, set up, and managed booths for all events.

➢ Conceived and coordinated highly successful co-marketing partnership with CAA Travel, highlighted by a BBQ event and drawing for a free trip to Paris, France.

➢ Key contributor to St. Augustine's recognition by Pinehurst Chamber of Commerce for business and operational excellence (placed second for all businesses throughout Pinehurst within that category).

ABC FINANCIAL, Pinehurst, Ontario

INDEPENDENT INSURANCE BROKER   1990–1998

Marketed and sold a full range of home and business insurance products, including life, health, casualty, and property insurance. Prospected new clients through targeted cold calling and direct-mail campaigns.

• Consistently maintained a high-standard performance and sales record through exceptional service and follow-through, strong product knowledge, and outstanding communications, sales, closing, and customer service skills.

VIDEO WORLD, Augusta, Ontario

OWNER / OPERATOR   1981–1990

Grew single video store into small seasonal chain with locations in Pinehurst, Kirkland, and Cobot Cove. Managed all retail operations, hired and trained staff, and personally oversaw all marketing, merchandising, purchasing, and business development. Sold business in 1990.

• First within market to offer VIP membership cards with prepaid values. Successfully captured return client base and significantly increased revenues.

• Recognized and capitalized on untapped opportunity within seasonal cottage market.

Previous experience includes successes in insurance sales and sales management.

PERSONAL INTERESTS & ACTIVITIES

• Actively purchase and renovate single and multiunit residential properties
• Enjoy fitness, swimming, and the performing arts

REFERENCES

• Provided upon request

the first main section. The applicant's strengths are grouped according to three categories presented as sub-headings. In the Work Experience section, a Key Achievements subheading directs the reader to accomplishments.

Susan Lee

Top performer
ready for a new challenge

PROFESSIONAL PROFILE

Positive attitude, committed to excellence, present
a strong **Sales / Marketing / Management**
background in the book industry and in private
store ownership.

Track record of continuous growth and customer
satisfaction in highly competitive and mature markets.
Consistently beat market trends.

Participative management style, with proven talent for
generating enthusiasm, motivating, achieving, and
maintaining high team morale. Instill confidence and
ensure highest level of productivity.

Relentless learner; value adaptability, innovation, and
flexibility. Highly intuitive with a keen instinct for and
genuine enjoyment of people.

#1 Funology Way
Circus City, WA 99999
(777) 777-7777

"I believe that the way you treat people, whether

employees or customers, is vital in creating

a successful business."

CAREER SUMMARY

Partner/General Manager, TEXTBOOK PALACE, Circus City, WA, 1996–present
Created and put into operation single family-owned retail store serving university and college students, teachers
and homeschoolers, and the general public. Sell course books, general books, office supplies, computer products,
university insignia clothing, and gifts. Annual sales approximately $3 million. Employees: 6–10 full-time and
15–25 part-time, depending on the season, with less than 10% employee turnover. Total P&L responsibility for
the entire store and operation.

- Statistically valid marketing research conducted by Cole-Geyer Marketing concluded "Textbook Palace has an
  incredible report card. In service, pricing, selection, and atmosphere, Textbook Palace excels."

- Secured 33–40% share of overall market and 50% in course books—exceeding national average of 20–25%
  market share—in less than 3 years from date of opening.

- Achieved levels of 56% gross sales in used textbooks—exceeding national average of 14%.

- Marketing research revealed 90% of the students surveyed said Textbook Palace was preferred overall to the
  campus store.

- Since store opening in 1996, sales in every quarter exceeded previous years' same-quarter sales without
  exception.

- Stun competition annually with new programs, services, and products.

- Negotiated smooth transfer of company ownership with no disruption of service to customers or public image.

171

Janice Shepherd, Bellingham, Washington

This resume begins with an unconventional, free-form, two-column layout, with the applicant's
name at the right and right-aligned, and a Professional Profile on the left and left-aligned.
The contact information is farther down and right-aligned in the right column. Farther down still

Susan Lee

CAREER SUMMARY CONTINUED

COLORADO BOOK COMPANY, INC., Boulder, CO, 1976–1996
The nation's largest used textbook wholesaler, providing innovative products and services that help bookstore managers run efficient and profitable operations.

Director, Canadian Division / Coordinator, Canadian Accounts, 1991–1996
Accepted challenge to expand Canadian market for Colorado Book Company. Trained and managed sales representatives. Trained and supervised company buyers. Wrote manuals and procedures for employees. Monitored monetary markets and strategically moved funds to take advantage of fluctuations. Arranged brokerage and shipping for international sales and purchases. Reviewed expenses and reports of Account Sales Representatives and provided basic bookkeeping functions consistent with management goals. Negotiated contracts with universities and college bookstores for purchasing and selling textbooks.

- Succeeded in establishing strong market presence in Canada.

- Reduced shipping costs by up to 50% by implementing system of national brokers and shippers and consolidating shipping points into larger shipments.

- Established Canadian national bank account to fund purchases, which reduced financing costs due to more-favorable exchange rates, less time lost setting up individual arrangements, and reduced travel and labor costs associated with such arrangements.

Account Representative, 1980–1991
Built relationships and created sales opportunities with new, existing, and prospective customers. Maintained accurate contact records and conscientiously followed up with clients and prospects. Represented company at trade shows and conferences.

- Consistently met or exceeded weekly, monthly, and annual sales goals.

- Collaborated with company accounting offices and software programming department to create a program that allowed prices to be adjusted instantly and made conversions from U.S. to Canadian values. Saved 5–10% on purchase prices while maintaining a favorable status for "fair market" with customers.

Buyer, 1976–1980
Purchased inventory for wholesale resale. Managed travel, funds, and shipping of books purchased. Entertained clients and represented company. Kept accurate records. Coordinated with banks and schools for cash transfers.

"...skills at selling are very good...certainly has a good work ethic...a woman of her word.... One of Susan's strong traits is her ability to get along with people." MWO, President/CEO, Colorado Book Co., Inc.

"...a person of high integrity, and she throws her whole being into whatever she undertakes....you'll recognize patience, sincerity, organization, and communication skills...." MOL, Commodity Broker

"...superior ability to train her employees in human resources, consumer behavior, and customer satisfaction...her motivation and willingness to work motivate her employees to work harder and more efficiently....a person with such motivation, dedication, and leadership skills is hard to come by, and Susan is one of those rare people." CK, Middle School Instructor

"...an intelligent person...good management skills...works well with people...a person of honesty and integrity. As an employer and business operator, she is well respected by her employees and customers alike." JOS, Attorney

is a quotation, double-spaced and right-aligned. The Career Summary is a page long, reporting on four positions at two employers. The resume ends with a strong set of four testimonials.

TIMOTHY DAWSON

469 Clover Pathway
Newmarket, Ontario
L3X 9T9

555–555–5555
Cell 555–555–6666
Email myname@mysite.com

GENERAL MANAGER • DIRECTOR OF SALES • SALES MANAGEMENT PROFESSIONAL

EXECUTIVE PROFILE

Solutions-driven, innovative, and results-oriented, offering the benefit of 18 years of success in leading teams that serve highly competitive and volatile markets. **Track record of strong and sustainable revenue gains based on talent for growing client base, developing productive sales and marketing programs, and maximizing behind-the-scenes administrative operations.** Excellent networking, presentation, and negotiation skills. A dynamic and persuasive communicator, able to cultivate and maintain long-lasting business ties with staff, management, and clients from all organizational levels and cultural backgrounds. Earlier professional experience includes more than 5 years of managing a catering firm; more than tripled business in 2 years. Speak conversational Italian. Computer knowledge includes MS Office (Word, Excel, PowerPoint) and Internet research.

Sales Management Expertise
Public Speaking • Account Development & Retention • Brand Management • Buyer Awareness
Sales Closing Techniques • Consultative Sales • Field Sales Management • Incentive Planning
Dealer Relationship Management • Customer Satisfaction Index Creation • Marketing Materials Creation
New-Business Development • Territory Penetration & Optimization • Trade Show Representation
Profitable Sales Strategy Conception • Trend & Competitive Analysis

General & Operations Management Expertise
Budgeting & Forecasting • Cost Avoidance & Reduction • Job Description Creation & Monitoring
Tactical Planning & Execution • Operational Troubleshooting • P&L Management
Policy & Procedure Formation • Staff & Dealer Training, Coaching, & Counseling
Team Building & Organizational Leadership • Transition Management

Manufacturing Management Expertise
Automated & Cell Manufacturing • Distribution Management • Ergonomic Efficiency
Inventory Planning & Control • JIT Processes & On-Time Delivery • Logistics Management
Master Scheduling • Materials Planning • Project Management • Safety Training

CAREER HIGHLIGHTS

General Manager—North America, Storage Products Division (report directly to the V.P. of Sales)
Cadbury Industrial, Toronto   2000–present
(Global leaders in metal manufacturing with 100,000 sq. ft. of factory space and annual revenues in excess of $20 million)
Recruited, based on Storage Products Division's aggressive expansion, with a mandate to build product awareness. Accountable for daily divisional operations that include on-time product delivery, product manufacture, high-expectation customer service, and quote and tender generation. Extensively interact with external distribution network in envisioning additional uses for a myriad of products. Create all presentations for dealers, sales representatives, and end-users. Supervise 3 Customer Service employees.
   Selected Achievements:
- Grew sales from $1.8 million to $2.3 million in a 6-month span.
- Nearly doubled client base for sales reps and dealers through tireless marketing and product awareness promotion.
- Led a 3-person team in the dramatic overhaul of back-office administrative functions. **Results:** Boosted quote turnaround time, streamlined commission pay-out procedure, and accelerated distribution network in an effort to enhance Company awareness and better promote services offered.
- Created numerous selling strategies, customized for 10 independent sales agencies. **Result:** Captured an additional 20% to 25% in yearly revenues.
- Expanded the concept and promotion of volume selling. **Result:** Generated—and continue to maintain—a heightened interest in product encompassing new and established markets.
- Customized client satisfaction index programs according to individual agency. **Result:** Obtained effective tracking results, which revealed agency strengths and areas for improvement.

172

Marian Bernard, Aurora, Ontario, Canada

The applicant, a top-flight executive, wanted to bid good-bye to the manufacturing industry. With each new company, he had earned promotions. He felt that his original resume did not do him justice. This new resume cites a wealth of achievements. For these, look at the

TIMOTHY DAWSON • 555-555-5555 • Cell 555-555-6666　　　　　　　**Page Two**

CAREER HIGHLIGHTS (continued)

National Sales Manager (reported directly to the V.P. of Sales)
Vita-Flow Industries, Ltd., Oshawa　　　　　　　　　　　　　　　1999–2000
(National automotive outfitters catering to trucks and vans)
Recruited to oversee daily sales and operations of the Sales Fleet Dept. and Commercial Sales Staff.
　Selected Achievements:
- Single-handedly captured 5 key accounts through extensive network relationship-building. **Result:** Dramatically grew sales levels from zero to $1.5 million in only 5 months.
- Designed and implemented a sales and marketing program geared toward service fleet. **Result:** Successfully elevated client base.
- Overhauled in-house collections and trimmed receivables to less than 30 days.
- Introduced new VIP card program designed to increase repeat customer usage.
- Elevated awareness of Aftermarket Product Division to promote added value to customers. **Result:** Grew revenues by 9% within 1 year.
- Pioneered Company's first Customer Satisfaction Index to determine overall Company performance.

National Sales Manager (reported directly to the V.P. of Sales & Marketing)
Quick-Fix Window Glass, Toronto　　　　　　　　　　　　　　　1995–1999
(A highly respected Canadian retailer and wholesaler with more than 175 locations in all 10 provinces and 3 territories)
Originally recruited as Account Executive and promoted in record time based on unprecedented and self-generated revenue growth. Assisted Sales and Service Depts. with calling on their client base.
　Selected Achievements:
- Extended current network with a mandate of expanding business activity. **Result:** Won most improved territory for 2 years based on commitment to exceed business targets and grew national revenues from $1.1 million to $3.9 million in less than 3 years.
- Elevated awareness of Aftermarket Product Division to promote added value to customers. **Result:** Realized noticeable increase in sales within 12 to 15 months.
- Introduced new VIP card program designed to increase repeat-customer usage.
- Pioneered Company's first Customer Satisfaction Index to determine overall Company performance.
- Overhauled in-house collections and trimmed receivables to less than 30 days.
- Appointed Chairman of Safety Committee for theNational Association of Fleet Admin. in Ontario.
- Earned recognition in the following areas:
  - Won 3 sales competitions for most product sold within a 4-month period.
  - Won most increased number of clients in 3 months / 1 year.
  - Won most organized territory.

General Manager
Blue Lion Auto Parts Sales, Toronto　　　　　　　　　　　　　　1986–1995
(A local mobile franchiser serving mechanics, gas stations, and the general public)
　Achievement:
- Improved territory ranking from 29th to 3rd in Ontario through aggressive marketing and sales programs

EDUCATION AND PROFESSIONAL DEVELOPMENT

Completed a variety of company-sponsored courses:
- Modern Manufacturing Management
- Delegation Management
- Project Management
- Accounting for Non-Financial Managers
- Fred Pryor Sales & People Management
- "Sell Like the Pros"
- "The 7 Habits Coach" (originated by Stephen Covey)
- Nonverbal Communication Training

Business Administration Certificate, Chincousy College

Selected Achievements subheadings in the Career Highlights section. Many of the achievements include a Result (or Results) statement. Areas of expertise are grouped according to three categories and are center justified.

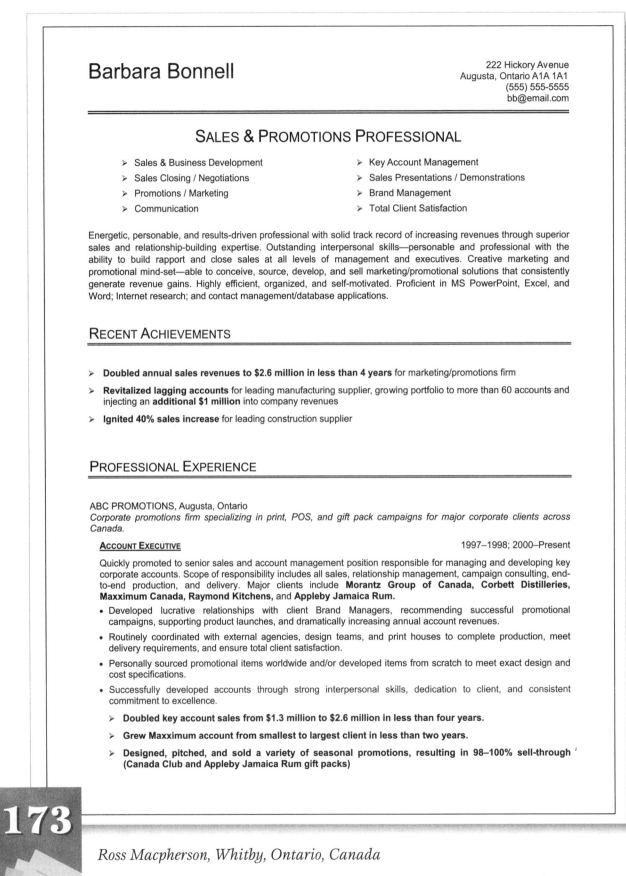

Barbara Bonnell

222 Hickory Avenue
Augusta, Ontario A1A 1A1
(555) 555-5555
bb@email.com

SALES & PROMOTIONS PROFESSIONAL

- ➢ Sales & Business Development
- ➢ Sales Closing / Negotiations
- ➢ Promotions / Marketing
- ➢ Communication

- ➢ Key Account Management
- ➢ Sales Presentations / Demonstrations
- ➢ Brand Management
- ➢ Total Client Satisfaction

Energetic, personable, and results-driven professional with solid track record of increasing revenues through superior sales and relationship-building expertise. Outstanding interpersonal skills—personable and professional with the ability to build rapport and close sales at all levels of management and executives. Creative marketing and promotional mind-set—able to conceive, source, develop, and sell marketing/promotional solutions that consistently generate revenue gains. Highly efficient, organized, and self-motivated. Proficient in MS PowerPoint, Excel, and Word; Internet research; and contact management/database applications.

RECENT ACHIEVEMENTS

- ➢ **Doubled annual sales revenues to $2.6 million in less than 4 years** for marketing/promotions firm
- ➢ **Revitalized lagging accounts** for leading manufacturing supplier, growing portfolio to more than 60 accounts and injecting an **additional $1 million** into company revenues
- ➢ **Ignited 40% sales increase** for leading construction supplier

PROFESSIONAL EXPERIENCE

ABC PROMOTIONS, Augusta, Ontario
Corporate promotions firm specializing in print, POS, and gift pack campaigns for major corporate clients across Canada.

ACCOUNT EXECUTIVE   1997–1998; 2000–Present

Quickly promoted to senior sales and account management position responsible for managing and developing key corporate accounts. Scope of responsibility includes all sales, relationship management, campaign consulting, end-to-end production, and delivery. Major clients include **Morantz Group of Canada, Corbett Distilleries, Maxximum Canada, Raymond Kitchens,** and **Appleby Jamaica Rum.**

- Developed lucrative relationships with client Brand Managers, recommending successful promotional campaigns, supporting product launches, and dramatically increasing annual account revenues.
- Routinely coordinated with external agencies, design teams, and print houses to complete production, meet delivery requirements, and ensure total client satisfaction.
- Personally sourced promotional items worldwide and/or developed items from scratch to meet exact design and cost specifications.
- Successfully developed accounts through strong interpersonal skills, dedication to client, and consistent commitment to excellence.

  - ➢ **Doubled key account sales from $1.3 million to $2.6 million in less than four years.**
  - ➢ **Grew Maxximum account from smallest to largest client in less than two years.**
  - ➢ **Designed, pitched, and sold a variety of seasonal promotions, resulting in 98–100% sell-through** (Canada Club and Appleby Jamaica Rum gift packs)

173

Ross Macpherson, Whitby, Ontario, Canada

In this resume, achievements and big-name clients are highlighted with boldfacing to show this candidate's performance. She left her company for two years and then returned. Dates for the current position show this gap in employment. Areas of expertise are put at the top

Barbara Bonnell

CENTURY ALLOYS & RESEARCH CO., Pinehurst, Ontario
Canadian arm of a leading international producer of high-grade welding rod for the manufacturing and industrial production industries.

SALES REPRESENTATIVE—OUTDOOR SALES   1998–2000

Hired to revitalize sales and manage existing accounts throughout Augusta-Pinehurst territory. Required extensive knowledge of more than 30 key products, including all technical specifications and related applications.

- Successfully rebuilt existing relationships, conducted onsite product demos and sales presentations, and further introduced and sold new clients.

  ➤ **Grew portfolio to more than 60 accounts, generating more than $1 million in sales within 10 months.**

  ➤ **Successfully rebuilt key 6-figure account with General Motors.**

SOUTHERN BUILDING, INC., West Pinellas, Florida
$20 million manufacturer and supplier of roof trusses and floor joists throughout the southern United States.

SALES REPRESENTATIVE—OUTDOOR SALES   1995–1997

Sold volume and custom-built trusses and joists to major builders and contractors throughout Florida. Additionally, consulted on technical specifications and repair issues and provided drafts of truss layouts.

  ➤ **Increased sales by 40% by effectively rebuilding key accounts, generating an additional $800,000 in annual revenues.**

PERRY & ASSOCIATES INSURANCE, Augusta, Ontario
Midsized home, auto, and farm insurance broker with 5 offices throughout Ontario.

INSURANCE BROKER   1993–1995

Promoted to assume one of only five broker positions. Responsible for all cold calling, walk-in sales, account maintenance, and customer service.

- Effectively sold and serviced more than 200 accounts. Secured sales, executed policy renewals and endorsements, and collected client premiums.

PROFESSIONAL DEVELOPMENT / TRAINING

Managing the Relationship—FRED PRINCE SEMINARS   2001
Managing Your Time—FRED PRINCE SEMINARS   2001

VOLUNTEER & COMMUNITY INVOLVEMENT

MEMBER / VOLUNTEER—LIONESS CLUB OF AUGUSTA   1999–Present
- Volunteer participant in a variety of community fund-raising and charitable events.

before a profile paragraph. The Recent Achievements section is a strong addition because of the "big numbers" it contains. A horizontal line under each main section heading makes it easy to see the overall design.

CHARLES FUNG

9 Greenway Crescent		Phone: (555) 555-5555
Augusta, Ontario A1A 1A1	cfung@email.com	Cellular: (222) 222-2222

SENIOR SALES EXECUTIVE
Specializing in High-Tech Business Development & Key Account Management

★ RECIPIENT OF MORE THAN 16 AWARDS FOR EXTRAORDINARY SALES PERFORMANCE ★

TOP-PRODUCING SALES EXECUTIVE with 25 years of professional experience in managing key accounts and generating outstanding revenue gains in the IT industry. Combine outstanding customer-needs assessment and solutions-selling skills with advanced negotiation and relationship-management capabilities. High-level understanding of complex systems management, networks, databases, mainframe and distributor products, and software. Outstanding leadership, communication, and presentation skills. Fluent English and French.

SALES ACHIEVEMENTS

➢ **5 "PRESIDENT'S CIRCLE" AWARDS, granted to top 10% for extraordinary sales achievement**

➢ **11 "100% CLUB" AWARDS for sales results above quota**

➢ *Recent sales results:*

YEAR	% OF QUOTA	YEAR	% OF QUOTA
2004	**143% YTD**	1999	**153%**
2002	**228%**	1997	**183%**
2001	**128%**	1996	**182%**

PROFESSIONAL EXPERIENCE

XYZ CORPORATION   **1980–Present**
Exemplary career in the sales and marketing of IT solutions across a wide variety of hardware and software lines. Rapid advancement through increasingly responsible sales account, executive, and leadership positions on the strength of solid relationship-building skills and consistent ability to exceed revenue targets.

CONSULTING SALES EXECUTIVE—Tripoli Systems, Inc., Augusta, Ontario (1997–Present)
Tripoli Systems, Inc., is a wholly owned XYZ subsidiary marketing integrated IT Systems Management software solutions.

Charged with the sale and account management of multimillion-dollar enterprise IT solutions to key corporate accounts across financial, insurance, and telecommunications industries. Promoted through Sales Executive (1997) and Senior Sales Executive (1998) positions. Scope of responsibility includes account ownership, business development, strategic sales planning, team leadership (10 direct reports), consultation on client business casing, and negotiations.

- Successfully built entire client base from scratch by establishing solid relationships with client executive team, selling expertise, and delivering powerful multimedia presentations on Tripoli's integrated solutions.
- Established key business relationships with XYZ Business Partners and XYZ Global Services to deliver complimentary services and technology components.

  ➢ **Within first year, single-handedly sold key corporate accounts and effectively realized 148% of sales targets.**

  ➢ **Continued to overachieve all targets in subsequent years—228% (2002), 143% YTD (2004).**

174

Ross Macpherson, Whitby, Ontario, Canada

This resume uses an eye-catching chart to highlight exceptional sales results. Awards and achievements also are highlighted to position the individual as a top candidate. Lines enclosing the profile make the information there highly visible. In the Professional Experience section, a statement

SOFTWARE ACCOUNT MANAGER, Augusta, Ontario (1996–1997)

Managed all sales, sales strategy, and account management of enterprise database and applications development software products (DB2, Java). Responsible for negotiating complex software solutions and supporting services to major players in the financial services industry. Focused on the development of solid client relationships and assistance with business case development to correctly identify specific client architecture, resource, and service requirements. Assembled and led a team of 6 Technical Specialists.

➢ **Achieved sales results of 182% (1996) and 183% (1997).**

PROGRAM MANAGER, NORTH AMERICA—Augusta Software Lab (1995)

Specifically recruited to manage internal sales and marketing of new database and AS/400 software applications throughout U.S. and Canadian markets. Developed and delivered highly effective sales presentations promoting software capabilities and illustrating sales potential.

➢ **Introduced creative incentive program, resulting in a significant sales increase across market.**

BUSINESS DEVELOPMENT MANAGER, Pinehurst, Ontario (1987–1994)

Promoted to run Pinehurst XYZ branch, focusing on the management and development of all mainframe and associated software sales to key government ministry accounts. Unique client group required patience; persistence; high degrees of creativity; and solid relationship-building, negotiation, and business casing skills. Success hinged on ability to recognize and market to unique government requirements, anticipate and work within strict budget restrictions, and negotiate creative leasing/financing options. Full management and leadership responsibilities for team of 10 System Engineers and 6 Sales Representatives.

➢ **Consistently exceeded sales targets, averaging 128% over six years.**

ACCOUNT MANAGER, Centennial, British Columbia (1980–1987)

Recruited to take over mainframe sales and manage multimillion-dollar financial and commercial accounts. Responsible for all front-end sales, relationship building, and account management.

➢ **Consistently exceeded targets, averaging 148% over six years.**

PROFESSIONAL DEVELOPMENT

- IBM Management Program—Levels I & II
- CRM Practices
- Solutions Selling Process
- Signature Selling Methodology
- Negotiation & Soft Selling
- Selling E-Business
- Messaging and Collaboration Sales—Lotus
- IT Systems Management Principles

PERSONAL ACHIEVEMENTS / ACTIVITIES

➢ Private Pilot's License—more than 5000 flying hours
➢ Skydiving—more than 350 jumps
➢ Additional interests include rock climbing (indoor and outdoor), equitation, mountain biking, and boating.

in italic describes the company. Arrow-tip bullets point to significant achievements for each of the positions held at this same company since 1980. At the end we learn that he is a pilot and skydiver.

CHRIS ANDERSON

698 Cranberry Street
Salt Lake City, UT 84117

Email: canderson@hotmail.com

Mobile: (801) 555-5555
Residence: (801) 277-5511

GENERAL MANAGER • SENIOR SALES MANAGER • BRANCH MANAGER

Profit & Loss Accountability

Consensus-driven senior executive, expert in delivering realistic, repeatable outcomes; driving spirited profit performances in declining markets; and sourcing the right solution for the right time. Considered an "enabler of success" with a clear resolve for quality, revenue growth, and cost containment, underpinned with integrity and big-picture vision. Proven track record of propelling startups to market prominence and restoring prosperity to ailing companies—applying a mix of innovation, fiscal accountability, and rational decision-making to the process of management.

Professional strengths:

- General Management
- Sales & Marketing Management
- Market Expansion Initiatives
- Profit Turnarounds
- Budget Management
- Staff Recruitment & Training
- Succession Planning & Motivation

- Strategic Planning
- Business Forecasting
- Vendor Relationship Building
- Process Reengineering
- Change Management
- Sales & Contract Negotiations
- Lead Generation/Prospecting
- Executive Presentations

- Distribution Channel Development
- VIP Client Management
- Cost Containment
- New Startups
- Technology Sales
- Business Operations

BENCHMARKS & MILESTONES

- Launched new IT startup in partnership, establishing a dealership network **delivering $3 million per annum in revenues by year three.** By year four, product **attained "Top 3" marketplace status.** (Pointer Research Corporation)

- Pioneered the first distribution network across three states for a software startup company targeting the accounting industry with the *DDA* product. From humble beginnings, the software enjoyed enormous market brand awareness, becoming the **leading product in its market segment by year three,** installed at more than 10,000 sites and boasting 100 dealerships nationwide. (Pointer Research Corporation)

- Spearheaded introduction of call center designed to arrest declining customer service rates and boost field consultants' productivity. **In three months, customer satisfaction rates rose by 242%,** and consultants' write-off time **was cut by 400%.** (Bill Dollar)

EMPLOYMENT CHRONOLOGY

ECLIPSE IT, Salt Lake City, UT   4/2000–11/2004
Reseller and installation provider of information systems to $5M–$50M SME market. $14 million turnover.
Director, New Business
Products: Account distribution costing software and reporting tools.
Transformed cold leads generated through telemarketing into firm prospects, entering into protracted sales cycles frequently spanning 12 months of negotiations and implementation works. Drove new business strategies across Utah, winning rare audiences with CFOs and project committees.

- Reversed a long-held history of heavy discounting negatively impacting profit margins; focused instead on winning the sale by emphasizing value-added services and quality.

- Despite a steeply declining IT market, secured multiple appointments and drove fledgling sales negotiations; interpreted business needs and provided cost-effective solutions. Active contributor to the business, achieving the "Microsoft Business Solutions Inner Circle" for 2002.

175

Gayle Howard, Chirnside Park, Melbourne, Victoria, Australia

A lack of education has not been a handicap for this Senior Business Development Executive who was seeking the next step on his career path to general management. Note in this resume the use of italic, boldfacing, font sizes, page borders, lines of different lengths, parentheses,

***

EMPLOYMENT CHRONOLOGY (continued)

BILL DOLLAR, Salt Lake City, UT   1/1998–4/2000
Software producer of information systems for the SME market.
Director, New Business
Reported to IT Partner; Direct Reports: 5; Operational Budget: $3 million.
Products: Account distribution costing software.

A short-term sales role transitioned to full divisional management upon request to arrest the swift decline of staff morale and eliminate increasingly unproductive work practices. **Restored operations to a tight, cost-effective operation** and spearheaded a series of infrastructure improvements designed to increase customer satisfaction, win new business, and increase market share.

Daily accountabilities included strategic sales planning and execution, contract negotiations/renewals, call center management, and consulting to business clients to devise a range of technology solutions and conduct full process reviews. **Consistently met all sales volume and profit targets.**

- Reengineered the entire sales cycle to maximize profits and eliminate the company-held belief in the value of price discounting. The cultural shift from "cheaper price wins the sale" to a renewed focus on value and quality was a new strategy that paid solid dividends, with the company achieving "President's Club" status—**one of only two U.S. companies to reach this benchmark.**

- Key contributor in elite three-person team **winning gross product sales of $1.3 million and service sales of $1.3 million**—including nabbing a "personal best" sale of $700K.

- Identified and attributed significant drops in customer satisfaction rates to slow service responses, which in turn affected the productivity of field staff restricted from sales activities by routine "customer service" matters. Spearheaded new call center initiative that **in just 3 months elevated customer service rates from 14% to 48%** and **cut field consultants' non-selling times from 25% to 5%.**

POINTER RESEARCH CORPORATION, Salt Lake City, UT   1/1990–12/1997
Startup software company distributing accounting software through a national dealership network.
Sales & Marketing Director
Reported to Board of Directors; Operational Budget: $3 million
Direct Reports: 6 (Managers: State, Sales, Marketing, Support, and Operations)

Formed startup enterprise with two partners to facilitate the distribution of the (then) newly developed Pointer Accounting software through a national dealership. From a market novice in 1990, the aggressive establishment of a dealership network combined with intense brand-awareness campaigns propelled the software to become **one of the top 3 products in the marketplace** by the company's fourth year, with more than 100 dealerships nationally, and to become **profitable in the first 12 months.**

- Influential contributor in all phases of the software's development from concept to reality to a marketplace leader, **generating $3 million in revenues by year 3.** By 1997, 22 product modules were successfully on the market, and the product was installed at more than 6000 sites.

- **Introduced revenue-generating** "enhancement fee" billed directly to end users requesting product customization. Revenues burgeoned **to cover fixed costs,** ensuring product's profitability.

***

TRAINING

Hundreds of hours of training throughout career via formal short-courses, workshops, conferences, information sessions, and on-the-job training. Topics included

Strategic Selling, Negotiation Skills, Project Management, Structured System Design, COBOL Programming, Advanced Crystal Reports Design, and Conflict Resolution.

Chris Anderson   Page 2   Confidential

quotation marks, and use of a page number. Blank lines ensure white space even though the resume is full of information. Center justification of the main headings makes the overall design easy to see.

DIANA RETT

25512 Drayton Way ● Santa Clarita, California 91350 661-333-5775

SALES/MARKETING/BUSINESS DEVELOPMENT/KEY ACCOUNT MANAGEMENT

Dynamic 16-year sales and management career marketing products, technologies, and artists within high-growth, emerging, mature, and competitive business markets. **Top-Producing Sales Professional** with strong presentation, negotiation, and sales-closing skills. Deliver outstanding customer service. Excellent analytical and organizational skills; meticulous, professional, articulate. Qualified for client interaction at all levels. Success in the training and development of other sales professionals. Delivered consistent revenue growth through expertise in

- ◆ Sales Planning and Strategy
- ◆ Sales Forecasting and Measurement
- ◆ Sales Training and Development
- ◆ Team Building and Leadership
- ◆ Dealing with Difficult People

- ◆ New-Product Introduction
- ◆ Key Account Relationship Management
- ◆ Multichannel Development and Management
- ◆ Consultative Solutions Selling

Proficient in Microsoft Word, Excel; versatile with WordPerfect.

PROFESSIONAL EXPERIENCE

Integrity is crucial to customer care, and customer care makes *the* difference.

NTT/VERIO ● Los Angeles, CA 2001–Present
Senior Account Executive

Research and identify sales leads and opportunities as well as customer requirements that necessitate customized and complex solutions from NTT/VERIO's eBusiness services; effective handling of entire sales cycle followed by comprehensive account management. Provide leading role in new-business negotiations requiring in-depth knowledge of product strategy and NTT/VERIO's sales objectives. Accounts average $10,000 a month.

WORLDCOM ● Los Angeles, CA 2000–2001
Major Account Executive

Prospected corporations in Southern California to develop partnerships by providing telecommunication solutions for Internet access, ATM, Frame Relay, managed web hosting services, colocation services, videoconferencing, and global applications as well as facility-based services. Researched and tailored proposals to clients' needs. Grew, maintained, and serviced all accounts. Networked with vendors and attended networking sessions and seminars.

SPRINT CORPORATION ● Universal City, CA 1999–2000
Business Account Manager

Analyzed, presented, and sold all aspects of telecommunications (long-distance services, voice, and data) to small and midsize businesses. Maintained and serviced all existing accounts. Continuously developed territory. Successfully utilized telemarketing techniques in setting appointments to increase market share.

Pinnacle Award for 1999 (outstanding sales achievement)

176

Myriam-Rose Kohn, Valencia, California

This applicant has a multifaceted life, being a Business Manager for an entertainment company while pursuing a professional career in sales and working on a bachelor's degree. You can gain a better sense of this individual's career path if you start at the end of the Professional Experience

DIANA RETT   Page 2

CONNECTION III ENTERTAINMENT, INC. ● Los Angeles, CA   1995–Present
Business Manager   (concurrently)
  Challenged to launch an entrepreneurial venture, combining expertise in sales, marketing, and
  general business management. Full responsibility for Ross Bagley's career. Manage legal, financial,
  and administrative affairs; develop organizational infrastructure (legal, accounting); establish goals;
  design staffing patterns and create sales functions. Keep all articles of incorporation current, file
  taxes, and set up trust account.

  Interface with acting/voice coaches, producers, studio moguls, and attorneys. Involved in theatrical
  contract negotiations.

SPRINT CORPORATION ● Gardena, CA   1991–1995
Account Manager Outside Sales (1993–1995)
Account Manager Inside Sales (1991–1993)
  In **Outside Sales,** analyzed market segments, developed marketing plans, and designed territory
  coverage. Key areas of management included sales/marketing, staff recruitment and supervision,
  employee training, scheduling, customer relations, and daily administrative affairs. Prospected
  tremendously to acquire new business. Developed, tailored, and wrote proposals to address clients'
  needs. Followed through on each account.

  Clients included mostly senior management in charge of telecommunications. Became valuable
  team asset.

  Accomplishment: Increased sales in territory by **25%** within first **6 months.**

  In **Inside Sales,** received several quarterly awards for **consistently exceeding revenue goals**.
  Requested by senior management to develop *The Revenuers* program for other employees to
  reach quota.

THOMAS SERVICES ● Los Angeles, CA   1988–1991
Account Manager
  Interfaced with middle to senior management and service coordinators to build strategic
  relationships, as well as to gain competitive advantage and market positioning for this temporary
  agency. Acquired thorough knowledge of government contracts (The Gas Company being one of
  many such clients), OSHA, and HAZMAT.

  Interviewed and placed temporaries. Handled disability and workman's compensation claims.

EDUCATION

  Working toward **Bachelor of Science, Health Administration;** Minor: Psychology; California State
  University, Northridge, CA

  Generation D Certification, WorldCom, January 2001

  Computer courses in Lotus 1-2-3, Microsoft Excel
  Technical Sales Training through Sprint Technical Support
  Day-Planner Course
  Courses in OSHA and HAZMAT regulations
  Numerous sales seminars
  Real estate training

section and read to the beginning. Note the design touch of the philosophical statement in a shaded box.
Boldfacing highlights an award and notable achievements.

PATRICIA J. LALLY

1515 Pinehurst Court • Augusta, Ontario A1A 1A1
Bus: (555) 555-5555 • Home: (222) 222-2222 • Cellular: (777) 777-7777

SENIOR SALES / MANAGEMENT / TRAINING
16 Years of Outstanding Sales Performance & Team Leadership
★ **WINNER OF MORE THAN 30 PRESTIGIOUS AWARDS FOR SALES ACHIEVEMENT** ★

HIGHLY RESPECTED SALES PROFESSIONAL skilled in high-level sales, account management, and team leadership. **Dynamic, aggressive, competitive, and driven to be the best.** Proven ability to pull together sales teams around a common goal and motivate to exceed expectations. Expertise includes

- **Key Account Management**
- **Sales Training & Development**
- **Team Building & Leadership**
- **Territory Management & Development**
- **Goal Setting & Achievement**
- **Labor Negotiations**

SALES AWARDS & ACCOMPLISHMENTS

- **Ranked #1 Sales Consultant 12 out of 16 years (out of 50 Sales Consultants)**
- **Achieved highest level within President's Gold Circle out of 300 Sales Consultants across company:**

  $3 Million Net Sales—fourth and highest plateau (2002)
  (highest level ever achieved by Sales Consultant)
  $2.5 Million Net Sales—third plateau (1999)
  $2 Million Net Sales—second plateau (1997)
  $1 Million Net Sales—first plateau (1993)

- **Winner of company Customer Service Award for 7 of the last 10 years:** 2003, 2002, 2000, 1999, 1997, 1996, & 1995
- **Earned 14 Canvass Awards for most advertising sold per geographic area**

SALES LEADERSHIP

- Successfully **led sales teams to exceed highest targets** within company.
- Consulted as **Sales Subject Matter Expert** for creation of seven in-house training courses on Professional Selling Skills.
- Chosen to participate in a variety of **Executive Focus Groups** developing and introducing new corporate products, incentives, business strategies, marketing, and training courses.
- Specifically requested to deliver **motivational sales presentations** for departments throughout company designed to ignite staff and model sales skills and excellence.
- Demonstrated **excellent communication and negotiation skills with all levels of management and executives,** including two collective agreement contracts as Chief Steward for OGEU, the only union representing $100,000+ Sales Consultants in Canada.

177

Ross Macpherson, Whitby, Ontario, Canada

This applicant was making a shift upward into sales management. A strong profile with keywords and a Sales Awards & Accomplishments section worked well to position this client as an expert in sales performance and leadership. The white-on-black graphic containing the individual's initials

PROFESSIONAL EXPERIENCE

YP ACTIMEDIA, INC. (Formerly TeleSales), Augusta, Ontario   1988–Present
$600+ million corporation specializing in database and directory publishing and e-commerce business solutions. Currently operating in nine countries across four continents worldwide.

BUSINESS SOLUTIONS CONSULTANT *(1997–Present)*
Sell print directory advertising, Internet, and e-commerce business solutions to highest-value client group throughout greater Augusta area. Maintain accounts, increase account revenues, and provide advanced consultative and strategic advice on most effective combinations of advertising media.

- Manage and increase exclusive high-value client base consisting of more than 200 accounts generating $1.7 million in existing revenue.
- Maintain highest level of customer service in high-stress environment, coordinating with client executive and meeting all publishing and artwork deadlines.

> **Currently maintaining a 91% renewal rate on a $1.7 million customer base.**
> **Currently generating a 14% net gain, exceeding department average of 9%.**

DIRECTORY ADVERTISING CONSULTANT *(1988–1992; 1994–1997)*
Directory advertising sales to medium to large corporate accounts throughout GTA and bonus canvass areas (London, Sarnia, Windsor, Thunder Bay, Kitchener)

- Managed and increased high-value accounts generating minimum $1,000–$20,000/month.
- Provided strategic advice on advertising methodology, design, and overall program.

> **Recognized 16 times as #1 Top Sales Performer.**
> **Generated more than $3 million in net sales, achieving highest level within prestigious President's Gold Club.**

BUSINESS MANAGER *(1993)*
Selected to lead teams of 10–14 Sales Reps to improve previous performance and meet highest sales targets within company.

- Applied years of sales expertise to coach, consult with, and mentor team on advanced sales techniques, encouraging individual goal setting, creativity, and calculated risk taking.
- Provided team and individual development through advanced sales and account management training.

> **Successfully led team to exceed 14% net gain target on $14 million client base.**
> **Consistently exceeded sales targets and modeled best team practice within company.**

TRAINING / PROFESSIONAL DEVELOPMENT

> **Xerox Training Courses I & II**
> **Richard Horne Selling Course**—4-day
> Numerous courses and workshops on topics including **Consultative Selling, Handling Objectives, Closing Techniques, Teamwork Development, Coaching, and Counseling**

catches attention immediately. The graphic is echoed in smaller form at the top of page 2. Note how bold-facing also captures attention. Follow the bold through the resume to the key information.

PETER J. PATEL

555 Southbridge Court
Chicago, IL 60185

pjpatel@aol.com

Cell (000) 000-0000
Home/Fax (555) 555-5555

AUTOMOTIVE SALES MANAGEMENT

*Extensive background in dealership management with a focus on
driving revenue growth and profitability to meet financial objectives.*

Plan, organize, coordinate, and measure the activities of new- and used-vehicle sales departments.

Strategic Planning—Forecast vehicle requirements by department for the immediate 90-day sales period. Prepare annual Operating Plans and Sales & Profit Forecasts. Project monthly and annual unit sales, gross profit, and departmental profit. Prepare the Plan of the Week.

Human Resources—Project staffing needs, design compensation plans, and evaluate performance of sales consultants. Review monthly commission sheets, productivity vs. forecast reports, and profit performance for each salesperson.

Staff Development—Develop and challenge sales consultants to meet or exceed monthly objectives for client traffic, closing ratios, time efficiency, prospecting, unit sales, and income. Review past performance and develop plans of action. Conduct sales meetings and provide on-the-job sales training.

Marketing—Contribute to short- and long-term advertising strategies, sales and lease promotional programs, and marketing initiatives.

Inventory Control—Maintain balanced new and used-vehicle inventory. Establish programs for moving new vehicles over 60 days and used vehicles over 45 days. Comply with dealer standards for displaying, merchandising, and maintaining new and used vehicles. Maintain dealership demonstrators.

Customer Service—Enforce strict customer service procedures to ensure a high level of customer satisfaction and client retention. Resolve customer issues personally to avoid escalation to senior management. Monitor salespeople in following up with prospective and delivered clients.

Areas of Automotive Expertise—

Sales Operations Management	Automotive Financing	Marketing & Advertising
Used Retail/Wholesale Operations	Substandard Financing	Training & Development
New Retail/Wholesale Operations	Inventory Management	Automobile Appraisals

PROFESSIONAL EXPERIENCE

BILL WILLIAMS AUTO GROUP   05/06–Present
General Sales Manager
Accountable for attaining dealership profitability, customer retention objectives, new and used car sales goals, and $4 million in new and $1.4 million in used inventory. Plan, motivate, and coordinate the activities of 10–12 professionals on the sales and finance team. Responsible for monthly and annual sales, profit, and expense forecasting, branding standards, best practices, business planning, trade-in appraisals, wholesale operations, and merchandising strategies.
- ✓ Increased new and used volume.
- ✓ Established the Finance Department that generated additional profit.
- ✓ Reduced aged inventory by 50% in five weeks.
- ✓ Initiated Internet e-commerce and hired and trained an Internet Manager.
- ✓ Increased the CSI (Customer Satisfaction Index).
- ✓ Trained three telephone-sales representatives and four direct-sales representatives.
- ✓ Improved reconditioning quality standards.
- ✓ Elevated marketing strategies by outsourcing advertising program.
- ✓ Implemented *Walk in My Shoes* cross-training initiative.

178

Rosemary Fish Justen, Schaumburg, Illinois

This individual had worked at several dealerships in the automotive sales industry and wanted to take his knowledge and skills to another auto dealer. In the opening section the writer focused on the range of the applicant's abilities and areas of expertise. In the Professional Experience

PETER J. PATEL   Page Two

JOHNSON PONTIAC—GMC/HYUNDAI   2001–05/06
Director of Used Operations
Directed sales, service, inventory, advertising, and wholesale operations with accountability for more than $2 million in inventory. Supervised 12 salespeople and three buyers to achieve 100+ retail sales and 100+ wholesale sales/purchases per month. Authorized all service work and reviewed and adjusted all vehicle appraisals. Authorized all wholesale negotiations. Negotiated all deals from inception to close to maximize sales associates' closing ratio.
- ✓ Increased gross and volume revenue more than 200% while decreasing operating expenses.
- ✓ Elevated department's ranking in volume and profit performance, from 5th to 1st position.
- ✓ Increased finance penetration and profits.
- ✓ Improved service income.
- ✓ Eliminated aged inventory to improve cash flow, update inventory choices, and increase revenue/profits.
- ✓ Established new standards of performance, quality, and customer service delivery.
- ✓ Developed innovative marketing initiatives to achieve higher sales volume in January than in June.

ANDREWS MOTOR SALES, INC.   1996–2001
Chief Financial Officer / Director of Operations
Directed operational and financial operations of retail, wholesale, and finance business. Managed vehicle reconditioning, marketing plans, sales, service, and customer service delivery. Created funds to finance inventory, oversaw purchasing functions, inspected vehicles, and monitored reconditioning.
- ✓ Created additional profit while increasing sales volume and profitability of existing operations.
- ✓ Trained managers to ensure attainment of financial objectives.
- ✓ Directed and approved all sales and finance initiatives.

MATTHEWS CHEVROLET   1990–1996
Senior Director of Used Operations (1993–1996)
Directed retail and wholesale operations and financial management. Directed and approved sales negotiations and contracts. Supervised 14 sales, finance, service, and administrative personnel.
- ✓ Increased finance penetration and gross profits by reviewing all financial contracts.
- ✓ Maintained $960,000 in inventory, managed reconditioning operations, and developed expert appraisals.
- ✓ Increased dealership sales through highly effective advertising and marketing programs.
- ✓ Achieved a 50% customer loyalty/repeat business rating against the 30% industry average.
- ✓ Attained highest finance profit, net profit, and sales volume in the dealership's 30-year history.
- ✓ Ranked #2 in 20-dealer group, elevating standing from 18th.
- ✓ Recognized as *Employee of the Year* and *Manager of the Year* in 1993, 1994, and 1995.

Director of Finance, New & Used (1990–1993)
Initiated strong and trusted relationships with banks and financial institutions.
- ✓ Increased finance income by 300% and insurance sales by 40%.
- ✓ Designed and implemented procedures that resulted in prompt and efficient flow of paperwork .

EDUCATION
Northwestern University • Business Management, HR, and Finance curriculum
University of Illinois • Finance curriculum

Licenses: Illinois Auto Dealer License, 1996–2001; Insurance producer, 1991–1997.
Computer Skills: Daily use of Microsoft business applications and operating systems. Proficient in finance communication software.
Interests / Affiliations: Diane's Designated Helpers, Cancer support organization; Long-distance English horseback riding.

section and for each position held, checkmark bullets point to significant achievements. Reading the resume from the end to the beginning shows a progression of solid work experiences.

John J. Withers

Senior Retail Executive

Operations ▪ Marketing ▪ Merchandizing ▪ Sales

Increasing Revenue ▪ Enhancing Profitability ▪ Maximizing Productivity
Capturing Market Share

Top-performing executive with impeccable ethics, integrity, and a keen desire to succeed. Respected for consistently delivering results and

- Reversing underperforming operations and transforming them into top operations.
- Attracting, hiring, challenging, and effectively utilizing talent; building cohesive organizations; facilitating ownership/pride; and motivating team members through shared vision.
- Driving market share and revenue growth.
- Reducing costs and expenses and managing budget.
- Defining and enhancing the customer experience.

Expertise

- Strategic Planning
- Revenue Growth
- Margin Improvement
- Expense Reduction

- P&L
- Operational Execution
- Budgeting/Forecasting
- Marketing/Merchandising

- Organizational Restructuring
- Relationship/Team Building
- Training/Mentoring
- Employee Development/Recognition

Professional Experience at Lowe's Home Improvement Warehouse 1988–2004

Regional Vice President 2002–2004

Directed retail sales for the Eastern Region of the Northwest Division (CO, WY, UT, ID, and NV) producing $2.5B of annual revenue. Accountable for P&L, strategic market planning, business development, sales, forecasting, marketing/merchandising activities, pricing, shrink/safety control, training, and personnel. Managed nine district managers and two remote division support partners as direct reports; supported by a regional team of 10,000 associates. Worked from Denver, CO.

Key 2003 and 2004 Results

- Achieved 12% increase in retail sales and 32% increase in profit over previous year.
- Exceeded sales-per-square-foot goals by $28.
- Recaptured $25M in annual profit through stringent shrink control—reduced shrink by 47% in 18 months.
- Achieved 86% customer service satisfaction rating, 8 points higher than company average.
- Increased operating profit in low-volume stores $1.2M over plan.
- Achieved the third-lowest operational expense in company and sixth-highest safety rating.
- Grew store count by 36% while reducing employee attrition by 37% in 18 months.
- Attained:
    #1 company-wide new-store performance ranking. Realized $1.4M over operating profit plan.
    #1 company-wide ranking for professional tool rentals, achieving 38% profit margins.
    #1 company-wide ranking for on-time training of associates (101% Curriculum Score).
- Finished 2003:
    $3.1M under Workman's Compensation and General Liability Plan.
    $0.10 under effective wage plan, reducing labor costs by $1.5M/year.

123 South Circle ▪ Highlands Ranch, CO 00000 ▪ 123.456.7890 ▪ jjw@warmail.net

179

Roberta F. Gamza, Louisville, Colorado

This applicant was an accomplished, top-performing executive who spent many years with one company and now was seeking employment with a new company. The writer stressed the individual's most recent accomplishments and impact on the bottom line in order to

John J. Withers

Page 2

Vice President Operations, Contractor Business 2000–2002

Assumed leadership for Lowe's Pro Initiative, a start-up program to increase revenues by capturing a greater share of annual spending from existing contractor base. Challenged to reduce the much-higher-than-anticipated program costs and to accelerate roll-out speed.

- Identified/resolved bottlenecks and unnecessary costs in the program. Reduced expenses by 40% and accelerated roll-out speed by 200% (30 stores in 2000; 335 stores in 2001; 512 stores in 2002).
- Developed additional services necessary to enable further sales, including contractor sales associates who were able to capture more products per sale than general sales associates.
- Pro Initiative stores realized $1.2–$2M more in incremental sales revenue and 10% higher profit margins than non-Pro stores.
- Restructured stores' G&A, resulting in $22M savings.
- Created "Walk the Talk" and "The Pro Show" live video training programs delivered via the Lowe's internal network. Personally scripted and anchored "The Pro Show."
- Developed labor model for the Lowe's Supply concept store and corporate staffing model for low-volume stores.

District Manager, San Francisco, CA 1998–2000

Promoted from store manager and challenged to turn around and return to profitability the worst-performing district in the division (highest shrink rate, worst safety and attrition record). First district manager to work from San Francisco location.

- Developed and executed strategic plan that reversed the district's overall performance, resulting in market growth of 167%, from 3 stores to 8 stores.
- Achieved 109% of sales plan and 159% of profit plan in 1999.
- Significantly reduced Workers Compensation and General Liability costs by finishing 33% under plan.
- Achieved the largest shrink reduction in the Western Division. Climbed from #21 of 21 to #2 in two years.
- Became the first test market for online business operations. Established staging areas, order fulfillment procedures, shipping stations, and UPS interface processes to facilitate e-commerce initiative.

Store Manager, San Jose, CA 1995–1998

Managed all phases of daily operations of this Bay-area store while maximizing store sales and profitability.

- Achieved 107% over sales plan and 140% of profit plan.
- Awarded Store Manager of the Year, 1997 (#1 of 160 store managers).

Education and Professional Development

Babson Executive Education, Retail Seminar, August 2003
Selected for the elite Lowe's Executive Learning Program, April 2003
Lowe's Regional Vice President Training, July 2002 (2-week intensive program)
Lowe's CEO Dinner Series Events (quarterly dinners/discussions with CEOs from outside companies)
    John Chambers, Cisco, August 2001
    Ram Charam, Charan Associates, Inc., April 2001
    David Glass, Walmart, January 2001

Mission College, Cerritos, CA 1987 (56 units in pre-med studies)

123 South Circle ▪ Highlands Ranch, CO 00000 ▪ 123.456.7890 ▪ jjw@warmail.net

demonstrate his value. The Key 2003 and 2004 Results section contains an impressive list of achievements. Bulleted items on the second page are a continuation of extraordinary accomplishments.

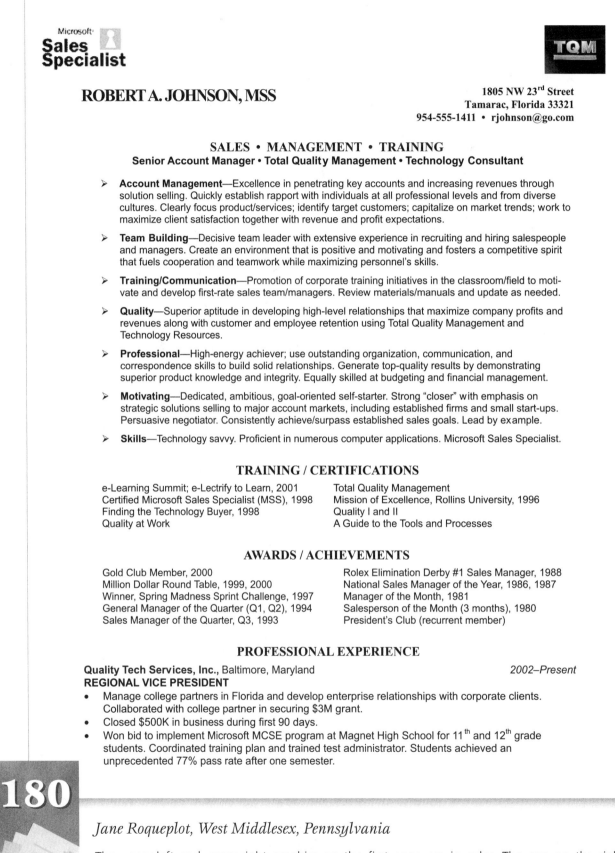

Microsoft
Sales
Specialist

TQM

ROBERT A. JOHNSON, MSS

1805 NW 23rd Street
Tamarac, Florida 33321
954-555-1411 • rjohnson@go.com

SALES • MANAGEMENT • TRAINING
Senior Account Manager • Total Quality Management • Technology Consultant

➢ **Account Management**—Excellence in penetrating key accounts and increasing revenues through solution selling. Quickly establish rapport with individuals at all professional levels and from diverse cultures. Clearly focus product/services; identify target customers; capitalize on market trends; work to maximize client satisfaction together with revenue and profit expectations.

➢ **Team Building**—Decisive team leader with extensive experience in recruiting and hiring salespeople and managers. Create an environment that is positive and motivating and fosters a competitive spirit that fuels cooperation and teamwork while maximizing personnel's skills.

➢ **Training/Communication**—Promotion of corporate training initiatives in the classroom/field to motivate and develop first-rate sales team/managers. Review materials/manuals and update as needed.

➢ **Quality**—Superior aptitude in developing high-level relationships that maximize company profits and revenues along with customer and employee retention using Total Quality Management and Technology Resources.

➢ **Professional**—High-energy achiever; use outstanding organization, communication, and correspondence skills to build solid relationships. Generate top-quality results by demonstrating superior product knowledge and integrity. Equally skilled at budgeting and financial management.

➢ **Motivating**—Dedicated, ambitious, goal-oriented self-starter. Strong "closer" with emphasis on strategic solutions selling to major account markets, including established firms and small start-ups. Persuasive negotiator. Consistently achieve/surpass established sales goals. Lead by example.

➢ **Skills**—Technology savvy. Proficient in numerous computer applications. Microsoft Sales Specialist.

TRAINING / CERTIFICATIONS

e-Learning Summit; e-Lectrify to Learn, 2001
Certified Microsoft Sales Specialist (MSS), 1998
Finding the Technology Buyer, 1998
Quality at Work

Total Quality Management
Mission of Excellence, Rollins University, 1996
Quality I and II
A Guide to the Tools and Processes

AWARDS / ACHIEVEMENTS

Gold Club Member, 2000
Million Dollar Round Table, 1999, 2000
Winner, Spring Madness Sprint Challenge, 1997
General Manager of the Quarter (Q1, Q2), 1994
Sales Manager of the Quarter, Q3, 1993

Rolex Elimination Derby #1 Sales Manager, 1988
National Sales Manager of the Year, 1986, 1987
Manager of the Month, 1981
Salesperson of the Month (3 months), 1980
President's Club (recurrent member)

PROFESSIONAL EXPERIENCE

Quality Tech Services, Inc., Baltimore, Maryland
REGIONAL VICE PRESIDENT
2002–Present

• Manage college partners in Florida and develop enterprise relationships with corporate clients. Collaborated with college partner in securing $3M grant.
• Closed $500K in business during first 90 days.
• Won bid to implement Microsoft MCSE program at Magnet High School for 11th and 12th grade students. Coordinated training plan and trained test administrator. Students achieved an unprecedented 77% pass rate after one semester.

180

Jane Roqueplot, West Middlesex, Pennsylvania

The upper-left and upper-right graphics on the first page are in color. The one on the right has multiple colors and different levels of shading. In addition, the person's name, the contact information, the centered headings, and both kinds of bullets are dark blue. The profile's content

ROBERT A. JOHNSON, 954-555-1411, *Page 2*

PROFESSIONAL EXPERIENCE, *continued*

Production Point International, Orlando, Florida   *1997–2002*
SENIOR ACCOUNT MANAGER / ENTERPRISE CONSULTANT
- Deliver Technology Learning Solutions and Workforce Performance Improvement Strategies for software, network OS, and business skills development to targeted customer base.
- Profitably direct account management programs for key customers in South Florida. Built account base from ground floor to more than $1M in revenue within 2 years. Increased customer satisfaction ratings with implementation of account management and retention strategies.
- Consistently maintain highest GM and lowest discount percentage in region.
- Gold Club Member 2000; consistently in top 10% in National Sales Ranking.

Professional Business Systems, Pompano Beach, Florida   *1996–1997*
MAJOR ACCOUNT MANAGER
- Sold digital imaging and reproduction software and hardware. Generated $500K in new gross revenue within first 12 months with $112K gross profit.

Barton Protective Services, Atlanta, Georgia   *1992–1996*
GENERAL MANAGER, Tampa, Florida (1995–1996)
GENERAL SALES MANAGER, Lanham, Maryland (1993–1995)
SALES MANAGER, Springfield, Virginia (1992–1993)
- Within one year turned around Tampa branch from 60% of sales and profit plan to 100% of sales and profit plan in Q1 1996.
- Managed first office to exceed $100K/month in sales in first year, March 1994.
- Achieved 117% Profit Plan, 1994. Recognized as #1 in company; President's Club 1994.
- Managed and motivated team members to achieve National Sales Champion, 1992, 1993, and #2 Rookie, 1993.

Production Resource Group, Greenwich, Connecticut   *1989–1992*
CONSULTANT / REGIONAL SALES MANAGER
- Oversaw sales and distribution of consumer products; provided management, marketing, and sales consulting in U.S. and internationally.
- Generated $500K in wholesale first-year sales for Environmental Products Division. Developed more than 350 new distributors through December 1990. Produced $150K annual revenue in Telecom Division in first six months.

ADT Security Systems, Greenwich, Connecticut   *1982–1989*
BRANCH MANAGER
- Built sales force, increased major accounts, spearheaded customer growth, and developed sales branches as profit centers in Westchester County, NY, and Fairfield County, CT. Grew office from 9 employees and less than $500K in annual sales to more than 60 employees and $2.5M in sales.
- Hired and trained salespeople who achieved National Sales Status in several divisions: Residential (1986, 1987, 1988), Commercial (1988), and Rookie (1985, 1987).

Copy Systems, Inc., Glastonbury, Connecticut   *1980–1982*
SALES MANAGER / SALESPERSON
- Increased territory production by 30% within one year. Ranked 2nd of 14 managers in average sales per man (1981) and 3rd of 14 managers in total sales ($1.1M).

EDUCATION

1977–1980, NORTHEASTERN UNIVERSITY, Boston, Massachusetts
Business Administration
Major: Marketing • *Minor:* New-Venture Management

is grouped according to categories in boldface. In the Professional Experience section, round bullets point to notable achievements.

— NANCY WILLIAMS —
455 Knots Lane
Kettering, Ohio 00000
(555) 555-5555

— PROFILE —

Capable and self-motivated professional with a strong desire to apply skills in sales, client relations and communications • Ability to coordinate people and activities • Special talent for relating easily to others and inspiring confidence • Equally effective in self-managed projects and as a team member • Creative, enthusiastic and positive • Computer-literate

— STRENGTHS —

Problem Solving ... Organizational Skills ... Communications
Interpersonal Effectiveness ... Bilingual ... Client Relations

— SUMMARY of SKILLS —

Sales / Business Development

- Developed and sold residential properties ranging from $50,000 to $350,000.
- Utilized cold calling, direct mail, promotions, open houses and advertising to develop new clients.
- Researched, prepared and presented market analyses to prospective clients based on current market data.
- Established partnership in a start-up wholesale craft supply business.

Customer Relations & Service

- Utilized strong client relations and problem-solving skills to ensure optimum service.
- Prepared contracts and managed all aspects of real estate transactions/negotiations through closing.

Communications / Languages

- Proficient in both English and German.
- Extensive knowledge of European cultures from experience in living and traveling abroad.
- Provided freelance translation services from German to English.

Community Service

- Served as volunteer assisting with programs provided at battered women's shelter in Bergen County.
- Contributed as volunteer during children's enrollment at Merritt Memorial School Library.

— EXPERIENCE —

Crafts Company • Kettering, Ohio • 1992 to Present
Business Partner/Full-Time Parent

Barnes Real Estate • Kettering, Ohio • 1991 to 1992
Real Estate Associate

Bordeaux Restaurant • Kettering, Ohio • 1986 to 1990
Hostess

— EDUCATION —

A.A. in **Liberal Arts,** Ohio Community College, Akron, Ohio

181

Louise Garver, Windsor, Connecticut

This person had combined a crafts business with full-time parenting. She wanted to return to the workforce full time in sales or customer service. Featuring related skills helped her win an offer.

Technology

Resumes at a Glance

LEONARD BAKER

10 Blackbird Lane • Bridgetown, Pennsylvania 16466

(555) 645-3219   **lbaker@hotmail.com**

MACHINIST • WELDER • FITTER

◆ Proficient and skilled in technical specialty. Recognized for dedicated work ethic and productivity. Capable of doing work that requires concentration, high degree of patience and attention to detail. Mechanically inclined. Able to work independently.

◆ Thrive in a team- and deadline-oriented environment. Exceptional organizational skills; capable of prioritizing, scheduling and managing heavy work flow.

◆ Proficiency in technical skills/machine operations/equipment processes:

✓ MIG	✓ Fluxcore	✓ Computer Numeric Control
✓ TIG	✓ Submerged Arc	✓ Gantry Crane
✓ Stick	✓ Inner Shield	✓ Tolerancing
✓ Pulse	✓ Drill Press	✓ Forklift Operator
✓ Aluminum	✓ Technical Math	✓ Machine Print Reading
✓ Blueprint Reading	✓ Applied Math	✓ Lathes and Milling Machines

PROFESSIONAL EXPERIENCE

CLASS A WELDER, Forker Industries, *Bridgetown, Pennsylvania*   *1988–Present*
- Fit and weld boxcars with Fluxcore and submerged arc welding. Examine welds to ensure they meet specifications.
- Instrumental on shift that slashed project hours from 11 (by another shift) to 8 hours while maintaining quality of workmanship.

WELDER ASSEMBLER, Sun Engineering, *Walton, Texas*   *1987–1988*
- Used spray arc welding equipment. Assembled dock levelers and functioned as a saw operator, forklift driver, truck driver and member of installation crew.

WELDER FITTER, Perfection Metal Products, *Hazen, Texas*   *1986–1987*
- Fitted and welded frames for the electronic industry using MIG and TIG welding. Recognized for outstanding workmanship by lead man.

LABORER, City of Wilding, *Wilding, Texas*   *1985–1986*
- Received commendation from mayor for exemplary service to the citizens of Wilding by working more than 96 hours during a winter storm to repair water main leaks.

CERTIFICATIONS

◆ Arc Welding	◆ Gas Metal Arc Welding, Advanced	◆ Plumbing and Pipefitting Fundamentals
◆ 1/8" LH	◆ AWS SMAW 3/8" Butt Weld	◆ Flat and Vertical, Inside Corner Filler
◆ 7018 AWS Structural	◆ Flat, 3/8" Dia. Plug Weld	◆ 75-Fillet Vertical and Overhead Positions
◆ Vertical Outside Corner	◆ Vertical, T-Butt Weld Vertical	◆ 86 GMAW, Spray Arc Single V Groove with Backing 1G-Flat
◆ AWS D1	◆ GMAW AWS D7.7	
◆ Code D1.1		

EDUCATION

A.S., Machine Technology, anticipated November 2004
Dean's Certificates; 3.94 GPA to date; Perfect Attendance; Class President
Capitol School of Trades, *Weathersfield, Pennsylvania*

182

Jane Roqueplot, West Middlesex, Pennsylvania

The overall design of this one-page, four-section resume is easily grasped at a glance. Boldfacing and three kinds of bullets ensure that the reader sees all of the most important information.

Fred G. Jamisen

9999 Abernethy Road • Oregon City, Oregon 99999
555-555-5555

Steamfitter

Professional Profile

Highly skilled, conscientious, and precise **Steamfitter** with more than 6 years of experience and more than 10,000 hours of training in all aspects of steam fitting. Familiar with all required codes, appropriate use of equipment, steam-fitting techniques, safety standards, and proper procedures to prevent injuries. Proficient in reviewing plans, blueprints, and specifications for steam-fitting projects with proven ability to provide expert recommendations. Well-developed troubleshooting skills with accurate and precise repairs. Experienced EMT willing to volunteer EMT services on the job. Excellent communication skills, personable, trustworthy, adaptable, and committed to a long-term career.

Expertise and Training:

- Air Conditioning and Refrigeration Systems and Equipment
- Boilers
- Commercial and Industrial
- Conduit Flex, Duct, and Controls
- Electrical and Electronic Contracting
- HVAC, Air Conditioning, and Refrigeration
- Instrumentation
- Outdoor Installations
- Overhead and Underground
- Process Systems and Equipment
- Steam and Heating Systems and Equipment
- Troubleshooting and Maintenance
- Welding Processes, Including Orbital Welder and Arc 207
- Wire Pulling, Wiring Devices, Removal and Finish

Licenses

Pressure Vessel and Boiler License Class V • *State of Oregon*
United Association of Steamfitters • *Local 290*

Employment History

Steamfitter • United Association of Steamfitters • Portland, Oregon • *6 years*
  Assigned to various companies and projects as needed.

Paper Machine Operator • Crown Zellerbach Corp. • West Linn, Oregon • *11 years*
  Previously owned by James River and Simpson Paper Company.
  EMT *(Emergency Medical Technician)* • Served as volunteer EMT for the paper mill.

Sales Representative • Pepsi Bottling Company • Portland, Oregon • *8 years*
  Beverage sales.

Military

U.S. Army • **Specialist E-4—Nuclear Missile Technician** • *Honorable Discharge* • *1976*

Education

Associate of Applied Arts • **Humanities**
  Carroll College • Helena, Montana, *and* Clackamas Community College • Oregon City, Oregon

183

Rosie Bixel, Portland, Oregon

This applicant's position was highly specialized. His resume was designed for an international job opening. Bold italic side headings indicate the resume's main sections.

RAYMOND FINNEGAN

887 Ballinger Road
Springfield, IL 00000
(555) 555-0789 • rayfin@aol.com

QUALIFICATIONS

Licensed Elevator Mechanic with specialized skills in hydraulics, motor controls, wiring controls, rigging, electrical print reading, solid-state computers and print boards.

➤ Experienced in troubleshooting, repair, installation and testing of electromechanical systems, including pumps, drives and reducers.

➤ Contributor in self-directed, high-performance team environment with proven ability to complete multiple projects in a timely, efficient manner.

➤ Skilled in welding (steel, aluminum and industrial equipment), pipe fitting, millwrighting and machining. Strong mathematical, organizational and time-management skills.

CURRENT EMPLOYMENT

BAYSTATE ELECTRO-MECHANICS, Springfield, IL
Overhead Crane Mechanic (1998 to present)

- Perform on-site service calls on overhead cranes for customers in the chemical, power and paper industries.
- Diverse responsibilities include repairing, troubleshooting, removing, installing and testing electromechanical equipment to ensure safe operations.
- Repair and install chemical processes and related equipment such as pumps, drives and reducers.

ELEVATOR SERVICE EXPERIENCE

VANGUARD ELEVATORS, Springfield, IL
Elevator Mechanic (1990 to 1998)

- Performed all aspects of elevator installations, from setting up and aligning brackets, rails and car, to setting up motors on tractions and wiring the elevators.
- Serviced contracts for elevator equipment at major area companies: American Technologies, Payne & Company, Montgomery Corp., Dover Enterprises and others.

INTERNATIONAL UNION OF OPERATING ENGINEERS, West Springfield, IL
Hoisting Engineer (1986 to 1990)

- Operated and maintained heavy equipment, including backhoes, cranes, bulldozers and rollers.

Additional Experience: Service Manager, MARLAND PROPERTIES, Chicopee, MA
Supervised staff of 9 in all aspects of property maintenance for 300 residential units. Ensured that repairs were completed in a timely, cost-effective manner while maintaining quality standards. Prepared and maintained up-to-date documentation on all repairs performed *(1984-1986)*.

EDUCATION

Electronics courses
Illinois Technical Community College, Westfield, IL

International Union of Elevator Constructors' School, Springfield, IL
Completed training in Elevator Mechanics, Electronics, Hydraulics, Motor Controls, Electrical Theory

184

Louise Garver, Windsor, Connecticut

This applicant wanted to return to his preceding occupation as an Elevator Mechanic. To emphasize his prior experience in relation to his goal, the writer created the heading Elevator Service Experience.

ALLEN AYERS

Cell: (804) 493-8672 | E-mail: AllAyers@Students.Lynchburg.edu

Film / Media / Production Intern

Raw Skills:
Energetic third-year student motivated by media technology and mass-media communication. Organized. Creative thinker. Strong attention to detail. Stimulated by use of media technologies and development of short films, clips, commercials, broadcasts, and movies. Well-traveled with exposure to many cultures. Fluent in English and Spanish.

Summer Focus:
Team player seeking an internship in movie production, filming, and/or editing. Strong interest in electronic media and leverage of media technologies.

College Career:
B.A., Communication (degree expected Dec 2009)—Lynchburg College (Lynchburg, VA).
➢ Emphasis on communication through electronic media (i.e., radio, TV, and film).
➢ Coursework in interpersonal communication, media and culture, writing for the media, research methods, persuasion, communication theory, and media law.
➢ Studies abroad in 2005 (Australia, New Zealand) and 2006 (England) on cultural differences and universal similarities.

Production Projects:
➢ Filmed and edited a 10-minute movie on virtual reality in the classroom. Used a P2 camera for filming. Edited with Adobe Premiere. *(Class: Intro to Media Technology)*
➢ Filmed a 5-minute session of an amateur artist playing guitar. Used a P2 camera for filming. Voted best of 20 submissions. *(Class: Intro to Studio Production)*
➢ Currently developing a 30-second TV commercial on Lynchburg College based on existing clips and new voiceovers. Using Avid Media Composer for filming and editing. Expect the piece to air on the campus TV station and the college news website this spring. *(Class: Principles of Media Production)*

Roles & Recognition:
➢ Honorable Mention, 2006—For promoting a fellow student in a 5-minute film that helped launch his first paying job in entertainment.
➢ On-Set Assistant, Drama Club
➢ Yearbook Photographer, Class of 2008
➢ Fund-raiser Photographer, 2005—Took 125 close-ups for students to purchase as holiday gifts.

PO Box 2457, Lynchburg College, Lynchburg, VA 24501

185

Helen Oliff, Reston, Virginia

This media-relevant resume is for a third-year college student wanting a specific summer internship to work on a film. The filmstrip image makes the resume look relevant at once.

Denise Sylvestor
467 Appleton Street
Dayton, OH 00000
(555) 555-5555

Summary

More than 13 years of experience in electronic assembly, quality-control inspection, shipping and receiving and production. Experience in leading and training other employees to perform productively.

Proficient in sub and final assembly, testing and inspection of electronic components, including printed circuit boards, wiring and other products.

Skilled in operating a variety of hand tools and machinery; able to assemble and handle simple to complex operations.

A team-oriented, dedicated, punctual employee recognized for the ability to learn quickly and produce quality work.

Computer skills include Microsoft Word for Windows.

Experience

Electronic Assembly/Machining

- Assemble and build printed circuit boards and automotive parts (exhaust and intake for Chrysler cars) from blueprints/schematics, using soldering iron, gauges and various other hand tools.
- Operate exhaust machine and make any necessary minor repairs/adjustments to Bradley Allen computer to maintain top production levels and minimize downtime.

Quality Control Inspection/Shipping & Receiving

- Inspect more than 340 boxes of electronic parts each day to ensure compliance with company standards, using chemicals and electric equipment.
- Record incoming and outgoing shipments as well as prepare items for shipment; verify information against bills of lading, invoices, orders and other records.

Team Leadership

- Selected by management in recognition of dependability and excellent performance as lead person on Cybex production line, overseeing team of 16 assemblers.
- Provide ongoing guidance, training and leadership to assembly team, maintaining top levels of productivity.

Employment History

Full-Time Caregiver, Dayton, OH (2002 to present)

AUTOMOTIVE CORPORATION, Dayton, OH (1994 to 2002)
Quality Control Inspector
Electronic Assembler
Machinist

WIRE COMPANY, Dayton, OH (1990 to 1994)
Automotive/Electronic Assembler

NEW VISIONS, Dayton, OH (1989 to 1990)
Electronic Assembler

Education

A.S. in Electronics Technology
Dayton Community College, Dayton, OH

186

Louise Garver, Windsor, Connecticut

This person's mother became ill, and the applicant served as a full-time caregiver. After her mother died, the applicant wanted to return to work. This skills-based resume helped her land a job.

James Karberg

11100 S.W. Cork Avenue • Trenchville, Georgia 99999
555-666-7777

Service Technician

Professional Profile

Energetic, self-motivated, and resourceful *Technician* offering a solid background in installations, service, and technical support of all security systems, as well as voice and data systems. Able to read blueprints, provide inconspicuous wiring, and supply efficient and accurate installations. Experienced working with Alarmnet cellular backup systems.

Possess outstanding "people skills," with strong customer-service abilities and strengths in working well with all types of personalities. Excellent troubleshooting and problem-solving skills. Learn quickly, work well independently and effectively as a team member. Career-oriented, honest, loyal, and committed to a job well done.

Projects Include

Prewire new construction, including retirement, condominium and apartment projects.
State of Georgia—Networked all buildings.
First Interstate Tower
One Financial Building
Nordstrom's

Related Employment History

Prewire Technician • 2002–2004
Century Cable Services • Trenchville, Georgia

Installation Manager • Service • 1998–2002
Great Western Security Systems • Los Angeles, California
(Satellite office—Trenchville, Georgia)
Supplied technical support, installation and service for security systems.
Maintained full operation of satellite office in Georgia.

Technician • 1984–1987; 1991–1997
Various temporary jobs.

Technician • 1987–1990
Christenson Electric • Lancaster, Georgia
Provided voice and data installations.

Installer • 1982–1984
TCI Cablevision of Georgia, Inc.
Installed broadband cable TV.

Community Service

Volunteer • Trenchville Food Bank • Trenchville, Georgia • *11 years*

Education

Machine Technology • Trenchville Community College, Trenchville, Georgia • *1989*
Electrical Codes • Landcaster Community College • Trenchville, Georgia • *1989*

187

Rosie Bixel, Portland, Oregon

The writer displayed projects and chronological information in a different format (centered) with a page border for emphasis. Centered section headings complement the center-justified information.

Roberto J. Sisti

5550 Oak Tree Court, Nashville, TN 37205

615-555-4629 (Home)   rjsisti@adelphia.net   615-555-8400 (Cell)

Professional Profile

Highly skilled mechanic with more than 20 years of experience maintaining, inspecting, troubleshooting, and repairing diesel- and gasoline-powered new and used vehicles, heavy duty and light trucks, off-road construction and excavation equipment. Methodical in gathering information and data to present logical solutions to technical problems. Emphatic about following policies and procedures to achieve positive outcomes. Excel at attending to detail and accuracy and producing high-quality work.

Technical Qualifications & Competencies

- Suspensions & Alignments
- Diagnostic Equipment
- Hydraulics
- Air Compressors
- Electrical Troubleshooting
- ABS Systems
- Body Control Systems
- Generators
- Welding (MIG) & Fabrication
- Engine & Transmission Controls
- Forklift Safety & Operation
- Two-Cycle Compactors

Hold Tennessee CDL—Tanker & Airbrake Endorsements

MACS (Mobile Air Conditioning Society) Refrigerant Air Conditioning & Service Certified

Recent Employment History

Automotive Technician, Jaguar Land Rover of Nashville, Nashville, TN   Jul 2002–Present
- Specialize in performing Tennessee State Safety Inspections on high-end luxury vehicles acquired from auctions and trade-ins; complete brake, suspension, steering, engine, mechanical, and interior repairs to ensure top dollar profits at resale.

Class-A Driver/Automotive Technician, Pete's Auto Brokers, Nashville, TN   Jul 2001–Jul 2002
- Transported vehicles to and from auctions in Nashville and Grant, TN. Completed repairs and prepared vehicles for resale, turning over as many as 50–60 vehicles per month. Provided backup coverage to owner by assessing customer needs, writing estimates, ordering parts, and dispatching repair orders to service mechanics.

Automotive Technician, Rollins Park Shell, Nashville, TN   Dec 2000–Jul 2001
- Performed diagnostic assessment of customer vehicles, prepared written estimates, and completed necessary repairs. Conducted Tennessee State Safety Inspections. Worked almost exclusively with repeat customers, ensuring ongoing maintenance and safety of owner vehicles.

Mechanic Foreman/Fuel Truck Driver, Elliott Contracting, Knoxville, TN   Mar 2000–Dec 2000
- Managed preventative maintenance program for multimillion-dollar vehicle and equipment inventory. Supervised three mechanics; repaired construction equipment and trucks. Drove fuel and mobile repair truck to multiple job sites throughout central Tennessee.

Automotive Technician, Discount Tire & Auto, Knoxville, TN   Aug 1997–Mar 2000
- Performed basic diagnostic, repair, and inspection work on customer vehicles; transitioned to store locations in Knoxville and Grant, TN.

Previous Automotive Technician Experience (10+ years)
- Milestone Exxon, Grant, TN; Century Ford, Grant, TN; Albert Ford; Grant, TN; Sears Automotive, Knoxville, TN. Owned and operated vehicle exhaust and repair shop.

Prior Certifications
- Master Certified Emissions Technician, State of Tennessee Vehicle Emissions Inspection Program
- ASE Master Mechanic

Sponsoring Member, **iATN international Automotive Technicians Network.** Former Member, **Military Vehicle Preservation Society**—Restored and sold a military "deuce and-a-half."

Graduate, **Richard Montgomery High School,** Knoxville, TN

188

Norine Dagliano, Hagerstown, Maryland

This individual had a lead on a mechanic position with his local fire department and needed a resume. The writer played up the diversity of the candidate's experience and strengths.

PAUL THOMAS

3 Etwell Court
Fairborn, OH 45324

Email: thomas_paul@bigpool.com

Telephone: (937) 855-3358
Fax: (937) 855-3351

PRODUCT SUPPORT FITTER • FIELD SERVICE FITTER • WORKSHOP FITTER

Equipment:

Blasthole drills D45K, D55K, D75K, D90K

Caterpillar off-highway trucks to 789B

All auxiliary plant

Dozers to D11 Series III

Loaders to 992G

Graders to 16G

Liebherr R994A, R994 200 series, R994B 200 series, R996

Komatsu—all equipment including excavators to PC1800

Hitachi excavators to EX2500 Super

Dragline Marion 8050

Licenses:

Licensed to drive forklifts, earthmovers, mobile equipment, passenger vehicles, and trucks.

Training:

- Workplace Health & Safety
- Safe Operating Procedures
- Coal Surface
- Generic Induction
- Codes of Conduct

Heavy equipment diesel fitter with expert technical troubleshooting and leadership capabilities. Acknowledged for capacity to juggle multiple projects and priorities simultaneously; restore order from chaos; and consistently reinforce the importance of quality, deadlines, and safety across multidisciplined teams. Competent technical lead, team member, or solo performer.

Vast experience working in inhospitable and remote terrains has sharpened talents in "making do"—fashioning tools and components using available resources for minimal downtime. Specialist experience in production blasthole drill rigs, air conditioning, electrics, hydraulics and pneumatics, engine, power train, final drive, hydraulic pumps, and full hydraulic tune-ups.

Professional strengths:

- Service Scheduling
- Hydraulic Faults: Diagnosis and Repair
- Preventive Maintenance Planning
- Component Records Management
- Parts & Component Procurement
- Time Management

- Workload Allocation & Direction
- Client Relationship Management
- Critical Problem Solving
- Staff Education & Awareness
- Workplace Health & Safety
- Safe Operating Procedures

Trade Qualifications

Qualified Heavy Equipment Diesel Mechanic

ISO 9002 (Hydraulics & Pneumatics)
Parker Jackson College (1995)

Certificate of Motor Mechanics
Ohio Community College (1988)

Project Highlights

- **Overcame stock availability issues** on 24-hour operation by analyzing regularly needed parts, stringently monitoring stock levels, and modifying equipment for longer equipment life.

- **Consistently passed exacting standards** enforced by independent product representatives inspecting maintenance works for compliance to product warranties.

- Completed drill rig rebuilds in 8 days, **saving 2 days from plant department's estimates.**

- Skirted major breakdown incidences by conducting a regime of regular inspections and identifying fault defects prior to negative impact. Careful recordkeeping of faults in drill rigs **drove plant availability from 40% to 90% in six months.**

- Delivered accountability to workshop operations by implementing 24-hour inspections.

189

Gayle Howard, Chirnside Park, Melbourne, Victoria, Australia

It takes some time to see all the information on this two-page resume. The Equipment, Trade Qualifications, and Project Highlights sections are different but particularly relevant to this individual's situation. In studying this resume, note the use of page borders, boxes, columns,

PAUL THOMAS

Employment Experiences

Computer Technologies:

- Microsoft Word
- PowerPoint
- Outlook
- Internet
- Email
- Windows 2000
- Caterpillar ET: engine power train software
- Caterpillar SIS (spare parts and electronic workshop manuals)
- PlantPac (component records management)

References

Ian Vincent
Support Supervisor / Consultant
Johnson Peck
Tel: (937) 555-6789
Ian.V@johnpeck.com

Peter Barrons
Workshop Foreman
RTG Pty Ltd
Bus: (937) 555-4433
pbarrons@rtg.com

George Barton
Product Support Manager
Mines Australia P/L
Tel: +61 3 9776 8112
gbarton@optus.com.au

ATC DIESEL SERVICE & REPAIRS P/L   1991–Present
Contractor
Projects: Major mining site projects.

Building a reputation as an accomplished diesel fitter with specialist talents in multimillion-dollar heavy earthmoving equipment. Successfully won long-term contracts to repair, rebuild, troubleshoot, and maintain project-critical equipment at several major mining sites in remote locations.

As an expert in fault-finding, diagnostic works, and full hydraulic tune-ups, recommendations to schedule equipment for repair or remove for immediate service are observed rigorously by management, with project costing relying heavily on sustained levels of productivity.

- **RTG Pty Ltd:** Leading contractors servicing 60% of mining contracts across the largest area of coal infrastructure in Australia, conducting full mining operations for major companies such as RAG Australia BHP Billiton, MIM, and Camel Resources on multimillion-dollar projects.

  With heavy emphasis on minimum equipment/machinery downtime and quick turnarounds, regular service checks to identify potential defects and assess risks are vital to sustaining production levels and circumventing costly lost equipment time and parts. With much of the repair/maintenance and troubleshooting tasks both unsupervised and solo assignments, performances are measured on the quick identification of problems, resolution, and turnaround of equipment to commission.

  Frequently achieved minimum downtime targets of 7 days each quarter.

- **EXEL Hydraulics, Mobile Hose Doctor and Contract Diesel Fitter.** Mount Isa, Queensland, Australia. Top 3 Australian company specializing in hydraulic and pneumatic service and repairs to plant and equipment in transportation and mining industries. On 24-hour call for machinery modifications and setups, shut-down maintenance, and component overhauls for Mount Isa Mines, Universal Transport Operations, Atlas Copco, Tamrock, and Selwyn Mines underground and surface. On-call 24/7 diesel fitting onsite and remote work.

  Workshop Manager & Contract Diesel Fitter. Supervised 5 staff (administrative, trades assistant, and customer service). Multifaceted role managing $1.1 million budget, overseeing daily workshop operations, customer and supplier liaison, scheduling servicing projects, and juggling "hands-on" technical diesel fitting projects. Trained workers in assembly line technique, time management, and order dispatch. Achieved 12-hour turnarounds from receipt to dispatch.

CARTERS EARTHMOVING, Fairborn, OH   1988–1991
Serviced and maintained plant and machinery in remote sites across the United States.
Contract Diesel Fitter
Repaired and restored mobile plant equipment and earthmoving machinery and equipment in remote locations. Designed, refurbished, and overhauled parts and components where immediate "fixes" and difficult terrain for transportation inhibited parts procurement and deliveries.

FRED SIVYER HOLDEN, Fairborn, OH   1984–1988
Apprentice Motor Mechanic

boldfacing, italic, short lines, very small type (for e-mail addresses), and reduced leading (less space between lines). Observe how some white space is achieved through some center justification.

Roberta Magnotti

Telecom Training Solutions

1234 Pinehurst Road
Augusta, Ontario A1A 1A1

Office: 444.555.8888
Home: 555.444.3333

Training Professional
Expert in Technical, Sales, and Product Training

Dynamic training professional skilled in providing top-quality training and learning programs to individual and corporate audiences throughout Canada and the United States. Outstanding reputation and success built on ability to design and deliver enriching and engaging learning programs focused on specific development needs and client objectives. Skilled in a wide variety of learning methodologies, including classroom, online, distance learning, and CBT. Motivating and enthusiastic facilitator.

- Learning Needs Assessment
- Program Facilitation
- Train-the-Trainer
- Curriculum Design & Development
- Consulting
- Assessment Strategies

Fully Certified in Adult Learning and Distance Education

"Best instructor ever!"
—Account Executive
Bell Telecom

"Fantastic! The instructor explained everything in a way that could be understood by everyone."
—Sales Representative
SaskTel

"Amazing instructor…kept the course alive and interesting. Was able to teach to entire class at their level of understanding."
—Service Director
Bell Nexxium

"This is by far the best course I've been on…[Instructor's] knowledge level is amazing. Speaks to you so you understand."
—Sales Associate
Bell Nexxium, Vancouver

"..excellent presentation and style."
—Account Consultant
SaskTel

"The instructor is really terrific! She made the course easy to understand."
—Business Office Rep
Bell Telecom

Training & Facilitation Expertise

- Personally trained more than 3000 employees for industry leaders throughout Canada and the United States.
- Solid reputation for outstanding program design and facilitation skills.
- Polished, professional, and personable training style. Innovative and flexible approach ensures success with both beginner and advanced audiences.
- Extremely self-motivated and customer-focused. Dedicated to providing first-rate service and guaranteeing client success.
- Polished consulting and learning needs assessment skills. Able to identify key learning need, design solution, and meet objectives.
- Advanced troubleshooting, analysis, and problem-solving skills. Able to accurately identify problems and implement effective solutions.

Training Experience

TELECOM TRAINING SOLUTIONS, *Augusta, Ontario*

President 2001–Present

Founded successful telecommunications training company offering more than 30 cutting-edge training courses and development programs to 35 leading Telcos throughout North America. Provide all learning consulting, design and develop curricula, and facilitate all programs.

- Train corporate telecom audiences throughout North America in data and voice technologies, product positioning and pricing, data sales training, and technology overviews.
- Consistently receive highest rating of participant and client feedback. Majority of business acquired through word of mouth and client recommendations.

continued...

190

Ross Macpherson, Whitby, Ontario, Canada

This unique format allows this Training Professional to show off some of the comments from her workshops. Furthermore, the two Experience sections, Training Experience and Additional

BELL TELECOM, *Augusta, Ontario*   1993–1999

TRAINING TEAM LEADER / DESIGNER—Bell Institute for Professional Development

Managed and led Bell's in-house training facility for Ontario & Quebec. Required to revise all outdated programs, introduce new learning technologies, and facilitate all courses. Managed team of 4 designers and training support staff.

- Revamped entire Bell curriculum, transferred all supporting materials to updated technologies, and revised 12 comprehensive in-house programs. Content covered Network Concepts, Data Network Protocols, New Emerging Technologies, ATM Concepts, DMS Family of Switches, and Frame Relay.
- Consistently received outstanding participant feedback for course design, content, and facilitation style.
- Liaised with product managers to ensure all product updates incorporated into state-of-the-art training modules.

Corporate clients:

Bell Nexxium

SaskTel

Bell Telecom

AT&T (TigerTel)

Qwest

Alaint

Northern Telephone

NWTel

USwest

IntrisHP

Newbell Networks

Dell Canada

ADDITIONAL TELECOM EXPERIENCE

BELL TELECOM, *Augusta, Ontario*   1988–2001

Rapid promotion through a series of increasingly responsible positions based on solid industry expertise, strong leadership and team development skills, and consistent ability to generate results.

DIRECTOR—Advanced Solutions (1999–2001)

- Led strategic development and growth of new corporate division mandated to protect Bell interests in the face of open telecom competition.

ACCOUNT EXECUTIVE—Bell Executive Service (1989–1993)

- Full key account management responsibilities for **$180 million CIBT account**. Sold full-scale data and voice systems in response to detailed needs analyses. Consulted on comprehensive technology solutions, designed and monitored blueprints, negotiated pricing, and managed account relationships with key lines of business.

NETWORK CONTROLLER (1988–1989)

- Contributed to the coordination and implementation of Canada's first Voice/Data Trans-Canada Megastream T1 Network.

PROFESSIONAL DEVELOPMENT

Distance Learning Certificate—Ohio State University   1997
Effective Planning—TICA Learning   1995
Project Management—TICA Learning   1995
Instructor Training—Lange Learning   1993
Seven Steps of Highly Effective People—Steven Covey   1990

Computer Communications—Electronic Engineering

- Senegal College of Applied Arts & Technology

Telecom Experience, allow her to clearly show both her training experience and her professional experience in her target industry. If you read the workshop comments, you can see how testimonials strengthen a resume, particularly if it—unlike this resume—has some conspicuous weaknesses.

ROBERT C. KELLY

1862 Glen Oaks Drive • Sacramento, CA 77777 • (555) 555–5555 • bobckelly@myexcel.com

PROFILE

More than 15 years of experience in troubleshooting and repairing electrical and electronic systems and equipment, including robotic, pneumatic, mechanical, control circuit, power supply, hydraulic, and vacuum systems. Adept at providing technical equipment support and developing new processes through ongoing maintenance, defect resolution, and enhancement solutions. Combine excellent technical, analytical, and engineering qualifications with outstanding customer-service skills. Expertise includes

- Customer Service, Support, & Communication
- Training & Team Leadership
- Blueprints & Schematics
- Problem Identification & Resolution
- Inspection & Maintenance

- Technical Documentation
- Project Scheduling & Management
- Systems Design & Installation
- Quality Control & Assurance
- Interpersonal Communications

PROFESSIONAL EXPERIENCE

EXTREME TECHNOLOGIES—Sacramento, CA   1989–2004
Senior Technician—Engineering Equipment Support

Conducted and scheduled investigative tests, repairs, and overhauls of robotic and automated manufacturing and processing equipment to ensure proper operation. Documented inspections, maintenance, repair work, and failures in maintenance logs and statistical process control charts. Trained employees on operational procedures with emphasis on quality, productivity, and overall equipment readiness.

- Designed and fabricated several equipment modifications, including a parts handler to prevent breaking of tie bars in encapsulated parts, which resulted in saving $40,000 per breakdown.

- Created and installed low-level alarm system for slurry barrels, preventing $80,000 in damage to machine and product by sounding an audible alarm when slurry was low.

- Developed and implemented wafer guide for the Westech 372 Planarizer. Ensured nonbreaking feed of wafers, saving up to $6,000 in materials cost.

- Reduced lot count time to seconds by designing electronic handheld lead frame counter.

- Selected to participate in Mirra Polisher installations and training located in Singapore. Created a team approach to problem solving and technical support.

ADDITIONAL EXPERTISE

Assembly Encapsulation

· Nickolet X-Ray Machine
· Lawton Encapsulation Press L.A. Rose Preheater
· AIS Automated Handler
· Blaser 5000 Laser
· Boschman & Fico Automold
· MTI Media Deflash
· Dia Ichi Seiko

Chemical Mechanical Planarization (CMP)

· Nel Taper & De-taper Ontrak Scrubbers (Series 0, 1, 2)
· Strasbaugh 6DS
· Applied Materials Mirra & Ebara Planarizers
· Ipec 676
· Westech 372
· Shibayama Back Grinder
· ADE Ultra Gauge 9500 NOVA Scan 210
· 420 Prometrix UV-1050

EDUCATION

Associate's Degree (1989), Electronics Engineering Technology, ITT Technical Institute—Sacramento, CA

191

Denette Jones, Mountain View, Hawaii

The horizontal lines before and after the Profile make it the first area of attention. Bulleted areas of expertise are listed after the descriptive Profile paragraph. The Additional Expertise section is a plus.

Transcription

Transportation

Resumes at a Glance

TERI REINHOLD

716-555-4629	5105 Oak Tree Court, Glenwood, NY 14069	t.reinhold@adelphia.net

PROFESSIONAL PROFILE

- Ambitious transportation professional offering more than 12 years of bus operator experience with Erie County Public Schools.
- Hold valid New York Class B CDL with passenger, air brakes and school bus endorsements; skilled in all aspects of vehicle safety and maintenance.
- Extensive knowledge of traffic safety rules and laws; recipient of "Ten Year Safe Driving Award."
- Outstanding reputation for positive work ethic and attitude; highly regarded by management, co-workers, school personnel, students, and parents.
- Excellent communication, customer service, troubleshooting, and problem-solving skills.
- Ability to lead by example; experience managing teams of up to 30 employees and delivering one-on-one training and mentoring support.
- Passionate commitment to the safety and security of each child; customer-service focus and quality conscious.

PROFESSIONAL EXPERIENCE

Bus Operator, Erie County Public Schools, Orchard Park, NY   Feb 1994–Present
(Erie South Depot, Wilson High School Cluster)

Operate a 55-passenger bus, safely transporting average of 160 students daily. Work collaboratively with team of 35 drivers, a dispatcher, and Transportation Cluster Supervisors (TCS) while consistently upholding high standards of SSPGS (Supporting Services Professional Growth System).

- Provide team support and assistance and demonstrate willingness to go the extra mile to ensure timely completion of every job.
- Demonstrate expertise in patching runs and frequently handle on-the-spot requests made by managers and dispatcher.
- Support dispatcher during breaks by answering phones and two-way radio. Troubleshoot problems and implement corrective actions making appropriate referrals to TCS or dispatcher intervention.
- Deliver buses for safety inspections and rearrange bus lots to clear paths for snow removal.

Key Contributions

- Selected by Depot Manager for **New Employee Coordinator** (Jan 2004). Provide orientation and oversight of all new hires to ensure exposure to all aspects of the job and smooth job transition.
- Maintained manual tracking of new employee hours for biweekly payroll; provided input to employee evaluations; recruited and assigned drivers for ride-alongs; provided ongoing support with personnel issues; served as liaison between new drivers and dispatcher.
- Mentored newly licensed drivers and prepared formal written evaluations.
- Served on Bus Discipline Review Board, a cross-functional team of school professionals exploring updates and revisions to disciplinary forms in response to "Ride by the Rules" campaign.
- Represented Erie South Depot in providing data to assist union and third-party consultant with preparing job reclassification recommendations.
- Took initiative to learn basic Transportation Information Management System (TIMS) applications and assist with inputting and extracting data from the system.

EDUCATION & PROFESSIONAL DEVELOPMENT

Advanced Microsoft Word & Working with Windows; "Delivering Unbeatable Customer Service over the Phone"; EAP Online Supervisors Training
Graduate, **Wilson High School,** Orchard Park, NY

192

Norine Dagliano, Hagerstown, Maryland

Applying for a promotion within her current company, the applicant found it difficult to identify her achievements. To offset this problem, the writer created the Key Contributions section.

Jason A. Zimmerman

2513 West Vista Lane   Miami, FL 33166   (cell) 786.522.9875   (home) 305.779.0036

> **Professional truck driver offers a winning combination to an organization that values stability, dependability, and timely deliveries**

- ❖ **3 Million Miles**
- ❖ **Multiple Safety Awards**
- ❖ **32 Years of Experience**

Single and Team Driver of the following rigs:

Vans	Step Deck	Reefers
Doubles	Flat Deck	Tankers

SAFETY AWARDS

SCHROEDER NATIONAL
6-Year Driver Safety Award
GREENWAY/LOADSTAR
5-Year Driver Safety Award
EAST POINT TRANSIT
800,000-Mile Driver Safety Award
SOUTHEAST EXPRESS
7-Year Driver Safety Award
PULMAN GROUP
2-Year Driver Safety Award

PROFESSIONAL EXPERIENCE

Nov 1996–Present
SCHROEDER NATIONAL
Richmond, Virginia

- Drive vans transporting general freight throughout the United States.
- Supervise the dock management of product: loading, unloading, and accounting.

Oct 1991–Oct 1996
GREENWAY/LOADSTAR
Buffalo, New York

- Drove single and double vans, flatbeds, and step decks transporting general freight throughout the United States.
- Supervised the dock management of product: loading, unloading, accounting, securing freight, and customer interaction.

Jan 1991–Oct 1991
GLOBAL MARINE
Charleston, South Carolina

- Drove specialized boat trailers transporting high-value yachts.
- Supervised the crane work and tie-down of the yachts.
- Coordinated delivery times with the customer.

1970–1991
**GLENDALE SHIPPING / REINOLD TRUCKING CO. / EAST POINT TRANSIT
INTERSTATE TRUCKING CO. / SOUTHEAST EXPRESS / COASTAL TRANSPORT
PULMAN GROUP**

193

MeLisa Rogers, Shiner, Texas

The original resume was a hodgepodge of company listings. The writer transformed it into a precise background document that emphasizes the person's tenure in the industry and his safety record.

Leroy Taylor

555 102nd St.
Forest Hills, NY 50505

555-505-5050
ltaylor@xxx.com

Summary

Experienced CDL-A truck driver with solid track record transporting, assembling, and installing computer equipment and peripherals. Excellent reputation for ensuring safe delivery and achieving high customer satisfaction and retention.

Work History

Computer Giant, New York, NY   1997 to 2009
Sales, delivery, and installation of computer equipment from the factory to companies throughout the Tri-State region. Clients included large organizations such as Apple Bank, Chase Manhattan, Yale University, Colgate-Palmolive, Merck & Co., as well as smaller companies and home offices.
Driver/Installer

- Drove tractor-trailers throughout the Tri-State area to make on-time deliveries and perform installations.
- Maintained perfect safety record and truck security, and ensured intact and on-time arrival of equipment.
- Loaded and unloaded equipment weighing up to 700 pounds, making certain of proper cargo weight and appropriate configuration on the truck to streamline deliveries.
- Ensured that trucks were fully equipped to pass safety inspection; reported maintenance problems.
- Kept accurate records of deliveries and documented shipping discrepancies.
- Worked in the warehouse, pulling orders, entering data in the computer, manually receiving and putting away stock, and maintaining warehouse safety.

New York Computer Warehouse, Queens, NY   1995 to 1997
Delivery and installation of computer peripherals, primarily for home office and small business settings.
Driver/Installer

- Drove 24-foot box trucks to deliver and install computer peripherals to companies on Long Island.
- Achieved perfect safety record and ensured that equipment arrived undamaged and on time.

Education

High School Diploma—Martin Van Buren High School, Queens Village, NY

194

Wendy Gelberg, Needham, Massachusetts

The resume showcases the applicant's strongest selling points: his CDL-A license, perfect safety record, on-time and intact delivery of equipment, and solid track record of handing vehicles.

SUSAN LONG

55555 East Harvard Drive #555
Aurora, Colorado 80000   susan4long@comcast.net   Home (303) 000.0000
      Cell (303) 000.0000

SUMMARY OF QUALIFICATIONS

Flight Attendant with practical, hands-on experience in providing exceptional, personalized service. Highly flexible, willing and able to be available for flights on short notice. Adept at utilizing available resources and paying close attention to details. React quickly and calmly to stressful situations. Function well unsupervised, as well as part of a team unit. Strong communication skills, polished skill relating to people with diverse backgrounds. Friendly and humorous contribution to team/work dynamic. Possess extensive worldwide travel and living experience. High degree of proficiency with food preparation and food safety.

FLIGHT ATTENDANT TRAINING

FAA Certification   **CPR Certification**

Safety, Service Training, Aircraft Knowledge

PROFESSIONAL EXPERIENCE

REGIONAL AIR, Ashland, Washington   2005–present
FLIGHT ATTENDANT

Provided excellent service for 1 to 70 passengers per flight. Performed safety procedures, inspected emergency equipment and carefully adhered to all safety regulations for carrier with renowned safety record. Greeted passengers and made public address announcements. Prepared cabin and passengers for takeoff and landing. Communicated with captain. Served refreshments. Responsible for numerous unaccompanied minors. Prepared, restocked and cleaned cabin.

- Relied upon for passenger safety in emergency medical situations, including situations that required paramedics upon landing and an aborted takeoff.
- Noted for ability to interact with passengers professionally as well as on personal level, including ability to console grieving passengers. Consistently served as a "go-to" resource for peers.

CREATIVE ORIGINALS, Tacoma, Washington
OWNER & MANAGER

Launched successful business in photographic backgrounds that was later expanded into mobile shave ice business to compensate for seasonal fluctuations in revenue.

Mobile Shave Ice Business   1998–2005

Solely responsible for all aspects of business operations. Hired and trained employees. Conducted daily business operations including sales, marketing, bookkeeping and obtaining permits. Trained personnel in proper safeguards against food contamination and importance of food safety. Ordered and managed inventory, profit/loss and purchasing.

- Selected as vendor for Tacoma Special Olympics.
- Attained record amounts of shared revenue for Bellingham and Burlington Soccer Leagues, resulting in soccer league administration purchasing a shave ice business.
- Assisted rehabilitation of auto accident victim with brain injuries with relearning motor skills.

Photographic Backgrounds   1991–2001

Manufactured photographic backgrounds for special high school events. Established business through attending trade shows and conducting advertising campaigns. Accountable for ensuring exceptional customer service, ordering supplies and bookkeeping. Completed nationwide sales, including scheduling orders and shipping.

- Built home-based business into six-figure income within eight years.

Possess additional 5-year background as travel agent that required first-class customer service.

195

Michele Angello, Aurora, Colorado

The applicant insisted that her resume be limited to one page because job postings specified one page. The writer therefore selected only high points of the applicant's qualifications.

Electronic Resumes

Resumes at a Glance

GARY RANDALL

5401 88ᵗʰ Street • Lubbock, TX 79424 • Phone: 555-555-5555 • E-mail: garyrandall4385@yahoo.com

CAREER PROFILE: SALES

15+ Years of Experience in All Sales Activities, with Consistent Success in Meeting Business Growth and Client Relationship Goals; Work Effectively in Non-Supervised Environments Requiring Frequent Travel

Solutions-focused professional able to increase sales and client bases through persistence, persuasion, and fulfillment of clients' needs. Effective communicator and presenter; strong research and analysis skills. More than 10 years in working with high-profile clients within the Lubbock area. Fluent in Spanish.

Core competencies include

New Product Introduction / Consultative Sales Approach / Customer Needs Assessment
Client Relationship Development / Product Analysis—Evaluation / Sales Development Life Cycle
Traditional & Online Research Strategies / Prospecting & Lead Generation / Relationship & Solutions Selling

PROFESSIONAL EXPERIENCE

Sales Representative—Wood Flooring Specialists—1996–Present—*Wood flooring installation business.*

Manage all business development activities, including prospecting/cold calling, lead generation and qualification, product presentations, and overall client service. Sell services to homeowners, business owners, and public institutions. Create and implement marketing strategies to build business, establishing and sustaining strong client relationships. Travel frequently to deliver on-site presentations and client projects. *Selected Accomplishments:*

- **Expanded business from Lubbock-only territory to region that includes Eastern New Mexico,** southern Oklahoma, and most of Texas. Grew client base from average of 3 to 16 per month.

- **Gained experience and skill in working with high-profile clients, including local physicians and** government leaders. Consistently met and exceeded client expectations, leading to repeat/referral business.

- **Demonstrated persistence and high tolerance for overcoming rejection through efforts in increasing** sales for start-up company. Excelled in convincing clients of product/service benefits.

Sales Representative—Ace Tile & Marble—1985–1996—*Tile and marble product/service business.*

Launched start-up distributorship, selling tile and working with homeowners, contractors, architects, and designers to specify products. Handled all phases of sales cycles, from prospect identification to closing and follow-up activities, with emphasis on consultative selling and relationship building. *Selected Accomplishments:*

- **Secured several lucrative projects for Accent, including largest job for Interceramic** (largest North American ceramic tile manufacturer) involving 480,000 sq. ft. Sheraton hotel (6-figure sale). Developed repeat business with builders, architects, and designers.

- **Gained expertise in product knowledge to drive sales growth, providing client recommendations** that led to satisfaction and referral business.

** Additional positions include Personnel Director with the Marriott Hotel and Owner of XYZ Service. For the Marriott Hotel, implemented Employee Relations and Spanish-Speaking programs to improve relations and service. For XYZ Service, grew customer base through on-site visits to businesses.

PROFESSIONAL DEVELOPMENT

Associate of Arts in Management
SOUTH PLAINS COLLEGE—Lubbock, TX—3.5, Major Studies

Language Skills—Fluent in Spanish and English
Computer Skills—Microsoft Office applications, Internet research
Community Involvement—Volunteer to support Boy Scouts and local church organizations

196

Daniel J. Dorotik, Jr., Lubbock, Texas

This is the first of two resumes with a companion electronic resume to show the difference between the two kinds of resumes. Study this resume and compare it with Resume 197.

GARY RANDALL
5401 88th Street
Lubbock, TX 79424
Phone: 555-555-5555
E-mail: garyrandall4385@yahoo.com

CAREER PROFILE: SALES

15+ Years of Experience in All Sales Activities, with Consistent Success in Meeting Business Growth and
Client Relationship Goals; Work Effectively in Non-Supervised Environments Requiring Frequent Travel

Solutions-focused professional able to increase sales and client bases through persistence, persuasion,
and fulfillment of clients' needs. Effective communicator and presenter; strong research and analysis
skills. More than 10 years in working with high-profile clients within the Lubbock area. Fluent in
Spanish.

Core competencies include:
New Product Introduction / Consultative Sales Approach / Customer Needs Assessment / Client Relationship
Development / Product Analysis - Evaluation / Sales Development Life Cycle / Traditional & Online
Research Strategies / Prospecting & Lead Generation / Relationship & Solutions Selling

PROFESSIONAL EXPERIENCE

Sales Representative - Wood Flooring Specialists - 1996-Present - Wood flooring installation business.

Manage all business development activities, including prospecting/cold calling, lead generation and
qualification, product presentations, and overall client service. Sell services to homeowners, business
owners, and public institutions. Create and implement marketing strategies to build business,
establishing and sustaining strong client relationships. Travel frequently to deliver on-site
presentations and client projects.

Selected Accomplishments:
+ Expanded business from Lubbock-only territory to region that includes Eastern New Mexico, southern
  Oklahoma, and most of Texas. Grew client base from average of 3 to 16 per month.
+ Gained experience and skill in working with high-profile clients, including local physicians and
  government leaders. Consistently met and exceeded client expectations, leading to repeat/referral
  business.
+ Demonstrated persistence and high tolerance for overcoming rejection through efforts in increasing
  sales for start-up company. Excelled in convincing clients of product/service benefits.

Sales Representative - Ace Tile & Marble - 1985-1996 - Tile and marble product/service business.

Launched start-up distributorship, selling tile and working with homeowners, contractors, architects, and
designers to specify products. Handled all phases of sales cycles, from prospect identification to
closing and follow-up activities, with emphasis on consultative selling and relationship building.

Selected Accomplishments:
+ Secured several lucrative projects for Accent, including largest job for Interceramic (largest North
  American ceramic tile manufacturer) involving 480,000 sq. ft. Sheraton hotel (6-figure sale). Developed
  repeat business with builders, architects, and designers.
+ Gained expertise in product knowledge to drive sales growth, providing client recommendations that led
  to satisfaction and referral business.

** Additional positions include Personnel Director with the Marriott Hotel and Owner of XYZ Service. For
the Marriott Hotel, implemented Employee Relations and Spanish-speaking programs to improve relations and
service. For XYZ Service, grew customer base through on-site visits to businesses.

PROFESSIONAL DEVELOPMENT

Associate of Arts in Management
SOUTH PLAINS COLLEGE - Lubbock, TX - 3.5, Major Studies

Language Skills - Fluent in Spanish and English
Computer Skills - Microsoft Office applications, Internet research
Community Involvement - Volunteer to support Boy Scouts and local church organizations

197

Daniel J. Dorotik, Jr., Lubbock, Texas

Compare this electronic resumes as a text (.txt) file with Resume 196. Note the absence of font
enhancements (bold, italic, greater font size, and small caps), bullets, lines, and centering.

PHYLLIS BOTKIN, CPA

2453 83rd Street, Lubbock, TX 79424 / Phone: 555-555-5555 / E-mail: pbotkin@cox.net

CAREER TARGET: ACCOUNTANT

More Than 15 Years of Experience in Finance-Accounting Specialist Positions
Consistent Success in Reducing Costs and Improving Financial Functions
Extensive Training Courses in Accounting and Other Financial Disciplines

Broad range of knowledge and skills in financial activities, including auditing, financial controls, budget management, and reporting processes. Skilled trainer, mentor, and motivator for diverse groups of individuals; recognized by upper management for ability to excel as both a leader and key contributor. Disciplined, meticulous approach to financial and accounting tasks; maintain the highest level of professional and personal ethics. Excellent technology background.

- ❏ Accounts Payable & Receivable
- ❏ General Ledger Reconciliation
- ❏ Financial Audits & Reporting
- ❏ Employee Training & Evaluations
- ❏ Staff Scheduling & Supervision
- ❏ Vendor/Partner Relationships
- ❏ Strategic Planning & Execution
- ❏ New Software Implementation
- ❏ Escalated Problem Resolution

PROFESSIONAL EXPERIENCE

GRAND SYSTEMS, Lubbock, TX

ACCOUNTANT, 2004–PRESENT

FINANCIAL FUNCTIONS—Manage all accounting and related functions, supervising team that includes Accountant and Accounting Clerks. Approve all A/Ps and A/Rs, oversee all G/L and payroll activities, and generate monthly financial statements. Participate in internal audits conducted by parent company. Plan and administer budgets, completing monthly analysis of financials vs. budget to determine areas for improvement.

KEY CONTRIBUTIONS & ACHIEVEMENTS

- **Cost Reduction & Avoidance**—Consolidated positions to reduce labor; conducted analysis and reports that illustrated spending activities and areas for cost reduction.

- **Financial Controls**—Assisted in creating internal controls within the company to achieve consistent financial data management and under-budget performance.

- **Technology Solutions**—Maintained IT performance following series of software implementations over extensive time period, including JD Edwards, Oracle Financials, Lotus 1-2-3/Notes, and Windows/MS Office.

- **Performance Recognition**—Earned recognition from supervisor on recent performance appraisal:
  "Phyllis' leadership abilities are outstanding…earned a promotion by showing her leadership through a tough transition time along with her technical abilities…has positive interpersonal relationships with her staff and her colleagues…has exceeded expectations in performing the duties of her position." —Reviewing Supervisor

PROFESSIONAL DEVELOPMENT

Certifications: Certified Public Accountant
Professional Training: 100+ hours in Accounting, Finance, Auditing, Compliance, and Office Management disciplines

198

Daniel J. Dorotik, Jr., Lubbock, Texas

This, a one-page version of Resume 6, is the second of two resumes with a companion electronic resume. Study this resume and compare it with Resume 199.

```
PHYLLIS BOTKIN, CPA
2453 83rd Street
Lubbock, TX 79424
Phone: 555-555-5555
Email: pbotkin@cox.net

CAREER TARGET: ACCOUNTANT

Over 15 Years of Experience in Finance-Accounting Specialist Positions
Consistent Success in Reducing Costs and Improving Financial Functions
Extensive Training Courses in Accounting and Other Financial Disciplines

Broad range of knowledge and skills in financial activities, including auditing,
financial controls, budget management, and reporting processes. Skilled trainer,
mentor, and motivator for diverse groups of individuals; recognized by upper
management for ability to excel as both a leader and key contributor. Disciplined,
meticulous approach to financial and accounting tasks; maintain the highest level of
professional and personal ethics. Excellent technology background.

* Accounts Payable & Receivable
* Employee Training & Evaluations
* Strategic Planning & Execution
* General Ledger Reconciliation
* Staff Scheduling & Supervision
* New Software Implementation
* Financial Audits & Reporting
* Vendor/Partner Relationships
* Escalated Problem Resolution

PROFESSIONAL EXPERIENCE

GRAND SYSTEMS, Lubbock, TX
ACCOUNTANT, 2004-PRESENT

FINANCIAL FUNCTIONS - Manage all accounting and related functions, supervising team
that includes Accountant and Accounting Clerks. Approve all A/Ps and A/Rs, oversee all
G/L and payroll activities, and generate monthly financial statements. Participate in
internal audits conducted by parent company. Plan and administer budgets, completing
monthly analysis of financials vs. budget to determine areas for improvement.

KEY CONTRIBUTIONS & ACHIEVEMENTS
* Cost Reduction & Avoidance - Consolidated positions to reduce labor; conducted
analysis and reports that illustrated spending activities and areas for cost
reduction.
* Financial Controls - Assisted in creating internal controls within the company to
achieve consistent financial data management and under-budget performance.
* Technology Solutions -  Maintained IT performance following series of software
implementations over extensive time period, including JD Edwards, Oracle Financials,
Lotus 1-2-3/Notes, and MS Windows/Office.
* Performance Recognition - Earned recognition from supervisor on recent performance
appraisal:
"Phyllis' leadership abilities are outstanding…earned a promotion by showing her
leadership through a tough transition time along with her technical abilities…has
positive interpersonal relationships with her staff and her colleagues…has exceeded
expectations in performing the duties of her position." - Reviewing Supervisor

PROFESSIONAL DEVELOPMENT

Certifications: Certified Public Accountant
Professional Training: 100+ hours in Accounting, Finance, Auditing, Compliance, and
Office Management disciplines
```

199

Daniel J. Dorotik, Jr., Lubbock, Texas

Compare this electronic resume as a text (.txt) file with Resume 198. Note the absence of font enhancements (bold, italic, greater font size, and small caps), bullets, lines, and centering.

3

P · A · R · T

Best Cover
Letter Tips

Best Cover Letter Tips at a Glance

Best Cover Letter Writing Tips

In an active job search, your cover letter and resume should complement one another. Both are tailored to a particular reader you have contacted or to a specific job target. To help you create the best cover letters for your resumes, this part of the book mentions and debunks some common myths about cover letters and presents tips for polishing the letters you write.

Myths About Cover Letters

1. **Resumes and cover letters are two separate documents that have little relation to each other.** The resume and cover letter work together in presenting you effectively to a prospective employer. The cover letter should mention the resume and call attention to some important aspect of it.

2. **The main purpose of the cover letter is to establish friendly rapport with the reader.** Resumes show that you *can* do the work required. The main purpose of cover letters is to express that you *want* to do the work required. But it doesn't hurt to display enthusiasm in your resumes and refer to your abilities in your cover letters.

3. **You can use the same cover letter for each reader of your resume.** Modify your cover letter for each reader so that it sounds fresh rather than canned. Chances are that in an active job search, you have already talked with the person who will interview you. Your cover letter should reflect that conversation and build on it.

4. **In a cover letter, you should mention any negative things about your education, work experience, life experience, or health to prepare the reader before an interview.** This is not the purpose of the cover letter. You might bring up these topics in the first or second interview, but only after the interviewer has shown interest in you or offered you a job. Even then, if you feel that you must mention something negative about your past, present it in a positive way, perhaps by saying how that experience has strengthened your will to work hard at any new job.

5. **It is more important to remove errors from a resume than from a cover letter because the resume is more important than the cover letter.** Both your resume and your cover letter should be free of errors. The cover letter is usually the first document a prospective employer sees. The first impression is often the most important one. If your cover letter has an embarrassing error in it, chances are good that the reader may not bother to read your resume or may read it with less interest.

6. **To make certain that your cover letter has no errors, you need just to proofread it or ask a friend to do so.** Trying to proofread your own cover letter is risky, even if you are good at grammar and writing. Once a

document is printed, it has an aura about it that may make it seem better written than it is. For this reason, you are likely to miss typos or other kinds of errors.

Relying on someone else is risky, too. If your friend is not good at grammar and writing, that person may not see any mistakes either. Try to find a proofreader, an editor, an English teacher, a professional writer, or an experienced secretary who can point out any errors you may have missed.

7. **After someone has proofread your letter, you can make a few changes to it and not have someone look at it again.** More errors creep into a document this way than you would think possible. The reason is that such changes are often done hastily, and haste can waste an error-free document. If you make *any* change to a document, ask someone to proofread it a final time just to make sure that you didn't introduce an error during the last stage of revision. If you can't find someone to help you, the next section gives you advice on how to eliminate common mistakes in cover letters.

Tips for Polishing Cover Letters

You might spend several days working on your resume, getting it just right and free of errors. But if you send it with a cover letter that is written quickly and contains even one conspicuous error, all your good efforts may be wasted. That error could be just the kind of mistake the reader is looking for to screen you out.

You can prevent this kind of tragedy by polishing your cover letter so that it is free of errors. The following tips can help you avoid or eliminate common errors in cover letters. If you become aware of these kinds of errors and know how to fix them, you can be more confident about the cover letters you send with your resumes.

Note that you can apply some of the following tips to your resume, especially the tips on grammar, punctuation, and word usage.

Using Good Strategies for Letters

1. **Use the postal abbreviation for the state in your mailing address.** See resume writing Tip 1 in Part 1.

2. **Make certain that the letter is addressed to a specific person and that you use this person's name in the salutation.** Avoid using such general salutations as Dear Sir or Madam, To Whom It May Concern, Dear Administrator, Dear Prospective Employer, and Dear Committee. In an active job search, you should do everything possible to send your cover letter and resume to a particular individual, preferably someone you've already talked with in person or by phone, and with whom you have arranged an interview. If you have not been able to make a personal contact, at least do everything possible to find out the name of the person who will read your letter and resume. Then address the letter to that person.

3. **Adjust the margins for a short letter.** If your cover letter is 300 words or longer, use left, right, top, and bottom margins of 1 inch. If the letter is shorter, you should increase the margins' width. How much to increase them is a matter of personal taste. One way to take care of the width of the top and bottom margins is to center a shorter letter vertically on the page. A maximum width

for a short cover letter of 100 words or fewer might be 2-inch left and right margins. As the number of words increases by 50 words, you might decrease the width of the left and right margins by two-tenths of an inch.

4. **If you write your letter with word-processing or desktop-publishing software, use left justification to ensure that the lines of text are readable and have fixed spacing between words.** The letter will have a "ragged right" look along the right margin, but the words will be evenly spaced horizontally. Don't use full justification (having each line end even with the right margin) in an attempt to give your letter a printed look. Unless you do other typesetting procedures, such as kerning and hyphenating words at the end of some lines, full justification can make your letter look worse by giving it some extra-wide and extra-narrow spaces between words.

Using Pronouns Correctly

5. **Use *I* and *My* sparingly.** When most of the sentences in a cover letter begin with *I* or *My*, you might appear self-absorbed, self-centered, or egotistical. If the reader is turned off by this kind of impression (even if it is a false one), you could be screened out without ever having an interview. Of course, you need to use these first-person pronouns sometimes because most of the information you put in your cover letter is personal. But try to avoid using *I* and *My* at the beginnings of sentences and paragraphs.

6. **Refer to a business, company, corporation, or organization as "it" rather than "they."** Members of the Board may be referred to as "they," but a company is a singular subject that requires a singular verb. Note this example:

> New Products, Inc., was established in 1980. It grossed more than $1 million in sales during its first year.

7. **If you start a sentence with *This,* be sure that what *This* refers to is clear.** If the reference is not clear, insert a word or phrase to clarify what *This* means. Compare the following:

> You should receive my revised application for the new position by fax on Friday. *This* should be acceptable to you.

> You should receive my revised application for the new position by fax on Friday. *This method of sending the application* should be acceptable to you.

A reader of the first sentence wouldn't know what *This* refers to. Friday? By fax on Friday? The revised application for the new position? The insertion after *This* in the second sentence, however, tells the reader that *This* refers to the use of faxing.

8. **Use *as follows* after a singular subject.** Literally, *as follows* means *as it follows,* so the phrase is illogical after a plural subject. Compare the following:

Incorrect:	My plans for the day of the interview are as follows:
Fixed:	My plans for the day of the interview are these:
Correct:	My plan for the day of the interview is as follows:
Better:	Here is my plan for the day of the interview:

The last version avoids a hidden reference problem—the possible association of the silent "it" with *interview*. Whenever you want to use *as follows,* check to see whether the subject that precedes *as follows* is plural. If it is, don't use this phrase.

Using Verb Forms Correctly

9. **Make certain that subjects and verbs agree in number.** Plural subjects require plural forms of verbs. Singular subjects require singular verb forms. Most writers know these things, but problems arise when subject-verb agreement gets tricky. Compare the following:

Incorrect:	My education and experience has prepared me....
Correct:	My education and experience have prepared me....

Incorrect:	Making plans plus scheduling conferences were....
Correct:	Making plans plus scheduling conferences was....

   In the first set, *education* and *experience* are two separate things (you can have one without the other) and therefore require a plural verb. A hasty writer might lump them together and use a singular verb. When you reread what you have written, look out for this kind of improper agreement between a plural subject and a singular verb.

   In the second set, *making plans* is the subject. It is singular, so the verb must be singular. The misleading part of this sentence is the phrase *plus scheduling conferences.* It may seem to make the subject plural, but it doesn't. In English, phrases that begin with such words as *plus, together with, in addition to, along with,* and *as well as* usually don't make a singular subject plural.

10. **Whenever possible, use active forms of verbs rather than passive forms.** Compare the following:

Passive:	My report will be sent by my assistant tomorrow.
Active:	My assistant will send my report tomorrow.

Passive:	Your interest is appreciated.
Active:	I appreciate your interest.

Passive:	Your letter was received yesterday.
Active:	I received your letter yesterday.

    Sentences with passive verbs are usually longer and clumsier than sentences with active verbs. Passive sentences often leave out the crucial information of who is performing the verb's action. Spot passive verbs by looking for some form of the verb *to be* (such as *be, will be, have been, is, was,* and *were*) used with another verb.

    In solving the passive-language problem, you might create another problem, such as using the pronouns *I* and *My* too frequently (see Tip 5 in this list). The task then becomes one of finding some other way to start a sentence while keeping your language active.

11. **Be sure that present and past participles are grammatically parallel in a list.** See Tip 50 in Part 1. What is true about parallel forms in resumes is true

also in cover letters. Present participles are action words that end in *-ing,* such as *creating, testing,* and *implementing.* Past participles are action words that usually end in *-ed,* such as *created, tested,* and *implemented.* These types of words are called *verbals* because they are derived from verbs but are not strong enough to function as verbs in a sentence. When you use a string of verbals, control them by keeping them parallel.

12. **Use split infinitives only when *not* splitting them is misleading or awkward.** An *infinitive* is a verb preceded by the preposition *to,* as in *to create, to test,* and *to implement.* You split an infinitive when you insert an adverb between the preposition and the verb, as in *to quickly create, to repeatedly test,* and *to slowly implement.* About 50 years ago, split infinitives were considered grammatical errors, but opinion about them has changed. Many grammar handbooks now recommend that you split your infinitives to avoid awkward or misleading sentences. Compare the following:

> Split infinitive: I plan to periodically send updated reports on my progress in school.
>
> Misleading: I plan periodically to send updated reports on my progress in school.
>
> Misleading: I plan to send periodically updated reports on my progress in school.

The first example is clear enough, but the second and third examples may be misleading. If you are uncomfortable with split infinitives, one solution is to move *periodically* further into the sentence: "I plan to send updated reports periodically on my progress in school."

Most handbooks that allow split infinitives also recommend that they not be split by more than one word, as in "to quickly and easily write." A gold medal for splitting an infinitive should go to Lowell Schmalz, an Archie Bunker prototype in "The Man Who Knew Coolidge" by Sinclair Lewis. Schmalz, who thought that Coolidge was one of America's greatest presidents, split an infinitive this way: "to instantly and without the least loss of time or effort find...."[1]

Using Punctuation Correctly

13. **Punctuate a compound sentence with a comma.** A compound sentence is one that contains two main clauses joined by one of seven conjunctions (*and, but, or, nor, for, yet,* and *so*). (A clause is a group of words containing a subject and a verb.) In English, a comma is customarily put before the conjunction if the sentence isn't unusually short. Here is an example of a compound sentence punctuated correctly:

> I plan to arrive at O'Hare at 9:35 a.m. on Thursday, and my trip by cab to your office should take no longer than 40 minutes.

The comma is important because it signals that a new grammatical subject (*trip,* the subject of the second main clause) is about to be expressed. If you use

---

[1] Sinclair Lewis, "The Man Who Knew Coolidge," *The Man Who Knew Coolidge* (New York: Books for Libraries Press, 1956), p. 29.

this kind of comma consistently, the reader will rely on your punctuation and be on the lookout for the next subject in a compound sentence.

14. **Be certain not to put a comma between compound verbs.** When a sentence has two verbs joined by the conjunction *and,* these verbs are called *compound verbs.* Usually, they should not be separated by a comma before the conjunction. Note the following examples:

> I *started* the letter last night *and finished* it this morning.

> I *am sending* my resume separately *and would like* you to keep the information confidential.

Both examples are simple sentences containing compound verbs. Therefore, no comma appears before *and.* In either case, a comma would send a wrong signal that a new subject in another main clause is coming, but no such subject exists.

15. **Use (or don't use) the serial comma consistently.** How should you punctuate a series of three or more items in a sentence? If, for example, you say in your cover letter that you increased sales by 100 percent, opened two new territories, and trained four new salespeople, the comma before *and* is called the *serial comma.* It is commonly omitted in newspapers, magazine articles, advertisements, and business documents. However, it is often used for precision in technical documents or for stylistic reasons in academic text, particularly in the Humanities.

16. **Avoid using *as well as* for *and* in a series.** Compare the following:

> | Incorrect: | Your company is impressive because it has offices in Canada, Mexico, as well as the United States. |
> |---|---|
> | Correct: | Your company is impressive because it has offices in Canada and Mexico, as well as in the United States. |

Usually, what is considered exceptional precedes the phrase *as well as,* and what is considered customary follows it. Note this example:

Your company is impressive because its managerial openings are filled by women as well as men.

17. **Put a comma after the year in a grouping of month, day, and year.** Similarly, put a comma after the state when it appears after the city. Compare the following pairs of examples:

> | Incorrect: | On January, 28, 2004 I was promoted to senior analyst. |
> |---|---|
> | Correct: | On January 28, 2004, I was promoted to senior analyst. |

> | Incorrect: | I worked in Springfield, Illinois before moving to Dallas. |
> |---|---|
> | Correct: | I worked in Springfield, Illinois, before moving to Dallas. |

18. **Put a comma after an opening dependent clause. An opening dependent clause often begins with a word such as "When," "If," "Because," or "Although" and cannot stand by itself as a separate sentence.** Compare the following:

> | Incorrect: | If you have any questions you may contact me by phone or e-mail. |
> |---|---|

Correct:	If you have any questions, you may contact me by phone or e-mail.

Actually, many writers of fiction and nonfiction don't use this kind of comma. The comma is useful, though, because it signals where the main clause begins. If you glance at the example with the comma, you can tell where the main clause is without even reading the opening clause. For a step up in clarity and readability, use this comma. It can give the reader a feel for a sentence even before he or she begins reading the words.

19. **Use semicolons when they are needed.** Semicolons are used to separate two main clauses when the second clause starts with a *conjunctive adverb* such as *however*, *moreover*, or *therefore*. Compare the following:

Incorrect:	Your position in sales looks interesting, however, I would like more information about it.
Correct:	Your position in sales looks interesting; however, I would like more information about it.

The first example is incorrect because the comma before *however* is a *comma splice,* which is a comma that joins two sentences. It's like putting a comma instead of a period at the end of the first sentence and then starting the second sentence. A comma may be a small punctuation mark, but a comma splice is a huge grammatical mistake. What are your chances of getting hired if your cover letter tells your reader that you don't recognize where a sentence ends, especially if a requirement for the job is good communication skills? Yes, you could be screened out because of one little comma!

20. **Avoid putting a colon after a verb or preposition to introduce information.** The reason is that the colon interrupts a continuing clause. Compare the following:

Incorrect:	My interests in your company are: its reputation, the review of salary after six months, and your personal desire to hire handicapped persons.
Correct:	My interests in your company are these: its reputation, the review of salary after six months, and your personal desire to hire handicapped persons.

Sometimes it is better to avoid the colon.

Better:	My interests in your company are its reputation, the review of salary after six months, and your personal desire to hire handicapped persons.

Although some people may say that it is OK to put a colon after a verb such as *include* if the list of information is long, it is better to be consistent and avoid colons after verbs altogether.

Incorrect:	My areas of expertise include: life insurance, health insurance, disability insurance, tax-deferred annuities, and retirement plans.
Correct:	My expertise includes these areas: life insurance, health insurance, disability insurance, tax-deferred annuities, and retirement plans.

Better:	My areas of expertise include life insurance, health insurance, disability insurance, tax-deferred annuities, and retirement plans.
Incorrect:	In my interview with you, I would like to: learn how your company was started, get your reaction to my updated portfolio, and discuss your department's plans to move to a new building.
Correct:	In my interview with you, I would like to discuss these issues: how your company was started, what you think of my updated portfolio, and when your department may move to a new building.
Better:	In my interview with you, I would like to discuss how your company was started, what you think of my updated portfolio, and when your department may move to a new building.

21. **Understand the use of colons.** People often associate colons with semicolons because their names sound alike, but colons and semicolons have nothing to do with each other. Colons are the opposite of dashes. Dashes look backward, whereas colons usually look forward to information about to be delivered.

Dash:	William joined the company—last week, I believe.
Colon:	Three items are on the agenda: a staff party, extended vacation time, and salary increases.

One common use of the colon does look backward, however. Here are two examples:

My experience with computers is limited: I have had only one course in programming, and I don't own a computer.

I must make a decision by Monday: that is the deadline for renewing the lease on my apartment.

In each example, what follows the colon explains what was said before the colon. Using a colon this way in a cover letter can impress a knowledgeable reader who is looking for evidence of writing skills.

22. **Use slashes correctly.** Information about slashes is sometimes hard to find because *slash* often is listed in grammar books under a different name, such as *virgule* or *solidus.* If you are unfamiliar with these terms, your hunt for advice on slashes may lead to nothing.

At least know that one important meaning of a slash is *or.* For this reason, you often see a slash in an expression such as ON/OFF. This usage means that a condition or state, such as that of electricity activated by a switch, is either ON *or* OFF but never ON *and* OFF at the same time. This condition may be one in which a change means going from the current state to the opposite (or alternate) state. If the current state is ON and there is a change, the next state is OFF, and vice versa. With this understanding, you can recognize the logic behind the following examples:

Incorrect:	ON-OFF switch (on and off at the same time!)
Correct:	ON/OFF switch (on or off at any time)
Correct:	his-her clothes (unisex clothes, worn by both sexes)
Correct:	his/her clothes (each sex had different clothes)

Note: Both his-her and his/her are clumsy. Try to find a way to avoid them. One way is to rephrase the sentence so that you use *their* or *your:*

> Campers should make their beds before breakfast.

> Please make your beds before breakfast.

Another way is to rephrase the sentence without possessive pronouns:

> Everyone should get dressed before going to breakfast.

23. **Think twice about using *and/or*.** This stilted expression is commonly misunderstood to mean *two* alternatives, but it literally means *three.* Consider the following example:

   If you don't hear from me by Friday, please call and/or e-mail me on Monday.

   What is the person at the other end to do? The sentence really states three alternatives: just call, just e-mail, or call *and* e-mail on Monday. For better clarity, use the connectives *and* or *or* whenever possible.

24. **Use punctuation correctly with quotation marks.** A common misconception is that commas and periods should be placed outside closing quotation marks, but the opposite is true. Compare the following:

Incorrect:	Your company certainly has the "leading edge", which means that its razor blades are the best on the market.
Correct:	Your company certainly has the "leading edge," which means that its razor blades are the best on the market.
Incorrect:	In the engineering department, my classmates referred to me as "the girl guru". I was the youngest expert in programming languages on campus.
Correct:	In the engineering department, my classmates referred to me as "the girl guru." I was the youngest expert in programming languages on campus.

   Note this exception: Unlike commas and periods, colons and semicolons go *outside* double quotation marks.

Using Words Correctly

25. **Avoid using lofty language in your cover letter.** A real turn-off in a cover letter is the use of elevated diction (high-sounding words and phrases) as an attempt to seem important. Note the following examples, along with their straight-talk translations:

Elevated:	My background has afforded me experience in…
Better:	In my previous jobs, I…
Elevated:	Prior to that term of employment…
Better:	Before I worked at…

Elevated:	I am someone with a results-driven profit orientation.
Better:	I want to make your company more profitable.
Elevated:	I hope to utilize my qualifications…
Better:	I want to use my skills…

In letter writing, the shortest distance between the writer and the reader is the most direct idea.

26. **Check your sentences for excessive use of compounds joined by *and*.** A cheap way to make your letters longer is to join words with *and* and to do this repeatedly. Note the following wordy sentence:

> Because of my background and preparation for work and advancement with your company and new enterprise, I have a concern and commitment to implement and put into effect my skills and abilities for new solutions and achievements above and beyond your dreams and expectations. [44 words]

Just one inflated sentence like that would drive a reader to say, "No way!" The writer of the inflated sentence has said only this:

> Because of my background and skills, I want to contribute to your new venture. [14 words]

If, during rereading, you eliminate the wordiness caused by this common writing weakness, an employer is more likely to read your letter completely.

27. **Avoid using abstract nouns excessively.** Look again at the inflated sentence in the preceding tip, but this time with the abstract nouns in italic:

> Because of my *background* and *preparation* for *work* and *advancement* with your *company* and new *enterprise*, I have a *concern* and *commitment* to implement and put into *effect* my *skills* and *abilities* for new *solutions* and *achievements* above and beyond your *dreams* and *expectations*.

Try picturing in your mind any of the words in italic. You can't because they are *abstract nouns*, which means that they are ideas and not images of things you can see, taste, hear, smell, or touch. One certain way to turn off the reader is to load your cover letter with abstract nouns. The following sentence, containing some images, has a better chance of capturing the reader's attention:

> Having created seven multimedia tutorials with my video camera and Gateway Pentium computer, I now want to create some breakthrough adult-learning packages so that your company, New Century Instructional Technologies, Inc., will exceed $50,000,000 in contracts by 2005.

Compare this sentence with the one loaded with abstract nouns. The one with images is obviously the better attention-grabber.

28. **Avoid wordy expressions in your cover letters.** Note the following examples in the first column and their shorter alternatives in the second column:

at the location of	at
for the reason that	because
in a short time	soon

in a timely manner	on time
in spite of everything to the contrary	nevertheless
in the event of	if
in the proximity of	near
now and then	occasionally
on a daily basis	daily
on a regular basis	regularly
on account of	because
one day from now	tomorrow
would you be so kind as to	please

Trim the fat wherever you can, and your reader will appreciate the leanness of your cover letter.

29. **At the end of your cover letter, don't make a statement that the reader can use to reject you.** For example, suppose that you close your letter with this statement:

   > If you wish to discuss this matter further, please call me at (555) 555-5555.

   This statement gives the reader a chance to think, "No, I don't wish to." Here is another example:

   > If you know of the right opportunity for me, please call me at (555) 555-5555.

   The reader may think, "I don't know of any such opportunity. How would I know what's right for you?" Avoid questions that prompt yes-or-no answers, such as, "Do you want to discuss this matter further?" If you ask this kind of question, you give the reader a chance to say no. Instead, make a closing statement that indicates your optimism about receiving a positive response from the reader. Such a statement might begin with one of the following clauses:

   > I am confident that....

   > I look forward to....

   In this way, you invite the reader to say yes to further consideration.

Exhibit of Cover Letters

The following Exhibit contains sample cover letters that were prepared by professional resume writers to accompany resumes submitted for this book. In most cases, the names, addresses, and facts have been changed to ensure the confidentiality of the original senders and recipients. For each letter, however, the essential substance of the original remains intact. Because each cover letter was written for a resume displayed in the Gallery, the resume number is indicated first, along with the name of the resume writer.

LAURI A. MARTINGALE

0000 Rising Sun Road ● **555-555-5555**
Salem, KY 55555 ● **martingale@email.com**

January 1, 2009

Ms. Gerri Smith
Equine Biomechanics
0000 Tennessee Lane, Suite 123
Lexington, Kentucky 55555

Dear Ms. Smith:

I am following up on my online submission regarding your organization's advertisement on Monster.com for an Equine Analyst. I was thrilled to find the Equine posting as my research background and equine skills meet your requirements for this position. Please allow me to briefly reiterate the positive qualities I can bring to Equine Biomechanics. I offer:

Superb administration, public relations and communications skills, developed through experience as a research analyst at the University of Kentucky.

Excellent analytical and organizational skills, demonstrated throughout my employment in data research, analysis and documentation.

Equine handling skills, established through years of experience in raising foals, training all age brackets (Quarter Horses and Thoroughbreds), serving as a handler/groomer for the Keeneland Yearling Sales (with most of the yearlings selling for more than $100K) and as barn manager and / or weekend caretaker for several farms in New York.

I am an individual who would bring a balance of analytical and nonanalytical skills to help your organization achieve success. I am self-motivated with an energetic style and quite eager to transition my skills to a position of responsibility within the equine industry.

Whatever task or project I undertake, I perform it to the best of my ability. My focus, drive and determination, coupled with my acute attention to detail, have progressed my career to date, and I intend to continue to apply this same level of expertise as a member of your team.

Since my resume is an overview of my background and accomplishments, I look forward to providing you with further insight into my professional value during a personal interview. Please contact me by phone or email to establish a mutually convenient time to meet.

Thank you in advance for your time and consideration. I look forward to speaking with you soon.

Sincerely,

Lauri A. Martingale

Enclosure

For Resume 12. *Tammy K. Shoup, Decatur, Indiana*

Horizontal lines enclosing the contact information make it easily seen. The letter expresses, in turn, the candidate's interest in the announced position, her focus, her credentials, and a probe for an interview.

William S. Beyer

78 Holcomb Drive • Franklin Park, NJ 08823 • 732-378-1972 • wsbeyer7@aol.com

DISTRIBUTION / WAREHOUSING SPECIALIST

Re: Distribution Position

Dear Sir or Madam:

Enclosed is my resume for your review. I am confident that my long-term chemical/food experience with various types of manufacturing positions would serve as an asset to an opening in your company.

I have 12 years of experience in working at Procter & Gamble as a Warehouse Specialist, Safety Leader, and Fork Lift driver. I have taken an early retirement package and would like to continue my manufacturing career with another company.

I am considered a quick learner with high concentration skills. As a Safety Leader, I have had the responsibility of making sure all plant personnel were properly trained and in compliance with OSHA guidelines. In addition, I feel that my interpersonal skills, honesty, and rapport with fellow employees will benefit the company.

Other skills that I have gained though my employment are ergonomics and shipping and receiving, as well as inventory control. I have always been known for my accuracy and hard-working attitude.

Thank you for your consideration. I look forward to speaking with you personally so that we may discuss my qualifications in greater detail.

Sincerely yours,

William S. Beyer

Enclosure

For Resume 63. *Beverly and Mitch Baskin, Marlboro, New Jersey*

The page border and bold, large type in the contact information complement the applicant's claim of being a confident, take-charge kind of employee. Short paragraphs make the reading tempo fast.

ANDREW G. LANE

0505 OLD MISSION DRIVE • KALAMAZOO, MICHIGAN 49505 • HOME: 505.555.0050 CELL: 505.005.5505

January 30, 2009

Mr. Jeremy Spears
Production Supervisor
Birmingham Automotive Corporation
55505 North Michigan
Dearborn, MI 45505

RE: Job Position of Supervising Welder (Job Posting 10045)

Dear Mr. Spears:

I think that you will agree that proper welding procedures and techniques are the most critical component of any automotive parts manufacturing operation. If you are interested in a professional supervising welder who can help you develop new welding standards and/or processes to improve the overall performance of your various product lines, we should talk.

Please consider my qualifications:

- Twelve years of experience as a lead welder/quality technician for a large, high-volume automotive parts corporation specializing in chassis and safety component manufacturing.
- Advanced MIG shop welding practices on automotive-grade steel and aluminum. A strong background in special welding processes, heat treatments, and nondestructive testing, which means I can bring immediate value to your company.
- An extensive background in ISO-9001/QS-9000 and Lean Manufacturing quality systems.
- Loyal, dedicated, and dependable hard worker.
- A strong team player with a knack for supervising others.

As you will note by the enclosed résumé, my career background is one of increasing responsibility, dedication, and solid accomplishments, especially in the areas of MIG welding processes and advanced welding techniques. While I am secure in my present position, I have reached a juncture in my career where I am highly motivated to look at other career opportunities that are available to me. I am most interested in a position that offers additional opportunities for advancement, a chance to lead and guide coworkers, and the ability to use my rich mix of skills to further serve an automotive company's needs.

It would be a pleasure to meet with you at your convenience to discuss the contributions I would make to your team. I am ready to put my energy and experience to work for you. I look forward to hearing from you soon.

Sincerely,

Andrew G. Lane

Encl.

3

For Resume 151. *Richard T. Porter, Portage, Michigan*

Boldfacing makes the target position stand out in the first paragraph. Diamond bullets call attention to achievements as work highlights after the second, main paragraph, which "sells" the candidate.

CHRISTOPHER STEPHENS

Eager to develop with new opportunities

c-stephens@ou.edu
Campus Address: 100 South Main Street, Ohio University, Athens, OH 45810 ▪ 937.306.1952
Permanent Address: 1864 Seneca Park Drive, Hamilton, OH 45504 ▪ 937.306.1948

September 8, 2009

PricewaterhouseCoopers LLP
Attention: Richard C. Stover
2080 Madison Tower
Dayton, OH 45423

Ladies and Gentlemen:

Passion: "Boundless enthusiasm."

As a freshman–year computer science major, I learned—too late in the semester to save my cumulative GPA—that this field was not my passion. Although freshman year may look like a disaster on paper, it was responsible for leading to my current major and a subsequent GPA reflective of **the right career choice.** As a result, I am finishing this quarter with a 3.75—the fifth quarter in a row above a 3.0. Because I enjoy Accounting and understand firsthand that **success and fulfillment stem from discovering and working in one's passion,** it is with great interest that I apply for the position of Staff 1 Accountant.

From hands-on internship experience, I understand that success boils down to three important factors in the Accounting industry:

- Structured goals and the implementation of a master plan to achieve those goals,
- Knowledge and transferable skills development to be successful, and
- Accurate, principled reporting and top-quality products and services to customers.

Transferable strengths offered to PricewaterhouseCoopers to meet these factors are the following:

☑ **Critical thinking** to gather, analyze, and disseminate decisive information regarding privacy, risk, internal controls, performance, and data analysis.

☑ **Positive communication** to foster collaborative working relationships and lend balance and structure to teams. I understand group dynamics, earn respect as a team member, and continually demonstrate the ability to use **well-honed speaking and listening skills.**

☑ **Mental toughness** to handle situations requiring determination and stress tolerance.

☑ **Energy** to multitask in fast–moving environments—structured or unstructured—to be productively competent.

Because proven skills are best explained in person, I look forward to discussing where your personnel needs and my qualifications intersect and can be reached at 937.306.1952 to arrange an interview. With a personal commitment to working with integrity and efficiency, I would relish the prospect of taking responsibility for a role where achievements are highly visible. I am confident you will find me to be versatile and 100% capable of contributing to PricewaterhouseCoopers' mission. Thank you for your professional courtesy in reviewing my résumé.

Sincerely,

Christopher Stephens

Encl: Résumé

4

Sharon Pierce-Williams, Findlay, Ohio

The letter makes clear the applicant's target position, recently acquired knowledge, plans for additional learning, experience and skills, and interest in contributing to the prospective company.

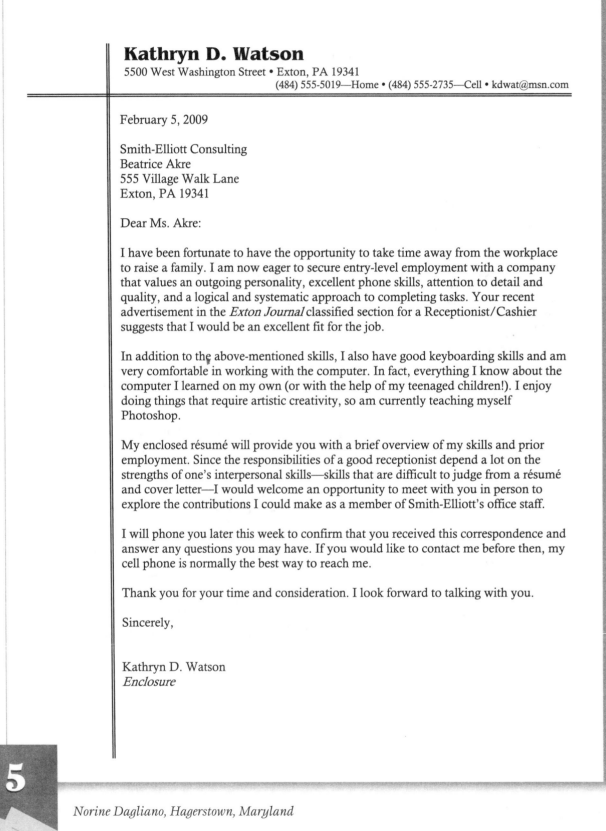

Kathryn D. Watson

5500 West Washington Street • Exton, PA 19341
(484) 555-5019—Home • (484) 555-2735—Cell • kdwat@msn.com

February 5, 2009

Smith-Elliott Consulting
Beatrice Akre
555 Village Walk Lane
Exton, PA 19341

Dear Ms. Akre:

I have been fortunate to have the opportunity to take time away from the workplace to raise a family. I am now eager to secure entry-level employment with a company that values an outgoing personality, excellent phone skills, attention to detail and quality, and a logical and systematic approach to completing tasks. Your recent advertisement in the *Exton Journal* classified section for a Receptionist/Cashier suggests that I would be an excellent fit for the job.

In addition to the above-mentioned skills, I also have good keyboarding skills and am very comfortable in working with the computer. In fact, everything I know about the computer I learned on my own (or with the help of my teenaged children!). I enjoy doing things that require artistic creativity, so am currently teaching myself Photoshop.

My enclosed résumé will provide you with a brief overview of my skills and prior employment. Since the responsibilities of a good receptionist depend a lot on the strengths of one's interpersonal skills—skills that are difficult to judge from a résumé and cover letter—I would welcome an opportunity to meet with you in person to explore the contributions I could make as a member of Smith-Elliott's office staff.

I will phone you later this week to confirm that you received this correspondence and answer any questions you may have. If you would like to contact me before then, my cell phone is normally the best way to reach me.

Thank you for your time and consideration. I look forward to talking with you.

Sincerely,

Kathryn D. Watson
Enclosure

5

Norine Dagliano, Hagerstown, Maryland

The first paragraph expresses the candidate's interest in the position, and the next three paragraphs show how she is the best match for the position. The last paragraph calls for an interview.

Michael J. Fisher, C.M.C.

56 Madison Avenue
Summit, New Jersey 07901
(908) 277-8796

Dear Sir/Madam:

Enclosed is my resume for your review. I am confident that my extensive experience as an executive chef and hotel/restaurant manager would serve as an asset to a position in your organization. My career began 23 years ago as an apprentice training under several internationally known chefs. Since that time I have been involved extensively in the area of food services management and marketing.

I am currently General Manager and Corporate Executive Chef of Hague Nieuw-York. In 1999 I was hired to start up this 225-seat restaurant. The casual dining establishment is part of Avanti Brands, Inc., USA. I am responsible for all financial reporting and instituted key control systems to meet the standards of the parent company. Additional achievements include gaining excellent media publicity, creative menu development, and directing on- and off-site catering for many New York City premiers. I was asked to coordinate all aspects of our new construction and to assist in the design aspects of the kitchen.

As Director of Operations for Town Square Katering and Times Square Restaurant in Hoboken, New Jersey, I expanded the business to accommodate parties ranging from 10 to 4,000 people and grossed more than $1.5 million in sales.

Working as Vice President of Operations and Executive Chef for Pine Ridge Country Club, I oversaw all profit-and-loss functions for a 165-seat a la carte restaurant and a 1,000-seat banquet facility. The club had an 18-hole Championship Golf Course that I managed, with an active membership of 1,000 members.

I gained extensive international experience working as Executive Chef for Ordini's, a five-star restaurant in New Zealand, where I prepared food for the Prime Minister, various heads of state, and visiting dignitaries. I obtained my New Zealand Master Chef's Certification. In addition, I served as an Executive Pastry Chef and Chef for a Hawaiian hotel owned and operated by the Sheraton Corporation.

Thank you for your consideration. I look forward to speaking with you personally regarding my qualifications and how I can contribute positively as a member of your management staff.

Sincerely yours,

Michael J. Fisher, C.M.C.

Enclosure

6

For Resume 100. *Beverly and Mitch Baskin, Marlboro, New Jersey*

The opening paragraph gives an overall picture of the candidate's career. The next four paragraphs express, in turn, the major positions, responsibilities, and achievements of his notable career.

PHYLLIS MARTIN, PHR

(555) 555-5555

5555 Maxwell, Clearview, Texas 79000

July 12, 2004

Sid Critefelder
Vice President of Human Resources
NATURAL GAS COMPANY
P.O. Box 5555
Panhandle, Texas 79408

RE: HUMAN RESOURCES GENERALIST

Dear Mr. Critefelder:

Your recent HR generalist vacancy has prompted me to send you my résumé for review. As you will discover, I offer the depth of experience necessary to successfully administer safety, benefits, and compensation programs; recruit, train, develop, and retain staff; build community relations; assess and fulfill staffing needs, and evaluate/revise policies and procedures. **My 14 years of collective HR experience** also indicates a comprehensive knowledge of state and federal personnel regulations. Additionally, my history reflects a loyal, stable employee who thrives on increasing responsibility and progressive learning. It would be an honor to contribute to a corporate culture, such as yours, that values people and appreciates differences.

The following attributes and well-developed skills are additional reasons to take a close look at my credentials:

HUMAN RESOURCES ADMINISTRATION
- Integrity, loyalty, and diligence earn respect and reflect distinction.
- Ownership of responsibility and accountability demonstrate leadership and character.
- Time-management and organization skills help streamline tasks and cultivate efficiency.
- Investigation and discernment foster effective problem resolution.
- Analysis and interpretation skills assist in understanding guidelines, policies, and procedures.

COMMUNICATION / INTERPERSONAL SKILLS
- Direct communication and appropriate interpersonal style enhance understanding.
- Enthusiastic presentation stimulates interest in and retention of material.
- Attentive listening enhances interviewing, counseling, and mediating.
- Professional/personal security reflect a genuine person who easily integrates into teams.
- Ability to build rapport strengthens community ties and maintains valuable resources.
- Persuasiveness sells ideas and promotes acceptance of change.

PERSONAL CHARACTERISTICS
- Friendly, personable, helpful attitude contributes to an accommodating environment.
- Attention to details and focus on excellence inspire others to excel.
- Capacity to easily learn and retain procedural information suggests decreased training time.
- Willingness to embrace challenging, changing situations indicates flexibility and adaptation.
- A sense of humor and positive outlook help ease stress in the workplace.

Experience, confidence, and drive will enable me to make significant contributions to your HR goals. Since a personal interview would benefit us both, I will contact you within the week to schedule an appointment at your convenience. In the meantime, thank you for your consideration.

Sincerely,

Phyllis Martin, PHR

Enclosure: Résumé

Edith A. Rische, Lubbock, Texas

Boldfacing in the first paragraph makes the applicant's experience stand out. Each bulleted item is a sentence indicating the person's value or potential benefit to the prospective company.

Robert Render
147 Englishtown Road ~ Old Bridge Township, NJ 08857
(732) 555-5555 (H) ~ E-mail: render538@aol.com

MAINTENANCE SPECIALIST

Dear Sir/Madam:

As a professional **Maintenance Specialist**, I understand that success depends on several factors. These include attention to detail during manufacturing, continual upkeep of machinery, supervision of maintenance programs, and monitoring outside contractors. My extensive work experience has allowed me to ensure product quality during production, timely completion of projects, and adherence to corporate safety requirements.

Throughout my career I have been promoted and have acquired increasing responsibilities within every position. In my latest position as a Maintenance Leader for Procter & Gamble, I had the reputation for excellent machinery knowledge.

Procter & Gamble is downsizing the plant in Dayton, New Jersey, and I have accepted a voluntary separation package from the company. I would like to continue my career with a different company offering me new challenges.

Thank you for your consideration. I possess excellent hands-on knowledge as well as supervisory expertise. I look forward to meeting with you personally so that we may discuss how I can make a positive contribution to your team.

Very truly yours,

Robert Render

Enclosure

8

For Resume 123. *Beverly and Mitch Baskin, Marlboro, New Jersey*

The first paragraph summarizes the candidate's success as a worker. The second and third paragraphs indicate his last position, his reason for leaving it, and his desire for a new position.

CONFIDENTIAL   *Ready to relocate to the Clovis area*

Charles Henry Kraft
2102 Sledgeway Street – Anchorage, Alaska 99517
☎ 907.555.5555 (Cell) – apmaster@whiz.att.net

November 26, 2004

Mr. Joe North
Director of Maintenance
TopLine Airlines, Inc.
500 Northridge Parkway
Suite 400
Clovis, New Mexico 87000

Dear Mr. North:

I want to make it easy for you to add me to your team as your newest aircraft maintenance supervisor.

As a first step, I thought you deserved to see more than the usual tired lists of jobs held and training completed. In their place you'll find a half dozen examples of maintenance teams motivated, productivity boosted, liability reduced—in short, problems solved. And, while a résumé format tailored to your needs is good at documenting results, it cannot tell you *how* I contribute to our leadership's peace of mind.

Therefore, as you read, I hope the following ideas stand out:

- ❏ I am only as good as the last job I signed off—conditions in the remote parts of Alaska leave even less room for maintenance errors.

- ❏ I am only as good as my last quarter's MX statistics. If I don't spot and correct trends, we'll lose time and money.

- ❏ I am only as good as the teams I attract, recruit, train, and retain. Our labor market is among the tightest in the nation.

I'm employed now, and my company likes my work. However, I want to relocate to be closer to my family. That's why I am testing the waters with this confidential application.

When it comes to something as important as finding TopLine Airlines's next aircraft maintenance supervisor, words on paper are no substitute for people speaking with people. So let me suggest a next step. I'd like to get on your calendar in a few days so we can explore how I might serve your special maintenance needs.

Sincerely,

Charles Henry Kraft

Encl.: Résumé

CONFIDENTIAL

9

For Resume 124. *Don Orlando, Montgomery, Alabama*

The writer of this letter is a master at avoiding the typical, the expected, and the dull. As you examine this letter, note the many ways it avoids being a conventional, ordinary cover letter.

James Howard

7777 Tracer Downs ◆ Perry, GA 00000 ◆ (H) 000–000–0000 ◆ (C) 000–000–0000

(Date)

Mr. (Ms.) _____
(Company)
(Address 1)
(Address 2)

Dear Mr. _____ :

(Insert 2-line paragraph about how you heard of the position and why you are applying for it. For example: "If the information in the *Times Courier* is still accurate, I am currently seeking to fill the position of Customer Service Manager. This letter is to introduce myself as a candidate for just such a position.")

I am an experienced and highly qualified management professional. My areas of expertise lie in operations management, facilities management, transportation and embarkation, inventory and logistics, purchasing and procurement, personnel and human resources, materials management, public and motivational speaking, written and oral communications, information gathering, data analysis, team coordination and budget administration. I accepted my current position with the Air Logistics Center at Robins AFB, GA, in an attempt to gain meaningful employment within the infrastructure of civil service. Because opportunities for advancement from this position are quite limited, I am seeking a position within the community at large where my wealth of knowledge and expertise can be fully utilized to the benefit of both my employer and myself.

The enclosed résumé briefly outlines my experience and accomplishments. If it appears that my qualifications meet your current needs, I would be happy to discuss my background in a meeting with you. Please feel free to contact me at the above telephone number.

Sincerely,

James Howard

Enclosure

10

For Resume 137. *Lea J. "Laila" Clark-Salaam, Atlanta, Georgia*

The letter begins with a "stage direction" for you to follow at the beginning if you adapt this letter to your own situation and job search. You would then tailor the next paragraph to your experience.

ELIZABETH GREEN

5555 Oak Tree Lane • Northridge, CA 55555
(818) 555-5555 • egreen@email.com

[Date]

[Name]
[Address]
[City, State Zip]

Dear [Salutation]:

If you are seeking a motivated and detail-oriented Purchasing Professional with a proven ability to streamline operations, motivate teams and achieve significant cost savings in a multimillion-dollar environment, my enclosed résumé should be of interest to you.

Common themes that have run throughout my professional career have included outstanding team-building and leadership strengths, as well as my ability to see the "big picture"—integrating the purchasing function into corporate goals. Representative of my past accomplishments are the following:

- Directed $200 million purchasing unit for West Coast Entertainment Company
- Hired, trained and motivated top-performing team members
- Consistently identified and developed talent in others
- Employed technology to streamline procedures, including automating the downloading of purchasing orders to the Letter of Credit system, improving on-time issuance from 20% to 75% within two years
- Consolidated supplier base from 1,200 to 650 within one year
- Sourced and developed excellent working relationships with outside and internal vendors
- Participated in key negotiations

I am currently seeking a new professional challenge where I can make a positive contribution to future goals and success. I possess a high level of energy and motivation, learn quickly, adapt well to new environments and enjoy challenges. I look forward to a personal meeting at which time we can discuss your needs and my qualifications in detail. Please don't hesitate to call me at the above number to set up a meeting. Thank you in advance for your time and consideration.

Sincerely,

Elizabeth Green

Enclosure

11

For Resume 156. *Vivian VanLier, Los Angeles, California*

This letter draws attention to the applicant's scope of responsibilities and strengths. Bullets point to achievements, enabling the reader to see at a glance what the applicant brings to the table.

Steven Brooks

1111 Lawrenceville Road ◆ Haven, CT 00000 ◆ 000–000–0000 ◆ user@adelphia.net

(Date)

(contact name)
(company name)
(street address)
(city, state, zip code)

Dear Hiring Professional (or insert contact name):

As a goal-oriented, progressive individual with more than 20 years of combined experience in positions that allowed for the development of diverse skills and proactive management in the areas of Recruiting and Information Technology, I feel my skills and qualifications are ideal to fill the position of (insert job title) in your (insert department), as listed with (insert source) on (insert date).

My background has positioned me to accept employment where I can make use of a wide range of skill sets within a small to midsized organization. The ideal position will allow me to provide a wealth of experience to employ a combination of strategic marketing, budget administration, and technological and sourcing skills to grow revenues and increase bottom-line profitability.

I have enclosed a copy of my résumé for your review. Please feel free to contact me, at your convenience, if you have any questions or would like to schedule an interview. I look forward to discussing the mutual benefit of our association.

Thank you for your time and consideration.

Sincerely,

Steven Brooks

12

For Resume 161. *Lea J. "Laila" Clark-Salaam, Atlanta, Georgia*

You can easily adapt this letter to your own job search by noting the information called for within parentheses and changing the language to match your worker traits, experience, skills, and goals.

List of Contributors

List of Contributors

The following professional resume writers contributed the resumes and cover letters in this book. All the contributors are professional resume writers. To include in this appendix the names of these writers and information about their businesses is to acknowledge with appreciation their voluntary submissions and the insights expressed in the e-mails that accompanied their submissions. Resume and cover letter numbers after a writer's contact information are the *numbers of the writer's resumes and cover letters* included in the Gallery, not page numbers.

Australia

New South Wales

Sydney

Jennifer Rushton
Keraijen
Level 14, 309 Kent St.
Sydney NSW 2000
Phone: 61 2 9994 8050
E-mail: info@keraijen.com.au
Web site: www.keraijen.com.au
Member: The Alliance, CDI, AORCP
Certifications: CARW, CERW, CEIC, CWPP
Resume: 113

Victoria

Hallum

Annemarie Cross
Advanced Employment Concepts
P.O. Box 91
Hallam, Victoria, 3803
Phone: 61 3 9708 6930
Fax: 61 3 9796 4479
E-mail: success@aresumewriter.com.au
Web site: www.aresumewriter.com.au
Member: The Alliance, CDI, CDAA
Certifications: CERW, CMRW, CPBS, CARW, CWPP, CCM, CPRW, CEIP
Resume: 9

Melbourne

Gayle Howard
Top Margin Career Marketing
P.O. Box 74
Chirnside Park, Melbourne, Victoria 3116
Phone: 61 3 9726 6694
E-mail: getinterviews@topmargin.com
Web site: www.topmargin.com
Member: The Alliance, CDI, AORCP, ACP
Certifications: MRW, CERW, CCM, MCP, RPBS, CRS + IT, CWPP
Resumes: 64, 108, 175, 189

Canada

Ontario

Aurora

Marian Bernard
Principal
The Regency Group (d.b.a. Regency Secretarial)
6 Morning Crescent
Aurora, Ontario
L4G 2E3
Phone: (905) 841-7120
Fax: (905) 841-1391
E-mail: marian@neptune.on.ca
Web site: www.resumeexpert.ca
Member: The Alliance, PARW/CC
Certifications: CPS, CPRW, JCTC, CEIP
Resumes: 146, 172

Whitby

Ross Macpherson
Career Quest
131 Kirby Crescent
Whitby, Ontario
L1N 7C7
Phone: (905) 438-8548
Toll-free: (877) 426-8548
Fax: (905) 438-4096
E-mail: ross@yourcareerquest.com
Web site: www.yourcareerquest.com
Member: The Alliance, PARW/CC, ACP
  International
Certifications: MA, CPRW, CJST, CEIP, JCTC
Resumes: 42, 50, 74, 84, 98, 110, 150, 170, 173,
  174, 177, 190

United States

Alabama

Montgomery

Don Orlando
The McLean Group
640 S. McDonough St.
Montgomery, AL 36104
Phone: (334) 264-2020
Fax: (334) 264-9227
E-mail: yourcareercoach@charterinternet.com
Member: The Alliance, PARW/CC
Certifications: CPRW, JCTC, CCM, CCMC, MBA
Resumes: 45, 78, 124, 135
Cover letter: 9

Arizona

Chandler

Wanda McLaughlin
Execuwrite
Chandler, AZ
Phone: (480) 732-7966
Toll-free (866) 732-7966
Member: PARW/CC, The Alliance, NRWA
Certifications: CPRW, CEIP
Resume: 60

Phoenix

Helen Oliff
Principal
Turning Point
Phoenix, AZ
Phone: (703) 346-8888

Fax: (801) 601-0077
E-mail: helen@turningpointnow.com
Web site: www.turningpointnow.com
Member: The Alliance, PARW
Certifications: CFRWC, CPRW, ECI
Resumes: 101, 115, 134, 185

Arkansas

Hot Springs Village

Beverley Drake
39 Reclamo Circle
Hot Springs Village, AR 71909
Phone: (501) 922-0893
E-mail: bdcprw@aol.com
Member: PARW
Certifications: CEIP, IJCTC, CPRW
Resume: 142

California

Los Angeles

Vivian VanLier
Advantage Career Services
6701 Murietta Ave.
Valley Glen, CA 91405
Phone: (818) 994-6655
Fax: (818) 994-6620
E-mail: vivianvanlier@aol.com
Web site: www.CareerCoach4U.com
Member: The Alliance, NRWA, PARW/CC
Certifications: CPRW, JCTC, CEIP, CCMC, CPRC,
  CRBS
Resumes: 7, 16, 87, 117, 156, 165
Cover letter: 11

San Jose

Georgia Adamson
A Successful Career
1096 N. Central Ave.
San Jose, CA 95128
Phone: (408) 244-6401
E-mail: success@ablueribbonresume.com
Web site: www.ABlueRibbonResume.com
Member: The Alliance, NRWA, PARW
Certifications: CCMC, CCM, CEIP, CPRW, JCTC,
  MRW
Resume: 158

Torrance

Gail Taylor
A Hire Power Résumé
21213-B Hawthorne Blvd., #5224

Torrance, CA 90503
Phone: (424) 247-9978
Fax: (310) 421-9213
E-mail: hirepwr@yahoo.com
Web site: www.call4hirepower.com
Member: EFA
Certifications: CEIP, CPRW
Resume: 38

Valencia

Myriam-Rose Kohn
JEDA Enterprises
27201 Tourney Rd., Ste. 201M
Valencia, CA 91355-1857
Phone: (661) 253-0801
Toll-free: (800) 600-JEDA
Fax: (661) 253-0744
E-mail: myriam-rose@jedaenterprises.com
Web site: www.jedaenterprises.com
Member: The Alliance, NRWA, PARW/CC
Certifications: CPRW, CEIP, IJCTC, CCM, CCMC
Resumes: 19, 33, 176

Colorado

Aurora

Michele Angello
Advance Your Career Resume
19866 E. Dickenson Place
Aurora, CO 80013
Phone: (303) 537-3592
Fax: (303) 537-3542
E-mail: michele@aycresume.com
Web site: www.advanceyourcareerresume.com
Member: PARW/CC, The Alliance
Certification: CPRW
Resumes: 21, 51, 66, 70, 91, 143, 195

Louisville

Roberta F. Gamza
Career Ink
Louisville, CO
Phone: (303) 955-3065
Fax: (303) 955-3065
E-mail: roberta@careerink.com
Web site: www.careerink.com
Member: The Alliance, NRWA
Certifications: CEIP, CTC, CJST
Resumes: 89, 167, 179

Connecticut

Wethersfield

Ross Primack
Connecticut Labor Department
200 Folly Brook Blvd.
Wethersfield, CT 06109
Phone: (860) 263-6041
Fax: (860) 263-6041
E-mail: rossprimackcprw@hotmail.com
Member: CMI, PARW
Certifications: CPRW, CEIP, GCDF
Resume: 147

Windsor

Louise Garver
Career Directions, LLC
Windsor, CT
Phone: (860) 623-9476
Fax: (860) 623-9473
E-mail: careerpro@cox.net
Web site: www.careerdirectionsllc.com
Member: The Alliance, NRWA, PARW/CC, ACA,
    NCDA, ACPI, CPADN
Certifications: MA, JCTC, CMP, CPRW, MCDP,
    CEIP, CPBS, CLBF, CRC
Resumes: 2, 69, 106, 128, 181, 184, 186

Florida

Bonita Springs

Edward Turilli
AccuWriter Resume Service
Bonita Springs, FL
Phone: (239) 298-9514
E-mail: edtur@cox.net
Web site: www.resumes4-u.com
Certifications: MA, CPRW
Resumes: 1, 32, 81

Tampa

Gail Frank
Employment U
10409 Greendale Dr.
Tampa, FL 33626
Phone: (813) 926-1353
Fax: (813) 926-1092
E-mail: gailfrank@post.harvard.edu
Web site: www.EmploymentU.com
Member: PARW, NRWA, PRWRA, CMI, SHRM,
    ASTD
Certifications: NCRW, CPRW, JCTC, CEIP, MA
Resumes: 31, 56, 65

Georgia

Atlanta

Lea J. "Laila" Clark-Salaam
ProWriter
116 Vanira Ave. SE
Atlanta, GA 30315
Phone: (770) 882-6196
Fax: (404) 963-6613
E-mail: lea@prowriter.us
Web site: www.prowriter.us
Certifications: CRW, BIT, Certified Editor
Resumes: 137, 161
Cover letters: 10, 12

Hawaii

Mountain View

Denette D. Jones
Jones Career Specialties
P.O. Box 711523
Mountain View, HI 96771
Phone: (808) 430-1177
E-mail: dj@jonescareerspecialties.net
Web site: www.jonescareerspecialties.net
Member: The Alliance, NRWA, CDI
Resumes: 18, 61, 109, 126, 168, 191

Illinois

Lincolnshire

Christine L. Dennison
Dennison Career Services
Lincolnshire, IL 60069
Phone: (847) 405-9775
E-mail: chris@thejobsearchcoach.com
Web site: www.thejobsearchcoach.com
Member: PARW/CC, The Alliance, Greater
   Lincolnshire Chamber of Commerce
Certification: CPC
Resume: 164

Schaumburg

Rosemary Fish Justen
Creative Communication Services, Inc.
1025 Southbridge Lane
Schaumburg, IL 60194-2265
Phone: (847) 490-8686
E-mail: rosemary@CCSResumes.com
Web site: www.CCSResumes.com
Member: PARW/CC

Certification: CPRW
Resumes: 62, 141, 160, 178

Waukegan

Eva Locke
Resource Specialist
Lake County Workforce Development
1 N. Genesee St.
Waukegan, IL 60085
Phone: (847) 377-3456
E-mail: elocke@co.lake.il.us
Web site: www.lakecountyjobcenter.com
Member: CDI
Resume: 71

Indiana

Decatur

Tammy K. Shoup
Breakthrough Resume Writing Service
Decatur, IN 46733
Phone: (260) 223-1821
E-mail: AWordpro@aol.com
Web site: www.breakthroughresumes.com
Member: PARW/CC
Certification: CPRW
Resumes: 12, 127, 153
Cover letter: 1

Maryland

Hagerstown

Norine Dagliano
ekm Inspirations
14 N. Potomac St., Ste. 200A
Hagerstown, MD 21740
Phone: (301) 766-2032
Fax: (301) 745-5700
E-mail: norine@ekminspirations.com
Web site: www.ekminspirations.com
Member: The Alliance, PARW/CC
Certifications: CPRW, CFRW/CC
Resumes: 14, 26, 41, 58, 68, 77, 188, 192
Cover letter: 5

Massachusetts

Concord

Jean Cummings
A Resume For Today
123 Minot Rd.

Concord, MA 01742
Phone: (978) 254-5492
E-mail: jc@YesResumes.com
Web site: www.aResumeForToday.com
Member: Reach, Inc.; NRWA, PARW/CC, The
  Alliance
Certifications: CPBS, CPRW, CEIP
Resumes: 107, 111, 159

Groton

Carol Nason
Career Advantage
95 Flavell Rd.
Groton, MA 01450-1536
Phone: (978) 448-3319
Fax: (978) 448-8948
E-mail: nason1046@aol.com
Web site: acareeradvantageresume.com
Member: The Alliance, PARW/CC, NRWA
Certifications: MA, CPRW
Resume: 95

Needham

Wendy Gelberg
Gentle Job Search
Advantage Resumes
21 Hawthorn Ave.
Needham, MA 02492
Phone: (781) 444-0778
Fax: (781) 455-0778
E-mail: WGelberg@aol.com
Member: NRWA, The Alliance
Certifications: M.Ed., CPRW, CEIP, IJCTC
Resumes: 3, 194

Westford

Jeanne Knight
Career and Job Search Coach
P.O. Box 162
Westford, MA 01886
Phone: (617) 968-7747
E-mail: jeanne@careerdesigns.biz
Web site: www.careerdesigns.biz
Member: The Alliance, NRWA, CCCNE
Certifications: JCTC, CCMC
Resume: 112

Michigan

Brighton

Lorie Lebert
Résumés For Results/The Loriel Group
P.O. Box 91
Brighton, MI 48116

Phone: (810) 229-6811
Toll-free: (800) 870-9059
Fax: (810) 222-0101
E-mail: Lorie@ResumeROI.com
Web sites: www.ResumeROI.com and
  www.CoachingROI.com
Member: The Alliance, PARW/CC, CDI
Certifications: CPRW, JCTC, CCMC
Resume: 88

Flint

Janet L. Beckstrom
Word Crafter
1717 Montclair Ave.
Flint, MI 48503-2074
Toll-free: (800) 351-9818
Fax: (810) 232-9257
E-mail: wordcrafter@voyager.net
Member: The Alliance, PARW/CC
Certification: CPRW
Resumes: 52, 73, 119

Portage

Richard T. Porter
CareerWise Communications, LLC
332 Magellan Ct.
Portage, MI 49002-7000
Phone: (269) 321-0183
Fax: (269) 321-0191
Toll-free fax: (888) 565-7109
E-mail: careerwise_resumes@yahoo.com
Member: The Alliance, PARW/CC
Resumes: 44, 151
Cover letter: 3

New Jersey

Edison

Patricia Duckers
Prism Writing Services, LLC
P.O. Box 6434
Edison, NJ 08818-6434
Phone: (732) 239-2240
Fax: (732) 906-5636
E-mail: sales@prismwritingservices.com
Web site: www.prismwritingservices.com
Member: CDI, The Alliance, PRWRA/CC, NAFE
Certifications: CPRW, CERW, CFRWC, CEIP,
  CFRW, CMRW, CWPP
Resume: 162

Flemington

Carol A. Altomare
World Class Résumés
P.O. Box 483

Three Bridges, NJ 08887-0483
Phone: (908) 237-1883
Toll-free: (877) 771-6170
Fax: (908) 237-2069
E-mail: caa@worldclassresumes.com
Web site: www.worldclassresumes.com
Member: PARW/CC, The Alliance
Certifications: CPRW, MRW
Resumes: 15, 105, 132

Mahwah

Igor Shpudejko
Career Focus
23 Parsons Ct.
Mahwah, NJ 07430
Phone: (201) 825-2865
Fax: (201) 825-7711
E-mail: Ishpudejko@aol.com
Web sites: www.careerinfocus.com and
www.anexecutiveresumewriter.com
Member: The Alliance, PARW/CC
Certifications: CPRW, JCTC, MBA, BSIE
Resume: 138

Marlboro

Beverly and Mitch Baskin
BBCS Counseling Services
6 Alberta Dr.
Marlboro, NJ 07746
Other offices: 33 Wood Ave. S., Ste. 400, Iselin, NJ
    08830; 4400 Rte. 9 S., Freehold, NJ 07728;
    Carnegie Center, Princeton, NJ 08540
Toll-free: (800) 300-4079
Fax: (732) 972-8846
E-mail: bbcs@att.net or info@bbcscounseling.com
Web sites: www.baskincareer.com,
    www.resumewriternj.com, and
    www.bbcscounseling.com
Member: NRWA, NCDA, NECA, MACCA,
    AMHCA, NJCA
Certifications: Ed.S, MA, MS, LPC, NCCC, CPRW,
    MCC, PE, NAJST
Resumes: 8, 59, 63, 100, 120, 123, 149, 157
Cover letters: 2, 6, 8

West Paterson

Melanie Noonan
Peripheral Pro, LLC
560 Lackawanna Ave.
West Paterson, NJ 07424
Phone: (973) 785-3011
Fax: (973) 256-6285
E-mail: PeriPro1@aol.com
Member: NRWA, PARW/CC

Certification: CPS
Resumes: 20, 25, 43, 46, 47, 76

New York

Altamont

John Femia
Custom Résumé & Writing Service
1690 Township Rd.
Altamont, NY 12009
Phone: (518) 872-1305
Fax: (518) 872-1305
E-mail: customresume1@aol.com
Web site: www.customresumewriting.com
Member: PARW/CC
Certification: CPRW
Resumes: 13, 55

East Islip

Ann Baehr
Best Resumes of New York
49 Fern Ave.
East Islip, NY
Phone: (631) 224-9300
Fax: (916) 314-6871
E-mail: resumesbest@earthlink.net
Web site: www.ebestresumes.com
Member: The Alliance, NRWA
Certification: CPRW
Resumes: 125, 155

Huntington

M J Feld, MS
Careers by Choice, Inc.
205 E. Main St., Ste. 2-4
Huntington, NY 11743
Phone: (631) 673-5432
Fax: (631) 673-5824
E-mail: mj@careersbychoice.com
Web site: www.careersbychoice.com
Member: PARW/CC
Certifications: MS, CPRW
Resumes: 17, 28, 39, 92

Poughkeepsie

Kristin M. Coleman
Kristin Coleman Career Services
44 Hillcrest Dr.
Poughkeepsie, NY 12603
Phone: (845) 452-8274
Fax: (845) 452-7789
E-mail: kristin@colemancareerservices.com
Member: The Alliance
Resumes: 10, 49, 121, 131, 154

Smithtown

Linda Matias
CareerStrides
37 E. Hill Dr.
Smithtown, NY 11787
Fax: (631) 382-2425
E-mail: linda@careerstrides.com
Web site: www.careerstrides.com
Member: The Alliance, NRWA, PARW/CC
Certifications: CEIP, JCTC
Resume: 30

North Carolina

Charlotte

Doug Morrison
Career Power
2915 Providence Rd., Ste. 250-B
Charlotte, NC 28211
Phone: (704) 365-0773
Fax: (704) 365-3411
E-mail: dmpwresume@aol.com
Web site: www.CareerPowerResume.com
Member: The Alliance, PARW/CC, CDI
Certification: CPRW
Resume: 152

Indian Trail

Nathan J. Adams
First Impressions Résumé & Career Management Center
P.O. Box 1653
Indian Trail, NC 28079
Phone: (704) 882-2839
Fax: (704) 322-4038
Email: rezumay4u@aol.com
Web site: www.firstimpressionscount.com
Certification: CPRW
Resume: 57

Ohio

Athens

Melissa L. Kasler
Résumé Impressions
306 W. Union St.
Athens, OH 45701
Phone: (740) 592-3993
Toll-free: (800) 516-0334
Fax: (740) 592-1352
E-mail: resume@frognet.net

Web site: www.resumeimpressions.com
Member: The Alliance, PARW/CC
Certification: CPRW
Resumes: 23, 48

Findlay

Sharon Pierce-Williams, M.Ed.
Job Rockit
609 Lincolnshire Lane
Findlay, OH 45840
Phone: (419) 422-0228
Fax: (419) 425-1185
E-mail: Sharon@JobRockit.com
Web site: www.JobRockit.com
Member: The Alliance, CDI, Findlay-Hancock
    County Chamber of Commerce
Certifications: M.Ed., CPRW
Resumes: 67, 80
Cover letter: 4

Springfield

Teena L. Rose
Résumé to Referral
1824 Rebert Pike
Springfield, OH 45506
Phone: (937) 325-2149
Fax: (937) 236-1351
E-mail: admin@resumetoreferral.com
Web site: www.resumebycprw.com
Member: The Alliance
Certifications: CPRW, CEIP
Resume: 96

Oregon

Portland

Rosie Bixel
A Personal Scribe Resume Writing & Design
13039 E. Burnside St.
Portland, OR 97233
Phone: (503) 254-8262
Fax: (503) 608-4065
Web site: www.apersonalscribe.com
E-mail: rosie@apersonalscribe.com or
    rosiebixel@yahoo.com
Member: NRWA, CDI
Resumes: 22, 29, 54, 83, 85, 86, 129, 130, 183, 187

Jennifer Rydell
Simplify Your Life Career Services
6327-C SW Capitol Hwy PMB 243
Portland, OR 97239-1937
Phone: (503) 977-1955

Fax: (503) 245-4212
E-mail: jennifer@simplifyyourliferesumes.com
Web site: www.simplifyyourliferesumes.com
Member: The Alliance, NRWA, PARW/CC
Certifications: CPRW, NCRW, CCM
Resume: 75

Pennsylvania

Media

Karen L. Conway
Premier Resumes
1008 N. Providence Rd.
Media, PA 19063
Phone: (610) 566-8422
Toll-free: (866) 241-5300
Fax: (610) 566-3047
E-mail: premresume@aol.com
Web site: www.ResumesInADay.com
Member: PARW/CC
Certifications: CPRW, CEIP
Resume: 24

Sinking Spring

Darlene Dassy
Dynamic Résumé Solutions
14 Crestview Dr.
Sinking Spring, PA 19608
Phone: (610) 678-0147
Fax: (714) 274-7191
E-mail: darlene@dynamicresumesolutions.com
Web site: www.dynamicresumesolutions.com
Member: NRWA, CDI
Certifications: CERW, CARW
Resume: 139

West Middlesex

Jane Roqueplot
JaneCo's Sensible Solutions
3493 Sharon Rd.
West Middlesex, PA 16159
Phone: (724) 528-1000
Toll-free: (888) 526-3267
Fax: (724) 346-5263
E-mail: jane@janecos.com
Web site: www.janecos.com
Member: The Alliance, NRWA, CDI, NRWA,
    PARW/CC, AORCP
Certifications: CPBA, CWDP, CECC
Resumes: 11, 72, 82, 90, 144, 180, 182

Rhode Island

North Kingstown

Edward Turilli
AccuWriter Resume Service
North Kingstown, RI
Phone: (401) 268-3020
E-mail: edtur@cox.net
Web site: www.resumes4-u.com
Certifications: MA, CPRW
Resumes: 1, 32, 81

Texas

Lubbock

Daniel J. Dorotik, Jr.
100PercentResumes
5401 68th St.
Lubbock, TX 79424
Phone: (806) 783-9900
Fax: (806) 993-3757
E-mail: dan@100percentresumes.com
Web site: www.100percentresumes.com
Member: NRWA
Certification: NCRW
Resumes: 6, 35, 79, 102, 116, 118, 133, 136, 196,
197, 198, 199

Edith A. Rische
Write Away Resume
5908 73rd St.
Lubbock, TX 79424-1920
Phone: (806) 798-0881
Fax: (806) 798-3213
E-mail: earische@suddenlink.net
Web site: www.writeawayresume.com
Member: NRWA
Certifications: NCRW, JCTC
Resume: 166
Cover letter: 7

Shiner

MeLisa Rogers, ed.d
Ultimate Career
P.O. Box 272
Shiner, TX 77984
Phone: (361) 594-8585
E-mail: mrogers@tisd.net
Web site: www.ultimatecareer.biz
Member: PARW/CC, SHRM, ASTD
Certifications: Ph.D. training and performance
    improvement, CPRW, CPBA, Achieve
    Global, Vital Learning
Resumes: 27, 36, 37, 122, 140, 145, 163, 193

Virginia

Reston

Helen Oliff
Principal
Turning Point
Reston, VA
Phone: (703) 346-8888
Fax: (801) 601-0077
E-mail: helen@turningpointnow.com
Web site: www.turningpointnow.com
Member: The Alliance, PARW
Certifications: CFRWC, CPRW, ECI
Resumes: 101, 115, 134, 185

Washington

Bellingham

Janice M. Shepherd
Write On Career Keys
Bellingham, WA 98226-4260
Phone: (360) 738-7958
Fax: (360) 306-8225
E-mail: Janice@writeoncareerkeys.com
Web site: www.writeoncareerkeys.com
Member: The Alliance, PARW/CC
Certifications: CPRW, JCTC, CEIP
Resumes: 104, 171

Seattle

Alice Hanson
Seattle, WA
Resumes: 94, 97

Woodland

Jennifer Anthony
1087 Lewis River Rd. #160
Woodland, WA 98674
Toll-free: (888) 295-4985
Fax: (503) 334-3930
E-mail: jenn@jennwrites.com
Web site: www.resumeasap.com
Member: NRWA
Resumes: 4, 53, 99, 103, 148, 169

Wisconsin

Glendale

Michele J. Haffner
Advanced Résumé Services
1314 W. Paradise Ct.
Glendale, WI 53209

Phone: (414) 247-1677
Fax: (414) 247-1808
E-mail: michelle@resumeservices.com
Web site: www.resumeservices.com
Member: PARW, Coachville
Certifications: CPRW, JCTC
Resumes: 5, 40, 93

Three Lakes

Susan Guarneri
Guarneri Associates
6670 Crystal Lake Rd.
Three Lakes, WI 54562
Phone: (715) 546-4449
E-mail: Susan@Resume-Magic.com
Web site: www.Resume-Magic.com
Member: ACA, NCDA, CDI, The Alliance,
   PARW/CC, WCDA, NBCC
Certifications: CPRW, MRW, CERW, NCC, NCCC,
   CCMC, CPBS, MBPS, COIS, CEIP, IJCTC, DCC
Resumes: 34, 77, 114

Professional Organizations

If you would like more recommendations of resume writers and career coaches in your area, see the following information.

Career Management Alliance

(A Division of Kennedy Information, Inc.)
1 Phoenix Mill Lane, Fl. 3
Peterborough, NH 03458
Phone: (603) 924-0900, ext. 617
Fax: (603) 924-4034
Web site: www.careermanagementalliance.com

National Résumé Writers' Association

Toll-free: (877) 843-6792
E-mail: AdminManager@nrwaweb.com
Web site: www.nrwaweb.com

Professional Association of Résumé Writers & Career Coaches

1388 Brightwaters Blvd., NE
St. Petersburg, FL 33704
Toll-free: (800) 822-7279
Fax: (727) 894-1277
E-mail: PARWhq@aol.com
Web site: www.parw.com

Career Directors International

Phone: (321) 752-0442
Toll-free: (888) 867-7972
Fax: (801) 752-7517
E-mail: info@careerdirectors.com
Web site: www.careerdirectors.com

www.CertifiedCareerCoaches.com
www.CertifiedResumeWriters.com

For information on the certification programs for
Certified Federal Job Search Trainer (CFJST) or
Certified Federal Resume Writer & Coach
(CFRWC), see the following information.

Ten Steps to a Federal Job™
The Resume Place, Inc.
89 Mellor Ave.
Baltimore, MD 21228
Phone: (410) 744-4324
Fax: (410) 744-0112
E-mail: kathryn@resume-place.com
Web sites: www.resume-place.com and
www.tensteps.com

Occupation Index

Note: Numbers are resume numbers in the Gallery, *not* page numbers.

Features Index

The following sections are common and therefore are not included in this Features Index: Work Experience, Work History, Professional Experience, Related Experience, Other Experience, Employment, Education (by itself), Student Teaching, Additional Information, and References. Variations of these sections, however, are included if they are distinctive in some way or have combined headings. As you look for features that interest you, be sure to browse through *all* the resumes. Some important information, such as Accomplishments, might not be listed here if it is presented as a subsection of another section.

Note: Numbers are resume numbers in the Gallery, *not* page numbers.